Solving Problems
On Concurrent Processors
Volume II

Software for Concurrent Processors

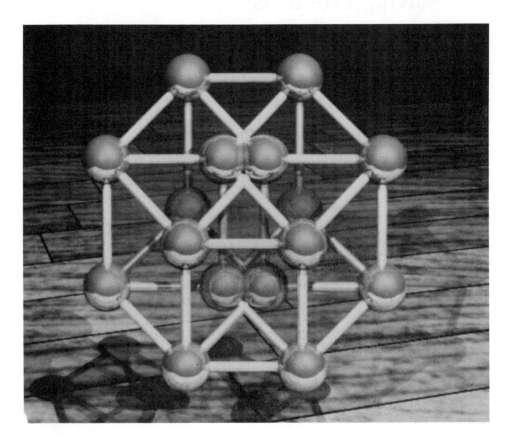

A four dimensional hypercube computed on a 512 node NCUBE using ray tracing. This picture was produced by S. Huang, J. Goldsmith, and J. Salmon at Caltech.

Solving Problems
On Concurrent Processors
Volume II

Software for Concurrent Processors

Ian G. Angus, Geoffrey C. Fox
California Institute of Technology

Jai Sam Kim
Pohang Institute of Technology

David W. Walker
University of South Carolina

PRENTICE HALL
Englewood Cliffs, New Jersey 07632

Library of Congress Cataloging-in-Publication Data
(Revised for vol. 2)

Solving problems on concurrent processors.
  Vol. 2 by Ian G. Angus...[et al.].
  Includes bibliographical references.
  Contents: v. 1. General techniques and regular
problems—v. 2. Software for concurrent processors.
  1. Parallel processing (Electronic computers)
2. Multiprocessors. I. Fox, Geoffrey C. II. Angus,
Ian G.
QA76.5.S6534   1988   004'.35   87–7288
  ISBN 0-13-823022-6 (v.1)
  ISBN 0-13-829714-2 (v.2)

Editorial/production supervision: Kerry Reardon
Manufacturing buyer: Ray Sintel

 © 1990 by Prentice-Hall, Inc.
A Division of Simon & Schuster
Englewood Cliffs, New Jersey 07632

The publisher offers discounts on this book when ordered
in bulk quantities. For more information, write:

    Special Sales/College Marketing
    College Technical and Reference Division
    Prentice Hall
    Englewood Cliffs, New Jersey 07632

Printed in the United States of America

10 9 8 7 6 5 4 3 2 1

ISBN 0-13-829714-2

Prentice-Hall International (UK) Limited, *London*
Prentice-Hall of Australia Pty. Limited, *Sydney*
Prentice-Hall Canada Inc., *Toronto*
Prentice-Hall Hispanoamericana, S.A., *Mexico*
Prentice-Hall of India Private Limited, *New Delhi*
Prentice-Hall of Japan, Inc., *Tokyo*
Simon & Schuster Asia Pte. Ltd., *Singapore*
Editora Prentice-Hall do Brasil, Ltda., *Rio de Janeiro*

Contents

Preamble

This book is the second in a two volume series dealing with the use of concurrent processors in science and engineering. Both volumes have a strong practical bias and emphasize the concurrent implementation of algorithms on real machines. This reflects the approach of the Concurrent Computation Program at Caltech and is founded on the belief that fundamental insights into how to exploit most effectively the full potential of parallel computation can be gained by this "problem-driven" approach.

Volume I discusses general techniques of communication and problem decomposition and describes their application to several important algorithms. The contents of Volume I are given after the index of this volume. This second volume focuses on software which explicitly implements the algorithms presented in Volume I. Chapter 1 of Volume II reviews the parallel hardware currently available and presents a survey of applications on several parallel machines. Chapter 2 gives an overview of the CrOS III communication system. The Virtual Machine Loosely Synchronous Communication System (VMLSCS) and the *Express* communication environment, which respectively generalize CrOS III for inhomogeneous and homogeneous multiprocessors, are also discussed. In Chapter 3 the details of the implementation of CrOS III on a number of concurrent machines are given. Chapter 4 describes the CUBIX concurrent I/O system. Some supplements to the CrOS III environment are presented in Chapter 5. These supplements deal mainly with the management of processing nodes and nonlocal communication and form the basis of an applications "toolkit." Chapter 6 describes a hypercube simulator which may be used to run the software presented in this volume. In Chapter 7 we discuss tutorial systems that may be used for educational purposes, or for developing concurrent applications that are to be run subsequently on larger systems. Chapter 8 forms the core of the book and describes 16 application codes in detail. Most of these applications are implementations of algorithms described in Volume I . The C and Fortran source code is given in the appendices of this volume. Chapter 9 describes a set of benchmark programs which have been used at Caltech to evaluate the performance of a number of advanced architecture computers. In Chapter 10 an overview is given, followed by a discussion of where we expect parallel processing to lead by the year 2000.

This volume also includes a tutorial for parallel systems using the CrOS III communication system. This tutorial is intended to help new users become familiar with the concurrent implementation of simple regular problems on such systems. The tutorial is independent of Volumes I and II in that it assumes no prior knowledge of concurrent computing, but directs the reader to certain key parts of the text of these volumes. In this way a practical knowledge of a particular approach to concurrent computation can be gained without having to read Volumes I/II from cover to cover.

Appendices A and B contain listings of the complete C and Fortran source code for the applications discussed in Chapter 8. C and Fortran source code listings for the exercises set in the Tutorial are given in Appendices C and D. Appendices E and F respectively contain C source code listings and manual pages for the supplements to CrOS III discussed in Chapter 5. The software presented in this volume, together with the hypercube simulator discussed in Chapter 6, may be obtained in computer-readable form as described in Appendix G. This code is in the public domain, although the authors would appreciate being acknowledged if it is used in published research. Although care has been taken to ensure that the code is correct and reliable it almost certainly contains bugs, and no doubt parts of it could be written more elegantly. The authors would be pleased to receive bug reports at the address listed in Appendix G, and would be even happier to receive bug fixes! Please note that we are a small (distributed) research group and cannot undertake to maintain the software provided. Furthermore the reader must use the code at his or her own risk – neither the authors nor Prentice Hall accept liability for any ill effects.

Many people have contributed to this volume. We would particularly like to thank Mark Johnson, Greg Lyzenga, Steve Otto, and John Salmon, and everyone else involved in producing Volume I. John Schiff, Elizabeth Scott, Alex Ho and Esther Williams helped in developing the hypercube simulator, which is based on an earlier implementation by Hiram Hunt. We are also grateful to Jon Flower and Adam Kolawa for commenting on early drafts.

This work is supported by many generous sponsors who are fully acknowledged in Volume I.

A Tutorial Introduction
to CrOS III

T-1 Overview

In this section we present a tutorial introduction to the use of the CrOS III communication system on concurrent processors. This tutorial does not cover all aspects of the use of CrOS III but, instead, has the more modest objective of helping potential users to become familiar with the most commonly used CrOS III routines. It is strongly recommended that the reader work through the exercises on a real concurrent processor or on a simulator, such as *nsim*, which is discussed in Chap. 6. After completing all the exercises successfully, the reader should be able to write simple concurrent programs and be able to understand most of the applications codes listed in Appendices A and B.

It is assumed that the reader has access to a concurrent processor running CrOS III, such as the NCUBE and INTEL iPSC/1,2 hypercubes, transputer arrays running *Express*, or to a PC-based hypercube (see Chap. 7), or to a sequential computer running the hypercube simulator, *nsim*. As an additional prerequisite the reader should also have a copy of Volume I of *Solving Problems on Concurrent Processors* ([Fox 88a]). It is also assumed that the reader knows how to compile, link, run, and edit CrOS III programs on whichever machine is to be used. If this is not the case before proceeding further with this tutorial, the reader should consult the appropriate manuals, seek the advice of an "expert," or use the on-line help/manual facility, *mann*, if this is available (see Sec. 6-2.2). Documentation on compiling, linking, and running on the commercial and PC-based hypercubes should have been received when the CrOS III system was installed. Details for the use of *nsim* are given in Chap. 6.

The tutorial consists of a number of tasks which should be executed in sequence. When referring to things such as the names of routines the C language name is used, and the Fortran equivalent is given in parentheses. Example codes for the programming tasks presented in this tutorial are given in Appendices C and D.

This tutorial begins with a set of tasks which involve the exchange of data between the control processor (CP) and the nodes of the concurrent processor. This is followed by examples of the use of simple communication routines for exchanging data between pairs of nodes, broadcasting data from one node to a set of nodes, and combining data from all nodes. The tasks also involve the use of the *gridmap* routines for mapping the nodes onto Cartesian meshes. The use of the CUBIX programming model (see Chap. 4) is then illustrated, and all the previous tasks are repeated using CUBIX.

T-2 Programs Involving CP-Node Communication

As explained in Chap. 4, in the CPNODE programming model a control processor (CP) program must be written to download the node program to the nodes and initiate its execution, and to mediate I/O between the nodes and peripherals such as disks, terminals, and so on. The user must therefore write one program for the CP and another for the nodes. This section consists of a number of tasks aimed at familiarizing the reader with the CPNODE style of programming.

Task 2.1 Preliminary Reading

Read the overview of CrOS III in Chap. 3. If you are not clear about how to use a routine, read the appropriate manual page in Appendix E of Volume I, or use the on-line help if your system has it installed. After completing this task, you should be familiar with at least the following most important CrOS III routines:

cubeld	(KCUBEL)	mload	(KMLOAD)
cparam	(KCPARA)	loadelt	(KLOADE)
cwrite	(KCWRIT)	mdumpcp	(KMDUMP)
cread	(KCREAD)	dumpelt	(KDUMPE)
bcastcp	(KBCSTC)	combcp	(KCOMBC)
bcastelt	(KBCSTE)	combelt	(KCOMBE)
broadcast	(KBROAD)	combine	(KCOMBI)
cshift	(KCSHIF)		

Task 2.2 Review of Wave Equation Application

Read Secs. 5-2 and 5-3 of Volume I about the parallel solution of the one-dimensional wave equation. Then look at the corresponding code in Appendix D-2 and D-3 of Volume I (D-6 and D-7 for Fortran), and understand the use of the CrOS III routines in this application.

Task 2.3 Communication Between the CP and Nodes

The next task is to write a simple CPNODE program. The CP program should first read in the hypercube dimension and download the node program to the hypercube using the routine *cubeld* (KCUBEL). You may find it useful to look at how this is done in the wave equation program in the routine *down_load* (DOWNLD). Be sure to check the value returned by *cubeld* (KCUBEL) – if an error occurs an error message should be output, and the program should be terminated. If the node program is successfully downloaded the CP program should next read in an integer, *intcp*, and use the routine *bcastcp* (KBCSTC) to send it to all the nodes. For the nodes to receive this integer, the node program should start with a call to *bcastelt* (KBCSTE). After receiving the integer *intcp* from the CP, the node program should next call the routine *cparam* (KCPARA) so that each node can determine its unique node number, *iproc*. Each node should then add together *intcp* and *iproc* to give *isum*, and return this to the CP by calling the routine *dumpelt*

(KDUMPE). The CP receives these integers by calling *mdumpcp* (KMDUMP) and outputs the different value of *isum* received from each node. The CP and node programs then terminate.

Task 2.4 Sending Different Data to Each Node

If you have successfully completed Task 2.3, modify the code so that each node receives a different integer from the CP. Thus if the dimension of the hypercube is d, then the CP should read in 2^d integers into an array and send the first to node 0, the second to node 1, and so on. The integers should be sent by calling the routine *mloadcp* (KMLOAD) in the CP program, and the node program should call the routine *loadelt* (KLOADE) to allow each node to receive its integer. As in Task 2.3, each node should return the value of *isum* to the CP to be output.

Task 2.5 Combining Data from Nodes

The program from Task 2.4 should next be modified to illustrate the use of the routine *combcp* and *combelt* (KCOMBC and KCOMBE). After evaluating *isum* in each node, the node program should divide this number by the number of nodes (obtained from the previous call to *cparam* (KCPARA)). The resulting floating-point number should then be summed over all nodes and the sum returned to the CP by calling *combelt* (KCOMBE) in the node program. The CP program should call the routine *combcp* (KCOMBC) to receive the summed quantity. In this way the CP and each of the nodes receive the value of *isum* averaged over all nodes.

T-3 The Use of the *gridmap* Routines

The *gridmap* routines can be used to map the nodes onto a rectangular (or Cartesian) mesh. In this section the use of the *gridmap* routines for performing one- and two-dimensional decompositions is illustrated.

Task 3.1 Preliminary Reading

Read the CrOS III manual pages for the *gridmap* routines in Appendix E of Volume I. Also look at the wave equation example in Appendix D-3 (D-7) to see how the nodes are mapped onto a line in this program. You may find Sec. 14-7 of Volume I useful as well.

Task 3.2 A One-Dimensional Example

Write a CPNODE program in which the node program first calls *cparam* (KCPARA) so that each node can determine its node number. Next call the routine *gridinit* (KGRDIN) to initialize the decomposition of the nodes onto a (one-dimensional) ring. Then call the routine *gridcoord* (KGRDCO) to allow each node to determine its position in the ring, and return this value to the CP program to be output. The number of the node in the clockwise and counterclockwise directions for each node should then be found by calling the routine *gridproc* (KGRDPR).

Return these node numbers to the CP and output them. Next call the routine *gridchan* (KGRDCH) to find the channel masks for communicating with the adjacent nodes, and return these values to the CP and output them. Make sure you understand the values returned by the *gridmap* routines and output by the CP program.

Next initialize the integer *imove* in each node to be equal to the node number. Then set up a loop in each execution of which each node passes its current value of *imove* to the next node in the ring in the clockwise direction. This should be accomplished by calling the routine *cshift* (KCSHIF) so that each node writes in the clockwise direction while reading from the anticlockwise direction. The integer received should overwrite the former value of *imove*. Thus in each pass through the loop the values of *imove* originating in each node get passed one step round the ring. In each pass through the loop the current value of *imove* should be returned by each node to the CP and output. The number of times the loop is executed should be read in near the start of the CP program and broadcast to the nodes.

Task 3.3 A Two-Dimensional Example

In this task you will decompose the nodes onto a two-dimensional mesh. After downloading the node program the CP program should next read in the number of nodes in each of the two directions, *npx* and *npy*. Thus the nodes will be arranged in a two-dimensional grid of *npx* by *npy* nodes. The product of *npx* and *npy* should equal the total number of nodes, and your CP program should check this. The values of *npx* and *npy* should then be broadcast from the CP to the nodes by calling *bcastcp* (KBCSTC) and *bcastelt* (KBCSTE) in the CP and node programs, respectively.

After receiving the values of *npx* and *npy* the node program should next call *cparam* (KCPARA) to determine the node number. The *gridmap* routines are then called to decompose the nodes onto a *npx* by *npy* grid. As in Task 3.2 the *gridmap* routines are initialized by calling *gridinit* (KGRDIN). The channel masks for communicating with the four nearest nodes (in the left, right, up and down directions) are found by calling the routine *gridchan* (KGRDCH) once for each direction. The position of each node in the grid should then be found by calling *gridcoord* (KGRDCO). Each node should return its position in the mesh to the CP program, where it should be output. This completes the decomposition for this task.

The node program should next determine the sum of the node numbers for each row of nodes as follows. Those nodes lying in the first column of nodes in the mesh send their node numbers to the node to the right by calling the routine *cwrite* (KCWRIT). Those nodes not lying in either the first or last columns receive an integer from the node to the left by calling *cread* (KCREAD) and add their own node number to this. The result is then sent to the node to the right, again by calling *cwrite* (KCWRIT). Those nodes lying in the last (rightmost) column of nodes receive an integer from the node to the left and add their node number to it. At this stage the nodes in the last column now contain the sum, *irsum*, of the node numbers for their respective rows. Clearly the action taken by each node will differ depending on which column of the mesh it lies in. The pseudocode for this part of the program is given in Code T-1. As it stands Code T-1 is incorrect since if there is only a single column of nodes the variable *irsum* will not be assigned a value. In particular, the code will fail if there is only one node. Write your code carefully so that it will work correctly for hypercubes of any dimension.

```
        ...
        if_begin ( node is in first column of nodes ) then
                [ send node number to right ]
        else_if ( node is in last column ) then
                [ receive sum of node numbers from left ]
                [ irsum ← irec + iproc ]
        else
                [ receive integer, irec, from left ]
                [ isend ← irec + iproc ]
                [ send isend to right ]
        if_end
        ...
```

Code T-1 Pseudocode for finding sum of node numbers in each column of nodes.

In the next stage of the program the sum for each row, *irsum*, contained in the nodes in the last column of nodes is passed back along each row to the left so that each node then contains the sum of the node numbers for its row. This is essentially the same as the previous stage of the algorithm, except that instead of reading from the left and writing to the right, nodes read from the right and write to the left. Thus the nodes in the last column send the value of *irsum* to the nodes on their left, and this is passed along the row until it reaches the node in the first column. Each node should then send the value of the sum of node numbers for its row to the CP program to be output.

Next the sums for each row are added together to give the total sum of all the node numbers. This is similar to the summation of the node numbers in each row, but instead the summation is done over the values of *irsum* in each column of nodes. Thus each node in the first (bottom) row sends its value of *irsum* to the node above. This node adds the value of *irsum* for the second row to the value received and sends the result to the node above. This process continues until the nodes in the last (top) row each contain the sum over all node numbers. This result should then be passed back down the columns so that every node contains the total sum. Each node should then send this value to the CP program to be output. The node and CP programs should then terminate.

Task 3.4 The Use of *broadcast*

Modify the program of Task 3.3 so that after finding the sum, *irsum*, in the nodes in the last column, the routine *broadcast* (KBROAD) is used to send *irsum* to the other nodes in the same row rather than explicitly passing the value back along the row. The routine *broadcast* (KBROAD) may be used to do this since the nodes in any one row form a subcube, and the mask specifying this subcube (see Sec. 5-2) is just $(npx - 1)$. You should also use *broadcast* (KBROAD) to broadcast the sum over all nodes from the nodes in the top row to the nodes in the same column. Again the nodes in each column form a subcube, and the mask which specifies this subcube is $npx * (npy - 1)$.

Task 3.5 Integration by Simpson's Rule

As a more practical problem we next consider the evaluation of a definite integral by Simpson's rule. Suppose we want to find the integral of some function $f(x)$ between $x = a$ and $x = b$. The x range is divided into an even number of n intervals of size h by the ordinates $x_0 = a, x_1, \ldots, x_{n-1}, x_n = b$, so that $x_k = a + kh$ and $h = (b - a)/n$. Simpson's rule approximates the integral over a pair of intervals by,

$$\int_{x_k - h}^{x_k + h} f(x)\, dx \approx \frac{h}{3}\left(f_{k-1} + 4f_k + f_{k+1}\right) \tag{T.1}$$

where $f_k = f(x_k)$ is the value of the function at x_k. Thus, summing over successive pairs of intervals we get the following approximation for the value of the integral between a and b,

$$\int_a^b f(x)\, dx \approx \frac{h}{3}[f_0 + f_n + 4(f_1 + f_3 + \cdots + f_{n-1})$$
$$+ 2(f_2 + f_4 + \cdots + f_{n-2})] \tag{T.2}$$

The CP program should begin by reading in the hypercube dimension and then downloading the node program. For a given function the inputs to the program are the limits a and b of the integral and the number of intervals used, n. These should be read in by the CP program and sent to the nodes by calls to the routine *bcastcp* (KBCSTC). The CP then waits for the answer from the nodes, which it will receive by a call to *combcp* (KCOMBC), and then outputs it.

The node program should first call the routine *cparam* (KCPARA) so that each node can determine its node number and the hypercube dimension. Then the limits a and b on the integral, and the number of intervals n, should be received from the CP by calling *bcastelt* (KBCSTE).

The problem should be decomposed by dividing the $n + 1$ ordinates into N_p groups of successive values, where N_p is the number of nodes, and assigning one group to each node. To ensure optimal load balance the number of ordinates in each node should be approximately equal. The assignment of groups of ordinates to nodes may be done in any way, provided each node knows the values of its x

ordinates. Each node must evaluate the contribution to the integral that arises from its ordinates according to Eq. (T.2), and so must also know the index value of its first ordinate (or, more precisely, whether it is odd or even). This will depend on how the ordinates are grouped together when assigning them to nodes. In addition, each node must know if it contains either the first or last ordinate. This is an example of an "embarrassingly parallel" algorithm, since no communication between the nodes is needed to evaluate the contribution from each node. After decomposing the problem the nodes can now evaluate their contributions to the integral without need for any communication. The node program then calls *combelt* (KCOMBE) to sum the contributions from all nodes and to return the value of the integral to the CP.

You might like to test your program by using it to evaluate the integral

$$\int_0^{\pi/2} \frac{dx}{\sqrt{1 - (\sin^2 x)/2}} \tag{T.3}$$

This is the complete elliptic integral of the first kind, $K(1/\sqrt{2})$, and its tabulated value is 1.85407.

T-4 CUBIX Applications

In the CUBIX programming model the user does not need to write a separate CP program for each application, thereby simplifying program development and debugging. CUBIX provides an uniform interface between the nodes and operating system utilities. In this section you will learn the basics of programming parallel processors using CUBIX.

Task 4.1 Preliminary Reading

Read Chap. 6 of Volume I, and try to understand the CUBIX version of the one-dimensional wave equation application in Appendix D-4 of Volume I (D-8 for Fortran). If you are using Fortran you should also read Appendix C of Volume I. Chapter 15 of Volume I gives more details of the implementation of CUBIX, but may be omitted.

Task 4.2 CUBIX Examples from Chapter 4

Read Chap. 4 of this volume, and run the example programs. Try to find a way to modify the example CUBIX bug in Code 4-4 so that the code executes correctly.

Task 4.3 More CUBIX Examples

Repeat the tasks in Secs. T-2 and T-3, using the CUBIX programming model. Which of the two programming models, CPNODE and CUBIX, makes programming the easiest?

T-5 Concluding Remarks

If you have followed through this tutorial and have successfully completed all of the tasks, you should now possess a good fundamental understanding of how to write parallel programs using the CrOS III communication system. However, some of the CrOS III routines, for example, *vread* (KVREAD) and *vwrite* (KVWRIT), have not been covered in this tutorial. If you wish to learn about these routines you should read the relevant manual pages in Appendix E of Volume I and look at some of the applications listed in Appendices A and B of this volume which use them, for example the LU decomposition program and the *indexx* routine. Finally, if you want to gain a more complete knowledge of programming concurrent processors it is suggested that you start by reading Volumes I and II, which contain references to other material to help you in your quest.

1

Introduction

1-1 Motivation

In Volume 1 of this series, *Solving Problems on Concurrent Processors* [Fox 88a], we described the decomposition and performance of many scientific problems on parallel machines. In this second volume, we present software to implement the explicit algorithms given in Volume 1. It is hoped that this software, which is presented in both C and Fortran, will have value as a tutorial, and perhaps as part of a base set used in benchmarking different parallel machines. This volume is intended to be used as a handbook for developing and running applications on concurrent computers and, therefore, differs in style from more traditional textbooks.

Unfortunately there are no generally accepted standards in the parallel computing field, and so we have been forced to choose a particular framework in which to develop our software. This is the so-called CrOS III Communication System used at Caltech and described in Volume 1. CrOS III is overviewed in Chap. 2, while in Chap. 3 we discuss its implementation on several commercial parallel computers: the INTEL and NCUBE hypercubes and the BBN Butterfly. As CrOS III is a simple system, we can expect it to be ported to future machines if it continues to be useful. CrOS III is only implemented directly and naturally on distributed memory machines with the hypercube topology or on a system whose interconnect, such as a full-bus connection, includes the hypercube. There is a natural generalization of this called VMLSCS, for Virtual Machine Loosely Synchronous Communication System, which was introduced in Volume 1. VMLSCS is discussed in Sec. 1-3 and Chap. 2. Chapter 2 also describes *Express*, a general asynchronous buffered communication system for homogeneous multiprocessors produced by Parasoft. *Express* generalizes CrOS III in a fashion different from VMLSCS and provides a vehicle for implementing CrOS III on systems such as transputer arrays whose hardware interconnect does not include the hypercube. *Express* also has the advantage of being a commercially supported version of CrOS III. Chapters 4 and 5 describe two important extensions of CrOS III in the areas of input/output (I/O) and a library of useful utilities. The latter manages subcubes of a full hypercube and implements several commonly used communication patterns. The CUBIX I/O system introduced in Volume 1 is now fully defined for both C and Fortran, and this extension is given in Chap. 4. Chapters 6 and 7 describe two simple ways of exploring parallel computing without the commitment and expense of acquiring dedicated hardware. Chapter 6 defines a simple simulator that allows sequential computers to emulate a parallel system and so execute the

1

parallel software in this supplement. The simulator runs under UNIX or Digital's
VMS operating system.

Chapter 7 describes tutorial systems for concurrent computers. Such systems
include add-on boards for PCs and workstations using parallel architectures and
distributed networks of sequential computers where, for example, several PCs can
be hooked together to form a parallel computer. For the case of IBM PCs, we use
serial (RS232) channels between PCs to form hypercube communications. We also
present a parallel system built around Apple Macintoshes in which an AppleTalk
connection connects the PCs together. In each case, we have a fully implemented
CrOS III communication system available. The IBM PC and MAC cubes should
run the standard CrOS III software presented in this volume. These systems also
have the interesting feature of possessing good graphics, for example, a monitor
attached to every processor in the parallel system. This is exploited in software
built specially for these systems and described in Chap. 7.

Chapter 8 is the heart of this book as it describes 16 parallel codes separately
for C and Fortran. This chapter gives function and use while appendices A and B
list the explicit C and Fortran code. Table 1-1 reviews the applications in Chap. 8
and also indicates where they are described in Volume 1. The software is designed
to run on

> Simulator
> UNIX
> VMS
> IBM PC-CUBE
> MAC-CUBE
> NCUBE/ten hypercube running CrOS III
> INTEL iPSC/1 hypercube running CrOS III
> BBN Butterfly running CrOS III
> Transputer arrays running *Express*

CrOS III and the *Express* enhancements will be available on more modern machines,
including the INTEL iPSC/2 and Symult S2010.

Chapter 9 describes a set of application codes that were an outgrowth of
Caltech research on the hypercube, and which has been used in a recent project
to evaluate the performance of several advanced architecture computers [Walker
88a; Messina 89]. The explicit codes are not recorded here, but may be obtained
electronically, as described shortly and in Appendix G.

Appendix A contains a full listing of the C code in Chap. 8, and Appendix
B contains listings of the Fortran versions. Appendices C and D list the code
associated with the tutorial section at the start of this volume. In Appendices E
and F the source code and manual pages are presented for a set of CrOS III utilities.
Appendix G describes how this software may be obtained from Caltech in computer-
readable form using standard network connections. Appendix H lists some suppliers
of hardware and software for distributed memory concurrent processors.

Application	Volume 1 Chapter	Volume 2 Chapter
Tutorial programs	—	8-2, C, D
Wave equation	5, 6	8-3, A-2, A-3, B-2, B-3
Finite difference solution of Laplace's equation	7	8-4, A-4, B-4
Finite element (conjugate gradient) solution of Laplace's equation	8	8-5, A-5, B-5
Long-range particle interactions	9	8-6, A-6, B-6
Matrix multiplication	10	8-7, A-7, B-7
Fast Fourier transform (Cooley-Tukey binary FFT)	11	8-8, A-8, B-8
Use of parallel random number generators	12	8-9, A-9, B-9
Particle dynamics with a Lennard-Jones potential	16	8-10, A-10, B-10
Ecological simulation — WATOR	17	8-11, A-11, B-11
Sorting on a hypercube (Bitonic Sort, Shell Sort, and Quick Sort)	18	8-12, A-12, B-12
Efficient calculation of multiple scalar products (*fold*)	19, 21	8-13, A-13, B-13
Banded matrix LU decomposition	20	8-14, A-14, B-14
Subcube management	—	5-2, 8-15, A-15
Communication utilities	14, 21	2, 5-3, 8-16, A-16, B-16
Crystal_Router	22	5-4, 8-17, A-17, B-17
Crystal_Accumulator	22	8-18, A-18, B-18
Quantum chromodynamics (high-energy physics)	13, 23	9-2
Multiple-target tracking (Kalman filtering)	22	9-3
Chemical reaction dynamics	21-5, 23-4.3	9-4
Fluid dynamics using vortex methods	9, 23-4.4	9-5
Plasma physics	—	9-6
Neural networks	22-4, 23-4.2	9-7

Table 1-1 Parallel Algorithms Implemented in Volume 2.

We note that all the software listed in this book has been placed in the public domain and may be freely used or modified. We would no doubt be gratified if you acknowledged this volume where appropriate. Some related or enhanced software is available for purchase from commercial sources — in particular a parallel software company Parasoft that can be contacted at the address given in Appendix H. This appendix also lists other relevant commercial contacts.

Our software surely has bugs and you may have other queries. Please send these to:

Software For Concurrent Processors
Caltech Concurrent Computation Program
Mail code 206-49
Pasadena, CA 91125

You may contact us by electronic mail at:

`c3prequest@hamlet.caltech.edu`   for INTERNET users

`c3prequest@hamlet`   for BITNET users

Further details are given in Appendix G.

Please note that we are a research group and cannot provide support consulting on material contained in this book. We have formed an industrial consortium that does allow members in depth access to our research. Please contact us, as instructed, if you are interested in this.

In the remainder of the introduction, we review some aspects of parallel processing so as to put the work presented here in context. Sections 1-2, 1-3, and 1-4 cover, respectively, hardware, systems software, and applications. The last section concludes with a table of computational science and engineering problems and an indication whether they can or cannot be tackled on parallel computers with the techniques given in the two volumes of our book. Where the simple techniques of Volumes 1 or 2 are applicable, we indicate which chapters cover relevant material.

1-2 Available Parallel Computer Architectures

Our books concentrate on the implementation of problems on currently available parallel computer hardware and we discuss this here. Chapter 2 of Volume 1 has a more general treatment and an elementary overview will be found in Messina [Messina 87].

Consider the six classes of parallel computer systems given in Tables 1-2, 1-3, and 1-4, where the last two classes in Table 1-3 represent simple options with tutorial value but are not true parallel architectures.

We used the conventional jargon

MIMD: for multiple instruction, multiple data to denote parallel machines with independent nodes operating asynchronously.

SIMD: for single instruction, multiple data to denote parallel machines whose nodes run synchronously while executing an identical instruction stream.

I:	Distributed memory MIMD multicomputer	Hypercube:	AMETEK S14 FPS T Series INTEL iPSC/1, iPSC/2 NCUBE System 10
		Other topologies:	AMETEK S2010 Transputer arrays (CSA, MEIKO) SUPRENUM, MYRIAS SPS-2
II:	Shared memory MIMD multiprocessor	BBN Butterfly Encore Multimax Sequent Balance/Symmetry Alliant FX CRAY X-MP, Y-MP, CRAY-2 ETA-10, Evans and Sutherland ES1 IBM 3090	
III:	Distributed memory SIMD	ICL DAP Goodyear MPP Thinking Machines CM-1, CM-2 AMT DAP	

Table 1-2 Commercial Parallel Computers.

IV:	Add-on boards for PCs and workstations using parallel architecture (see appendix H and Chap. 7)	Four- to 16-node NCUBE hypercube for PC/AT. Transputer-based boards for Macintosh (LEVCO), IBM PC (DEFINICON and others), SUN (TOPOLOGIX and MEIKO).
V:	Linked collection of sequential computers (distributed computer systems)	Typically communication bandwidth too small for "true" parallel computing. • IBM PC-CUBE — a set of IBM PCs with added card containing several serial ports that provide RS232 links between PCs that form a hypercube (Fig. 1.1(a)) • MAC-CUBE — set of Apple Macintoshes linked by AppleTalk network (Fig. 1.1(b))
VI:	Simulator on sequential computer	Each process represents a node of a parallel computer. Available for UNIX and VMS in this book (Chap. 6)

Table 1-3 Tutorial Parallel Computers.

We can expect a continuing set of machines of the three architectures given in Table 1-2 with a range of models up to supercomputer performance.

Class II could be further divided into those like Butterfly, RP3, Ultracomputer, and CEDAR, which scale to systems with many nodes, and the remainder, which are effective parallel systems but limited to a modest number ($\lesssim 32$) of nodes. We have separated from the first three classes small parallel systems that can be added to a conventional PC or workstation. These class IV systems can be viewed as PC "power boosters," where they compete with vector and RISC architecture coprocessors. For the purpose of this book, we view them as cheap, convenient tutorial systems. They can be used to develop and test code for larger systems. Alternatively they can be used in an instructional setting to teach the fundamentals of parallel processing. The simulators of class VI are also of instructional value but not of course useful as a computational tool. Finally, class V considers distributed systems or networks of conventional computers. There is no fundamental difference between such a network and the machines of class I. There is, however, a quantitative difference, since in the notation of Volume 1,

$$t_{comm}/t_{calc} \qquad \text{(Class I)} \qquad \leq 10 \qquad\qquad (1.1)$$

where t_{comm} and t_{calc} are typical node-to-node communication and internal node calculation times. On the other hand, one typically finds

$$t_{comm}/t_{calc} \qquad \text{(Class V)} \qquad \geq 100 \qquad\qquad (1.2)$$

In spite of this performance difference, it is clear that one can expect software developed for class I to run on class V systems. Thus class V systems certainly have tutorial and perhaps greater significance [Furmanski 88c]. At Caltech we have developed two special instructional systems of this type which can be assembled from popular IBM and Apple PCs [Ho 88a,d]. These are explained in Chap. 7, and the modest power of the basic nodes allows reasonable performance. For instance, one finds

$$t_{comm}/t_{calc} \qquad \text{(IBM PC-CUBE)} \qquad \sim 12 \qquad\qquad (1.3)$$

corresponding to $t_{calc} = 50~\mu\text{sec}$ for the INTEL 8087 floating-point chip and $t_{comm} = 600~\mu\text{sec}$ corresponding to 50-kilobit/sec serial transmission over the RS232 links between the PC nodes in Fig. 1-1(a). Note that t_{comm} is the time to transmit a full 32-bit word.

I: Multicomputer	Hypercube: Caltech Cosmic Cube, JPL Mark II, Mark III, Mark IIIfp
II: Shared memory multiprocessors	IBM Yorktown RP3, NYU Ultracomputer, Illinois CEDAR

Table 1-4 Related University Machines.

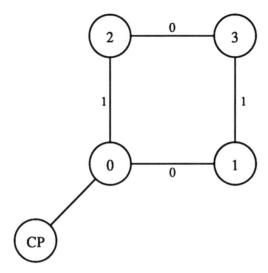

Figure 1-1(a) A 4-node PC-CUBE. Each numbered circle represents a node of the hypercube. The control processor is labeled "CP." One IBM PC is used for each of the nodes and CP, and the hypercube communication channels are RS-232 links between the nodes. Node 0 also communicates with the CP via an RS-232 link. The hypercube communication channels are shown labeled by the channel number.

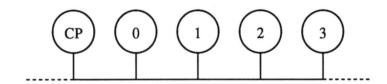

Figure 1-1(b) A 4-node MAC-CUBE. The nodes communicate via an AppleTalk network, and the hypercube communication channels are emulated in software.

The codes in this book cannot be used for the SIMD machines listed as class III. As described in Volume 1 and Fox [Fox 87a,88b], SIMD and MIMD architectures often have similar algorithmic issues and problem domains but currently offer very different programming environments. In principle the software codes in this volume can be executed on machines in the remaining five classes. We detail the practical restrictions to this in Table 1-5.

Note that Volume 1 introduces the concept of loose synchronicity, which is briefly reviewed in Sec. 1-4. Both VMLSCS and CrOS III are only applicable to loosely synchronous problems, and one needs more general communication systems to describe asynchronous problems. In a recent review we estimated that about

I: Distributed memory MIMD	CrOS III suitable for hypercube (or richer) topology; VMLSCS and *Express* for other topologies.
II: Shared memory MIMD	CrOS III, VMLSCS and *Express* can be easily implemented on these machines, which have a full interconnect for message passing. VMLSCS exploits the full interconnect; CrOS III does not, but is sufficient for many problems which only need a hypercube or lower interconnect. Use of collective communication utilities avoids the limitations of CrOS III. Neither CrOS III, VMLSCS, nor *Express* exploit the full power of the architecture (see Sec. 1-3).
III: Distributed memory SIMD	Not applicable.
IV: Add-on boards	Applicability as for architecture I, II, III of add-on board.
V: Distributed computer network	In general applicability as for Class I. This volume only presents CrOS III for IBM PC and MAC cubes.
VI: Simulator	Only a CrOS III simulator available (see Chap. 6). A VMLSCS or *Express* simulator would be straightforward to build.

Table 1-5 CrOS III, VMLSCS, and *Express* Communication Systems on Six Classes of Parallel Systems.

85% of large-scale scientific and engineering computations fell into the loosely synchronous class. All the problems described in Volume 1 and Chaps. 8 and 9 of this book are loosely synchronous.

1-3 Programming Models

Here we will put CrOS III and VMLSCS in the context of a simple taxonomy of programming models. Currently SIMD parallel computers (class III) support a very different model from CrOS III, and we will not consider these further; some remarks on this will be found in Fox [Fox 87a,88e]. Classes IV and V reduce to the earlier classes as shown in Table 1-5. Class VI is not a true parallel machine. Thus we will discuss classes I and II here. These naturally support:

Class I — Distributed Processing of Distributed Data

Class II — Distributed Processing of Shared Data

The shared memory of the class II systems allows programming models where the user and/or compiler does not need to "worry" about the location of data. For example, one can take conventional Fortran code and either automatically, or with user directives, obtain concurrency from parallel execution of separate iterations of a DO loop. This model can probably be implemented on class I machines, but this has yet to be demonstrated in practice [Callahan 88b;Zima 88]. Presently one cannot "hide" communication on a multicomputer as you can with a shared memory machine, but rather communication has to be made explicit by the user. A natural class I programming model is that of Communicating Sequential Processes, and this was the basis of Hoare's pioneering paper on CSP [Hoare 78]. CrOS III and VMLSCS implement this style, but here there are many variations, and typically our systems have traded away functionality in favor of simplicity and performance. This is detailed in Table 1-6, which lists nine features in approximate order of increasing generality. VMLSCS is a strict superset of CrOS III; in the last column of Table 1-6, we give examples of parallel operating systems implementing features not offered by VMLSCS.

CrOS III and VMLSCS are certainly limited, but this does allow efficient portable implementations on a variety of target machines. The features of these systems have been designed to suit loosely synchronous problems, which are, as indicated in the previous section, the large majority of scientific and engineering problems. There is some reason to believe that many of the problems needing the additional features (d) and (e) in Table 1-6 may in fact not parallelize well [Fox 88b]. The algorithmic synchronization of loosely synchronous problems naturally allows many nodes to work efficiently on the same problem.

1-4 Applications

In Volume 1 and extensions given in Fox [Fox 88b], we have classified the computational structure of problems into three types:

$$
\left.
\begin{array}{l}
\text{Synchronous} \\
\text{Properly loosely synchronous} \\
\text{Properly asynchronous}
\end{array}
\right\}
\quad
\begin{array}{l}
\text{Together called loosely} \\
\quad \text{synchronous}
\end{array}
\qquad (1.4)
$$

The computation in loosely synchronous problems can be labeled by a global parameter that naturally synchronizes the individual node calculations "every now and then." This global parameter would be time in a physical simulation or an iteration count in iterative calculations. In this language, one can summarize the lessons of Volume 1 as:

Large loosely synchronous problems run well on current parallel machines and this success should continue to larger systems.

In Volume 1 we explained in detail the importance of *large* in terms of the minimum value of a *grain size, n*.

Using the notation t_{comm}, t_{calc} defined in Sec. 1-2, we found a typical fractional communication overhead, f_C ;

$$
f_C \sim \frac{\text{constant}}{n^{1/d_s}} \cdot \frac{t_{comm}}{t_{calc}}
\qquad (1.5)
$$

Feature	CrOS III	VMLSCS	More General Systems
(a) Communication synchronous between source and destination	Yes	Yes	Yes
(b) Communication concurrent (i.e., occurs at macroscopic synchronization points)	Yes, but only here	Yes, but only here	Yes
(c) General topologies	Only with *crystal_router* unless hypercube	Yes	Yes
(d) General synchronous communication	No	No	CSP [Hoare 78]
(e) Asynchronous communication	No	No	INTEL, NCUBE and other commercial hypercube systems; *Express* on a variety of distributed memory parallel machines [Parasoft 88a,b,c,d,e]
(f) Multitasking in nodes	No	Yes	Reactive kernel on Caltech and AMETEK hypercubes [Seitz 88] MOOSE [Salmon 88a], [Koller 88a, 88c] *Express*, Linda
(g) Full object-oriented environment	No	No	(Concurrent) Smalltalk [Dally 88]
(h) Efficient portability between hierarchical and distributed memory machines	No	Yes	Typically not available
(i) Shared memory model for messages	No	No	Linda [Whiteside 88] [Dally 88]

Table 1-6 Features of Message Passing Systems.

where d_S measures the system dimension of the problem.

Equation (1.4) divides the loosely synchronous class into two: *synchronous* and *properly loosely synchronous*. Synchronous problems not only satisfy a macroscopic but also a microscopic synchronization condition and map well onto SIMD machines. MIMD architecture computers are appropriate for the full loosely synchronous class, but only the *proper* subset takes complete advantage of the MIMD flexibility.

In Chap. 8, the examples of Secs. 8-3, 8-4, 8-5, 8-6, 8-7, 8-8, 8-13, and 8-14 are synchronous, while those in Secs. 8-10, 8-11, and 8-12 are properly loosely synchronous. In the cases like 8-4 and 8-5, our examples use a regular geometry and are synchronous but would become properly loosely synchronous if the geometry is irregular. In Chap. 9 the applications of Secs. 9-2, 9-4, 9-5, 9-6, and 9-7 are synchronous, and only 9-3 is properly loosely synchronous. The algorithms and codes given in this book easily generalize to irregular geometries using either CrOS III or VMLSCS.

This is not the only possibility of generalizing simplifying features of the codes given in this volume. For instance, the simple time evolution algorithm in Sec. 8-4 illustrates the parallelization issues in many regular Monte Carlo problems such as those discussed in Chap. 13 of Volume 1 and Sec. 9-2 of this volume. Again the long-range particle dynamics method in Sec. 8-6 contains the "essential" parallelization idea for some integral equation problems characterized by a complete interconnect between elements. We finish this section by introducing two tables adapted from Fox [Fox 88b], which reviews many existing parallel applications for a variety of MIMD and SIMD machines. We indicate where in our two volumes to find relevant discussion or whether one needs new ideas not covered here.

1-4.1 Tables 1-7 and 1-8: Parallel Applications

These tables are abstracted from Fox [Fox 88b,89i,n], which gives more detail and also further parallel applications. Fox [Fox 88b] also attempts to give an unbiased survey and interpretation of applications on several parallel machines: hypercubes, the arrays, the Goodyear MPP, Thinking Machines CM-1 and 2, and the ICL DAP. Further information may be found in the Caltech Concurrent Computation Program annual reports [Fox 87b,88v] and in the Proceedings of the first four conferences on Hypercube Concurrent Computers and Applications [Fox 88c], [Gustafson 89a], [Heath 86,87].

Synchronicity Abbreviations

- **S** Synchronous (lockstep)
- **PLS** Loosely synchronous, but not synchronous
- **LS** Typically synchronous if regular geometry, but irregularities in system can make properly loosely synchronous
- **A** Asynchronous
- **A(E-P)** Asynchronous, but "embarrassingly parallel" — different components are executed independently as spatially disconnected

S(E-P) Synchronous, and also "embarrassingly parallel"

Notes on Other Columns

1. Volume 1 is Fox [Fox 88a].
2. "(Alg. only)" implies similar algorithms are discussed in the indicated section of Fox [Fox 88a].
3. Volume 2 is this book.
4. A "Y" in the column labeled "Application Present in HCCA3" indicates that this application is covered in a paper contained in Fox [Fox 88c], the Proceedings of the Third Hypercube Conference held in Pasadena, 19–20 January 1988.

Label	Application	Machine	Researchers	References
A1	Biological neural networks	Hypercube	Bower, Furmanski (Caltech)	[Bower 88b] [Koch 89]
A2	Artificial (applied) "learning" neural networks	Hypercube	Furmanski, Ho, Otto, Koch (Caltech) Joe, Mori (Kyoto) Allen, Saha (MCC) Horvath (JPL) Huntsberger (S. Carolina)	[Ho 88c] [Otto 88] [Joe 89a] [Allen 89a] [Newhall 89a] [Ajjimarangsee 89a]
		MPP	Hastings, Waner (Hofstra)	[Fischer 87]
		CM-1 CM-2	Blelloch (MIT) Rogers (NASA, Ames) TMC Staff	[Blelloch 87b] [Rogers 89] [Waltz 88]
A3	Early vision algorithms	Hypercube	Furmanski, Bond, Battiti, Koch (Caltech) Choudhary, Das (Illinois) Celenk, Lim (Ohio) Baek, Teague (Oklahoma) Parikh (S. Conn, Bridgeport) Huntsberger (S. Carolina) Ranka, Sahni (Minnesota)	[Furmanski 88c] [Battiti 88, 89b] [Bond 88b] [Choudhary 89a] [Celenk 89a] [Baek 89a, 89b] [Parikh 89a] [Huntsberger 89a] [Ranka 88]
		Warp Transputer	Wallace, Webb (CMU) Sarnoff Center Edinburgh	[Wallace 88b] [Tinker 88] [Wallace 88a]
		CM-1	Little, Poggio (MIT)	[Little 87] [Waltz 88]
		MPP	Po (North Carolina) Strong (Goddard)	[Fischer 87]
A4	Complex neuron models	Hypercube	Furmanski, Koch (Caltech)	[Fox 87b] [Koch 89]

Table 1-7(a) Nine Parallel Applications in Biology and Machine Intelligence.

Label	Application	Machine	Researchers	References
A5	Higher vision	MPP	Barnden (Indiana)	[Fischer 87]
			Hambrusch (Purdue)	[Hambrusch 88]
		Hypercube	Furmanski,	[Fox 87b]
			Battiti (Caltech)	[Furmanski 88c]
			Willebeek (Cornell)	[Willebeek 88]
			Soh, Huntsberger	[Soh 89a]
			(S. Carolina)	
			Daniel, Teague	[Daniel 89a]
			(Oklahoma)	
		Transputer	Ward, Roberts	[Ward 88, Hey 88b]
			(RSRE,UK)	
		Butterfly	Brown (Rochester)	[Brown 88]
		CM-2	TMC Staff	[Waltz 88, Tucker 88]
A6	Speech recognition	Butterfly	Kimball (BBN)	[Kimball 87]
A7	Medical imaging	Transputer	Norman	[Norman 87]
			(Edinburgh)	[Wallace 88a]
A8	Human genome (Protein sequence analysis)	Hypercube	Furmanski,	[Fox 87b]
			Hood (Caltech)	[Barnes 88a]
			Huntsberger, Soh	[Huntsberger 89b]
			(S. Carolina)	
			Bjornson (Yale)	[Bjornson 89a]
		DAP	Lyall (Edinburgh)	[Lyall 86]
		Transputer	Pawley (Edinburgh)	[Pawley 88, Wallace 88a]
		CM-2	Lander (Harvard)	[Lander 88a,b]
A9	WaTOR — an ecological simulation	Hypercube	Otto (Caltech)	[Fox 88a]

Table 1-7(a) Nine Parallel Applications in Biology and Machine Intelligence (continued).

Label	Application	Machine	Researchers	References
B1	Three- or 4-body chemical reactions	Hypercube	Kuppermann, Hipes (Caltech)	[Hipes 88a] [Hipes 88b] [Cuccaro 88a]
B2	Protein mechanics	Hypercube	Goddard, Ding (Caltech)	[Ding 88a]
B3	Chemical engineering simulation	Hypercube	Morari, Skjellum (Caltech)	[Skjellum 88]
B4	High T_C superconductivity	Hypercube	Ding (Caltech) Barnes (Toronto)	[Fox 87b] [Barnes 88b,c,d]
B5	Molecular electronic structure	Hypercube	Eggers (Buffalo)	[Eggers 89]

Table 1-7(b) Five Parallel Applications in Chemistry and Chemical Engineering.

Label	Application	Machine	Researchers	References
C1	Plasma physics	Hypercube	Liewer (JPL)	[Liewer 88b,e,89a]
			Walker	[Walker 89a]
			(South Carolina)	
			Azari (Cornell)	[Azari 89]
		MPP	Gledhill (Stanford)	[Fischer 87]
			Lin	[Lin 89a,b]
			(SW Research Inst.)	
			Vonhaven (KMS,	[Fischer 87]
			Michigan Tech.)	
C2	Vortex	Hypercube	Leonard (Caltech)	[Leonard 87]
	dynamics			[Catherasoo 87],
				[Harstad 87],[Fox 87b]
			Baden (UCB)	[Baden 87]
C3	Cellular	CM-1	Wolfram (Illinios)	[Wolfram 86]
	automata		Lubachevsky (AT&T)	[Lubachevsky 87]
	for fluids	CM-2	United Technologies	[Egolf 88]
			Boghosian (TMC)	[Boghosian 88]
		Hypercube	Hayot (Ohio State)	[Hayot 87]
			Sturtevant (Caltech)	
		Transputer	Kenway (Edinburgh)	[Wallace 87,88a]
C4	Flux-corrected	Hypercube	Walker (Caltech)	[Walker 88b]
	transport		Montry (SANDIA)	[Gustafson 88]
			Tripathi (Oak Ridge)	[Tripathi 88]
C5	Monte Carlo	MPP	Earl (Maryland)	[Fischer 87]
	transport			
C6	Lagrangian	Hypercube	Williams (Caltech)	[Williams 87]
	fluid dynamics			[Williams 88a,c]
C7	Image	DAP	Forrest (Edinburgh)	[Forrest 87]
	processing by	Transputer	Roweth (Edinburgh)	[Wallace 87]
	neural networks	Hypercube	Thakoor (JPL)	[Sammes 87]
	(See also A3,A5)			
C8	Convolutional	Hypercube	Pollara (JPL)	[Pollara 86]
	decoding			

Table 1-7(c) Fifteen Parallel Applications in Engineering and Applied Science.

Label	Application	Machine	Researchers	References
C9	Computational fluid dynamics (Navier-Stokes, Euler)	Hypercube	Weissbein (Northrop)	[Weissbein 88]
			Bruno (UCSB)	[Bruno 88]
			Chu, Magnus (Northrop)	[Chu 89]
			Ecer (Purdue)	[Ecer 88,89]
			Angus (Northrop)	[Angus 89]
			Williams (Caltech)	[Williams 89b]
			Barszcz (NASA), Chan (UCLA)	[Barszcz 89]
			McDonnell Douglas	[Catherasoo 89]
			Jameson (Princeton)	[Chesshire 89]
			Wu (Michigan)	[Wu 89a]
		CM-2	United Technologies	[Wake 89, Egolf 88]
			Lockheed	[Long 89a,b]
			McDonnell Douglas	[Agarwal 89a,b]
			General Electric	[Braaten 88,89]
			Tomboulian (MassPar, NASA Langley)	[Tomboulian 88]
		MPP	Grosch (Old Dominion)	[Fatoohi 88]
C10	Structural analysis	Hypercube	Lyzenga (JPL)	[Lyzenga 88]
			Gustafson (SANDIA)	[Gustafson 88]
			Malone (GM)	[Malone 87,89a,b]
			Martin (UES)	[Martin 89a]
			Fulton (Georgia)	[Fulton 88]
		Transputer	Cosnuau (ONERA)	[Cosnuau 89]
		Butterfly	O'Neil (BBN)	[O'Neil 87]
		CM-2	United Technologies	[Egolf 88]
			Sandia Livermore	[Cline 89a]
			Farhat, Sobh, Park (Boulder)	[Farhat 89]
C11	E-M fields	Hypercube	Patterson (JPL)	[Calalo 88]
			Barton (INTEL)	[Barton 89a]
		CM-2	United Technologies	[Egolf 88]

Table 1-7(c) Fifteen Parallel Applications in Engineering and Applied Science (continued).

Label	Application	Machine	Researchers	References
C12	Control systems	Hypercube	Gardiner (UCSB)	[Gardiner 88]
C13	Robotics	Hypercube	Jones (Oak Ridge)	[Barhen 87]
				[Jones 88]
		General	Kurdila (Texas A&M)	[Kurdila 89]
C14	Battle and other management tasks (See H14, H15)	Hypercube	Curkendall (JPL)	[Warren 88a] [Gottschalk 87,88a,b] [Meier 89a]
			Glover (Oak Ridge)	[Glover 88]
			Carpenter, Davis (AFIT)	[Carpenter 88]
			Walsh (R&D Ass.)	[Walsh 89]
C15	Dynamical systems, Invariant manifolds	Hypercube	Lorenz, Van de Velde Beigie (Caltech)	[Lorenz 89] [Beigie 89]

Table 1-7(c) Fifteen Parallel Applications in Engineering and Applied Science (continued).

Label	Application	Machine	Researchers	References
D1	Seismic modeling	Hypercube CM-1	Clayton (Caltech) Kao (Houston) Renault (Norway) Baker (Exxon) Fiebrich (TMC)	[Clayton 87,88] [Kao 87] [Renault 88] [Baker 88] [Fricke 87]
D2	Geophysical normal modes	Hypercube	Tanimoto (Caltech)	[Clayton 87]
D3	Simulation of the earth's mantle	Hypercube	Hager (Caltech) Lyzenga (JPL)	[Lyzenga 88] [Gurnis 88]
D4	Large-scale oceanography	MPP Hypercube CM-2	Grosch (Old Dominion) Halpern (JPL) Kolawa (Parasoft) Sato, Schwarztrauber (NCAR)	[Fischer 87] [Fox 87b] [Fox 89p] [Sato 88], [McBryan 89]
D5	Hydrology	MPP	Gurney (Goddard)	[Fischer 87]
D6	Meteorology	MPP CM-2	Suarez (Goddard) Carmichael (Iowa) Truccillo (National Weather Center)	[Fischer 87] [Fischer 87] [Truccillo 89]
D7	LANDSAT data processing	MPP	Ozga (U.S. Dept. Agriculture)	[Fischer 87]
D8	Synthetic aperture radar (SAR)	Hypercube MPP	Aloisio (Italian Space Agency) Childress (TRW) Simoni, Zimmerman (JPL) Ramapriyan (Goddard)	[Aloisio 87,88,89a] Private comm. [Simoni 89a] [Fischer 87]

Table 1-7(d) Thirteen Parallel Applications in Geology and Earth (and Space) Science.

Label	Application	Machine	Researchers	References
D9	Seismic data analysis	Hypercube	Clayton (Caltech) Shell Corp. (Houston) Madisetti (UCB) Addison (Norway)	Private comm. Private comm. [Madisetti 88a] [Addison 88]
D10	Image processing (See also A3, A5 catagories)	Hypercube DAP CM-2	Lee, Groom, Mazer Solomon (JPL) Synnott, Reidel (JPL) Sammur, Hagan (Oklahoma) RSRE, UK MRJ Ltd.	[Groom 88] [Lee 89b] [Synnott 89a] [Sammur 89a] [Merrifield 88] [Opsahl 88]
D11	Reservoir simulation	CM-2	McBryan (Boulder)	[McBryan 89]
D12	Wave motion on offshore structures	—	Sclavounos, Newman (MIT)	[Newman 88]
D13	Optical diffraction simulation	CM-2	Firestone (MRJ Ltd.)	[Firestone 89]

Table 1-7(d) Thirteen Parallel Applications in Geology and Earth (and Space) Science (continued).

Label	Application	Machine	Researchers	References
E1	Lattice gauge theory	DAP Hypercube CM-1/2	Wallace (Edinburgh) Baillie (Caltech) Otto, Flower, Chiu Baillie, Ding, Walker (Caltech) Baillie (Caltech) Brickner, Gupta (Los Alamos)	[Wallace 87] [Baillie 88b] [Brooks 84] [Fox 88a] [Flower 88b] [Chiu 88c] [Walker 88c] [Apostolakis 88c] [Baillie 88g,89g] [Ding 89a,b] [Baillie 88b,d] [Baillie 89e, Brickner 89, Fox 89n]
E2	Coulomb gas	Hypercube	Fucito, Solomon (Caltech)	[Fucito 85]
E3	Liquid-solid phase transitions	Hypercube	Johnson (Caltech)	[Johnson 86]
E4	Liquid molecular dynamics	DAP Butterfly Hypercube CM-2	Pawley (Edinburgh) Pawley (Edinburgh) Salmon (Caltech) Flinn (INTEL) Argonne	[Pawley 84,88] [Pawley 87,88] [Fox 88a] [Flinn 88] [Greenwell 89]
E5	Solid molecular dynamics	DAP	Pawley (Edinburgh)	[Pawley 82]
E6	Structure of low-temperature helium	Hypercube	Callahan (Caltech)	[Callahan 88a]
E7	Ising and related spin models	DAP MPP Transputer Hypercube	Wall (Edinburgh) Suranyi (Cincinnati) Sullivan (NBS) Hey (Southampton) Gupta (Los Alamos)	[Wall 86] [Fischer 87] [Hey 88] [Gupta 88]
E8	Turbulence in Jupiter's red spot	Hypercube	Miller, Cross (Caltech)	[Fox 88v]
E9	Granular physics	Hypercube	Haff, Werner, Gutt (Caltech)	[Werner 88] [Fox 88v] [Gutt 89a] [Fox 89n]

Table 1-7(e) Fourteen Parallel Applications in Physics.

Label	Application	Machine	Researchers	References
E10	Boltzmann equation for fluid flow	MPP	White (Space Telescope)	[Fischer 87]
E11	Percolation	DAP	Dewar (Edinburgh)	[Dewar 87]
E12	Neutron scattering	DAP	Mitchell (Edinburgh)	[Mitchell 85] [Wallace 87]
E13	High-energy physics data analysis	Transputer	Hey (Southampton)	[Glendinning 87] [Hey 88]
E14	Subatomic string dynamics	Hypercube	Baillie (Caltech)	[Fox 89n] [Baillie 89h]

Table 1-7(e) Fourteen Parallel Applications in Physics (continued).

Label	Application	Machine	Researchers	References
F1	Gravitational lensing	Hypercube	Apostolakis (Caltech)	[Apostolakis 88d]
F2	Evolution of the universe, Collision of galaxies	Hypercube CM-1 CM-2	Salmon (Caltech) Cooper, Orcutt (Las Vegas) Barnes, Hut (Princeton) Katzenelson (MIT)	[Warren 88b] [Fox 88a] [Salmon 89a] [Cooper 89] [Hillis 87b] [Barnes 86,89b] [Katzenelson 89]
F3	Astronomical data analysis	Hypercube	Prince (Caltech)	[Gorham 88a,b] [Fox 89n]
F4	Image deconvolution	MPP Hypercube	Heap (Goddard) Yin (Goddard) Prince (Caltech)	[Fischer 87] [Nakajima 89a]
F5	VLBI parameter determination	Hypercube	Patterson (JPL) Henkel (NCSU)	[Patterson 86] [Henkel 88]
F6	Astrophysical fluid dynamics	Hypercube	Meier (JPL)	[Meier 84]

Table 1-7(f) Six Parallel Applications in Astronomy and Astrophysics.

Label	Application	Machine	Researchers	References
G1	Graphics ray tracing	MPP	Dorbard (Goddard)	[Fischer 87]
			Treinish (Goddard)	
		Hypercube	Goldsmith (JPL)	[Goldsmith 88]
			Salmon (Caltech)	[Warren 88a]
			Orcutt (Las Vegas)	[Orcutt 88]
		Transputer	Edinburgh	[Wallace 88a]
		CM-1	Delany (MIT)	[Delany 88]
G2	Computer circuit simulation	Butterfly Alliant	Jacob (UCB)	[Jacob 86]
			Sadayappan (Ohio),	[Sadayappan 88]
			Visvanatha (Bell)	
		Hypercube	Mattisson (Lund),	[Mattisson 86,89]
			Seitz (Caltech)	[Peterson 89]
			Raman (Illinois)	[Raman 89]
			Ozguner (Ohio State)	[Ozguner 88]
		CM-1	Webber (TMC)	[Fiebrich 87a]
		MPP	O'Donnel (Indiana)	[Fischer 87]
G3	Optimizing circuit layout	CM-1	Casotto (UCB)	[Casotto 86]
				[Fiebrich 87b]
		Hypercube	Furmanski (Caltech)	[Fox 88v]
G4	Event-driven simulations	Butterfly Hypercube	Jefferson (UCLA)	[Jefferson 88]
			Wieland (JPL)	[Wieland 88,89a]
			Reynolds (Virginia)	[Sammes 87]
			Madisetti (UCB)	[Madisetti 88b]
			Hartrum (AFIT)	[Hartrum 88]
G5	Compiling	Hypercube	Fox, Koller (Caltech)	[Koller 88b] [Fox 88x]
G6	Full tree search	—	—	—

Table 1-7(g) Eleven Parallel Applications in Computer Science.

Label	Application	Machine	Researchers	References
G7	Computer chess	Hypercube	Felten, Otto (Caltech)	[Felten 88g]
		CM-2	Stiller (Boston)	[Waltz 88]
G8	Distributed artificial intelligence	Hypercube	Bond (UCLA) Gasser (USC) Lamont (AFIT)	[Bond 88a] [Gasser 88] [Lamont 88]
		CM-1	Morgan (GE)	[Morgan 88]
		CM-2	TMC Staff	[Waltz 88]
G9	Document search	CM-1	TMC Staff	[Stanfill 86] [Waltz 87a,88]
G10	Transaction analysis	Hypercube	Frey (IBM)	[Fox 87b]
G11	Full database	Hypercube	Pfaltz (Virginia)	[Pfaltz 88] [Son 88]
			Kolawa (Caltech)	[Kolawa 88a]
		Specialized hardware	Teradata	[Schemer 84]

Table 1-7(g) Eleven Parallel Applications in Computer Science (continued).

Label	Application	Machine	Researchers	References
H1	Full-matrix algorithms (e.g., multiplication, LU decomposition, inversion, eigenvalues, eigenvectors) Penn State, Rutgers, Yale	Hypercube	Workers at Argonne, Austin, Caltech, Cornell, INTEL, Minneapolis, Norway, Oak Ridge,	[Bischof 88,89] [Aldcroft 88] [Furmanski 88b] [Hipes 88a,89a], [Fox 88a],[Van de Velde 89a] [Bojanczyk 89] [Moler 86], [Heath 87b] [Geist 88], [de Pillis 88] [Pothen 88], [Gerasoulis 88] [Johnsson 85,87] [van de Geijn 89a] [Park 89]
		CM-2	Tichy (NASA, Ames)	[Tichy 89]
		MPP	Ida (Akron)	[Fischer 87]
H2	Banded matrix algorithms	Hypercube	Workers at Caltech and Oak Ridge	See above
H3	Sparse-matrix PDE algorithms (e.g., multigrid, domain decomposition, conjugate gradient)	Hypercube	Keller, Van de Velde (Caltech) Almeida (Vanderbilt) Haghoo (USC) Houstis, Rice (Purdue)	[Fox 88a],[Van de Velde 87a,b] [Almeida 88] [Haghoo 88] [Houstis 88], [Mu 89], [Christara 88,89]
			Olesen (Norway) Aykanat (Ohio State) Abe (Japan) Baxter (Yale) Amin (UES) Zhang, Schnabel (Boulder) Brochard (IBM) Vandewalle, Roose (Leuven)	[Olesen 88] [Aykanat 88] [Abe 88] [Baxter 88] [Amin 89] [Zhang 89] [Brochard 89b] [Vandewalle 89]
		MPP CM-1,2	Reif (Duke) McBryan (Boulder) Frederickson (NASA)	[Fischer 87] [McBryan 87,89] [Frederickson 88, 89a,b]
		CM-2	Fonseca (MIT) Tong (UCLA) Saltz (Yale)	[Fonseca 89] [Tong 89] [Berryman 89]

Table 1-7(h) Seventeen General Parallel Algorithms.

Label	Application	Machine	Researchers	References
H4	Tridiagonal matrices (e.g., QR and Cuppen's algorithms)	Hypercube	Fox (Caltech) Egecioglu (UCSB) Cox (Clemson) Ipsen (Yale) Geist (Oak Ridge)	[Fox 84] [Egecioglu 88] [Jackson 88] [Ipsen 87] [Geist 89]
H5	Linear programming (assignment, scheduling)	Butterfly Hypercube	Jeffrey (Harvard) Felten (Caltech) Stunkel (Illinois) Noetzel (Brooklyn) Rosen, Maier (Minnesota) Bailor, Seward (AFIT) Ho (Taiwan)	[Jeffrey 87] Private Comm. [Stunkel 88a,b,89] [Noetzel 89] [Rosen 89] [Bailor 89] [Ho 88k]
		Butterfly CM-2	Sheu (Penn State) Zenios (Wharton)	[Sheu 88] [Zenios 88]
H6	Optimization — branch and bound	Hypercube	Felten (Caltech) Ma (Aerospace) Mudge (Michigan) Schwan (Ohio State) Pargas (Clemson)	[Felten 88c] [Ma 88] [Abdelrahman 88] [Schwan 88] [Pargas 88]
		Butterfly Transputer	Rao (Texas) McBurney (U.K.)	[Rao 87] [McBurney 88]
H7	Optimization — neural networks [Hopfield 86]	Hypercube	Furmanski, Fox (Caltech) Toomarian (Oak Ridge)	[Fox 88e] [Toomarian 88]
		Transputer	Durbin (Edinburgh)	[Durbin 87]
H8	Optimization — simulated annealing	Hypercube	Felten, Karlin, Otto (Caltech) Flower (Caltech) Braschi (Grenoble)	[Felten 85b] [Flower 86] [Braschi 89]
H9	Genetic and other multiple choice search algorithms	Hypercube	Allison (Virginia)	[Allison 88]
		Butterfly	O'Neil (BBN)	[O'Neil 88]
H10	Sorting	Hypercube	Felten, Otto (Caltech) Seidel (Michigan Tech.) Nayudu (Oklahoma)	[Felten 85a] [Fox 88a,b] [Seidel 88] [Nayudu 89]

Table 1-7(h) Seventeen General Parallel Algorithms (continued).

Label	Application	Machine	Researchers	References
H11	Binary fast Fourier transform (FFT)	Hypercube VMLSCS Hypercube Hypercube CM-2 CM-2	Salmon (Caltech) Walker (Caltech) Chu (Northrop) Lin (UCLA) Bershader (MRJ Ltd.) Kamin (Purdue)	[Fox 88a,b] [Walker 88d] [Chu 88] [Lin 88] [Bershader 89a] [Bershader 89b] [Kamin 89]
H12	Nonbinary FFT	Hypercube	Aloisio (Italy) Kim (Caltech) Desbat, Trystram (Grenoble)	[Aloisio 87,88,89b] [Fox 88a] [Desbat 89]
H13	Computational geometry	Hypercube	Miller, Boxer (Buffalo)	[Miller 88], [Boxer 88],
H14	Kalman multitarget filtering	Hypercube Warp	Gottschalk (Caltech) General Dynamics General Electric	[Gottschalk 87] [Gottschalk 88a,b] [Baillie 88f] [Barstad 89a] [O'Hallaron 88]
H15	Assignment	Hypercube	Carpenter, Davis (AFIT) Oak Ridge	[Carpenter 88] [Culioli 89]
H16	Factoring Large Numbers	Hypercube	Holdridge (Sandia)	[Holdridge 89]
H17	Number theory (Fermat's theorem)	CM-1	Frye (TMC)	[Frye 88]

Table 1-7(h) Seventeen General Parallel Algorithms (continued).

Label	Algorithm	Synchr-onicity	Volume 1 Reference	Volume 2 Reference	Application in HCCA3
A1	Circuit simulation	LS	Sec. 22-4	Sec. 9-7	Y
A2	Circuit simulation (complete interconnect)	S	Chap. 9 (alg. only)	Sec. 8-6	Y
A3	Local iteration and neural networks	S	Chaps. 5, 7 (alg. only)	Sec. 9-7	Y
A4	Finite elements	PLS	Chap. 8 (alg. only)	—	N
A5	Neural networks to expert systems	PLS	—	—	N
A6	Signal processing	PLS	—	—	N
A7	Detection of surfaces	A	—	—	N
A8	Database and pattern recognition. Neural nets or traditional AI	S or A	—	—	N
A9	Irregular time simulation	PLS	Chap. 17	Sec. 8-11	N

Table 1-8(a) Nine Parallel Applications in Biology and Machine Intelligence.

Label	Algorithm	Synchr-onicity	Volume 1 Reference	Volume 2 Reference	Application in HCCA3
B1	Multichannel Schrödinger equation Matrix inversion, finite elements	S	Matrix: Sec. 21-5 FEM: Chap. 8	Matrix: similar to Sec. 8-14 FEM: Sec. 8-5 Sec. 9-4	Y
B2	Long-range Monte Carlo	S	Chap. 12, 13	—	Y
B3	Circuit simulation	PLS	Chap. 22 (alg. only)	—	Y
B4	Monte Carlo	S	Chap. 12, 13	Similar to Sec. 9-2	N
B5	Eigenvalue	S	Sec. 21-5	—	N

Table 1-8(b) Five Parallel Applications in Chemistry and Chemical Engineering.

Label	Algorithm	Synchr-onicity	Volume 1 Reference	Volume 2 Reference	Application in HCCA3
C1	Particle-in-cell with PDE and particle evolution	LS	—	Sec. 9-6	Y
C2	Long-range interaction between vortices; $O(N \log N)$ Clustering method possible	S	Chap. 9	Sec. 8-6 Sec. 9-5	Y
C3	Local iteration	S	—	—	N
C4	Finite difference	S	Chap. 7 (alg. only)	Sec. 8-4	Y
C5	Independent particle evolution	S	Chap. 12	—	N
C6	Finite elements with mesh refined on hypercube	PLS	Chap. 8 (alg. only)	Sec. 8-5	Y
C7	Iterative local algorithms	S	—	Sec. 9-7	N
C8	Similar to FFT for Viterbi method	S	Chap. 11 Sec. 23-4 (alg. only)	—	N
C9	Local PDEs	LS	Chap.8 (alg. only)	Sec. 8-4 Sec. 8-5	Y
C10	Finite elements for PDE	LS	Chap. 8	Sec. 8-5	Y
C11	Finite difference,element evolution Full matrix algebra (Green's Function)	LS	Chap. 7,8 (alg. only) Chap. 20	Sec. 8-4 Sec. 8-5	Y
C12	Nonlinear matrix solution	PLS	—	—	Y
C13	See A3, C10, C12	PLS	—	—	Y
C14	Asynchronous control algorithms such as H14, H15	A	—	—	Y
C15	Surfaces from PDE Solution	LS	Chap. 20	Sec. 8-14	N

Table 1-8(c) Fifteen Parallel Applications in Engineering and Applied Science.

Label	Algorithm	Synchr- onicity	Volume 1 Reference	Volume 2 Reference	Application in HCCA3
D1	Finite difference or ray tracing	S	Chap. 7	Sec. 8-3,4	Y
D2	Independent calculation of modes	S(E-P)	—	—	N
D3	Finite elements	LS	Chap. 8	Sec. 8-5	Y
D4	Finite difference	LS	Chap. 7 (alg. only)	Sec. 8-4	N
D5	Finite difference	LS	Chap. 7 (alg. only)	Sec. 8-4	N
D6	Finite difference	LS	Chap. 7 (alg. only)	Sec. 8-4	N
D7	Independent classification of pixels	S(E-P)	—	—	N
D8	FFT	S	Chap. 11	Sec. 8-8	Y
D9	Finite difference	PLS	—	—	Y
D10	Local and nonlocal FFT convolutions	S	Chaps. 3, 11 (FFT alg. only)	Sec. 8-8	Y
D11	Finite elements	LS	Chap. 8 (alg. only)	Sec. 8-5	N
D12	Integral equation linking nodes of finite element grid	S	Chap. 9 (alg. only)	Sec. 8-6	N
D13	Independent Rays	S(E-P)	—	—	N

Table 1-8(d) Thirteen Parallel Applications in Geology and Earth (and Space) Science.

Label	Algorithm	Synchr-onicity	Volume 1 Reference	Volume 2 Reference	Application in HCCA3
E1	Monte Carlo on a regular lattice	S	Chap. 13	Sec. 9-2	Y
E2	Long-range Monte Carlo	S	Chap. 13	—	N
E3	Monte Carlo of an irregular 2-D or 3-D system	PLS	Chap. 13	—	N
E4	Time evolution of an irregular system of particles	PLS	Chap. 16	Sec. 8-10	Y
E5	Time evolution of a regular system of particles	S	Chap. 16	Sec. 8-10	N
E6	Irregular Monte Carlo	PLS	Chap. 12	—	Y
E7	Local Monte Carlo on single-bit or continuous variables in a regular 2-D or 3-D lattice	S	Chap. 13 (alg. only)	—	Y
E8	See C2	PLS	Chap. 12	—	N
E9	Evolution of sand grains under wind, gravity, and mutual contact	PLS	Chap. 16 (alg. only)	—	Y
E10	Local update in phase space	S	—	—	N
E11	Neural network type of algorithm	PLS	—	—	N
E12	Independent convolution of theory with experimental resolution	S(E-P)	—	—	N
E13	Indepedent analysis of events on separate nodes	A(E-P)	—	—	Y
E14	Independent Monte Carlo of Random Surfaces	A(E-P)	—	—	N

Table 1-8(e) Fourteen Parallel Applications in Physics.

Label	Algorithm	Synchr-onicity	Volume 1 Reference	Volume 2 Reference	Application in HCCA3
F1	Independent calculation and storage in large database	A(E-P)	—	—	Y
F2	Particle dynamics solved by FFT or O($N \log N$) clustering	LS	Chap. 11 Sec. 9-5	Sec. 8-8	Y
F3	Multiple binary FFT	S	Chap. 11	Sec. 8-8	Y
F4	Pattern recognition, perhaps neural networks	PLS	—	Sec. 9-7	N
F5	Matrix (Householder)	S	Sec. 21-5	—	Y
F6	Finite difference, or elements, with plasma effects	LS	Chap. 7 (alg. only)	Sec. 8-4	N

Table 1-8(f) Six Parallel Applications in Astronomy and Astrophysics.

Label	Algorithm	Synchron-icity	Volume 1 Reference	Volume 2 Reference	Application in HCCA3
G1	Independent rays traversing distributed database	A(E-P)	—	—	Y
G2	Circuit simulation	LS	Sec. 22-3	—	Y
G3	Simulated annealing or neural networks	LS	Chap. 13	—	N
G4	Independent connected time lines for distributed simulation	A	—	—	Y
G5	Conventional compilers hard to parallelize; neural networks or simulated annealing easier	A or PLS	— —	— —	N
G6	Independent search of leaves of tree	S(E-P)	—	—	N
G7	Irregular dynamic tree search	A	—	—	Y
G8	Traditional AI; agents, expert systems	A	—	—	Y
G9	Synchronous matching of phrases to many independent documents	S(E-P)	—	—	N
G10	Distributed database; irregular access by independent users	A(E-P)	—	—	Y
G11	Asychronous control of reading and writing	A	—	—	Y

Table 1-8(g) Eleven Parallel Applications in Computer Science.

Label	Algorithm	Synchr-onicity	Volume 1 Reference	Volume 2 Reference	Application in HCCA3
H1	Full-matrix algorithms	S	Chaps. 10, 20 Sec. 21-5	Sec. 8-7, 8-14 Sec. 9-4	Y
H2	Banded-matrix algorithms	S	Chap. 20	Sec. 8-14	Y
H3	Sparse-matrix PDE algorithms	LS	Chap. 8 Sec. 8-7	Sec. 8-5	Y
H4	Tridiagonal-matrix algorithms	S	Sec. 21-5	—	Y
H5	Linear programming	S	—	—	Y
H6	Optimization — branch and bound	A	—	—	Y
H7	Optimization — neural networks	S	—	Sec. 9-7	Y
H8	Optimization — simulated annealing	LS	Chap. 13	—	Y
H9	Genetic and other multiple-search algorithms	A(E-P)	—	—	Y
H10	Sorting	PLS	Chap. 18	—	Y
H11	Binary fast Fourier transform	S	Chap. 11	Sec. 8-8	Y
H12	Nonbinary FFT	PLS	Sec. 22-3	—	Y
H13	Computational geometry	PLS	—	—	Y
H14	Kalman multitarget filtering	PLS	Sec. 22-2	Sec. 9-3	Y
H15	Assignment	LS	Chap. 13 (alg. only)	—	Y
H16	Quadratic sieve	A(E-P)	—	—	N
H17	Tree search	S(E-P)	—	—	N

Table 1-8(h) Seventeen General Parallel Applications.

2

Communication Environments

2-1 General Remarks

In this chapter three related communication environments for concurrent multiprocessors will be described. The first of these is CrOS III, which has been dealt with at length in Volume 1. CrOS III is a synchronous communication environment for homogeneous hypercubes and for types of computer capable of emulating the hypercube topology. An overview of the CrOS III environment is given in Sec. 2-2, and Chap. 3 describes its implementation on a number of hypercubes and on the BBN Butterfly. The software available with this book (see Appendices A and B for details), and described in Chaps. 8 and 9, is written using CrOS III routines and makes use of the CUBIX I/O system reviewed in Chap. 4.

CrOS III and its extensions (see Chap. 5) provides an adequate environment for homogeneous hypercubes, but in general cannot be implemented efficiently on multiprocessors, such as shared memory machines, which have hierarchical memories. Section 2-3 describes the Virtual Machine Loosely Synchronous Communication System (VMLSCS). This is a loosely synchronous, object-oriented communication environment for MIMD multiprocessors which allows applications to be ported between different types of MIMD multiprocessors without sacrificing performance.

The third communication environment discussed in this chapter is the *Express* system produced by Parasoft. *Express* is a general, asynchronous, buffered communication system for homogeneous multiprocessors, which contains CrOS III and CUBIX as a subset.

2-2 An Overview of the CrOS III Communication System

2-2.1 Blocking and Loose Synchronicity

CrOS III is a crystalline communication system for passing messages between the nodes of a concurrent computer. Here the term "crystalline" is synonymous with "synchronous," since when a message is sent from one processor to one or more other processors, all the processors involved must anticipate the communication. Thus, when a processor sends a message by executing a call to a *write* routine, the destination processor(s) must be prepared to receive it by calling a *read* routine. These *write* and *read* routines for sending and receiving messages constitute the communication primitives of any message-passing system, and their CrOS III specifications will be presented in Sec. 2-2.3.

An important characteristic of CrOS III is that all communication is blocking. This means that when a processor sends a message, it will not continue execution until all the message has been received by the destination processor. Similarly, when a processor calls a *read* routine to receive a message, it will wait until a message is received before continuing execution. Thus, in CrOS III two processors are synchronized when they communicate. Blocking communication permits the occurrence of deadlock, which occurs when calls to send and receive messages are not properly matched. For example, if a processor writes a message for which there is no corresponding read in the destination processor, then that processor will deadlock (or "hang"), since it cannot continue execution until the destination processor reads the message. Conversely, if a processor makes a call to read a message which is never sent, deadlock will also occur. In CrOS III the occurrence of deadlock is usually due to a programming error, since it is the responsibility of the user to ensure that the exchange of messages is performed using correctly matched read and write routines in the destination and source processors.

As mentioned in Sec. 1-4, loosely synchronous problems are characterized by calculation interspersed with need-predictable communication phases. The communication synchronizes the processors; however, between successive communication phases the individual processors can execute completely asynchronously. Since CrOS III is a synchronous communication system, it can be used to perform the communication in loosely synchronous problems. A large class of problems of interest to scientists and engineers are loosely synchronous in nature, and all the applications in Chap. 8 fall into this class. It should be noted that loosely synchronous problems do not require a general-purpose asynchronous communication system. In fact, a simple crystalline system such as CrOS III may be preferable since it generally entails less overhead and is therefore more efficient.

2-2.2 The CrOS III Programming Model

In the CrOS III programming model we assume there is a control processor (CP) and a set of node processors. The CP performs two main tasks:

1. To download the program to be executed to the node processors and initiate its execution. This is done using one of the family of *cubeld* routines described in detail in Appendix E of Volume 1.
2. To mediate I/O between the nodes and the "outside world" (disks, printers, terminals, etc.).

The CP may also play a role in the computation itself, although in our experience we have found that it is generally more efficient to perform all calculations on the node processors. Since the processing power of the CP is usually no greater than that of the individual nodes, it is generally best to perform inherently sequential portions of an algorithm on all node processors rather than to waste time performing the communication between the CP and node processors necessary to perform the calculation on the CP. The realization that the CP need not play any computational role has led to the development of the CUBIX I/O system, which will be discussed in more detail in Chap. 4 and is also described in

Chaps. 6 and 15 of Volume 1. CUBIX consists of two parts: (1) a general-purpose CP program that downloads the node program and acts as a server for I/O requests made by the nodes and (2) a set of routines and/or language constructs for use in the node program to make I/O requests to the server running on the CP.

In most cases it is more convenient to use the CUBIX CP program, and this is recommended. Most of the examples in Chap. 8 make use of CUBIX. If for some reason the use of CUBIX is not appropriate, the user must write his or her own CP program in addition to the node program. An example of a user-written CP program is given in Sec. 8-3, and C and Fortran versions of the code are listed in Appendices A and B.

2-2.3 CrOS III Communication Primitives

The CrOS III communication primitives have been discussed in detail in Sec. 14-3 of Volume 1, and full specifications are given in the CrOS III manual pages that make up Appendix E of Volume 1. However, for clarity we will describe here their important features.

CrOS III is implemented in terms of two pairs of communication primitives. The first pair, *cread* and *cwrite*, exchange a message consisting of a number of contiguous data items. In the case of the second pair, *vread* and *vwrite*, the message consists of data items spaced at regular intervals in computer memory. The calling syntax of *cwrite* and *cread* is given in Code 2-1 and Code 2-2, respectively, for the C programming language. The syntax for the Fortran equivalents is very similar and is given explicitly in Appendix E of Volume 1.

The communication channels on which messages are written and read are specified in CrOS III by means of channel masks. A processor's communication channels are numbered 0, 1, 2, ..., and so on. A channel mask is a binary number in which the ith bit is set to 1 if channel number i is specified and is zero otherwise. For example, if we wish to specify channels 0, 2, and 3, the binary representation of the channel mask is 1101, corresponding to a value of 13.

When *cwrite* is called a message consisting of the *nbytes* bytes of contiguous memory starting at the location pointed to by *buffer* is sent out on the communication channels specified in the channel mask *out_mask*. The value returned by *cwrite* is the number of bytes sent or, if an error occurs, a negative error code.

The routine *cread* reads a message from the communication channel specified by the channel mask *in_mask* and stores it in memory at the location pointed to by *buffer*. No more than *max_bytes* bytes are stored in *buffer*, and if the message is longer than this, the extra bytes are discarded and *cread* returns a negative value to indicate an error. Otherwise the actual number of bytes read is returned. The channel mask *out_mask* specifies the communication channels on which the message is to be forwarded. If *out_mask* is zero the message is not forwarded.

The calling syntax for *vwrite* and *vread* is given in Codes 2-3 and 2-4, respectively, and is similar to that of *cwrite* and *cread*. The message sent by *vwrite*

```
int cwrite ( buffer, out_mask, nbytes )
char *buffer;     /* pointer to storage for message          */
int out_mask;     /* mask specifying destination processors   */
int nbytes;       /* length of message in bytes               */
```

Code 2-1 The routine *cwrite*.

```
int cread ( buffer, in_mask, out_mask, max_bytes )
char *buffer;     /* pointer to storage for message          */
int in_mask;      /* mask specifying source processor         */
int out_mask;     /* mask specifying processors to forward to */
int max_bytes;    /* maximum length of message in bytes       */
```

Code 2-2 The routine *cread*.

consists of *nitems* data items, each *size* bytes in length. The first item is located at the position pointed to by *buffer*. The start of the second item is offset by *offset* bytes from the start of the first item. Similarly, subsequent data items are also offset by *offset* bytes from the start of the previous item.

The routine *vread* reads the message on the communication channel specified by the channel mask *in_mask* and stores it with a format similar to that used by *vwrite*. Like *cread*, *vread* can also forward messages on the communication channels specified by *out_mask*.

The last of the CrOS III communication primitives is the routine *rdstat*, shown in Code 2-5. This routine checks the channels specified by *mask* and returns a value of 1 if all channels are ready to receive data, or 0 if this is not the case. A negative integer is returned in the event of an error. The routine *rdstat* is useful for determining whether a message is ready to be received on a particular channel without actually having to read and store it.

2-2.4 CrOS III Collective Communication Routines

All communication between the control processor and the node processors, and between the node processors themselves, can be performed using the two pairs of communication primitives described in Sec. 2-2.3. However, there are a number of common communication tasks which are most conveniently performed as a single unit. CrOS III therefore includes a set of *collective communication routines*. The reader is referred to Chap. 14 and Appendix E of Volume 1 for a full discussion. Here we will mention only briefly the most useful of the collective communication routines.

We will first review the routines for performing collective communication between the node processors. The routine *cshift* allows a processor to send a message out on a set of communication channels, while at the same time receiving a message on a single channel. Thus, *cshift* can be thought of as a call to *cwrite* to send the outgoing message, followed by a call to *cread* to receive the incoming

```
int vwrite ( buffer, out_mask, size, offset, nitems )
char *buffer;     /* pointer to storage for message          */
int out_mask;     /* mask specifying destination processors  */
int size;         /* the size of each data item in bytes     */
int offset;       /* the offset in bytes between data items   */
int nitems;       /* the number of data items                */
```

Code 2-3 The routine *vwrite*.

```
int vread ( buffer, in_mask, out_mask, size, offset, max_items )
char *buffer;     /* pointer to storage for message          */
int in_mask;      /* mask specifying source processor        */
int out_mask;     /* mask specifying processors to forward to */
int size;         /* size of each data item in bytes         */
int offset;       /* offset in bytes between data items       */
int max_items;    /* maximum number of data items            */
```

Code 2-4 The routine *vread*.

```
int rdstat ( mask )
int mask;   /* channel mask specifying channels to be checked */
```

Code 2-5 The routine *rdstat*.

message. As explained in Sec. 14-5.1 of Volume 1, because of the possibility of deadlock, the actual implementation of *cshift* is rather more complicated than this.

The routine *vshift* is similar to *cshift*, except that the message consists of data items regularly spaced in memory rather than being contiguous. Conceptually *vshift* is equivalent to a call to *vwrite* followed by a call to *vread*.

The routine *broadcast* is another important collective communication routine that sends a message from a source processor to a set of other processors. The destination processors are specified by means of a channel mask, and the message is sent to all processors connected by the channels specified in the mask. For the hypercube topology, the destination processors make up a subcube whose dimension equals the number of channels specified in the mask, as shown by the examples in Fig. 2-1.

The *combine* routine takes a data item from each of the node processors and combines them in a pairwise manner using a commutative and associative function supplied by the user. The result is returned to all nodes. Thus, if $a(i)$ denotes the data item in processor i, and the combining function is $\oplus$, the *combine* routine evaluates

$$b = a(0) \oplus a(1) \oplus a(2) \oplus \cdots \oplus a(N_p - 1) \qquad (2.1)$$

where N_p is the number of processors.

Routines for performing collective communication between the control processor and the node processors will now be discussed. These consist of pairs

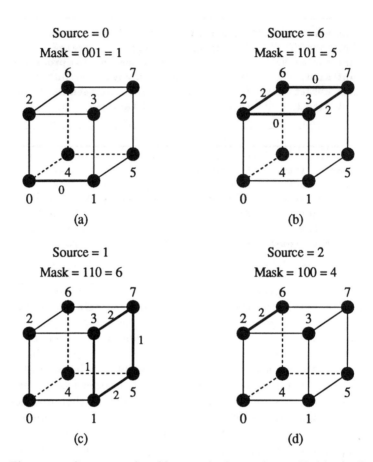

Figure 2-1 Some examples of how a subcube can be specified in a call to *broadcast* by giving the number of the source processor and a channel mask. In each case the subcube involved in the broadcast is shown by thick solid lines.

of routines, one of which is called on the control processor and the other on the node processors. For historical reasons the control processor routines generally have the suffix "cp," and the node processor routines the suffix "elt." These routines are only for use in a non–CUBIX environment.

The *bcastcp/bcastelt* pair of routines permit a common message to be sent from the control processor to all the node processors. If a different message is to be sent from the control processor to each of the node processors, then the *mloadcp/loadelt* pair of routines may be used. The converse function of sending a unique message from each of the node processors to the control processor is performed by the *mdumpcp/dumpelt* routines. Quite often we wish to perform a combine operation over all the node processors and send the result to the control process. This may be done using the *combcp/combelt* pair of routines.

The total size of the data sets input and output by the node processors often exceeds the memory limits of the control processor. CrOS III therefore provides routines for exchange data between the control processor's file system and the node processors. Data may be loaded from a file into the nodes by calling *floadcp* and may be written to a file using *fdumpcp*. The complementary routines that must be run on the node processors are *loadelt* and *dumpelt*, respectively.

2-3 Portable Programming for Inhomogeneous Multiprocessors

2-3.1 The Need for VMLSCS

The success of civilization spawned many nations with the strengths of diversity and the weaknesses symbolized by the tower of Babel. The success of parallel processing has produced a Babel of architectures and an even greater diversity and inconsistency of user environments. We expect the number of parallel architectures offered commercially to increase in the near future as the market expands and new ideas or refinements of old ideas struggle for market share. We need to protect the application programmer from unnecessary burdens stemming from this diversity. We may have learned that "parallel processing works" and persuaded many leading computational scientists to use parallel machines. However, it is only reasonable to expect each user to develop perhaps one parallel code, and certainly not to recode it for each new parallel machine. Thus we believe it is essential to develop portable environments that allow a user code to be moved between machines without a major sacrifice in performance.

CrOS III was developed historically as an optimized environment for hypercube multicomputers. It is not an appropriate portable system as it unnecessarily reflects details of the hypercube topology. In Volume 1, we have proposed VMLSCS as a possible portable environment for distributed and shared memory MIMD parallel computers. In a perfect world with no historical constraints, both volumes should have perhaps used VMLSCS throughout and not just in Chaps. 4 and 22. However, VMLSCS supports the same *loosely synchronous* problem class as CrOS III and is a superset of it. Thus, one can easily either convert CrOS III programs into VMLSCS or less efficiently implement CrOS III on top of a native VMLSCS.

The essential features of the programming model supported by VMLSCS are given in Table 1-6 and are summarized in a different form as follows:

- Explicit message passing occurs between coarse grain processes.
- Synchronous communication is initiated and completed at globally macroscopic synchronization points.
- Source and destination for messages are arbitrary.
- Communication and calculation can be overlapped.

VMLSCS is not *the* portable programming environment but rather one specialized to the special (but numerous) problems satisfying the loose synchronization condition. As discussed in Chap. 22 of Volume 1, it can be implemented in terms of an underlying synchronous or asynchronous message delivery and buffering system.

VMLSCS not only supports distributed memory systems and shared memory emulating (or restricted to) distributed memory, but also hierarchical memory. As described in Fox [Fox 87c] and Walker [Walker 88d,e], one can exploit a natural analogy between hierarchical memory (minimize cache misses or paging) and distributed memory (minimize communication).

2-3.2 Description of VMLSCS

VMLSCS is based on a loosely synchronous, object–oriented, message-passing programming paradigm in which processes cooperating on a common task communicate during loosely synchronous communication phases, but otherwise run independently. The fact that VMLSCS deals with *processes* rather than *processors* implies some form of multitasking on the node processors. Implementing this strongly machine-dependent aspect of VMLSCS in many cases represents a formidable task. However, we believe that VMLSCS can be efficiently implemented on a broad range of MIMD concurrent architectures, provided that the amount of computation performed by each process per context switch is sufficiently large. In the nomenclature of Volume 1, VMLSCS will work efficiently if the granule size of each process is sufficiently large. The maximum permitted granule size is determined by the nature of the problem and by the machine hardware. For a homogeneous hypercube, such as the NCUBE/10, the hardware limit on the granule size is just the maximum amount of memory available on each node processor. In this case we need only one process per processor. For inhomogeneous hypercubes, such as the Caltech/JPL Mark IIIfp and shared memory machines with cache, the relevant hardware limit on granule size is the capacity of the cache. In such cases more than one process will reside on each processor.

In this section we will concentrate on the specifications of the VMLSCS environment and will consider the implementation of the multitasking system necessary to manage the VMLSCS processes. A discussion of the implementation of VMLSCS on shared memory multiprocessors, and on the Caltech/JPL Mark IIIfp hypercube, is given in Walker [Walker 88e]. In general, communication between processes can be regarded as being handled by having a separate child process, called the VM process (VMP), running in each process, the purpose of which is to communicate messages between the parent processes. Communication is always performed in nonblocking mode so there is no possibility of deadlock. Each loosely synchronous phase may be divided into two stages. In the first stage processors pass read and write requests to their associated VMP and perform calculation and I/O. These communication requests are not, in general, serviced immediately, but instead are deferred until the second part of the cycle when messages are actually exchanged. On some advanced architecture machines calculation can be overlapped with communication in the second stage of the cycle, allowing a more efficient use of the hardware. The VMLSCS communication routines can be divided into three sets:

1. Initialization, setup, and overall control.
2. Basic message passing.
3. Collective communication.

We describe these in the following three subsections which use a slight evolution of the nomenclature introduced in Chap. 22 of Volume 1.

2-3.2.1 Initialization, Setup, and Overall Control

A part of a typical VMLSCS application program is shown schematically in Fig. 2-2, in which it is assumed that the problem has already been decomposed into processes, each of which has been assigned a unique ID number. The program represented in Fig. 2-2 should be regarded as running in each process, and all the routines shown in shaded boxes are called loosely synchronously in all processes.

All processes first call the routine *vm_setup* that takes as its only input the character string *options*. The *options* string contains machine-dependent information and other details, such as the size of each VMPs communication buffer. The routine *vm_exit* has functionality similar to the UNIX *exit* routine and ensures that all processes terminate correctly, returning a status integer to their parent process. The calling syntax of *vm_setup* and *vm_exit* is given in Code 2-6.

After calling *vm_setup* the routine *vm_init* must next be called with loose synchrony in all processes to initialize the VMPs in each process. If an error occurs, then *vm_init* returns a negative error code; otherwise the total number of processes is returned. The routine *vm_kill*, when called loosely synchronously, terminates all VMPs, and releases their resources to the system.

```
int vm_setup ( options )
char options[256];   /* options string */

void vm_exit ( status )
int status;          /* exit status */

int vm_init ( )

int vm_kill ( )
```

Code 2-6 The routines *vm_setup*, *vm_exit*, *vm_init*, and *vm_kill*.

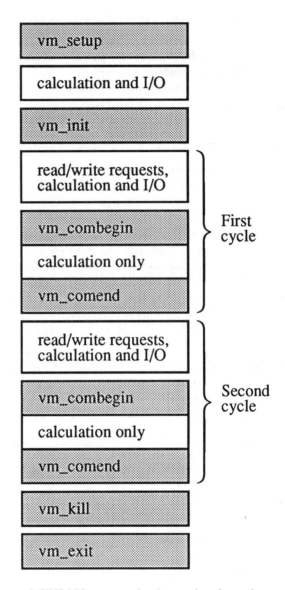

Figure 2-2 An example VMLSCS program showing two loosely synchronous cycles. The calls shown in shaded boxes must be performed loosely synchronously.

2-3.2.2 Basic Message Passing

Once *vm_init* has been called, processes can begin to exchange messages. Messages have four characteristics — length, type, destination, and source — and may be read and written in nonblocking mode using the routines *vm_read* and *vm_write*. If necessary, messages can be sent in blocking mode using the routine *vm_transfer* described later.

A write request can either be serviced in buffered or unbuffered mode. In buffered mode the message is copied to a communication buffer, set up during the call to *vm_init*, and is subsequently sent to its destination during the communication phase. In unbuffered mode a pointer to the message is stored in a special array, called the *write array*, together with other information characterizing the message. The write array is also set up by the earlier call to *vm_init*. The most efficient way of writing messages is determined by the machine architecture and message-passing system, so the write mode (buffered or unbuffered) is specified in the *options* string of *vm_setup*. For example, if messages are passed by a DMA mechanism, then unbuffered mode is appropriate, whereas on packetizing machines, buffered mode may be best. The Mark IIIfp hypercube has a special communications processor (see Sec. 3-2) that can perform the necessary memory-to-memory copies while the Weitek processor is performing calculations, so unbuffered mode is particularly advantageous on the Mark IIIfp. It should be noted that if unbuffered mode is used, then it is possible for a message to be corrupted by the user overwriting its storage location before the write request is serviced. Thus portability issues arise, and it is possible for a program that works when writing in buffered mode to fail in unbuffered mode.

Write requests are made by calling *vm_write*, which is specified in Code 2-7. The first argument, *buf*, is a pointer to the start of the message. The ID number of the destination process is given by *dest_id*, the message type is *mtype*, and the length of the message is *nbytes* bytes. If an error occurs in *vm_write* a negative error code is returned; otherwise the number of bytes in the message is returned.

```
int vm_write ( buf, dest_id, nbytes, mtype )
char *buf;        /* pointer to start of message      */
int dest_id;      /* ID number of destination process */
int nbytes;       /* length of message in bytes       */
int mtype;        /* message type                     */
```

Code 2-7 The routine *vm_write*.

Read requests can be of two types: queued and nonqueued. If a read request is queued, details of the process ID — message type, maximum message length, and the location at which the message is to be stored if and when it arrives — are copied to a special array, called the *read queue*. This array is allocated in the previous call to *vm_init*. During the next communication cycle the messages received are checked to see if they correspond to any of the queued read requests, and if a match is found, the message is copied to the storage location given by the corresponding entry in the read array. The read array is overwritten during successive communication cycles, so read requests queued in one cycle are destroyed at the start of the next cycle.

A read request made in nonqueued mode checks if any unread messages of a specific type and source process have been received in a previous communication cycle. If such a message is found it is copied to the appropriate location.

Read requests are made by calling the routine *vm_read*, which is shown in Code 2-8. The routine *vm_read* requests a message from source process *source_id* of message type *mtype*, and of maximum length *max_bytes* bytes. When the message is read it is stored at location *buf*. In queued mode the actual length of the message is stored at the location pointed to by *len_ptr*, unless no corresponding message is received in the next communication cycle, in which case the value stored at *len_ptr* is the macro value NONE. In nonqueued mode *vm_read* returns the length of the message, or the macro NONE if no message matches the specifications. In nonqueued mode *len_ptr* is irrelevant. If *flag* is 1, the message is read in queued mode; if *flag* is 2, an attempt is made to read the message in nonqueued mode, but if no valid message has been received, the read request is switched to queued mode; finally, if *flag* is 3, the read is performed in nonqueued mode. If an error is encountered in *vm_read*, a negative error code is returned.

```
int vm_read ( buf, source_id, max_bytes, mtype, flag, len_ptr )
char *buf;          /* pointer to storage for message       */
int source_id;      /* ID number of source process          */
int max_bytes;      /* maximum length of message in bytes */
int mtype;          /* message type                         */
int flag;           /* queued=1, Q-switch=2, nonqueued=3  */
int *len_ptr;       /* pointer to message length            */
```

Code 2-8 The routine *vm_read*.

The routine *vm_query* can be used to check whether a message of a given type has been received from a specified process. As shown in Code 2-9, the arguments to *vm_query* are pointers to integers specifying the source processor ID and message type, either or both of which may have a "wild card" value to indicate that any value for the corresponding quantity is acceptable. If an unread message satisfying the source process ID and message type constraints has been received in a previous communication cycle, then the actual source process ID and message type are stored at the locations pointed to by the routine's arguments. If an error occurs in *vm_query*, a negative error code is returned. Otherwise if no valid message has been received, the value NONE is returned, and if there is a valid message, its length in bytes is returned.

The actual exchange of messages between processes is initiated by the routine *vm_combegin*, which must be called loosely synchronously by all processes. If an error occurs in *vm_combegin*, a negative error code is returned; otherwise

```
int vm_query ( source_ptr, mtype_ptr )
int *source_ptr;    /* pointer to desired source process ID */
int *mtype_ptr;     /* pointer to desired message type      */
```

Code 2-9 The routine *vm_query*.

0 is returned. The routine *vm_comend* ensures that all messages have been delivered to their destination processes. The routine *vm_comend* must also be called loosely synchronously and blocks further execution until all communication has been completed. No communication calls may be made between a call to *vm_combegin* and the corresponding call to *vm_comend*. In addition no I/O may be performed since on many machines this implicitly involves communication. Thus only calculation is permitted between calls to *vm_combegin* and *vm_comend*, shown in Code 2-10.

```
int vm_combegin ( cmask )
int cmask;  /* channel mask (only for hypercubes ) */

int vm_comend ( )
```

Code 2-10 The routines *vm_combegin* and *vm_comend*.

In *vm_combegin* the value of *cmask* is only relevant on hypercubes that actually perform the requested communication by means of the *crystal_router* algorithm (see Sec. 5-4). In such cases *cmask* is the channel mask specifying which channels will be used in the *crystal_router*. Thus, if it is known a priori that only a few of the available channels are needed to do the requested communication, unnecessary overhead can be avoided.

2-3.2.3 VMLSCS Collective Communication Routines

In addition to the read and write primitives VMLSCS also supports a set of collective communication routines which are essentially identical to the node-based CrOS III collective communication routines reviewed in Sec. 2-2.4, that is, *vm_shift*, *vm_broadcast*, and *vm_combine*. The VMLSCS routines, of course, communicate between processes rather than processors. VMLSCS includes two additional routines. The routine *vm_transfer* sends a message from one process to another. The routine *vm_index* takes an array of data items in each process and redistributes them so that the jth item in process number i is exchanged with the ith item of process j. The VMLSCS collective communication routines may be regarded as special versions of the routine *vm_combegin* for performing particular communication tasks. As with *vm_combegin*, each of the collective communication routines must be called in loose synchrony in all processes and initiates the exchange of messages between processes. After initiating communication the routines return, thereby allowing communication to be overlapped with calculation on certain machines. A subsequent loosely synchronous call to the routine *vm_comend* ensures that all communication has been completed. As we become more familiar with the use of VMLSCS, we expect additional collective communication routines to be added at a later date.

In VMLSCS I/O is performed according to the CUBIX model, described in Chap. 4. At the user level CUBIX is identical in VMLSCS and CrOS III.

2-4 Portable Programming for Homogeneous Multiprocessors

2-4.1 An Overview of the *Express* Communication Environment

Express is a flexible communication environment produced by Parasoft for homogeneous MIMD multiprocessors. In this section we will describe the main features of *Express*; a full description may be found in the *Express* manual [Parasoft 88a].

The *Express* environment is made up of three layers. The lowest level provides support for allocating processors, loading programs, and asynchronous message passing between arbitrary nodes. At a higher level are utilities to aid in the decomposition of problems with regular structure, and routines for communicating among the nodes and between the nodes and the control processor (CP). At this level CrOS III is available as a subset of the *Express* environment, however, *Express* permits communication between any two processors, thereby allowing the user to ignore the underlying topology of the hardware. At the highest level is a complete I/O system allowing parallel node programs uniform access to the operating system facilities of the CP. This I/O system incorporates the CUBIX system reviewed in Chap. 4 and discussed in detail in Chaps. 6 and 15 of Volume 1. Thus both CUBIX and non–CUBIX CrOS III programs will run in the *Express* environment. In fact, at Caltech several of the codes in Chap. 8 have been run without modification on a Definicon transputer array running *Express* (see Sec. 7-2.2). The only parts of CrOS III that *Express* does not currently support are some of the extensions to CrOS III presented in Chap. 5.

Each of the levels just described is logically distinct and builds only on those below it. The flexibility of *Express* allows an application to make use of the level most suited to its needs. Thus, most of the loosely synchronous applications in Chap. 8 would make use of the highest level, whereas applications such as computer chess [Felten 88g], which require asynchronous communication, would use the lowest level.

2-4.2 Processor Allocation and Program Loading

Express provides high-level routines for loading programs from the CP into the nodes which are very similar to the *cubeld* family of routines in CrOS III (see Appendix E of Volume 1). However, *Express* also provides a set of allocation and loading routines at a much lower level for applications that need special control over system resources. These routines allow a single CP program to access multiple groups of nodes, or for multiple CP programs to share access to a single group of nodes.

A *processor group* is a collection of nodes specified by a call to the routine *pgopen*, shown in Code 2-11. The value returned by *pgopen* is the *processor group index* which may be used subsequently to indicate the particular set of nodes to which an operation should apply. The routine *pgopen* causes *nnodes* nodes to be allocated on the device indicated by the first argument. The last argument, *start_node*, specifies exactly which nodes are required. This feature is useful in allowing applications built around custom-designed networks to place certain applications physically on certain nodes. The macro value DONTCARE may be used to indicate no interest in the physical placement of the program.

```
int pgopen ( device, nnodes, start_node )
char *device;        /* device on which nodes are to be allocated */
int nnodes;          /* number of nodes in processor group       */
int start_node;      /* node at which loading starts             */
```

Code 2-11 The routine *pgopen*.

The flexibility provided by processor groups becomes important in certain types of large application. For example, it may be convenient to have one group of nodes running a tightly coupled synchronous calculation, while another group of nodes in the same application asynchronously processes a dynamically varying database.

A program may be downloaded from the CP to a processor group by the routines *pgload* and *pgloadp*, which are shown in Code 2-12. Both routines load the program *progname* into the processor group *pgroup*. The additional third argument of *pgopenp* allows different programs to be loaded into different nodes in the same processor group.

```
int pgload ( pgroup, progname )
int pgroup;          /* processor group index       */
char *progname;      /* name of program to be loaded */

int pgloadp ( pgroup, progname, node )
int pgroup;          /* processor group index             */
char *progname;      /* name of program to be loaded      */
int node;            /* node to which program is to be loaded */
```

Code 2-12 The routines *pgload* and *pgloadp*.

Once a program has been downloaded to a processor group, it is started running by calling *pgstart*, which takes the processor group index as its only argument. If necessary a program can be loaded in a "stopped" state by calling the routine *pgpause* at any time between allocating a processor group and loading a program into it. This facility is particularly useful in debugging programs since it allows a program to be executed under user control by means of a parallel debugger such as *ndb* [Parasoft 88b]. The specifications of *pgstart* and *pgpause* are given in Code 2-13.

```
void pgstart ( pgroup )
int pgroup;          /* processor group index        */

void pgpause ( )

int pgshare ( device, pid, numptr )
char *device;        /* device on which nodes are to be allocated */
int pid;             /* process ID number of processor group       */
int *numptr;         /* pointer to integer to hold number of nodes */
```

Code 2-13 The routines *pgstart*, *pgpause*, and *pgshare*.

So far we have described how a single CP program can control several processor groups. However, *Express* also allows multiple CP processes to share access to the same set of nodes. This might be necessary, for example, if each CP process were acting as an interface to a peripheral device such as a disk. A CP process can share access to a processor group by calling the routine *pgshare*, also shown in Code 2-13. The first argument is the name of the device, and the second is the process ID number of the processor group to be shared. The last argument is a pointer used to return the number of nodes in the shared group. The value returned by *pgshare* is the processor group index.

While the flexibility of processor groups may be necessary in some applications, it may be a needless bother in others. Thus *Express* provides versions of the allocation and loading routines that may be used when only one processor group is used by an application. These routines — *exopen*, *exload*, *exstart*, *expause*, and *exshare* — are shown in Code 2-14 and are similar to their *pg* counterparts but omit arguments referring to processor groups.

2-4.3 Asynchronous Communication Under *Express*

The lowest level of the *Express* environment is based on an asynchronous, point-to-point communication system. This may be used to send messages from one node to any other node (including the CP) at any time. The *Express* kernel is responsible for any necessary intermediate buffering and routing.

The asynchronous communication primitives are *exwrite*, *exread*, and *extest*, shown in Code 2-15. The routine *exwrite* is nonblocking and sends a message pointed to by *buf* to node number *dest*. The length of the message is *nbytes* bytes and its type is *type*. The message type is a positive integer that allows readers to

```
int exopen ( device, nnodes, start_node )
char *device;      /* device on which nodes are to be allocated */
int nnodes;        /* number of nodes in processor group         */
int start_node;    /* node at which loading starts               */

int exload ( progname )
char *progname;    /* name of program to be loaded               */

int exloadp ( progname, node )
char *progname;    /* name of program to be loaded               */
int node;          /* node to which program is to be loaded      */

void exstart ( )

void expause ( )

int exshare ( device, pid, numptr )
char *device;      /* device on which nodes are to be allocated */
int pid;           /* process ID number of processor group       */
int *numptr;       /* pointer to integer to hold number of nodes */
```

Code 2-14 The ex- versions of the allocation and load routines.

differentiate between various messages and (in a multitasking node environment) permits multiple readers on the same node to access different message streams.

The routine *exread* blocks until a suitable message has been read. The number of the source node is pointed to by *src_ptr*, and the required message type by *type_ptr*. If either *src_ptr* or *type_ptr* is the NULL pointer, then the corresponding value is considered a match. If *src_ptr* or *type_ptr* point to the macro value DONTCARE, then any value is considered a match, and the actual value for the message read is stored at the corresponding pointer location. If more than one message meets the selection criteria, then the first one that arrived is accepted. The maximum acceptable message length is given by *max_bytes*, and *exread* returns the actual number of bytes read or a negative value if an error occurs. The special macro value HOST is available to indicate the CP as either the source or destination of a message.

The nonblocking routine *extest* checks whether a message of a given type has been received from a given source node. As with the routine *exread*, NULL and DONTCARE may be used to indicate that any match is acceptable. If an acceptable message has been received the length of the message is returned; otherwise a negative value is returned.

```
int exwrite ( buf, nbytes, dest,  type )
char *buf;      /* pointer to start of message */
int nbytes;     /* length of message in bytes  */
int dest;       /* destination node number     */
int type;       /* message type                */

int exread ( buf, max_bytes, src_ptr, type_ptr )
char *buf;      /* pointer to where message is to be stored  */
int max_bytes;  /* maximum message length                    */
int *src_ptr;   /* pointer to value of required source node  */
int *type_ptr;  /* pointer to value of required message type */

int extest ( src_ptr, type_ptr )
int *src_ptr;   /* pointer to value of required source node  */
int *type_ptr;  /* pointer to value of required message type */
```

Code 2-15 Primitives of the *Express* asynchronous communication environment.

2-4.4 Decomposition Tools

Express uses the same *gridmap* routines as CrOS III to decompose the nodes onto a Cartesian mesh (see Chap. 14 of Volume 1). There is an important difference, however, in the meaning of a "mask" in the CrOS III and *Express* environments. As explained in Sec. 2-2.3, in CrOS III a mask (or channel mask) is a binary number whose 1's bits indicate the physical channels on which a message is to be sent. In the *Express* environment the user is not concerned with the underlying physical topology of the machine, and the concept of a "communication channel" is not required by the *Express* programming model. In *Express* a mask is merely a means of specifying to the kernel a particular node. The kernel then uses the information in the mask to ensure that a message to the corresponding node is correctly routed.

We believe that this generalization of the CrOS III channel mask is very elegant and allows an immediate execution of CrOS III programs on arbitrary distributed memory concurrent processors. There is an analogy to the UNIX I/O system, in which the *read, write* primitives access an explicit file *number* returned by *open*. The more elegant and user-friendly *fread* and *fwrite* routines access a pointer of type FILE returned by *fopen*. In a similar fashion, *Express* has changed an explicit and inflexible numerical labeling by a mask to what is essentially a pointer whose significance or value is immaterial to the user. It is found by calling the *gridmap* family of decomposition routines.

In *Express* the routine *exgridmask* is used in place of the CrOS III routine *gridchan* to obtain the mask for a node at a particular position in the Cartesian mesh. The specification of *exgridmask* is given in Code 2-16. The routine *exgridmask* returns the mask necessary to send a message from node *proc* to the node located *dist* nodes away in direction *dir*.

Express also provides an additional *gridmap* routine called *exgridsize* not found in CrOS III. This routine, shown in Code 2-16, is used to distribute an array of data over a Cartesian mesh of nodes. The first argument of *exgridsize* is a node number, and the second is an array containing the total number of array elements in each dimension. After the call the third argument is an array containing the number of elements in each dimension in the node specified.

```
int exgridmask ( proc, dir, dist )
int proc;      /* number of source node                      */
int dir;       /* direction in Cartesian mesh                */
int dist;      /* number of mesh spacings to destination node */

int exgridsize ( proc, g_size, l_size )
int proc;      /* node number                                */
int *g_size;   /* integer array giving global size of array   */
int *l_size;   /* integer array giving local size of array in proc */
```

Code 2-16 The routines *exgridmask* and *exgridsize*.

3

The Implementation of CrOS III
on Concurrent Processors

3-1 General Remarks

The CrOS III communication system has been implemented on several concurrent computers. For commercial hypercubes, such as the NCUBE and iPSC/1 discussed in the sections that follow, CrOS III can be implemented simply, but inefficiently, in terms of the native message-passing primitives. More efficient implementations make direct use of the hardware. The Caltech/JPL Mark III hypercube and CrOS III were designed to be compatible, so CrOS III runs particularly efficiently on the Mark III. On machines with other architectures, such as shared memory multiprocessors, CrOS III is implemented by simulating the hypercube communication channels in software.

All the high-level CrOS III routines are written in terms of the CrOS III communication primitives described in Sec. 2-2.3, namely, *cread*, *cwrite*, *rdstat*, *vread*, and *vwrite*. Thus, implementing CrOS III only requires these primitives to be successfully ported. In fact, the problem is simpler even than this, since the CrOS III primitives themselves are written in terms of the *rd* and *wt* primitives that read and write a certain number of bytes on a specified communication channel.

3-2 The Implementation of CrOS III on the Mark III Hypercube

The architecture of the Mark III hypercube was designed with the efficient implementation on the CrOS III communication routines specifically in mind. The CrOS III routines are implemented in terms of the assembly-coded CrOS III primitives. A unique feature of the implementation of CrOS III on the Mark III is that messages that are to be forwarded by *cread* are automatically forwarded by the hardware. Thus routines such as *broadcast*, which rely heavily on message forwarding, are very efficiently implemented on the Mark III.

To explain the implementation of the CrOS III primitives on the Mark III better, an overview of the hardware will first be given. Each node of the Mark III contains two MC68020 processors — one for data processing (the DP) and one for I/O processing (the IOP) [Tuazon 88]. The nodes of the Mark IIIfp also contain the Weitek W8000 chip set for enhanced floating-point performance, but this has no bearing on the implementation of CrOS III. The DP has two daughter processors: an MC68882 floating-point unit and an MC68851 memory management unit. The IOP controls 8 unidirectional communication channels, each with a 64-byte FIFO buffer at either end. The DP and IOP (and the Weitek on the Mark IIIfp) have access to 4 Mbytes of shared DRAM on each node, as shown in Fig. 3-1.

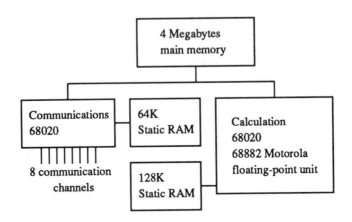

Figure 3-1 The basic Mark III node board.

When a CrOS III communication routine is executed on the DP (or Weitek) a token is written to a predefined block of shared memory called the "mailbox." The DP then places the arguments to the CrOS III routine on a stack in shared memory and sends an interrupt to the IOP. The IOP responds to the interrupt by entering an interrupt handler routine which takes the arguments off the stack and jumps to the address given by the token in the mailbox. The IOP then manages the transmission of data between two nodes as follows. The IOP of the transmitting node fills the FIFOs of the channels on which it is writing and sends an interrupt to the IOP of the node at the other end of each channel. Upon receipt of this interrupt the receiving IOPs empty the FIFOs of the transmitting IOP. When a FIFO becomes empty an interrupt is sent from the transmitting IOP to the receiving IOP, and the next packet is loaded into the FIFO of the transmitting IOP. FIFO's can be loaded and unloaded directly into shared memory using DMA transfers.

3-3 The Implementation of CrOS III on the NCUBE/10 Hypercube

Two versions of CrOS III have been implemented on the NCUBE/10 hypercube at Caltech [Baillie 87a]. "Slow CrOS" is implemented on top of the native VERTEX node operating system in terms of the VERTEX primitives *nread* and *nwrite* [NCUBE 87], and "fast CrOS" directly addresses the DMA hardware. Slow CrOS III is easily (but inefficiently) implemented by writing the CrOS III primitives *cread*, *cwrite*, *rdstat*, *vread*, and *vwrite* in terms of *nread*, *ntest*, and *nwrite*. The CrOS III routines *fcread* and *fcwrite* must also be modified so that they interact appropriately with the AXIS operating system on the NCUBE host.

All the high-level CrOS III routines are written in terms of these primitives, and so little further effort is required to implement them.

The VERTEX operating system permits asynchronous communication between arbitrary pairs of nodes. The CrOS III communication system requires synchronous communication between neighboring nodes. Hence, fast CrOS is implemented by disabling VERTEX and running the CrOS III primitives directly on the hardware. A complication arises from the specification of the *cread* routine which requires that *cread* be able to forward messages to other nodes. Since messages may be of any length, it is not practical to store messages on intermediate forwarding nodes. Therefore, forwarded messages are sent as a series of fixed-length packets. The transmission of packetized messages is not done very efficiently by the NCUBE since each packet incurs a high latency. Thus, messages which do not have to be forwarded are sent in nonpacketized mode.

An NCUBE node has 11 input and 11 output DMA channels, each of which has an address register and a count register associated with it. To transmit a message from one node to another using the primitives *rd* and *wt*, the two nodes do an initial "handshake" in which the transmitting node sends a 2-byte integer giving the length of the message to the receiving node. The receiving node evaluates the minimum of the message length and the maximum space available (from the argument list of *cread*) and stores this in the count register of the receiving node. This is the actual number of bytes that will be communicated. The receiving node returns this as a 2-byte integer to the transmitting node to indicate that it is ready to receive data. In packetizing mode this handshake must be performed for each packet, and it is this that makes packetized communication on the NCUBE inefficient. The address register of the receiving channel holds the address at which the incoming message is to be stored (this comes from the argument list of the *rd* routine). The transmitting node stores the address of the start of the message in the address register of the transmitting channel, and the number of bytes to be sent in the count register. Once the count register is set to a nonzero value, the DMA channels operate independently of instruction processing. The handshake protocol works because the DMA channel itself is able to buffer one half word (2 bytes), thereby enabling the transmitting node to send a half word to the receiving node even if its count register contains zero.

In fast CrOS the receiving node must decide whether the message is to be sent in packetizing mode, since the transmitting node does not know if the message is to be forwarded. In the handshake procedure the 2-byte integer giving the message length has its sign bit set to 1 if packetizing mode is to be used. In this way the receiving node is able to tell the transmitting node to send the message in packets. This restricts the length of messages in fast CrOS to fewer than 32 Kbytes. An additional restriction of fast CrOS is that the hardware forces the lowest-order bit of the address and count registers to be zero so that messages must start at a half word boundary and be an even number of bytes in length. The fast CrOS implementations of *cread* and *cwrite* are shown in pseudocode in Codes 3-1 and

3-2, in which the routine *initrd* and *initwt* are used to inform all nodes involved in the communication whether or not to packetize.

```
proc_begin cread ( read from node A, optionally forward to F 1, F2,... )
        if_begin ( forwarding ) then
                proc_call initrd ( tell node A to packetize )
                proc_call initwt ( tell node F1, F2,... to packetize )
                for_begin ( each packet )
                        proc_call rd ( read packet from node A )
                        proc_call wt ( write packet to F1, F2,... )
                for_end
        else
                proc_call initrd ( tell node A not to packetize )
                proc_call rd ( read entire message from node A )
        if_end
proc_end
```

Code 3-1 The fast CrOS implementation of *cread*.

```
proc_begin cwrite ( write to nodes B1, B2,... )
        for_begin ( each destination node, Bi, i = 1, 2,... )
                proc_call initwt ( find out if node Bi says packetize )
                if_begin ( packetizing ) then
                        for_begin ( each packet )
                                proc_call wt ( write packet to Bi )
                        for_end
                else
                        proc_call wt ( write entire message to Bi )
                if_end
        for_end
proc_end
```

Code 3-2 The fast CrOS implementation of *cwrite*.

Before a fast CrOS program can be run on the nodes, VERTEX must first be disabled by turning off communication interrupts on channels within the user's subcube. Since the NCUBE is a multiuser system problems can arise when a VERTEX (or slow CrOS) program tries to perform I/O to the host through a subcube running a fast CrOS program. This situation can be avoided by ensuring that fast CrOS and VERTEX programs never run on the same 64-node NCUBE board.

The fast CrOS protocol just described is not the only way of implementing

CrOS III efficiently on the NCUBE. In fact, CrOS III can be made even faster if we do not allow *cread* to forward messages [Baillie 87b,c].

3-4 The Implementation of CrOS III on the iPSC/1 Hypercube

The implementation of CrOS III on the INTEL iPSC/1 hypercube exploits the internal 128-bit (16-bytes) buffer of the INTEL 82586 LAN chip associated with each communication channel [Fox 86]. As on the NCUBE hypercube, the CrOS III primitives are implemented on the iPSC/1 in terms of the routines *rd* and *wt*, which read and write on a specified physical communication channel. However, unlike the NCUBE implementation, all CrOS messages on the iPSC/1 are packetized, and the packet size of 16 bytes is determined by the size of the FIFO buffer on the LAN chip. When a message is to be transmitted over a channel by the routine *wt*, a flag is set in a special area of memory called the LAN control area. The address of the start of the message and the message length are also stored in the LAN control area. Each LAN chip continuously checks its control area, and when it sees that a message is to be sent, it transmits the first packet of the message. The corresponding call to *rd* in the receiving node also sets a flag in the appropriate LAN control area and instructs the LAN to receive up to a certain number of bytes and store them at a specified address. When the receiving LAN receives the first packet from the transmitting LAN, it sends an acknowledgment and stores the packet at the appropriate memory location. Upon receipt of the acknowledgment, the transmitting LAN sends the next packet. In this way the entire message is sent one packet at a time, with the receipt of each packet being acknowledged before the next one is sent. When the whole message has been sent the hardware of the transmitting LAN sends a checksum which is checked in hardware by the receiving LAN. While communication is taking place the 80286 node processor polls an area of memory. The LAN sets a flag at this location when communication is complete, and the 80286 processor then continues execution.

3-5 The Implementation of CrOS III on the BBN Butterfly

The Butterfly is a MIMD, homogeneous, shared memory concurrent computer made by Bolt, Beranek and Newman, Inc. [BBN 87], consisting of up to 256 identical nodes connected by the "Butterfly switch." Each node contains an MC68020 processor plus an MC68881 coprocessor, and 4 Mbytes of local memory. Each node has a "processor node controller" which manages references through the switch to other nodes' memory. Thus, collectively the local memory on each node constitutes a global shared memory. The Chrysalis operating system runs on the Butterfly and provides a UNIX-like environment. An implementation of the shared memory programming model, called the Uniform System, runs on top of Chrysalis.

CrOS III is implemented on the Butterfly by designating one of the nodes as the control processor and simulating the hypercube connection topology between the other 2^d nodes that constitute the hypercube. Each hypercube channel is simulated as a bidirection link; that is, if nodes A and B are connected in the hypercube topology, there is a path from A to B and another from B to A. The path from A to B is simulated by means of a buffer in the local memory of node A, and the path from B to A by a buffer in the local memory of node B. The packet size is, by definition, the length of the buffer. When data are sent from node A to node B, node A writes the data one packet at a time into its buffer, from which node B reads them. Each buffer is assigned a unique number so that the number of the buffer in node p corresponding to channel c is:

$$bufnum = p * d + c \tag{3.1}$$

where d is the dimension of the hypercube. The CP has a bidirectional channel connecting it to node 0. Each node knows the number of the buffers at each end of its channels.

Versions of CrOS III have been implemented on top of both the Uniform System and Chrysalis [Baillie 87d,e], and we will now describe each of these. Currently, BBN is switching its operating environment to one based on MACH UNIX, and we expect similar CrOS III and *Express* implementations to be available under this new environment.

3-5.1 CrOS III on the Uniform System

The Uniform System does not support multitasking on the Butterfly nodes, so each node of the simulated hypercube and the CP must be assigned to different Butterfly nodes. The Uniform System's memory management function *AllocScatterMatrix* is used to locate storage for the channel buffers. Each node of the d-dimensional hypercube is allocated d channel buffers, as follows:

```
chan_bufs = (char **)AllocScatterMatrix(n,d,packet_size)
```

An additional channel buffer is allocated to allow bidirectional communication between node 0 and the CP. All the channel buffers have the same size, which by definition is the packet size. A flag is associated with each buffer and is used to synchronize communication over the corresponding channel. In UsCrOS the routines *rd* and *wt* are used in transmit packetized messages as shown in the pseudocode in Codes 3-3 and 3-4.

Each pass through the **for** loop by the communicating nodes occurs in loose synchronization. The channel flag *flag_on_Abuf* is initialized to 0. On each pass through the loop the transmitting node A waits until the channel flag is 0 and then copies a packet of the message into the channel buffer, *Abuf*. Once this is done node A sets the channel flag to 1 to indicate that the packet is ready to be read. Node B, which has been waiting for the channel flag to be set to 1, reads the packet from the channel buffer and sets the channel flag to 0. This indicates to node A that the packet has been read, and that the next packet can now be copied to the channel buffer. This process of coordinated copying continues until all the packets have been transmitted from node A to node B.

```
proc_begin rd ( read message on specified channel )
      for_begin ( each packet )
             [ wait until flag_on_Abuf = 1 ]
             [ copy next packet from Abuf ]
             [ flag_on_Abuf ← 0 ]
      for_end
proc_end
```

Code 3-3 The implementation of rd under the Uniform System.

```
proc_begin wt ( write message on specified channel )
      for_begin ( each packet )
             [ wait until flag_on_Abuf = 0 ]
             [ copy next packet into Abuf ]
             [ flag_on_Abuf ← 1 ]
      for_end
proc_end
```

Code 3-4 The implementation of wt under the Uniform System.

3-5.2 CrOS III Under Chrysalis

The main advantage of Chrysalis over the Uniform System is that it is a multitasking operating system and can therefore run more than one process at a time on each Butterfly processor. An arbitrarily large hypercube can therefore be emulated (subject to memory limitations). The implementation of CrOS under Chrysalis, ChrysCrOS, emulates a hypercube by first grabbing all the free Butterfly processors (some may be in use by other users) and spreading the hypercube nodes and the CP over them. Channel buffers are allocated as in the implementation of UsCrOS discussed in Sec. 3-5.1. Their use under Chrysalis may be synchronized by a number of different methods which will now be described.

One way in which to communicate synchronously is to create a flag for each buffer and to poll it as was done in UsCrOS. The main disadvantage of this method is that polling a flag in a remote memory location can saturate the Butterfly's switching network. A better way to synchronize communication is to make use of events or dual queues.

An *event*, in this context, is a Chrysalis object which informs a process that something has occurred. An event is created for each channel buffer, and a message is sent from node A to node B as shown in Code 3-5 and 3-6.

The reader (node B) posts *event_A* to indicate that it is ready to read the data. Node A, which has been waiting for this event, copies a packet into the channel buffer and then posts *event_B* to indicate that the packet is ready to be

```
proc_begin rd ( read message on specified channel )
        for_begin ( each packet )
                [ post event_A ]
                [ wait event_B ]
                [ copy next packet from Abuf ]
                [ reset event_B ]
        for_end
proc_end
```

Code 3-5 The implementation of rd under Chrysalis using events.

```
proc_begin wt ( write message on specified channel )
        for_begin ( each packet )
                [ wait event_A ]
                [ copy next packet into Abuf ]
                [ post event_B ]
                [ reset event_A ]
        for_end
proc_end
```

Code 3-6 The implementation of wt under Chrysalis using events.

read. When this occurs node B copies the data from the channel buffer. Finally, both *event_A* and *event_B* are reset by node A and B, respectively, so they are ready for the communication of the next packet. The basic mechanism is similar to that used in UsCrOS. However, in Chrysalis a process is put to sleep while it is waiting for an event, and is woken up when the event is posted. Thus processes do not continuously poll memory and clog up the switching network.

A third method used to synchronize CrOS communications involves the use of *dual queues*. Suppose we have a queue of tasks waiting for processes to service them. This leads to the problem of what a process should do when the task queue is empty. Polling the queue in a loop wastes resources, and putting processes to sleep between tests of the task queue impairs performance time. The alternate approach of having a queue of idle processes awaiting tasks leads to the problem of what to do if the process queue is empty. A natural solution is to have a task queue *and* a process queue. If there are more tasks than processes then the extra tasks are put on the task queue, and if there are more processes than tasks, the idle processes are put on the process queue. At any moment either the task queue or the process queue (or both) is empty. Thus there is really no need for two distinct queues — they can be merged into a *dual queue*, which at some instant either contains tasks or processes, or is empty. The dual queue mechanism simply and efficiently allocates tasks to processes. When a process becomes idle, it either gets a task from the queue, or if there are none, it goes onto the queue itself. Similarly, when a task is ready to be serviced it looks for an idle process on the queue, and if there is none it goes onto the queue. The use of the dual queue mechanism to synchronize communication between two nodes is shown in Code 3-7 and 3-8.

```
proc_begin rd ( read message on specified channel )
       for_begin ( each packet )
               [ enqueue dual_q_A ]
               [ wait dual_q_B ]
               [ copy next packet from Abuf ]
       for_end
proc_end
```

Code 3-7 The implementation of rd under Chrysalis using dual queues.

```
proc_begin wt ( write message on specified channel )
       for_begin ( each packet )
               [ wait dual_q_A ]
               [ copy next packet into Abuf ]
               [ enqueue dual_q_B ]
       for_end
proc_end
```

Code 3-8 The implementation of wt under Chrysalis using dual queues.

4

The CUBIX Concurrent I/O System

4-1 Concurrent I/O Paradigms

In this chapter the use of the CUBIX system for performing concurrent input and output will be reviewed. A more detailed discussion of the specifications and implementation of the C language version of CUBIX is given in Chaps. 6 and 15 of Volume 1. Similar details are given for Fortran CUBIX (FCUBIX) in Appendix C of Volume 1 and in Angus [Angus 88]. A more tutorial approach will be taken in this chapter.

Most distributed memory, concurrent processors currently available are interfaced to disks, terminals, and other peripherals, by means of a single host computer, which is often referred to as the control processor. A programming model commonly applied to such systems is the master/slave paradigm in which a program called the control process runs on the host computer and supervises the node processors. In the master/slave model the host computer schedules the work performed on the nodes, and also does any inherently sequential parts of the algorithm. In this scenario the host computer (the master) plays the central role, while the nodes (the slaves) act only as high-speed peripherals for performing computations under the host's direct control. Since nodes can perform I/O only indirectly via the control process, the nodes and I/O peripherals can only interact via the coordinated exchange of messages between the host and nodes. The CrOS III communication system provides the pairs of communication routines *mdumpcp/dumpelt* and *mloadcp/loadelt* for performing collective communication between the nodes and the host. However, the necessity of writing a host and a node program for every application, and having to coordinate the exchange of messages carefully between them, places a burden on the application programmer, thereby slowing down program development and providing a potential source for many bugs.

In the CUBIX programming model the relationship between the host and nodes is reversed, with the nodes now controlling the host, which merely acts as a file server for the nodes. A universal program (called *cubix*) runs on the host so a different host program does not have to be written for each application. The nodes perform I/O by using the appropriate constructs of the programming language being used, for example, *printf* and *scanf* in C and WRITE and READ in Fortran. CUBIX removes the logical necessity of having a host program, that is, within the CUBIX paradigm the performance of I/O can be described without reference to a host program (although such a program does exist — at least on all currently available systems). Future machines may have full node-based operating systems with each node attached to a disk, making a host computer physically as well as logically unnecessary for certain applications. The PC-CUBE of Sec. 7-3 may be regarded as a prototype of such a system.

4-2 The Design and Implementation of FCUBIX

Before beginning the CUBIX tutorial we will first consider some important details of the design and implementation of FCUBIX. A more complete discussion is given in Angus [Angus 88]. In the C language I/O is performed by means of subroutine or function calls. In contrast, I/O in Fortran is an integral part of the language. This fact, coupled with the versatility of Fortran I/O, makes the implementation of FCUBIX more complex than for the C version. Of course, it is possible to compromise and perform I/O in FCUBIX by means of C-like subroutine calls. For example, a function KPRNTF could be called to perform output, and would have an argument list similar to the corresponding C routine *printf*. Similarly, input could be performed by calling the function KSCANF, and so on. This approach, although simpler to implement, is less elegant and requires the Fortran programmer to be familiar with the performance of I/O in the C language. A further disadvantage of using subroutine and function calls to do I/O in FCUBIX is that many of the routines would have to have a variable number of arguments to be compatible with their equivalent in C.

FCUBIX is therefore implemented in a natural way by extending the grammar of the Fortran language, as specified in Appendix C of Volume 1. A simple, but not very portable, method of implementing these extensions on a given machine would be to modify the compiler. However, often the compiler source code is not available. Instead the application program is first run through a preprocessor that parses the code and produces a new Fortran program with each FCUBIX I/O statement replaced by a set of function calls. These functions (which the application programmer need not be aware of) are written in C and are contained in a set of FCUBIX libraries. The program produced by the preprocessor is then compiled using a standard Fortran compiler, and the FCUBIX libraries are linked in.

At the time of writing FCUBIX has a few important restrictions, which may be relaxed in the future.

1. The preprocessor expands each I/O statement into several function calls, so statement labels should not be associated with I/O statements.

2. For similar reasons statements of the form,

```
if ( expression ) I/O statement
```

are forbidden.

3. Internal I/O is not supported.

4-3 A Tutorial Overview of CUBIX

In the CUBIX programming model file streams (or units in Fortran) have an attribute known as *multiplicity*, which can either be *singular* or *multiple*. In singular-input mode the same data are input to all the nodes. Similarly, in singular-output mode all nodes output the same single set of data. I/O in singular mode must be performed in loose synchronization. However, in multiple-input mode, different nodes read in different data. In multiple-output mode each node may output different data, or no data at all. Thus in multiple mode there is no need for I/O to be done loosely synchronously. The multiplicity of a file stream can be changed by means of loosely synchronous calls to the routines *fsingl* and *fmulti* (SINGLE and MULTIPLE). Here and throughout this chapter we use the C names of the routines and give the Fortran equivalents in parentheses.

In multiple I/O mode the data to be output by each node is copied into a buffer and is not actually output until a loosely synchronous call is made to one of *fflush*, *fclose*, and *exit* (FLUSH, CLOSE, and STOP). The default size of this buffer is usually between 512 and 4096 bytes and may be changed by the routine *setbuffer* (BUFFER).

The use of CUBIX will now be illustrated with a number of examples. In the first example, shown in Code 4-1, the nodes perform a *printf* (WRITE) in singular mode to output the message "Hello world!" Note that since singular mode is the default I/O mode, no call to *fsingl* (SINGLE) is necessary.

```
#include <stdio.h>
#include <cros.h>

main()
{
    printf("\n Hello world!");
    exit(0);
}
```

```
        PROGRAM HWRLD1

        WRITE (6,100)
100     FORMAT(' Hello world!')

        STOP
        END
```

Code 4-1 Output in singular mode.

The program shown in Code 4-1 outputs the string "Hello world!" once only; however, if a *fmulti* (MULTIPLE) statement were placed before the *printf* (WRITE), then each processor would output the string once on a separate line. In Code 4-2 we give an example of multiple-mode output. The program begins with a call to *cparam* (KCPARA) to determine the processor number. This is followed by a call to *fmulti* (MULTIPLE) to switch the I/O mode from the default singular mode to multiple mode. Each node then calls a routine, *iwork*, and upon completion checks the value returned. If a negative value is returned, signifying that an error occurred in *iwork*, an appropriate message is output. Otherwise no message is output. The program then terminates. It should be noted that the call to *exit* (STOP) causes the CUBIX buffers to be flushed, and so if it is omitted no output will be seen, regardless of the value returned by *iwork*.

```c
#include <stdio.h>
#include <cros.h>

main()
{
    struct cubenv env;
    int iresp;

    cparam(&env);
    fmulti(stdout);
    iresp = iwork();
    if ( iresp < 0 )
        printf("\n Error: %d returned by node %d",iresp,env.procnum);
    exit(0);
}
```

```fortran
      PROGRAM HWRLD2
      INTEGER IENV(5)
      CALL KCPARA(IENV)
      MULTIPLE(6)
      IRESP = IWORK(0)
      IF ( IRESP.LT.0 ) THEN
          WRITE (6,100) IRESP,IENV(2)
      ENDIF
100   FORMAT(' Error: ',I6,' returned by node ',I6)
      STOP
      END
```

Code 4-2 Output in multiple mode.

In the example program in Code 4-2, the nodes in general will not perform output in loose synchrony. However, the CUBIX buffers are flushed in loose synchrony when all nodes execute *exit* (STOP). When in multiple mode the buffers are flushed in order of increasing processor number. Thus if in Code 4-2 the routine *iwork* returned a value of −1 in nodes 0, 3, and 6, and a value of 0 in the other nodes, then the following would be output:

```
Error:      -1 returned by node    0
Error:      -1 returned by node    3
Error:      -1 returned by node    6
```

The order in which data are output can be critically affected by when the CUBIX buffers are flushed. As an example, consider Code 4-3. This code first calls *cparam* (KCPARA) to determine the processor number and the total number of nodes, and then calls *gridinit* (KGRDIN) and *gridcoord* (KGRDCO) to decompose the nodes onto a ring. Next each node performs output in multiple mode and outputs two lines of data and flushes the CUBIX buffers. Actually, the *fflush* (FLUSH) could be omitted since the *exit* (STOP) which immediately follows will also flush the buffers. If the number of processors is four, then the following output will be produced by Code 4-3:

```
Hello world! This is node     0
I am at position      0 in the ring
Hello world! This is node     1
I am at position      1 in the ring
Hello world! This is node     2
I am at position      3 in the ring
Hello world! This is node     3
I am at position      2 in the ring
```

In this output the first two lines are output by node 0, the next two by node 1, and so on. Note that the ring positions are given by the Gray code ordering which ensures that each node is connected to the neighboring nodes in the ring by a communication channel.

Now consider the effect of moving the *fflush* (FLUSH) in Code 4-3 to before the preceding line, so that it lies between the two *printf* (WRITE) lines. Now the CUBIX buffers are flushed after each line of output so the modified code will produce the following:

```
Hello world! This is node     0
Hello world! This is node     1
Hello world! This is node     2
Hello world! This is node     3
I am at position      0 in the ring
I am at position      1 in the ring
I am at position      3 in the ring
I am at position      2 in the ring
```

Perhaps the most common bug made in CUBIX programs is that of not flushing the buffers loosely synchronously. This type of error can easily slip into a program if care is not taken. For example, the code fragment shown in Code 4-4 is incorrect and will probably cause the program to deadlock. In Code 4-4 a loop is performed in which a random number is generated. The loop terminates

```
#include <stdio.h>
#include <cros.h>

main()
{
    struct cubenv env;
    int ipos,iresp;

    cparam(&env);
    iresp = gridinit(1,&env.nproc);
    iresp = gridcoord(env.procnum,&ipos);

    fmulti(stdout);
    printf("\n Hello world! This is node %d",env.procnum);
    printf("\n I am at position %d in the ring",ipos);
    fflush(stdout);

    exit(0);
}
```

```
      PROGRAM HWRLD3
      INTEGER IENV(5)

      CALL KCPARA(IENV)
      IRESP = KGRDIN(1,IENV(3))
      IRESP = KGRDCO(IENV(2),IPOS)

      MULTIPLE(6)
      WRITE(6,100) IENV(2)
      WRITE(6,101) IPOS
      FLUSH(6)

      STOP
100   FORMAT(' Hello world! This is node ',I6)
101   FORMAT(' I am at position ',I6,' in the ring')
      END
```

Code 4-3 The use of *fflush* (FLUSH).

when a random number greater than or equal to some lower limit is found. In each pass through the loop, the random number is output, and the CUBIX buffers are flushed. Clearly the intent of the programmer is to have each node output its random number on each pass through the loop. However, if the random number generator in each node has been seeded with a different integer (as would normally be the case), then the nodes will not all perform the loop the same number of times. This means that, in general, *fflush* (FLUSH) will be called a different number of times in each node, thereby contravening the constraint of loose synchrony.

```
    ....
    do{
        ptemp = pranf();
        printf("\n ptemp = %f",ptemp);
        fflush(stdout);
    } while (ptemp<plimit)
    ....
```

```
       ....
   10  CONTINUE
       PTEMP = PRANF(IDUMMY)
       WRITE (6,100) PTEMP
  100  FORMAT(' ptemp = ',F8.6)
       FLUSH(6)
       IF (PTEMP.LT.PLIMIT) GOTO 10
       ....
```

Code 4-4 A common CUBIX bug.

Now we will consider the singular- and multiple-input modes of the CUBIX system. In singular mode all nodes perform input loosely synchronously, and each receives the same input data. As in the example of singular mode output in Code 4-1, the CUBIX code is the same as that for a sequential computer. An example of input in singular mode is given in Code 4-5. Code 4-5 begins by opening the files **input.dat** and **output.dat** using *fopen* (OPEN), and the node number is found by calling *cparam* (KCPARA). A single integer is then read from the input file in singular-input mode and is written to the output file, also in singular mode. The output mode is then switched to multiple by calling *fmulti* (MULTIPLE), and the product of the input and the node number is output by each node to the output file. This must be done in multiple mode since each node is outputting a different number. If the input file contains the single integer 6, say, then for a 4-node hypercube the following will be output:

```
The input integer is      6
In node     0 nprod =      0
In node     1 nprod =      6
In node     2 nprod =     12
In node     3 nprod =     18
```

Code 4-6 illustrates input in multiple mode. This example is similar to that in Code 4-5, except that in Code 4-6 all I/O is performed in multiple mode. Each

```
#include <stdio.h>
#include <cros.h>

main()
{
    struct cubenv env;
    int nin, nprod;
    FILE *inptr, *outptr, *fopen();

    inptr  = fopen("input.dat","r");
    outptr = fopen("output.dat","w");

    cparam(&env);

    fscanf(inptr,"%d",&nin);
    nprod = nin*env.procnum;

    fprintf(outptr,"\n The input integer is %d",nin);
    fmulti(outptr);
    fprintf(outptr,"\n In node %d nprod = %d",env.procnum,nprod);

    exit(0);
}
```

```
      PROGRAM ILOOP1
      INTEGER IENV(5)

      OPEN(UNIT=5,FILE='input.dat')
      OPEN(UNIT=6,FILE='output.dat')

      CALL KCPARA(IENV)

      READ(5,*) NIN
      NPROD = NIN*IENV(2)

      WRITE(6,100) NIN
      MULTIPLE(6)
      WRITE(6,101) IENV(2),NPROD

      STOP
100   FORMAT(' The input integer is ',I6)
101   FORMAT(' In node ',I6,' nprod = ',I6)
      END
```

Code 4-5 Input in singular mode.

node now receives a unique input integer, and the input file contains one integer for each node. It should be noted that in the Fortran code the I/O mode associated with the two files is specified in the OPEN statement using the MODE parameter. In multiple input mode data is passed to the nodes in order of increasing node number, and there is no need to flush the input stream. If, for example, the input file contains the numbers 5, 3, 7, 2, then the output from a 4-node hypercube would be :

```
The input integer is    5 in node    0
In node       0 nprod =    0
The input integer is    3 in node    1
In node       1 nprod =    3
The input integer is    7 in node    2
In node       2 nprod =    14
The input integer is    2 in node    3
In node       3 nprod =    6
```

4-4 Extensions to CUBIX

In this chapter we have reviewed the essential features of the basic CUBIX system in a series of examples. The version of CUBIX described here and in Volume 1 is the same as that used in the application programs described in Chap. 8. However, versions of CUBIX are commercially available that provide enhancements to the system described here. In the version marketed by Parasoft Corporation [Parasoft 88c], the CUBIX buffers are managed by the system so that in singular output mode they are flushed automatically when they become full. In multiple-output mode, however, the user must still flush the buffers as in the original Caltech version of CUBIX. The UNIX–like routine *setvbuf* is used to change the method by which buffers are flushed. Another feature of the Parasoft version is that the user can specify the order in which nodes are to perform I/O. This is performed using a new routine, *forder*.

As described so far, CUBIX can only be used in a loosely synchronous fashion, and many of its most powerful and elegant features require this. However, it is sometimes very useful to use CUBIX asynchronously; this can occur while debugging even when the underlying application is loosely synchronous. A mixture of asynchronous and loosely synchronous operation is possible in *Express*, which simultaneously supports both styles of message transfer. *Express* allows a new CUBIX file stream attribute termed *asynchronous*, in addition to *singular* and *multiple*. This is set by calling a new routine *fasync*, which corresponds to *fmulti* and *fsingl*.

```c
#include <stdio.h>
#include <cros.h>
main()
{
    struct cubenv env;
    int nin, nprod;
    FILE *inptr, *outptr, *fopen();

    inptr  = fopen("input.dat","r");
    outptr = fopen("output.dat","w");
    fmulti(inptr);
    fmulti(outptr);

    cparam(&env);

    fscanf(inptr,"%d",&nin);
    nprod = nin*env.procnum;

    fprintf(outptr,"\n The input integer is %d in node %d",nin,
                                                env.procnum);
    fprintf(outptr,"\n In node %d nprod = %d",env.procnum,nprod);

    exit(0);
}
```

```fortran
      PROGRAM ILOOP1
      INTEGER IENV(5)

      OPEN(UNIT=5,FILE='input.dat',MODE='multi')
      OPEN(UNIT=6,FILE='output.dat',MODE='multi')

      CALL KCPARA(IENV)

      READ(5,*) NIN
      NPROD = NIN*IENV(2)

      WRITE(6,100) NIN,IENV(2)
      WRITE(6,101) IENV(2),NPROD

      STOP
100   FORMAT(' The input integer is ',I6,' in node ',I6)
101   FORMAT(' In node ',I6,' nprod = ',I6)
      END
```

Code 4-6 Input in multiple mode.

5

Extended CrOS III

5-1 Supplements to the CrOS III Programming Environment

The basic CrOS III environment introduced in Sec. 2-2, and described in detail in Chap. 14 of Volume 1, provides routines for performing a set of simple communication tasks. CrOS III also includes the *gridmap* routines for mapping the processing nodes onto a Cartesian grid. Although it is adequate for many problems, it is desirable to enhance the basic CrOS III environment to improve programmability and increase functionality. In Chap. 4 we described a supplement to the CrOS III environment called CUBIX that provides I/O utilities to the nodes. CUBIX removes from the application programmer the burden of having to write a separate host and node program for every application, thereby simplifying the task of program development. PLOTIX [Flower 86b, Parasoft 88d] is a further supplement to the CrOS III programming environment that permits the nodes to generate graphical output. A source level debugger, *ndb*, has also been developed for use with CrOS III [Parasoft 88b]. In this chapter we will describe some further additions to the CrOS III environment, finishing with a review of the Parasoft extensions.

The *submap* library consists of a set of utilities for managing subcubes within an application program. The *submap* routines allow the user to partition a hypercube into subcubes, so that, if necessary, each subcube can perform a separate task. The *comutil* library provides routines for performing common nonnearest neighbor communication tasks. These routines were mentioned in Chap. 2, and have been described in Chap. 21 of Volume 1. The *comutil* library includes, for example, the routines *transpose*, which transposes data distributed on a two-dimensional array of processors and *index* which is of use in FFT algorithms. Last, in this chapter, we describe a version of the *crystal_router* algorithm which provides a loosely synchronous mechanism for transmitting messages of arbitrary length between arbitrary nodes of a hypercube. The C language source code and the manual pages for these utilities are presented in Appendices E and F.

5-2 The *submap* Subcube Management Library

The *submap* library is a supplement to the CrOS III programming environment which allows the user to split a hypercube into subcubes within an application program. Each subcube can then work independently on different aspects of a problem. It should be emphasized that the *submap* routines are intended for use within a single application program. Thus all nodes execute the same code, but nodes within different subcubes may perform different, but related,

subtasks. The *submap* routines are not intended to allow *distinct* applications
to run in different subcubes — the *Express* processor allocation and program
loading routines described in Sec. 2-4.2 can be used to do this. Alternatively, on
"space-sharing" hypercubes, such as the NCUBE, systems software permits several
applications to run independently in different subcubes.

As an example, suppose we wish to find the convolution of two images. This
requires the Fourier transform of each image to be evaluated and multiplied together
to give the Fourier transform of the convolved image. The required convolution is
then found by taking the inverse Fourier transform. This problem could be tackled
by distributing both images over the hypercube and finding the Fourier transform
of each in turn. These transforms can then be multiplied together, and the inverse
transform evaluated to give the convolved image. An alternative approach is to
use the *submap* routines to split the hypercube into two subcubes, each of which
evaluates the Fourier transform of one of the images. Once this has been done
the subcubes can then cooperate first to multiply the Fourier transforms together
and then to find the inverse transform. The main advantage of using *submap* in
this problem is that it allows each node to operate on a larger data set since both
Fourier transforms are evaluated concurrently by the two subcubes. This larger
grain size yields a higher concurrent efficiency.

The *submap* routines allow the user to partition any previously defined
subcube by applying a channel mask. A hypercube can be partitioned using a
channel mask simply by removing those channels for which the corresponding bits
in the channel mask are zero. For example, consider the application of the channel
mask 5 to a three-dimensional hypercube. The binary representation of 5 is 101,
of which bit number 1 is zero. Thus the cube is partitioned by removing channel
number 1, as shown in Fig. 5-1, into the two-dimensional subcubes $(0, 1, 5, 4)$ and
$(2, 3, 7, 6)$. If we denote the ID number of a processor by *procnum* then those
processors for which bit number 1 of *procnum* is 0 make up subcube 0, and those
for which it is 1 make up subcube 1. Thus each subcube has a unique ID number.

The subcubes produced by the partitioning in the example have a dimension
of 2. To allow the subcubes to be used independently, it is necessary to renumber
the processors as 0, 1, 2, and 3 and the channels as 0 and 1, in each subcube. This
renumbering is illustrated in Fig. 5-2. A partitioning therefore involves the mapping
of the processor and channel numbers onto those of a subcube. In general, given
some hypercube of dimension d, and a channel mask, c, the processor numbers are
mapped by discarding those bits of *procnum* for which the corresponding bits of
c are zero. Thus, in the example in which the channel mask is 5, bit number 1
of *procnum* is discarded. Furthermore, the ID number of the subcube to which a
particular processor belongs is obtained by concatenating the discarded bits. The
mapping of processors numbers for a three-dimensional cube and a channel mask
of 5 is summarized in Table 5-1.

The channels are mapped so that channel number i in the subcube corresponds
to channel number j in the parent hypercube, where j is the ith nonzero bit in the

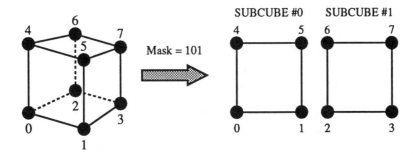

Figure 5-1 An example of the partitioning of a hypercube by a mask. In this case a three-dimensional hypercube is split into two two-dimensional subcubes by the mask 5 (=101 in binary).

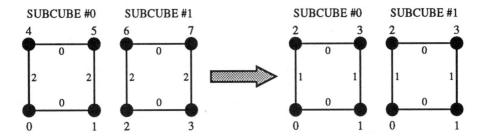

Figure 5-2 After splitting the hypercube as in Fig. 5-1 the processor and channel numbers must be renumbered as appropriate for the new subcubes. Thus the processor numbers are mapped to 0, 1, 2, and 3 and the channel numbers to 0 and 1.

procnum	Mapped *procnum*	Subcube number
000	00	0
001	01	0
010	00	1
011	01	1
100	10	0
101	11	0
110	10	1
111	11	1

Table 5-1 The mapping of a three-dimensional hypercube into a pair of two-dimensional subcubes by the channel mask 5. (The first column gives the original processor number, and the second column the processor number within the subcube. The last column gives the subcube ID number.)

channel mask. Thus in our example, channels 0 and 1 of the subcubes correspond to channels 0 and 2, respectively, in the original hypercube.

The *submap* library allows the user to arbitrarily partition a hypercube. Given a particular partitioning, we will call the subcube to which a processor belongs the *current subcube*, and the mapping of processor and channel numbers associated with the partitioning the *current mapping*. The *submap* routines can be used to change the current mapping, either by partitioning the current subcube further, or by restoring some previously defined mapping.

It is useful to regard a partitioning of a hypercube as a tree in which each node of the tree corresponds to a subcube. Each subcube has an ID number that is unique within the level of the tree in which it is found. This ID number is constructed by taking the ID number of the parent subcube and shifting its bits d positions to the left, where d is the dimension of the parent subcube. Adding this to the bits discarded in mapping the processor number, the ID number of the child subcube in which each processor lies is obtained. For concreteness we will consider the example shown in Fig. 5-3. The root of the tree is in level 0 and has ID number 0. This corresponds to the entire hypercube, which is here assumed to be of dimension 3. This is partitioned by the mask 5 into two subcubes of dimension 2 with ID numbers 0 and 1. The subcube with ID number 0 is further partitioned into four subcubes of dimension 0 by the mask 0. In this partitioning each of the four processors in the parent subcube are mapped to processor number 0. The four new subcubes are labeled 0, 1, 2, and 3 and lie in level 2 of the tree. The subcube at level 1 with ID number 1 is split by mask 1 into two one-dimensional subcubes. Each processor in these subcubes can determine the ID number of the subcube in which it lies by shifting the ID number of the parent subcube two bits to the left (giving 4), and then adding the bits discarded in mapping the processor numbers, namely, 0 and 1. Thus the new level 2 subcubes have ID numbers 4 and 5. Finally, these two subcubes are split into zero-dimensional subcubes by the mask 0. The ID numbers of these subcubes are 8, 9, 10, and 11.

The routine *partition_subcube* is used to partition the current subcube. It must be called loosely synchronously by all processors involved in the partitioning. For each of these the subcube produced by this partitioning becomes the current subcube. The only argument to *partition_subcube* is the mask to be applied in the partitioning. If no errors occur, then the ID number of the subcube in which the processor now lies is returned; otherwise a negative error code is returned.

A partitioning at a lower level in the tree can be restored by calling the routine *restore_subcube* with loose synchrony in all processors in the subcube being restored. The only argument to *restore_subcube* is the level of the subcube to be restored. If no errors occur then the ID number of the restored subcube is returned; otherwise a negative error code is returned.

After partitioning or restoring a subcube the CrOS III routine *cparam* can be used to give information on the new subcube, such as its dimension and the numbers of the nodes.

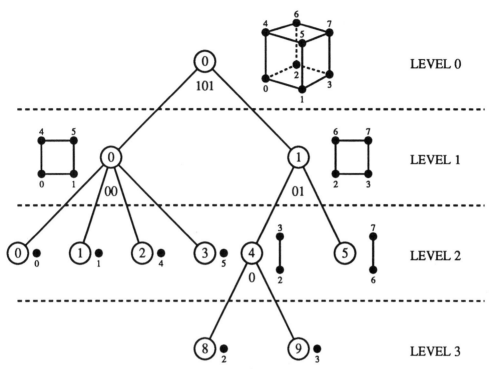

Figure 5-3 An example partitioning tree for a three-dimensional hypercube (see text for details). At each level of the tree the nodes are labeled by the subcube number. The masks for each partitioning are shown below the parent tree nodes. The processing nodes making up each subcube are shown in terms of their original unmapped processor numbers.

As an example of the use of the *submap* routines consider the section of C code in Code 5-1.

The first 13 lines of Code 5-1 partition a three-dimensional hypercube as shown in Fig. 5-3. The zero-dimensional subcubes numbered 0, 1, 2 and 3 in Fig. 5-3 each independently perform the routine *do_work1*. The subcubes numbered 8 and 9 call the routine *do_work2*, while the two nodes in subcube number 5 call *do_work3*. Once the nodes in subcubes 5, 8 and 9 have completed their respective tasks they call *restore_subcube* and are reconfigured as a two-dimensional, level 1 subcube. In this subcube the routine *do_work4* is performed. Finally, *restore_subcube* is called in all nodes to reconfigure them as the original three-dimensional hypercube, and all nodes call the routine *do_work5*.

The way in which I/O is performed when using the *submap* routines is, in general, constrained by how CUBIX is implemented. If an asynchronous message-passing system is used then it is possible to perform I/O independently in each

```
    ....
    ID = partition_subcube(5);
    if (ID==0){
         ID    = partition_subcube(0);
         iresp = do_work1();
    }
    else{
         ID = partition_subcube(1);
         if (ID==4){
              ID    = partition_subcube(0);
              iresp = do-work2();
         }
         else    iresp = do_work3();
    }
    if (ID>4){
         ID    = restore_subcube(1);
         iresp = do_work4();
    }
    ID    = restore_subcube(0);
    iresp = do_work5();
    ....
```

Code 5-1 An example of the use of the *submap* routines.

subcube. However, if the underlying message-passing protocol is synchronous this is not possible, and calls to CUBIX routines such as *fflush*, *fmulti* and *fsingl* must be made loosely synchronously in all nodes of the hypercube. In the *Express* communication environment discussed in Sec. 2-4, CUBIX is implemented in terms of an asynchronous message-passing system, and this may be used to permit different subcubes to perform I/O independently. It should be noted that the order in which different subcubes perform I/O is indeterminate, although this is unlikely to create any problems provided that each subcube accesses different I/O streams.

5-3 The *comutil* Global Communication Library

In Sec. 2-2.4 an overview of the CrOS III collective communication routines was given. The routines for communicating between the processing nodes either involve only local "nearest-neighbor" communication (e.g., *cshift*, *vshift*) or a simple type of global communication (e.g., *broadcast*, *combine*). In this section we introduce a more sophisticated set of global communication routines which make up the *comutil* library. The *comutil* routines were originally formulated for use in matrix algorithms [see Fox 88h; Furmanski 88b], but have also been found to have applications in other fields, such as the evaluation of fast Fourier transforms [Walker 88d].

The *comutil* routines generally act on a one-dimensional array of P data items distributed over the N processing nodes. It will be assumed, without loss of generality, that P is divisible by N, $p = P/N$. The term *global index* will be used to refer to the index of a data item within the complete array, while the term *local index* will denote the index of a data item within a particular processor. All indices are assumed to start from 0. The *comutil* routines transform data between different types of decompositions. The following are five common data decompositions and are illustrated in Fig. 5-4.

1. In the I ("I" for *inhomogeneous*) decomposition all the data resides in one processor.
2. In the D_1 ("D" for *domain*) decomposition each processor contains all the data array.
3. In the D_N decomposition the first p items in the data array are stored in processor 0, the next p items in processor 1, and so on.
4. In the S_1 ("S" for *scattered*) decomposition the data item with global index J is stored in processor number $J \bmod N$ at local index J.
5. In the S_N decomposition the data item with global index J is stored in processor number $J \bmod N$ at local index $N * \lfloor r/N \rfloor + t$, where $r = J \bmod p$ and $t = \lfloor J/p \rfloor$.

The implementation of the *comutil* routines on hypercubes has been discussed in Chap. 21 of Volume 1, and so here we will just describe what each of the routines does. Manual pages for each of the *comutil* routines are given in Appendix D.

5-3.1 The *indexx* Routine

The *indexx* routine transforms the data decomposition between types D_N and S_N. Two successive applications of *indexx* recovers the original data decomposition, so *indexx* is its own inverse. The data item with local index j in processor i is exchanged with the data item with local index $i + N * \lfloor j/N \rfloor$ in processor $j \bmod N$, as illustrated in Fig. 5-5.

Another way to view the effect of *indexx* is to consider how the global index is transformed. If the array originally has decomposition type D_N, then the number of the processor in which the data item with global index J is stored is given by the upper d bits of J, where $d = \log_2 N$. The local index is given by the lower q bits of J, where $q = \log_2 p$ (see Fig. 5-6).

The effect of *indexx* is to exchange the upper and lower d bits of the global index. Thus the item with global index J is sent to the processor given by the lower d bits of J. In this processor its local index is given by the lower q bits of J, after replacing the lower d bits by the upper d bits of J. This is shown schematically in Fig. 5-7.

5-3.2 The *fold* and *expand* Routines

The *fold* routine combines all data items with the same local index, j, and stores the result in processor $j \bmod N$ with the local index j. Thus *fold* changes the

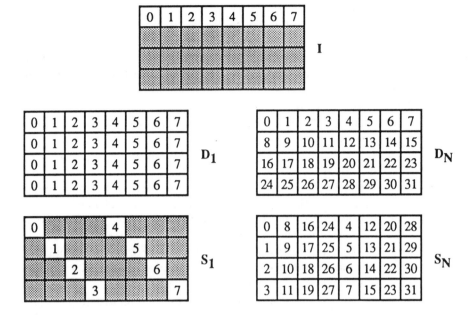

Figure 5-4 The five data decomposition types, illustrated for a two-dimensional hypercube. Each row of squares represents the data array in one processing node. Shaded squares indicate that the decomposition does not assign any particular value to that item in the data array. In the I, D_1, and S_1 cases an array of 8 data items is decomposed over the nodes. In the D_N and S_N cases an array of 32 data items is decomposed over the nodes.

data decomposition from type D_N to type S_1, as shown in Fig. 5-8. The combining function must be associative and commutative.

The *expand* routine transforms the data decomposition from type S_1 to type D_1, as shown in Fig. 5-9. Thus the item with local index j in processor $j \bmod N$ is sent to all other processors where it is stored with the same local index. The application *fold* followed by *expand* has the same effect as the routine *combine* mentioned in Sec. 2-2.4.

5-3.3 The *transpose* Routine

The *transpose* routine can only be used when the number of processors is a perfect square, that is, $N = D^2$. This restricts us to hypercubes of even dimension. The processors are assumed to be arranged on a two-dimensional grid of D rows and D columns. The lower D bits of *procnum* give the position of a processor on the mesh in one direction, while the upper D bits give the position in the second direction. The *transpose* routine exchanges the data in the processor at position (i, j) on the mesh with the data in the processor at position (j, i), as illustrated in

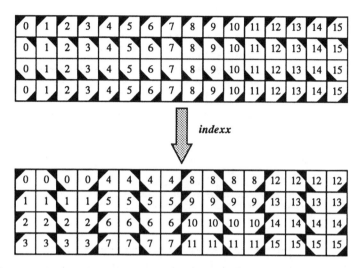

Figure 5-5 The effect of the *indexx* routine on an array of 64 data items distributed over 4 nodes. Each row of boxes represents the 16 data items held in one node. The initial distribution of the data is shown in the upper part of the figure. After applying *indexx* the data is distributed as shown in the lower part of the figure. Data items are labeled by their local index in the initial distribution, and each box has one corner shaded to identify the node in which that data item originated.

Fig. 5-10. The data decomposition type is left unchanged by *transpose*.

5-3.4 The *bcast* Routine

The standard tree-based CrOS III *broadcast* routine, described in Sec. 14-5.3 of Volume 1, performs a common communication task. For this reason *broadcast* was "discovered" before the other *comutil* routines and, hence, for historical reasons is usually included in the set of collective communication routines reviewed in Sec. 2-2.4. The function of *broadcast*, however, is to change the data decomposition type from I to D_1, and so it is more natural to classify it as a *comutil* routine. For compatibility we retain the original CrOS III *broadcast* routine and introduce a new *comutil* version called *bcast*. In Sec. 21-4.1 of Volume 1 three different broadcast algorithms were discussed, each of which was the most efficient for certain combinations of hypercube dimension and message size. Ideally, the *bcast* routine should be implemented so that it will automatically use the most efficient broadcast algorithm for a given machine size and message length.

5-3.5 The *scatter* Routine

The *scatter* routine transforms the data decomposition from I to S_1. The data is assumed to lie initially in processor 0 (other cases can be dealt with by temporarily relabeling processors). The *scatter* routine sends the item with local

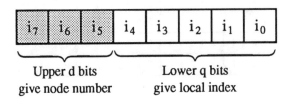

Figure 5-6 In the D_N decomposition of an array the upper d bits of the global index of a data item give the number of the node in which that item lies, and the remaining lower q bits give the local index. Figure 5-6 illustrates the case in which the global index ranges from 0 to 255, and the hypercube dimension, d, is 3. Each box represents a single bit.

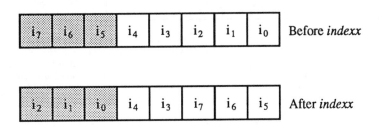

Figure 5-7 The *indexx* routine has the effect of exchanging the upper and lower d bits of the global index. The lower d bits of the local index of a data item give the number of the node to which it is sent, while the bits of the node number in which the data item initially lies become the lower d bits of the local index.

index j in processor 0 to processor $j \bmod N$ where it has the same local index. This is shown in Fig. 5-11.

5-3.6 The *transfer* Routine

The *transfer* routine sends data from one processor to another. The initial decomposition is of type I and remains unchanged.

5-4 A Buffered Crystal Router

The dynamic *crystal_router* routine, when called with loose synchrony, allows messages of any length (subject to buffer size limitations) to be sent between arbitrary nodes of a hypercube. The *crystal_router* algorithm is closely related to the *crystal_accumulator* algorithm, and both are discussed in Secs. 22-2, 3, and 4 of Volume 1. The *crystal_router* algorithm described next is not necessarily the fastest or most memory-efficient version. For example, Warren [Warren 88b] uses a modified algorithm which avoids the need for very large buffers. Instead we

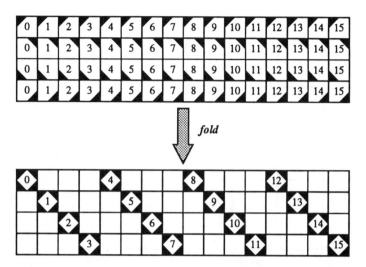

Figure 5-8 The effect of the *fold* routine on an array of 64 data items distributed over 4 nodes. As in Fig. 5-5, each row of boxes represents the 16 data items held in one node. After applying *fold* the corresponding data items in each node have been summed, and these sums are distributed over the nodes as shown in the lower part of the figure.

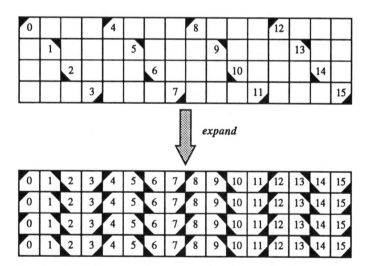

Figure 5-9 The effect of the *expand* routine on an array of 64 data items distributed over 4 nodes. As in Fig. 5-5, each row of boxes represents the 16 data items held in one node. The *fold* routine sends the data items labeled in the upper part of the figure to all processors, so the final distribution of data items is as shown in the lower part of the figure. Note that the effect of applying *fold* and then *expand* is the same as that of the CrOS III routine *combine*, but avoids some redundant calculation.

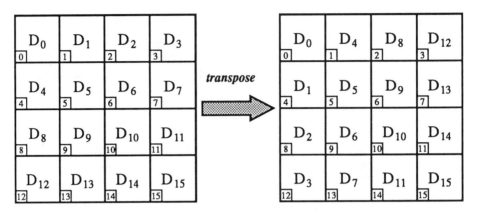

Figure 5-10 The effect of the *transpose* routine for a 16-node concurrent processor. Each box labeled by D_i represents some data in a particular node. The node number is given in the lower left-hand corner of each of these boxes. After applying *transpose* the data have been transposed on the two-dimensional mesh of processors.

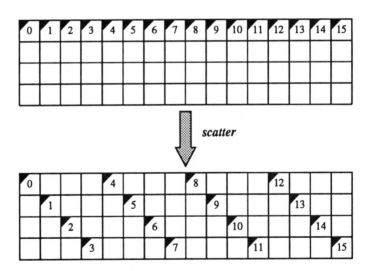

Figure 5-11 The effect of the *scatter* routine on an array of 64 data items distributed over 4 nodes. As in Fig. 5-5, each row of boxes represents the 16 data items held in one node. The *scatter* routine distributes the data items in one node over the other nodes. In the case shown, node 0 is the source node, and its data items are distributed by *scatter* as shown in the lower part of the figure.

describe here a relatively simple version of the *crystal_router* which illustrates the basic methodology.

The basic crystal router algorithm for sending a message from one processor to another is very simple. Each of the hypercube communication channels is considered in turn, and the message is sent on a particular channel if the destination processor lies in the subcube at the other end of the channel. More precisely, the bitwise XOR of the source and destination processor numbers is found, and the message is sent on channel number i if the ith bit of this quantity is set.

The operation of the crystal router may be divided into three phases.

1. In the first phase each processor specifies the messages that it wants to send.
2. In the second phase the messages are sent to their destinations. Messages destined for nonneighboring processors are automatically forwarded by the intermediate processors.
3. In the third phase the messages received are read; that is, they are copied from a *crystal_router* buffer to a location in memory specified by the user.

In phase 1 of the algorithm the messages to be sent may be stored in basically two ways. In the unbuffered crystal router a list is maintained which specifies the destination processor, message length, and the location in memory of the start of each message. In the buffered crystal router, however, when a message is specified it is immediately copied to a crystal router buffer. In general, the most efficient type of crystal router depends on the message routing mechanism used by a particular machine. Another factor to be considered is the memory required — the buffered crystal router needs more memory. However, since it is not possible to maintain a list of pointers in Fortran, we will describe here a buffered crystal router.

There are a number of ways in which the crystal router buffers can be managed. One possibility is to have a buffer for each of the communication channels and to place the outgoing messages in the buffer of the channel on which the message must next be sent. This is quite an efficient strategy, but wastes memory, since the buffers must be assigned a certain size before knowing the maximum size needed for each. If the message traffic is unbalanced, it is possible for some buffers to be empty most of the time, while others may become full. This memory-balance problem can be avoided (at the expense of efficiency) if there is just a single buffer in which all outgoing messages are stored. This results in a more robust algorithm, and so will be the one described here. Thus in each processor there is an outgoing message buffer (OMB) and a received message buffer (RMB). The RMB is used to store messages which have reached their final destination.

In phase 1 of the algorithm messages may be queued for transmission by copying them to the OMB using the routine *send_message*, shown in Code 5-2. The routine *send_message* sends the message in *buf* to each of the *ndest* destination processors listed in the array *dest*. The message is *nbytes* bytes in length.

```
int_fun send_message ( buf, nbytes, ndest, dest )
declare_buf buf;        /* buffer containing message */
declare_int nbytes;     /* length of message in bytes */
declare_int ndest;      /* number of destination processors */
declare_int dest;       /* integer array of destination processors */
```

Code 5-2 The *send_message* Routine.

An index, *OMB_index*, into the OMB is maintained which gives the location of the next available space in the buffer. Initially this is set to the start of the OMB. When *send_message* is called a message header is placed in the OMB at the position pointed to by *OMB_index*. This is followed by the actual message. The *OMB_index* is then set to the start of the next word following the end of the message data. The message header consists of the following integers, so the structure of the OMB is as shown in Fig. 5-12.

ndest   . . . . . . the number of destination processors
source . . . . . . the source processor number
nbytes . . . . . . the length of the message in bytes
flag   . . . . . . a flag to indicate if the message should
                     be deleted from the OMB
dest   . . . . . . a list of the destination processors

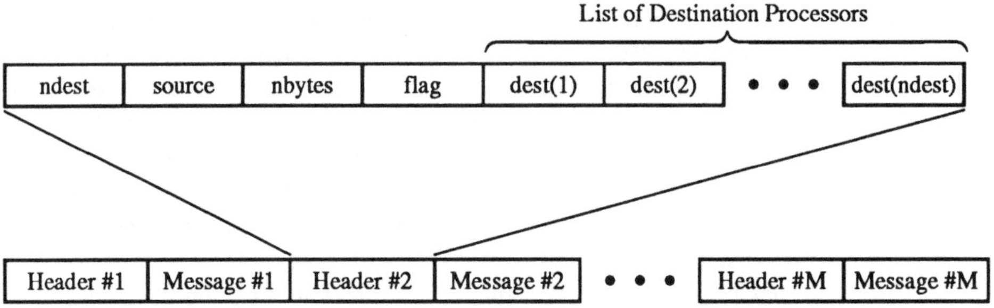

Figure 5-12 The upper part of the figure shows the structure of a message header. The lower part of the figure shows how messages and their respective headers are arranged in the outgoing message buffer (OMB).

In the second phase of the algorithm, messages are actually sent to their destinations by calling the routine *crystal_router*. This routine, which has no arguments, first compresses the RMB to remove any messages flagged for deletion (i.e., any messages delivered by a previous call to *crystal_router* which have already been read). The algorithm then checks through the messages in the OMB and copies any messages that a processor may have sent to itself to the RMB. Each time a message is copied to the RMB, the corresponding entry in the list of destination processors (*dest*) is set equal to the macro value DONE. When all the entries in *dest* for a message equal DONE, the message has been delivered to all its destination processors and is flagged for deletion from the OMB by setting the value of *flag* in the message header to the macro value DELETE.

The algorithm then loops over the communication channels, and for each channel, *c*, checks each message in the OMB to see if it must be sent on this channel. This is decided by evaluating the route mask for each destination processor. If bit number *c* of the route mask for one or more destination processors is 1, then the message (including the header) is copied to a communication buffer. After this, all entries in *dest* for which bit number *c* of the route mask is 1 are set equal to the macro value DONE, and if all the entries are DONE, the message is flagged for deletion from the OMB. The communication buffer begins immediately after the last message in the OMB, that is, it starts at the location pointed to by *OMB_index* at the start of each communication channel loop. An index, *COM_index*, indicates where the next message is to be placed in the communication buffer, and at the start of each loop is set equal to *OMB_index*. Each processor calls *cshift* to exchange the data in its communication buffer with that of the processor on the other end of the current channel. The received data overwrites that sent. The messages received in the communication buffer are checked, and any that have arrived at one of their destination processors (given in *dest*) are copied to the RMB of that processor. The header data are also copied, except for *ndest* and the list of destination processors, *dest*. When a message is copied to the RMB, the corresponding entry in *dest* (in the communication buffer header) is set to DONE, and, as usual, if all the entries are DONE, the message is flagged for deletion. The communication buffer is then merged with the OMB by setting *OMB_index* equal to *COM_index*, and the resulting buffer is compressed, thereby removing all messages flagged for deletion. After this the loop over the next communication channel is performed.

After calling *crystal_router* the messages received can be read by the routine *get_message*, shown in Code 5-3. The routine *get_message* extracts from the RMB the next message from a specified source and copies it (without the header) to the buffer *buf*. The length of the message is returned in the variable *nbytes*. It is also possible to supply a "wild card" value for the source processor, in which case the next message regardless of source will be returned, and the number of the actual source processor will be returned in *source*. Since values are returned via *nbytes* and *source* in the C language version of the crystal router, these are pointers to variables of C-type int. Once a message has been read, it is flagged for deletion, and the deletion actually takes place on the next call to *crystal_router*. A value of 0 is returned by *get_message* if an unread message from the requested source is found, 1 is returned if the RMB is empty, 2 is returned if there are no messages from the specified source processor, and 3 is returned if all messages in the RMB have been read, that is, if they are all flagged for deletion.

The three routines *send_message*, *crystal_router*, and *get_message* just described provide a basic implementation of the crystal router algorithm. In

```
int_fun get_message ( buf, max_bytes, source, nbytes )
declare_buf buf;         /* buffer to hold message */
declare_int max_bytes;   /* maximum length of message in bytes */
declare_int source;      /* number of required source processor */
declare_int nbytes;      /* actual length of message */
```

Code 5-3 The *get_message* routine.

addition, we will present a few routines which are useful in using the crystal router. These routines are shown in Code 5-4, and manual pages for these and additional routines are presented in Appendix F. The routine *set_cr_buf* may be used to change the size of the OMB or the RMB. All the messages in the OMB or the RMB may be deleted using the routine *clear_cr_buf*. Finally, the routine *error_messages* may be called with loose synchrony in CUBIX programs to output a summary of any errors that may have occurred in the crystal router routines.

```
int_fun set_cr_buf ( buf_size, OMB_or_RMB )
declare_int buf_size;   /* required buffer size in bytes */
declare_int OMB_or_RMB; /* 0 for OMB, 1 for RMB */

int_fun clear_cr_buf ( OMB_or_RMB )
declare_int OMB_or_RMB; /* 0 for OMB, 1 for RMB */

int_fun error_messages ( stream )
declare_file stream;    /* File pointer in C, unit number in Fortran */
```

Code 5-4 Additional crystal router routines.

In designing the crystal router algorithm described in this section efficiency has been sacrificed in the interests of generality and robustness. In applications in which this generality is not required, a different implementation of the crystal router may be more appropriate. Another problem that must be addressed in any practical crystal router is how to avoid buffer overflow. In languages such as Fortran, which do not allow memory to be allocated dynamically, imbalanced or high-volume message traffic can lead to unavoidable buffer overflows. In C programs similar problems can occur if a call to *malloc* is unable to allocate sufficient buffer space for messages. Our approach is therefore to anticipate such problems and alert the user by means of a negative return code. When copying to a message buffer, overflow can be avoided by checking if there is enough space for the message and header before copying it into the buffer. Buffer overflow can also occur when *cshift* receives a set of messages into the communication buffer. However, once again the potential problem can be handled since *cshift* takes the maximum size of the incoming data as one of its input arguments. If the size of the incoming data exceeds this limit the extra bytes are discarded and *cshift* returns a negative value. If this occurs in the *crystal_router* routine any incomplete message that may have been received is discarded. The only other place that buffer overflow can occur is in copying a message from the RMB to a user-supplied buffer by means of the *get_message* routine. One of the input arguments to *get_message* is the maximum size of the message that will be accepted, and if a valid message is found which exceeds this limit, then *get_message* returns a negative value and the message is not copied. With this approach messages may be lost when buffer limits are reached, and the user is informed of this possibility. However, such an implementation is safe in the sense that deadlock can only be caused by hardware failure, and buffers never overflow their bounds. A more sophisticated crystal router would save any messages that caused buffer overflow problems, and attempt to process them later. A description of such a router is beyond the scope of this discussion.

5-5 CrOS III Extensions Under *Express*

5-5.1 PLOTIX

PLOTIX was originally developed at Caltech [Flower 86b] and represents a straightforward extension of CUBIX to provide graphical output from a parallel computer [Parasoft 88d]. PLOTIX views a graphics screen or a plotter as a file to be manipulated in the same way as other files in CUBIX. It can currently support Tektronix terminals, Hewlett-Packard compatible plotters, SUN and IBM-PC screens, and Postscript devices. PLOTIX provides a conventional plot interface mapping user space to device space with the novel concept of naturally dividing the plotting surface between processors in an arbitrary fashion. It supports overlapping or distinct plot regions assigned to different processors. A full range of vector drawing commands are available as well as a contouring package.

5-5.2 A Parallel Debugger *ndb*

Parasoft's parallel debugger was originally developed by Flower at Caltech for the NCUBE hypercube. Parasoft has subsequently improved it, and it is currently available for the NCUBE (PC or full version), transputer arrays, and the Caltech/JPL Mark III hypercube [Parasoft 88b]. *ndb* is basically similar to conventional symbolic debuggers on sequential machines. A key new idea is a simple, but powerful, way of specifying groups of one or more processors for which a particular debugging command is applicable. This allows practical debugging even on systems like the NCUBE with 1024 nodes.

5-5.3 Profiling and Performance Monitoring

Express allows several types of profiling to measure system performance, and to understand sequential and other bottlenecks in parallel programs [Parasoft 88e].

As on a sequential machine, *Express* allows execution profiling with a simple parallel
extension of the UNIX *profil* command. Furthermore, one can tag events and
produce graphically for each processor a time sequence of the occurrence of events
flagged in the user node program. Similar features are found in SEECUBE [Couch
88], and other performance monitoring systems [Malony 89].

A new feature which is only present due to the parallel nature of the machine
is the profiling of communication activity, which can be done at various levels.
Information includes message length, frequency of traffic, and the nature of the
communication routine used.

6

NSIM: A Hypercube Simulator

6-1 Introduction

The purpose of this chapter is to describe the *nsim* package and to explain how to install the software and use the basic commands that are provided by the package. We will also indicate how to extend the simulator and, for some applications, to improve its performance greatly.

A common problem with the introduction of any new technology has been that its availability has often lagged behind the interest in its application. This has been the case with concurrent computation. The simulator which we will describe here is meant to ameliorate this problem partially. It is designed to run on an IBM-PC/AT and up. While it does not, and cannot, provide a replica of a concurrent machine to the last detail, at the level of the applications programmer it will deliver an excellent alternative to actually having a real parallel machine. If you already have a concurrent computer, then it is hoped that this system, or a modified version of it, will aid in applications software development.

6-2 Installation

In this section we describe how to build *nsim* on your local system. While considerable effort has been put into ensuring that the package is reasonably portable within the UNIX and VMS family, we make no promises. What we expect to be the most likely trouble spots will be pointed out in the subsection dedicated to portability. The installation of the VMS version will be dealt with separately in Sec. 6-7.

In this description of the installation we have assumed that there are no complications, such as the sharing of code between machines of different architectures via an NFS or similar network, or the use of the code as both a simulator and an actual cube environment residing on a cube's host. These issues have been addressed, however, for simplicity we defer them until later (see Sec. 6-8).

This section is also intended to be a partial road map of where everything is within the software package. All UNIX pathnames are given either as absolute pathnames, or as paths relative to the root directory of *nsim* which is called *NSIM*. There is also a directory *NSIM* that is a subdirectory of the root. There are no absolute pathnames coded into *nsim* so it does not matter where in the directory structure it is installed.

Once it has been determined where the *nsim* package is to be located, the command search variable *PATH* must be modified to include the directory *bin*. This is necessary even if the executable files are to be relocated after installation.

6-2.1 The C compiler: *ccc*

Due to variations among the available C compilers, it is not possible to provide a generic driver for compilation. However, we are able to deliver a reasonably general framework for the driver script that enables necessary customization to be done easily. All the files pertaining to the C compiler are located in the directory *ccc*. The discussion of this section is confined to that directory.

The file that contains the bulk of the compile driver is the Bourne shell script `ccc.template`. All the options that control the hypercube-specific compilation are defined in this file along with many options that were considered to be universal among UNIX systems. For future reference the hypercube switches are *-cros3*, *-cubix*, *-ih*, *-plotix*, *-cl ...*, and *-LD arg*. The meaning of these options will be described in a later section.

In the following discussion, *system* is taken to be the name used to identify the machine or operating system that the compiler script is intended for. There are three sections that have been separated to facilitate customization:

- `system.head`

  This file contains system specific initializations and default flags. In particular this specifies all flags that are always set for either the host or element programs and the names of the low-level libraries. These are denoted by the shell variables:

  * *ccc* — The name of the C compiler. Usually this would be *cc*. Similar macros may be employed to denote nonstandard names for other commands such as the stream editor *sed*.
  * *LMACH_IH* — The library for low-level CP routines.
  * *LMACH_ELT* — The library for low-level element routines.
  * *CFLAGS* — These flags are used for *all* compilations. Typically these are switches that are recognized by the preprocessor.
  * *C_EFLAG* — Flags that are always passed to the compiler for element programs. These flags, and those for the remaining variables, usually will pertain to floating-point specifications such as the type of coprocessor.
  * *C_HFLAG* — Flags that are always passed to the compiler for host programs.
  * *L_EFLAG* — Flags that are always passed to the linker for element programs.
  * *L_HFLAG* — Flags that are always passed to the linker for host programs.

- `system.opts`

  This file contains flags that are specific to the local driver, such as floating-point options. This is the file that will most often be modified. The way which the script handles switches that were not recognized by the body of the script in `system.template` can be specified by the user in this file. The provided default is that such flags are passed to both the compiling and linking phases of the script through the shell variables $COPT$ and $LOPT$. Note that this file fits into a *case – esac* statement within the main script so the syntax must be strictly correct.

- **system.link**
  This is the command line used for linking. There is likely to be a lot of variation in this file. Several important variables need to be noted:
  * $LOPT$ — Options passed to the link phase.
  * $OBJS$ — All object files.
  * $LIBS$ — The system and *nsim* libraries.
  * $ULIB$ — All user libraries.
  * L_EFLAG and L_HFLAG — These flags are defined in **system.head**.

The files described that contain special options are included into the file **ccc.template** to make the basic compiling script **ccc.system**. Once these files have been edited, the source script for the driver can be generated with

$$make\ MACH{=}system\ ccc$$

This produces the compiler script **ccc.system**. The remaining steps of producing the driver are either handled by the automatic installation or, if *ccc* is being upgraded, can be invoked with

$$make\ MACH{=}system\ install$$

This is the way in which this makefile is used by the installation script. This final step inserts into the compiler the knowledge of where all include files and libraries can be found. As absolute path names are used nothing should be moved around after the completion of this step. The compile driver *ccc* is then placed in the NSIM directory *bin* where all other executables will also be installed.

To get started, a pregenerated script **ccc.nsim** was generated from the files with *system* set to be *nsim*. This is intended only to get the user started. While this compiler will probably suffice for many applications, we expect that ultimately the user will want to customize it.

In a few situations, the provided **ccc.template** will be unable to utilize fully the features of the local compiler. In that case you may develop your own script and place it in **ccc.system**. In this case the makefile will bypass the use of **system.head**, and so on, if dummy entries are provided for these files. It is also possible that the central **Makefile** will need to be edited if you chose a name for *system* that is not currently supported. It should be remembered that this script is used to compile almost all the libraries, so the switches that correspond to hypercube usage must not be redefined. As a working rule, the addition of new switches to the scripts via **system.opts** is permitted; however, the removal of existing options from **ccc.template** should be strictly avoided.

6-2.2 C, Commands, Utilities, Installation

The installation of the *nsim* package is very simple. In the root directory of the package there is a central **Makefile**. From here the entire installation of *nsim* for C programming is controlled. For reasons that will be described later, the Fortran interface has to be built from the directory *FORTRAN*.

In brief, the complete installation could be executed by the command line:

make init system commands lint manual

where *system* could stand for any one of *xenix*, *bsd*, or *unix* or a system name that the user has implemented the needed support for. In this section we will walk the reader through what each of the dependencies on that command line stands for, and how the system may be extended to support a machine environment other than the three mentioned.

A summary, but not an exhaustive list, of the provided dependencies reads as:

help	– Provides a brief summary of the makefile dependencies.
init	– Several basic initializations.
xenix	– Install full XENIX system.
bsd	– Install on a Berkeley UNIX system.
unix	– Install under UNIX System 5.
commands	– Compile all user commands.
lint	– Install the lint libraries.
manual	– Install all manual cat and index files.

Typing "*make help*" will provide a very terse statement of the component commands required to build the system. Following these steps will install the basic *nsim* package.

The first step of installation is

make init

This ensures that the directories *bin*, *LIBS*, and *MANN/cat?* have been created and that the file **setup** has the correct permissions (executable by the installer). You will also see a message telling you which version of *nsim* you have. If you don't see such a message, then you have one of the very early versions. The discussion in this book is relevant to version 1.0 and later. The version label is contained in the file **version.c** if it exists. For future reference this version number is installed into all the libraries.

To install the software package fully, it is necessary to know which breed of UNIX you are using. For example, if you are on a XENIX system, all you need to do is type

make xenix

This process takes the most time. There is always the possibility that *nsim* will not compile on your system due to variations of definitions within include files or differences in their locations. If so these will need to be fixed. In Sec. 6-3 we will describe the most likely forms of problems that might arise. Assuming that no such problems are encountered, the net effect of this step is to install all the linkable libraries in the directory *LIBS*. Installation on a Berkeley or System 5 UNIX is executed in the same way. It has been implicitly assumed that that XENIX runs on 16-bit machines and that all other systems are on 32-bit computers. The XENIX implementation supports the four models of compilation.

The provided options for what systems can be built are intended in part to be exemplary. If a different name is desired, or required, then all that needs to be done is for a new entry to be made in the root **Makefile** and a similar entry to be made in the file **setup**. An example is provided under the name *ex_sys*. The value provided for *MACH* used in the construction of *ccc* must be set appropriately. The default is *MACH=nsim*.

The file **setup** contains all of the default options for compilers, system labels, and so on, that are defined in most subordinate makefiles. The major flags are:

SYSM   This is the name that you have elected to call this system.

ARCV   This defines the way in which library files are to be constructed. The important feature is that the macros $(OBJS) and $(LIBR) cannot be renamed.

CFLG   This relates to any special flags that should be passed to all uses of the C compiler. There is a choice as to whether flags are defined here or in the compiler script. There is no preference as to which is used.

MAKE   Sets the macro of the same name in makefiles. It is usually unnecessary to need to set this macro. The default setting is **/bin/make**.

SHELL   All makefiles must use **/bin/sh** as the shell. Setting this is also usually unnecessary, the default being **/bin/sh**.

Modifications to the file **setup** have the potential to be somewhat involved. An example entry is provided that corresponds to the example *ex_sys* in the main makefile. Several flags are set, all of which mean something to most of the makefiles within *nsim* so the variable names cannot be changed without severe consequences. A partial list of such flags includes *CMDD, SUFX, PREF, INCL, EXEC, PROF*. Any of these flags could be set from the file **setup**; however, this is not advisable unless you really know what you are doing. We have enforced the rule that all *nsim* makefile macro variables are denoted by four uppercase letters, so user variables other than of this specification are guaranteed to be safe.

The one variable that deserves special mention is *PREF*. This is the prefix letter for all files that are kept in *LIBS*. By default it will be an uppercase *S*. This letter takes on significance in the case of a XENIX implementation or if the code is shared over a network. The meaning of this prefix will be described more fully in the section on code sharing (Sec. 6-8).

The libraries that are installed are derived from code in the source directories:

CROS3/IH   Contains the CrOS III CP routines.

CROS3/ELT   Contains the CrOS III node routines and a few general utility functions.

CUBIX/IH   Contains the CUBIX interface between the CP and the UNIX system calls. These functions implement most of the server function that the host fulfills under CUBIX.

CUBIX/C   Contains the CUBIX equivalents to the standard I/O library and UNIX system calls.

NSIM   Contains the low-level functions that actually implement the simulator.

It should also be noted that the libraries with profiling turned on are not installed by this step. If these libraries are desired, then the command must be modified to, for example,

make PROF=1 xenix

This will install both the profiled and standard libraries in a single step. This uses the makefile macro $*(SUFX)* which is set to *_p* for profiled libraries; otherwise it is null. The profiled libraries are also placed in *LIBS*.

The next step is to install all the executable commands in *bin*. This step is invoked by

make commands

This compiles and installs all the commands in *EXEC* and *CUBIX/EXEC* into *bin*. This step must be done after the installation of the libraries has been successfully completed. Problems that could be encountered in linking the commands will be discussed in the section on portability (Sec. 6-3).

If you use *lint*, and we strongly recommend that you do, then the lint libraries can be installed with

make lint

It is a good bet that you will see a few error messages appear when the lint libraries are compiled; however, these should be fairly harmless. The lint libraries must be installed after the commands have been because the libraries are compiled with *clint*. The lint libraries have the form `$(PREF)llib-l{name}.ln` and have been placed in *LIBS*.

The next step after all the libraries and executable programs have been compiled is to set the users' path to search the directory *bin* or to move all these programs to an appropriate directory. We strongly discourage the latter unless *nsim* is being used in an environment where there is no sharing of code. Moving pieces of *nsim* around is also risky because of the existence of absolute pathnames that get encoded into commands during installation.

If you are going to install the Fortran package, then that should be done now, otherwise proceed with the installation of the manual.

The final step for the installer would be to build and then peruse the on-line manual that is provided. To construct the manual entries and the indices fully, the command is

make manual

All the commands that you will need to know about are documented in the manual along with documentation for all of the system calls and a few other things that were deemed important. The manual will be described in more detail in Sec. 6-4.1. For the moment, to get started, type:

mann mann

This will tell you about the *mann* command. *mann* is intended to have the same general functionality as the UNIX command *man*. In particular, it enables the user to peruse the indices. Once all of this has been done, the *nsim* package is ready for use.

There are also several dependencies that can be used to clean out the directory structure of *nsim*. These are all invoked with:

make clean

Do not use these unless their function is understood because they will undo most of what you will have done up to now. Their main function is for preparing a clean distribution file. The many object and other temporary files that are created during installation are all cleaned out automatically as installation proceeds.

6-2.3 Installing Fortran

If you do not wish to use Fortran, then this section may be skipped. All *nsim* has been written in C to enhance portability. However, in deference to the fact that most scientific computing is done in Fortran, a Fortran interface to the C code has been provided. Because of the variety of Fortran compilers even within the UNIX family, this installation step cannot in general be automatic.

If you are on a UNIX machine that has a standard implementation of Fortran and are in the NSIM/FORTRAN directory then the installation process is single step:

make unix

When this has completed, the only thing left to do is to install the manual pages pertinent to this Fortran. This can be done with the command:

make manual

The manual is built automatically from *MANN* directory and then linked into the standard manual directories. It is because of this that it is best to leave the full installation of the manual until last.

If you have a standard Fortran implementation, then you are lucky and can directly install your Fortran and return to the last part of the *nsim* installation. Otherwise, a substantial amount of work needs to be done to build a Fortran simulator environment. The rest of this section is devoted to this endeavor.

6-2.4 FORTRAN-C Interface

The major problem that must be addressed is how the Fortran routines call C and vice versa. The interface between the two languages is notorious for not having universal portability. Unless you are using one of the compilers for which we have provided interfaces, then you will have to write your own. To simplify the conversion to the local system, we have attempted to keep all nonportable constructions bottled up in specific libraries. The inevitable downside of this arrangement is that efficiency is lost. For any single case, one could always do much better.

If you need to write your own Fortran-C interfaces then the routines that need to be written correspond to those in the directories *CROS3/IH*, *CROS3/ELT*, and *CROS3/CUBIX*, all these pathnames being given relative to *FORTRAN/UNIX*. It is suggested that the makefiles from these directories be used without modification so as to ensure that everything that is needed will be done. When these routines and script have been written along with their makefiles, modify the makefile in *FORTRAN* to accommodate your new codes.

An important technical issue is whether a Fortran program can be called from a C main program and contain IO statements. In general it is not possible to do this. Surmounting this problem will not be difficult, just annoying. The obvious solution is to write the main program in Fortran although this is typically not a very convenient thing to do.

6-2.5 Fortran Libraries

The locally provided Fortran libraries may need to be modified to allow for successful linking. The best way is to copy the library and then link the simulator programs using the specially prepared version. It is not possible to say in advance what gymnastics will be necessary here.

6-2.6 Compile Driver

To compile Fortran programs a compiler script will need to be written. Unfortunately, due to the variety of Fortrans, a canned tool such as was provided for the C compiler is not a viable product. However, the model provided by `FORTRAN/UNIX/cf77.sh` is likely to be a good start.

The script `cf77.sh` which is aimed at the UNIX Fortran will support the implied use of the C preprocessor */lib/cpp* as indicated by the `.F` suffix and the use of *ratfor* as specified by the filename extension `.r`. The flags pertaining to the hypercube are the same as for the C compiler *ccc*.

6-2.7 Installation

The `Makefile` in the directory FORTRAN will need to be edited. The only point to keep in mind is that the contents of the directories *FORTRAN/CF77PP* and *CUBIX* must be included. All the code here is in C and is portable between Fortran implementations. The new Fortran may now be installed just as for the provided versions.

6-3 Portability Issues

This subsection is a compendium of some of the things that might go wrong and so prevent the installation of *nsim* from completing normally. We will also point out several known sections of code that rely on special features of the C language implementation.

6-3.1 Shell Scripts and Makefiles

There is a possibility that some of the shell scripts will not work as they should. Under the most common versions of UNIX this is unlikely to occur; however, with UNIX lookalikes, anything could happen. The main vulnerability is in the C compiler *ccc*. It should be noted that everything was designed to be run under */bin/sh* so make sure that the environment variable *SHELL* is set appropriately.

Throughout *nsim*, use is made of the UNIX utilities, in no particular order: *awk, sed, ed, sort, /lib/cpp, test, cut, paste, split, basename, tr,* and of course, *make*. The syntax of the shell */bin/sh* is also assumed to be standard. Variations in the switches and usage of any of these utilities are likely to cause trouble. The manual is also dependent upon *nroff, ptx,* and *fgrep*.

Problems with *make* and *sed*, or the shell, are likely to show up very quickly. Makefile problems will occur if the command *make* is not located at */bin/make* or the shell is not */bin/sh*. These problems can be fixed by setting the macro variables *MAKE* and *SHELL* via the mechanism of **setup** as discussed in the previous section.

If trouble is encountered at this level, there is no solution that we can suggest here except to work around each problem as it is encountered.

6-3.2 Library Archives

Some machines require archives to have a random library format while others require the libraries to have a strict ordering of the external references, while still others repeatedly search the libraries until all external references have either been resolved or obviously cannot be. We have tried to ensure that everything will work whichever archival scheme you have. The form of the archiving command is controlled from the file **setup** by setting the makefile macro *ARCH*.

6-3.3 Includes Files

There tends to be some variation among UNIX and VMS systems as to the exact form and location of definitions in include files. Important points to note are that *nsim* tries to use its own include files where possible and only uses "well known" standard include files otherwise. The *nsim* specific files are located in the directories *INCL, INCL/sys,* and *INCL/CUBIX*.

The file **errno.h** is not used, rather, the system include file **sys/errno.h** is included by the *nsim* **INCL/errno.h**. This in particular means that the values that *errno* can take are always consistent with the local system. This is vital to ensure that CUBIX will work properly.

CUBIX has its own `stdio.h`, which has small, but critical, differences from the `stdio.h` in *usr/include*. If the incorrect file is picked up, the *CUBIX/C* library will fail to compile.

Other perennial problems such as whether it is `string.h` or `strings.h` may or may not cause you grief; however, at least these failings are easy to fix.

6-3.4 Functions Taking a Variable Number of Arguments

Several functions within *nsim* (*cubeldl*, *cubeldle*, *printf*, *fprintf*, *sprintf*, and *scanf*, *fscanf*, *sscanf*) take a variable number of arguments and so are vulnerable to portability problems.

These functions all assume that the C compiler pushes the arguments of a function onto the stack. If your compiler uses a different method such as passing a fixed number of arguments through registers; then these programs may require modification. The functions that assume the stack layout are *cubeldve*, *_xprint*, and *_xscan*.

All these functions have been written using `varargs` macros. For the functions *cubeldl* and *cubeldle*, the standard include file is used; however, for *_xprint* and *_xscan*, the macro definitions (but not the usage) are not standard. The way to "standardize" these definitions would be, for example, to promote *_xprint* to be *printf*.

This will be less efficient on the reuse of code but may be necessary. At least it should avoid the need to provide a new *printf*. Another possibility is to make use of the local system's *vsprintf* family of functions. The code to do this is provided but is currently commented out. The only trick if this is the desired solution is that some *vsprintf* implementations return an integer, others return a pointer to a character. The user will also have to be careful to avoid buffer overflow in this case.

6-4 Utilities

Next we discuss in more detail the layout and usage of the utilities. They are described in the order that they are likely to be first needed by the user. Hence, initially we will get the user acquainted with the manual; then we will progress to compiling, running, and debugging parallel programs.

We will assume that the reader has some familiarity of what is involved in programming under the crystalline system and that he or she has a reference of some form available. This section is not intended to teach concurrent programming.

6-4.1 The NSIM Programmers Manual

For help on-line a fairly comprehensive version of the manual is accessible using the command *mann*. The syntax for the command and the arrangement of the manual pages is very similar to those of the UNIX manual. The manual is stored in the directory *MANN* and has the standard subdirectories *MANN/man?* and *MANN/cat?* where

- *cat1 cat2* hold the processed outputs of the manual sections.
- *man1 man2* hold the raw forms suitable for input to nroff or troff.

Within the *MANN/man?* directories, the manual is organized roughly as

- *man0*, which holds incidental pages — title page, indexes, and so on.
- *man1*, which holds commands.
- *man2*, which holds system calls.
- *man3*, which holds user subroutines.
- *man4*, which holds miscellaneous stuff.

Into which section one places the documentation for some items is often a matter of personal preference. Within sections 2 and 3 of the manual, there are subsections that are denoted by the letters *e* and *h*. These denote entries that, respectively, pertain to either the node or CP functions alone. Those functions that do not belong to either of these subsections are relevant to both node and CP programs.

The index is constructed automatically from the raw manual pages using

make manual

in the root directory. There is no problem regarding the inclusion of new manual pages if you so wish. Just add the new pages and remake the manual as before. Like the UNIX manual, the entries tend to be rather terse.

For each command referenced within the manual, the pathname for the source code, and the location of the library module is given relative to the root of the NSIM directory. The user is warned that not all routines are documented, in particular, some of those within the *nsim* kernel are omitted.

The only annoying feature to beware of is that *mann* will not deal with standard UNIX manual entry requests. If your local command *man* is reasonably good (supports an option to specify the directories that are searched for manual entries), then the use of *mann* can probably be dispensed with altogether. When *mann* is compiled, the absolute pathname of where the manual pages and indices are located is included so the formatted pages cannot be moved around within the system without adverse consequences.

6-4.2 Compiling

To make the compiling of programs easier, a shell script *ccc* has been provided. As long as one does not wish to do anything really clever, then this command will be all that is needed. The form of a typical compilation is

ccc [options] file1 ...

The files are all assumed to be C source with a `.c` suffix or object files with a `.o` suffix. The inclusion of assembly source files is not permitted. Otherwise the compiling steps are intended to be as close as possible to those that would be used in any other application. If an error is detected during compilation, *ccc* returns a (potentially meaningless) nonzero exit code; otherwise zero is returned to indicate success. The flags that are special to *ccc* are

-ih   Compile this program as a CP program. This flag currently must appear with (and preceding) the **-cros3** switch and must never be used in conjunction with the **-cubix** switch. The variable _IH is set as defined.

-cros3   Compile as a CP program if the **-ih** switch has been set, otherwise compile as a node program.

-cubix   Assume that the program employs CUBIX. Compile and link (if requested) using the appropriate include files and libraries. This also sets the preprocessor variable _CUBIX to be defined.

-plotix   Compiles allowing a crude plotting utility from the nodes. This option will only be usable if the utility libraries supporting plotting commands have been installed in *UTIL/LIBS*. The variable *plotix* is defined for the preprocessor.

-cllib   Search the library lib, which may be located in either *LIBS* or UTIL/LIBS for resolution of external references. The library is assumed to have the name $(PREF)lib.a.

-M   Use this switch to generate dependency lists of include files. The shell script that supports this option is the most vulnerable to variations among UNIX system commands in *ccc*.

-LD   Pass the following argument to the loader. With this mechanism one can utilize the full capability of the local linker without having to modify the internal details of *ccc*. With this option an unusual switch may be passed to the linker without the local compiler having to figure out what it might be. If *ccc* has been properly customized, there should be no need for this flag.

A few common switches are supported directly by *ccc*. It is possible to obtain preprocessor and assembly listings in the usual way. It is also possible to incrementally compile programs. The only caveat is that the order in which options are specified can alter the outcome. In particular, all the options mentioned should be specified (if they are required) before any source files are entered.

We should note that the scripts that are used to compile Fortran programs support the same switches with the same requirements of usage. The generic Fortran compilation would be :

$$cf77 \; [options] \; file1 \; ..$$

where the example has been taken from the UNIX Fortran implementation. The cf77 script expects Fortran source files to have either an .f or a .for extension. If the file has the suffix .F, then it will be passed through the C-preprocessor /lib/cpp before being passed to the compiler. Ratfor programs are also permitted and are recognized by the extension .r. Not all permutations of the foregoing can be supported on all systems. We also note that the Fortran compiler may have a name other than cf77; for instance, the script for Ryan-McFarland Fortran is invoked with crmf.

6-4.3 Executing a simulation

To run a program requires use of the *nsim* command. The format of the most general command is:

nsim [NSIM_options ...] progIH [IH_options ...]   \

progELT [ELT_options] [ELT_args ...]

The important point is that what the user types is identical to the command line that would be typed on a real hypercube except for the text prior to *progIH*, the CP program. The text beyond the *progIH* will depend strongly upon how the program has been written, but not at all on what *nsim* options are being used. When using CUBIX then *progIH* simply becomes *cubix*.

The options that *nsim* currently supports (representing **NSIM_options** in the command line above) are:

-s# file   This option is used for debugging and will be described later. It should be pointed out that this *special process* could be used in other circumstances, for instance, a program compiled using *ctrace*. The number # following the **s** corresponds to the node designated to be the special process. **file** is an executable file that will be loaded instead of the node program *progELT* at the special node. If the special node number is set equal to -1 then the special process is run instead of the CP program. This is typically used for debugging CP programs.

-p[csilfd][0-7]   This option defines the communications debugging to be done on this run. The letter specifies the type description of the data that will represent the data packets if relevant. The digit indicates the debugging level. This feature will be described later. If the switch is omitted, the communications debugging is completely turned off. If the communications debugging was disconnected during installation, then this switch will have no effect.

-m   This option produces the profile output for this run. If this flag is not specified, all profiling information is suppressed. Compile all programs with the **-p** option if this feature is to be used. The output will be decoded by *cprof*. For systems other than XENIX, this utility will need to be modified.

-c[int]   This option controls the core dumps. The default is to produce a core file for each node and the CP in the case of a fatal error or a quit signal initiated by the user. This option is only likely to be useful if file system space is at a premium.

There are several other less important options that do not need to be discussed here. These may be removed in later versions of *nsim*.

6-4.4 Debugging

Perhaps the most important function of any simulator is that it provides a capacity for expediting the chore of debugging.

The *nsim* simulator provides us with several forms and levels of debugging that will be described shortly. At the lowest level is the use of an assembly, or symbolic, debugger on an individual node. Then several facilities of varying usefulness are provided to enable us to get some handle on problems related to the internode communications and program performance.

We would like to point out that obtaining the information to support debugging of a parallel machine is not particularly difficult. The truly important issue is to decide how to display that data in a form that is useful to the user. We will make no contribution to the solution of this problem here. Rather, we provide a set of utilities that bring some of the tools designed for sequential programming to bear on concurrent debugging.

6-4.4.1 Symbolic Debugging

Within any individual node, including the CP, we can use the available debuggers that are provided by the local system. These utilities, such as *adb*, were of course designed for use with sequential programs, and so they may not tell us much (or anything) about communications bugs. However, for many purposes this facility will be sufficient. The major downfall here is that one can only examine one node at a time. These debuggers are invoked as the name of the local debugger prefixed with the letter *c*, for instance, *adb* becomes *cadb*. For this discussion, we will denote the debugger utility with the generic label *debug*.

The use of the local debuggers is provided through the special process. To prevent the debugger from being totally messed up by the signals that are used in the communications routines, the special process continuously polls the locations at which it expects to receive data.

When the provided debugger is used on an element node, the command line will have the appearance

$$nsim\ [\ NSIM\_options\ ]\ -s\#\ debug\ progIH\ ...$$

The relative order of the **NSIM_options** and the debugging option that we are highlighting is unimportant.

The other node programs all begin executing and will continue until they attempt a communication function that requires the cooperation of the special node. Only now is the simulation under control of the debugger. When the simulation finishes, as defined by the end of the CP program, the node process and the debugger will be killed. This can be annoying, however, it is necessary to prevent the CP returning to the invoking shell and so leaving the debugger process in limbo. When the CP is being debugged, the command line has the form

$$nsim\ [\ NSIM\_options\ ]\ -s\#\ debug\ progIH$$

In this case the debugger will not die; however, you cannot restart a second simulation from the debugger. Note that when the CP is being debugged, the name of the host program must still appear. The rest of the command line is not specified until the program is actually executed from within the debugger environment.

All the debuggers are derived from the common format of one particular file: *EXEC/debug.c*. Experienced users may want to provide specialized options regarding paths to search to find source files, and so on. The important point is that options cannot be passed to the special process (debugger in this case) on the command line. They have to either be hard coded or read in from a command file once the debugger is running under the user's control. The reason for not providing command line arguments was simply the expedient of avoiding a potentially hideous syntax to disentangle debugger from program switches and arguments.

Because the UNIX kernel shares the text of executing programs, for the debugging of node programs the node program is physically copied to a file that is called **debugNODE**. This is necessary to thwart the sharing of text. This additional file will be removed upon termination of the debugging session.

6-4.4.2 Communication Debugging

This is the most poorly implemented function. Each node prints out a report of entry, and exit, from the various communication functions. By default these files are created as **node?.out** where the question mark stands for a node number corresponding to that node of the simulation. This utility is invoked with:

nsim [NSIM_options] -p[uilfdc]# progIH ...

The second field of the switch specifies the output form of any data that is written to the debugging files. The letters specify the types as: *u* for shorts, *i* for integers, and so on.

The second field is an integer from 0 to 7 that determines the debugging level. Of the eight levels of complexity possible, only four are actually used by the system. The user is free to make use of the others. For languages other than C the debugging facility will realize that, for example, Fortran is being used.

The major problem with this utility is that it produces large files which make it difficult to find what you want. The functions that control this facility could probably be much more profitably used to deliver output to a utility such as SEECUBE [Couch 88].

Communications debugging, and the overhead associated with it, can be excised from the system by setting the *DEBUG* variable appropriately in the file **INCL/sys/debugsys.h**.

6-4.4.3 Core Dumps

nsim has been implemented so that the user can retrieve the core image files from all of the nodes. This option should be used with care if you have severely limited disk space as one gets an image for each node, **core#** (# being the node number), plus one for the CP which is **core**. Other options permit the suppression of the dumps. The communication file is not removed in the case of an abnormal termination. A single file **nsim.dump** is written for all crashes. This file contains a few useful returns from each node such as the status of the communication channels, the abort code, the current value of *errno* for the user's program, but not for *nsim*'s code.

It is not guaranteed that the core files will be correctly written in the event of a fatal error. The code and data that handles the needed synchronization is not separated from the user's program so it could become corrupted by an error. A more reliable way to handle the core dumps would be to cause each node to execute in a separate directory. Even this is not guaranteed to provide for a graceful crash. Often user intervention via an interrupt will be required.

It is possible to suppress the production of core files with the -c switch.

6-4.4.4 Profiling

Profiling is primarily of use in improving algorithm performance, rather than in debugging. In addition to the ability to retrieve a monitor profile from each node, called mon#.out (# is the node number), and the CP (mon.out), there is a simple utility *cprof* that combines the results for all the node programs and displays them side by side. The results are sorted in the order of the function name. Because of variation among local profiling utilities, the user will probably need to modify this function. The documented form of this utility is:

> *cprof -elt progELT*

One problem with profiling will be that the timings that one receives for functions that involve communications will most likely be completely useless. The reason is that a lot of system time gets tied up in the communication routines waiting for some other node (process) to write to the appropriate channel. Much work needs to be done if *cprof* is to become a truely useful product.

6-4.4.5 Lint

One of the most useful utilities that is provided with UNIX is *lint*. For *nsim* we have provided libraries which permit the checking of node programs. It should be pointed out that this will not detect any communications bugs such as possible deadlocks; rather, it is an application of sequential facilities and so will be of greatest utility in preventing bugs that are of a sequential nature. The flags that *clint* accepts are essentially the same as for *ccc*. Lint library entries are provided for all the CrOS III and CUBIX functions. Libraries for some of the utility functions may also be provided. The form of a typical *clint* command is:

> *clint [options] file1 ...*

where the options can be basically the same as for *ccc*. *Clint* can also be used to build user lint libraries, and the syntax is defined in the on-line manual.

6-4.4.6 Comments

Obviously, much work needs to be done in the direction of developing useful debugging tools that can aid in program and algorithm development on parallel machines. It should be pointed out that *clint*, and so on, will suffer from all of the bugs that your system does. These utilities are only shell scripts or simple C programs that ultimately call the local version of *lint*, and so on.

6-5 Utility Libraries

This section of *nsim*, consisting of the files in *UTIL*, stands alone from the rest of the *nsim* package and must be installed separately as such. The contents are likely to change with time and so will not be described in detail.

All of the directories deliver either executables that are placed in *bin* or libraries that are placed in UTIL/LIBS. All these libraries may be linked with the **-cl ...** switch to *ccc*.

To install the utility libraries and commands, the single step is

make install

invoked from the directory *UTIL*. The directory *UTIL* is also provided as the place that the user can put locally designed utilities.

6-6 Implementation Details

The main point we want to make (indirectly) in this section is that it is actually very simple to implement and use *nsim* as a real environment on a real parallel machine.

Most of the code that is included within *nsim* is independent of whether we are using a simulator or a real hypercube. In fact, a good implementation of the crystalline environment can be achieved by customizing only the routines in the directory *NSIM* to a real cube and, perhaps, but not necessarily, the routines *cread*, *cwrite*, *vread*, and *vwrite*. The intent was to confine all machine-dependent code to this directory.

With this in mind, the rest of this discussion is related to the contents of *NSIM*. We would like to point out that for optimal performance on a hypercube, or mesh, or any other machine for which a crystalline environment makes sense, that the functions such as *cread* should be optimized for that machine architecture.

The internal details of *nsim* will be left to the reader perusing the code; however, we will describe in brief the hooks that are used to connect the machine-dependent *nsim* code to the relatively portable code elsewhere. For almost all nonsystem applications, the user will never need to be concerned with calling these functions. Some, but not all, of them are documented in the on-line manual. These hooks are

initELT, which sets up the internal variables that define an individual node. It may also call routines that initialize communications.

initIH, which performs the same functions for the CP as _initELT_ does for the nodes.

downld, which loads the node program into the nodes. For the case of *nsim*, this is done in a sequential fashion. If you are using the TCP/socket implementation, then the download is done in parallel. If the user wished to load distinct programs into separate groups of nodes, then this is the routine that would need to be modified.

_rd,_wt,_pipe,_shift,_exch, which handle communication. Not all these will be used in any one implementation. For the standard *nsim* package, only _rd and _wt are fundamental, with the others all being defined in terms of these two functions. If a careful implementation of CrOS III was to be done on specific hardware, then there would be some value in promoting some of the other routines to the level of "fundamental."

_simexit, which for *nsim* controls the overall shutdown of a simulation. The node programs will wait in a pause until the CP reaches its exit and then kills the node programs.

_cread_HOST,_cwrite_HOST,_cread_CUBE,_cwrite_CUBE, which enable communication between the CP and the nodes. These routines were separated from the node-node communications protocol for a good reason; you may wish to use distinct methods of communications for the CP-node communications as opposed to the node-node. Indeed this is the way that the communications for the simple iPSC interfaces are handled. For *nsim* itself, the division is artificial.

_cread_NODE,_cwrite_NODE, which can be used if a nonpacketized method of communications is intended.

abort, _abort, which (the first calls the second within the nodes) are used to crash the simulation because of some user-defined error. Core dumps should be produced.

rdrdy, wtrdy, which provide a low-level means to determine if a given channel can be read from or written to.

There are also several parameters that protrude out of the *nsim* code. They are _hprocnum, _hnproc, and for convenience, _hdoc; these correspond to the node number, number of nodes, and the dimension of the cube.

The porting of the *nsim* environment to any other machine is quite straightforward and has been done (but is not being distributed) for both the iPSC and the iPSC2. There are several variables and functions that implement the debugging features of *nsim*. These additional variables are *nsim* specific and do not appear in the true parallel machine implementations. The user may wish to make use of the communications debugging hooks. If so, then versions of the functions _ENTER_ and _EXIT_ must be provided.

6-6.1 Communications

There are several implementations of the communication technology:

Common file — the most basic, undoubtedly the slowest, but also the most likely to work on an arbitrary UNIX system. The file is always called ns im.comm; hence, only one simulation can be executed in a given directory at any one time. This is the default implementation.

Shared memory — for both UNIX and VMS. The layout of the shared memory segment is identical to that of the common file. Under UNIX if the shared memory system calls are supported then this implementation can be used by compiling the code in directory *NSIM* with *-D_SHM* added to the compile flags. The commands must then be recompiled with the same flag set. No other libraries will need to be updated.

Message Passing/Sockets — Other possible methods of implementation could employ the UNIX facility of message passing, or the use of sockets. The design of such codes is as difficult (or as easy) as porting NSIM directly to machines such as the Intel hypercubes.

In addition to these strategies that have all been implemented in one form or another, the code can be installed on a real hypercube either through the use of a compatibility library or by customizing the basic communications calls.

6-6.2 Extension to General Topologies

Although the implementation that we have provided is for a hypercube topology, we will not be dogmatic about this configuration. In fact, the actual structure of *nsim* allows for the straightforward implementation of any connection topology including a fully connected machine.

For all current implementations of *nsim* each node is treated as a separate process. For the rest of this discussion, we will talk in terms of the common file or shared memory implementations. To some degree the same arguments will carry over to the message passing version. The applicability to the socket version is more problematic.

All the communications are routed through a file that is shared by the element nodes and the CP processes. Within this file separate read and write buffers are provided for each channel emanating from each individual node. Each node maintains two tables, _r_tab, _w_tab, which define the locations of the read/write buffers within the communications file corresponding to a particular channel. The channels are ordered sequentially starting with zero. Channels to the CP can be denoted by any value that is not a valid channel to another element node. This arrangement is general enough to permit any topology the user wants. Obviously, should another topology be desired, many of the higher-level functions would require some modification. The code that is specific to topology has been mainly isolated in the program _tables.c.

The lengths of these buffers have initially been defined to be 64 bytes plus 1 byte to denote the read/write status; however, this length is an arbitrary parameter. On a real hypercube, the length of this buffer may be fixed by the nature of the hardware. For the purpose of *nsim*, this is just a parameter that we can choose arbitrarily. Typically, the longer the message length, the better the performance, for most applications with medium-size message lengths. The value of the packet lengths can be changed by redefining *PKSIZE* in INCL/sys/packet.h. If you make this change, you must recompile all the *nsim* libraries that are defined in *CROS3/IH*, *CROS3/ELT*, and *NSIM* and all the binary executables.

The nodes (and for this discussion the CP is just another node) do not continuously poll the buffer but wait on signals from the other nodes. The exception for this rule is the special process which polls continuously. This allows the debuggers to work on this node without being constantly interrupted by the signals. For the message-passing and socket simulators, there need be no exchange of signals and no polling.

6-6.3 Undocumented Features

In addition to what is documented, we warn the enthusiastic reader who also takes the time to rummage through the code that there are several undocumented features to *nsim*. These were not documented because they fall outside the framework of a discussion on the crystalline system. We are not going to discuss these features here because then they would no longer be undocumented.

6-7 VMS Simulator

There is a VMS version of *nsim* that was derived from an early version of the UNIX implementation of *nsim*. User programs are portable between the UNIX and VMS simulators.

6-7.1 VMS Installation

The installation is directed from the root directory just as for UNIX except that Fortran is now installed directly without any intervention from the user. The command to install is:

> @*makevms*

When the installation is complete there will be a file in the root directory called `nsim.com`. This file defines the absolute pathnames for all the executable images that are provided by *nsim*. These definitions should be included with one's login definitions. Otherwise this command file will need to be executed before each session for which the simulator is to be used.

6-7.2 Differences from UNIX

Externally the VMS simulator is almost identical to the UNIX version. Because the VMS implementation was derived almost directly from the UNIX version some of the function of the latter was lost in the process. These problems are primarily confined to the utilities like *clint* and *mann*. Debugging using a special process is still possible, but it requires two compilations for each run. The process with the debug information needs to be executed as the special process.

The main feature of the VMS version is that shared memory was used instead of a commonly accessed file. The layout of the data within the shared memory section is identical to that in the common file implementation.

Another superficial difference is that VMS uses the character / to indicate a switch on a particular command line as opposed to the - of UNIX. Spaces are also often important for delimiting switches in UNIX, whereas VMS is insensitive to such white space. The compiling and linking commands have been altered to allow for these differences; otherwise the qualifiers are the same between the two operating systems.

There are a few technical changes that had to be made to CUBIX and Fortran CUBIX to deal with the way VMS deals with files. No extensions were made to CUBIX to give the user access to the **RMS** system. All operations are done via the UNIX file operations.

6-8 Code Sharing

As was mentioned earlier, it is possible to share the *nsim* source code over a heterogeneous network and compile and run the simulator from individual workstations. It is also possible to use the same code as both a simulator on a host and as the corresponding programming environment on a real parallel machine.

There are only two issues that need to be addressed: how to select the correct executables and how to link with the appropriate libraries. The first is achieved by the use of the shells *nsh* and *ncsh* corresponding to the Bourne shell, /bin/sh, and C-shell, /bin/csh. These commands modify the command search path in an appropriate way. There are some complications that affect the C-shell. In particular the user needs to modify his or her .cshrc so that the path is only read if the flag _path_flag is not set (otherwise the effect of using *ncsh* will be undone) and to set some special environment variables. The following environment variables need to be set.

LIB_PREF, which controls the prefix letter that is attached to the library so that the correct archives can be accessed from a common directory location. The default of S is used if this variable is not set. For XENIX systems, the prefix on the library is any of S,M,L, corresponding to small, medium, and large model libraries, respectively.

arch, *arch_id*=$arch/, which specifies the type of CPU that the user is currently executing on. The former variable needs to be set when the user logs in independently of *nsim*. The latter is set in *nsh*. This variable is used to place the executables in a subdirectory of *bin*. If not set these variables are defaulted to null.

For the case of sharing file systems between machines of differing architectures over a network, the problem of identifying which libraries and executables to use can be hidden completely within the user's environment, thereby avoiding the need to use *nsh* or *ncsh*. However, given the host of a cube and the desire to run the same environment both as a simulator or on the cube, the use of *nsh* is necessary.

6-8.1 Installation

To install *nsim* allowing for code sharing, first set up the environment variables for the archive prefixes and the machine architecture. The source code for *nsh* will also need to be edited to ensure that the appropriate value for *LIB_PREF* will be propagated. Then from the *nsim* root directory, type

make nsh

The command *nsh* is placed in the directory *bin*. To perform the installation, all that needs to be done is to invoke *nsh* and then proceed with the installation as for the simple case. If the code is being installed onto the host of a real hypercube, then *nsh* needs to be called with a single argument

nsh system

where system corresponds to either *nsim* or *cube* or whatever other name you wish to use. If *system* is not specified, it is defaulted to *nsim*. The effect of these options is to place the executables in the directory *bin/$arch/_system* (or *bin/_system* if *arch* is undefined) so that they can be accessed when those commands are invoked from *nsh* with the appropriate arguments.

The environment variable *PATH* for each user should only include the directories *bin* and *bin/$arch*, the pathnames being relative to the *nsim* root directory. If only *nsh* is to be used, then no more modifications to the user environment will be needed. If however, *ncsh* is favored, then `.cshrc` will need to be modified to permit conditional redefinition of the *path* variable.

From the user's point of view, all that needs to be done is the invocation of either *nsh* or *ncsh* before beginning an *nsim* session. The user should refrain from attempting to set either *NPATH* or *_path_flag*, the results of which will be unpredictable. The invocation of *nsh* and *ncsh* can be nested without consequence.

7

Tutorial Systems
for Concurrent Computation

7-1 The Benefits of Tutorial Systems

In Table 1-3 three different classes of tutorial systems for parallel computers were presented. To reiterate, these classes were

1. Add-on boards for PCs and workstations using parallel architectures.
2. A distributed network of linked sequential computers.
3. A simulator running on a sequential computer.

The main benefit of these types of tutorial systems is to allow students the opportunity to gain practical experience in the use of concurrent computers. Some systems, such as the NCUBE PC systems discussed in Sec. 7-2, can also be used to develop and debug parallel application codes before running "production" versions on larger systems such as the NCUBE/ten. The PC-CUBE and MAC-CUBE systems in Sec. 7-3 can be readily assembled, and since many educational institutions already possess the necessary hardware (IBM or Apple PCs), "hands-on" experience of programming hypercube concurrent processors can be made available at a modest cost. Moreover, CrOS III programs, such as those in Chap. 8, developed on any of the tutorial systems discussed in this chapter, or on the hypercube simulator, *nsim*, described in Chap. 6, can be directly ported to larger machines running CrOS III, such as those discussed in Chap. 3.

The hypercube simulator, *nsim*, together with the tutorial systems described in Secs. 7-2 and 7-3, make concurrent programming generally accessible to large numbers of students, scientists, and engineers in high schools, colleges, and universities. As more people gain expertise in concurrent programming techniques we expect that research in this area will progress at a faster rate and that the commercial infrastructure necessary to promote the use of concurrent computers to become established more quickly.

The *nsim* simulator has already been extensively discussed in Chap. 6. In this chapter we will describe two different add-on boards for IBM PCs, namely, the NCUBE PC hypercube systems and the transputer-based boards. These were pioneered by Definicon Systems, Inc., but as shown by Appendix H-2, there are now many vendors. In addition, Sec. 7-3 will describe distributed concurrent systems formed by linking together IBM or Apple personal computers with a hypercube topology.

7-2 Add-on Boards for Personal Computers

7-2.1 The NCUBE PC Systems

The NCUBE/four system consists of an IBM PC/AT (or compatible) host and between 1 and 4 processor cards. Each processor card contains 4 NCUBE nodes, so that 4, 8, and 16 node hypercube systems are possible and can be plugged into a standard PC/AT expansion slot which provides a 16-bit connection to the PC/AT backplane. Systems that contain more than one processor card require an expansion cabinet to provide extra power and cooling. Each NCUBE node has 512 Kbytes of memory and a peak speed of 350 Kflops (250 Kflops) for 32-bit (64-bit) arithmetic. An additional plug-in Graphics/four card provides a graphical interface for the NCUBE nodes which is compatible with the graphics on larger NCUBE systems.

NCUBE Corporation also markets the NCUBE 386-AT system, which, like the NCUBE/four system, can accommodate up to 4 NCUBE processors cards, but is equipped with a system board with a 16-MHz INTEL 80386 processor and either an INTEL 80287 or 80387 math coprocessor. Thus the host computer of the NCUBE 386-AT system is more powerful than that of the NCUBE/four system.

The NCUBE PC systems run AXIS and VERTEX, the standard NCUBE host and node operating systems. However, to run the CrOS III application codes described in Chap. 8 on the NCUBE PC systems, it is necessary to use the XENIX-based driver produced by Parasoft Corporation. The *Express* communication system described in Sec. 2-4 can be run on NCUBE PC systems running the PC-XENIX operating system on the host computer. Since all the application codes in Chap. 8 use the CrOS III communication system, which is a subset of *Express*, it follows that all of these codes can be run on an NCUBE PC system running under PC-XENIX. Full details of how to install and use *Express* on such a system are given in Parasoft's *Express* manual [Parasoft 88a].

NCUBE announced a follow-on system, the NCUBE-2 with a similar architecture but a faster processor and much more memory per node. *Express* will be ported to these new systems.

7-2.2 The Transputer Systems

A growing number of companies are now producing plug-in transputer boards for PC and workstation systems. Currently Transputer boards are available for the Apple Macintosh II, IBM PC/AT, and SUN workstations using the proprietary Macintosh, DOS, or UNIX operating systems. A list of the vendors known to us is given in Appendix H. The transputer chip, manufactured by INMOS, consists of a fast RISC-architecture processor with four serial links which can be used to connect it to other transputers or to a host computer. A typical add-on transputer board contains four T414 or T800 transputer chips, and boards can be connected together to form a multiprocessor network, the size and topology of which is largely up to the user. The T800 transputer has the advantage of an on-board floating-point unit with a peak performance of 1.5 Mflops at 20-MHz. The 30-MHz version of the T800 is 50% faster. We have benchmarked a 20-MHz transputer at about four times the performance of the original NCUBE-1 processor; we expect the new NCUBE-2 node to be about twice the speed of a 20-MHz transputer. The 1989 version of these add-on systems have typically one to four megabytes of memory for each transputer. This will naturally increase as higher density DRAMS become available.

Parasoft Corporation has implemented the C and more recently Fortran version of the *Express* communication environment for transputer systems [Parasoft 88b] produced by the vendors in Appendix H. Thus all the applications presented in Chap. 8 can be run on the transputer systems for IBM, Apple and SUN systems. In addition, the performance monitor, parallel debugger, and PLOTIX graphics library, described in Sec. 5-5, can also be used with these transputer systems. Since *Express* allows communication between arbitrary pairs of nodes, doing any necessary message forwarding automatically, the actual topology of the transputer network is not important. However, it has been found that communication is generally efficient if transputer networks of 16 or fewer nodes are connected as a hypercube, and larger networks as a two-dimensional mesh.

7-3 Distributed Networks of Personal Computers

7-3.1 The PC-CUBE

The PC-CUBE is an ensemble of IBM PCs connected with the hypercube topology via RS-232 serial links [Ho 88a]. The hardware-limited communication rate of 115.2 Kbaud is obtained over these links by using low-level routines written to address the UART (Universal Asynchronous Receiver/Transmitter) chip on the serial board.

The CrOS III communication environment and the CUBIX parallel I/O system, described in Sec. 2-2 and Chap. 4, respectively, have been implemented on the PC-CUBE system, as has the asynchronous Mercury operating system [Lee 86]. CrOS communications are implemented using a synchronous communication protocol giving an effective data transmission rate of 47 Kbaud. This leads to the estimate of t_{comm} given in Eq. (1.3).

In addition, a CrOS III performance monitor has been developed for the PC-CUBE system. This can be used to record the amount of calculation, idle, and communication time in a particular segment of a program, and a summary of these statistics is output to a specified file stream. The performance monitor also has a real-time mode in which the current state of each node is displayed graphically on the node's display monitor. The performance monitor gives easily understood information on load imbalance and communication inefficiencies in a parallel program and is therefore useful both as a program development and educational tool.

A general execution profiler for determining the time spent in each subroutine has also been developed for the PC-CUBE system and may be used for both parallel and sequential programs. This is primarily of use in program development and gives an indication of which parts of an application should be parallelized or fine-tuned to achieve optimum performance.

Graphics may be performed using a version of the PLOTIX system referred to in Sec. 5-5.1 or by using the Grafix library, which contains routines to emulate a subset of the commercially available HALO graphics package.

Each node of the PC-CUBE is a complete PC/XT or AT with a keyboard, a floppy and/or hard disk drive, and a display monitor. These I/O devices are useful in debugging codes and also can be used to allow each node to display its output independently. Thus in this regard the PC-CUBE has an advantage over most currently available commercial hypercubes, which, in general, must route their I/O to the host computer or peripherals through intermediate nodes. Another advantage is that given a set of PCs, the cost of linking them into a PC-CUBE is small (~$1,000) compared with the cost of purchasing a small commercial hypercube, though, of course, the PC-CUBE is intended as an educational tool rather than as a high-performance parallel computer.

The following hardware is needed to construct a PC-CUBE:

1. One IBM PC (or compatible) for each node of the hypercube, plus one for the control processor (CP). Thus, a PC-CUBE of dimension d requires $(n + 1)$ PCs, where $n = 2^d$.

2. d standard RS-232 serial ports for each node, except for node 0, which requires $(d + 1)$ ports (the extra one is used to communicate with the CP). The CP requires just one serial port to communicate with node 0.

3. $1 + (n*d)/2$ ordinary computer cables, with at least seven wires, to connect the nodes and the CP.

The minimum software requirements to run a PC-CUBE are DOS version 2.0 or higher (although the execution profiler requires version 3.0 or higher) and a C compiler. In the development of the PC-CUBE at Caltech the Microsoft C compiler version 4.0 was used. Fortran versions of the CrOS III communication routines have not been written, however, the Microsoft mixed language interface can be used to access the C CrOS III routines from MS-FORTRAN or MS-PASCAL programs.

At Caltech, PC-CUBEs with up to 8 nodes have been built. Details of the construction of a PC-CUBE are given in the PC-CUBE User's Guide [Ho 88g], which is available electronically as described in Appendix G. A PC-CUBE package consisting of all the software and application development tools mentioned in this section, together with instructions on the assembly of a PC-CUBE, is available from Parasoft (see Appendix H).

Concurrent XLISP (CXLISP) has also been implemented on the PC-CUBE system, but is not currently available for distribution.

7-3.2 The MAC-CUBE

The MAC-CUBE is a Macintosh-based hypercube, using AppleTalk hardware and software to emulate communication channels between nodes [Ho 88d]. The AppleTalk local area network has a ring topology, and since only one message can travel on the bus at one time, the MAC-CUBE is inherently less efficient than the PC-CUBE, described in Sec. 7-3.1, in which messages can travel between nodes concurrently. On the other hand, unlike the PC-CUBE, which requires extra cables and serial ports for its construction, no additional hardware is needed to build a MAC-CUBE.

CrOS III communications are implemented using the link access routines (ALAP). The CrOS III primitives described in Sec. 2-2.3 (*cread*, *cwrite*, *vread*, and *vwrite*) are written in assembly language and interact with the asynchronous AppleTalk drivers.

The control processor of the MAC-CUBE must be a Macintosh Plus, SE, or II Personal Computer with at least a 10 Mbyte hard disk (preferably 20 Mbytes). The node processors should be a Macintosh Plus or SE Personal Computer with one disk drive. Both the CP and the nodes require System version 4.1 and Finder version 5.5 software and the MAC-CrOS routines. In addition, the CP must have the Macintosh Programmer's Workshop version 2.0. All nodes and the CP must lie in the same AppleTalk zone. Other Macintosh, MAC-CUBE, and AppleTalk gateways can also be in the same local zone.

CrOS III application programs may be developed and compiled on the CP. Before running a CrOS program the user "collects" a hypercube by running *boot* on the CP and *bootelt* on the 2^d nodes. This procedure configures a MAC-CUBE, and it is then ready to run the application. The Macintosh assembly-level debugger (Macsbug or TMON) and AppleTalk Peek have been found to be useful in debugging CrOS applications.

7-4 Parallel Computation on a Distributed Network

In Sec. 7-3 ensembles of personal computers connected by RS-232 serial links or via an AppleTalk network were discussed. Such ensembles may be used for educational purposes and provide a relatively inexpensive way of introducing students to concurrent processing.

More recently progress has been made in implementing parallel application programs on a local area network (LAN) of computers. These types of distributed computing systems are potentially very powerful, and have uses extending beyond the tutorial and educational benefits of the distributed systems of personal computers discussed in Sec. 7-3. For example, a network of VAX VMS computers connected by Ethernet has been used to run parallel programs written in the LINDA-C language [Whiteside 88]. Not surprising, the types of applications termed "embarrassingly parallel" in Sec. 1-4.1 run with high efficiency on such distributed networks of computers and can achieve supercomputer performance. However, for the class of loosely synchronous problems the communication speed over the network is too slow to allow efficient implementation of most concurrent algorithms.

Another interesting, and somewhat worrisome, aspect of this type of work is the possibility of writing a "worm" program capable of propagating itself through a network and running iterates of an embarrassingly parallel program on underutilized machines. Each instance of the worm program would return its results to a master program via electronic mail. If such a worm program could be written and escape detection, it could arguably constitute the highest performance system in existence. However, we do not advocate this type of "Internet piracy" as it is almost certainly illegal (or soon will be).

8

The Application Programs

8-1 General Remarks

This chapter presents a set of concurrent application programs that may be run in any CrOS III environment. Most of the applications are implementations of algorithms described in Volume 1 [Fox 88a], which should be consulted for a full description of the algorithms used. For each of the applications we give a concise description of the problem, followed by a discussion of the C and Fortran implementations. The actual C and Fortran source code for each application is listed in Appendices A and B and may be obtained by computer mail as described in Appendix G. The code listed in Appendices A and B undoubtedly contains errors and inefficiencies. Such problems will be fixed in the electronically distributed software as we become aware of them, and so this will differ after a time from the code listed in the appendices. This chapter is intended for those who wish to run and understand the application programs — it is not recommended for the casual reader.

For portability reasons the applications generate only rudimentary graphical output (if any!). Users are encouraged to interface the application codes with graphics packages on their local systems. This is particularly useful if the applications are to be used in a teaching environment.

As mentioned in Chap. 3, the CrOS III communication system has been implemented on a number of different concurrent processors, including the PC-CUBE described in Chap. 7. In addition, we have developed a hypercube simulator, *nsim*, details of which are given in Chap. 6. The application codes presented in this chapter may be run in any of these environments. In addition the CUBIX codes can also be run on sequential computers. However, in general the method of compiling, linking, and running the code will differ from machine to machine. Since it is not practical to describe how to compile, link, and run the codes in all the CrOS III environments, we will just give details for two specific cases, namely, the *nsim* simulator, and the NCUBE hypercube. The software described in this chapter is available electronically as described in Appendix G and includes "make" files (for use on UNIX and XENIX systems) and "command" files (for VMS systems) for compiling and linking the codes to execute on *nsim*, and in the case of CUBIX code, on sequential computers as well. The reader may find it useful to refer to these files. The compilation and linking of code for *nsim* is also discussed in Chap. 6, but will be repeated here for the sake of completeness. The NCUBE handbook [NCUBE 87] gives a complete description of the commands for compiling and linking on the NCUBE.

121

```
UNIX and XENIX nsim
      ccc -ih -cros3 -c -I../INCS progCP.c
      ccc -ih -cros3 -o progCP progCP.o ../LIBS/CPlib.a -lm
      ccc -cros3 -c -I../INCS progNODE.c
      ccc -cros3 -o progNODE progNODE.o ../LIBS/NODElib.a -lm
VMS nsim
      ccc /ih /cros3 /include=[.-.INCS] progCP.c
      clink /ih /cros3 progCP.obj, [.-.LIBS]CPlib.olb/LIB
      ccc /cros3 /include=[.-.INCS] progNODE.c
      clink /cros3 progNODE.obj, [.-.LIBS]NODElib.olb/LIB
NCUBE
      ucc -c -kNH -I~/INCS -o progCP.o progCP.c
      ucc -kNH -o progCP.ltl progCP.o ~/LIBS/CPlib.a
      lc -e progCP progCP.ltl
      ucc -c -kNN -o progNODE.on -I~/INCS progNODE.c
      ucc -LA450k -kNN -o progNODE.ltl progNODE.on ~/LIBS/NODElib.a
      lcn -e progNODE progNODE.ltl
```

Box 8-1 Compiling and linking CP and node C programs.

We assume for concreteness that the directory structure is the same as that specified in Appendix G; that is, there is a directory, CODE, that has two subdirectories, CDIR and FDIR, that contain the C and Fortran codes, respectively. CDIR and FDIR each contain a separate subdirectory for each application and also a subdirectory LIBS containing libraries of commonly used routines. CDIR also has a subdirectory INCS containing commonly used include files. This allows the libraries and include files to be conveniently accessed by means of relative path names. ANSI standard Fortran 77 does not permit the use of include files or conditional compilation statements; however, if necessary Fortran 77 source code can be run through the C preprocessor. Also many Fortran compilers, such as f77 on the NCUBE, incorporate a C-like preprocessor. For the purposes of this discussion, however, we will assume that these extended Fortran features are not present.

We will first consider the compilation and linking of the control process (CP) and node source programs. As discussed in Chap. 2, the main tasks of the CP are to download the node program to the concurrent processor and initiate its execution, and to perform I/O services for the nodes. The bulk of the computation is usually performed by the nodes. In Box 8-1 we show how CP and node programs are typically compiled and linked for the C language. The corresponding commands for Fortran are shown in Box 8-2.

```
UNIX nsim
        cf77 -ih -cros3 -o progCP progCP.f
        cf77 -cros3 -o progNODE progNODE.f
XENIX nsim
        crmf -g -ih -cros3 progCP.f
        crmf -g -cros3 progNODE.f
VMS nsim
        ccc /fort /ih /cros3 progCP.f,
        clink /fort /ih/cros3 progCP.obj
        ccc /fort /cros3 progNODE.f
        clink /fort /cros3 progNODE.obj
NCUBE
        f77 progCP.f
        ld -g -x1 -o progCP.ltl progCP.q /lib/f77.lib
        lc -e progCP progCP.ltl
        f77 -N progNODE.f
        ldn -b -A450k -o progNODE.ltl progNODE.qn /lib/f77n.lib
        lcn -e progNODE progNODE.ltl
```

Box 8-2 Compiling and linking CP and node Fortran programs.

```
UNIX and XENIX nsim
        ccc -cubix -c -I../INCS progCUB.c
        ccc -cubix -o progCUB progCUB.o ../LIBS/CUBlib.a -lm
VMS nsim
        ccc /CUBIX /include=[.-.INCS] progCUB.c
        clink /CUBIX progCUB.obj, [.-.LIBS]CUBlib.olb/LIB
NCUBE
        ucc -c -kcubix -I^/INCS -o progCUB.o progCUB.c
        ucc -LA450k -kcubix -o progCUB.ltl progCUB.o ^/LIBS/CUBlib.a
        lcn -e progCUB progCUB.ltl
```

Box 8-3 Compiling and linking CUBIX C programs.

A particular characteristic of CUBIX programs is that the same source code can be made to run on both concurrent and sequential machines. All that is necessary in the sequential case is to provide "dummy" CrOS III routines that perform that same functions as the corresponding routines on a single node concurrent machine. For example, the sequential version of *cshift* merely copies the contents of the output buffer to the input buffer. The situation is slightly more complicated for Fortran CUBIX programs since some of the CUBIX extensions are statements rather than subroutine calls. However, conditional compilation statements can be used to omit these statements when compiling for sequential computers, as shown in Box 8-6 for UNIX and XENIX systems. Boxes 8-3 and 8-4 show how to compile and link CUBIX programs for C and Fortran languages, respectively.

We now describe each of the applications. Note that throughout this chapter we shall use N_p to denote the number of processing nodes.

```
UNIX nsim
        cf77 -cubix -o progCUB progCUB.f
XENIX nsim
        crmf -g -cubix progCUB.f
VMS nsim
        ccc /fort /CUBIX progCUB.f
        clink /fort /CUBIX progNODE.obj
```

Box 8-4 Compiling and linking Fortran CUBIX programs.

```
UNIX and XENIX nsim
        cc -DSEQ -c -I../INCS progCUB.c
        cc -o progSEQ progCUB.o ../LIBS/SEQlib.a -lm
VMS nsim
        cc /define=(SEQ) /include=[.-.INCS] progCUB.c
        link /obj=progSEQ progCUB.obj, [.-.LIBS]SEQlib.olb/LIB
NCUBE
        ucc -c -DSEQ -kNH -I^/INCS -o progSEQ.o progCUB.c
        ucc -kNH -o progSEQ.ltl progSEQ.o ^/LIBS/SEQlib.a
        lc -e progSEQ progSEQ.ltl
```

Box 8-5 Compiling and linking CUBIX C programs for sequential execution.

```
UNIX nsim
        /lib/cpp progCUB.f progSEQ.f
        f77 -o progSEQ progSEQ.f ../LIBS/SEQlib.a
XENIX nsim
        /lib/cpp progCUB.f | grep -v "^#" >progSEQ.f
        rmfort -g progSEQ.f
VMS nsim
        f77 progCUB.f, [.-.LIBS]SEQlib.olb/LIB
```

Box 8-6 Compiling and linking CUBIX Fortran programs for sequential execution.

8-2 Tutorial Programs

Refer to	: Chapters 4 and 6 of Volume 1, Tutorial of Volume 2
C Directory	: $TUTORIAL/CDIR
Fortran Directory	: $TUTORIAL/FDIR

We consider first the programs in the Tutorial section of this volume that illustrate the use of some of the most important CrOS III communication routines. Details of these programs are given in the Tutorial and so will not be further discussed here. The tutorial codes are listed in Appendices C and D.

8-3 The One-Dimensional Wave Equation

Refer to	: Chapters 5 and 6 of Volume 1
C Directory	: $CODE/CDIR/WAVE/CPNODE
	$CODE/CDIR/WAVE/CUBIX
Fortran Directory	: $CODE/FDIR/WAVE/CPNODE
	$CODE/FDIR/WAVE/CUBIX

8-3.1 Purpose

This program solves the one-dimensional wave equation on the domain $0 \leq x \leq L$;

$$\frac{\partial^2 \psi}{\partial t^2} = c^2 \frac{\partial^2 \psi}{\partial x^2} \tag{8.1}$$

with fixed end points and given initial form of $\psi = \psi(x, t)$. That is;

$$\psi(0,t) = \psi(L,t) = 0 \tag{8.2}$$
$$\psi(x,0) = f(x) \tag{8.3}$$

This problem corresponds to finding the displacement of a vibrating string fixed at both ends, given some arbitrary initial configuration.

We consider the two cases in which (1) the string is initially a sine wave and (2) the string is plucked. For the sine wave case $f(x) = \sin(2\pi P x / L)$, and the analytical solution is:

$$\psi(x,t) = \sin\left(\frac{2\pi P}{L}x\right) \cos\left(\frac{2\pi P}{L}ct\right) \tag{8.4}$$

After j time steps the solution at the ith point is given by:

$$\psi(x_i, t_j) = \sin\left(\frac{2\pi P}{(N_x - 1)}i\right) \cos\left(\frac{2\pi P}{(N_x - 1)}\tau j\right) \tag{8.5}$$

where $\tau = c\Delta t / \Delta x$. The analytic solution for the plucked string case is

$$\psi(x,t) = \sum_{n=1}^{\infty} A_n \sin(\pi n x / L) \cos(\pi n c t / L) \tag{8.6}$$

where

$$A_n = \frac{2}{\pi^2 a(1-a)} \frac{\sin(\pi n a)}{n^2} \tag{8.7}$$

After j time steps the solution at the ith point is given by

$$\psi(x,t) = \sum_{n=1}^{\infty} A_n \sin\left(\frac{\pi n}{(N_x - 1)}i\right) \cos\left(\frac{\pi n}{(N_x - 1)}\tau j\right) \tag{8.8}$$

8-3.2 C Implementation

Both CPNODE and CUBIX versions of this code are provided in the software release. As explained in Chap. 5 of Volume 1, the problem is solved by employing a uniform discretization in the spatial and temporal domains. That is, we seek an approximate solution at the set of N_x points $x = 0, \Delta x, 2\Delta x, \ldots, (N_x-1)\Delta x = L$ at times $t = \Delta t, 2\Delta t, \ldots, N_t \Delta t$. The solution is advanced in time using the relation:

$$\psi_i(t + \Delta t) = 2\psi_i(t) - \psi_i(t - \Delta t) + \tau^2[\psi_{i-1}(t) - 2\psi_i(t) + \psi_{i+1}(t)] \tag{8.9}$$

where $\tau = c\Delta t/\Delta x$ is the dimensionless *time advance parameter* and $\psi_i(t)$ is the value of ψ at the point $x_i = i\Delta x$ at time t.

The problem is spatially decomposed by mapping the nodes onto the discretized x domain so that each node is responsible for a set of points. This mapping is done using the *gridmap* routines to ensure that adjacent nodes are directly connected by a communication channel. The arrays *old_values*, *values*, and *new_values* are used to hold the values of the displacement at the previous, current and next time steps, and hence are distributed over the hypercube. If node number p contains n_p points then each of these arrays is $n_p + 2$ elements long. In each node displacement values are stored at element numbers $1, 2, \ldots n_p$. To update the first and last points in each node, the displacements of the points to the left and right must be known and these reside in the neighboring nodes. Thus at the start of each time step the CrOS III routine *cshift* is called twice to communicate the necessary values between the nodes. On the first call, each node sends the displacement of its last point (element number n_p of the array *values*) to the node on the right while receiving the corresponding value from the node on the left. This is stored as element number 0 of *values*. On the second call to *cshift*, each node sends the displacement of its first point (element number 1 of *values*) to the node on the left while receiving the corresponding value from the node on the right. This is stored as element number $n_p + 1$ of *values*. The displacements at points $1, 2, \ldots n_p$ in each node are then updated using the displacements held in *old_values* and *values* by means of Eq. (8.9). The updated values are stored in *new_values*. Since the displacements of the first and last points are held fixed at zero, those two points are treated differently using an **if** statement within the loop over points. The code would run faster if this statement were taken out of the loop and the loop indices

were adjusted to leave out the first and last points in the nodes responsible for the
two ends of the domain.

To initialize the problem the user must specify the total number of discrete
points, N_x, in the x direction. The user must also specify the initial displacement,
$f(x_i)$, at each point by choosing either a sine wave or a plucked string as the initial
configuration. In both cases the maximum initial amplitude is Δx. If a sine wave is
chosen, the user must give the integer number of periods between $x = 0$ and $x = L$.
In the plucked string case the point at which the string is plucked must be specified
as a fraction of the length, L, of the string. In addition the user must specify the
time advance parameter, τ, in Eq. (8.9). Values of the order of 0.1 give reasonable
results. The values of $\psi(x_i,\ t)$ may either be listed or displayed graphically. Output
may either be sent to the standard output, or to a user-specified disk file.

The maximum total number of points must not exceed 1,500, and the number
of points in any node must not exceed 500. If the initial configuration is a plucked
string, then a must lie between 0 and 1. If a lies outside this range, it is set equal to
0.5. Finally, to ensure an accurate solution the value of the time advance parameter,
τ, should be less than about 0.5.

8-3.3 Fortran Implementation

Apart from the naming of variables, arrays, and subroutines, and differences
between the C and Fortran versions of CUBIX, the essential features of the Fortran
code are the same as those of the C code.

8-4 Solution of the Laplace Equation by the Finite Difference Method

Refer to : Chapter 7 of Volume 1
C Directory : $CODE/CDIR/SOR_LAPLACE
Fortran Directory : $CODE/FDIR/SOR_LAPLACE

8-4.1 Purpose

To solve the two-dimensional Laplace equation on the domain $0 \le x \le L_x$,
$0 \le y \le L_y$

$$\frac{\partial^2 \psi}{\partial x^2} + \frac{\partial^2 \psi}{\partial y^2} = 0 \tag{8.10}$$

subject to boundary conditions on $x = 0$, $x = L_x$, $y = 0$, and $y = L_y$. The domain
may also contain regions on which ψ is fixed.

This problem corresponds to finding the equilibrium temperature distribution
within a box containing objects at a fixed temperature and whose edges are also
kept at a fixed temperature. Another corresponding problem is that of determining
the distribution of electrical potential within a box containing objects at a fixed
potential and whose edges are also held at a fixed potential.

8-4.2 C Implementation

As explained in Chap. 7 of Volume 1, the problem is solved using an iterative successive over relaxation (SOR) scheme according to the formula

$$\psi_i^{(k)} = \frac{\omega}{4}\left[\psi_{i-x}^{(k)} + \psi_{i-y}^{(k)} + \psi_{i+x}^{(k-1)} + \psi_{i+y}^{(k-1)}\right] + (1-\omega)\psi_i^{(k-1)} \qquad (8.11)$$

where k is the iteration number, ω is the overrelaxation parameter, and the neighboring grid points in the x and y directions are designated by the $\pm x$, $\pm y$ subscripts.

The problem is decomposed by means of a spatial block decomposition. That is, the nodes of the concurrent processor are mapped onto the two-dimensional discrete grid of the rectangular problem domain so that each node is responsible for the grid points within a rectangular subdomain. The *gridmap* routines are used to map the nodes onto the plane so that the nodes responsible for adjacent blocks of grid points are directly linked by a communication channel. Within each node the problem domain is further subdivided into a 2×2 grid of subblocks. The lower left and upper right blocks are designated as "red" blocks, while the other two blocks are "black." As explained in Chap. 7 of Volume 1, the grid points lying in the red and black blocks are updated separately to preserve as closely as possible the update order of the corresponding sequential algorithm.

The two fundamental data structures of this problem are a two dimensional array of floats, *psi*, and a two-dimensional array of integers, *color*. These arrays are decomposed over the nodes as described earlier. In each node the solution at point number (i, j) is stored at *psi(i, j)*, and *color(i, j)* indicates the color of the subblock in which the point lies. In each iteration the red points are updated first, followed by the black points. A 5-point stencil is used to perform the update [see Eq. (8.11)]; thus to update the points lying on the edges of a node's subdomain values must be obtained from the four neighboring nodes. Before the red points are updated, each node calls *cshift* four times. On the first call, each node sends the solution for the red points lying on the right-hand edge of its subdomain to the node on the right, while receiving the corresponding values from the node on the left. These values are stored in the zeroth column of the array *psi*. On the second call to *cshift*, the solutions for the red points lying on the left-hand edge of the subdomain are sent to the node on the left while the corresponding values are received from the node on the right. These values are stored in column number $n_x + 1$ of *psi*. The two other calls to *cshift* communicate the solution for red points lying on the top and bottom edges of each nodes subdomain, with the values received being stored in rows number 0 and $n_y + 1$. The red points in each node are then updated according to Equation (8.11), and the process is then repeated for the black points.

To initialize the problem the user must first specify P_x and P_y, the number of nodes in the x and y directions, respectively. P_x and P_y do not have to be powers of two, however, the following relationship must hold:

$$d \geq \lceil \log_2 P_x \rceil + \lceil \log_2 P_y \rceil \tag{8.12}$$

where d is the dimension of the hypercube and $\lceil x \rceil$ is the smallest integer greater than or equal to x.

The user next specifies the number of grid points per node n_x and n_y in the x and y directions, followed by the value of the successive overrelaxation parameter, ω, which should lie in the range $1 < \omega < 2$. The boundary conditions may either be read from a disk file or keyed in at the terminal. In either case the user must first give the values of ψ on each of the edges of the domain. The user then gives the number of interior grid points whose values are fixed. For each of these points the user gives the grid point number in the x and y directions, and the fixed value at the grid point. Grid point numbers range from 0 to $n_x P_x - 1$ in the x direction and from 0 to $n_y P_y - 1$ in the y direction.

There are three types of output which may either be sent to the standard output or to a user-specified disk file:

1. The values of the solution ψ at a set of grid points may be listed.
2. The values of ψ at a set of grid points may be displayed in a hex plot. That is, the range of ψ values is divided into 16 bins, each of which is labeled by the corresponding hex number (0, 1, 2,..., a, b, c, d, e, f). The numerical grid is then displayed with the value of ψ at each grid point being represented by the appropriate hex number.
3. The grid point type can be displayed. In this case, each grid point is represented by a character. Boundary points are represented by "E," black points in the checkerboard ordering by "B," red points by "R," and fixed interior grid points are left blank.

If either the maximum or minimum column number for which output is requested is negative, then output is given for all column numbers. Similarly, if the maximum or minimum row number is negative output is given for all rows. The number of grid points per node in the x and y directions must not exceed 30. The overrelaxation parameter, ω, should lie in the range $1 < \omega < 2$.

8-4.3 Fortran Implementation

Apart from the naming of variables, arrays, and subroutines, and differences between the C and Fortran versions of CUBIX, the essential features of the Fortran code are the same as those of the C code.

8-5 Solution of the Laplace Equation by the Finite Element Method

Refer to	: Chapter 8 of Volume 1
C Directory	: $CODE/CDIR/FEM_LAPLACE
Fortran Directory	: $CODE/FDIR/FEM_LAPLACE

8-5.1 Purpose

This program finds the solution of the two-dimensional Laplace equation Eq. (8.10) in a rectangular region subject to given boundary conditions, using the finite element method. Decomposition of the region into a mesh of quadrilateral or triangular elements and quantifying them is very laborious. Since our main goal is to demonstrate the use of the parallel conjugate gradient algorithm in solving finite element problems, rather than meshing schemes, we use a simple mesh of rectangular elements.

For the specific problem considered in this code the problem domain is bounded by $x = 0$, $x = 1$ and $y = 0$, $y = 1$, and the boundary conditions are

$$\begin{aligned} \psi &= 1 \qquad \text{if} \quad y = 0, & \psi = -1 \quad \text{if} \quad y = 1 \\ \psi &= 1 - 2y \quad \text{if} \quad x = 0 \quad \text{or} \quad x = 1 \end{aligned}$$

The solution to this simple example problem is $\psi(x,y) = 1 - 2y$.

Following the Galerkin approximation [see Strang 73], the original PDE is recast in the form of a variational equation, which in turn reduces the problem to that of solving a sparse linear system, $\mathbf{K\Psi} = \mathbf{b}$. The example program described next solves this system of equations by the conjugate gradient method, which for an M by M system is as follows,

1. Initialize:
   a.) Assemble $\mathbf{K}$ and $\mathbf{b}$.
   b.) Set $\mathbf{\Psi}_0 = \mathbf{0}$, $\mathbf{r}_0 = \mathbf{b}$, $\beta_1 = 0$.

2. Iterate: For $k = 1, 2, \ldots, M$

Projection vector	$\mathbf{p}_k = \mathbf{r}_{k-1} + \beta_k \mathbf{p}_{k-1}$
Matrix-vector product	$\mathbf{q}_k = \mathbf{K}\mathbf{p}_k$
Solution update length	$\alpha_k = (\mathbf{r}_{k-1}^T . \mathbf{r}_{k-1})/(\mathbf{p}_k^T . \mathbf{q}_k)$
Solution vector	$\mathbf{\Psi}_k = \mathbf{\Psi}_{k-1} + \alpha \mathbf{p}_k$
Residual vector	$\mathbf{r}_k = \mathbf{r}_{k-1} - \alpha_k \mathbf{q}_k$
Convergence test	if $|\mathbf{r}_k| < \delta$ set $\mathbf{\Psi} = \mathbf{\Psi}_k$ and quit
Projection length	$\beta_{k+1} = (\mathbf{r}_k^T . \mathbf{r}_k)/(\mathbf{r}_{k-1}^T . \mathbf{r}_{k-1})$

3. Terminate: $\mathbf{\Psi} = \mathbf{\Psi}_M$ (if arithmetic exact)

8-5.2 C Implementation

The C code is a straightforward adaption of the Fortran code that is described next.

8-5.3 Fortran Implementation

The routine SETELT maps the hypercube onto a two-dimensional mesh and identifies the location of each processing node in the mesh and the channel masks for communicating with its neighbors. The x and y positions of a node in the mesh are stored in the variables MX and MY, respectively. For simplicity, we assume the number of processing nodes, N_p, to be a square of an integer.

The routine IDELEM sets up and initializes the finite element arrays. Each element has a list of the finite element nodes it contains in the array *EDGE*, and each finite element node has a list of the nodes with which it shares elements in the array *NGHBOR*. The nodal values are stored in the array *PHI*, which has "guard cell" entries to hold the nodal values of elements lying along the boundaries of the neighboring processors. Those nodes belonging to other processors are flagged in the array *YOURS*. In the processors containing a boundary of the problem domain, the entries in *PHI* corresponding to nodes on the domain boundary are flagged in the array *BND*. The routine IDELEM initializes the arrays *PHI*, *YOURS*, *NGHBOR*, and *BND*.

The routine STIFF computes the stiffness matrix and stores it in the array *KE*. Due to the simplicity of the mesh in our example problem this is a straightforward procedure, although for a more complex problem the contributions to entries in the stiffness matrix would have to determined for each element in turn, and would depend on the geometry of the elements. An important difference between the algorithm described in Chap. 8 of Volume 1 and the algorithm used here is that the stiffness matrix is fully assembled.

The routine GETBND computes the force term, **b**, and identifies the nodes that belong to each processor by means of a flag in the array *INTR*.

The routine CONGRA finds the unknown values of *PSI* at the nodes using the conjugate gradient method. The routine begins by initializing the vectors **r** and **p**. Each processor then exchanges those entries in **p** corresponding to nodes lying along the boundaries between processors. This is done by the routine COMMUN, which calls the CrOS III routines KCSHIF and KVSHIF. The evaluation of the matrix-vector product **Kp** then proceeds as in the sequential case. Global scalar products are calculated by the routine SCALAR. Each processor computes its share of the scalar product and these results are summed by calling the CrOS III routine KCOMBI. The conjugate gradient loop is executed until either the length of the residual vector, **r**, is less than the user-supplied value of *ALLOW*, or when M iterates have been performed.

8-6 The Long-Range Force Problem

Refer to	: Chapter 9 of Volume 1 and Sec. 9-5 of Volume 2
C Directory	: $CODE/CDIR/LONG_RANGE
Fortran Directory	: $CODE/FDIR/LONG_RANGE

8-6.1 Purpose

This program finds the gravitational potential energy of a group of particles at positions r_i and with masses m_i, $i = 1, \ldots, N$. In addition, the gravitational force, F_i, on each particle is also found.

The gravitational potential energy is given by

$$V = -\sum_{i=1}^{N} \sum_{j=i+1}^{N} \frac{m_i m_j}{r_{ij}}$$ (8.13)

where r_{ij} is the distance between particles i and j.

The force on each particle is

$$\mathbf{F}_i = \sum_{\substack{j=1 \\ j \neq i}}^{N} \frac{m_i m_j}{r_{ij}^3} \mathbf{r}_{ij}$$ (8.14)

8-6.2 C Implementation

As explained in Chap. 9 of Volume 1, approximately equal numbers of particles are assigned to each node. The particles in each node are stored in an array, *objarr*, of data type OBJECT. This data type is defined by means of a *typedef* statement and consists of a struct containing the x, y, and z coordinates of the position, the components of the force in each direction, and the mass. The nodes are mapped into a ring and a copy of the particles resident in each node is stored in the OBJECT array *obj_copy*. At each step round the ring, the interaction between the particles in *objarr* and *obj_copy* is calculated; the force on each particle is updated, and the contribution to the potential energy is summed. At the end of each step the data in *obj_copy* is rotated one step clockwise around the ring of nodes. This is done using *cshift*, which writes to the node in the clockwise direction while reading from the counterclockwise node. The data received overwrites the data formerly stored in *obj_copy*. After each set of traveling particles has been rotated around the ring the total potential energy is found by summing the contributions of all nodes, and the force on each particle is found by summing the force on the corresponding traveling and resident particles. Newton's third law is used to reduce the number of calculations necessary by a factor of 2.

To initialize the problem the user must specify the total number of particles. The particle positions and masses may be read from the standard input or a disk file or random data may be used. In the last case the x, y, and z coordinates and the mass are chosen at random from a uniform distribution between 0 and 1. Output may either be sent to the standard output, or to a user-specified disk file. When outputting the force on each particle the components in each direction are summed as a check on the results. These sums, of course, should all be zero. The number of particles per node must not exceed 128.

8-6.3 Fortran Implementation

Apart from the naming of variables, arrays, and subroutines and differences between the C and Fortran versions of CUBIX, the essential features of the Fortran code are the same as those of the C code.

8-7 Matrix Multiplication

Refer to	: Chapter 10 of Volume 1
C Directory	: $CODE/CDIR/MATMULT
Fortran Directory	: $CODE/FDIR/MATMULT

8-7.1 Purpose

This program multipies two real $M \times M$ matrices, A, B, to form $C = AB$.

8-7.2 C Implementation

As explained in Chap. 10 of Volume 1, each node is assigned a square subblock of the input matrices, A and B, so the nodes are arranged as a two-dimensional grid. If necessary the matrices are padded with zeros. At the end of the algorithm each node contains a subblock of the resultant matrix, C. The ith step of the algorithm consists of three stages: (1) in each row of nodes the ith node to the right of the diagonal pipes its subblock of A to all the other nodes in the same row. We denote this subblock by A_{pipe}. (2) A_{pipe} is multiplied by B_{roll} and is added to C in each node. For the zeroth step of the algorithm B_{roll} is just B. (3) Each node sends its B_{roll} subblock to the node above. Periodic boundary conditions apply so the nodes in the top row send their values of B_{roll} to the nodes in the bottom row. Each node overwrites its previous B_{roll} subblock with the new subblock. After $\sqrt{N_p}$ steps, where N_p is the number of nodes, each node contains a subblock of the matrix C.

To initialize the problem the user must first specify the order of the matrices to be multiplied. The matrices may either be read from the standard input or a disk file, or random matrices may be used. In the last case the elements of the matrices are taken from a uniform random distribution between -0.5 and $+0.5$. The order of the subblock matrices in each node must not exceed 30.

8-7.3 Fortran Implementation

For simplicity, it is assumed in the Fortran implementation that the number of nodes is a perfect square, that is, that the hypercube dimension is even. Furthermore, the size of the subblocks in each node is set by a PARAMETER statement to be 4 by 4.

The Fortran code begins by calling the routine SETELT to map the nodes onto a two-dimensional mesh. The CrOS III *gridmap* routines are used to find the location of each node in the mesh and the masks required to communicate with the neighboring nodes in the four directions.

The routine INPUT is called to initialize the matrices, A and B, that are to be multiplied. The user is prompted to either read the matrix elements in from the files **INPUT.A** and **INPUT.B** or to use demonstration matrices computed within the routine. If the matrices are read from a file, they must be given in row order.

The multiplication of the two input matrices is performed in the routine MATMUL. At each step of the algorithm this routine calls PIPEA to pipe the appropriate subblock of the matrix A to all processors in the same row of the processor mesh. After the product of the subblock of A broadcast in each row with the current B subblock has been accumulated in C, the program then calls the routine ROLLB to replace each node's current B subblock with that of the node below. After $\sqrt{N_p}$ steps, where N_p is the number of nodes, each node contains a subblock of the matrix C.

Upon completion of the matrix multiplication, the routine VIEWMT is called to output the matrices A, B, and C. The user is asked which matrix is to be displayed and is then prompted to specify which subblock is to be output.

8-8 Fast Fourier Transforms

Refer to	: Chapter 11 of Volume 1
C Directory	: \$CODE/CDIR/FFT
Fortran Directory	: \$CODE/FDIR/FFT

8-8.1 Purpose

This program evaluates the discrete Fourier transform, $\mathbf{F(x)}$, of a one-dimensional array of $N = 2^M$ complex data points, $\mathbf{x} = (x_0, x_1, \ldots, x_{N-1})$ using the Cooley-Tukey FFT algorithm.

$$F_k(\mathbf{x}) = \sum_{j=0}^{N-1} x_j \exp\left(\frac{2\pi i j k}{N}\right) \tag{8.15}$$

In the C code either the recursive or the iterative algorithm may be used, the details of which are explained in Chap. 11 of Volume 1. The Fortran code uses only the iterative algorithm. The algorithm used here is not necessarily the most efficient, particularly on machines with a high message latency, since the communication is performed one floating-point number at a time within the inner loop of the algorithm. A more efficient algorithm, due to Furmanski and described in Walker [Walker 88d], performs the communication outside the outer loop using the *index* algorithm described in Sec. 5-3.

8-8.2 C Implementation

To initialize the problem the user must specify the number of points, N, in the data, and choose one of three functions to transform. These functions are all real-valued and are defined as follows:

- Top-hat function:

$$x_j = \begin{cases} 0 & \text{if } 0 \le j < N/4 \\ 1 & \text{if } N/4 \le j < 3N/4 \\ 0 & \text{if } 3N/4 \le j < N \end{cases} \tag{8.16}$$

- Ramp function:

$$x_j = j/(N-1) \tag{8.17}$$

- Triangle function:

$$x_j = \begin{cases} 2j/(N-1) & \text{if } 0 \le j < N/2 \\ 2(N-1-j)/(N-1) & \text{if } N/2 \le j < N \end{cases} \tag{8.18}$$

The real and imaginary parts of the discrete Fourier transforms of the three example functions just defined are as follows:

- Top-hat function:

$$\Re(F_k(\mathbf{x})) = \begin{cases} \frac{N}{2} & \text{if } k = 0 \\ 0 & \text{if } k \ne 0 \text{ is even} \\ (-1)^{(k+1)/2} \cot(\frac{\pi k}{N}) & \text{if } k \text{ is odd} \end{cases} \tag{8.19}$$

$$\Im(F_k(\mathbf{x})) = \sin(\tfrac{\pi k}{2}) \tag{8.20}$$

- Ramp function:

$$\Re(F_k(\mathbf{x})) = \begin{cases} \frac{N}{2} & \text{if } k = 0 \\ -\frac{N}{2(N-1)} & \text{if } k \ne 0 \end{cases} \tag{8.21}$$

$$\Im(F_k(\mathbf{x})) = \begin{cases} 0 & \text{if } k = 0 \\ -\frac{N}{2(N-1)} \cot(\frac{\pi k}{N}) & \text{if } k \ne 0 \end{cases} \tag{8.22}$$

- Triangle function:

$$\Re(F_k(\mathbf{x})) = \begin{cases} \frac{N}{2}(\frac{N-2}{N-1}) & \text{if } k = 0 \\ 0 & \text{if } k \ne 0 \text{ is even} \\ -\frac{2}{N-1}\cot^2(\frac{\pi k}{N}) & \text{if } k \text{ is odd} \end{cases} \tag{8.23}$$

$$\Im(F_k(\mathbf{x})) = \begin{cases} 0 & \text{if } k \text{ is even} \\ \frac{2}{N-1} \cot(\frac{\pi k}{N}) & \text{if } k \text{ is odd} \end{cases} \tag{8.24}$$

The original data are overwritten by the transformed data. However, the kth element of the transform is not stored at location number k in the data array, but instead is at location $\overline{k}$, where $\overline{k}$ is the number obtained by writing the $\log_2 N$ bits of k in reverse order. Element number k of the transform is moved to location k in the data array by applying the routine *global_reverse*.

The contents of the current data array may be listed to the terminal screen. Each element of the data array is a complex number, $a + ib$, and is represented as (a, b). The number of data points per processor must lie between 4 and 512. The number of data points per processor must not be less than the number of processors. This constraint arises from the fact the *global_reverse* algorithm requires a grain size that is at least as large as the number of processors.

8-8.3 Fortran Implementation

Apart from the naming of variables, arrays, and subroutines and differences between the C and Fortran versions of CUBIX, the essential features of the Fortran code are the same as those of the C code.

8-9 The Generation of Random Numbers

Refer to	: Chapters 12 and 13 of Volume 1, Sec. 9-2 of Volume 2
C Directory	: \$CODE/CDIR/RANDOM
Fortran Directory	: \$CODE/FDIR/RANDOM

8-9.1 Purpose

This program illustrates the use of a linear congruential random number generator on a concurrent processor. Although this algorithm is simple to implement, it has a relatively short period, and there exist short-range correlations between the numbers generated. For many scientific applications, such as lattice gauge theory, the shift-register algorithm provides a more suitable means of generating random numbers. This algorithm has been implemented on the hypercube by Ding [Ding 88d] and Chiu [Chiu 88b]. The program allows a set of random numbers to be listed and uses Monte Carlo methods to estimate the value of π and evaluate the integral:

$$y = \int_0^1 x^2 dx \tag{8.25}$$

8-9.2 C Implementation

In the generation of a simple sequence of random numbers a "leapfrog" scheme is adopted in which node number P evaluates the numbers at positions $P, P + N_p, P + 2N_p, \ldots$, in the sequence, where N_p is the number of processors. This algorithm ensures that the sequence of pseudorandom numbers generated is independent of the number of nodes and is used in listing the set of random numbers and in evaluating the integral in Eq. (8.25). Each node evaluates the multiplicative and additive parameters, A and B, of the linear congruential generator and also finds the seed integer for its subsequence of random numbers. This is done in the routine *prand_setB*. Subsequent calls to the function *prandB* return the value of the next random number in the sequence. In evaluating the integral in Eq. (8.25), each node records its own estimate of the integral, and after the specified number of trials, the global estimate is found by taking the average of all the individual nodes' estimates. This is done using the CrOS III *combine* routine.

In evaluating π, points are generated at random within a square with corners at $(-1, -1)$, $(-1, 1)$, $(1, -1)$, and $(1, 1)$. The fraction, f, of the points lying within unit distance of the origin is recorded. This ratio is statistically asymptotic to $\pi/4$, and hence π can be approximated by $4f$. For the answer to be independent of the number of nodes, we want processor P to take the numbers at positions $2P$

and $2P + 1$ in the sequence as the x and y coordinates of the first random point in processor P. The coordinates of the second point are at positions $2P + 2N_p$ and $2P + 2N_p + 1$ in the sequence, and those of the third point are at positions $2P + 3N_p$ and $2P + 3N_p + 1$, and so on. Thus each node evaluates the x coordinate and then jumps one step in the sequence to evaluate the y coordinate, after which a jump of $2N_p$ steps takes place to evaluate the x coordinate of the next point. The x coordinates are evaluated by the routine $prandS$, which performs the single step jump necessary for the subsequent evaluation of the y coordinate, which is performed by the routine $prandB$. At the end of $prandB$ the big jump of $2N_p$ steps is performed ready for the evaluation of the next x coordinate. As in the evaluation of the integral, each node independently evaluates its own estimate of π, and at the end of the program a global estimate is found by averaging the individual estimates by means of the *combine* routine. The total number of trials over all nodes must not exceed the largest integer allowed on the machine.

The source code and manual pages for the routines $prand\_setB$, $prandS$, and $prandB$ are presented in Appendices E and F, respectively.

8-9.3 Fortran Implementation

Apart from the naming of variables, arrays, and subroutines, and differences between the C and Fortran versions of CUBIX, the essential features of the Fortran code are the same as those of the C code.

8-10 The Medium-Range Force Problem

Refer to   : Chapter 16 of Volume 1
C Directory   : \$CODE/CDIR/LENNARD_JONES
Fortran Directory   : \$CODE/FDIR/LENNARD_JONES

8-10.1 Purpose

This program evaluates the interaction potential of a set of particles interacting via the Lennard-Jones potential. For simplicity the particles are assumed to lie in the (x, y) plane, although the algorithm is readily generalized to three dimensions. For a pair of particles at positions $\mathbf{r}_i$ and $\mathbf{r}_j$ the interaction potential is:

$$U_{ij} = U(r_{ij}) = -\frac{U_0}{4}\left[\left(\frac{\sigma}{r_{ij}}\right)^{12} - \left(\frac{\sigma}{r_{ij}}\right)^{6}\right] \tag{8.26}$$

where $r_{ij} = |\mathbf{r}_i - \mathbf{r}_j|$ is the distance between the two particles and U_0 and σ are constants.

The program only includes in the total potential, U_{TOT}, contributions from pairs of particles whose separation, r_{ij}, is less than 3σ.

8-10.2 C Implementation

The (x, y) domain is divided into cells of size 3σ by 3σ. A spatial block decomposition is used to map the nodes onto this grid of cells. As usual, the *gridmap* routines are used to ensure that nodes assigned to adjacent regions of the problem domain are directly linked by a communication channel. If each node contains $n_x \times n_y$ cells and the nodes are decomposed onto a $N_x \times N_y$ mesh, then the size of the problem domain is $3\sigma n_x N_x \times 3\sigma n_y N_y$, and any particles outside of this region are ignored. The particle positions are either read from a disk file or from the standard input, or they are generated at random. In the last case the particles all lie within a unit square with its lower left corner at the origin. In each node the particles are stored in the array *part_arr*, which is of data type PARTICLE. The particles in any one cell are inserted into a linked list each entry of which is of data type LIST. Both the PARTICLE and LIST data types are defined by a *typedef*. The PARTICLE data type consists of a struct containing the coordinates of the particle, and the LIST data type consists of a pointer to the particle's entry in *part_arr* and a pointer to the next entry in the list. A pointer to the start of the list of each cell is kept in the two-dimensional array *cell_arr*. If a cell is at coordinate position (i, j) in a particular node, where i may run from 1 to n_x and j from 1 to n_y, then the pointer to the start of that cell's list is stored in *cell_arr(i,j)*. To find the contribution to the interaction energy from a single particle, only those particles in the same cell and the eight neighboring cells need to be examined since particles in other cells lie at distances greater than 3σ. Those cells lying on the edge of a node need to examine the boundary cells of neighboring nodes, thus information about the particles lying in these cells must be exchanged between nodes.

The interaction energy is evaluated by the routine *compute_energy*. This routine first calls *make_list* to create pointers to the start of each cell's list and stores them in the array *cell_arr*. The particles are then inserted into the appropriate list by the routine *insert*. Next the routine *bound_exchg* is called to exchange information about the particles in boundary cells. The PARTICLE array *edge_particle* serves two purposes. First, it is used to hold the positions of the boundary particles of the neighboring nodes. In addition it also is used as a communication buffer in exchanging data between nodes. In each node the routine *bound_exchg* first calls *list_exchg* for each of the cells along the left-hand boundary. The routine *list_exchg* calls *contents* which takes the information for the particles in the cell and copies it to the array *edge_particle*. These data are then sent to the neighboring node on the left, while the corresponding data are received from the node on the right. The data received overwrite the data sent in *edge_particle*, and a counter, *n_edge_parts*, is set to indicate the next unused slot in *edge_particle*. The particles received are inserted into cell lists pointed to by the entries in column number $n_x + 1$ of the array *cell_arr*. Thus around the lists of the cells resident in a node, a "border" of lists is maintained for the boundary cells of the neighboring nodes.

The particles in the cells along the right-hand boundary are next sent to the node on the right, while the corresponding data are received from the left-hand node. In this case the outgoing data are stored in *edge_particle* on top of the data received in the previous communication; that is, the outgoing data start at element number *n_edge_parts*. The data received again overwrite those sent, and *n_edge_parts* is again set to the next unused slot in *edge_particle*. The particles received are inserted into cell lists pointed to by entries in column number 0 of *cell_arr*. The routine *bound_exchg* continues with similar calls to *list_exchg* to exchange data for the particles in cells lying along the upper and lower boundaries of the nodes.

After calling *bound_exchg* the program evaluates the node's contribution to the interaction energy by looping over each of the resident cells. For each particle in each of these cells, the energy of interaction due to all other particles in the same cell and 8 neighboring cells is found by calling the routine *interact*. Since the border cells for the particles from the neighboring nodes have all been set up in the previous call to *bound_exchg*, the routine *interact* is the same as that used in the sequential algorithm. The total interaction energy is then found by summing the contributions from each node using the CrOS III routine *combine*.

Finally, the routine *compute_energy* calls *delete_list* to free the memory allocated to the members of each list. Then *unmake_list* is called to free the pointer to the head of each list.

8-10.3 Fortran Implementation

Since the Fortran language does not permit the explicit manipulation of memory addresses, the management of linked lists in Fortran requires sophisticated buffer management routines. These routines have little direct bearing on the parallel issues that arise in the medium-range interaction problem, and so the development and use of such routines for this illustrative code is not warranted. For these reasons the C and Fortran versions of the code differ substantially. Also since the Fortran language does not permit memory to be dynamically allocated, the arrays associated with each cell should be dimensioned to hold data for the maximum number of particles that could ever lie in the same cell. Thus, memory is inefficiently utilized in the Fortran code, although the situation could be improved by more sophisticated buffer management.

In the Fortran version of the code, the routine GETENV is first called to spatially decompose the problem domain. Each node contains 256 particles which are initially distributed at random over 16 cells arranged in a 4 by 4 subblock. The program then performs ten iterates of a loop in which the positions of the particles are randomly perturbed, and the potential energy for the resulting new configuration is evaluated. At each iterate the total potential energy is output, together with the number of pairs of particles that contributed to this energy.

Each of the ten iterates begins by calling the routine UPDATE. This routine takes each particle in turn and moves it at random by a small amount. The cell in which the particle now lies is determined. If that cell lies in another node, the particle's position is loaded into the appropriate export buffer. If the cell still lies in the same node, it is put into the list for that cell by the routine INSERT. The INSERT routine manages an array *INVENT*. Element *INVENT(I,J,K)* gives the particle number of the Ith particle in the cell at location $(J - 1, K - 1)$ in a given node. The indexing of cell locations in each direction begins at 0. The number of particles in the cell at (J, K) is stored in the two-dimensional array L. The INSERT routine also stores the x and y coordinates of the cell in which the particle lies in the arrays $IDOMX$ and $IDOMY$, respectively. The arrays $INVENT$ and L are dimensioned so that in addition to holding lists for the cells in a node, they also can store the lists for the cells lying along the boundaries of neighboring nodes. Thus each node can be imagined to have a "guard ring" of cells that surrounds the cells for which it is responsible.

The UPDATE routine then sends the export buffers in each of the four directions, while receiving particle data into the corresponding four import buffers. Particles that have arrived at their destination nodes, are inserted into the list for the appropriate cell. Some particles may have to be sent to diagonally adjacent nodes, and these are removed from the import buffer and copied to the correct export buffer. A second communication cycle then sends these particles to their final destinations.

At this stage all particles lie in the correct node, and have been put into the list of the cell in which they lie. The routine EXCHG is then called to send the data for particles lying in cells along node boundaries to the neighboring nodes. The particles received are inserted in the list of the appropriate guard ring cell, and their position coordinates are appended to the X and Y arrays. As in the UPDATE routine, some particles need to travel to diagonally adjacent nodes, and again a two-pass communication strategy is employed.

After calling EXCHG each node has all the information needed to evaluate the potential energy. The algorithm used to do this is essentially that shown in Code 16-6 of Volume 1. To avoid counting interactions twice, the interaction between two particles, p_1 and p_2, only contributes to the potential energy if the x coordinate of p_1 is greater than that of p_2. The total potential energy is found by summing the contributions from all nodes using the CrOS III routine KCOMBI. Each of the ten iterates concludes by outputting the potential energy.

Upon completion of the ten iterates the minimum total potential energy over the iterates is output.

8-11 WaTor — An Ecological Simulation

Refer to	: Chapter 17 of Volume 1
C Directory	: $CODE/CDIR/WATOR
Fortran Directory	: $CODE/FDIR/WATOR

8-11.1 Purpose

The domain of WaTor is a rectangular mesh with periodic boundaries that represents a toroidal ocean in which minnows and sharks struggle for survival according to a set of simple rules [Dewdney 84]. Each mesh location either contains a minnow or a shark or else is empty. For convenience we shall refer to the minnows and sharks collectively as fish, although of course minnows belong to the class Pisces and sharks to the class Selachii. The simulation progresses in a series of discrete time steps, at each of which all the fish are updated. For each type of fish there are a number of input parameters which determine their behavior. A fish breeds if its age is greater than or equal to a specified number of updates. In general, minnows and sharks have different breeding ages. Sharks starve to death if they have not eaten any minnows within a certain number of updates. Minnows eat universally available plankton and so never starve. The rules for updating minnows are as follows:

> Increase the age of the minnow by 1. Select a direction at random (up, down, left, or right), and if the neighboring location in that direction is vacant, then move the minnow to it. If that location is not vacant, continue selecting different directions until a vacant neighboring location is found and move the minnow there. If the minnow is able to move, and if its age is greater than or equal to the minnow breeding age, then a new minnow of age 0 is left in the original location. If the minnow is unable to move, it stays where it is and cannot breed regardless of its age.

The rules for updating sharks are a little more complicated since they have to find minnows to eat in order to survive;

> Increase the age of the shark and the time since the shark last ate a minnow by 1. If the time since the shark last ate is greater than the shark starvation time, then the shark dies. If the shark does not starve it checks its four neighboring locations in random order, and if it finds a minnow at a location, it eats it and moves to that location. If there are no neighboring minnows, the shark moves in a random direction in the same way that the minnows move. If the shark moves to a new location and if its age is greater than or equal to the shark breeding age, then a new shark of age 0 is left in the original location.

8-11.2 C Implementation

As explained in Volume 1, if the ocean is decomposed by means of a block decomposition consistency problems arise when 2 (or even 3 or 4) nodes try to change the status of the same location in the ocean in the same update. For example, a fish in one node could move to a location on the boundary, and a fish in the neighboring could simultaneously try to move to the same location. In Volume 1 a scattered decomposition and rollback were suggested as ways of avoiding conflicts of this sort. The scattered decomposition is particularly attractive as it also ensures statistical load balance. In our implementation, however, conflicts are avoided by dividing the subdomains allocated to each node into cells each containing a rectangular grid of locations. The corresponding cells in all nodes are updated loosely synchronously, thereby avoiding conflicts provided there are at least two cells per processor in each coordinate direction. This is essentially a "red/black" strategy similar to that adopted (for different reasons) in the SOR solution of the Laplace equation in Sec. 8-4. The red/black approach avoids the need for rollback, but is not load balanced. Statistical load balance could be achieved by using a scattered red/black decomposition, but this more sophisticated approach is not used here.

Each node contains a grid of $ncells\_x$ by $ncells\_y$ cells, each of which contains $cell\_sizex$ times $cell\_sizey$ ocean locations. Thus each node's ocean mesh is $xsize = cell\_sizex \times ncells\_x$ by $ysize = cell\_sizey \times ncells\_y$ in size. The characteristics of a fish, such as its type, age, position, et cetera, are stored in a variable of data type FISH. For each cell there is a doubly linked list of all the fish in that cell. Each entry is of type LIST, which is a struct consisting of a variable of type FISH and pointers to the previous and next fish in the list. The two-dimensional array $ocean$ of data type OCC is used to record the status of the ocean locations in each node. Each location in $ocean$ is a struct containing an integer to specify the type of fish (if any) at that location, and a pointer of type LIST to the fish's entry in the linked list. The data types FISH, OCC and LIST are all defined by typedefs. The two-dimensional array $cell\_arr$ of type LIST is used to store pointers to the start of each cell's linked list.

The ocean locations in each node are numbered 1 through $xsize$ in the x direction, and 1 through $ysize$ in the y direction. Data about location (i, j) are stored at $ocean(i, j)$. Column number 0 of $ocean$ is used to store data from column $xsize$ of the neighboring node on the left, while column $xsize + 1$ is used to store data from column 1 of the node to the right. Similarly, rows 0 and $ysize + 1$ are used to store data from rows $ysize$ and 1 of the neighboring nodes below and above.

The WaTor program begins by reading in the problem parameters, and then calling the routine $setup\_grid$ to decompose the nodes onto a two-dimensional grid. Next the routine $setup\_problem$ initializes the $ocean$ matrix and the linked lists for each cell. The fish are then updated a specified number of times, each update being performed by a call to the routine $move\_fish$. After each update the routine $output\_results$ is called to allow the user to view the current state of the ocean.

In each node $move\_fish$ performs a loosely synchronous loop over the cells. Since no two adjacent cells are ever updated in the same loosely synchronous step, no conflicts can occur. For a cell not on the boundary of a node all the information needed to update that cell resides in the same node, and so the cell can simply be updated by a call to the routine $update\_fish$, which is essentially the same as that used in the sequential case. For a cell which is on the boundary of a node information must be received from one or more neighboring nodes before doing the update. In addition information must also be sent to neighboring nodes. This exchange of information between nodes is performed by the routine $send\_bound$ and the routines $xstrip\_exchg$ and $ystrip\_exchg$, which are called by $send\_bound$. These routines send and receive data about the fish in the appropriate strips of the $ocean$

matrix. The fish received are inserted into the cells' linked list. After returning from *send_bound*, all the information necessary to update the fish in the cell is in place, and the routine *update_fish* is called. After updating the fish any changes affecting the ocean locations residing in adjacent nodes must be communicated to those nodes. For example, a fish may have moved from the boundary of one node into the boundary of a neighboring node. Once again communication between the nodes is necessary, and this is performed by the routine *return_bound*, which, like *send_bound*, also calls *xstrip_exchg* and *ystrip_exchg*. These routines remove from the *ocean* matrix and cell list details of any fish that need to be sent to another node. Details of such fish are then sent to the node in which they reside. Details of any fish received from neighboring nodes are inserted into the *ocean* matrix and cell list. After returning from *return_bound* the fish in the next cell can be updated. The method of exchanging fish between nodes is similar to that used in Sec. 8-10.2 to exchange particles, and so will not be discussed in detail here. The only significant difference is that in the latter case a single buffer, *edge_particles*, is used, whereas in WaTor separate buffers, *edge_send* and *edge_return*, are used by the routines *send_bound* and *return_bound*.

8-11.3 Fortran Implementation

As in the medium-range interaction problem discussed in Sec. 8-10, the C and Fortran versions of WaTor are very different since the C code makes use of linked lists. The Fortran code also uses a different way of avoiding site conflicts.

The Fortran code begins by calling the routine SETELT to decompose spatially the rectangular grid that represents the ocean. This determines the location of each node in the node mesh and the masks required to communicate with neighboring nodes in the mesh.

The routine SETUP is then called to populate the ocean with sharks and minnows. The x and y coordinates of a fish are recorded in the arrays *FISHX* and *FISHY*. The arrays *BREED* and *STARVE* give the number of iterates since the fish last reproduced and ate. Finally, *FSKIND(I)* is 1 if fish number I is a minnow and is 2 if it is a shark. If fish number I is at position (J, K) then the value of *MESH(J,K)* is I; otherwise it is 0. The total number of fish (minnows plus sharks) is stored in the variable *NOFISH*.

The user is then prompted to give the number of intervals, *FBREED* and *SBREED*, after which minnows and sharks reproduce, and the number of iterations, *DEADAG*, after which the shark starves if it has not eaten.

The simulation then begins and runs for 10 iterations. In each iteration the minnows are updated first, and then the sharks.

The routine SNDBND is called to exchange details of the types of fish lying along boundaries between neighboring nodes. This ensures that each node knows whether the boundary grid points of its neighbors contain a minnow or a shark or are empty. The arrays *UBUF*, *DBUF*, *LBUF*, and *RBUF* store this information for the four directions and are used in subsequent calls to the routine NXTDIR.

For each fish in turn the routine UPDATE is called to update the state of the fish according to the rules given in Sec. 8-11.1. The routine NXTDIR is called to select an adjacent grid point to move to. If there is no move possible the fish stays at its current site; otherwise the routine CHKMOV is called to determine if the new site lies in the jurisdiction of a neighboring node. If this is the case, the routine MOVOUT is called to place the fish in the appropriate communication buffer, and the routine REMFIS is called to remove the fish. A list of removed fish is kept in the array *DEADFS*, and the total number of such fish is stored in the variable *DEADNO*. If the fish remains in the same node and has a valid site to move to, the *FISHX, FISHY*, and *MESH* arrays are updated by the routine MVFISH. If the fish moves to a new site and it has reached breeding age, a new fish is created at the current site by the routine MAKEFS. If the fish remains in the same node and is a shark, the routine MOVEAT is called to determine if there is a minnow at site to which it is moving, in which case the shark eats the minnow. If there is no minnow to eat and the shark has reached its starvation age, then it dies and is removed by a call to REMFIS.

After calling UPDATE for every fish of a given type, the routine RTNBND is called to send the fish placed in the communications buffers by MOVOUT to the neighboring nodes. It is possible that a fish moving to a site in a different node may not be able to do so if that node has already moved one of its own fish to that site. The routine PUTSND is called to determine if an incoming fish has a vacant site to move to. If the incoming fish is a shark and there is a minnow at the disputed site, then the shark simply eats the minnow. In all other cases of dispute, the incoming fish is left in the communication buffer.

When RTNBND has finished trying to move fish to neighboring node, the routine RESOLV is called to determine the fate of the fish that were unable to find a vacant site. The routine RESOLV sends back the unwelcome fish to their original node. If the original site is still vacant, then the routine PUTBAK is called to reestablish the fish there. Otherwise it is assumed that the fish has been caught by a fisherman, and it is discarded.

In the update procedure a number of fish are eaten, starved, or caught, and their entries in the fish data arrays can be reused for new fish in the next iteration. The routine REARRN rearranges the fish data arrays so that the entries for the dead fish can be reused. In addition, a summary of the changes in the fish population for the current iteration is output.

8-12 Distributed Sorting Algorithms

Refer to	: Chapter 18 of Volume 1
C Directory	: $CODE/CDIR/SORTING
Fortran Directory	: $CODE/FDIR/SORTING

8-12.1 Purpose

This section describes three programs to demonstrate distributed sorting algorithms: (1) the bitonic sort, (2) the quicksort, and (3) the Shell sort. The programs listed in Appendices A and B sort integers, but could be modified to permit the sorting of other data types. The parallel bitonic and quicksort algorithms sort the data according to node number; that is, the data are sorted so that it is in ascending order in each node, and all the data in a particular node are less than the data in all higher-numbered nodes. In the parallel Shell sort algorithm, the data are not globally sorted into node number order. Instead, the nodes are mapped onto a ring using the *gridmap* routines, and each node is assigned a position, *ringpos* in this ring. The data are sorted so that globally they end up in *ringpos* order; that is, the nodes with the smallest values of *ringpos* contain the smallest items.

8-12.2 C Implementation

In all cases the data to be sorted are initially distributed over the nodes. We will consider each of the three algorithms separately. The bitonic algorithm first adds very large positive and negative numbers to the list in each node to ensure that the subsequent sorting strategy terminates correctly. These extra numbers are discarded later. The next step is to sort each list locally in each node. This is done with a sequential quicksort, followed by an insertion sort, as described in Knuth [73a]. The routine *bitonic_merge* is then called. As described in Sec. 18-4 of Volume 1, this routine repeatedly compares the lists of pairs of nodes connected by a communication channel and exchanges data items so that the smaller end up in one node and the larger in another. This action is performed by the routines *cmp_ex_high* and *cmp_ex_low*. For any particular communication channel, one node calls *cmp_ex_high* and receives the larger items, while the node at the other end of the channel calls *cmp_ex_low* and receives the smaller items.

The parallel Shell sort algorithm begins in the same way as the parallel bitonic algorithm by locally sorting the lists in each node (see Sec. 18-6 of Volume 1). The routine *shell_merge* is then called, which globally sorts the data in two phases. The first phase is similar to the start of the *bitonic_merge* routine and calls *cmp_ex_high* and *cmp_ex_low* for each communication channel. This imposes an approximate global order in which the data are almost sorted but have a few items in the wrong place. In the second phase of the *shell_merge* routine, the nodes again call *cmp_ex_high* and *cmp_ex_low* to exchange items with their neighbors in the ring decomposition. This "mop-up" phase continues until the data are correctly sorted.

The quicksort algorithm, described in Sec. 18-8 of Volume 1, begins by calling the routine *distrib*. In the first part of *distrib* the data are sampled, and a set of N_p splitting keys is generated. This is done by first calling the routine *sample_data* to select *nsample* items at random from the list in each node. These sampled items are then globally sorted using the parallel bitonic algorithm described earlier. In each node the smallest item in the sorted list of samples is chosen as a splitting key for use in the second part of *distrib*. The splitting keys are communicated to all nodes by means of the CrOS III routine, *concat*. The second part of *distrib* consists of a loop over all communication channels. The items in the two nodes connected by a particular channel are sorted so that those greater than the appropriate splitting key end up in one node, while the rest of the items end up in the other node. This action is performed by the routines *high_dist* and *low_dist*, which are analogous to the routines *cmp_ex_high* and *cmp_ex_low* called in the bitonic and Shell sort algorithms.

The sorting codes listed in Appendices A and B will fail if any of the nodes initially contain no data items. In fact, the bitonic algorithm will not work in certain cases in which one node has very much fewer data items than another. These shortcomings could be removed, for example, by performing an initialization phase to balance approximately the number of items in each node.

8-12.3 Fortran Implementation

The Fortran versions of the parallel bitonic, Shell sort, and quicksort algorithms are illustrated in three separate programs, all of which are similar to the C implementation.

The parallel bitonic sort program, BITMRG, calls the routine SHELL to produce a locally sorted list in each node. The basic merging routines CMPEXH and CMPEXL are then used to compare and exchange items repeatedly between pairs of neighboring nodes. For any particular pair of nodes, one node calls CMPEXH and receives the larger items, while the other node calls CMPEXL and receives the smaller items.

The parallel Shell sort program, SHLMRG, begins by calling the CMPEXH and CMPEXL routines once for each pair of neighboring nodes to produce an almost sorted list. The nodes are then configured as a ring, and out-of-order items are passed round the ring (again using the routines CMPEXH and CMPEXL), until the list is globally sorted.

Apart from the naming of variables, arrays, and subroutines, and differences between the C and Fortran versions of CUBIX, the essential features of the Fortran version of the parallel quicksort code, QKSORT, are the same as those of the C code, and so will not be discussed further.

8-13 Global Scalar Products

Refer to	: Chapter 19 of Volume 1
C Directory	: $CODE/CDIR/ADDVEC
Fortran Directory	: $CODE/FDIR/ADDVEC

8-13.1 Purpose

Suppose we have M vectors of dimension N distributed across the N_p nodes, and we wish to sum the components of each of the M vectors leaving the result available to each node. The first step would be for each node to sum the components of each of the M vectors that it contains. After this stage, each node would contain partial sums for each vector. This program assumes that these partial sums have already been evaluated and sums them over all nodes for each vector. In each node the partial sums of the vectors are stored in an array B so that in each node the ith element of B is that node's partial sum for vector number i. This program evaluates the sum over all nodes of the elements of each of the M vectors and stores the result for vector number i in the ith element of some other array C in each node. Thus;

$$C_i \leftarrow \sum_{P=0}^{N_p-1} B_P(i) \tag{8.27}$$

where $B_P(i)$ is the partial sum of vector i in node P.

8-13.2 C Implementation

The program contains three main routines. The routine *setup_vectors* initializes the vectors to be summed, either by generating random vectors or by reading them from the standard input or a disk file. The routine *addvec* sums the vectors in two stages, and since the algorithm is fully described in Sec. 19-3 of Volume 1, we will not go into details here. In the first stage of *addvec* each vector is summed and the result is stored in a single node. In the second stage the sums are distributed to all nodes. Results are output by the routine *output_results*.

8-13.3 Fortran Implementation

Apart from the naming of variables, arrays, and subroutines and differences between the C and Fortran versions of CUBIX, the essential features of the Fortran code are the same as those of the C code.

To improve portability, some bit manipulation routines are included with the Fortran code. These routines assume that integers are 4 bytes long. Some systems with extended Fortran features already have these bitwise routines, and users may wish to use them instead of the ones supplied in this code.

8-14 LU Decomposition and the Solution of Linear Systems

Refer to	: Chapter 20 of Volume 1
C Directory	: $CODE/CDIR/LU_DECOMP
Fortran Directory	: $CODE/FDIR/LU_DECOMP

8-14.1 Purpose

This program solves linear systems of equations of the type

$$A\mathbf{x}_k = \mathbf{b}_k \tag{8.28}$$

where the coefficient matrix, A, is an $M \times M$ nonsymmetric, narrow-banded matrix (i.e., bandwidth, $w \ll M$), and $\mathbf{x}_k$ and $\mathbf{b}_k$ $(k = 0, 1, \ldots, n_b - 1)$ are vectors. For convenience Eq. (8.28) will be rewritten in the form

$$AX = B \tag{8.29}$$

where X is an $M \times n_b$ matrix the columns of which are simply the vectors $\mathbf{x}_k$ and B is an $M \times n_b$ matrix whose columns are the vectors $\mathbf{b}_k$. The need to solve such systems of equations arises, for example, when solving a partial differential equation for a number of different boundary conditions.

Equation (8.29) is solved using LU decomposition, followed by forward reduction and back-substitution. Both the nonpivoting and partial pivoting cases are considered.

8-14.2 C Implementation

Since the matrix A is a banded rather than a full matrix a block decomposition of the matrix is not appropriate since this would result in excessive load imbalance. Instead a scattered decomposition is used. The N nodes are mapped onto a square two-dimensional grid, or template, by means of the *gridmap* routines. The fact that we assume a *square* template implies that the code will only work for hypercubes of even dimension. Elements of the matrix A are then assigned to nodes by placing this decomposition template periodically over the matrix, as shown in Fig. (8-1). In this way the elements assigned to a particular node are not contiguous subblocks of A, but instead are scattered periodically over A. The matrix, B, of right-hand sides, and the solution matrix, X, are decomposed in a similar fashion.

For narrow-banded systems most of the elements of A are zero, and it would be a great waste of memory to store them all. Instead the following scheme is used to store A efficiently. We first assume that the order M is exactly divisible by $\sqrt{N}$. If this is not the case then A is padded with the appropriate elements of the identity matrix. The decomposition template is then stamped periodically over the matrix, as in Fig. 8-1, thereby defining a mesh of $\sqrt{N}$ by $\sqrt{N}$ subblocks. In the nonpivoting case, the first row of such subblocks can cover all the nonzero elements of A with a minimum of $\lceil m/\sqrt{N} \rceil + 1$ subblocks. The second row requires at least $\lceil m/\sqrt{N} \rceil + 2$ subblocks, and so on for other rows of subblocks. The minimum number of subblocks needed to cover all the nonzero elements in an arbitrary row of subblocks is $2\lceil m/\sqrt{N} \rceil + 1$. This is the case for all but the first and last $\lceil m/\sqrt{N} \rceil$ rows of subblocks, which we extend to the same size as the other rows of subblocks by adding subblocks to the start or end of the rows, as shown in Fig. 8-2. Next we slide the rows of subblocks horizontally so they form a rectangle. In our implementation of the algorithm we also add an extra row of subblocks to the beginning and end of the rectangle to properly deal with end effects encountered later in the algorithm, as shown in Fig. 8-3. These extra rows are not strictly necessary and could be avoided by inserting conditional statements at the appropriate points. The subblocks are then numbered in a columnwise manner as shown in Fig. 8-3. In each subblock precisely one element of A is stored in each node. We set the "elements" in the extra subblocks that have been added to zero. In each node the element stored in subblock number i is stored as element number i of the array *Aspace*. In the partial pivoting case, the width of the window varies as the algorithm progresses and can be up to $3\lceil m/\sqrt{N} \rceil - 1$ subblocks wide. This

0	1	3	2	0	1	3	2	0	1	3	2	0	1	3	2	0	1	3	2
4	5	7	6	4	5	7	6	4	5	7	6	4	5	7	6	4	5	7	6
12	13	15	14	12	13	15	14	12	13	15	14	12	13	15	14	12	13	15	14
8	9	11	10	8	9	11	10	8	9	11	10	8	9	11	10	8	9	11	10
0	1	3	2	0	1	3	2	0	1	3	2	0	1	3	2	0	1	3	2
4	5	7	6	4	5	7	6	4	5	7	6	4	5	7	6	4	5	7	6
12	13	15	14	12	13	15	14	12	13	15	14	12	13	15	14	12	13	15	14
8	9	11	10	8	9	11	10	8	9	11	10	8	9	11	10	8	9	11	10
0	1	3	2	0	1	3	2	0	1	3	2	0	1	3	2	0	1	3	2
4	5	7	6	4	5	7	6	4	5	7	6	4	5	7	6	4	5	7	6
12	13	15	14	12	13	15	14	12	13	15	14	12	13	15	14	12	13	15	14
8	9	11	10	8	9	11	10	8	9	11	10	8	9	11	10	8	9	11	10
0	1	3	2	0	1	3	2	0	1	3	2	0	1	3	2	0	1	3	2
4	5	7	6	4	5	7	6	4	5	7	6	4	5	7	6	4	5	7	6
12	13	15	14	12	13	15	14	12	13	15	14	12	13	15	14	12	13	15	14
8	9	11	10	8	9	11	10	8	9	11	10	8	9	11	10	8	9	11	10
0	1	3	2	0	1	3	2	0	1	3	2	0	1	3	2	0	1	3	2
4	5	7	6	4	5	7	6	4	5	7	6	4	5	7	6	4	5	7	6
12	13	15	14	12	13	15	14	12	13	15	14	12	13	15	14	12	13	15	14
8	9	11	10	8	9	11	10	8	9	11	10	8	9	11	10	8	9	11	10

Figure 8-1 The scattered decomposition of matrix A. In this case the order of A is $M = 20$, and the full bandwidth is $w = 11$. The band is shown shaded. The matrix is decomposed onto a 16-node hypercube, for which the corresponding decomposition template is 4×4 grid of cells. Each cell in the template represents a matrix element, and the number in the cell is the number of the node in which that element is stored.

variation can be accommodated by adding extra columns of subblocks to the matrix A.

The matrix of right-hand sides, B, is also decomposed using a scattered decomposition. In this case the subblocks stamped out by the decomposition template naturally form a rectangle so it is not necessary to slide the rows of subblocks as in the case of the matrix A. The subblocks of B are numbered columnwise, and subblock number i is stored in the appropriate node as element i of the array *bspace*. In each node the element in the ith subblock row and jth subblock column of the current window of A is accessed by the macro $a(i, j)$. Similarly, in each node the element at the corresponding position in the current window of B is accessed by the macro $b(k, i, j)$, where k is the row number of the subblock at which the node's elements first appear in the window.

The program calls the routine *decompose* to map the nodes onto the decomposition template. The row and column of the template occupied by each node is stored in the variables PI and PJ, respectively, which range from 1 to $\sqrt{N}$. The program then enters the main command loop which allows matrices to

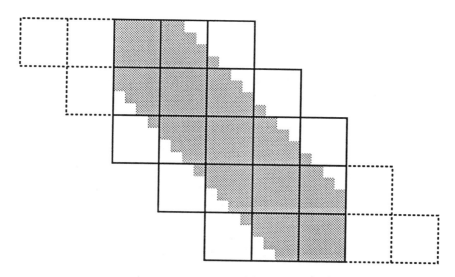

Figure 8-2 This figure shows the subblocks stamped out by periodically superimposing the decomposition template over the matrix. As in Fig. 8-1, the order, M, is 20, and the bandwidth, w, is 11. The subblocks containing non-zero elements are drawn with solid lines, and the extra subblocks added at the beginning and end are drawn with dashed lines.

be initialized and examined, and also finds the solution. Solving the system of equations consists of three stages: (1) LU decomposition, (2) forward reduction, and (3) back-substitution. These algorithms are described into detail in Secs. 20-2 through 20-5 of Volume 1 and in Aldcroft [Aldcroft 88] and so will not be fully discussed here.

We first consider the nonpivoting case. The matrix A is decomposed into lower and upper triangular matrices, L and U, by the routine $LU\_decompose$. This routine loops over the M stages of the algorithm. At each stage, k, only the elements of A within a computational window of size $\lceil m/\sqrt{N} \rceil + 1$ by $\lceil m/\sqrt{N} \rceil + 1$ subblocks are updated, and the kth row of U and the kth column of L are evaluated. The variables PI and PJ are used to keep track of where a particular node's elements appear in the window. At each stage a node calls one of four routines. If the node contains the element in the upper left-hand corner of the current window it calls LU_corner; otherwise if it contains elements lying in the first row or column of the window it calls LU_top or LU_left, respectively. Finally, if a node does not contain elements in the first row or column of the current window it calls LU_middle. The routines LU_corner and LU_top first send the elements in the top row of the current window to the other nodes in the same column of the decomposition template. This is done by first calling the routine v_to_c to copy the elements to be sent to a communication buffer $combuf$. This buffer is then

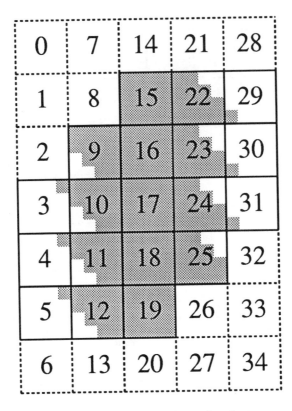

Figure 8-3 In the scattered decomposition each node stores one element of
A from each of the subblocks. The number of the subblocks is the array index
at which the element is stored in *Aspace*. The elements in the band are shown
shaded. In the unshaded parts of the subblocks the elements are set equal to
zero.

passed to the *split_pipe* routine, described in Sec. 20-4 of Volume 1. The routine
split_pipe is also called in loose synchrony by *LU_left* and *LU_middle* to receive
the data in the nodes not containing elements in the first row of the window. The
routines *LU_corner* and *LU_left* next evaluate the *k*th column of *L*, overwriting the
corresponding elements of *A* in the process. The first column of the current window
is then sent by the routines *LU_corner* and *LU_left* to the nodes lying in the same
row of the decomposition template. As before, the data are sent by calling *v_to_c*
and *split_pipe*, and in the nodes not containing elements in the first column of the
window, the routines *LU_top* and *LU_middle* call *split_pipe* loosely synchronously
to receive and forward the data. Finally, all nodes update the elements in the
current window, except for those in the first row and column.

Similar techniques are used to update the matrix *B* in the forward reduction and back-substitution stages to get the final solution. Once again each node calls one of four routines depending on where its elements lie in the current window. An important difference is that in the back substitution algorithm the window of A moves up the main diagonal starting at the lower right-hand corner of the matrix, and the window of B moves vertically up, starting at the bottom of B, whereas in the forward reduction algorithm the window of A moves diagonally down and the window of B moves vertically down. Thus in the back-substitution algorithm it is the right-hand column of the current window of A and the bottom row of the current window of B that must be communicated.

If partial pivoting is used, the algorithms are not fundamentally altered. At the start of each step of the LU decomposition algorithm the routine *find_pivot* is called in all nodes to locate the position of the pivot row, as described in Sec. 20-5 of Volume 1. The pivot row is determined by the node containing the element in the top left-hand corner of the current window, and its position is stored in that node in the arrays *blockno* and *rowno*. The position of the pivot row is communicated to the other nodes using the CrOS III routine *broadcast*. The routine *pivot_A* is then called in all nodes to communicate the pivot row elements to all nodes with the *split_pipe* routine and to transfer the first row of the window to the former position of the pivot row via the shortest geodesic pipe. The pivoting causes the width of the window to vary in size from m to $2m-1$ columns. At each stage the current size (in subblocks) of the window is stored in the array *nblocks* by the node containing the element in the lower right-hand corner of the window. After completing the pivoting the LU decomposition algorithm continues as in the nonpivoting case, except that the new window width is used. The forward reduction algorithm is also very similar to the nonpivoting case, except that at each stage the routine *pivot_B* is called to perform on matrix B the same exchange as rows that occurred for matrix A in the LU decomposition algorithm. This exchange could have been performed in the LU decomposition phase at the same time that A was being pivoted. In fact, the algorithm would be more efficient, but probably less easy to understand, if the LU decomposition and forward reduction stages were merged into a single step. The back-substitution algorithm is also identical to the nonpivoting case, except that each stage is preceded by a communication phase in which the node containing the element in the lower right-hand corner of the current window broadcasts the width of the window to the other nodes using the data stored in *nblocks*.

8-14.3 Fortran Implementation

Apart from the naming of variables, arrays, and subroutines, and differences between the C and Fortran versions of CUBIX, the essential features of the Fortran code are the same as those of the C code.

8-15 Subcube Allocation and Management

Refer to   : Chapter 5 of this volume
C Directory   : $CODE/CDIR/SUBCUBE

8-15.1 Purpose

This program demonstrates the use of the *submap* subcube management routines discussed in Sec. 5-2. The source code and manual pages for the *submap* utilities are presented in Appendices E and F.

8-15.2 C Implementation

The program presents the user with a menu which allows the *submap* routines *partition_subcube* and *restore_subcube* to be run on a specified subcube, and also permits information on the current partitioning to be output.

8-15.3 Fortran Implementation

The *submap* routines have not yet been implemented in Fortran.

8-16 The Communication Utility Routines

Refer to   : Chapter 5 of this volume and Chapter 21 of Volume 1
C Directory   : $CODE/CDIR/COMUTIL
Fortran Directory   : $CODE/FDIR/COMUTIL

8-16.1 Purpose

This program illustrates the use of the *comutil* communication utility routines, discussed in Sec. 5-3. The source code and manual pages for the *submap* utilities are presented in Appendices E and F.

8-16.2 C Implementation

The C code is a straightforward implementation of the *comutil* routines described in Chap. 21 of Volume 1 and Sec. 5-3 of this volume. The user is presented with a menu which allows five different functions to be performed.

1. A set of labels may be initialized. A label in this context is a pair of integers (j, i), where i is the node number, and j represents an array index. Initially the labels in some node , P, are just $(0, P), (1, P), (2, P), \ldots, (J-1, P)$, where J is the number of labels in the node. When these labels are passed as input to the *comutil* routines, they provide a convenient way of showing the effect of the routines on a data array.

2. The labels may be transformed by any of the *comutil* routines, i.e., *expand*, *fold*, *index*, *global_reverse*, *scatter*, *transfer* and *transpose*. In some cases, such as *global_reverse* and *index*, the number of labels in each node must be a power of 2 and exceed the number of nodes. In general, however, there may be an arbitrary number of labels in each node.

3. The labels may be output.

4. The program may be terminated.

8-16.3 Fortran Implementation

The Fortran code is made up of seven programs, each of which demonstrate the use of one of the *comutil* routines.

The program that illustrates the EXPAND routine first prompts the user to supply the number of elements, *NDIM*, in the vector. The vector is distributed across the nodes so that element number I of the global vector is also element number I in the local vector of node I. The vector is initialized so that element I of the vector is $(I - J)^2 + 2J$, where $J = N_p \lfloor (I - 1)/N_p \rfloor$ and $I = 1, 2, \ldots, NDIM$. After calling the EXPAND routine each node contains all the elements of the vector, and the vector is output by each node in turn.

The program that illustrates the FOLD routine begins by asking the user to supply the number of vectors, *NVEC*, distributed across the hypercube. Each vector contains N_p elements, and element number I is in node number I. The vectors are initialized so that the elements of vector number J are all equal to J. After calling the FOLD routine each node contains the sum over all elements for each vector. The program ends by outputting the sums for each node in turn.

The program that illustrates the INDEX routine does not prompt the user for any input. In each node the code initializes an array in which element number I equals $I * (P + 1)$, where P is the node number. Each node then outputs this array. The array is then passed to the INDEX routine, after which each node outputs the transformed array.

The program that illustrates the MTRANS routine for transposing data on a square two-dimensional mesh of nodes begins by calling the *gridmap* routines to ascertain the position of the nodes in the mesh, and the masks needed to communicate with neighboring nodes. In each node the variable $IVAR$ is set equal to the node number and is passed to the routine MTRANS. Upon return the value of $IVAR$ for the node at position (I, J) in the mesh equals the original value for the node at position (J, I). Each node outputs its value of $IVAR$, and the program terminates.

The program that illustrates the SCATER routine begins by initializing the array V in node 0 so that $V(I) = I$, for $I = 1, 2, \ldots, 12$. The elements of V are initialized to 0 in all other nodes. All nodes then pass V to the routine SCATER, specifying node 0 as the source node. Upon return from SCATER the array V is unchanged in node 0, but in the other nodes the elements of V are scattered as in Fig. 5-11. That is, in node P element $V(P + N_p * I)$ now equals the corresponding element in node 0, where $I = 0, 1, \ldots$. The program concludes by outputting the elements of V for each node.

The program that illustrates the TRANFS routine begins by initializing an array, V, in each node so that element number I equals $I * (P + 1)$, where P is the node number and $I = 1, 2, \ldots, 8$. The user is then prompted to supply the number of the source and destination nodes between which data are to be transferred. These numbers, together with the array V, are passed to the routine TRANSF. Upon return the elements of V in the destination node have been overwritten by the corresponding elements of V in the source node. The program concludes by outputting the elements of V for each node.

8-17 The Crystal Router

Refer to	: Chapter 22 of Volume 1, Chapter 5 of this volume
C Directory	: $CODE/CDIR/ROUTER
Fortran Directory	: $CODE/FDIR/ROUTER

8-17.1 Purpose

This program demonstrates the use of a buffered crystal router for communicating messages of arbitrary length between arbitrary nodes of a hypercube concurrent processor.

8-17.2 C Implementation

The main menu of this program allows messages to be created, sent, and received and also allows the contents of the outgoing and incoming message buffers to be examined. In addition, message buffers can be cleared, or their size altered, and error messages may be listed.

Each node maintains two main buffers: *in_default_buf* is used to store unread messages sent to the node from other nodes, and *out_default_buf* is used to store messages to be sent or forwarded to other nodes. Both these buffers are 10,000 bytes in size, but if necessary, larger buffers may be allocated by calling the routine *set_cr_buf*. A message consists of a header followed by the data to be sent. The first item in the header is an integer giving the number of nodes to which the message is to be sent. The second item is the node number of the source node which is sending the message. Next comes the number of bytes in the data to be sent. This is just the total message size minus the header size. The next item is the deletion flag, which is 1 if the message is flagged for deletion from the message buffer, and is 0 if the message is still current. The final part of the header is a list of integers specifying the nodes to which the data are to be sent, following which comes the data itself. Messages are added to the outgoing message buffer by calling the routine *send_message* described in Sec. 5-4. This routine first checks the arguments passed to it and, if they are valid, places the message header and data into the outgoing message buffer. A pointer, *out_buf_ptr*, is maintained which on exiting *send_message* points to the next byte in the outgoing message buffer directly after the last message. If there is not enough room in the outgoing message buffer for the message the appropriate bit of *cr_error* is set.

Messages are actually sent to their destinations by the routine *crystal_router*. This, first of all, compresses the buffer of received messages. This is done by the routine *compress_in_buf*, which looks at each message in the received message buffer.

Messages that have already been read, that is, have their deletion flag set to 1, are discarded, and the buffer is rewritten so that the current messages form a contiguous data block. The routine *copy_to_in_buf* is then called to scan the outgoing message buffer for any messages that the node has sent to itself. Any such messages are copied to the received message buffer and are marked for deletion from the outgoing message buffer.

The main component of the *crystal_router* routine is a loop over the channels of the hypercube, starting with channel 0. Each of these loops performs the following tasks. First, for all channels except channel 0, the routine *compress_out_buf* is called to compress the outgoing message buffer. This operation is similar to that performed by *compress_in_buf* on the received message buffer and discards all messages flagged for deletion and rewrites the buffer as a contiguous data block. Next the routine *check_buffer* is called. This scans the outgoing message buffer and copies any current messages which are to be sent on the communication channel to a communication buffer. Once a message has been copied to the communication buffer, it is flagged for deletion from the outgoing message buffer. In node P a message must be sent on some channel c if bit number c of at least one of the message's destination nodes differs from bit number c of P. The start of the communication buffer is the first byte directly after the last message in the outgoing message buffer, and messages are copied to the communication buffer by the routine *add_to_com_buf*. The communication buffer is exchanged with the corresponding buffer from the node at the other end of the communication channel by means of the CrOS III routine *cshift*. A check is made to see if there is enough space to receive the incoming data, and if there is not the routine *rescue_com_buf* is called to discard any incomplete messages that may have been received and to set the appropriate bit of *cr_error*. The received data in the communication buffer is then examined by calling the routine *copy_to_in_buf*, and any messages destined for this node are copied to the received message buffer. If a message is to be forwarded to another node, it is left unaltered in the communication buffer; otherwise it is flagged for deletion. After returning from *copy_to_in_buf*, the only current messages in the communication buffer are those that are to be forwarded. The communication buffer therefore becomes part of the outgoing message buffer. Since the communication buffer is next to the outgoing message buffer in memory, all that is required is to reset the pointer *out_buf_ptr* to the next byte after the end of the communication buffer and to increment the counter, *out_bytes*, which records the size of the outgoing message buffer, by *rec_bytes* (the size of the communication buffer). These operations are repeated for each of the channels of the hypercube, and at the end of this process, all nodes contain the messages addressed to them in their respective received message buffers. Finally, before exiting, *crystal_router* calls *compress_out_buf* one last time to compress the outgoing message buffer.

After calling *crystal_router* the received messages may be read by calling the routine *get_message*. This routine circularly scans the received message buffer for the next unread message from a particular source. It is also possible to request the next message from any source. If a valid message is found its data are copied to a user-supplied buffer, and it is flagged for deletion. If no valid message is found a nonzero value is returned.

8-17.3 Fortran Implementation

The Fortran version illustrates the use of the *crystal_router* by having each processor send a set of integers to every other processor. The user is not required to supply any input. The dimension of the hypercube is set equal to 2 by means of a PARAMETER statement, although this can be changed if necessary.

The program begins by setting up the data to be communicated. The array *NITEM* is used to store the number of integers to be sent to each processor. The integers themselves are stored in the two-dimensional array *OTMAIL*, so that *OTMAIL(J,I)* is the *J*th integer to be sent to processor number *I*. The data to be sent by each processor are then output. Next the routine CRYSRT is called which returns the number of integers received (or -1 if an error is detected) and stores them in the array *INMAIL*. Finally, the integers received by each processor are output.

The routine CRYSRT begins by initializing the two-dimensional array *ITHBIT*, so that *ITHBIT(I,N)* is bit number *I* of the integer *N*. In an application which calls CRYSRT several times this initialization is only performed on the first call. Next a DO loop is performed (DO 10 ...) which examines the mail to be sent to each processor in turn. This loop does three main things:

1.) Any integers that a processor has sent to itself are put into the array *INMAIL*. The variable *K* is used to keep a count of the number of integers that have been put into *INMAIL*.

2.) If the messages for a given processor does not have to be sent over channel number 0, then these messages are put into the array *TMPBUF*. Each destination processor has its own chunk of *TMPBUF* capable of holding up to *MAXBUF* integers. The array *IHOLD* is used to store the index of the start of each processor's chunk of *TMPBUF*.

3.) The messages that must be sent on channel 0 are copied into the array *TOMBUF*. The number of integers to be sent is stored in the array *AITEM*, and the ID number of the destination processor is stored in the array *BITEM*.

After completing the first DO loop the main *crystal_router* loop (DO 40 ...) over each of the hypercube communication channels may begin. The arrays *AITEM*, *BITEM*, and *TOMBUF* lie in the COMMON block /TOM/ and therefore occupy contiguous locations in memory. Thus in the first pass through the loop, the call to the CrOS III routine KCSHIF at the start of the loop sends the arrays *AITEM*, *BITEM*, and *TOMBUF* out on channel 0, while the corresponding data received on channel 0 are stored in the arrays *CITEM*, *DITEM*, and *COMBUF*, which also lie in the COMMON block /TOM/. The rest of the loop is similar to the initialization loop described in the previous paragraph. The data received in *COMBUF* are examined, and any messages that have arrived at their destination are copied into the array $INMAIL$. Messages in $COMBUF$ which do not have to be forwarded on the next iterate of the loop are stored in $TMPBUF$, and those which are to be forwarded are copied to $TOMBUF$. Finally, the messages in $TMPBUF$ are checked, and any that must be sent over the next channel are also copied to $TOMBUF$. The arrays $AITEM$ and $BITEM$, which store the number of integers to be sent to each destination processor and the IDs of those processors, are also modified. The next iterate of the $crystal\_router$ loop can then be performed.

After exchanging data over each of the communication channels, each processor has received all the data sent to it. These data are stored in the array $INMAIL$. The CRYSRT routine then returns, and each processor outputs the messages that it has received.

8-18 The Crystal Accumulator

Refer to	: Chapter 22 of Volume 1, Chapter 2 of this volume
C Directory	: $CODE/CDIR/CRYACC
Fortran Directory	: $CODE/FDIR/CRYACC

8-18.1 Purpose

This program demonstrates the use of the crystal accumulator routine for globally combining data distributed in sparse data structures over the nodes of a concurrent processor. In the case considered here each node contains an array of integers the elements of which are to be combined across the hypercube using some associative and commutative operator, which is taken to be addition. If the data to be combined are denoted by $V_j(i)$, where i is the node number and j is the array index $(j = 0, 1, \ldots, J - 1)$, then the program combines these data into an array, S, the decomposition of which is arbitrary:

$$S_{q(j)} = V_j(0) \oplus V_j(1) \oplus \cdots \oplus V_j(N_p - 1) \tag{8.30}$$

where the combining operation in our case is addition and $q(j)$ maps the ordering of the elements of S to that of the $V(i)$.

8-18.2 C Implementation

An array, Vx, of random integers is generated within each node by the routine $initialize$. The number of times that the identity element of the combining operator appears in Vx is determined by the user-supplied sparsity factor. The mapping $q(j)$ of the ordering of the elements of S to that of the $V(i)$ is generated at random and stored in the integer array qx. The final decomposition of S over the nodes is also generated at random and stored in the array px. Thus $qx(j)$ is the element number of S at which the combined jth elements of the $V(i)$ is stored, and $px(i)$ is the number of the node in which S_i is stored.

After initializing the problem, the routine $crystal\_accumulator$ is called to do the combining. The routine packages the input array Vx into an array, $data\_buf1$, of data type DSTRUCT by the routine $set\_up\_data\_buf$. This routine also sorts the elements of *data_buf1* with the *quicksort* and *insertion* routines, using the channel mask as the primary key and *qorder* (the final ordering of elements in S) as the secondary key. Each variable of type DSTRUCT is a struct containing three items. The first item is an integer that initially equals the channel mask necessary to send the corresponding element of Vx to the node that will contain that element combined over all nodes. For element number j this is node number $p(q(j))$. The second item of the structure is the index $q(j)$, and the third item is the input array element, V_j. Most of the *crystal_accumulator* routine consists of a loop over the channels of the hypercube, starting with the highest numbered. At the start of the loop for channel i the routine *high_pts* is called to determine how many data items are to be sent over this channel. This is just the number of items for which the channel mask is greater than 2^i. These data items are then exchanged with the corresponding items from the node at the other end of channel i by means of the CrOS III *cshift* routine. The routine *merge_lists* is then called to perform the combine/merge step in which those items received which correspond to elements already resident in the node are combined, and those which do not are inserted into the array, maintaining the ordering by channel mask and *qorder*.

8-18.3 Fortran Implementation

The program used to illustrate the Fortran version of the *crystal_accumulator* routine uses a somewhat different algorithm from the C version described in Sec. 8-18.2. The main differences are in how the various communications buffers are handled.

The Fortran program additively accumulates an array, V, of eight integers over the nodes of a two-dimensional hypercube. Results are accumulated in the array, S, which is decomposed over the hypercube nodes according to the array P. The array Q holds the mapping of the ordering of V to that of S. Thus after applying the *crystal_accumulator* algorithm, $S(I)$ contains the sum over all nodes of the $V(Q(I))$, and lies in processor number $P(I)$.

The *crystal_accumulator* algorithm is implemented by the routine CRACUM, which is really just a modified form of the *crystal_router* routine CRYSRT described in Sec. 8-17.3. CRACUM first initializes a two-dimensional array, $ITHBIT$, so that $ITHBIT(I,N)$ holds the Ith bit of the integer N. This initialization avoids some redundant calculation later in the algorithm. Next a loop over all the items in V is performed (DO 10 ...). This puts items of V that are already in the correct processor (according to the array P) into the array $INMAIL$. The corresponding values in Q are stored in the array $JNMAIL$, and the variable K is used to count the number of items in the $INMAIL$ and $JNMAIL$ arrays. Of the remaining items of V, those which do not have to be sent on channel 0 are copied to the array $TMPBUF$, and the corresponding values in Q are copied to the array $SMPBUF$. The variable JC is used to record the number of items copied to $TMPBUF$ and $SMPBUF$. Those items of V that are to be sent on channel 0 are copied to the array $TOMBUF$, and the corresponding values of Q are copied to $SOMBUF$. The number of items copied to $TOMBUF$ and $SOMBUF$ is stored in the variable MC. At this stage all the buffers have been initialized for the first communication phase over channel 0.

As in the *crystal_router* routine, CRACUM next performs a loop over each channel of the hypercube in turn, starting with channel 0 (DO 40 ...). At the start of each iterate, the arrays $TOMBUF$ and $SOMBUF$ are sent out on the current channel, and the corresponding data received on the same channel are stored in the arrays $COMBUF$ and $DOMBUF$, respectively. This is done by two calls to the CrOS III routine KCSHIF. Following this a loop is performed (DO 50 ...) which processes each of the items received in $COMBUF$. If an item has arrived at its final destination, it is copied into the arrays $INMAIL$ and $JNMAIL$. If there is no slot already for this item in these arrays then one is created, and K is incremented; otherwise, the item is accumulated at a pre-existing slot. If an item in $COMBUF$ has not reached its final destination, then we check to see if it must be sent on the channel in the next iterate. If this is not the case, then the item's details are copied to $TMPBUF$ and $SMPBUF$. Again, if no slot exists for an item, then one is created, otherwise the item is accumulated in a preexisting slot. If the item must be sent on the channel of the next iterate, then it is copied or accumulated into the arrays $TOMBUF$ and $SOMBUF$. If an item is accumulated, this frees up a slot in the arrays $TMPBUF$ and $SMPBUF$, and these arrays are tidied up by copying the last item to the newly freed slot.

This completes the processing of the data received into $COMBUF$ and $DOMBUF$. The last task to do before performing the next iterate is to check through the array $TMPBUF$ to see which items must be sent on the next iterate (DO 60 ...). Any items to be sent on the next iterate are copied from the arrays $TMPBUF$ and $SMPBUF$ to the arrays $TOMBUF$ and $SOMBUF$. This frees up slots in $TMPBUF$ and $SMPBUF$, and a record of these is kept in the array $LIST$. The number of freed-up slots is stored in the variable LC. Finally, the freed up slots in $TMPBUF$ and $SMPBUF$ are re-utilized by copying items from the end of the arrays to the free slots. The next iterate in the loop over channels can now be performed.

After performing the loop over each of the channels, all the items have been accumulated and sent to the correct processor. CRACUM concludes by using the index information in $JNMAIL$ to copy the items in $INMAIL$ to the correct location in the final array S. After returning from CRACUM the program outputs the array S in each processor.

9

A Suite of
Parallel Benchmark Programs

9-1 General Remarks

In recent years a growing number of advanced architecture computers have become commercially available. These diverse types of machine promise to provide high performance at a unit cost lower than that of traditional computers and may soon also surpass them in terms of absolute performance. It is therefore important to assess the performance of advanced architecture computers and to determine the suitability of a given machine for a specific class of application [NAS 86, Martin 87].

In this chapter we describe a suite of benchmark programs for evaluating the performance of advanced architecture computers. In addition, we also include in the benchmarking suite the matrix multiplication and LU decomposition programs described in Secs. 8-7 and 8-14, respectively. This suite of programs has been used in the Caltech Performance Evaluation Project to conduct a pilot study of the performance of the machines listed in Table 9-1 [Walker 88a], and the results are presented in [Messina 89]. The source code and I/O files have been placed in the public domain and may be accessed electronically as described in Appendix G. We encourage people to use these benchmarks to evaluate the performance of new machines as they become available and any existing machines of interest not listed in Table 9-1. Some of the scientific calculations using these benchmarks are reviewed in Fox [Fox 89i,n,p].

The benchmark programs have been chosen to be representative of the types of scientific codes typically used in university and research environments and are capable of producing results of scientific interest. Thus, these benchmarks are to be distinguished from computational kernels, such as the Livermore loops, which in some instances may not be fully representative of actual programs. The benchmarks also differ from larger "production" codes, such as NASTRAN and SPICE, which typically have many thousands of lines of code. These more substantial codes are often difficult to port to certain types of machine, such as hypercubes, and so are not suitable for a preliminary performance study. However, a study of the performance of large-scale codes on mainly vector and shared memory multiprocessors has been made [Berry 89], and this may be extended to distributed memory machines in the future.

Machine	Description
NCUBE	Hypercube with custom scalar processors
Mark III	Hypercube with MC68020/68882 processors
Mark IIIfp	Mark III hypercube with XL Weitek chip set
INTEL iPSC/1	Intel 80286/80287-based hypercube
BBN Butterfly	MIMD network of MC68020/68881-based processors
Alliant FX/8	Shared memory vector multiprocessor
Sequent Balance	NS32032/32081-based shared memory multiprocessor
Sequent Symmetry	Intel 80386-based shared memory multiprocessor with optional scalar Weitek chips
Encore Multimax	NS32332-based shared memory multiprocessor
Cydrome Cydra 5	Very Long Instruction Word machine
Cray X/MP	4-node vector supercomputer
Cray 2	4-node vector supercomputer with large memory
SCS-40	Vector mini-supercomputer, Cray X/MP compatible
ETA-10 E	4 vector processors with shared memory
Connection Machine 2	Massively parallel SIMD machine with 16K nodes and Weitek chips

Table 9-1 Advanced Architecture Computers Studied in the Caltech Performance Evaluation Project.

9-2 Quantum Chromodynamics

Quantum chromodynamics (QCD) is the gauge theory of the strong interaction which binds quarks and gluons into hadrons, which in turn make up the constituents of nuclear matter. Analytical perturbation methods can be applied to QCD only at small distances (or equivalently at high energies); hence computer simulations are necessary to study long-range effects in QCD theory (i.e., at lower energies). In these lattice gauge theory simulations, the quantum field is discretized onto a periodic, four-dimensional, space-time lattice. Quarks are located at the lattice sites, and the gluons that bind them are associated with the lattice links. The gluons are represented by SU(3) matrices, which are a particular type of 3 by 3 complex matrix. A major component of the QCD code involves updating these matrices. A number of different methods have been proposed for updating the SU(3) matrices; see Otto [Otto 87] for a summary. The QCD benchmark uses the Cabbibo-

Marinari pseudoheat-bath algorithm [Cabbibo 82] to update the SU(3) matrices on the lattice links. This algorithm uses a Monte Carlo technique to generate a chain of configurations which are distributed with a probability proportional to $\exp[-S(U)]$, where $S(U)$ is the action of configuration U. If the only contributions to the action come from the gauge field, then the action is local. The effects of dynamical fermions give rise to a nonlocal action, which complicates the algorithm considerably [Apostolakis 88c]. However, in the QCD code the effects of dynamical fermions are ignored. The code therefore represents a pure-gauge model in the "quenched" approximation.

Lattice QCD problems are among the most computationally intensive large-scale scientific computations [Baillie 89g]. In fact, it was the need for a cost-effective means of seriously addressing lattice QCD computations that spurred the development of the early hypercubes at Caltech in 1981 to 1983. The QCD code has its origins in the work of Otto and coworkers at Caltech. In his Ph.D. thesis Otto used a small prototype of the 64-node Cosmic Cube hypercube to investigate the mass of the O^{++} glueball for SU(2) theory [Otto 83]. The Caltech group then used the full Cosmic Cube to study SU(3) lattice theory [Brooks 84; Otto 84a, 85]. This work was developed further by Flower and Stolorz [Flower 85, 87; Stolorz 87] who used the 128-node Caltech/JPL Mark II hypercube to measure the mesonic and baryonic potential on a 20^4 lattice. Recent calculations have used a version of this code on the Mark IIIfp hypercube which achieved 0.5 gigaflop performance in production mode [Ding 89a,b]. This version of the pure gauge SU(3) code, which was written in C, was subsequently ported to the NCUBE, iPSC/1, and Mark III hypercubes. In 1987 to 1988 sequential and parallel FORTRAN versions of the code were developed [Baillie 88g]. Since the QCD code was developed originally on hypercubes with only a small amount of memory per node, care was taken to minimize the memory used to store the SU(3) matrices associated with each lattice link. For SU(3) matrices only two of the columns are independent, so each matrix can be specified by 6 complex numbers. Moreover, the real and imaginary parts of each number always lie between -2 and $+2$ and can therefore be stored as 2-byte integers in the C version of the code. In this case each matrix can be stored as 12 short integers.

A major component of the QCD code is the updating of the SU(3) matrices associated with each link in the lattice, and it is this operation that is benchmarked in the timings. Two basic operations are involved in updating the lattice, namely, the multiplication of SU(3) matrices, and the generation of pseudorandom numbers with the desired distribution.

9-3 Target Tracking

The TRACKER code was developed at Caltech by Gottschalk and coworkers to determine the course of a set of an unknown number of targets, such as rocket boosters, from observations of the targets taken by sensors at regular time intervals (see Gottschalk [Gottschalk 88a,b] and references therein). The targets may be

launched from a number of different sites. Gottschalk's code was originally written
in C for the Caltech/JPL Mark II and III hypercubes and has also been ported
to the iPSC/1 and NCUBE hypercubes [Baillie 88f]. The sequential FORTRAN
version used for benchmarking was written by Gottschalk at the start of 1988.

If the target's acceleration is assumed to be known then the path of an
individual object is described fully by a four-component launch vector made up
of the latitude and longitude of the launch site, the time of launch, and the initial
launch azimuth relative to due north. At each time step a simple linear Kalman
filter is first used to estimate the position, velocity, and acceleration of the targets
from the noise-corrupted sensor data, using an underlying kinematical model with
a stochastic acceleration component developed by Gottschalk. The output from
this phase is then passed to the precision parameter estimation module which uses
Newton-Raphson iteration to solve an equation giving a more precise estimate of
the launch parameter vector.

In a multitarget scenario the assignment of sensor data points are associated
with tracks by means of the "track-splitting" algorithm described in Gottschalk
[Gottschalk 87]. In general this association will not be unique, and a single sensor
point may at some stage of processing be associated with more than one track. This
is particularly true at the early stages of processing when the number of possible
valid tracks may be large. The problem of a potential combinatoric explosion in the
number of valid tracks is dealt with by a track pruning algorithm which discards
the poorer of any duplicate tracks. The initialization of new tracks is managed by
a separate module called the "batch mode initializer," which limits possible new
tracks to a reasonably plausible set.

9-4 Chemical Reaction Dynamics

This application studies the quantum mechanical reactive scattering of an
atom and a diatomic molecule by calculating the differential cross-section as a
function of energy. In the past lack of convergence, and other numerical problems,
in the solution of the Schrödinger equation have hindered these types of ab initio
quantum chemical calculations, even for very simple systems. A recent significant
advance in chemical dynamics is the use of symmetrized hyperspherical coordinates
[Kuppermann 75] in the solution of reactive scattering problems. Symmetrized
hyperspherical coordinates (SHC) are used to specify the geometrical configuration
of triatomic systems in terms of the hyperspherical radius, ρ, and a set of five
hyperspherical angles collectively denoted by ω. The use of SHC avoids the
numerical problems inherent in the earlier methods.

As explained in Hipes [Hipes 87; 88b], the SHC method first expands the
scattering wave function in terms of a separable basis set, namely, the local
hyperspherical surface functions (LHSF), $\Phi_n^{J,M}(\omega; \rho)$, which are defined to be
the simultaneous eigenfunctions of the surface Hamiltonian and the total angular

momentum operators. Thus for ρ in some neighborhood of $\overline{\rho}_j$ we write,

$$\Psi^{J,M}(\rho,\omega) = \rho^{-5/2} \sum_{n'=1}^{N} f_{n'}^{J}(\rho;\overline{\rho}_j)\Phi_{n'}^{J,M}(\omega;\overline{\rho}_j) \qquad (9.1)$$

This expansion is then substituted into the Schrödinger equation to yield a set of coupled ordinary differential equations known as the coupled channel Schrödinger equation, from which the coefficients $f_{n'}^{J}(\rho;\overline{\rho}_j)$ can be derived,

$$\sum_{n'=1}^{N} \left[\delta_{n'}^{n} \frac{d^2}{d^2\rho} + V_{n,n'}^{J}(\rho,\overline{\rho}_j) \right] f_{n'}^{J}(\rho;\overline{\rho}_j) = 0 \qquad (9.2)$$

where $\delta_{n'}^{n}$ is the Kronecker delta function, and V^J is the interaction matrix, which depends upon the total energy, integrals over pairs of LHSFs, and the potential energy function.

The system of coupled ODEs in Eq. (9.2) is solved using the logarithmic derivative integrator of Johnson [Johnson 73] and Mrugala [Mrugala 83]. This fourth-order integrator is based on the Ricatti form of the coupled channel Schrödinger equation. In addition to having good stability, the logarithmic derivative method has the additional advantage of being straightforward to implement, since the principal algorithm involved is matrix inversion.

Different sets of LHSFs are needed for each neighborhood, $\overline{\rho}_j$. Thus it is necessary to be able to transform coefficients in Eq. (9.1) for one set of LHSFs to those corresponding to the LHSFs of an adjacent neighborhood. The main operation involved in such transformations is matrix multiplication. Thus the implementation of the logarithmic derivative method requires matrix inversion and matrix multiplication algorithms.

The complete reactive scattering problem is performed in three stages. First, the LHSFs are determined; then, the interaction matrices are calculated using numerical quadrature; and last, the coupled Schrödinger equation is solved by the logarithmic derivative method. The benchmark program used in the Caltech Performance Evaluation Project only performs the last of these stages. The input to the program is the set of interaction matrices, which have previously been calculated on a Cray X/MP. 65 terms are used in the expansion of the scattering wave function, and the input set contains several hundred 67 by 67 matrices, resulting in a very large input file of approximately 24 Mbytes. The matrix inversion required in the logarithmic derivative method is performed using the Gauss-Jordan algorithm, and this dominates the calculation time.

The parallel implementation of the logarithmic derivative method on the hypercube is discussed in Hipes [Hipes 88b], and the matrix inversion is performed using the parallel Gauss-Jordan algorithm described in Hipes [Hipes 88a, 89a]. A local rectangular sub-block decomposition is used for both the Gauss-Jordan and matrix multiplication algorithms. Initially on the Mark III hypercube it was found that I/O dominated the run time due to the large size of the input data file. However, after extensive modifications, the I/O time become slightly less than the calculation time.

The problem addressed in the benchmark program is the reactive scattering in three-dimensional space of $H + H_2 \rightarrow H_2 + H$. The number of neighborhoods used is 30, and the calculation is performed for 300 time steps.

9-5 Fluid Dynamics Using the Vortex Method

The vortex method is used to model the flow of incompressible, inviscid fluids. The method is particularly useful for studying turbulent flows at high Reynolds number, since such flows often are characterized by regions of concentrated vorticity (eddies) embedded in an otherwise irrotational fluid. Applications of the vortex method include the simulation of the flow past bluff bodies, helicopter blades, and stalled airfoils [Spalart 83, 84] and the interaction of colliding smoke rings [Chua 88]. Reviews of the method may be found in Leonard [Leonard 80, 85] and Aref [Aref 83].

The vortex method rests on the fact that in an inviscid flow the fluid vorticity moves with the local velocity. If the flow is incompressible then the velocity field can be determined from the vorticity distribution. In other words, the incompressible Navier-Stokes equations can be replaced by the vorticity equation, which in two dimensions is

$$\frac{\partial \boldsymbol{\omega}}{\partial t} + (\mathbf{u} \cdot \nabla)\boldsymbol{\omega} = 0 \tag{9.3}$$

Since the vorticity is defined as $\boldsymbol{\omega} = \nabla \times \mathbf{u}$, the velocity field can be determined from the Poisson equation:

$$\nabla^2 \mathbf{u} = -\nabla \times \boldsymbol{\omega} \tag{9.4}$$

Writing the solution to Eq. (9.4) in terms of the Biot-Savart integral we have

$$\mathbf{u}(\mathbf{r}, t) = -\frac{1}{2\pi} \int \frac{(\mathbf{r} - \mathbf{r}') \times \mathbf{k}}{|\mathbf{r} - \mathbf{r}'|^2} \boldsymbol{\omega}(\mathbf{r}', t) d\mathbf{r}' \tag{9.5}$$

where $\mathbf{k}$ is the unit vector in the z direction.

If the vorticity field is represented by a set of N point vortices; that is,

$$\boldsymbol{\omega}(\mathbf{r}, t) = \sum_{j=1}^{N} \Gamma_j \delta\left[\mathbf{r} - \mathbf{r}_j(t)\right] \tag{9.6}$$

where Γ_j is the circulation of the jth vortex and δ is the two-dimensional Dirac delta function. Then the velocity can be written as

$$\mathbf{u}(\mathbf{r}, t) = -\frac{1}{2\pi} \sum_{j=1}^{N} \frac{(\mathbf{r} - \mathbf{r}_j) \times \mathbf{k}}{|\mathbf{r} - \mathbf{r}_j|^2} \Gamma_j \tag{9.7}$$

This expression leads to a set of $2N$ coupled, nonlinear, first-order, differential equations, which can be integrated to give the vortex positions as a function of time.

The vortex method as outlined is static in the sense that the number of vortices is constant. However, in many applications of interest the number of vortices is allowed to change dynamically as the fluid flow evolves. For example, in simulating the flow past a bluff body, in which the fluid flow separates from the surface, vortices are created at specific points on the surface to satisfy the boundary conditions. Downstream, suitable pairs of vortices are merged to limit the total number of vortices and vortices colliding with walls are removed.

The use of the point vortex method, however, often leads to numerical instabilities for fluid flows of interest. This instability arises from the singularity of the point vortices. This problem can be overcome by spreading the vortices out so that each has a finite core size [Chorin 73]. Thus in the "vortex blob method" the vorticity field is represented by

$$\omega(\mathbf{r}, t) = \sum_{j=1}^{N} \Gamma_j \gamma_j \left(\mathbf{r} - \mathbf{r}_j(t) \right) \tag{9.8}$$

where γ_j is the vorticity distribution of the vortex centered at $\mathbf{r}_j$.

Other modifications to the vortex method, such as the vortex-in-cell algorithm [Christiansen 73], have sought to reduce the operation count. As may be seen from Eq. (9.7), each vortex contributes to the velocity of all other vortices. The vortex method is, therefore, a form of long-range interaction algorithm in which each vortex interacts with all other vortices. Thus, for a system of N vortices, the standard vortex method has a complexity varying as N^2. This currently limits the number of vortices to a few thousand, whereas the simulation of flows of engineering interest requires 10^5 to 10^6 vortices. Recent advances in particle interaction algorithms may be applicable to the vortex method. For example, Appel [Appel 85] has used an algorithm similar to that of Barnes [Barnes 86], in which distant particles (or vortices) are clumped together, leading to an algorithm of complexity $N \log_2 N$. A multipole expansion algorithm developed by Greengard [Greengard 86] for use in particle simulations has a complexity of N and may also be applicable to the vortex method. This clustering algorithm has been successfully implemented on the hypercube for astrophysical particle dynamics simulations by [Warren 88b] and [Salmon 89a].

In three-dimensional problems the vorticity field is represented by vortex filaments instead of blobs. For a review of three-dimensional problems the reader is referred to Leonard [Leonard 85].

The VORTEX code used in the Caltech Performance Evaluation Project makes use of the standard, two-dimensional, vortex blob algorithm. The problem considered is the evolution of a vortex sheet in which vortices are initially located at regular intervals, Δ, in the x direction. Successive vortices alternate at a distance

Δ above and below the x axis, and also alternate in the sign of their circulation. Thus initially,

$$\mathbf{r}_j = \left(j\Delta, (-1)^j \Delta \right), \qquad \Gamma_j = (-1)^j \tag{9.9}$$

The velocity of the ith vortex induced by the other vortices is given by

$$\frac{d\mathbf{r}_i}{dt} \equiv \mathbf{u}_i = -\frac{1}{2\pi} \sum_{j=1}^{N} (-1)^j \frac{(\mathbf{r}_i - \mathbf{r}_j) \times \mathbf{k}}{\sigma^2 + |\mathbf{r}_i - \mathbf{r}_j|^2} \tag{9.10}$$

where σ represents the size of each vortex blob. This set of nonlinear, first-order, differential equations is solved for the vortex positions using a third-order Runge-Kutta integrator with a fixed time step, δt. In the Caltech benchmark a constant number of 5000 vortex blobs were used with the following model parameters:

$$\Delta = 0.1, \quad \sigma^2 = 0.0043, \quad \delta t = 0.025 \tag{9.11}$$

Since the vortex method is essentially a long-range force type of problem it can be implemented on a hypercube using an algorithm similar to that discussed in Chap. 9 of Volume 1 and Sec. 8-6 of this volume. Catherasoo [Catherasoo 87] has discussed the performance of the vortex method on the AMETEK System 14 hypercube, and Harstad [Harstad 87] has compared the performance of the Caltech/JPL Mark II hypercube with that of the Cyber 205 vector computer for a problem similar to that used in the benchmark described here. Since the concurrent overhead of the parallel long-range force algorithm on the hypercube is inversely proportional to the grain size (the number of vortices per processing node), it was found that the vortex method can be efficiently implemented on the hypercube for sufficiently large problems.

9-6 Plasma Physics

Plasma particle simulations have important applications in many areas of physics, such as space plasma physics, electron and ion beam propagation, microwave generation by gyrotrons, and magnetic and inertial fusion. In plasma simulations we seek to determine the orbits self-consistently of up to 10^6 charged particles as they move under the influence of an electromagnetic field, which is generated (or modified) by the plasma particles themselves. The motion of each particle is governed by the equation

$$\frac{d^2\mathbf{x}_i}{dt^2} \equiv \frac{d\mathbf{v}_i}{dt} = \frac{q_i}{m_i} \left(\mathbf{E} + \frac{\mathbf{v}_i \times \mathbf{B}}{c} \right) \tag{9.12}$$

where $\mathbf{x}_i$, $\mathbf{v}_i$, q_i, and m_i are the position, velocity, charge, and mass of the ith particle. $\mathbf{E}$ and $\mathbf{B}$ represent the electric and magnetic fields and are determined by Maxwell's equations, with the charge and current densities generated by the plasma particles being given by

$$\rho(\mathbf{x}, t) = \sum_{i=1}^{N} q_i \delta(\mathbf{x} - \mathbf{x}_i)$$

$$\mathbf{j}(\mathbf{x}, t) = \sum_{i=1}^{N} q_i \mathbf{v}_i \delta(\mathbf{x} - \mathbf{x}_i) \tag{9.13}$$

Since each particle influences the motion of all other particles through the Lorentz force, $\mathbf{F} = q(\mathbf{E} + \mathbf{v} \times \mathbf{B}/c)$, a naive solution for a system of N plasma particles would have a computational complexity proportional to N^2. To allow simulations involving large numbers of particles a faster algorithm is required. The particle-in-cell (PIC) method avoids the "N^2 problem" by solving for the electromagnetic field on a discrete numerical grid, using either a fast Fourier transform or finite difference technique.

The particles themselves are not constrained to lie at the grid points, thus before the electromagnetic field can be calculated the charge and current densities are interpolated onto the grid. Then, after Maxwell's equations have been used to solve for the electromagnetic field on the grid, the force on a particle at a particular location is found by interpolation from the values of $\mathbf{E}$ and $\mathbf{B}$ at nearby grid points. The particle position and velocity can then be updated according to Eq. (9.12).

The BEPS1 code benchmarked in the Caltech Performance Evaluation Project is a one-dimensional, electrostatic, PIC simulation model. The electromagnetic field is neglected, and the code self-consistently calculates the motion of the plasma particles in the electric field generated by their charge densities.

Equation (9.12) is integrated using a simple leapfrog scheme to give the velocity and position of each particle.

$$\mathbf{v}_i(t + \Delta t/2) = \mathbf{v}_i(t - \Delta t/2) + \frac{q_i}{m_i} \mathbf{F}_i \Delta t$$

$$\mathbf{x}_i(t + \Delta t) = \mathbf{x}_i(t) + \mathbf{v}_i(t + \Delta t/2) \Delta t \tag{9.14}$$

The domain of the problem is divided into intervals of equal length, and the net charge density at each point on the resulting one-dimensional grid is obtained by interpolating the charge of each particle onto the nearest grid points. The electric field, $\mathbf{E} = (E, 0, 0)$, is then determined on the grid by solving

$$\frac{dE}{dx} = 4\pi\rho \tag{9.15}$$

by a fast Fourier transform technique. The force, $q_i\mathbf{E}_i$, on each particle is then found by quadrupole interpolation of the electric field values at the nearest grid points.

The parameters of the benchmark program were taken to be the same as those used by Decyk [Decyk 88] in his extensive evaluation of plasma simulation codes on predominantly shared memory and vector supercomputers. The total number of plasma particles (electrons and ions) was 11,264, 128 spatial grid points were used, and the benchmark code was run for 2,500 time steps. Initially, the particles are spaced at regular intervals and have Maxwellian velocity distributions.

The implementation of plasma PIC simulation codes on hypercube concurrent computers has been described in Liewer [Liewer 88b, 89]. Two different decompositions are used: one to update the particle positions and velocities and another to solve the electromagnetic field equations. In the first of these decompositions, the spatial domain of the computation is divided into subdomains and one is assigned to each processing node so that initially each processing node is responsible for approximately equal numbers of plasma particles. In the second decomposition, equal numbers of grid points are placed in each nodes, and distributed among the nodes as required by the hypercube FFT algorithm described in Chap. 11 of Volume 1.

As the system evolves, particles will move from one processing node's subdomain to another, requiring the data for that particle to be communicated between the two nodes. Each processing node contains all the data for the particles which lie within its subdomain. In addition, it contains the electromagnetic field values for the grid points that lie within its subdomain and also the values for the grid points lying along the boundaries of the neighboring subdomains. Thus, each node is able to update all the particles for which it is responsible without additional internode communication. The charge and current densities at the grid points in each subdomain can also be calculated without internode communication. After the charge and current densities are calculated, the nodes communicate to distribute this information over the nodes, as required in the decomposition used to solve for the electromagnetic fields. After solving for the electric and magnetic fields on this grid, the nodes again communicate so that each node stores the field values appropriate to the first decomposition.

As the system evolves, particles will move from one processing node's subdomain to another, so that after a time the number of particles in each node will differ, and hence the load balance will become uneven. When this occurs, the computational domain should be subdivided anew, so that each node again contains approximately the same number of particles. This technique is called dynamic load balancing. In the version of the code that was benchmarked dynamic load balancing was not implemented.

An alternative decomposition strategy that would avoid the difficulties associated with dynamic load balancing would be to replace the first decomposition described above by a nonspatial decomposition [Walker 89]. In this decomposition equal numbers of particles are assigned to each processor, and this assignment of particles to processors does not change throughout the computation. The *crystal_accumulator* algorithm described in Sec. 22.4 of Volume 1 is used to interpolate the charge and current densities onto the regular grid used in the second decomposition. A number of strategies could be used to distribute field values on the grid to the processors that need them. The simplest solution is to send the values for each grid point to all processors. A more sophisticated approach would involve communication in two phases. In the first phase each processor generates a list of the grid points it needs, and this information is distributed to the processors containing those grid points. At the end of this phase each processor knows where it needs to send the field values for the grid points that it contains. In the second communication phase the field values are distributed to the processors that requested them in the first phase. This may be done using the *crystal_router* algorithm of Sec. 8-17.

9-7 Neural Networks

This application is an implementation of a neuro-physiological model of the piriform cortex — a part of the cerebral cortex in mammals involved in processing olfactory data. Details of the model and its biological basis are given in Wilson [Wilson 88]. The implementation on the hypercube is discussed in Bower [Bower 88b] and makes use of the *fold* communication routine described in Sec. 21-3.3 of Volume 1. A scattered decomposition of neurons over the hypercube is used to ensure approximate load balance. This code is a useful benchmark as it is representative of more general neural networks.

A neural network consists of a number of independent processing elements (the neurons). These neurons can send information to other nodes along individual communication lines (the axons) to form, in general, a network of arbitrary complexity. Each neuron may process input data in a different way and sends its output to the other neurons to which it is connected. Typically, a neuron's output is zero if a certain function of its input is less than some threshold value. If the threshold is exceeded a spike is propagated with finite velocity down the axons to the connected neurons. After this happens the neuron will not signal again within a time period known as the absolute refractory period.

The piriform cortex is modeled by a two-dimensional array of essentially fully interconnected neurons. The benchmark program has been used to simulate up to 3,000 moderately complex neurons, which may be of three basic types. One type has an excitory effect on other neurons, and the other two types have inhibitory effects. When a shock is used to stimulate the network a pattern of rhythmic, long-lasting activity is observed, which is similar to the behavior seen in the olfactory system of mammals.

10

Wrap-up

10-1 What Have We Done?

In Volume 1 of this series we discussed the implementation of several problems on concurrent processors. These basic principles are backed up in Volume 2, which presents explicit code in C and Fortran for these examples, as well as additional problems given in Chap. 9. This set of codes is not hailed as possessing great brilliance or completeness, but rather should be viewed as a tutorial and benchmark suite. Our goal in presenting the codes in Chap. 8 is to help others learn how to use parallel machines. In Chap. 9 we have selected some typical scientific problems which we have already implemented on several conventional and novel computers. We hope these may form a benchmark set to help understand the performance and design trade-offs in current and future high-performance computers [Walker 88a; Messina 89]. In Appendix G we describe how to obtain the software contained in this book in computer-readable form. This facility will also incorporate extensions and corrections to the software. We urge the reader to use this mechanism to obtain the "best available" copy of the software and also to communicate to us bugs and suggested improvements to the codes. We note that all software presented in Volume 2, or obtained via the mechanism of Appendix G, has been placed in the public domain to facilitate its convenient use. We would be grateful if you acknowledge its source when using the software in published material.

Volume 2 also discusses several explicit realizations of CrOS III on different machines, as well as extensions that we have found helpful. We have indicated how communication and I/O in CrOS III can be implemented in high-performance mode, or (with more overhead) on top of other more general communication systems. In particular we have discussed the BBN Butterfly, INTEL iPSC, and NCUBE commercial communication systems. Particular emphasis has been given to *Express* since this Parasoft product offers commercial support for CrOS III and CUBIX.

10-2 What Haven't We Done?

In Chap. 1 of this volume we have described a taxonomy of problems and computers and indicated how the techniques of Volumes 1 and 2 of this series are restricted to what we have termed *loosely synchronous* problems. These appear to constitute the majority of scientific and engineering computations, and so our methods are quite general. A good example of an application that is *asynchronous* and needs more sophisticated techniques is the parallel computer chess program of Felten and Otto [Felten 88g].

Even in the *loosely synchronous* class most of our examples are relatively simple and lack the sophistication of "real" problems. References to such "serious" parallel applications are given in Table 1-7, while the proceedings of hypercube conferences, Heath [Heath 86, 87], Fox [Fox 88c], and Gustafson [Gustafson 89a] are good general references. The Caltech Concurrent Computation Program annual reports [Fox 87b,88v] are also helpful, and Fox [Fox 89i, 89n, 89p] review several recent major parallel computations at the supercomputer performance level.

The topic of load balancing, or distributing the work equally between the nodes, is typically straightforward in the regular problems studied in Volumes 1 and 2. Substantial progress has been made in this area using powerful optimization methods such as neural networks and simulated annealing [Flower 86; Lyzenga 88; Nicol 88; Fox 88e]. Several references are also contained in Fox [Fox 88c], and we optimistically consider this as a "solved problem" for an application class that Koller calls adiabatic [Koller 88a]. Most scientific problems are indeed adiabatic, or in other words may be irregular, but this irregularity changes slowly with time. Currently there are only initial implementations of these load balancing ideas [Koller 88c; Saltz 87], but we can expect the successful basic research to beget usable systems in the near future.

10-3 The Future

We can expect that the year 2000 will see commercial parallel supercomputers with performance in the 1 to 10 teraflop range. As shown in Fig. 10-1, adapted by Fox and Messina [Walker 88f] from an earlier plot by Buzbee [Buzbee 85], both conventional (CRAY, ETA, IBM, and Japanese vendors) and novel architectures should realize this performance. Whether one has 1,000 powerful processors, or 100,000 processors of relatively modest power, parallel processing will be needed to use these machines and realize their full potential.

Current research has shown that "parallel processing works" but, as shown by our two volumes, this is currently quite painful for the user. The problems must be decomposed by hand and software written that reflects this particular decomposition. This was an appropriate approach to "get going quickly" and effective for the modest-sized problems (measured by number of lines of code) treated here. However, a more productive software environment will be needed to exploit future high-performance parallel machines. These include parallelizing compilers, system utilities, and new languages [DeBenedictis 88; Callahan 88b; Zima 88; Fox 88e, 88f; Mirchandaney 88]. We have not addressed these issues at all in these volumes, although we do believe the lessons summarized here will be important in designing a better software environment. We expect this to be a key component of future parallel computing research. This software environment should be portable between different machine architectures and preserve good performance. An example of this is the VMLSCS system described in Chap. 2 which exploits the special features of loosely synchronous problems.

Our books have specialized in detail to the hypercube, but our techniques

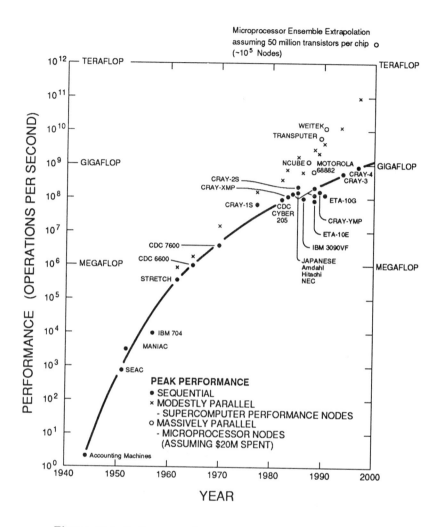

Figure 10-1 Performance of computers as a function of time.

and codes are simply transportable to other MIMD architectures. This is illustrated by the discussion of the BBN Butterfly (Chap. 3) and the distributed memory transputer arrays (Chap. 7), which, respectively, have a richer or simpler interconnection topology than the hypercube. In the near future we expect to use the ideas of Fox [Fox 88b] and extend the portability to include both MIMD and SIMD machines such as the Connection Machine. This will probably involve a rather different approach to parallel programming than that adopted with CrOS III and *Express*. A style similar to C* [Rose 87] or Coherent Parallel C [Felten 88a] or as discussed in [Angus 89] seems possible. Alternatively, a decomposing compiler [AMT 88; Callahan 88b; Zima 88] should be able to support SIMD and MIMD architectures simultaneously.

References

The labeling of these references has been chosen to be consistent with that used in Volume 1 and with the C^{3}P bibliographic database. For this reason, the sequence of letters appended to a reference to distinguish multiple publications by an author in a particular year may contain gaps. Moreover, the letter appended to a reference does not indicate where in the text the work was first cited relative to other publications by the same author in the same year. More information on Caltech references may be found using the *citlib* facility described in Appendix G.

Abdelrahman 88   Abdelrahman, Tarek, S., and Mudge, Trevor N. 1988, "Parallel Branch and Bound Algorithms on Hypercube Multiprocessors." In *Proceedings of the Third Conference on Hypercube Concurrent Computers and Applications*, edited by G. C. Fox, published by ACM, New York, [Fox 88c].

Abe 88   Abe, G., and Hane, K. 1988, "The Preconditioned Conjugate Gradient Method on the Hypercube." In *Proceedings of the Third Conference on Hypercube Concurrent Computers and Applications*, edited by G. C. Fox, published by ACM, New York, [Fox 88c].

Addison 88   Addison, C. A., Cook, J. M., and Hagen, L. R. 1988, "An Interactive System for Seismic Velocity Analysis." In *Proceedings of the Third Conference on Hypercube Concurrent Computers and Applications*, edited by G. C. Fox, published by ACM, New York, [Fox 88c].

Agarwal 89a   Agarwal, R. K. 1989, "Development of a Navier-Stokes Code on a Connection Machine," to be published in *Proceedings of the Fourth Conference on Hypercube Concurrent Computers and Applications*, March 6–8, 1989, Monterey, CA, edited by J. L. Gustafson.

Agarwal 89b   Agarwal, R. K., and Richardson, J. L. 1989, "Development of an Euler Code on a Connection Machine." In *Proceedings of the Conference on Scientific Applications of the Connection Machine*, September 12–14, 1988, p. 27, edited by Horst D. Simon, published by World Scientific Publishing Co., Ltd, 687 Hartwell Street, Teaneck, NJ 07666.

Ajjimarangsee 89   Ajjimarangsee, P., and Huntsberger, T. L. 1989, "Unsupervised Pattern Recognition Using Parallel Self-Organizing

Feature Maps," to be published in *Proceedings of the Fourth Conference on Hypercube Concurrent Computers and Applications*, March 6–8, 1989, Monterey, CA, edited by J. L. Gustafson.

Aldcroft 88   Aldcroft, T., Cisneros, A., Fox, G. C., Furmanski, W., and Walker, D. W. 1988, "LU Decomposition of Banded Matrices and the Solution of Linear Systems on Hypercubes." In *Proceedings of the Third Conference on Hypercube Concurrent Computers and Applications*, edited by G. C. Fox, published by ACM, New York, [Fox 88c]. Caltech report C^3P-348B.

Allen 89a   Allen, W., and Saha, A. 1989, "Parallel Neural-Network Simulation Using Back-propagation for the ES-Kit Environment," to be published in *Proceedings of the Fourth Conference on Hypercube Concurrent Computers and Applications*, March 6–8, 1989, Monterey, CA, edited by J. L. Gustafson.

Allison 88   Allison, D. C. S., Chakraborty, A., and Watson, L. T. 1988, "Granularity Issues for Solving Polynomial Systems via Globally Convergent Algorithms on a Hypercube." In *Proceedings of the Third Conference on Hypercube Concurrent Computers and Applications*, edited by G. C. Fox, published by ACM, New York, [Fox 88c].

Almeida 88   Almeida, V. A. F., Dowdy, L. W., and Leuze, M. R. 1988, "An Analytic Model for Parallel Gaussian Elimination on a Binary N-Cube Architecture." In *Proceedings of the Third Conference on Hypercube Concurrent Computers and Applications*, edited by G. C. Fox, published by ACM, New York, [Fox 88c].

Aloisio 87   Aloisio G., Fox, G. C., Kim, J. S., and Veneziani, N. 1987, "A Concurrent Implementation of the Prime Factor Algorithm on the Hypercube." Caltech report C^3P-468.

Aloisio 88   Aloisio, G., Veneziani, N., Fox, G. C., and Kim, J. S. 1988, "The Prime Factor Non-Binary Discrete Fourier Transform and Use of Crystal_Router as a General Purpose Communication Routine." In *Proceedings of the Third Conference on Hypercube Concurrent Computers and Applications*, edited by G. C. Fox, published by ACM, New York, [Fox 88c]. Caltech report C^3P-523.

Aloisio 89a   Aloisio, G., Veneziani, N., Fox, G. C., Milillo, G. 1989, "X-SAR Digital Processor: Computational Load for Real-

Time." Caltech report C^{3}P-submitted to *Space Technology Journal.* Caltech report C^{3}P-740.

Aloisio 89b   Aloisio, G., Lopinto, E., and Fox, G. C. 1989, "A Method to Reduce the Inter-node Communications for a Concurrent Implementation of the Prime Factor Algorithm," to be published in *Proceedings of the Fourth Conference on Hypercube Concurrent Computers and Applications*, March 6–8, 1989, Monterey, CA, edited by J. L. Gustafson. Caltech report C^{3}P-773.

Amin 89   Amin, A., Mohanachandran, S., and Martin, S. 1989, "The Incomplete Cholesky Conjugate Gradient Method on a Vector Hypercube," to be published in *Proceedings of the Fourth Conference on Hypercube Concurrent Computers and Applications*, March 6–8, 1989, Monterey, CA, edited by J. L. Gustafson.

AMT 88   Active Memory Technology, October 1987, *Fortran-Plus Language*, published by AMT, 16802 Aston Street, Suite 103, Irvine, CA 92714.

Angus 88   Angus, I. G. 1988, "Fortran CUBIX: Definition and Implementation." In *Proceedings of the Third Conference on Hypercube Concurrent Computers and Applications*, edited by G. C. Fox, published by ACM, New York, [Fox 88c]. Caltech report C^{3}P-575.

Angus 89   Angus, I. G., and Thompkins, W. T. 1989, "Data Storage, Concurrency, and Portability: An Object-Oriented Approach to Fluid Mechanics," to be published in *Proceedings of the Fourth Conference on Hypercube Concurrent Computers and Applications*, March 6–8, 1989, Monterey, CA, edited by J. L. Gustafson.

Apostolakis 88c   Apostolakis, J., Baillie, C. F., Ding, H.-Q., and Flower, J. W. 1988, "Lattice Gauge Theory on the Hypercube." In *Proceedings of the Third Conference on Hypercube Concurrent Computers and Applications*, edited by G. C. Fox, published by ACM, New York, [Fox 88c]. Caltech report C^{3}P-605.

Apostolakis 88d   Apostolakis, J., and Kochanek, C. 1988, "Statistical Gravitational Lensing on the Mark III Hypercube." In *Proceedings of the Third Conference on Hypercube Concurrent Computers and Applications*, edited by G. C.

Fox, published by ACM, New York, [Fox 88c]. Caltech report C^3P-581.

Appel 85   Appel, W. A. 1985, "An Efficient Program for Many-Body Simulation." *SIAM J. Sci. Stat. Comput.*, **6**:85.

Aref 83   Aref, H. 1983, "Integrable, Chaotic and Turbulent Vortex Motion in Two-Dimensional Flows." *Ann. Rev. Fluid Mech.*, **13**:345.

Aykanat 88   Aykanat, C., Ozguner F., and Scott, D. S. 1988, "Implementation of the Conjugate Gradient Algorithm on a Vector Hypercube Multiprocessor." In *Proceedings of the Third Conference on Hypercube Concurrent Computers and Applications*, edited by G. C. Fox, published by ACM, New York, [Fox 88c].

Azari 89   Azari, N. G., Lee S.-Y., and Otani, N. F. 1989, "Parallel Gather-Scatter Algorithms for Particle-in-Cell Simulation," to be published in *Proceedings of the Fourth Conference on Hypercube Concurrent Computers and Applications*, March 6–8, 1989, Monterey, CA, edited by J. L. Gustafson.

Baden 87   Baden, S. B. 1987, "Run-Time Partitioning of Scientific Continuum Calculations Running on Multiprocessors." Ph.D. Thesis, University of California, Berkeley.

Baek 89a   Baek, J. H., and Teague, K. A. 1989, "Parallel Edge Detection on the Hypercube," to be published in *Proceedings of the Fourth Conference on Hypercube Concurrent Computers and Applications*, March 6–8, 1989, Monterey, CA, edited by J. L. Gustafson.

Baek 89b   Baek, J. H., and Teague, K. A. 1989, "Parallel Object Representation using Straight Lines on the Hypercube Multiprocessor Computer," to be published in *Proceedings of the Fourth Conference on Hypercube Concurrent Computers and Applications*, March 6–8, 1989, Monterey, CA, edited by J. L. Gustafson.

Baillie 87a   Baillie, C. F., and Flower, J. W. 1987, "CrOS III and CUBIX and NCUBE." Caltech report C^3P-432.

Baillie 87b   Baillie, C. F., Felten, E. W., Flower, J. W., and Otto, S. W. 1987, "CrOS III+ on the NCUBE — CrOS III Plus a Library of Super-fast Functions." Caltech report C^3P-434.

Baillie 87c   Baillie, C. F., and Flower, J. W. 1987, "CrOS III on the NCUBE — the Limits." Caltech report C^3P-492.

Baillie 87d Baillie, C. F. 1987, "The BBN Butterfly Operating System." *The Caltech Concurrent Computation Program Technical Bulletin*, **10**:13.

Baillie 87e Baillie, C. F. 1987, "CrOS on the BBN Butterfly." *The Caltech Concurrent Computation Program Technical Bulletin*, **11**:13.

Baillie 88b Baillie, C. F., and Pawley, G. S. 1988, "A Comparison of the CM with the DAP for Lattice Gauge Theory." to appear in *Parallel Computing*. Caltech report C³P-530.

Baillie 88d Baillie, C. F., Johnsson, S. L., Ortiz, L., and Pawley, G. S. 1988, "QED on the Connection Machine." In *Proceedings of the Third Conference on Hypercube Concurrent Computers and Applications*, edited by G. C. Fox, published by ACM, New York, [Fox 88c]. Caltech report C³P-572.

Baillie 88f Baillie, C. F., Gottschalk, T., and Kolawa, A. 1988, "Comparisons of Concurrent Tracking on Various Hypercubes." In *Proceedings of the Third Conference on Hypercube Concurrent Computers and Applications*, edited by G. C. Fox, published by ACM, New York, [Fox 88c]. Caltech report C³P-568.

Baillie 88g Baillie, C. F., and Walker, D. W. 1988, "Lattice QCD — as a Large Scale Scientific Computation," to be published in *Proceedings of the International Conference on Vector and Parallel Computing*. Caltech report C³P-641.

Baillie 89e Baillie, C. F., Brickner, R. G., Gupta, R., and Johnsson, L. 1989, "QCD with Dynamical Fermions on the Connection Machine," to be presented at the *Supercomputing 89*, Reno, Nevada. Caltech report C³P-786.

Baillie 89g Baillie, C. F., Johnston, D. A., and Kilcup, G. W. 1989, "Status and Prospects of the Computational Approach to High Energy Physics," submitted to *J. Supercomput.* Caltech report C³P-800.

Baillie 89h Baillie, C. F., Johnston, D. A., and Williams, R. D. 1989, "Crumpling in Dynamically Triangulated Random Surfaces with Extrinsic Curvature," submitted to *Nucl. Phys. B*, Caltech report C³P-807.

Bailor 89 Bailor, Paul D. and Seward, W. D. 1989, "A Distributed Computer Algorithm for Solving Integer Linear Programming Problems," to be published in *Proceedings of the Fourth*

Conference on Hypercube Concurrent Computers and Applications, March 6–8, 1989, Monterey, CA, edited by J. L. Gustafson.

Baker 88
Baker, L. J. 1988, "Hypercube Performance for 2-D Seismic Finite-Difference Modeling." In *Proceedings of the Third Conference on Hypercube Concurrent Computers and Applications*, edited by G. C. Fox, published by ACM, New York, [Fox 88c].

Barhen 87
Barhen, J., Einstein, J. R., and Jorgensen, C. C. 1987, "Advances in Concurrent Computation for Machine Intelligence and Robotics." In *Proceedings of the Second International Conference on Supercomputing*, published by the International Supercomputing Institute, Inc., St. Petersburg, FL. Caltech report C^3P-418.

Barnes 86
Barnes, J., and Hut, P. 1986, "A Hierarchical O(NlogN) Force Calculation Algorithm." *Nature*, **324**:446.

Barnes 88a
Barnes, C., Farber, R., and Lapedes, A. 1988, "Applications of New Neural Net Methods to Genetic Database Analysis," Los Alamos report.

Barnes 88b
Barnes, T. 1988, "Numerical Solution of High Temperature Superconductor Spin Systems." In *Proceedings of the Oak Ridge Meeting on "Computational Atomic and Nuclear Physics at One Gigaflop."* Also available as University of Toronto preprint UTPT-88-07.

Barnes 88c
Barnes, T., and Swanson, E. S. 1988, "The Two-Dimensional Heisenberg Antiferromagnet: A Numerical Study." *Phys. Rev.*, **B37**:9405.

Barnes 88d
Barnes, T., Kotchan, D., and Swanson, E. S. 1989, "Evidence of a Phase Transition in the Zero Temperature Anisotropic 2D Heisenberg Antiferromagnet." *Phys. Rev.*, **B39**:4357.

Barnes 89b
Barnes, J. E. 1989, "The Paradox of Tree Codes for Gravitational N-Body Problems." In *Proceedings of the Fourth International Conference on Supercompting*, Volume II, April 30–May 5, 1989, Santa Clara, CA, edited by Lana P. Kartashev and Steven I. Kartashev, p. 327, published by International Supercomputing Institute, Inc., Suite B-309, 3000-34th Street, South, St. Petersburg, FL 33711.

Barstad 89a   Barstad, D., Hines, J., and O'Leary, B. 1989, "Multiple Target Tracking using Multiple-Hypothesis Sensor Fusion with Pairwise Pattern Recognition," to be published in *Proceedings of the Fourth Conference on Hypercube Concurrent Computers and Applications*, March 6–8, 1989, Monterey, CA, edited by J. L. Gustafson.

Barszcz 89   Barszcz, E., Chan, T. F., Jespersen, D. C., and Tuminaro, R. S. 1989, "Performance of an Euler Code on Hypercubes," to be published in *Proceedings of the Fourth Conference on Hypercube Concurrent Computers and Applications*, March 6–8, 1989, Monterey, CA, edited by J. L. Gustafson.

Barton 89a   Barton, M. 1989, "Three-Dimensional Magnetic Field Computation on the iPSC/2 Distributed Memory Multiprocessor," to be published in *Proceedings of the Fourth Conference on Hypercube Concurrent Computers and Applications*, March 6–8, 1989, Monterey, CA, edited by J. L. Gustafson.

Battiti 88   Battiti, R. 1988, "Collective Stereopsis on the Hypercube." In *Proceedings of the Third Conference on Hypercube Concurrent Computers and Applications*, edited by G. C. Fox, published by ACM, New York, [Fox 88c]. Caltech report C^{3}P-583.

Battiti 89b   Battiti, R. 1989, "Surface Reconstruction and Discontinuity Detection: A Fast Hierarchical Approach on a Two-Dimensional Mesh," to be published in *Proceedings of the Fourth Conference on Hypercube Concurrent Computers and Applications*, March 6–8, 1989, Monterey, CA, edited by J. L. Gustafson. Caltech report C^{3}P-732.

Baxter 88   Baxter, D., Saltz, J., Schultz, M., Eisenstat, S., and Crowley, K. 1988, "An Experimental Study of Methods for Parallel Preconditioned Krylov Methods." In *Proceedings of the Third Conference on Hypercube Concurrent Computers and Applications*, edited by G. C. Fox, published by ACM, New York, [Fox 88c].

BBN 87   *Butterfly Products Overview*, BBN Advanced Computers, Inc., 10 Fawcett Street, Cambridge, MA, 1987.

Beigie 89   Beigie, D., Leonard, A., and Wiggins, S. 1989, "Chaotic Advection and Dynamical Systems Analysis Using Caltech/JPL Hypercubes," to be published in *Proceedings of the Fourth*

Conference on Hypercube Concurrent Computers and Applications, March 6–8, 1989, Monterey, CA, edited by J. L. Gustafson. Caltech report C³P-752.

Berry 89   Berry, M., Chen, D., Koss, P., Kuck, D., Lo, S., Pang, Y., Roloff, R., Sameh, A., Clementi, E., Chin, S., Scheider, D., Fox, G., Messina, P., Walker, D., Hsiung, C., Schwarzmeier, J., Lue, K., Orszag, S., Seidl, F., Johnson, O., Goodrum, R., and Martin, J. 1989, "The Perfect Club Benchmarks: Effective Performance Evaluation of Supercomputers." *Int. J. of Supercomputer Applications* Vol. 3, No. 3.

Berryman 89   Berryman, H., Gropp, W., and Saltz, J. 1989, "Krylov Methods and the CM-2." In *Proceedings of the Fourth International Conference on Supercomputing, Volume I,* April 30–May 5, 1989, Santa Clara, CA, edited by Lana P. Kartashev and Steven I. Kartashev, p. 106, published by International Supercomputing Institute, Inc., Suite B-309, 3000-34th Street, South, St. Petersburg, FL 33711.

Bershader 89a   Bershader, S., Kraay, T., and Holland, J. 1989, "The Giant-Fourier-Transform," to be published in *Proceedings of the Fourth Conference on Hypercube Concurrent Computers and Applications*, March 6–8, 1989, Monterey, CA, edited by J. L. Gustafson.

Bershader 89b   Bershader, S., Kraay, T., and Holland, J. 1989, "The Giant-Fourier-Transform." In *Proceedings of the Conference on Scientific Applications of the Connection Machine,* September 12–14, 1988, p. 129, edited by Horst D. Simon, published by World Scientific Publishing Co., Ltd, 687 Hartwell Street, Teaneck, NJ 07666.

Bischof 88   Bischof, C. H. 1988, "A Parallel QR Factorization Algorithm Using Local Pivoting." In Proceedings of Supercomputing '88, November 14–18, 1988, Orlando, FL, p. 400, published by IEEE Computer Society Press, 1730 Massachusetts Avenue, NW, Washington, DC 20036-1903.

Bischof 89   Bischof, C. H. 1989, "A Parallel QR Factorization Algorithm with Controlled Local Pivoting," to be published in *Proceedings of the Fourth Conference on Hypercube Concurrent Computers and Applications*, March 6–8, 1989, Monterey, CA, edited by J. L. Gustafson.

Bjornson 89a   Bjornson, R. 1989, "Experience with Linda on the iPSC/2," to be published in *Proceedings of the Fourth Conference on Hypercube Concurrent Computers and Applications*, March 6–8, 1989, Monterey, CA, edited by J. L. Gustafson.

Blelloch 87b   Blelloch, G. E., and Rosenberg, C. R. 1987, "Network Learning on the Connection Machine." In *Proceedings IJCAI*, 323.

Boghosian 88   Boghosian, B. M., Taylor, IV, W., and Rothman, D. H. 1988, "A Cellular Automata Simulation of Two-Phase Flow on the CM-2 Connection Machine Computer." In *Proceedings of Supercomputing 88, Volume II: Science and Applications*, edited by Joanne L. Martin and Stephen F. Lundstrom, p. 34, published by IEEE Computer Society Press, 1730 Massachusetts Avenue, NW, Washington, DC 20036-1903.

Bojanczyk 89   Bojanczyk, A. W., and Choi, J. 1989, "Implementations of Three QR Algorithms of the Toeplitz Matrix on a Hypercube," to be published in *Proceedings of the Fourth Conference on Hypercube Concurrent Computers and Applications*, March 6–8, 1989, Monterey, CA, edited by J. L. Gustafson.

Bond 88a   Bond, A. H., and Gasser, L. 1988, *Readings in Distributed Artificial Intelligence*, published by Morgan-Kaufmann, San Mateo, CA.

Bond 88b   Bond, A. H., and Fashena, D. 1988, "Parallel Vision Techniques on the Hypercube Computer." In *Proceedings of the Third Conference on Hypercube Concurrent Computers and Applications*, edited by G. C. Fox, published by ACM, New York, [Fox 88c]. Caltech report C[3]P-632.

Bower 88b   Bower, J. M., Nelson, M. E., Wilson, M. A., Fox, G. C., and Furmanski, W. 1988, "Piriform (Olfactory) Cortex Model on the Hypercube." In *Proceedings of the Third Conference on Hypercube Concurrent Computers and Applications*, edited by G. C. Fox, published by ACM, New York, [Fox 88c]. Caltech report C[3]P-404B.

Boxer 88   Boxer, L., and Miller, R. 1988, "Dynamic Computational Geometry on Parallel Computers." In *Proceedings of the Third Conference on Hypercube Concurrent Computers and Applications*, edited by G. C. Fox, published by ACM, New York, [Fox 88c].

Braaten 88   Braaten, M. E. 1988, "Solution of Viscous Fluid Flows on a Distributed Memory Concurrent Computer." In *Proceedings of the 1988 International Conference on Parallel Processing*, Volume III, August 15–19, 1988, edited by David H. Bailey, p. 243, published by Penn State University Press, 215 Wagner Building, University Park, PA 16802.

Braaten 89   Braaten, M. E. 1989, "Computational Fluid Dynamics on Hypercube Parallel Computers," to be published in *Proceedings of the Fourth Conference on Hypercube Concurrent Computers and Applications*, March 6–8, 1989, Monterey, CA, edited by J. L. Gustafson.

Braschi 89   Braschi, B. 1989, "Solving the Traveling Salesman Problem Using the Simulated Annealing on a Hypercube," to be published in *Proceedings of the Fourth Conference on Hypercube Concurrent Computers and Applications*, March 6–8, 1989, Monterey, CA, edited by J. L. Gustafson.

Brickner 89   Brickner, R. G., and Baillie, C. F. 1989, "Pure Gauge QCD on the Connection Machine." In *Proceedings of the Conference on Scientific Applications of the Connection Machine*, September 12–14, 1988, p. 234, edited by Horst D. Simon, published by World Scientific Publishing Co., Ltd, 687 Hartwell Street, Teaneck, NJ 07666.

Brochard 89b   Brochard, L. 1989, "Implementation and Performance Evaluation of Multigrid Methods on Hypercubes," to be published in *Proceedings of the Fourth Conference on Hypercube Concurrent Computers and Applications*, March 6–8, 1989, Monterey, CA, edited by J. L. Gustafson. Caltech report C^{3}P-772.

Brooks 84   Brooks, E., Fox, G. C., Johnson, M., Otto, S. W., Stolorz, P., Athas, W., DeBenedictis, E., Faucette, R., Seitz, C., and Stack, J. 1984, "Pure Gauge SU(3) Lattice Gauge Theory on an Array of Computers." *Phys. Rev. Lett.*, **52**:2324. Caltech report C^{3}P-65.

Brown 88   Brown, C. M. 1988, "Parallel Vision with the Butterfly™ Computer." In *Proceedings of the Third International Conference on Supercomputing, Volume III*, May 15–20, 1988, Boston, MA, edited by Lana P. Kartashev and Steven I. Kartashev, p. 54, published by International Supercomputing Institute, Inc., Suite B-309, 3000-34th Street, South, St. Petersburg, FL 33711.

Bruno 88   Bruno, J., and Cappello, P. R. 1988, "Implementing the Beam and Warming Method on the Hypercube." In *Proceedings of the Third Conference on Hypercube Concurrent Computers and Applications*, edited by G. C. Fox, published by ACM, New York, [Fox 88c].

Buzbee 85   Buzbee, B. L., and Sharp D. H. 1985, "Perspectives on Supercomputing." *Science*, **227**:591.

Cabbibo 82   Cabbibo, N., and Marinari, E. 1982, "A New Method of Updating SU(N) Matrices in Computer Simulations of Gauge Theories." *Phys. Lett.*, **119B**:387.

Calalo 88   Calalo, R. H., Lyons, J. R., and Imbriale, W. A. 1988, "Finite Difference Time Domain Solution of Electromagnetic Scattering on the Hypercube." In *Proceedings of the Third Conference on Hypercube Concurrent Computers and Applications*, edited by G. C. Fox, published by ACM, New York, [Fox 88c]. Caltech report C^3P-596.

Callahan 88   Callahan, S. 1988, "Non-Local Path Integral Monte Carlo on the Hypercube." In *Proceedings of the Third Conference on Hypercube Concurrent Computers and Applications*, edited by G. C. Fox, published by ACM, New York, [Fox 88c]. Caltech report C^3P-589.

Callahan 88b   Callahan, D., and Kennedy, K. 1988, "Compiling Programs for Distributed Memory Multiprocessors." In *Proceedings of the 1988 Workshop on Programming Languages and Compilers for Parallel Computing*, August 2–5, 1988, published by Cornell University Press, Ithaca, NY.

Carpenter 88   Carpenter, Barry A., and Davis, Nathaniel J. 1988, "Implementation and Performance Analysis of Parallel Assignment Algorithms on a Hypercube Computer." In *Proceedings of the Third Conference on Hypercube Concurrent Computers and Applications*, edited by G. C. Fox, published by ACM, New York, [Fox 88c].

Casotto 86   Casotto, A., and Sangiovanni-Vincintelli, A. 1986, "Placement of Standard Cells Using Simulated Annealing on the Connection Machine." EECS Department, University of California at Berkeley report.

Catherasoo 87   Catherasoo, C. J. 1987, "The Vortex Method on a Hypercube Concurrent Processor." In *Hypercube Multiprocessors,*

1987, edited by M. T. Heath, published by SIAM, Philadelphia, PA.

Catherasoo 89   Catherasoo, C. J. 1989, "Implementation of a Three-Dimensional Navier-Stokes Code on the Symult Series 2010," to be published in *Proceedings of the Fourth Conference on Hypercube Concurrent Computers and Applications*, March 6–8, 1989, Monterey, CA, edited by J. L. Gustafson.

Celenk 89a   Celenk, M. 1989, "Hypercube Mapped Ring and Mesh Implementations of Low-Level Vision Algorithms," to be published in *Proceedings of the Fourth Conference on Hypercube Concurrent Computers and Applications*, March 6–8, 1989, Monterey, CA, edited by J. L. Gustafson.

Chesshire 89   Chesshire, G., and Jameson, A. 1989, "FLO87 on the iPSC/2: A Parallel Multigrid Solver for the Euler Equations," to be published in *Proceedings of the Fourth Conference on Hypercube Concurrent Computers and Applications*, March 6–8, 1989, Monterey, CA, edited by J. L. Gustafson.

Chiu 88b   Chiu, T.-W. 1988, "Shift Register Sequence Random Number Generators on the Hypercube Concurrent Computer." In *Proceedings of the Third Conference on Hypercube Concurrent Computers and Applications*, edited by G. C. Fox, published by ACM, New York, [Fox 88c]. Caltech report C^3P-526.

Chiu 88c   Chiu, T.-W. 1988, "Fermion Propagations on a Four-Dimensional Random Block Lattice." *Phys. Lett.*, **B206**:510. Caltech report C^3P-507.

Chorin 73   Chorin, A. J. 1973, "Numerical Study of Slightly Viscous Flow." *J. Fluid Mech.*, **57**:785.

Choudhary 89a   Choudhary, A. N., Das, S., Ahuja, N., and Patel, J. H. 1989, "Surface Reconstruction from Stereo Images: An Implementation on a Hypercube Multiprocessor," to be published in *Proceedings of the Fourth Conference on Hypercube Concurrent Computers and Applications*, March 6–8, 1989, Monterey, CA, edited by J. L. Gustafson.

Christara 88   Christara, C. C., Houstis, E. N., and Rice, J. R. 1988, "A Parallel Spline Collocation-Capacitance Method for Elliptic Partial Differential Equations." In *Proceedings of the*

1988 International Conference on Supercomputing, July 4–8, 1988, St. Malo, France, pp. 659–667, published ACM, 11 West 42nd Street, New York 10036.

Christara 89 Christara, C. C., and Houstis, E. N. 1989, "A Domain Decomposition Spline Collocation Method for Elliptic Partial Differential Equations," to be published in *Proceedings of the Fourth Conference on Hypercube Concurrent Computers and Applications*, March 6–8, 1989, Monterey, CA, edited by J. L. Gustafson.

Christiansen 73 Christiansen, J. P. 1973, "Numerical Solution of Hydrodynamics by the Method of Point Vortices." *J. Comp. Phys.*, **13**:363.

Chu 88 Chu, C. Y. 1988, "Comparison of Two-Dimensional FFT Methods on the Hypercube." In *Proceedings of the Third Conference on Hypercube Concurrent Computers and Applications*, edited by G. C. Fox, published by ACM, New York, [Fox 88c].

Chu 89 Chu, C., and Mangus, J. 1989, "Hypercube Implementation of a 3-D Euler Solver for Aircraft Configurations." to be published in *Proceedings of the Fourth Conference on Hypercube Concurrent Computers and Applications*, March 6–8, 1989, Monterey, CA, edited by J. L. Gustafson.

Chua 88 Chua, K., Leonard, A., Pepin, F., and Winckelmans, G. 1988, "Robust Vortex Methods for Three-Dimensional Incompressible Flows." In *Proceedings of the Symposium on Recent Developments in Computational Fluid Dynamics*, ASME 1988 Winter Annual Meeting, Chicago, November 27 – December 2, 1988, edited by T. E. Tezduyar and T. J. R. Hughes, published by ASME, New York.

Clayton 87 Clayton, R., Hager, B., and Tanimoto, T. 1987, "Applications of Concurrent Processors in Geophysics." In *Proceedings of the Second International Conference on Supercomputing*, published by the International Supercomputing Institute Inc., St. Petersburg, FL. Caltech report C^3P-408.

Clayton 88 Clayton, R. 1988, "Acoustic Wave Field Propagation Using Paraxial Extrapolators." In *Proceedings of the Third Conference on Hypercube Concurrent Computers and Applications*, edited by G. C. Fox, published by ACM, New York, [Fox 88c]. Caltech report C^3P-613.

Cline 89a   Cline, Jr., R. E., Meza, J. C., Boghosian, B. M., and Walker, B. 1989, "Towards the Development of Engineering Production Codes for the Connection Machine," to be published in *Proceedings of the Fourth Conference on Hypercube Concurrent Computers and Applications*, March 6–8, 1989, Monterey, CA, edited by J. L. Gustafson.

Cooper 89   Cooper, Y. S., and Orcutt, D. E. 1989, "Galaxy Modeling in a Hypercube Environment," to be published in *Proceedings of the Fourth Conference on Hypercube Concurrent Computers and Applications*, March 6–8, 1989, Monterey, CA, edited by J. L. Gustafson.

Cosnuau 89   Cosnuau, A., and Leca, P. 1989, "Scientific Parallel Computing with Transputers Networks." In *Proceedings of the Fourth International Conference on Supercompting*, Volume II, April 30–May 5, 1989, Santa Clara, CA, edited by Lana P. Kartashev and Steven I. Kartashev, p. 216, published by International Supercomputing Institute, Inc., Suite B-309, 3000-34th Street, South, St. Petersburg, FL 33711.

Couch 88   Couch, A. L. 1988, "Seecube Users' Manual." Department of Computer Science, Tufts University, Medford, MA 02155. Caltech report C^3P-501.

Cuccaro 88a   Cuccaro, S. A., Hipes, P. G., and Kuppermann, A. 1989, "Hyper-spherical Coordinate Reactive Scattering Using Variational Surface Functions." *Chem. Phys. Letters*, **154(2)**:155.

Culioli 89   Culioli, J. C., Glover, C. W., Jones, J. P., and Roe, C. 1989, "$NCUBE^{TM}$ Implementation of Some Heuristics and an Optimal Algorithm for Large-Scale Assignment Problems," to be published in *Proceedings of the Fourth Conference on Hypercube Concurrent Computers and Applications*, March 6–8, 1989, Monterey, CA, edited by J. L. Gustafson.

Dally 88   Dally, W. J., and Chien, A. A. 1988, "Object-Oriented Concurrent Programming in CST." In *Proceedings of the Third Conference on Hypercube Concurrent Computers and Applications*, edited by G. C. Fox, published by ACM, New York, [Fox 88c].

Daniel 89a   Daniel, Jr., R., Carter, M., and Teague, K. 1989, "A Parallel Image Processing System for the iPSC/2," to be published in *Proceedings of the Fourth Conference on*

Hypercube Concurrent Computers and Applications, March 6–8, 1989, Monterey, CA, edited by J. L. Gustafson.

DeBenedictis 88   DeBenedictis, E. P. 1988, "Distributed Programs and Subroutines for Multiprocessors." In *Proceedings of the Third Conference on Hypercube Concurrent Computers and Applications*, edited by G. C. Fox, published by ACM, New York, [Fox 88c].

Decyk 88   Decyk, V. K. 1988, "Benchmark Timings with Particle Plasma Simulation Codes." *Supercomputer*, **27**:33.

Delany 88   Delany, H. C. 1988, "Ray Tracing on a Connection Machine." In *Proceedings of the 1988 International Conference on Supercomputing*, July 4–8, St. Malo, France, pp. 659–667, published ACM, 11 West 42nd Street, New York 10036.

de Pillis 88   de Pillis, L., Petersen, J., and de Pillis, J. 1988, "An Iterative Solution to Special Linear Systems on a Vector Hypercube." In *Proceedings of the Third Conference on Hypercube Concurrent Computers and Applications*, edited by G. C. Fox, published by ACM, New York, [Fox 88c].

Desbat 89   Desbat, L., and Trystram, D. 1989, "Implementing the Discrete Fourier Transform on a Hypercube Vector-Parallel Computer," to be published in *Proceedings of the Fourth Conference on Hypercube Concurrent Computers and Applications*, March 6–8, 1989, Monterey, CA, edited by J. L. Gustafson.

Dewar 87   Dewar, R., and Harris, C. K. 1987, "Parallel Computation of Cluster Properties: Application to 2-D Percolation." *J. Phys.*, **A20**:985.

Dewdney 84   Dewdney, A. K. December 1984, "Computer Recreations." *Scientific American*.

Ding 88a   Ding, H.-Q., and Goddard, W. A. 1988, "Polymer Simulation on the Hypercube." In *Proceedings of the Third Conference on Hypercube Concurrent Computers and Applications*, edited by G. C. Fox, published by ACM, New York, [Fox 88c]. Caltech report C^3P-574.

Ding 88d   Ding, H.-Q. 1988, "A Fast Random Number Generator for Mark IIIfp." Caltech report C^3P-629.

Ding 89a   Ding, H.-Q., Baillie, C. F., and Fox, G. C. 1989, "Heavy Quark Potential at Large Distances." Caltech report C^3P-779.

Ding 89b   Ding, H.-Q. 1989, "Performance of a QCD Code on Mark IIIfp Hypercube: II." Caltech report C^3P-799.

Durbin 87   Durbin, R., and Willshaw, D. J. 1987, "An Analogue Approach to the Travelling Salesman Problem Using an Elastic Net Method." *Nature*, **326**:689.

Ecer 88   Ecer, A., Akay, H. U., Rubek, V., Gurdogan, O., and Geddes, B. 1988, "Passage: A Finite Element Program for Analysis of Internal Flows." In *Proceedings of the Third Conference on Hypercube Concurrent Computers and Applications*, edited by G. C. Fox, published by ACM, New York, [Fox 88c].

Ecer 89   Ecer, A., Akay, H. U., and Erwin, S. 1989, "A Parallel Algorithm for the Solution of 3-D Euler Equations in Turbomachinery," to be published in *Proceedings of the Fourth Conference on Hypercube Concurrent Computers and Applications*, March 6–8, 1989, Monterey, CA, edited by J. L. Gustafson.

Egecioglu 88   Egecioglu, O., Koc, C. K., and Laub, A. J. 1988, "Prefix Algorithms for Tridiagonal Systems on Hypercube Multiprocessors." In *Proceedings of the Third Conference on Hypercube Concurrent Computers and Applications*, edited by G. C. Fox, published by ACM, New York, [Fox 88c].

Eggers 89   Eggers, W., Rico, R., McIver, Jr., J. W., and Eberlein, P. J. 1989, "MNDO on the iPSC/2," to be published in *Proceedings of the Fourth Conference on Hypercube Concurrent Computers and Applications*, March 6–8, 1989, Monterey, CA, edited by J. L. Gustafson.

Egolf 88   Egolf, T. A. 1989, "Scientific Applications of the Connection Machine at the United Technologies Research Center." In *Proceedings of the Conference on Scientific Applications of the Connection Machine*, September 12–14, 1988, p. 38, edited by Horst D. Simon, published by World Scientific Publishing Co., Ltd, 687 Hartwell Street, Teaneck, NJ 07666.

Farhat 89   Farhat, C., Sobh, N., and Park, K. C. 1989, "Dynamic Finite Element Simulations on the Connection Machine." In *Proceedings of the Conference on Scientific Applications of the Connection Machine*, September 12–14, 1988, p. 217, edited by Horst D. Simon, published by World Scientific Publishing Co., Ltd, 687 Hartwell Street, Teaneck, NJ 07666.

Fatoohi 88   Fatoohi, R., and Grosch, C. E. 1988, "Implementation and Analysis of a Navier-Stokes Algorithm on Parallel Computers." In *Proceedings of the 1988 International Conference on Parallel Processing*, Volume III, August 15–19, 1988, edited by David H. Bailey, p. 235, published by Penn State University Press, 215 Wagner Building, University Park, PA 16802.

Felten 85a   Felten, E., Karlin, S., and Otto, S., 1985. "Sorting on a Hypercube," to appear in *Journal of Parallel and Distributed Computing*. Caltech report C^3P-244.

Felten 85b   Felten, E., Karlin, S., and Otto, S. 1985, "The Traveling Salesman Problem on a Hypercube MIMD Computer." In *Proceedings of 1985 International Conference of Parallel Processing*, pp. 6–10, St. Charles, IL. Caltech report C^3P-93B.

Felten 88a   Felten, E. W., and Otto, S. W. 1988, "Coherent Parallel C." In *Proceedings of the Third Conference on Hypercube Concurrent Computers and Applications*, edited by G. C. Fox, published by ACM, New York, [Fox 88c]. Caltech report C^3P-527.

Felten 88c   Felten, E. W. 1988, "Best-First Branch-and-Bound on a Hypercube." In *Proceedings of the Third Conference on Hypercube Concurrent Computers and Applications*, edited by G. C. Fox, published by ACM, New York, [Fox 88c]. Caltech report C^3P-590.

Felten 88g   Felten, E. W., and Otto, S. W. 1988, "Chess on a Hypercube." In *Proceedings of the Third Conference on Hypercube Concurrent Computers and Applications*, edited by G. C. Fox, published by ACM, New York, [Fox 88c]. Caltech report C^3P-579.

Fiebrich 87a   Fiebrich, R. D. 1987, "The Connection Machine — A General Purpose Accelerator for VLSI CAD." Rev. version of paper in *IEEE Proceedings* of COMPCON 87, San Francisco, February 1987.

Fiebrich 87b   Fiebrich, R. D. 1987, "Data Parallel Algorithms for Engineering Applications." In *Proceedings of Second International Conference on Supercomputing*, Vol. II, p. 17. International Supercomputing Institute, Inc., St. Petersburg, FL.

Firestone 89   Firestone, R. M. 1989, "Application of Supercomputer
                          Methods to Optical Diffraction Analysis," to be published
                          in *Proceedings of the Fourth Conference on Hypercube
                          Concurrent Computers and Applications*, March 6–8, 1989,
                          Monterey, CA, edited by J. L. Gustafson.

Fischer 87   "Frontiers of Massively Parallel Scientific Computation,"
                          Proceedings of September 24–25, 1986, Goddard Space
                          Flight Center Symposium, edited by J. R. Fischer, NASA
                          Conference Publication 2478.

Flinn 88   Flinn, Paul A. 1988, "Molecular Dynamics Simulation on
                          an iPSC of Defects in Crystals." In *Proceedings of the
                          Third Conference on Hypercube Concurrent Computers and
                          Applications*, edited by G. C. Fox, published by ACM, New
                          York, [Fox 88c].

Flower 85   Flower, J. W., and Otto, S. W. 1985, "The Field
                          Distribution in SU(3) Lattice Gauge Theory." *Phys. Lett.*,
                          B160:128. Caltech report C^3P-178.

Flower 86   Flower, J. W., Otto, S. W., and Salama, M. 1986,
                          "A Preprocessor for Finite Element Problems."   In
                          *Proceedings of the Symposium on Parallel Computations
                          and Their Impact on Mechanics*, ASME Winter Meeting,
                          December 14–16, Boston, Caltech report C^3P-292.

Flower 86b   Flower, J. W., and Williams, R. D. 1986, "PLOTIX —
                          A Graphical System to Run CUBIX and UNIX." Caltech
                          report C^3P-285.

Flower 87   Flower, J. W. 1987, "Lattice Gauge Theory on a
                          Parallel Computer," Ph.D. Thesis, California Institute of
                          Technology, Pasadena, Caltech report C^3P-411.

Flower 87c   Flower, J. W. 1987, "An Introduction to Debugging with
                          NDB." Caltech report C^3P-489.

Flower 87d   Flower, J. W. 1987, "Debugging Aids on the NCUBE."
                          Caltech report C^3P-491.

Flower 88b   Flower, J., Apostolakis, J., Ding, H., and Baillie,
                          C. 1988, "Lattice Gauge Theory on the Hypercube."
                          In *Proceedings of the Third Conference on Hypercube
                          Concurrent Computers and Applications*, edited by G. C.
                          Fox, published by ACM, New York, [Fox 88c]. Caltech report
                          C^3P-605.

Fonseca 89
Fonseca, Jr., A. 1989, "An Adapted Finite Element Method for Massively Parallel Processors," to be published in *Proceedings of the Fourth Conference on Hypercube Concurrent Computers and Applications*, March 6–8, 1989, Monterey, CA, edited by J. L. Gustafson.

Forrest 87
Forrest, B. M. 1988, *Proceedings of Parallel Architectures and Computer Vision Workshop*, edited by Ian Page, published by Oxford University Press.

Fox 84
Fox, G. C. 1984, "Eigenvalues of Symmetric Tridiagonal Matrices." Caltech report C^3P-95.

Fox 86
Fox G. C., and Kolawa, A. 1986, "Implementation of the High Performance Crystalline Operating System on the INTEL iPSC Hypercube." Caltech report C^3P-247.

Fox 87a
Fox, G. C., and Frey, A. 1987, "High Performance Parallel Supercomputing Application, Hardware, and Software Issues for a Teraflop Computer." Caltech report C^3P-451B.

Fox 87b
Fox, G. C., and Messina, P. 1987, "The Caltech Concurrent Computation Program Annual Report 1986–1987." Caltech report C^3P-487.

Fox 87c
Fox, G. C. 1987, "Domain Decomposition in Distributed and Shared Memory Environment — I: A Uniform Decomposition and Performance Analysis for the NCUBE and JPL Mark IIIfp Hypercubes." Invited Paper at ICS 87, International Conference on Supercomputing, June 8–12, 1987, Athens, Greece. In *Lecture Notes in Computer Science*, Vol. 297, pp. 1042–1073, edited by E. N. Houstis, T. S. Papatheodorou, and C. D. Polychronopoulos, Springer-Verlag. Caltech report C^3P-392.

Fox 88a
Fox, G. C., Johnson, M. A., Lyzenga, G. A., Otto, S. W., Salmon, J. K., and Walker, D. W. 1988, *Solving Problems on Concurrent Processors*, Volume I: *General Techniques and Regular Problems*, published by Prentice Hall, Englewood Cliffs, NJ.

Fox 88b
Fox, G. C. 1988, "What Have We Learned from Using Real Parallel Machines to Solve Real Problems." In *Proceedings of the Third Conference on Hypercube Concurrent Computers and Applications*, edited by G. C. Fox, published by ACM, New York, [Fox 88c]. Caltech report C^3P-522.

Fox 88c   Fox, G. C. 1988, *The Third Conference on Hypercube Concurrent Computers and Applications*, Volumes I and II of the *Proceedings of the Third Hypercube Conference*, January 19–20, 1988, Pasadena, CA, edited by G. C. Fox, published by ACM, New York.

Fox 88e   Fox, G. C., and Furmanski, W. 1988, "Load Balancing Loosely Synchronous Problems with a Neural Network." In *Proceedings of the Third Conference on Hypercube Concurrent Computers and Applications*, edited by G. C. Fox, published by ACM, New York, [Fox 88c]. Caltech report C^3P-363B.

Fox 88f   Fox, G. C., and Furmanski, W. 1988, "A String Theory for Time Dependent Complex Systems and Its Application to Automatic Decomposition." In *Proceedings of the Third Conference on Hypercube Concurrent Computers and Applications*, edited by G. C. Fox, published by ACM, New York, [Fox 88c]. Caltech report C^3P-521.

Fox 88h   Fox, G. C., and Furmanski, W. 1988, "Optimal Communication Algorithms for Regular Decompositions on the Hypercube." In *Proceedings of the Third Conference on Hypercube Concurrent Computers and Applications*, edited by G. C. Fox, published by ACM, New York, [Fox 88c]. Caltech report C^3P-314B.

Fox 88u   Fox, G. C. 1988, "Issues in Software Development for Concurrent Computers." In *Twelfth Annual International Computer Software and Applications Conference*, edited by G. J. Knafl, published by the Computer Society Press of the IEEE, 1730 Massachusetts Ave., NW, Washington, DC 20036-1903. Caltech report C^3P-640.

Fox 88v   Fox, G. C., and Messina, P. 1988, "The Caltech Concurrent Computation Program Annual Report 1987–1988." Caltech report C^3P-685.

Fox 88w   Fox, G. C. 1988, "Theory and Practice of Concurrent Systems." In *Proceedings of the International Conference on Fifth Generation Computer Systems*, November 28 – December 2, 1988, pp. 157–160, ICOT Press, Tokyo. Caltech report C^3P-664.

Fox 88x   Fox, G. C., Furmanski, W., and Koller, J. 1988, "The Use of Neural Networks in Parallel Software Systems." In *Proceedings of the Conference on Expert Systems for*

Numerical Computing, December 5–7, 1988, at Purdue University, Lafayette, IN. Caltech report C^3P-642B.

Fox 89i Fox, G. C. 1989, "1989 – The First Year of the Parallel Supercomputer." to be published in *Proceedings of the Fourth Conference on Hypercube Concurrent Computers and Applications*, March 6–8, 1989, Monterey, CA, edited by J. L. Gustafson. Caltech report C^3P-769.

Fox 89n Fox, G. C. 1989, "Parallel Computing Comes of Age: Supercomputer Level Parallel Computations at Caltech." submitted to *Concurrency: Practice and Experience*. Caltech report C^3P-795.

Fox 89p Fox, G. C. 1989, "Applications of Parallel Supercomputers: Scientific Results and Computer Science Lessons." Invited presentation at the *Inaugural Symposium for the Center for Science and Technology*, March 2, 1989, Syracuse, NY. Caltech report C^3P-806.

Frederickson 88 Frederickson, P., and McBryan, O. 1988, "Intrinsically Parallel Multiscale Algorithms for Hypercubes." In *Proceedings of the Third Conference on Hypercube Concurrent Computers and Applications*, edited by G. C. Fox, published by ACM, New York, [Fox 88c].

Frederickson 89a Frederickson, P. O. 1989, "Totally Parallel Multilevel Algorithms for Sparse Elliptic Systems," to be published in *Proceedings of the Fourth Conference on Hypercube Concurrent Computers and Applications*, March 6–8, 1989, Monterey, CA, edited by J. L. Gustafson.

Frederickson 89b Frederickson, P. O. 1989, "Totally Parallel Multilevel Algorithms." In *Proceedings of the Conference on Scientific Applications of the Connection Machine*, September 12–14, 1988, p. 161, edited by Horst D. Simon, published by World Scientific Publishing Co., Ltd, 687 Hartwell Street, Teaneck, NJ 07666.

Fricke 87 Fricke, J. 1987, "Reverse Time Migration in Parallel." Thinking Machines Corporation report, 245 First Street, Cambridge, MA 02142.

Frye 88 Frye, R. E. 1988, "Finding $95800^4 + 217519^4 + 414560^4 = 422841^4$ on the Connection Machine." In *Proceedings of Supercomputing 88, Volume II: Science and Applications*, edited by Joanne L. Martin and Stephen F. Lundstrom,

p. 106, published by IEEE Computer Society Press, 1730 Massachusetts Avenue, NW, Washington, DC 20036-1903.

Fucito 85   Fucito, F., and Solomon, S. 1985, "Monte Carlo Parallel Algorithm for Long-Range Interaction." *Computer Physics Communication* 34:225. Caltech report C^3P-79B.

Fulton 88   Fulton, R. E., and Chiang, K.-N. 1988, "Comparison of Shared Memory and Hypercube Architectures for Structural Dynamics." In *Proceedings of the Third International Conference on Supercomputing,* Volume I, May 15–20, 1988, Boston, MA, edited by Lana P. Kartashev and Steven I. Kartashev, p. 418, published by International Supercomputing Institute, Inc., Suite B-309, 3000-34th Street, South, St. Petersburg, FL 33711.

Furmanski 88b   Furmanski, W., Fox, G. C. and Walker, D. 1988, "Optimal Matrix Algorithms on Homogeneous Hypercubes." In *Proceedings of the Third Conference on Hypercube Concurrent Computers and Applications,* edited by G. C. Fox, published by ACM, New York, [Fox 88c]. Caltech report C^3P-386B.

Furmanski 88c   Furmanski, W., and Fox, G. C. 1988, "Integrated Vision on a Network of Computers." Invited paper at the Fourth International Symposium on Biological and Artificial Intelligence Systems, published in *Biological and Artificial Intelligence Systems,* edited by E. Clementi and S. Chin, published by ESCON Science Publishers B.V., P.O. Box 214, 2300 AE Leiden, The Netherlands.

Gardiner 88   Gardiner, J. D., and Laub, A. J. 1988, "Solving the Algebraic Riccati Equation on a Hypercube Multiprocessor." In *Proceedings of the Third Conference on Hypercube Concurrent Computers and Applications,* edited by G. C. Fox, published by ACM, New York, [Fox 88c].

Gasser 88   Gasser, L. 1988, "Large-Scale Concurrent Computing in Artificial Intelligence Research." In *Proceedings of the Third Conference on Hypercube Concurrent Computers and Applications,* edited by G. C. Fox, published by ACM, New York, [Fox 88c].

Geist 88   Geist, G. A., Ward, R. C., Davis, G. J., and Funderlic, R. E. 1988, "Finding Eigenvalues and Eigenvectors of Unsymmetric Matrices Using a Hypercube Multiprocessor." In *Proceedings of the Third Conference on Hypercube*

Concurrent Computers and Applications, edited by G. C. Fox, published by ACM, New York, [Fox 88c].

Geist 89   Geist, G. A. 1989, "Reduction of a General Matrix to Tridiagonal Form Using a Hypercube Multiprocessor," to be published in *Proceedings of the Fourth Conference on Hypercube Concurrent Computers and Applications*, March 6–8, 1989, Monterey, CA, edited by J. L. Gustafson.

Gerasoulis 88   Gerasoulis, A., Missirlis, N., Nelken I., and Peskin R. 1988, "Implementing Gauss Jordan on a Hypercube Multicomputer." In *Proceedings of the Third Conference on Hypercube Concurrent Computers and Applications*, edited by G. C. Fox, published by ACM, New York, [Fox 88c].

Glendinning 87   Glendinning, I., and Hey, A. J. G. 1987, "Transputer Arrays as Fortran Farms for Particle Physics." *Computer Physics Comm.*, **45**:367.

Glover 88   Glover, Charles W. 1988, "Multi-sensor Integration on the NCUBE Hypercube Computer." In *Proceedings of the Third Conference on Hypercube Concurrent Computers and Applications*, edited by G. C. Fox, published by ACM, New York, [Fox 88c].

Goldsmith 88   Goldsmith, J., and Salmon, J. 1988, "A Hypercube Ray-Tracer." In *Proceedings of the Third Conference on Hypercube Concurrent Computers and Applications*, edited by G. C. Fox, published by ACM, New York, [Fox 88c]. Caltech report C^3P-592.

Gorham 88a   Gorham, P. W., and Prince, T. A. 1988, "Hypercube Data Analysis in Astronomy: Optical Interferometry and Millisecond Pulsar Searches." In *Proceedings of the Third Conference on Hypercube Concurrent Computers and Applications*, edited by G. C. Fox, published by ACM, New York, [Fox 88c]. Caltech report C^3P-571.

Gorham 88b   Gorham, P. W. 1988, "Computational Aspects of Bispectral Analysis in Interferometric Imaging." In *Proceedings of the NOAO-ESO Conference on High Resolution Imaging by Interferometry*. Caltech report C^3P-637.

Gottschalk 87   Gottschalk, T. D. 1987, "Multiple-Target Track Initiation on a Hypercube." In *Proceedings of the Second International Conference on Supercomputing*, published by the International Supercomputing Institute, Inc., St. Petersburg, FL. Caltech report C^3P-398.

Gottschalk 88a   Gottschalk, T. D. 1988, "A New Multi-Target Tracking Model." In *Proceedings of the Third Conference on Hypercube Concurrent Computers and Applications*, edited by G. C. Fox, published by ACM, New York, [Fox 88c]. Caltech report C^3P-480.

Gottschalk 88b   Gottschalk, T. D. 1988, "Concurrent Multiple Target Tracking." In *Proceedings of the Third Conference on Hypercube Concurrent Computers and Applications*, edited by G. C. Fox, published by ACM, New York, [Fox 88c]. Caltech report C^3P-567.

Greengard 86   Greengard, L., and Rokhlin, V. 1986, "A Fast Algorithm for Particle Simulation." Yale Report YALEU/DCS/RR-459, New Haven, CT.

Greenwell 89   Greenwell, D. L., Kalia, R. K., Patterson, J. C., and Vashishta, P. D. 1989, "Molecular Dynamics Algorithm on the Connection Machine." In *Proceedings of the Conference on Scientific Applications of the Connection Machine*, September 12–14, 1988, p. 252, edited by Horst D. Simon, published by World Scientific Publishing Co., Ltd, 687 Hartwell Street, Teaneck, NJ 07666.

Groom 88   Groom, S. L., Mazer, A. S., and Lee, M. 1988, "Design and Implementation of a Concurrent Image-Processing Workstation Based on the Mark III Hypercube." In *Proceedings of the Third Conference on Hypercube Concurrent Computers and Applications*, edited by G. C. Fox, published by ACM, New York, [Fox 88c]. Caltech report C^3P-599.

Gupta 88   Gupta, R., De Lepp, J., Batrouni, G., Fox, G. C., Baillie, C. F., and Apostolakis, J. 1988, "The Phase Transition in the 2-D XY Model." *Phys. Rev. Lett.*, 61:1996.

Gurnis 88   Gurnis, M., Raefsky, A., Lyzenga, G. A., and Hager, B. H. 1988, "Finite Element Solution of Thermal Convection on a Hypercube Concurrent Computer." In *Proceedings of the Third Conference on Hypercube Concurrent Computers and Applications*, edited by G. C. Fox, published by ACM, New York, [Fox 88c]. Caltech report C^3P-595.

Gustafson 88   Gustafson, J. L., Montry, G. R., and Benner, R. E. 1988, "Development of Parallel Methods for a 1024-Processor Hypercube." *SIAM Journal on Scientific and Statistical Computing*, 9:609.

Gustafson 89a   Gustafson, J. L., editor, 1989, *Proceedings of the Fourth Conference on Hypercube Concurrent Computers and Applications*, March 6–8, 1989, Monterey, CA.

Gutt 89a   Gutt, G. M. 1989, "The Physics of Granular Systems," Ph.D. Thesis, California Institute of Technology, Pasadena. Caltech report C^3P-785.

Haghoo 88   Haghoo, M., and Proskurowski, W. 1988, "Parallel Implementation of Domain Decomposition Techniques on Intel's Hypercube." In *Proceedings of the Third Conference on Hypercube Concurrent Computers and Applications*, edited by G. C. Fox, published by ACM, New York, [Fox 88c].

Hambrusch 88   Hambrusch, S., and TeWinkel, L. 1988, "A Study of Connected Component Labeling Algorithms on the MPP." In *Proceedings of the Third International Conference on Supercomputing*, Volume I, May 15–20, 1988, Boston, MA, edited by Lana P. Kartashev and Steven I. Kartashev, p. 477, published by International Supercomputing Institute, Inc., Suite B-309, 3000-34th Street, South, St. Petersburg, FL 33711.

Harstad 87   Harstad, K. 1987, "Performance of Vortex Flow Simulations on the Hypercube." Caltech report C^3P-500.

Hartrum 88   Hartrum, T. C., and Donlan, B. J. 1988, "Hypersim: Distributed Discrete-Event Simulation on an iPSC." In *Proceedings of the Third Conference on Hypercube Concurrent Computers and Applications*, edited by G. C. Fox, published by ACM, New York, [Fox 88c].

Hayot 87   Hayot, F., Mandal, M., and Sadayappan, P. 1989, "Implementation and Performance of a Binary Lattice Gas Algorithm on Parallel Processor Systems." *J. Comput. Ph.*, **80**:2, 277-287.

Heath 86   Heath, M. T. 1986, "Hypercube Multiprocessors, 1986." In *Proceedings of the First Hypercube Conference*, Knoxville, TN, August 26–27, 1985, edited by M. T. Heath, published by SIAM, Philadelphia.

Heath 87   Heath, M. T. 1987, "Hypercube Multiprocessors, 1987." In *Proceedings of the Second Hypercube Conference*, Knoxville, TN, September 29–October 1, 1986, edited by M. T. Heath, published by SIAM, Philadelphia.

Heath 87b   Heath, M. T. 1987, "Hypercube Applications at Oak Ridge National Laboratory." In *Hypercube Multiprocessors, 1987*, edited by M. T. Heath, published by SIAM, Philadelphia, PA.

Henkel 88   Henkel, C. S., Heath, M. T., and Plemmons, R. J. 1988, "Cholesky Downdating on a Hypercube." In *Proceedings of the Third Conference on Hypercube Concurrent Computers and Applications*, edited by G. C. Fox, published by ACM, New York, [Fox 88c].

Hey 88a   Hey, A. J. G. 1988, "Practical Parallel Processing with Transputers." In *Proceedings of the Third Conference on Hypercube Concurrent Computers and Applications*, edited by G. C. Fox, published by ACM, New York, [Fox 88c].

Hey 88b   Hey, A. J. G., and Pritchard, D. J. 1988, "Parallel Applications on the RTP Supernode Machine." In *Proceedings of the Third International Conference on Supercomputing, Volume II*, May 15–20, 1988, Boston, MA, edited by Lana P. Kartashev and Steven I. Kartashev, p. 264, published by International Supercomputing Institute, Inc., Suite B-309, 3000-34th Street, South, St. Petersburg, FL 33711.

Hillis 87b   Hillis, D., and Barnes, J. 1987, "Programming a Highly Parallel Computer." *Nature*, **326**:27.

Hipes 87   Hipes, P. G., and Kuppermann, A. 1987, "Lifetime Analysis of High-Energy Resonances in Three-Dimensional Reactive Scattering." *Chem. Phys. Letters*, **133**:1.

Hipes 88a   Hipes, P. G., and Kuppermann, A. 1988, "Gauss-Jordan Inversion with Pivoting on the Caltech Mark II Hypercube." In *Proceedings of the Third Conference on Hypercube Concurrent Computers and Applications*, edited by G. C. Fox, published by ACM, New York, [Fox 88c]. Caltech report C^3P-578.

Hipes 88b   Hipes, P. G., Mattson, T., Wu, M. Y.-S., and Kuppermann, A. 1988, "Chemical Reaction Dynamics: Integration of Coupled Sets of Ordinary Differential Equations on the Caltech Hypercube." In *Proceedings of the Third Conference on Hypercube Concurrent Computers and Applications*, edited by G. C. Fox, published by ACM, New York, [Fox 88c]. Caltech report C^3P-570.

Hipes 89a   Hipes, P. G. 1989, "Comparison of LU and Gauss-Jordan System Solvers for Distributed Memory Multicomputers." submitted to *Concurrency: Practice and Experience.* Caltech report C^3P-652b.

Ho 88a   Ho, A., Fox, G. C., Walker, D. W., Snyder, S., Chang, D., Chen, S., and Breaden, M. 1988, "PC-CUBE: The IBM PC-Based Hypercube." In *Proceedings of the Third Conference on Hypercube Concurrent Computers and Applications*, edited by G. C. Fox, published by ACM, New York, [Fox 88c]. Caltech report C^3P-587.

Ho 88c   Ho, A., and Furmanski, W. 1988, "Pattern Recognition by Neural Networks on Hypercubes." In *Proceedings of the Third Conference on Hypercube Concurrent Computers and Applications*, edited by G. C. Fox, published by ACM, New York, [Fox 88c]. Caltech report C^3P-528.

Ho 88d   Ho, A., Fox, G. C., Walker, D. W., Breaden, M., Chen, S., Knutson, A., and Kuwamoto, S. 1988, "MAC-CUBE: The Macintosh-Based Hypercube." In *Proceedings of the Third Conference on Hypercube Concurrent Computers and Applications*, edited by G. C. Fox, published by ACM, New York, [Fox 88c]. Caltech report C^3P-544.

Ho 88g   Ho, A., Snyder, S., and Chang, D. 1988, "Users' Guide for PC-CUBE, the IBM PC-Based Hypercube." Caltech report C^3P-563.

Ho 88k   Ho, H. F., Chen, G.-H., Lin, S. H., and Sheu, J. P. 1988, "Solving Linear Programming on Fixed-Size Hypercubes." In *Proceedings of the 1988 International Conference on Parallel Processing*, Volume III, August 15–19, 1988, edited by David H. Bailey, p. 112, published by Penn State University Press, 215 Wagner Building, University Park, PA 16802.

Hoare 78   Hoare, C. A. R. 1978, "Communicating Sequential Processes." *Communications of the ACM*, 21:666.

Holdridge 89   Holdridge, D. B., and Davis, J. A. 1989, "Factoring Very Large Numbers Using a Massively Parallel Computer," to be published in *Proceedings of the Fourth Conference on Hypercube Concurrent Computers and Applications*, March 6–8, 1989, Monterey, CA, edited by J. L. Gustafson.

Houstis 88   Houstis, E. N., Rice, J. R., and Vavalis, E. A. 1988, "A Schwarz Splitting Variant of Cubic Spline Collocation

Methods for Elliptic PDEs." In *Proceedings of the Third Conference on Hypercube Concurrent Computers and Applications*, edited by G. C. Fox, published by ACM, New York, [Fox 88c].

Huntsberger 89a   Huntsberger, B. A., and Huntsberger, T. L. 1989, "Hypercube Algorithms for Multi-spectral Texture Analysis," to be published in *Proceedings of the Fourth Conference on Hypercube Concurrent Computers and Applications*, March 6–8, 1989, Monterey, CA, edited by J. L. Gustafson.

Huntsberger 89b   Huntsberger, T. L., and Soh, Y. 1989, "Hypercube Algorithms for Syntactic Pattern Recognition Analysis of DNA Sequences," to be published in *Proceedings of the Fourth Conference on Hypercube Concurrent Computers and Applications*, March 6–8, 1989, Monterey, CA, edited by J. L. Gustafson.

Ipsen 87   Ipsen, I. C. F., and Jessup, E. 1987, "Two Methods for Solving the Symmetric Tridiagonal Eigenvalue Problem on the Hypercube." In *Hypercube Multiprocessors, 1987*, edited by M. T. Heath, published by SIAM, Philadelphia, PA.

Jackson 88   Jackson, J. A., Liebrock, L. M., and Ziegler, L. R. 1988, "A Hybrid Hypercube Algorithm for the Symmetric Tridiagonal Eigenvalue Problem." In *Proceedings of the Third Conference on Hypercube Concurrent Computers and Applications*, edited by G. C. Fox, published by ACM, New York, [Fox 88c].

Jacob 86   Jacob, G., Newton, R., and Pederson, D. 1986, "An Empirical Analysis of the Performance of a Multiprocessor-Based Circuit Simulator." In *Proceedings of the 23rd ACM/IEEE Design Automation Conference*, June 29–July 2, Las Vegas, Nevada. IEEE Computer Society Press, Washington, DC.

Jefferson 88   Jefferson, D. 1988, "The Status of the Time Warp Operating System." In *Proceedings of the Third Conference on Hypercube Concurrent Computers and Applications*, edited by G. C. Fox, published by ACM, New York, [Fox 88c]. Caltech report C^3P-627.

Jeffrey 87   Jeffrey, W., Simon, R., Celmaster, W., Tenenbaum, E., and Rosner, R. 1987, "Functional Optimization and Pattern Selection in Rayleigh-Benard Convection: An

Implementation on the BBN Butterfly Parallel Processor." Harvard University preprint.

Joe 89a
Joe, K., Mori, Y., and Miyake, S. 1989, "Simulation of a Large-Scale Neural Network on a Parallel Computer," to be published in *Proceedings of the Fourth Conference on Hypercube Concurrent Computers and Applications*, March 6–8, 1989, Monterey, CA, edited by J. L. Gustafson.

Johnson 73
Johnson, B. R. 1973, "The Multichannel Log-Derivative Method for Scattering Calculations." *J. Comput. Phys.*, **13**:445.

Johnson 86
Johnson, M. A. 1986, "Concurrent Computation and Its Application to the Study of Melting in Two Dimensions." Ph.D. Thesis, California Institute of Technology, Pasadena. Caltech report C^3P-268.

Johnsson 85
Johnsson, S. L. 1985, "Band-Matrix Systems Solvers on Ensemble Architectures." In *Supercomputers—Algorithms, Architectures and Scientific Computation,* eds. T. Tajima and F. A. Matsen, University of Texas Press, Austin (1987).

Johnsson 87
Johnsson, S. L., and Ho, C-T. 1987, "Matrix Multiplication on Boolean Cubes Using Generic Communication Primitives." In *Proceedings of the ARO Workshop on Parallel Processing and Medium-Scale Multiprocessors.*

Jones 88
Jones, J. P. 1988, "A Concurrent On-Board Vision System for a Mobile Robot." In *Proceedings of the Third Conference on Hypercube Concurrent Computers and Applications*, edited by G. C. Fox, published by ACM, New York, [Fox 88c].

Kamin 89
Kamin, III, R. A, and Adams, III, G. B. 1989, "Fast Fourier Transform Algorithm Design and Tradeoffs on the CM-2." In *Proceedings of the Conference on Scientific Applications of the Connection Machine*, September 12–14, 1988, p. 134, edited by Horst D. Simon, published by World Scientific Publishing Co., Ltd, 687 Hartwell Street, Teaneck, NJ 07666.

Kao 87
Kao, S. T., and Leiss, E. L. 1987, "An Experimental Implementation of Migration Algorithms on the INTEL Hypercube." *The Int. Journal of Supercomputing Appls.*, **1**:75.

Katzenelson 89
Katzenelson, J. 1989, "Computational Structure of the N-Body Problem." *SIAM J. Sci. Stat. Comput.*, **20**:4787-815.

Kimball 87   Kimball, O., Cosell, L., Schwartz, R., and Krasner, M. 1987, "Efficient Implementation of Continuous Speech Recognition on a Large Scale Parallel Processor." IEEE International Conference on Acoustics, Speech and Signal Processing, Dallas, TX, April 1987.

Knuth 73a   Knuth, D. E.   1973, *Sorting and Searching, the Art of Computer Programming, Volume 3*, published by Addison-Wesley, Reading, MA.

Koch 89   Koch, C., and Segev, I.   1989, *Computational Methods in Neuroscience*, published by MIT Press, Cambridge, MA.

Kolawa 88a   Kolawa, A., and Fox, G. C. 1988, "Use of the Hypercube for Symbolic Quantum Chromodynamics." In *Proceedings of the Third Conference on Hypercube Concurrent Computers and Applications*, edited by G. C. Fox, published by ACM, New York, [Fox 88c]. Caltech report C^3P-182C.

Koller 88a   Koller, J. 1988, "A Dynamic Load Balancer on the Intel Hypercube." In *Proceedings of the Third Conference on Hypercube Concurrent Computers and Applications*, edited by G. C. Fox, published by ACM, New York, [Fox 88c]. Caltech report C^3P-497.

Koller 88b   Koller, J., and Fox, G. C. 1989, "Code Generation by a Generalized Neural Network: General Principles and Elementary Examples." *Journal of Parallel and Distributed Computing*, 6:388. Caltech report C^3P-650B.

Koller 88c   Koller, J., Fox, G. C., and Furmanski, W. 1988, "Physical Optimization and Dynamical Load Balancing." Caltech report C^3P-670.

Kuppermann 75   Kuppermann, A. 1975, "A Useful Mapping of Triatomic Potential Energy Surfaces." *Chem. Phys. Lett.*, 32:374.

Kurdila 89   Kurdila, A. J. 1989, "A Review of Concurrent Multiprocessing Methods for Flexible, Multibody Systems." In *Proceedings of the Fourth International Conference on Supercomputing,* Volume II, April 30–May 5, 1989, Santa Clara, CA, edited by Lana P. Kartashev and Steven I. Kartashev, p. 421, published by International Supercomputing Institute, Inc., Suite B-309, 3000-34th Street, South, St. Petersburg, FL 33711.

Lamont 88   Lamont, G. B., and Shakley, D. J. 1988, "Parallel Expert System Search Techniques for a Real-Time Application."

In *Proceedings of the Third Conference on Hypercube Concurrent Computers and Applications*, edited by G. C. Fox, published by ACM, New York, [Fox 88c].

Lander 88a   Lander, E., Mesirov, J. P., and Taylor, IV, W. 1988, "Study of Protein Sequence Comparison Metrics on the Connection Machine CM-2." In *Proceedings of Supercomputing 88, Volume II: Science and Applications*, edited by Joanne L. Martin and Stephen F. Lundstrom, p. 2, published by IEEE Computer Society Press, 1730 Massachusetts Avenue, NW, Washington, DC 20036-1903.

Lander 88b   Lander, E., Mesirov, J. P., and Taylor, IV, W. 1988, "Protein Sequence Comparison on a Data Parallel Computer." In *Proceedings of the 1988 International Conference on Parallel Processing*, Volume III, August 15–19, 1988, edited by David H. Bailey, p. 257, published by Penn State University Press, 215 Wagner Building, University Park, PA 16802.

Lee 86   Lee, R. 1986, "Mercury I/O Library Users' Guide, C Language Edition." Caltech report C^3P-301.

Lee 89b   Lee, M., Groom, S., Mazer, A., and Williams, W. 1989, "Concurrent Image Processing Executive (CIPE)," to be published in *Proceedings of the Fourth Conference on Hypercube Concurrent Computers and Applications*, March 6–8, 1989, Monterey, CA, edited by J. L. Gustafson. Caltech report C^3P-810.

Leonard 80   Leonard, A. 1980, "Vortex Methods for Flow Simulation." *J. Comp. Phys.*, **37**:289.

Leonard 85   Leonard, A. 1985, "Computing Three-Dimensional Incompressible Flows with Vortex Elements." *Ann. Rev. Fluid Mech.*, **17**:523.

Leonard 87   Chua, K., and Leonard, A. 1987, "Three Dimensional Vortex Methods and the Vortex Reconnection Problem." In *Bulletin of the American Physical Society*, AIP Press, New York.

Liewer 88b   Liewer, P. C., Gould, R. W., Fox, G. C., Decyk, V. K., and Dawson, J. D. 1988, "A Universal Concurrent Algorithm for Plasma Particle-in-Cell Simulation Codes." In *Proceedings of the Third Conference on Hypercube Concurrent Computers and Applications*, edited by G. C.

Fox, published by ACM, New York, [Fox 88c]. Caltech report C^3P-562.

Liewer 88e Liewer, P. C., and Decyk, V. K. 1988, "A General Concurrent Algorithm for Plasma Particle-in-Cell Simulation Codes." to be published in *J. Comput. Phys.* in 1989. Caltech report C^3P-649b.

Liewer 89a Liewer, P. C., and Zimmerman, B. A., Decyk, V. K., and Dawson, J. M. 1989, "Application of Hypercube Computers to Plasma Particle-in-Cell Simulation Codes." Paper presented at the *Fourth International Conference on Supercomputing*, April 30–May 5, 1989, Santa Clara, CA. Caltech report C^3P-717.

Lin 88 Lin, X., Chan, T. F., and Karplus, W. J. 1988, "The Fast Hartley Transform on the Hypercube Multiprocessors." In *Proceedings of the Third Conference on Hypercube Concurrent Computers and Applications*, edited by G. C. Fox, published by ACM, New York, [Fox 88c].

Lin 89a Lin, C. S. 1989, "Simulations of Beam Plasma Instabilities Using a Parallel Particle-in-Cell Code on the Massively Parallel Processor," to be published in *Proceedings of the Fourth Conference on Hypercube Concurrent Computers and Applications*, March 6–8, 1989, Monterey, CA, edited by J. L. Gustafson.

Lin 89b Lin, C. S. 1989, "Particle-in-Cell Simulations of Wave Particle Interactions Using the Massively Parallel Processor." In *Proceedings of the Fourth International Conference on Supercompting,* Volume II, April 30–May 5, 1989, Santa Clara, CA, edited by Lana P. Kartashev and Steven I. Kartashev, p. 287, published by International Supercomputing Institute, Inc., Suite B-309, 3000-34th Street, South, St. Petersburg, FL 33711.

Little 87 Little, J. J., Blelloch, G. E., and Cass, T. 1987, "Parallel Algorithms for Computer Vision on the Connection Machine." In *Proceedings of the First International Conference on Computer Vision*, June 8-11, London, Computer Society Press of the IEEE.

Long 89a Long, L., Khan, M., and Sharp, H. 1989, "A Massively-Parallel Three Dimensional Euler/Navier-Stokes Method." Presented at the *AIAA 9th Computational Fluid Dynamics Conference*, June 13–15, Buffalo, NY, Report number

AIAA-89-1937, published by the American Institute of Aeronautics and Astronautics, 370 L'Enfant Promenade, SW, Washington, DC 20024.

Long 89b   Long, L. N. 1989, "A Three-Dimensional Navier-Stokes Method for the Connection Machine." In *Proceedings of the Conference on Scientific Applications of the Connection Machine*, September 12–14, 1988, p. 64, edited by Horst D. Simon, published by World Scientific Publishing Co., Ltd, 687 Hartwell Street, Teaneck, NJ 07666.

Lorenz 89   Lorenz, J. and Van de Velde, E. F. 1989, "Concurrent Computations of Invariant Manifolds," to be published in *Proceedings of the Fourth Conference on Hypercube Concurrent Computers and Applications*, March 6–8, 1989, Monterey, CA, edited by J. L. Gustafson. Caltech report C^3P-759 and CRPC-89-3.

Lubachevsky 87   Lubachevsky, B. D. 1987, "Efficient Parallel Simulations of Asynchronous Cellular Arrays." *Complex Systems*, 1:1099.

Lyall 86   Lyall, A., Hill, C., Collins, J. F., and Coulson, A. F. W. 1986, *Parallel Computing 1985*, edited by M. Feilmeier, G. Joubert, and U. Schendel, p. 235, North Holland, Amsterdam.

Lyzenga 88   Lyzenga, G., Raefsky, A., and Nour-Omid, B. 1988, "Implementing Finite Element Software on Hypercube Machines." In *Proceedings of the Third Conference on Hypercube Concurrent Computers and Applications*, edited by G. C. Fox, published by ACM, New York, [Fox 88c]. Caltech report C^3P-594.

Ma 88   Ma, R. P., Tsung, F.-S., and Ma, M.-H. 1988, "A Dynamic Load Balancer for a Parallel Branch and Bound Algorithm." In *Proceedings of the Third Conference on Hypercube Concurrent Computers and Applications*, edited by G. C. Fox, published by ACM, New York, [Fox 88c].

Madisetti 88a   Madisetti, V. K., and Messerschmitt, D. G. 1988, "Seismic Migration Algorithms on Parallel Computers." In *Proceedings of the Third Conference on Hypercube Concurrent Computers and Applications*, edited by G. C. Fox, published by ACM, New York, [Fox 88c].

Madisetti 88b   Madisetti, V., Walrand, J., and Messerschmitt, D. 1988, "WOLF: A Rollback Algorithm for Optimistic Distributed

Simulation Systems." the Society for Computer Simulation Conference, Seattle, 1988.

Malone 87   Malone, J. G. 1987, "Automated Mesh Decomposition and Concurrent Finite Element Analysis for Hypercube Multiprocessors Computers." *Comput. Meths. Appl. Mech. Engrg.*, **70**:27-58 (1988). General Motors Research Laboratory report GMR-5893, Detroit, MI, October 1, 1987.

Malone 89a   Malone, J. G. 1989, "Nonlinear Dynamic Finite Element Analysis of Three-Dimensional Shell Structures using Parallel Processing," to be published in *Proceedings of the Fourth Conference on Hypercube Concurrent Computers and Applications*, March 6–8, 1989, Monterey, CA, edited by J. L. Gustafson.

Malone 89b   Malone, J. G. 1989, "High Performance Using a Hypercube Architecture for Parallel Nonlinear Dynamic Finite Element Analysis." In *Proceedings of the Fourth International Conference on Supercompting,* Volume II, April 30–May 5, 1989, Santa Clara, CA, edited by Lana P. Kartashev and Steven I. Kartashev, p. 434, published by International Supercomputing Institute, Inc., Suite B-309, 3000-34th Street, South, St. Petersburg, FL 33711.

Malony 89   Malony, A., Arendt, J. W., Aydt, R. A., Reed, D. A., Grabas, D. and Totty, B. K. 1989, "An Integrated Performance Data Collection, Analysis, and Visualization System." to be published in *Proceedings of the Fourth Conference on Hypercube Concurrent Computers and Applications*, March 6–8, 1989, Monterey, CA, edited by J. L. Gustafson.

Martin 87   Martin, J. L., and Mueller-Wichards, D. 1987, "Supercomputing Performance Evaluation: Status and Directions." *J. Supercomput.*, Vol. 1, May.

Martin 89a   Martin, S. A. 1989, "HALPID: A Program for Finite Element Analysis of Nonlinear Deformation of Materials," to be published in *Proceedings of the Fourth Conference on Hypercube Concurrent Computers and Applications*, March 6–8, 1989, Monterey, CA, edited by J. L. Gustafson.

Mattisson 86   Mattisson, S. 1986, "CONCISE, A Concurrent Circuit Simulation Program." Ph.D. Thesis, Department of Applied Electronics, Lund Institute of Technology, Sweden.

Mattisson 89   Mattisson, S., Peterson, L., Skjellum, A., and Seitz, C. L. 1989, "Circuit Simulation on a Hypercube," to be published in *Proceedings of the Fourth Conference on Hypercube Concurrent Computers and Applications*, March 6–8, 1989, Monterey, CA, edited by J. L. Gustafson.

McBryan 87   McBryan, O. 1987, "The Connection Machine: PDE Solution on 65,536 Processors." Los Alamos report, to be published in *Parallel Computing*.

McBryan 89   McBryan, O. A. 1989, "Connection Machine Application Performance." In *Proceedings of the Conference on Scientific Applications of the Connection Machine*, September 12–14, 1988, p. 94, edited by Horst D. Simon, published by World Scientific Publishing Co., Ltd, 687 Hartwell Street, Teaneck, NJ 07666.

McBurney 88   McBurney, D., and Sleep, M. R. 1988, "Transputers + Virtual Tree Kernel = Real Speedups." In *Proceedings of the Third Conference on Hypercube Concurrent Computers and Applications*, edited by G. C. Fox, published by ACM, New York, [Fox 88c].

Meier 84   Meier, D. 1984, "Two-Dimensional, One-Fluid Hydrodynamics: An Astrophysical Test Problem for the Nearest Neighbor Concurrent Processor." Caltech report C^3P-90.

Meier 89a   Meier, D. L., Cloud, K. C., Horvath, J. C., Allan, L. D., Hammond, W. H., and Maxfield, H. A. 1989, "A General Framework for Complex Time-Driven Simulations on Hypercubes," to be published in *Proceedings of the Fourth Conference on Hypercube Concurrent Computers and Applications*, March 6–8, 1989, Monterey, CA, edited by J. L. Gustafson. Caltech report C^3P-761.

Merrifield 88   Merrifield, B. C., Roberts, J. B. G., Simpson, P., and Stanley, A. 1988, "Real Time Applications of DAP." In *Proceedings of the Third International Conference on Supercomputing,* Volume I, May 15–20, 1988, Boston, MA, edited by Lana P. Kartashev and Steven I. Kartashev, p. 54, published by International Supercomputing Institute, Inc., Suite B-309, 3000-34th Street, South, St. Petersburg, FL 33711.

Messina 87   Messina, P., and Fox, G. C. 1987, "Advanced Architecture Computers." *Scientific American*, **255**:67. Caltech report C^3P-476.

Messina 89   Messina, P., Walker, D. W., Pfeiffer, W., Baillie, C. F.,
                        Felten, E. W., Hipes, P. G., Williams, R. D., Alagard, A.,
                        Kamrah, A., Leary, R., and Rogers, J. 1989, "Benchmarking
                        Advanced Architecture Computers." to be published in
                        Concurrency: Practice and Experience. Caltech report C^3P-
                        712.

Miller 88   Miller, R., and Stout, Q. F. 1988, "Computational
                        Geometry on Hypercube Computers." In *Proceedings of the
                        Third Conference on Hypercube Concurrent Computers and
                        Applications*, edited by G. C. Fox, published by ACM, New
                        York, [Fox 88c].

Mirchandaney 88   Mirchandaney, R., Saltz, J., Smith, R., Nicol, D.,
                        and Crowley, K. 1988, "Principles of Runtime Support
                        for Parallel Processors." In *Proceedings of the 1988
                        International Conference on Supercomputing*, July 4–8,
                        St. Malo, France, p. 140, published by ACM, 11 West 42nd
                        Street, New York 10036.

Mitchell 85   Mitchell, P. W., and Dove, M. T. 1985, "SHAMGAR's
                        OXGOAD: A New Approach to the Problem of Resolution
                        Corrections for Triple-Axis Neutron Inelastic Scattering
                        Data Using Parallel Processors." *J. Appl. Cryst.*, **18**:493.

Moler 86   Moler, C. 1986, "Matrix Computation on Distributed
                        Memory Multiprocessors." In *Hypercube Multiprocessors,
                        1986*, edited by M. T. Heath, published by SIAM,
                        Philadelphia, PA.

Morgan 88   Morgan, Keith 1988, "Blitz: A Rule-Based System for
                        Massively Parallel Architectures." In *Proceedings of the
                        Third Conference on Hypercube Concurrent Computers and
                        Applications*, edited by G. C. Fox, published by ACM, New
                        York, [Fox 88c].

Mrugala 83   Mrugala, F., and Secrest, D. 1983, "The Generalized Log-
                        Derivative Method for Inelastic and Reactive Collisions."
                        J. Chem. Phys., **78**:5954.

Mu 89   Mu, M., and Rice, J. R. 1989, "LU Factorization and
                        Elimination for Sparse Matrices on Hypercubes," to be
                        published in *Proceedings of the Fourth Conference on
                        Hypercube Concurrent Computers and Applications*, March
                        6–8, 1989, Monterey, CA, edited by J. L. Gustafson.

Nakajima 89a   Nakajima, T., Kulkarni, S. R., Gorham, P. W., Ghez, A. M.,
                        Neugebauer, G., Oke, J. B., Prince, T. A., and Readhead,

A. C. S. 1989, "Diffraction-Limited Imaging II: Optical Aperture-Synthesis Imaging of Two Binary Stars." *Astron. J.*, **97**:5. Caltech report C^3P-805.

NAS 86   "An Agenda for Improved Evaluation of Supercomputer Performance," Report to the National Academy of Sciences, published by National Academy Press, Washington, DC, 1986.

Nayudu 89   Nayudu, S. K., and Teague, K. A. 1989, "Parallel Sorting on the iPSC/2 Hypercube Computer," to be published in *Proceedings of the Fourth Conference on Hypercube Concurrent Computers and Applications*, March 6–8, 1989, Monterey, CA, edited by J. L. Gustafson.

NCUBE 87   NCUBE Corporation, 1987, *NCUBE Users' Handbook*, published by NCUBE Corporation, Beaverton, OR.

Newhall 89a   Newhall, D. S., and Horvath, J. C. 1989, "Analysis of Text Using a Neural Network: A Hypercube Implementation," to be published in *Proceedings of the Fourth Conference on Hypercube Concurrent Computers and Applications*, March 6–8, 1989, Monterey, CA, edited by J. L. Gustafson. Caltech report C^3P-770.

Newman 88   Newman, J. N., and Sclavounos, P. D. 1988, "The Computation of Wave Loads on Large Offshore Structures." Paper presented at the Conference on the Behavior of Offshore Structures, Trondheim, June 1988.

Nicol 88   Nicol, D., and Saltz, J. 1988, "Dynamic Remapping of Parallel Computations with Varying Resource Demands." *IEEE Trans. Computers*, **37**:1073.

Noetzel 89   Noetzel, A. 1989, "Hypercube Implementations of Neural Networks for Combinatorial Optimization," to be published in *Proceedings of the Fourth Conference on Hypercube Concurrent Computers and Applications*, March 6–8, 1989, Monterey, CA, edited by J. L. Gustafson.

Norman 87   Norman, M. G. 1987, "A Three-Dimensional Image Processing Program for a Parallel Computer." M.Sc. Thesis, Dept. of Artificial Intelligence, University of Edinburgh.

Olesen 88   Olesen, T.-H., and Petersen, J. 1988, "Vectorized Dissection on the Hypercube." In *Proceedings of the Third Conference on Hypercube Concurrent Computers and Applications*, edited by G. C. Fox, published by ACM, New York, [Fox 88c].

O'Hallaron 88   O'Hallaron, D. R., and Baheti, R. S. 1988, "Parallel Implementation of a Kalman Filter on the Warp Computer." In *Proceedings of the 1988 International Conference on Parallel Processing*, Volume III, August 15–19, 1988, edited by David H. Bailey, p. 108, published by Penn State University Press, 215 Wagner Building, University Park, PA 16802.

O'Neil 87   O'Neil, E., Allik, H., Moore, S., and Tenebaum, E. 1987, "Finite Element Analysis on the BBN Butterfly Multiprocessor." In *Proceedings of the Second International Conference on Supercomputing,* published by the International Supercomputing Institute, Inc., St. Petersburg, FL, May.

O'Neil 88   O'Neil, E. J., and Shaefer, C. G. 1988, "The ARGOT Strategy III: The BBN Butterfly Multiprocessor." In *Proceedings of Supercomputing 88, Volume II: Science and Applications*, edited by Joanne L. Martin and Stephen F. Lundstrom, p. 214, published by IEEE Computer Society Press, 1730 Massachusetts Avenue, NW, Washington, DC 20036-1903.

Opsahl 88   Opsahl, T., Steck, R. R., and Kuszmaul, C. L. 1988, "Advanced Image Processing Applications on the Connection Machine." In *Proceedings of the Third International Conference on Supercomputing,* Volume I, May 15–20, 1988, Boston, MA, edited by Lana P. Kartashev and Steven I. Kartashev, p. 463, published by International Supercomputing Institute, Inc., Suite B-309, 3000-34th Street, South, St. Petersburg, FL 33711.

Orcutt 88   Orcutt, D. E. 1988, "Implementation of Ray Tracing on the Hypercube." In *Proceedings of the Third Conference on Hypercube Concurrent Computers and Applications*, edited by G. C. Fox, published by ACM, New York, [Fox 88c].

Otto 83   Otto, S. W. 1983, "Monte Carlo Methods in Lattice Gauge Theories," Ph.D. Thesis, California Institute of Technology, Pasadena.

Otto 84a   Otto, S. W., and Stack, J. 1984, "The SU(3) Heavy Quark Potential with High Statistics." *Phys. Rev. Lett.*, **52**:2328. Caltech report C^3P-67.

Otto 85   Otto, S. W., and Stolorz, P. 1985, "An Improvement for
                     Glueball Mass Calculations on a Lattice." *Phys. Lett.*,
                     B151:428. Caltech report C^{3}P-343.

Otto 87   Otto, S. W., Baillie, C. F., Ding, H-Q., Apostolakis, J.,
                     Gupta, R., Kilcup, G., Patel, A., and Sharpe, S. 1987,
                     "Lattice Gauge Theory Benchmarks." Caltech report C^{3}P-
                     450R.

Otto 88   Otto, S. W., Felten, E. W., and Martin, O. 1988, "Multiscale
                     Training of Large Back-Propagation Networks."   to be
                     published in *Biological Cybernetics*. Caltech report C^{3}P-
                     608.

Ozguner 88   Ozguner, F., Aykanat, C., and Khalid, O. 1988, "Logic
                     Fault Simulation on a Vector Hypercube Multiprocessor."
                     In *Proceedings of the Third Conference on Hypercube
                     Concurrent Computers and Applications*, edited by G. C.
                     Fox, published by ACM, New York, [Fox 88c].

Parasoft 88a   "EXPRESS: A Communication Environment for Parallel
                     Computers," Parasoft, 27415 Trabuco Circle, Mission Viejo,
                     CA 92692.

Parasoft 88b   "NDB: A Source Level Debugger for Parallel Computers,"
                     Parasoft, 27415 Trabuco Circle, Mission Viejo, CA 92692.

Parasoft 88c   "CUBIX: Programming Parallel Computers Without Pro-
                     gramming Hosts," Parasoft, 27415 Trabuco Circle, Mission
                     Viejo, CA 92692.

Parasoft 88d   "PLOTIX: A Graphical System for Parallel Computers,"
                     Parasoft, 27415 Trabuco Circle, Mission Viejo, CA 92692.

Parasoft 88e   "PROFILE: A Profiling System for Parallel Computers,"
                     Parasoft, 27415 Trabuco Circle, Mission Viejo, CA 92692.

Pargas 88   Pargas, R. P., and Wooster, D. E. 1988, "Branch-and-
                     Bound Algorithms on a Hypercube." In *Proceedings of the
                     Third Conference on Hypercube Concurrent Computers and
                     Applications*, edited by G. C. Fox, published by ACM, New
                     York, [Fox 88c].

Parikh 89a   Parikh, J. A., Damodaran, M., and Charnsuwannachot,
                     V. 1989, "Detection of Linear Features in Images using
                     Hopfield Neural Networks on the Intel Hypercube," to
                     be published in *Proceedings of the Fourth Conference on*

Hypercube Concurrent Computers and Applications, March 6–8, 1989, Monterey, CA, edited by J. L. Gustafson.

Park 89   Park, H., and Eberlein, P. J. 1989, "Eigensystem Computation on Hypercube Architectures," to be published in *Proceedings of the Fourth Conference on Hypercube Concurrent Computers and Applications*, March 6–8, 1989, Monterey, CA, edited by J. L. Gustafson.

Patterson 86   Patterson, J. 1986, "Householder Transformation, Decomposition, Results, Some Observations." Caltech report C^3P-297.5.

Pawley 82   Pawley, G. S., and Thomas, G. W. 1982, "Computer Simulation of the Plastic-to-Crystalline Phase Transition in SF_6." *Phys. Rev. Lett.*, **48**:410.

Pawley 84   Pawley, G. S., and Dove, M. T. 1984, "A Molecular Dynamics Simulation Study of the Orientationally Disordered Phase of Sulphur Hexafluoride." *J. Phys. C.*, **17**:6851.

Pawley 87   Pawley, G., Baillie, C., Jenerbaum, E., and Celmaster, W. 1987, "The BBN Butterfly Used to Simulate a Molecular Liquid." to be published in *Parallel Computing*, Caltech report C^3P-529.

Pawley 88   Pawley, G. S., Stroud, N., and Collins, J. 1988, "Experiences with Computers of Highly Parallel Architectures." In *Biological and Artificial Intelligence Systems*, edited by E. Clementi and S. Chin, published by ESCON Science Publishers B.V., P.O. Box 214, 2300 AE Leiden, The Netherlands.

Peterson 89   Peterson, L., and Mattisson, S. 1989, "Circuit Partitioning and Iteration Scheme for Waveform Relaxation used in Circuit Simulation," to be published in *Proceedings of the Fourth Conference on Hypercube Concurrent Computers and Applications*, March 6–8, 1989, Monterey, CA, edited by J. L. Gustafson.

Pfaltz 88   Pfaltz, J. L., Son, S. H., and French, J. C. 1988, "ADAMS Interface Language." In *Proceedings of the Third Conference on Hypercube Concurrent Computers and Applications*, edited by G. C. Fox, published by ACM, New York, [Fox 88c].

Pollara 86   Pollara, F. 1986, "Concurrent Viterbi Algorithm with Trace-Back." In August Conference of International Society of

Optical Engineering, *Advanced Algorithms and Architectures for Signal Processing,* Vol. 696 of SPIE Proceedings, 204. Caltech report C^3P-462.

Pothen 88   Pothen, A. 1988, "Distributed Orthogonal Factorization." In *Proceedings of the Third Conference on Hypercube Concurrent Computers and Applications*, edited by G. C. Fox, published by ACM, New York, [Fox 88c].

Raman 89   Raman, S., and Patnaik, L. M. 1989, "HIRECS: Hypercube Implementation of Relaxation-Based Circuit Simulation," to be published in *Proceedings of the Fourth Conference on Hypercube Concurrent Computers and Applications*, March 6–8, 1989, Monterey, CA, edited by J. L. Gustafson.

Ranka 88   Ranka, S., and Sahni, S. 1988, "Image Template Matching on MIMD Hypercube Multicomputers." In *Proceedings of the 1988 International Conference on Parallel Processing*, Volume III, August 15–19, 1988, edited by David H. Bailey, p. 92, published by Penn State University Press, 215 Wagner Building, University Park, PA 16802.

Rao 87   Rao, V. N., Kumar, V., and Ramesh, K. 1987, "Parallel Heuristic Search on Shared Memory Multiprocessors: Preliminary Results." In *Proceedings of the MCC University Symposium*, Austin, TX, July.

Renault 88   Renault, R., and Petersen, J. 1988, "Evaluation of a Vector Hypercube for Seismic Modelling." In *Proceedings of the Third Conference on Hypercube Concurrent Computers and Applications*, edited by G. C. Fox, published by ACM, New York, [Fox 88c].

Rogers 89   Rogers, D. 1989, "Kanerva's Sparse Distributed Memory: An Associative Memory Algorithm Well-Suited to the Connection Machine." In *Proceedings of the Conference on Scientific Applications of the Connection Machine*, September 12–14, 1988, p. 282, edited by Horst D. Simon, published by World Scientific Publishing Co., Ltd, 687 Hartwell Street, Teaneck, NJ 07666.

Rose 87   Rose, J., and Steele, C. April 1987, "C*: An Extended C Language for Data Parallel Programming." Thinking Machines Corporation report PL 87-5, 245 First Street, Cambridge, MA 02142.

Rosen 89   Rosen, J. B., and Maier, R. S. 1989, "Parallel Solution of Large-Scale, Block-Diagonal Linear Programs on a

Hypercube Machine," to be published in *Proceedings of the Fourth Conference on Hypercube Concurrent Computers and Applications*, March 6–8, 1989, Monterey, CA, edited by J. L. Gustafson.

Sadayappan 88   Sadayappan, P. 1988, "Parallelization and Performance Evaluation of Circuit Simulation on a Shared-Memory Multiprocessor." In *Proceedings of the 1988 International Conference on Supercomputing*, July 4–8, St. Malo, France, pp. 254–272, published by ACM, 11 West 42nd Street, New York 10036.

Salmon 88a   Salmon, J., Callahan, S., Flower, J., and Kolawa, A. 1988, "MOOSE: A Multi-Tasking Operating System for Hypercubes." In *Proceedings of the Third Conference on Hypercube Concurrent Computers and Applications*, edited by G. C. Fox, published by ACM, New York, [Fox 88c]. Caltech report C^3P-586.

Salmon 89a   Salmon, J., Quinn, P., and Warren, M. 1989, "Using Parallel Computers for Very Large N-body Simulations: Shell Formation Using 180K Particles," to appear in *Proceedings of the Heidelberg Conference on the Dynamics and Interactions of Galaxies*, edited by A. Toomre and R. Wieland, Springer-Verlag.

Saltz 87   Saltz, J., Mirchandaney, R., Smith, R., Nicol, D., and Crowley, K. 1987, "The PARTY Parallel Runtime System." In *Proceedings of the SIAM Conference on Parallel Processing for Scientific Computing*, Los Angeles, published by the Society for Industrial and Applied Mathematics.

Sammes 87   Sammes, A. J., editor,   October 1987, *First US/UK Workshop Parallel Processing*, Vol. 1, Royal Military College of Science, Shrivenham, U.K., 13–17 July 1987.

Sammur 89a   Sammur, N. M., and Hagan, M. T. 1989, "Mapping Signal Processing Algorithms on the Hypercube," to be published in *Proceedings of the Fourth Conference on Hypercube Concurrent Computers and Applications*, March 6–8, 1989, Monterey, CA, edited by J. L. Gustafson.

Sato 88   Sato, R. K., and Swarztrauber, P. N. 1988, "Benchmarking the Connection Machine 2." In *Proceedings of Supercomputing '88, Volume I*, November 14–18, 1988, Orlando, FL, p. 304, published by IEEE Computer Society Press, 1730 Massachusetts Avenue, NW, Washington, DC 20036-1903.

Schemer 84   Schemer, J., and Neches, P. 1984, "The Genesis of a
                    Database Computer." *IEEE Computer Magazine*, **19**.

Schwan 88   Schwan, K., Gawkowski, J., and Blake, B. 1988, "Process
                    and Workload Migration for a Parallel Branch-and-Bound
                    Algorithm on a Hypercube Multicomputer." In *Proceedings
                    of the Third Conference on Hypercube Concurrent Comput-
                    ers and Applications*, edited by G. C. Fox, published by
                    ACM, New York, [Fox 88c].

Seidel 88   Seidel, S. R., and George, W. L. 1988, "Binsorting on
                    Hypercubes with d-port Communication." In *Proceedings of
                    the Third Conference on Hypercube Concurrent Computers
                    and Applications*, edited by G. C. Fox, published by ACM,
                    New York, [Fox 88c].

Seitz 88   Seitz, C. L., Seizovic, J., and Su, W.-K. 1988, "The
                    C Programmer's Abbreviated Guide to Multicomputer
                    Programming." Caltech Computer Science Technical Report
                    CS-TR-88-1.

Sheu 88   Sheu, T.-L., and Lin, W. 1988, "Mapping Linear
                    Programming Algorithms onto the Butterfly Parallel
                    Processor." In *Proceedings of the Third International
                    Conference on Supercomputing, Volume II*, May 15–20,
                    1988, Boston, MA, edited by Lana P. Kartashev and
                    Steven I. Kartashev, p. 452, published by International
                    Supercomputing Institute, Inc., Suite B-309, 3000-34th
                    Street, South, St. Petersburg, FL 33711.

Simoni 89a   Simoni, D. A., Zimmerman, B. A., Patterson, J. E., Wu,
                    C., and Peterson, J. C. 1989, "Synthetic Aperture Radar
                    Processing Using the Hypercube Concurrent Architecture,"
                    to be published in *Proceedings of the Fourth Conference on
                    Hypercube Concurrent Computers and Applications*, March
                    6–8, 1989, Monterey, CA, edited by J. L. Gustafson. Caltech
                    report C^3P-775.

Skjellum 88   Skjellum, A., and Morari, M. 1988, "Waveform Relaxation
                    for Concurrent Dynamic Simulation of Distillation Columns."
                    In *Proceedings of the Third Conference on Hypercube Con-
                    current Computers and Applications*, edited by G. C. Fox,
                    published by ACM, New York, [Fox 88c]. Caltech report
                    C^3P-588.

Soh 89a   Soh, Y., and Huntsberger, T. L. 1989, "Hypercube
                    Algorithms for Dynamic Scene Analysis," to be published

in *Proceedings of the Fourth Conference on Hypercube Concurrent Computers and Applications*, March 6–8, 1989, Monterey, CA, edited by J. L. Gustafson.

Son 88   Son, S. H., and Pfaltz, J. L. 1988, "Reliability Mechanisms for ADAMS." In *Proceedings of the Third Conference on Hypercube Concurrent Computers and Applications*, edited by G. C. Fox, published by ACM, New York, [Fox 88c].

Spalart 83   Spalart, P. R., Leonard, A., and Baganoff, D. 1983, "Numerical Simulations of Separated Flows." NASA Report TM-84328, NASA/AMES, Moffett Field, CA.

Spalart 84   Spalart, P. R. 1984, "Two Recent Extensions of the Vortex Method." American Institute of Aeronautics and Astronautics Paper 84-0343, AIAA, New York.

Stanfill 86   Stanfill, C., and Kahle, B. 1986, "Parallel Free-Text Search on the Connection Machine System." *Comm. ACM*, 29:1229.

Stolorz 87   Stolorz, P. E. 1987, "Numerical Simulations of Lattice QCD," Ph.D. Thesis, California Institute of Technology, Pasadena, CA.

Strang 73   Strang, G., and Fix, G. J. 1973, *An Analysis of the Finite Element Method*, published by Prentice Hall, Englewood Cliffs, NJ.

Stunkel 88a   Stunkel, C. B., and Reed, D. A. 1988, "Hypercube Implementation of the Simplex Algorithm." In *Proceedings of the Third Conference on Hypercube Concurrent Computers and Applications*, edited by G. C. Fox, published by ACM, New York, [Fox 88c].

Stunkel 88b   Stunkel, C. B. 1988, "Linear Optimization Via Message-Based Parallel Processing." In *Proceedings of the 1988 International Conference on Parallel Processing*, Volume III, August 15–19, 1988, edited by David H. Bailey, p. 264, published by Penn State University Press, 215 Wagner Building, University Park, PA 16802.

Stunkel 89   Stunkel, C. B., Fuchs, W. K., Rudolph, D. C., and Reed, D. A. 1989, "Linear Optimization: A Case Study in Performance Analysis," to be published in *Proceedings of the Fourth Conference on Hypercube Concurrent Computers and Applications*, March 6–8, 1989, Monterey, CA, edited by J. L. Gustafson.

Synnott 89a   Synnott, S. P., Riedel, J. E., Stuve, J. A., Halamek, P., and Lehr, W. J. 1989, "Three Dimensional Geometry from Image Processing on the JPL/CIT Hypercube," to be published in *Proceedings of the Fourth Conference on Hypercube Concurrent Computers and Applications*, March 6–8, 1989, Monterey, CA, edited by J. L. Gustafson. Caltech report C^3P-763.

Tichy 89   Tichy, W. F. 1989, "Parallel Matrix Multiplication on the Connection Machine." In *Proceedings of the Conference on Scientific Applications of the Connection Machine*, September 12–14, 1988, p. 174, edited by Horst D. Simon, published by World Scientific Publishing Co., Ltd, 687 Hartwell Street, Teaneck, NJ 07666.

Tinker 88   Tinker, M. 1988, "The Implementation of Parallel Image Compression Techniques." In *Proceedings of the Third International Conference on Supercomputing, Volume II*, May 15–20, 1988, Boston, MA, edited by Lana P. Kartashev and Steven I. Kartashev, p. 209, published by International Supercomputing Institute, Inc., Suite B-309, 3000-34th Street, South, St. Petersburg, FL 33711.

Tomboulian 88   Tomboulian, S., Streett, C., and Macaraeg, M. 1988, "Spectral Solution of the Incompressible Navier-Stokes Equations on the Connection Machine 2." In *Proceedings of Supercomputing 88, Volume II: Science and Applications*, edited by Joanne L. Martin and Stephen F. Lundstrom, p. 45, published by IEEE Computer Society Press, 1730 Massachusetts Avenue, NW, Washington, DC 20036-1903.

Tong 89   Tong, C. 1989, "The Preconditioned Conjugate Gradient Method on the Connection Machine." In *Proceedings of the Conference on Scientific Applications of the Connection Machine*, September 12–14, 1988, p. 188, edited by Horst D. Simon, published by World Scientific Publishing Co., Ltd, 687 Hartwell Street, Teaneck, NJ 07666.

Toomarian 88   Toomarian, N. 1988, "A Concurrent Neural Network Algorithm for the Traveling Salesman Problem." In *Proceedings of the Third Conference on Hypercube Concurrent Computers and Applications*, edited by G. C. Fox, published by ACM, New York, [Fox 88c].

Tripathi 88   Tripathi, V. S., Drake, J. B., Asbury, R., and Yeh, G. T. 1988, "Hypercube Computers Outperform the Cray X-MP Supercomputer in Contaminant Transfer Simulations."

In *Proceedings of the Third International Conference on Supercomputing,* Volume I, May 15–20, 1988, Boston, MA, edited by Lana P. Kartashev and Steven I. Kartashev, p. 170, published by International Supercomputing Institute, Inc., Suite B-309, 3000-34th Street, South, St. Petersburg, FL 33711.

Trucillo 89   Trucillo, J. J. 1989, "Numerical Weather Prediction on the Connection Machine." In *Proceedings of the Fourth International Conference on Supercompting,* Volume II, April 30–May 5, 1989, Santa Clara, CA, edited by Lana P. Kartashev and Steven I. Kartashev, p. 334, published by International Supercomputing Institute, Inc., Suite B-309, 3000-34th Street, South, St. Petersburg, FL 33711.

Tuazon 88   Tuazon, J., Peterson, J., and Pniel, M. 1988, "Mark IIIfp Hypercube Concurrent Processor Architecture." In *Proceedings of the Third Conference on Hypercube Concurrent Computers and Applications*, edited by G. C. Fox, published by ACM, New York, [Fox 88c]. Caltech report C^3P-602.

Tucker 88   Tucker, L. W. 1988, "Data Parallelism and Computer Vision Using the Connection Machine." In *Proceedings of the Third International Conference on Supercomputing, Volume III*, May 15–20, 1988, Boston, MA, edited by Lana P. Kartashev and Steven I. Kartashev, p. 35, published by International Supercomputing Institute, Inc., Suite B-309, 3000-34th Street, South, St. Petersburg, FL 33711.

van de Geijn 89   van de Geijn, R. A., and Hudson, III, D. G. 1989, "Efficient Parallel Implementation of the Nonsymmetric QR Algorithm," to be published in *Proceedings of the Fourth Conference on Hypercube Concurrent Computers and Applications*, March 6–8, 1989, Monterey, CA, edited by J. L. Gustafson.

Van de Velde 87a   Van de Velde, E. F., and Keller, H. B. 1987, "The Design of a Parallel Multigrid Algorithm." In *Proceedings of the Second International Conference on Supercomputing at Santa Clara,* published by the International Supercomputing Institute, Inc., St. Petersburg, FL, Caltech report C^3P-406.

Van de Velde 87b   Van de Velde, E. F., and Keller, H. B. 1987, "The Parallel Solution of Nonlinear Elliptic Equations." Caltech report C^3P-447.

Van de Velde 89a   Van de Velde, E. 1989, "Experiments with Multicomputer LU-Decomposition." Submitted to *Concurrency: Practice and Experience*, Caltech reports C^{3}P-725 and CRPC-89-1.

Vandewalle 89   Vandewalle, S., Roose, D., and Piessens, R. 1989, "A Comparison of Two Parallel Multigrid Methods for the Numerical Solution of Parabolic Partial Differential Equations," to be published in *Proceedings of the Fourth Conference on Hypercube Concurrent Computers and Applications*, March 6–8, 1989, Monterey, CA, edited by J. L. Gustafson.

Wake 89   Wake, B. E., and Egolf, T. A. 1989, "Implementation of a Rotary-Wing Three-Dimensional Navier-Stokes Solver on a Massively Parallel Computer." Presented at the *AIAA 9th Computational Fluid Dynamics Conference*, June 13–15, Buffalo, NY, published by the American Institute of Aeronautics and Astronautics, 370 L'Enfant Promenade, SW, Washington, DC 20024.

Walker 88a   Walker, D. W., Messina, P., and Baillie, C. F. 1988, "Performance Evaluation of Scientific Programs on Advanced Architecture Computers." In *Proceedings of the Third Conference on Hypercube Concurrent Computers and Applications*, edited by G. C. Fox, published by ACM, New York, [Fox 88c]. Caltech report C^{3}P-580.

Walker 88b   Walker, D. W., Fox, G. C., and Montry, G. R. 1988, "The Flux-Corrected Transport Algorithm on the NCUBE Hypercube." In *Proceedings of the Third Conference on Hypercube Concurrent Computers and Applications*, edited by G. C. Fox, published by ACM, New York, [Fox 88c]. Caltech report C^{3}P-495.

Walker 88c   Walker, D. W. 1988, "Performance of a QCD Code on the NCUBE Hypercube." In *Proceedings of the Third Conference on Hypercube Concurrent Computers and Applications*, edited by G. C. Fox, published by ACM, New York, [Fox 88c]. Caltech report C^{3}P-490B.

Walker 88d   Walker, D. W. 1988, "Portable Programming Within a Message-Passing Model: The FFT as an Example." In *Proceedings of the Third Conference on Hypercube Concurrent Computers and Applications*, edited by G. C. Fox, published by ACM, New York, [Fox 88c]. Caltech report C^{3}P-631.

Walker 88e   Walker, D. W., and Fox, G. C. 1988, "A Portable Program-
                        ming Environment for Concurrent Multiprocessors." Paper
                        presented at the 12th *IMACS World Congress on Scientific
                        Computing*, July 18–22, 1988, Paris, France. Caltech report
                        C^3P-496.

Walker 88f   Walker, D. W., and Fox, G. C. 1988, "Concurrent
                        Supercomputers in Science." Paper presented at the 1988
                        Conference on Computers in Physics Instruction, August 1–
                        5, 1988, North Carolina State University, Raleigh, Caltech
                        report C^3P-646.

Walker 89a   Walker, D. W. 1989, "The Implementation of a Three-
                        Dimensional PIC Code on a Hypercube Concurrent
                        Processor," to be published in *Proceedings of the Fourth
                        Conference on Hypercube Concurrent Computers and
                        Applications*, March 6–8, 1989, Monterey, CA, edited by
                        J. L. Gustafson. Caltech report C^3P-739.

Wall 86   Wall, C. E. 1986, "Numerical Investigation of Hyperscaling
                        and Real Space Renormalization Group Transformations
                        in the Three-Dimensional Ising Model." Ph.D. Thesis,
                        University of Edinburgh.

Wallace 87   Wallace, D. J. 1987, "Scientific Computation on SIMD and
                        MIMD Machines." Edinburgh preprint 87/429, Invited Talk
                        at Royal Society Discussion Meeting, London, December 9–
                        10, 1987.

Wallace 88a   Bowler, K., Kenway, R., and Wallace, D. 1988, "The Ed-
                        inburgh Concurrent Supercomputer: Project and Applica-
                        tions." In *Proceedings of the Third International Conference
                        on Supercomputing, Volume II*, May 15–20, 1988, Boston,
                        MA, edited by Lana P. Kartashev and Steven I. Kartashev,
                        p. 200, published by International Supercomputing Insti-
                        tute, Inc., Suite B-309, 3000-34th Street, South, St. Peters-
                        burg, FL 33711.

Wallace 88b   Wallace, R. S., Webb, J. A., and Wu, I.-C. 1988, "Machine-
                        Independent Image Processing: Performance of Apply
                        on Diverse Architectures." In *Proceedings of the Third
                        International Conference on Supercomputing, Volume III*,
                        May 15–20, 1988, Boston, MA, edited by Lana P. Kartashev
                        and Steven I. Kartashev, p. 25, published by International
                        Supercomputing Institute, Inc., Suite B-309, 3000-34th
                        Street, South, St. Petersburg, FL 33711.

Walsh 89   Walsh, G. 1989, "A Hypercube-Based Command and Control Information Management System," to be published in *Proceedings of the Fourth Conference on Hypercube Concurrent Computers and Applications*, March 6–8, 1989, Monterey, CA, edited by J. L. Gustafson.

Waltz 87a   Waltz, D., Stanfill, C., Smith, S., and Thau, R. 1987, "Very Large Database Applications of the Connection Machine Systems." Thinking Machines Corporation report, 245 First Street, Cambridge, MA 02142.

Waltz 88   Waltz, D. L., and Stanfill, C. 1988, "Artificial Intelligence Related Research on the Connection Machine." In *Proceedings of the International Conference on Fifth Generation Computer Systems*, November 28–December 2, 1988, Tokyo, Volume 3, p. 1010, published by OHMSHA, Ltd., 3-1 Kanda Nishiki-cho, Chiyoda-ku, Tokyo 101, Japan..

Ward 88   Ward, J. S., and Roberts, J. B. G. 1988, "Optimising a Reconfigurable MIMD Transputer Machine for Line-of-Sight Calculations on Large Digital Maps." In *Proceedings of the 1988 International Conference on Parallel Processing*, Volume III, August 15–19, 1988, edited by David H. Bailey, p. 230, published by Penn State University Press, 215 Wagner Building, University Park, PA 16802.

Warren 88a   Warren, V. 1988, "Graphics Techniques in Concurrent Simulation." In *Proceedings of the Third Conference on Hypercube Concurrent Computers and Applications*, edited by G. C. Fox, published by ACM, New York, [Fox 88c]. Caltech report C^3P-600.

Warren 88b   Warren, M., and Salmon, J. 1988, "An O(NlogN) Hypercube N-body Integrator." In *Proceedings of the Third Conference on Hypercube Concurrent Computers and Applications*, edited by G. C. Fox, published by ACM, New York, [Fox 88c]. Caltech report C^3P-593.

Weissbein 88   Weissbein, D. A., Mangus, J. F., and George, M. W. 1988, "Solution of the 3-D Euler Equations for the Flow About a Fighter Aircraft Configuration Using a Hypercube Parallel Processor." In *Proceedings of the Third Conference on Hypercube Concurrent Computers and Applications*, edited by G. C. Fox, published by ACM, New York, [Fox 88c].

Werner 88   Werner, B. T., and Haff, P. K. 1988, "Dynamical Simulations of Granular Materials Using the Caltech Hypercube."

In *Proceedings of the Third Conference on Hypercube Concurrent Computers and Applications*, edited by G. C. Fox, published by ACM, New York, [Fox 88c]. Caltech report C^3P-612.

Whiteside 88   Whiteside, R. A., and Leichter, J. S. 1988, "Using Linda for Supercomputing on a Local Area Network." In *Proceedings of Supercomputing '88*, November 14–18, 1988, Orlando, FL. IEEE Computer Society Press, 1730 Massachusetts Avenue, NW, Washington, DC 20036-1903.

Wieland 88   Wieland, F., Hawley, L., and Feinberg, A. 1988, "Implementing a Distributed Combat Simulation on the Time Warp Operating System." In *Proceedings of the Third Conference on Hypercube Concurrent Computers and Applications*, edited by G. C. Fox, published by ACM, New York, [Fox 88c]. Caltech report C^3P-601.

Wieland 89a   Wieland, F., Hawley, L., Feinberg, A., DiLoreto, M., Blume, L., Ruffles, J., Reiher, P., Beckman, B., Hontalas, P., Bellenot, S., and Jefferson, D. 1989, "The Performance of a Distributed Combat Simulation with the Time Warp Operating System." to be published in *Concurrency: Practice and Experience* Caltech C^3P-798.

Willebeek 88   Willebeek-LeMair, M., and Reeves, A. P. 1988, "Region Growing on a Hypercube Multiprocessor." In *Proceedings of the Third Conference on Hypercube Concurrent Computers and Applications*, edited by G. C. Fox, published by ACM, New York, [Fox 88c].

Williams 87   Williams, R. D. 1987, "Dynamical Grid Optimization for Lagrangian Hydrodynamics." Caltech report C^3P-424.

Williams 88a   Williams, R. D. 1988, "DIME: A Programming Environment for Unstructured Triangular Meshes on a Distributed-Memory Parallel Processor." In *Proceedings of the Third Conference on Hypercube Concurrent Computers and Applications*, edited by G. C. Fox, published by ACM, New York, [Fox 88c]. Caltech report C^3P-502.

Williams 88c   Williams, R. D. 1988, "Free-Lagrange Hydrodynamics with a Distributed Memory Parallel Processor." *Parallel Computing*, **7**:439.

Williams 89b   Williams, R. D. 1989, "Supersonic Flow in Parallel with an Unstructured Mesh." to be published in *Concurrency: Practice and Experience*, Caltech report C^3P-636b.

Wilson 88 Wilson, M. A., and Bower, J. M. 1988, "A Computer Simulation of the Olfactory Cortex with Functional Implications for Storage and Retrieval of Olfactory Information." In *Proceedings of the IEEE Conference on Neural Information Processing Systems*, AIP Press, New York.

Wolfram 86 Wolfram, S. 1986, "Cellular Automaton Fluids 1: Basic Theory." *J. Stat. Phys.*, **45**:471.

Wu 89a Wu, E.-S., Calahan, D. A., and Wesley, R. 1989, "Performance Analysis and Projections for a Massively-Parallel Navier-Stokes Implementation," to be published in *Proceedings of the Fourth Conference on Hypercube Concurrent Computers and Applications*, March 6–8, 1989, Monterey, CA, edited by J. L. Gustafson.

Zenios 88 Zenios, S. A., and Lasken, R. A. 1988, "The Connection Machines CM-1 and CM-2: Solving Nonlinear Network Problems." In *Proceedings of the 1988 International Conference on Supercomputing*, July 4–8, St. Malo, France, pp. 648–658, published by ACM, 11 West 42nd Street, New York 10036.

Zhang 89 Zhang, X., Byrd, R. H., and Schnabel, R. B. 1989, "Solving Nonlinear Block Bordered Circuit Equations on a Hypercube Multiprocessor," to be published in *Proceedings of the Fourth Conference on Hypercube Concurrent Computers and Applications*, March 6–8, 1989, Monterey, CA, edited by J. L. Gustafson.

Zima 88 Zima, H. P., Bast, H. J., and Gerndt, M. 1988, "SUPERB: A Tool for Semi-Automatic MIMD/SIMD Parallelization." *Parallel Computing*, **6**:1.

A

Appendix A:
C Application Programs

This appendix lists the C source code for the application programs described in Chapter 8. Most of the algorithms are also dealt with in Volume 1. Although a reasonable effort has been made to ensure that the code is correct and reliable, there are, no doubt, bugs. If you encounter any bugs, or have constructive suggestions for improving the code, please write to the address given in Appendix G. When filing a bug report, please give full details of the problem and the input data.

A-1 A Library of Commonly Used Routines

A-1.1 Program Listings

```
int add_double(d1,d2,size)
double *d1,*d2;
int size;
{
    *d1 += *d2;

    return 0;
}


/*********************** end of routine add_double ************************/

int add_int(i1,i2,size)
int *i1,*i2,size;
{
    *i1 += *i2;

    return 0;
}


/************************ end of routine add_int ************************/

#include <stdio.h>

#define MINBUF 128
extern int std_flag,procnum;

change_buf(promptf,outf,inf,buf_flag)
FILE *promptf,*outf,*inf;
int *buf_flag;
{
    static char *IO_buf;
    char *malloc();
    int buf_size,check,add_int();

    for(;;){
        fprintf(promptf,"\n\nPlease give the size of the buffer ==> ");
        if(std_flag) fflush(stdout);
        fscanf(inf,"%d",&buf_size);

        if(buf_size<MINBUF){
            printf("\n\n**** Buffer must be >= %d bytes ****\n",
                    MINBUF);
            continue;
```

```
        }

        if(*buf_flag && IO_buf!=NULL) free(IO_buf);
        IO_buf = malloc(buf_size);

        check = IO_buf==NULL ? 1 : 0;
        combine(&check,add_int,sizeof(int),1);
        if(check)
            printf("\n\n**** Unable to allocate buffer ****\n");
        else{
            setbuffer(outf,IO_buf,buf_size);
            printf("\n\n Buffer allocated successfully\n");
            *buf_flag = 1;
            break;
        }
    }
    if(std_flag || outf==stdout) fflush(stdout);
}

/*********************** end of routine change_buf ***********************/

#include <stdio.h>
extern int init_status,std_flag;

int check_init()
{
    if(!init_status){
        printf("\n\n*** You must initialize the problem first ***\n");
        if(std_flag) fflush(stdout);
        return -1;
    }
    else return 0;
}

/*********************** end of routine check_init ***********************/

#include <stdio.h>

extern int std_flag;

dw_pause()
{
    char input[5];

    for(;;){
        if(ismulti(stdout)) fsingl(stdout);
        printf("\n<<<< Please enter c to continue >>>> ==> ");
```

```
        if(std_flag) fflush(stdout);
        scanf("%s",input);
        if(input[0]=='c') break;
    }
    printf("\n");
    return;
}
```

/*********************** end of routine dw_pause ************************/

```
#include <stdio.h>
#include "cubdefs.h"

extern int std_flag;

FILE *efopen(file,mode,error_action)
char *file,*mode;
int error_action;
{
    FILE *fp,*fopen();

    if((fp = fopen(file,mode)) == (FILE *)NULL){
        fprintf(stderr,"\nCan't open %s in mode %s\n",
        file,mode);
        if(error_action==KILL_ON_ERR) exit(1);
        else if (error_action==OK_ON_ERROR){
            fp=stdin;
            printf("\n\nInput will be read from terminal\n");
        }
    }
    if(std_flag) fflush(stdout);
    return fp;
}
```

/*********************** end of routine efopen ************************/

```
#include <cros.h>

extern int procnum,doc,nproc;

get_param()
{
    struct cubenv env;

    cparam(&env);

    procnum = env.procnum;
```

```
    doc     = env.doc;
    nproc   = env.nproc;
}


/************************ end of routine get_param ************************/

#include <stdio.h>
#include "cubdefs.h"

extern int nproc,left_chan,right_chan,std_flag;

line_plot(plot_array,ntotal,max_cols,max_rows,max_val,min_val,npts,location,
        global_start,x_axis_option,plot_sym,x_off,init_flag,filename)
double plot_array[],max_val,min_val;
int ntotal,max_cols,max_rows,npts,location,x_axis_option,x_off,init_flag;
int global_start;
char plot_sym;
FILE *filename;
{
    int bufpos,arrpos,max_plot,i,j,k,nplot,n_average;
    int count,row,left_margin,nbytes,add_int();
    int first_point,point_start,actual_start,point_end,nsend,nrec,error;
    double sum,plot_val,line_width,*inbuf;
    char *malloc();
    char line[ROW_MAX][COL_MAX];

    n_average   = 1 + (ntotal-1)/max_cols;
    line_width = (max_val-min_val)/(double)max_rows;
    max_plot    = 1 + (npts-1)/n_average + x_off;

    point_start = global_start/n_average;
    actual_start = n_average*point_start;
    first_point = (global_start==actual_start) ? actual_start:actual_start
                            + n_average;
    nsend = first_point - global_start;
    error = (nsend>npts) ? 1 : 0;
    combine(&error,add_int,sizeof(int),1);
    if(error){
        printf("\n\nThe averaging process spans more than 2 processors"
                    );
        printf("\nUnable to do plot\n");
        return;
    }
    point_end = global_start + npts - 1;
    if(point_end<first_point){
        nrec  = 0;
        nplot = 0;
```

```
}
else{
    nplot = 1 + (point_end-first_point)/n_average;
    if(location==(nproc-1)) nrec = 0;
    else nrec = n_average*nplot - (point_end-first_point+1);
}

nbytes = (nrec==0) ? 1 : sizeof(double)*nrec;
inbuf = (double *)malloc(nbytes);

cshift(inbuf,right_chan,nrec*sizeof(double),plot_array,
            left_chan,nsend*sizeof(double));

left_margin = (location==0) ? x_off : 0;
if(init_flag == ZERO_OUT){
    for(i=0;i<max_rows;++i)
        for(j=0;j<max_plot;++j) line[i][j] = ' ';

    if(x_axis_option == NATURAL_ORIGIN){
        row = max_val/line_width;
        if(row>max_rows) row = max_rows;
    }
    else row = max_rows;

    for(i=0;i<nplot;++i) line[row][i+left_margin] = '-';

    if(location == 0)
        for(i=0;i<max_rows;++i) line[i][x_off] = '|';
}

bufpos = 0;
arrpos = nsend;
for(i=0;i<nplot;++i){
    count = 0;
    sum = 0.0;
    for(j=0;j<n_average;++j){
        count++;
        if(arrpos>=npts){
            if(location == (nproc-1)) break;
            sum += inbuf[bufpos++];
        }
        else sum += plot_array[arrpos++];
    }
    plot_val = sum/(double)count;
    row = (max_val - plot_val)/line_width;
    line[row][i+left_margin] = plot_sym;
}
```

```
        if(location==0) nplot += x_off;
        if(!ismulti(filename)) fmulti(filename);
        for(i=0;i<max_rows;++i){
            if(location == 0) fprintf(filename,"\n");
            for(j=0;j<nproc;++j){
                if(location == j){
                    for(k=0;k<nplot;++k)
                        fprintf(filename,"%c",line[i][k]);

                }
                fflush(filename);
            }
        }
        fsingl(filename);

        fprintf(filename,"\ny axis from %g to %g",min_val,max_val);
        nplot = 1 + (ntotal-1)/n_average;
        fprintf(filename,"     %d out of %d points plotted",nplot,ntotal);
        fflush(filename);

        free(inbuf);
        printf("  Plot done");
        if(std_flag) fflush(stdout);
}


/*********************** end of routine line_plot ************************/

int log2_next(n)
int n;
{
    int x,m;

    x = n;
    m = 0;
    while(n>1){
        m += 1;
        n /= 2;
    }
    if(x>(1<<m)) m++;
    return (m);
}


/*********************** end of routine log2_next ************************/
```

```c
int max_double(d1,d2,size)
double *d1,*d2;
int size;
{
    *d1 = (*d1 > *d2) ? *d1 : *d2;

    return 0;
}

/*********************** end of routine max_double ***********************/

int min_double(d1,d2,size)
double *d1,*d2;
int size;
{
    *d1 = (*d1 < *d2) ? *d1 : *d2;

    return 0;
}

/*********************** end of routine min_double ***********************/

#include <stdio.h>

extern int nproc,doc;
extern FILE *in_file;

set_param(node_prog,max_dims)
char *node_prog;
int max_dims;
{
    int status,ok;
    char input[10];

    ok = 0;
    while(!ok){
        printf("\n\nPlease give the dimension of the hypercube ==> ");
        fscanf(in_file,"%s",input);

        doc = atoi(input);
        if(doc>=0 &&doc<=max_dims) ok=1;
        else printf("\n\nDimension must be between 0 and %2d",max_dims);
    }

    nproc   = 1<<doc;
    printf("\n\nBeginning download...\n\n");
```

```
        cubeld(doc,node_prog);
        printf("\n...download completed");
        printf("\n\nA hypercube of dimension %d is running (%d processors)\n",
                   doc,nproc);
}

/************************** end of routine set_param *************************/

#include <stdio.h>
#include "cubdefs.h"

FILE *setup_in(chrstr)
char chrstr[];
{
        char filename[40];
        FILE *efopen();

        getchar();
        printf("\nPlease give the name of the input file %s ",chrstr);
        printf("\n(default = screen) ==> ");
        gets(filename);

        if(strcmp("SCREEN",filename)==0||strcmp("screen",filename)==0||
                     filename[0]=='\n'||filename[0]=='\0')
            return stdin;
        else
            return efopen(filename,"r",OK_ON_ERROR);
}

/************************** end of routine setup_in *************************/

#include <stdio.h>
#include "cubdefs.h"

extern int file_status,std_flag;
extern FILE *in_file;

FILE *setup_out(safe_file)
char *safe_file;
{
        FILE *efopen(),*fptr;
        int i;
        char filename[40];

        getchar();
        for(;;){
        printf("\n\nPlease give the name of the output file <screen> ==> ");
```

```
            if(std_flag) fflush(stdout);
            fgets(filename,40,in_file);
            if(filename[0]=='\n'||filename[0]=='\0'){
                fptr = stdout;
                break;
            }
            for(i=0;filename[i]!='\n';++i) continue;
            filename[i] = '\0';
            if(strcmp("screen",filename)==0||strcmp("SCREEN",filename)==0){
                fptr = stdout;
                break;
            }
            else{
                if(strcmp(safe_file,filename)==0){
                    printf("\n\n%s is a protected file and ");
                    printf("cannot be used\n",filename);
                    if(std_flag) fflush(stdout);
                }
                else{
                  fptr = efopen(filename,"w",OK_ON_ERROR);
                  if(fptr != (FILE *)NULL){
                    file_status = OPEN;
                    printf("\n\n%s opened successfully\n",filename);
                    break;
                  }
                }
            }
        }
        if(std_flag) fflush(stdout);
        return fptr;
    }


    /*********************** end of routine setup_out ***********************/
```

A-1.2 Include File cubdefs.h

```
    #define SINGLE 0
    #define MULTI  1
    #define KILL_ON_ERR 0
    #define OK_ON_ERROR 1
    #define OPEN   0
    #define CLOSED 1
    #define ZERO_OUT    0
    #define NATURAL_ORIGIN 0
    #define ROW_MAX 21
    #define COL_MAX 80
```

A-2 The One-Dimensional Wave Equation: CPNODE Version

A-2.1 CP Program

```c
#include <stdio.h>
#include <cros.h>
#include "cubdefs.h"
#include "wavedef.h"

int doc,my_position,left_chan,right_chan,nproc,nprocs;
int n,nmax,ntot,file_status,init_status,std_flag;
double values[MAX_TOT];
FILE *in_file,*out_file,*save_out,*efopen();

main(argc,argv)
int argc;
char *argv[];
{
    int len,task,get_task();

    welcome();

    file_status = CLOSED;
    init_status = 0;

    if(argc == 1) in_file = stdin;
    else if((in_file = efopen(argv[1],"r",KILL_ON_ERR))==(FILE *)NULL){
        printf("\n\nProgram terminated\n\n");
        exit(1);
    }

    set_param("waveNODE",MAX_DIM);
    nprocs = nproc;

    setup_IH();

    while((task=get_task()) != STOP){
        switch(task){
            case INITIALIZE:
                initialize(&len);
                break;
            case UPDATE:
                do_steps();
                break;
            case OUTPUT:
                output_results(len);
                break;
```

```
            }
        }
        fprintf(out_file,"\nFinished\n");
        if(file_status == OPEN && out_file != stdout) fclose(out_file);
        exit(0);
    }


/**************************** end of routine main ****************************/
    int do_steps()
    {
        int nstep,check;
        char input[5];

        if(check_init()<0) return -1;

        for(;;){
            printf("\n\nPlease give the number of time steps ==> ");
            fscanf(in_file,"%s",input);
            nstep = atoi(input);
            if(nstep>=0) break;
            else printf("\n**** Invalid input - try again ****\n");
        }

        bcastcp(&nstep,sizeof(int));

        combcp(&check,sizeof(int),1);

        if(!check){
            printf("\n\n%d updates completed",nstep);
            return 0;
        }
        else return -1;
    }


/************************** end of routine do_steps **************************/
    int get_task()
    {
        int task;
        char input[40];

        for(;;){
            printf("\n\nPlease select one of the following :\n");
            printf(  "\n    1...to initialize a new problem");
            printf(  "\n    2...to do some updates");
            printf(  "\n    3...to output solution");
            printf(  "\n    4...to terminate program");
            printf("\n\n==> ");
```

```
        fscanf(in_file,"%s",input);

        task = atoi(input);

        printf("\n");
        if(task>0 && task<5) break;
        else printf("\n**** Invalid input - please try again ****\n");
    }
    bcastcp(&task,sizeof(int));

    return task;
}


/*********************** end of routine get_task ***********************/
get_values(max_bytes)
int max_bytes;
{
    int i,j,k,length,bufmap[1+MAX_PROCS];
    double *valbuf;
    char *malloc();

    valbuf = (double *)malloc(max_bytes);

    for(i=0,k=0;i<nprocs;++i){
        combcp(&length,sizeof(int),1);
        mdumpcp(valbuf,max_bytes,bufmap);
        for(j=0;j<length;++j,++k) values[k] = valbuf[j];
    }
    free(valbuf);
}


/*********************** end of routine get_values ***********************/
initialize(len)
int *len;
{
    double x,sin(),a,delt;
    int i,j,k,npts,periods,init_config;
    char input[10];

    for(;;){
        printf("\n\nDo you want the initial shape of the string to be :\n");
        printf("\n    1...a sine wave\n    2...a plucked string\n\n==> ");
        fscanf(in_file,"%s",input);

        init_config = atoi(input);
        if(init_config>0 && init_config<3) break;
```

```
            else printf("\n\n**** Invalid input - please try again ****\n");
    }
    bcastcp(&init_config,sizeof(int));

    for(;;){
        printf("\n\nPlease give the number of points ==> ");
        fscanf(in_file,"%s",input);
        ntot = atoi(input);
        if(ntot > MAX_TOT)
            printf("\n\n**** Too many points ****\n");
        else if(ntot<nprocs)
            printf("\n\n**** Too few points ****\n");
        else{
            n    = ntot/nprocs;
            nmax = n+1;
            if(nmax <= MAX_POINTS) break;
            else printf("\n\n**** Unable to allocate storage ****\n");
        }
    }
    bcastcp(&ntot,sizeof(int));

    if(init_config == SINE){
        printf("\n\nPlease give the integer number of periods on the ");
        printf("string ==> ");
        fscanf(in_file,"%d",&periods);
        bcastcp(&periods,sizeof(int));
    }
    else{
        printf("\n\nPlease give the point at which the string is ");
        printf("plucked (between 0 and 1) ==> ");
        fscanf(in_file,"%lf",&a);
        if(a<0.0||a>1.0) a = 0.5;
        bcastcp(&a,sizeof(double));
    }

    printf("\n\nPlease give the time advance parameter, tau ==> ");
    fscanf(in_file,"%lf",&delt);
    bcastcp(&delt,sizeof(double));

    init_status = 1;
}

/*********************** end of routine initialize ************************/
output_results(len)
int len;
{
    int i,j,k,npts,output_type;
```

```
        char input[40];
        FILE *setup_out();

        if(check_init()<0) return;

        for(;;){
            printf("\n\nPlease select type of output :\n");
            printf( "\n     1...numbers to screen");
            printf( "\n     2...plot string on screen");
            printf( "\n     3...dump numbers to file");
            printf( "\n     4...plot string in file\n\n==> ");

            fscanf(in_file,"%s",input);
            printf("\n");

            output_type = atoi(input);
            if(output_type>0 && output_type<5) break;
            else printf("\n**** Invalid input - please try again ****\n");
        }

        if(output_type==3 || output_type==4){
            if(file_status==CLOSED)
                out_file = save_out = setup_out("waveCP.c");
            else out_file = save_out;
        }
        else out_file = stdout;

        get_values(nmax*sizeof(double));

        fprintf(out_file,"\n");
        if(output_type==1 || output_type==3){
            for(i=0;i<ntot;++i)
                fprintf(out_file,"%7.4f%c",values[i],(i%10==9) ? '\n' : ' ');
        }
        fprintf(out_file,"\n");
        if(output_type==2 || output_type==4) plot_results(ntot);
}

/********************* end of routine output_results *********************/
plot_results(len)
int len;
{
        int global_start;
        char plot_sym;

        plot_sym = '*';
        global_start = my_position*n;
```

```
        line_plot(values,ntot,72,21,1.0,-1.0,len,my_position,global_start,
                  NATURAL_ORIGIN,plot_sym,1,ZERO_OUT,out_file);
        if(out_file == stdout) dw_pause();
        else fprintf(out_file,"\n");
    }


/*********************** end of routine plot_results **********************/
setup_IH()
{
    nproc = 1;
    my_position = 0;
    left_chan   = 0;
    right_chan  = 0;
}


/************************** end of routine setup_IH *************************/
welcome()
{
    printf("\n\n        ******************************************** ");
    printf(  "\n        *                                          * ");
    printf(  "\n        *    Welcome to the concurrent version of   * ");
    printf(  "\n        *    the wave equation solver. This program * ");
    printf(  "\n        *    solves the wave equation on a string   * ");
    printf(  "\n        *    fixed at both ends.                     * ");
    printf(  "\n        *                                          * ");
    printf(  "\n        ******************************************** ");
    printf("\n");
}


/************************** end of routine welcome *************************/
```

A-2.2   NODE Program

```
    #include <cros.h>
    #include "wavedef.h"

    int nproc,doc,procnum;
    int chan_mask,my_bytes,my_position,left_chan,right_chan;
    int n,nmax,ntot,init_status;
    double values[MAX_POINTS+2],oldval[MAX_POINTS+2],newval[MAX_POINTS+2];

    main()
    {
        int len,task,get_task();
        double delt;
```

```
        init_status = 0;

        get_param();

        decompose();

        while((task=get_task()) != STOP){
            switch(task){
                case INITIALIZE:
                    initialize(&len,&delt);
                    break;
                case UPDATE:
                    do_steps(len,delt);
                    break;
                case OUTPUT:
                    output_results(len);
                    break;
            }
        }
}

/*************************** end of routine main ***************************/
decompose()
{
    gridinit(1,&nproc);
    gridcoord(procnum,&my_position);
    left_chan  = gridchan(procnum,0,-1);
    right_chan = gridchan(procnum,0,1);
    if(my_position == 0)left_chan = 0;
    if(my_position == (nproc-1))right_chan = 0;

}

/************************* end of routine decompose ************************/
int do_steps(len,del)
double del;
int len;
{
    double c,delx,pfac;
    int i,j,size,nstep,check,add_int();

    if(!init_status) return;

    bcastelt(&nstep,sizeof(int));

    c = 1.0;
    delx = 1.0;
```

```
        pfac =c*del/delx;
        pfac *= pfac;

        size = sizeof(double);

        for(i=0;i<nstep;++i){

            cshift(&values[0],left_chan,size,&values[len],right_chan,size);
            cshift(&values[len+1],right_chan,size,&values[1],left_chan,size);

            for(j=1;j<=len;++j){
                if(my_position==0 && j==1) newval[j] = 0.0;
                else if(my_position==(nproc-1) && j==len) newval[j] = 0.0;
            else newval[j] = 2.0*values[j]-oldval[j]+
                    (values[j-1]-2.0*values[j]+values[j+1])*pfac;
            }

            for(j=1;j<=len;++j){
              oldval[j] = values[j];
                values[j] = newval[j];
                }
        }
        check = 0;
        combelt(&check,add_int,sizeof(int),1);
}

/************************* end of routine do_steps *************************/
int get_task()
{
        int task;

        bcastelt(&task,sizeof(int));

        return task;
}

/************************* end of routine get_task *************************/
initialize(len,delt)
int *len;
double *delt;
{
        double x,sin(),a,disp,fac;
        int i,j,k,npts,periods,init_config;

        bcastelt(&init_config,sizeof(int));
        bcastelt(&ntot,sizeof(int));
```

```
n    = ntot/nproc;
nmax = n+1;

if(init_config == SINE) bcastelt(&periods,sizeof(int));
else{
    bcastelt(&a,sizeof(double));
    disp = 1.0;
}

fac = 2.0*PI*periods;
for(i=0,k=0;i<nproc;++i){
    npts = (i < ntot%nproc) ? nmax : n;
    for(j=1;j<=npts;++j,++k){
        if(my_position==i){
            *len = npts;
            x = (double)k/(double)(ntot-1);
            if(init_config==SINE) values[j] = sin(fac*x);
            else{
                if(a==0) values[j] = disp*(1.0-x);
                else if(a==1) values[j] = disp*x;
                else{
                    if(x<a) values[j] = disp*x/a;
                    else values[j] = disp*(1.0-x)/(1.0-a);
                }
            }
        }
    }
}
for(i=1;i<=*len;++i) oldval[i]=values[i];

bcastelt(delt,sizeof(double));

init_status = 1;
}

/*********************** end of routine initialize ***********************/
output_results(len)
int len;
{
    int i,msend,nsend,nbytes,add_int();

    if(!init_status) return;

    for(i=0;i<nproc;++i){
        msend = nsend = i==my_position ? len : 0;
        combelt(&nsend,add_int,sizeof(int),1);
        nbytes = msend*sizeof(double);
```

```
            dumpelt(&values[1],nbytes);
        }
    }
```

/*********************** end of routine output_results ***********************/

A-2.3 Include File wavedef.h

```
#define MAX_POINTS 500
#define INITIALIZE   1
#define UPDATE       2
#define OUTPUT       3
#define STOP         4
#define SINE         1
#define PLUCKED      2
#define MAX_DIM     10
#define MAX_PROCS 1024
#define MAX_BUFF    33
#define PI    3.1415926
#define MAX_TOT    1500
```

A-3 The One-Dimensional Wave Equation: CUBIX Version

```c
#include <cros.h>
#include <stdio.h>
#include "cubdefs.h"
#include "wavedef.h"

int nproc,doc,procnum;
int chan_mask,my_bytes,my_position,left_chan,right_chan;
int n,nmax,ntot,file_status,std_flag=0,file_flag=0,init_status;
double values[MAX_POINTS+2],oldval[MAX_POINTS+2],newval[MAX_POINTS+2];
FILE *pfile,*save_out,*in_file,*out_file,*efopen();

main(argc,argv)
int argc;
char *argv[];
{
    int len,task,get_task();
    double delt;

    pfile = stdout;

    welcome();

    file_status = CLOSED;
    init_status = 0;

    fsingl(stdout);

    if(argc == 1) in_file = stdin;
    else          in_file = efopen(argv[1],"r",KILL_ON_ERR);

    get_param();

    decompose();

    while((task=get_task()) != STOP){
        switch(task){
            case INITIALIZE:
                initialize(&len,&delt);
                break;
            case UPDATE:
                do_steps(len,delt);
                break;
            case OUTPUT:
                output_results(len);
```

```
                    break;
            }
    }
    fprintf(out_file,"\nFinished\n");
    if(file_status == OPEN && out_file != stdout) fclose(out_file);
    exit(0);
}


/*************************** end of routine main ***************************/
decompose()
{
    gridinit(1,&nproc);
    gridcoord(procnum,&my_position);
    left_chan  = gridchan(procnum,0,-1);
    right_chan = gridchan(procnum,0,1);
    if(my_position == 0)left_chan = 0;
    if(my_position == (nproc-1))right_chan = 0;


}


/************************* end of routine decompose ************************/
int do_steps(len,del)
double del;
int len;
{
    double c,delx,pfac;
    int i,j,size,check,nstep,add_int();

    if (check_init()<0) return -1;

    printf("\n\nPlease give the number of time steps ==> ");
    if(std_flag) fflush(stdout);
    fscanf(in_file,"%d",&nstep);

    c = 1.0;
    delx = 1.0;

    pfac =c*del/delx;
    pfac *= pfac;

    size = sizeof(double);

    for(i=0;i<nstep;++i){
        cshift(&values[0],left_chan,size,&values[len],right_chan,size);
        cshift(&values[len+1],right_chan,size,&values[1],left_chan,size);
        for(j=1;j<=len;++j){
            if(my_position==0 && j==1) newval[j] = 0.0;
```

```
                else if(my_position==(nproc-1) && j==len) newval[j] = 0.0;
                else newval[j] = 2.0*values[j]-oldval[j]+
                            (values[j-1]-2.0*values[j]+values[j+1])*pfac;
        }

        for(j=1;j<=len;++j){
            oldval[j] = values[j];
            values[j] = newval[j];
        }
    }
    check = 0;
    combine(&check,add_int,sizeof(int),1);
    if(!check){
        printf("\n\n%d updates completed",nstep);
        if(std_flag) fflush(stdout);
        return 0;
    }
    else return -1;
}


/************************ end of routine do_steps ************************/
int get_task()
{
    int task,atoi();
    char input[40];

    for(;;){
        printf("\n\nPlease select one of the following :\n");
        printf( "\n   1...to initialize a new problem");
        printf( "\n   2...to do some updates");
        printf( "\n   3...to output solution");
        printf( "\n   4...to terminate program");
        printf("\n\n==> ");
        if(std_flag) fflush(stdout);

        fscanf(in_file,"%s",input);
        task = atoi(input);

        printf("\n");
        if(task>0 && task<5) break;
        else printf("\n**** Invalid input - please try again ****\n");
    }

    return task;
}


/************************ end of routine get_task ************************/
```

```c
initialize(len,delt)
int *len;
double *delt;
{
    double x,sin(),a,disp,fac;
    int i,j,k,npts,periods,init_config;
    char input[10];

    for(;;){
       printf("\n\nDo you want the initial shape of the string to be :\n");
       printf("\n    1...a sine wave\n    2...a plucked string\n\n==> ");
       if(std_flag) fflush(stdout);
       fscanf(in_file,"%s",input);

       init_config = atoi(input);
       if(init_config>0 && init_config<3) break;
       else printf("\n\n**** Invalid input - please try again ****\n");
    }

    for(;;){
        printf("\n\nPlease give the number of points ==> ");
        if(std_flag) fflush(stdout);
        fscanf(in_file,"%d",&ntot);

        n    = ntot/nproc;
        nmax = n+1;
        if(ntot<nproc) printf("\n\n*** Too few points ***\n");
        else if(nmax <= MAX_POINTS) break;
        else printf("\n\n**** Unable to allocate storage ****\n");
    }

    if(init_config == SINE){
        printf("\n\nPlease give the integer number of periods on the ");
        printf("string ==> ");
        if(std_flag) fflush(stdout);
        fscanf(in_file,"%d",&periods);
    }
    else{
        printf("\n\nPlease give the point at which the string is ");
        printf("plucked (between 0 and 1) ==> ");
        if(std_flag) fflush(stdout);
        fscanf(in_file,"%lf",&a);
        disp = 1.0;
        if(a<0.0 || a>1.0) a = 0.5;
    }

    fac = 2.0*PI*periods;
```

```
        for(i=0,k=0;i<nproc;++i){
            npts = (i < ntot%nproc) ? nmax : n;
            for(j=1;j<=npts;++j,++k){
                if(my_position==i){
                    *len = npts;
                    x = (double)k/(double)(ntot-1);
                    if(init_config==SINE) values[j] = sin(fac*x);
                    else{
                        if(a==0) values[j] = disp*(1.0-x);
                        else if(a==1) values[j] = disp*x;
                        else{
                          if(x<a) values[j] = disp*x/a;
                          else values[j] = disp*(1.0-x)/(1.0-a);
                        }
                    }
                }
            }
        }
    }

        for(i=1;i<=*len;++i) oldval[i]=values[i];

        printf("\n\nPlease give the time advance parameter, tau ==> ");
        if(std_flag) fflush(stdout);
        fscanf(in_file,"%lf",delt);

        init_status = 1;
}

/*********************** end of routine initialize ***********************/
output_results(len)
int len;
{
    int i,j,k,npts,output_type,maxi;
    char input[40];
    FILE *setup_out();

    if(check_init()<0) return;

    for(;;){
        printf("\n\nPlease select type of output :\n");
        printf( "\n     1...numbers to screen");
        printf( "\n     2...plot string on screen");
        printf( "\n     3...dump numbers to file");
        printf( "\n     4...plot string in file");
        printf( "\n     5...change buffer size for terminal output");
        printf( "\n     6...change buffer size for file output\n\n==> ");
        if(std_flag) fflush(stdout);
```

```
            fscanf(in_file,"%s",input);
            printf("\n");

            output_type = atoi(input);

            if(output_type==5) change_buf(stdout,stdout,in_file,&std_flag);
            else if(output_type==6){
                    if(file_status==CLOSED)
                            save_out = out_file = setup_out("waveCUB.c");
                    change_buf(stdout,out_file,in_file,&file_flag);
            }
            maxi = 7;
            if(output_type>0 && output_type<maxi) break;
            else printf("\n**** Invalid input - please try again ****\n");
    }

    if(output_type==3 || output_type==4){
            if(file_status==CLOSED)
                    save_out = out_file = setup_out("waveCUB.c");
            else out_file = save_out;
    }
    else out_file = stdout;

    if(output_type==1 || output_type==3){
            fmulti(out_file);

            for(k=0,i=0;i<nproc;++i){
                    npts = (i < ntot%nproc) ? nmax : n;
                    for(j=1;j<=npts;++j,++k){
                            if(my_position == i)
                                    fprintf(out_file,"%7.4f%c",values[j],
                                                        (k%10==9) ? '\n' : ' ');
                    }
                    fflush(out_file);
            }
    }
    if(output_type==2 || output_type==4) plot_results(len);
    fsingl(out_file);
}

/********************* end of routine output_results ***********************/
plot_results(len)
int len;
{
    int gtemp,global_start;
    char plot_sym;
```

```
    plot_sym = '*';
    gtemp        = my_position*n;
    global_start = my_position < ntot%nproc ? my_position+gtemp :
                          gtemp + ntot%nproc;

    line_plot(&values[1],ntot,72,21,1.0,-1.0,len,my_position,global_start,
              NATURAL_ORIGIN,plot_sym,1,ZERO_OUT,out_file);
    if(out_file == stdout) dw_pause();
    else fprintf(out_file,"\n");
}

/*********************** end of routine plot_results ************************/
welcome()
{
    printf("\n\n        ******************************************** ");
    printf(  "\n        *                                          * ");
    printf(  "\n        *    Welcome to the wave equation program.  * ");
    printf(  "\n        *    This program solves the wave equation  * ");
    printf(  "\n        *    on a string fixed at both ends.        * ");
    printf(  "\n        *                                          * ");
    printf(  "\n        ******************************************** ");
    printf("\n");
}


/************************* end of routine welcome *************************/
```

A-4 The Laplace Equation and the Finite Difference Method

A-4.1 CUBIX Program

```c
#include <cros.h>
#include <stdio.h>
#include "sordef.h"
#include "cubdefs.h"

#define min(A,B) ((A) < (B) ? (A) : (B))

int nproc,doc,procnum;
double values[MAX_SIZE+2][MAX_SIZE+2],omega,val_min,val_max,val_step;
int nx,ny,nprocx,nprocy,left_chan,right_chan,up_chan,down_chan,my_posit[2];
int nxpts,nypts,left_pts,right_pts,top_pts,bottom_pts,nxtot,nytot;
int use_status,ybytes,xbytes,file_status,niter,std_flag=0,init_status;
short ibc[MAX_SIZE+2][MAX_SIZE+2];
FILE *in_file;

main()
{
    int command,cycles;

    in_file    = stdin;
    file_status = CLOSED;
    init_status = 0;

    get_param();

    decompose();

    while( (command=get_task()) != STOP ){
        switch(command){
            case INITIALIZE:
                initialize();
                break;
            case UPDATE :
                cycles = get_cycles();
                update_sor(cycles);
                break;
            case OUTPUT:
                output_results();
                break;
            case QUERY:
                list_menu();
                break;
            case WRONG:
```

```
                        printf("\n**** Unrecognized command ****\n");
                        break;
                }
        }
        printf("\n\nFinished\n");
        exit(0);
}


/*************************** end of routine main ***************************/
clean_up(buffer,direction,color)
int direction,color;
double buffer[];
{
        int i,offset,npts;

        switch(direction){
            case LEFT:
                if(color==RED){
                        offset = 0;
                        npts   = bottom_pts;
                }
                else{
                        offset = bottom_pts;
                        npts   = top_pts;
                }
                for(i=1;i<=npts;++i)
                        values[i+offset][0] = buffer[i-1];
                break;
            case RIGHT:
                if(color==RED){
                        offset = bottom_pts;
                        npts   = top_pts;
                }
                else{
                        offset = 0;
                        npts   = bottom_pts;
                }
                for(i=1;i<=npts;++i)
                        values[i+offset][nxpts+1] = buffer[i-1];
                break;
            case BOTTOM:
                if(color==RED){
                        offset = 0;
                        npts   = left_pts;
                }
                else{
                        offset = left_pts;
```

```
                    npts    = right_pts;
              }
              for(i=1;i<=npts;++i)
                    values[0][i+offset] = buffer[i-1];
              break;
         case TOP:
              if(color==RED){
                    offset = left_pts;
                    npts    = right_pts;
              }
              else{
                    offset = 0;
                    npts    = left_pts;
              }
              for(i=1;i<=npts;++i)
                    values[nypts+1][i+offset] = buffer[i-1];
              break;
    }
}

/************************* end of routine clean_up *************************/
decompose()
{
    int i,j,k,num[2],status,logx,logy,log2_next();
    char active[10],dead[10];

    strcpy(active,"used");
    strcpy(dead,"not used");

    status = 0;
    while(!status){
         if(nproc>1){
              printf("\nNumber of processors in the x-direction ==> ");
              scanf("%d",&nprocx);
              printf("\nNumber of processors in the y-direction ==> ");
              scanf("%d",&nprocy);
              printf("\n");
         }
         else{
              nprocx = 1;
              nprocy = 1;
         }
         logx = log2_next(nprocx);
         logy = log2_next(nprocy);
         if((1<<(logx+logy))>nproc)
              printf("\nToo many processors specified\n");
         else
```

```
            status = 1;
    }
    nx = 1<<logx;
    ny = 1<<logy;
    while(nx*ny != nproc) nx *= 2;

    num[0] = ny;
    num[1] = nx;
    gridinit(2,num);

    gridcoord(procnum,my_posit);
    if(my_posit[1]>(nprocx-1) || my_posit[0]>(nprocy-1))
            use_status = NOT_USED;
    else  use_status = USED;

    left_chan   = gridchan(procnum,1,-1);
    right_chan  = gridchan(procnum,1, 1);
    down_chan   = gridchan(procnum,0,-1);
    up_chan     = gridchan(procnum,0, 1);

    if(my_posit[1]==0)           left_chan = 0;
    if(my_posit[1]==(nprocx-1)) right_chan = 0;
    if(my_posit[0]==0)           down_chan = 0;
    if(my_posit[0]==(nprocy-1))    up_chan = 0;

    if(nproc==1) return;

    fmulti(stdout);
    for(i=0,k=0;i<ny;++i){
        for(j=0;j<nx;++j,++k){
            if((i==my_posit[0])&&(j==my_posit[1])){
                printf("\nLocation (%d,%d) is processor %2d",
                    i,j,procnum);
                printf(" %8s",use_status==USED ? active:dead);
            }
            if(k%20==19||(i==(ny-1)&&j==(nx-1))){
                fsingl(stdout);
                dw_pause();
                fmulti(stdout);
            }
            fflush(stdout);
        }
    }

    fsingl(stdout);
}
```

```c
/************************* end of routine decompose *************************/
int get_cycles()
{
    int cycles;

    printf("\n\nPlease give the number of update cycles ==> ");
    scanf("%d",&cycles);

    return cycles;
}

/************************* end of routine get_cycles *************************/
get_edge(buf,color)
double buf[];
int color;
{
    get_ready(buf,LEFT,color);
    cshift(buf,right_chan,ybytes,buf,left_chan,ybytes);
    clean_up(buf,RIGHT,color);

    get_ready(buf,RIGHT,color);
    cshift(buf,left_chan,ybytes,buf,right_chan,ybytes);
    clean_up(buf,LEFT,color);

    get_ready(buf,TOP,color);
    cshift(buf,down_chan,xbytes,buf,up_chan,ybytes);
    clean_up(buf,BOTTOM,color);

    get_ready(buf,BOTTOM,color);
    cshift(buf,up_chan,xbytes,buf,down_chan,ybytes);
    clean_up(buf,TOP,color);
}

/************************* end of routine get_edge *************************/
int get_level(xval)
double xval;
{
    int result;

    result = (int)((xval-val_min)/val_step);
    result = result>15 ? 15 : result;
    result = result<0  ?  0 : result;

    return result;
}

/************************* end of routine get_level *************************/
```

```
get_ready(buffer,direction,color)
int direction,color;
double buffer[];
{
    int i,npts,offset;

    switch(direction){
        case LEFT:
            if(color==RED){
                offset = bottom_pts;
                npts   = top_pts;
            }
            else{
                offset = 0;
                npts   = bottom_pts;
            }
            for(i=1;i<=npts;++i)
                buffer[i-1] = values[i+offset][1];
            break;
        case RIGHT:
            if(color==RED){
                offset = 0;
                npts   = bottom_pts;
            }
            else{
                offset = bottom_pts;
                npts   = top_pts;
            }
            for(i=1;i<=npts;++i)
                buffer[i-1] = values[i+offset][nxpts];
            break;
        case BOTTOM:
            if(color==RED){
                offset = left_pts;
                npts   = right_pts;
            }
            else{
                offset = 0;
                npts   = left_pts;
            }
            for(i=1;i<=npts;++i)
                buffer[i-1] = values[1][i+offset];
            break;
        case TOP:
            if(color==RED){
                offset = 0;
                npts   = left_pts;
```

```
                    }
                    else{
                        offset = left_pts;
                        npts   = right_pts;
                    }
                    for(i=1;i<=npts;++i)
                        buffer[i-1] = values[nypts][i+offset];
                    break;
            }
    }

/************************* end of routine get_ready *************************/
int get_task()
{
    char ctemp[4];

    printf("\nPlease input command or ? ==> ");
    scanf("%s",ctemp);

    if(ctemp[0]=='i'||ctemp[0]=='I') return INITIALIZE;
    else if(ctemp[0]=='u'||ctemp[0]=='U') return UPDATE;
    else if(ctemp[0]=='o'||ctemp[0]=='O') return OUTPUT;
    else if(ctemp[0]=='s'||ctemp[0]=='S') return STOP;
    else if(ctemp[0]=='?')return QUERY;
    else return WRONG;
}

/************************* end of routine get_task *************************/
initialize()
{
    int i,j,nbc,ftype,xhalf,yhalf;
    int irow,icol,row,col,row_local,col_local;
    double left_edge,right_edge,bottom_edge,top_edge,bval;
    FILE *file_in,*setup_in();

    for(;;){
        printf("\nPlease give the number of points per processor ");
        printf("in the x direction ==> ");
        scanf("%d",&nxpts);

        printf("\nPlease give the number of points per processor ");
        printf("in the y direction ==> ");
        scanf("%d",&nypts);

        if(nxpts>=2 && nxpts<=MAX_SIZE && nypts>=2 && nypts<=MAX_SIZE)
            break;
        else
```

```
                  printf("\n\n**** Invalid number of points ****");
     }

     nxtot = nxpts*nprocx;
     nytot = nypts*nprocy;
     xbytes = nxpts*sizeof(double);
     ybytes = nypts*sizeof(double);
     niter  = 0;

     printf("\nPlease give the SOR parameter, omega ==> ");
     scanf("%lf",&omega);

     left_pts   = nxpts/2;
     right_pts  = nxpts - left_pts;
     bottom_pts = nypts/2;
     top_pts    = nypts - bottom_pts;

     for(i=1;i<=nypts;++i){
         yhalf = (i>bottom_pts) ? TOP : BOTTOM;
         for(j=1;j<=nxpts;++j){
             values[i][j] = 0.0;
             xhalf = (j>left_pts) ? RIGHT : LEFT;
             if( (xhalf==RIGHT && yhalf==BOTTOM) ||
                 (xhalf==LEFT  && yhalf==TOP) ) ibc[i][j] = BLACK;
             else ibc[i][j] = RED;
         }
     }

     file_in = setup_in("containing the boundary conditions");
     if(file_in==stdin) ftype=1;
     else ftype = 0;

     if(ftype){
         printf("\nPlease give the values on the left, right,");
         printf(" bottom and top edges ==> ");
     }
     fscanf(file_in,"%lf %lf %lf %lf",&left_edge,&right_edge,&bottom_edge,
                     &top_edge);

     if(ftype)
       printf("\nPlease give the number of fixed interior grid points ==> ");
     fscanf(file_in,"%d",&nbc);

     for(i=0;i<nbc;++i){
         if(ftype){
             printf("\nPoint %d : ",i);
             printf("Please give the column, row, and boundary value ==> ");
```

```
        }
        fscanf(file_in,"%d %d %lf",&icol,&irow,&bval);

        row = irow/nypts;
        col = icol/nxpts;
        if((my_posit[0]==row)&&(my_posit[1]==col)){
                row_local = irow - nypts*row + 1;
                col_local = icol - nxpts*col + 1;
                ibc[row_local][col_local]    = INTERIOR_BC;
                values[row_local][col_local] = bval;
        }
    }

    if(my_posit[0] == 0)
        for(i=1;i<=nxpts;++i){
                ibc[1][i]      = EDGE;
                values[1][i] = bottom_edge;
        }
    if(my_posit[0] == (nprocy-1))
        for(i=1;i<=nxpts;++i){
                ibc[nypts][i]      = EDGE;
                values[nypts][i] = top_edge;
        }
    if(my_posit[1] == 0)
        for(i=1;i<=nypts;++i){
                ibc[i][1]      = EDGE;
                values[i][1] = left_edge;
        }
    if(my_posit[1] == (nprocx-1))
        for(i=1;i<=nypts;++i){
                ibc[i][nxpts]      = EDGE;
                values[i][nxpts] = right_edge;
        }

    init_status = 1;
}

/*********************** end of routine initialize ***********************/
list_menu()
{
    printf("\nYou must input one of the following:");
        printf("\n    i...to read in bc's and initialize problem");
        printf("\n    u...to perform update cycles");
        printf("\n    o...to output results");
        printf("\n    s...to terminate program");
        printf("\n    ?...to display this message\n");
}
```

```
/*************************** end of routine list_menu **************************/
list_values(out_file)
FILE *out_file;
{
    int i,j,k,xmin,xmax,ymin,ymax,row,col,row_local,col_local,count;
    int lines,l_per_row;

    select_area(&xmin,&xmax,&ymin,&ymax);

    fmulti(out_file);

    l_per_row = (xmax-xmin)/7 + 2;
    lines = 0;

    for(i=ymin;i<=ymax;++i){
        count = xmin;
        row = i/nypts;
        row_local = i - row*nypts;
        for(j=xmin,k=0;j<=xmax;++j,++k){
            count++;
            col = j/nxpts;
            col_local = j - col*nxpts;
            if(my_posit[0]==row && my_posit[1]==col)
            out_value(i,j,k,xmin,xmax,row_local,col_local,out_file);
            if(count==nxpts){
                count = 0;
                fflush(out_file);
            }
        }
        if(count!=0) fflush(out_file);
        lines += l_per_row;
        if(out_file==stdout && lines>20 && i != ymax){
            lines = 0;
            fsingl(out_file);
            dw_pause();
            fmulti(out_file);
        }
    }
    fsingl(out_file);

    fprintf(out_file,"\nArea defined by (%d,%d) and (%d,%d)",ymin,xmin,
                ymax,xmax);
    if(out_file==stdout) dw_pause();
}


/*********************** end of routine list_values **********************/
```

```
minmax(xmin,xmax)
double *xmin,*xmax;
{
     int i,j,min_double(),max_double();
     double low,high,val;

     low  =  0.1e+30;
     high = -0.1e+30;

     if(use_status==USED){
          for(i=1;i<=nypts;++i)
               for(j=1;j<=nxpts;++j){
                    val  = values[i][j];
                    low  = (val<low)  ? val : low;
                    high = (val>high) ? val : high;
               }
     }

     *xmin = low;
     *xmax = high;

     combine(xmin,min_double,sizeof(double),1);
     combine(xmax,max_double,sizeof(double),1);
}


/************************* end of routine minmax *************************/
output_results()
{
     static FILE *out_file;
     FILE *setup_out();
     int output_type;
     char input[5];

     if(check_init()<0) return;

     if(file_status==CLOSED || out_file==stdout)
          out_file = setup_out("sorCUB.c");

     for(;;){
          printf("\nPlease select one of the following :");
          printf("\n   1...to list current values");
          printf("\n   2...to plot current values");
          printf("\n   3...to plot mesh point type");
          printf("\n   4...to quit this menu\n\n==> ");
          scanf("%s",input);

          output_type = atoi(input);
```

```
            if(output_type==1) list_values(out_file);
            else if(output_type==2 || output_type==3)
                plot_results(out_file,output_type);
            else if(output_type==4) break;
            else printf("\n\n**** Invalid input - try again ****\n");
        }
    }


/********************* end of routine output_results *********************/
    out_value(i,j,k,xmin,xmax,row_local,col_local,out_file)
    int i,j,k,xmin,xmax,row_local,col_local;
    FILE *out_file;
    {
        if(j==xmin) fprintf(out_file,"Row number %d\n",i);
        fprintf(out_file,"%10.4e%c", values[row_local+1][col_local+1],
                    (k%7==6 || j==xmax) ? '\n' : ' ');
    }


/************************ end of routine out_value ************************/
    plot_mesh(row_local,col_local,out_file)
    int row_local,col_local;
    FILE *out_file;
    {
        static char mesh_type[] = { ' ', 'R', 'B', 'E','\0' };
        int ival;

        ival = ibc[row_local+1][col_local+1];
        fprintf(out_file,"%c ",mesh_type[ival]);
    }


/************************ end of routine plot_mesh ************************/
    plot_results(out_file,output_type)
    FILE *out_file;
    int output_type;
    {
        int i,j,xmin,xmax,ymin,ymax,row,col,row_local,col_local,count;

        select_area(&xmin,&xmax,&ymin,&ymax);

        fmulti(out_file);

        if(output_type==2) set_up_range();

        xmax = min(xmax,SCREEN_WIDTH+xmin-1);

        for(i=ymax;i>=ymin;--i){
            count = xmin%nxpts;
```

```
            row = i/nypts;
            row_local = i-row*nypts;
            for(j=xmin;j<=xmax;++j){
                count++;
                col = j/nxpts;
                col_local = j-col*nxpts;
                if(my_posit[0]==row && my_posit[1]==col){
                    if(j==xmin) fprintf(out_file,"\n");
                    if(output_type==3)
                        plot_mesh(row_local,col_local,out_file);
                    else if(output_type==2)
                        plot_val(row_local,col_local,out_file);
                }
                if(count == nxpts){
                    count = 0;
                    fflush(out_file);
                }
            }
            if(count != 0) fflush(out_file);
        }

        fsingl(out_file);

        fprintf(out_file,"\nArea defined by (%d,%d) and (%d,%d)",ymin,xmin,
                    ymax,xmax);
        if(output_type==2){
            fprintf(out_file,"   Iteration %d",niter);
            fprintf(out_file,"\nmin = %g   max =%g   step=%g",val_min,
                val_max,val_step);
        }

        if(out_file==stdout) dw_pause();
}

/*********************** end of routine plot_results ************************/
plot_val(row_local,col_local,out_file)
int row_local,col_local;
FILE *out_file;
{
    int ival;

    ival = get_level(values[row_local+1][col_local+1]);
    fprintf(out_file,"%1x ",ival);
}


/*********************** end of routine plot_val ************************/
```

```
select_area(xmin,xmax,ymin,ymax)
int *xmin,*xmax,*ymin,*ymax;
{
    for(;;){
      printf("\nPlease give the minimum and maximum column numbers ==> ");
      scanf("%d %d",xmin,xmax);
      if( *xmin<0 || *xmax<0 ){
         *xmin = 0;
         *xmax = nxtot-1;
         break;
      }
      else if(*xmax>=nxtot || *xmin>*xmax)
         printf("\n\n**** Invalid input - try again ****\n");
         else break;
    }

    for(;;){
      printf("\nPlease give the minimum and maximum row numbers ==> ");
      scanf("%d %d",ymin,ymax);
      if( *ymin<0 || *ymax<0 ){
         *ymin = 0;
         *ymax = nytot-1;
         break;
      }
      if(*ymax>=nypts*ny || *ymin>*ymax)
         printf("\n\n**** Invalid input - try again ****\n");
      else break;
    }
}

/*********************** end of routine select_area ***********************/
set_up_range()
{
    minmax(&val_min,&val_max);

    val_step = (val_max - val_min)/16.0;

}

/********************** end of routine set_up_range **********************/
update_sor(cycles)
int cycles;
{
    int i,j,k;
    double edge_buf[MAX_SIZE],A,B,t1,t2;

    if(check_init()<0) return;
```

```
        if(use_status==NOT_USED) return ;

    A = omega/4.0;
    B = (1.0-omega);

    for(i=0;i<cycles;++i){
        niter++;

        get_edge(edge_buf,RED);
        for(j=1;j<=nypts;++j)
            for(k=1;k<=nxpts;++k){
                if(ibc[j][k]==RED){
                    t1 = values[j][k-1]+values[j-1][k];
                    t2 = values[j][k+1]+values[j+1][k];
                    values[j][k]=A*(t1+t2)+B*values[j][k];
                }
            }

        get_edge(edge_buf,BLACK);
        for(j=1;j<=nypts;++j)
            for(k=1;k<=nxpts;++k){
                if(ibc[j][k]==BLACK){
                    t1 = values[j][k-1]+values[j-1][k];
                    t2 = values[j][k+1]+values[j+1][k];
                    values[j][k]=A*(t1+t2)+B*values[j][k];
                }
            }

    }
}

/*********************** end of routine update_sor ***********************/
```

A-4.2 Include File sordef.h

```
#define INITIALIZE 1
#define UPDATE     2
#define OUTPUT     3
#define STOP       4
#define QUERY      5
#define WRONG     -99
#define MAX_PROCS 32
#define LEFT       0
#define RIGHT      1
#define BOTTOM     2
#define TOP        3
```

```
#define SIZE        4
#define USED        0
#define NOT_USED    1
#define DUMPED      0
#define NOT_DUMPED  1
#define INTERIOR_BC 0
#define RED         1
#define BLACK       2
#define EDGE        3
#define MAX_SIZE    40
#define SCREEN_WIDTH 39
```

A-5 The Laplace Equation and the Finite Element Method

A-5.1 Cubix Program

```c
#include <cros.h>
#include <stdio.h>
#include <math.h>
#define NROW  10
#define MAXNOD     (NROW+2)*(NROW+2)
#define MAXELM     (NROW+1)*(NROW+1)
#define  TRUE 1
#define  FALSE    0
int  lmask,rmask,dmask,upmask,procnum,nproc,mx,my;
float     ke[MAXNOD+1][MAXNOD+1],phi[MAXNOD+1],b[MAXNOD+1],allow;
int  edge[5][MAXELM+1],nghbor[10][MAXNOD+1],iter;
int  bnd[MAXNOD+1],yours[MAXNOD+1],intr[MAXNOD+1];


main()
{
    float     c1,c2;

    setelt();
    printf("\nNumbering elements and nodes and setting boundary values\n");
    idelem();
    c1=0.25;
    c2=0.25;
    printf("\nComputing the stiffness matrix...\n");
    stiff(c1,c2);
    printf("\nComputing the force terms...\n");
    getbnd();
    printf("\n\nHow many iterations?  ");
    scanf("%d",&iter);
    printf("Allowance?  ");
    scanf("%f",&allow);
    congra();
    printf("\n\n    Total number of iterations: %3d\n",iter);
    dump();
    printf("\n\nFinished\n\n");
    exit(0);
}


/*************************** end of routine main ***************************/
setelt()
{
    struct    cubenv env;
    int  doc,numdim[2],mypost[2],nprocx,nprocy;
```

```
        message();
        cparam(&env);
        procnum=env.procnum;
        doc=env.doc;
        nproc=env.nproc;
        nprocx=1<<(doc/2);
        nprocy=1<<(doc/2);
        numdim[0]=nprocy;
        numdim[1]=nprocx;
        gridinit(2,numdim);
        gridcoord(procnum,mypost);
        mx=mypost[1];
        my=mypost[0];
        lmask=gridchan(procnum,1,-1);
        rmask=gridchan(procnum,1,1);
        dmask=gridchan(procnum,0,1);
        upmask=gridchan(procnum,0,-1);
        if (mypost[1]==0) lmask=0;
        if (mypost[1]==nprocx-1) rmask=0;
        if (mypost[0]==0) upmask=0;
        if (mypost[0]==nprocy-1) dmask=0;
        fmulti(stdout);
        printf("            Processor %2d is working on region [X=%1d,Y=%1d]\n",
                procnum,mypost[1],mypost[0]);
        fsingl(stdout);
}


/************************* end of routine setelt *************************/
idelem()
{
    int   i,j,k,nproch,mproch,mrow;
    float    delphi,phiref;

    nproch=nproc/2;
    mproch=nproch-1;
    mrow=NROW+1;
    for(i=0;i<=MAXNOD;++i){
        phi[i] = 0.0;
        b[i]   = 0.0;
    }
    for(i=0;i<=MAXNOD;++i){
        yours[i] = FALSE;
        bnd[i]   = FALSE;
    }
    for(i=1;i<=NROW+2;++i) yours[i]=TRUE;
    for(i=MAXNOD-NROW-1;i<=MAXNOD;++i) yours[i]=TRUE;
    for(i=NROW+2;i<=MAXNOD-NROW-2;i=i+NROW+2){
```

```
            yours[i]=TRUE;
            yours[i+1]=TRUE;
      }
      for(i=1;i<=MAXELM;++i){
            j=(i-1)/mrow+i;
            k=j+mrow+1;
            edge[1][i]=j;
            edge[2][i]=j+1;
            edge[3][i]=k;
            edge[4][i]=k+1;
            nghbor[5][j]=j;
            nghbor[6][j]=j+1;
            nghbor[8][j]=k;
            nghbor[9][j]=k+1;
            nghbor[4][j+1]=j;
            nghbor[5][j+1]=j+1;
            nghbor[7][j+1]=k;
            nghbor[8][j+1]=k+1;
            nghbor[2][k]=j;
            nghbor[3][k]=j+1;
            nghbor[5][k]=k;
            nghbor[6][k]=k+1;
            nghbor[1][k+1]=j;
            nghbor[2][k+1]=j+1;
            nghbor[4][k+1]=k;
            nghbor[5][k+1]=k+1;
      }
      if(my==0){
            for(i=1;i<=NROW+2;++i){
                  bnd[i]=TRUE;
                  phi[i]=1.0;
            }
            for(i=2;i<=NROW+1;++i) yours[i]=FALSE;
            if(mx==0)
                  for(i=1;i<=MAXNOD-NROW-2;i=i+NROW+2) yours[i]=FALSE;
            if(mx==mproch)
                  for(i=NROW+2;i<=MAXNOD-NROW-2;i=i+NROW+2) yours[i]=FALSE;
      }
      if(my==mproch){
            for(i=MAXNOD-NROW-1;i<=MAXNOD;++i){
                  bnd[i]=TRUE;
                  phi[i]= -1.0;
            }
            for(i=MAXNOD-NROW;i<=MAXNOD-1;++i) yours[i]=FALSE;
            if(mx==0)
                  for(i=NROW+3;i<=MAXNOD;i=i+NROW+2) yours[i]=FALSE;
            if(mx==mproch)
```

```
                for(i=2*(NROW+2);i<=MAXNOD;i=i+NROW+2) yours[i]=FALSE;
        }
        delphi=2.0/(NROW*nproch+1);
        phiref=1.0-delphi*my*NROW;
        if(mx==0){
            for(i=1;i<=MAXNOD;i=i+NROW+2){
                bnd[i]=TRUE;
                phi[i]= -((float)(i/(NROW+2)))*delphi+phiref;
            }
            if(my!=0 || my!=mproch)
                for(i=NROW+3;i<=MAXNOD-NROW-2;i=i+NROW+2) yours[i]=FALSE;
        }
        if(mx==mproch){
            for(i=NROW+2;i<=MAXNOD;i=i+NROW+2){
                bnd[i]=TRUE;
                phi[i]= -((float)((i-1)/(NROW+2)))*delphi+phiref;
            }
            if(my!=0 || my!=mproch)
                for(i=2*(NROW+2);i<=MAXNOD-NROW-2;i=i+NROW+2) yours[i]=FALSE;
        }
}


/*************************** end of routine idelem ***************************/
stiff(c1,c2)
float   c1,c2;
{
    float   kn[5][5],xk[5],yk[5],r;
    int  i,j,k,l,id;

    xk[1]= -1.0;xk[2]=1.0;xk[3]= -1.0;xk[4]=1.0;
    yk[1]=1.0;yk[2]=1.0;yk[3]= -1.0;yk[4]= -1.0;
    r=c1/c2;
    for(i=1;i<=4;++i)
        for(j=i;j<=4;++j)
            kn[i][j]=0.25*r*xk[i]*xk[j]+0.25/r*yk[i]*yk[j]+
                        xk[i]*xk[j]*yk[i]*yk[j]*(r+1.0/r)/12.0;
    for(id=1;id<=MAXELM;++id){
        i=edge[1][id];
        j=edge[2][id];
        k=edge[3][id];
        l=edge[4][id];
        ke[i][i]=ke[i][i]+kn[1][1];
        ke[i][j]=ke[i][j]+kn[1][2];
        ke[j][i]=ke[i][j];
        ke[i][k]=ke[i][k]+kn[1][3];
        ke[k][i]=ke[i][k];
        ke[i][l]=ke[i][l]+kn[1][4];
```

```
        ke[l][i]=ke[i][l];
        ke[j][j]=ke[j][j]+kn[2][2];
        ke[j][k]=ke[j][k]+kn[2][3];
        ke[k][j]=ke[j][k];
        ke[j][l]=ke[j][l]+kn[2][4];
        ke[l][j]=ke[j][l];
        ke[k][k]=ke[k][k]+kn[3][3];
        ke[k][l]=ke[k][l]+kn[3][4];
        ke[l][k]=ke[k][l];
        ke[k][k]=ke[k][k]+kn[4][4];
    }
}


/*************************** end of routine stiff ***************************/
getbnd()
{
    int  nproch,n1,n2,i,j,k;

    nproch=nproc/2;
    n1=NROW+2;
    n2=(NROW+2)*(NROW+1);
    for(i=1;i<=MAXNOD;++i){
        if(i<=n1 || i>n2 || (i-1)%n1==0 || i%n1==0)
            intr[i]=FALSE;
        else{
            intr[i]=TRUE;
            for(k=1;k<=9;++k){
                j=nghbor[k][i];
                if(bnd[j]==TRUE) b[i]=b[i]-ke[i][j]*phi[j];
            }
        }
    }
}


/************************** end of routine getbnd **************************/
congra()
{
    float    p[MAXNOD+1],q[MAXNOD+1],r[MAXNOD+1];
    float    newnom,oldnom,alpha,beta,scalar();
    int  mrow,ilow,ihih,mstop,i,j,l,m;

    mrow=NROW+2;
    ilow=mrow+2;
    ihih=MAXNOD-mrow-1;
    mstop=iter/2;
    for(i=0;i<=MAXNOD;++i) {p[i]=q[i]=r[i]=0.0;}
    for(i=ilow;i<=ihih;++i)
```

```
            if(intr[i]==TRUE){ r[i]=b[i]; p[i]=b[i]; }

    oldnom=scalar(r,r);
    for(m=1;m<=iter;++m){
        commun(p);
        for(i=ilow;i<=ihih;++i)
            if(intr[i]==TRUE){
                q[i]=0.0;
                for(l=1;l<=9;++l){
                    j=nghbor[l][i];
                    if(j!=0 && bnd[j]==FALSE)
                        q[i]=ke[i][j]*p[j]+q[i];
                }
            }
        newnom=scalar(p,q);
        alpha=oldnom/newnom;
        for(i=ilow;i<=ihih;++i)
            if(intr[i]==TRUE){
                phi[i]=phi[i]+alpha*p[i];
                r[i]=r[i]-alpha*q[i];
            }
        newnom=scalar(r,r);
        beta=newnom/oldnom;
        if(m>=mstop && abs(newnom-oldnom)<=allow) break;
        oldnom=newnom;
        for(i=ilow;i<=ihih;++i)
            if(intr[i]==TRUE) p[i]=r[i]+beta*p[i];
    }
    if(m<iter) iter=m;
}


/*************************** end of routine congra ***************************/
int add(x,y,size)
float    *x,*y;
int size;
{
    *x += *y;
    return 0;
}


/*************************** end of routine add ***************************/
float scalar(a1,a2)
float    a1[],a2[];
{
    int add(),i,ierr;
    float    rn;
```

```
    rn=0.0;
    for(i=1;i<=MAXNOD;++i)
        if(intr[i]==TRUE) rn += a1[i]*a2[i];

    ierr=combine(&rn,add,sizeof(float),1);
    return rn;
}


/************************** end of routine scalar **************************/
commun(p)
float *p;
{
    int mrow,irow,jrow,lrow,ierr;

    mrow=NROW+2;
    irow=mrow+1;
    jrow=2*mrow;
    lrow=MAXNOD-mrow+1;
    ierr=vshift(p+irow,lmask,sizeof(float),mrow*sizeof(float),mrow,
                p+jrow-1,rmask,sizeof(float),mrow*sizeof(float),NROW);
    ierr=vshift(p+jrow,rmask,sizeof(float),mrow*sizeof(float),mrow,
                p+mrow+2,lmask,sizeof(float),mrow*sizeof(float),NROW);
    ierr=cshift(p+lrow,dmask,mrow*sizeof(float),
                p+irow,upmask,mrow*sizeof(float));
    ierr=cshift(p+1,upmask,mrow*sizeof(float),
                p+lrow-mrow,dmask,mrow*sizeof(float));
}


/************************** end of routine commun **************************/
message()
{
    printf("\n\nThis program will solve a Laplace equation in a ");
    printf("two-dimensional rectangular\nregion.\n");
}


/************************** end of routine message **************************/
dump()
{
    int mstart,mfini,myproc,j,k;

    fmulti(stdout);
    for(myproc=0;myproc<=nproc-1;++myproc){
        if(procnum==myproc)
            printf("\nProcessor #:%2d  Quadrant:[%2d,%2d]\n",
                                procnum,mx,my);
        fflush(stdout);
        for(j=2;j<=NROW-1;++j){
```

```
            mstart=(j-1)*(NROW+2)+2;
            mfini=mstart+NROW-1;
            if(procnum==myproc){
                for(k=mstart;k<=mfini;++k)
                    printf("%8.4f",phi[k]);
                printf("\n");
            }
            fflush(stdout);
        }
    }
    fsingl(stdout);
}


/*************************** end of routine dump ***************************/
```

A-6 The Long-Range Force Problem

A-6.1 CUBIX Program

```c
#include <cros.h>
#include <stdio.h>
#include "particle.h"
#include "cubdefs.h"

#define min(A,B) ((A) < (B) ? (A) : (B))

int nproc,doc,procnum;
OBJECT objarr[MAX_PARTICLES],obj_copy[MAX_PARTICLES];
int ringpos,c_clock_neigh,clock_neigh,file_status,std_flag=0,init_status;
int nleft,nmin,nlocal,ntotal;
FILE *fildat,*in_file,*out_file;

main()
{
    int command;

    in_file     = stdin;
    fildat      = stdin;
    out_file    = stdout;
    file_status = CLOSED;
    init_status = 0;

    welcome();

    get_param();

    ring_setup();

    while( (command=get_task()) != STOP ){
        switch(command){
            case INITIALIZE:
                initialize();
                break;
            case FIND_POT:
                find_potential();
                break;
            case FIND_FORCE:
                lr_force(objarr,nlocal);
                break;
            case OUTPUT_PART:
                output_particles();
                break;
```

```
                        case OUTPUT_FORCE:
                            output_force();
                            break;
                }
        }
        printf("\nFinished\n");
        exit(0);
}


/*************************** end of routine main **************************/
find_potential()
{
        double pot,lr_par();
        int add_double();

        if(check_init()<0) return;

        pot = lr_par(objarr,nlocal);
        combine(&pot,add_double,sizeof(double),1);

        fprintf(out_file,"\n\nThe potential of the %d particles is %13.5e\n",
            ntotal,pot);
}

/********************** end of routine find_potential ********************/
get_particles(option)
int option;
{
        double x,y,z,mass;
        int np,position,index;

        index=0;
        for(np=0;np<ntotal;++np){
            if(option==2 && fildat!=stdin)
                fscanf(fildat,"%lf %lf %lf",&x,&y,&z);
            else{
                printf("\n\nPlease give the x, y, and z co-ordinates ");
                printf("for particle %d ==> ",np+1);
                scanf("%lf %lf %lf",&x,&y,&z);
            }

            if(option==2 && fildat!=stdin)
                fscanf(fildat,"%lf",&mass);
            else{
                printf("\n\nPlease give the mass for particle %d ==> ",
                    np+1);
                scanf("%lf",&mass);
```

```
        }

        position = (np < (nmin+1)*nleft) ? np/(nmin+1):(np-nleft)/nmin;
        if(ringpos==position){
            objarr[index].x     = x;
            objarr[index].y     = y;
            objarr[index].z     = z;
            objarr[index].mass = mass;
            objarr[index].fx    = 0.0;
            objarr[index].fy    = 0.0;
            objarr[index].fz    = 0.0;
            index++;


        }
    }
}


/*********************** end of routine get_particles **********************/
int get_task()
{
    int task;
    char input[5];

    for(;;){
        printf("\n\nPlease choose one of the following :\n");
        printf("    1...to initialize a new particle configuration\n");
        printf("    2...to evaluate the potential\n");
        printf("    3...to evaluate the force on each particle\n");
        printf("    4...to output particle positions and masses\n");
        printf("    5...to output force on each particle\n");
        printf("    6...to terminate the program\n==> ");

        scanf("%s",input);

        task = atoi(input);

        if(task>0 && task<7) break;
        else printf("\n\n**** Invalid input - try again ****\n");
    }
    return task;
}


/*********************** end of routine get_task ***********************/
initialize()
{
    int option1,seed;
    char input[5];
```

```
FILE *setup_in();

for(;;){
    printf("\n\nPlease choose one of the following:\n");
    printf("   1...to input particles from terminal\n");
    printf("   2...to input particles from a disk file\n");
    printf("   3...to generate random particles\n");
    printf("   4...to exit this menu\n==> ");

    scanf("%s",input);

    option1 = atoi(input);

    if(option1>0 && option1<5) break;
    else printf("\n\n**** Invalid input - try again\n");
}

if(option1==2 && fildat==stdin)
    fildat = setup_in("containing particle data");
else if(option1==3){
    printf("\n\nPlease give a seed integer ==> ");
    scanf("%d",&seed);
    prand_setB(seed,JUMP,ringpos);
}
else if(option1==4) return;

for(;;){
    if(option1==2 && fildat!=stdin)
        fscanf(fildat,"%s",input);
    else{
        printf("\n\nPlease give the total number of particles ==> ");
        scanf("%s",input);
    }
    ntotal = atoi(input);

    nmin   = (ntotal-1)/nproc;
    if((nmin+1)<=MAX_PARTICLES) break;
    else printf("\n\n**** Too many particles - try again ****\n");
}

nleft  = ntotal-nmin*nproc;
nlocal = ringpos < nleft ? nmin+1 : nmin;
           /
if(option1==1 || option1==2) get_particles(option1);
else if(option1==3) ran_particles();

init_status = 1;
```

```
}

/*********************** end of routine initialize ***********************/
int is_even(i)
int i;
{
    return !(i&1);
}

/*********************** end of routine is_even ***********************/
lr_f_2(arr1,arr2,n1,n2,step)
OBJECT *arr1,*arr2;
int n1,n2,step;
{
    int i,j;

    for(i=0;i<min(n1,n2);++i){
        if(should_self_interact(i,step)) pair_force(&arr1[i],&arr2[i]);
        for(j=i+1;j<n2;++j) pair_force(&arr1[i],&arr2[j]);
    }
}

/*********************** end of routine lr_f_2 ***********************/
lr_force(residents,nres)
OBJECT *residents;
int nres;
{
    int i,nmovers,step;

    if(check_init()<0) return;

    nmovers = nres;
    for(i=0;i<nres;++i) obj_copy[i] = residents[i];

    for(step=0;step<nproc;++step){
        lr_f_2(residents,obj_copy,nres,nmovers,step);
        rotate(obj_copy,&nmovers);
    }
    recombine(residents,obj_copy,nres);
}

/*********************** end of routine lr_force ***********************/
double lr_par(residents,nres)
OBJECT *residents;
int nres;
{
    double sum,lr_sym_par();
```

```
    int nmovers,i,step;

    nmovers = nres;
    for(i=0;i<nres;++i) obj_copy[i] = residents[i];

    sum = 0.0;
    for(step=0;step<nproc;++step){
        sum += lr_sym_par(residents,obj_copy,nres,nmovers,step);
        rotate(obj_copy,&nmovers);
    }
    return sum;
}

/*********************** end of routine lr_par **************************/
double lr_sym_par(arr1,arr2,n1,n2,step)
OBJECT *arr1,*arr2;
int n1,n2,step;
{
    double pair_potential(),sum;
    int i,j;

    sum = 0.0;
    for(i=0;i<min(n1,n2);++i){
        if(should_self_interact(i,step)
            sum += pair_potential(arr1[i],arr2[i]);
        for(j=i+1;j<n2;++j) sum += pair_potential(arr1[i],arr2[j]);
    }
    return sum;
}

/********************* end of routine lr_sym_par *********************/
output_force()
{
    int np,npts,i,j,add_double();
    double sumx,sumy,sumz;
    FILE *setup_out();

    if(check_init()<0) return;

    if(file_status==CLOSED) out_file=setup_out("lrCUB.c");

    fprintf(out_file,"\n\nNumber     x force          y force");
    fprintf(out_file,"          z force\n");
    fmulti(out_file);
    sumx = sumy = sumz = 0.0;
    for(i=0,np=1;i<nproc;++i){
            npts = i<nleft ? nmin+1 : nmin;
```

```
        for(j=0;j<npts;++j,++np){
            if(ringpos==i){
                fprintf(out_file,"%4d %15.5e %15.5e %15.5e\n",np,
                objarr[j].fx,objarr[j].fy,objarr[j].fz);
                sumx += objarr[j].fx;
                sumy += objarr[j].fy;
                sumz += objarr[j].fz;
            }
            if(out_file==stdout && np%21==0 && np!=ntotal){
                fsingl(out_file);
                dw_pause();
                fmulti(out_file);
            }
            if(j%7==6) fflush(out_file);
        }
        fflush(out_file);
    }
    fsingl(out_file);

    combine(&sumx,add_double,sizeof(double),1);
    combine(&sumy,add_double,sizeof(double),1);
    combine(&sumz,add_double,sizeof(double),1);

    fprintf(out_file," ----    ------------    ------------    ");
    fprintf(out_file,"------------\n Sums %14.5e %15.5e %15.5e\n",sumx,
                            sumy,sumz);
    fprintf(out_file," ----    ------------    ------------    ");
    fprintf(out_file,"------------\n");

    if(out_file==stdout) dw_pause();
}

/*********************** end of routine output_force ***********************/
output_particles()
{
    int np,npts,i,j;
    FILE *setup_out();

    if(check_init()<0) return;

    if(file_status==CLOSED) out_file=setup_out("lrCUB.c");

    fprintf(out_file,"\n\nNumber          x               y");
    fprintf(out_file,"              z               mass\n");
    fmulti(out_file);
    for(i=0,np=1;i<nproc;++i){
            npts = i<nleft ? nmin+1 : nmin;
```

```
        for(j=0;j<npts;++j,++np){
            if(ringpos==i)
                fprintf(out_file,"%4d %15.5e %15.5e %15.5e %15.5e\n",np,
                    objarr[j].x,objarr[j].y,objarr[j].z,objarr[j].mass);
            if(out_file==stdout && np%21==0 && np!=ntotal){
                fsingl(out_file);
                dw_pause();
                fmulti(out_file);
            }
            if(j%7==6) fflush(out_file);
        }
        fflush(out_file);
    }
    fsingl(out_file);
    if(out_file==stdout) dw_pause();
}


/******************** end of routine output_particles ********************/
pair_force(obj1,obj2)
OBJECT *obj1,*obj2;
{
    double factor,distance,diffx,diffy,diffz,dsquared,sqrt();
    double forcex,forcey,forcez;

    diffx    = obj1->x-obj2->x;
    diffy    = obj1->y-obj2->y;
    diffz    = obj1->z-obj2->z;
    dsquared = diffx*diffx + diffy*diffy + diffz*diffz;

    if(dsquared==0.0) return;

    distance = sqrt(dsquared);

    factor = obj1->mass*obj2->mass/(distance*dsquared);
    forcex = factor*diffx;
    forcey = factor*diffy;
    forcez = factor*diffz;

    obj1->fx -= forcex;
    obj1->fy -= forcey;
    obj1->fz -= forcez;
    obj2->fx += forcex;
    obj2->fy += forcey;
    obj2->fz += forcez;
}


/*********************** end of routine pair_force ***********************/
```

```
double pair_potential(obj1,obj2)
OBJECT obj1,obj2;
{
    double diffx,diffy,diffz,dsquared,sqrt();

    diffx    = obj1.x-obj2.x;
    diffy    = obj1.y-obj2.y;
    diffz    = obj1.z-obj2.z;
    dsquared = diffx*diffx + diffy*diffy + diffz*diffz;

    return (dsquared==0 ? 0.0 : -obj1.mass*obj2.mass/sqrt(dsquared));
}

/*********************** end of routine pair_potential **********************/
ran_particles()
{
    int i;
    double prandB(),prandS();

    for(i=0;i<nlocal;++i){
        objarr[i].x    = prandS();
        objarr[i].y    = prandS();
        objarr[i].z    = prandS();
        objarr[i].mass = prandB();
        objarr[i].fx   = 0.0;
        objarr[i].fy   = 0.0;
        objarr[i].fz   = 0.0;
    }
}

/*********************** end of routine ran_particles **********************/
recombine(arr1,arr2,n)
OBJECT *arr1,*arr2;
int n;
{
    int i;

    for(i=0;i<n;++i){
        arr1[i].fx += arr2[i].fx;
        arr1[i].fy += arr2[i].fy;
        arr1[i].fz += arr2[i].fz;
    }
}

/*********************** end of routine recombine **********************/
```

```
ring_setup()
{
    gridinit(1,&nproc);
    gridcoord(procnum,&ringpos);

    c_clock_neigh = gridchan(procnum,0,-1);
    clock_neigh   = gridchan(procnum,0, 1);
}

/*********************** end of routine ring_setup ***********************/
rotate(arr,narr)
OBJECT *arr;
int *narr;
{
    int nrec,nbytes,space;

    nbytes = (*narr)*sizeof(OBJECT);
    space  = (nmin+1)*sizeof(OBJECT);
    nrec   = cshift(arr,clock_neigh,space,arr,c_clock_neigh,nbytes);
    *narr  = nrec/sizeof(OBJECT);
}

/*********************** end of routine rotate ***************************/
int should_self_interact(i,step)
int i,step;
{
    if(step<nproc/2) return 0;
    else if(step>nproc/2) return 1;
    else if(ringpos<nproc/2) return is_even(i);
    else return !is_even(i);
}

/******************* end of routine should_self_interact *****************/
welcome()
{
    printf("\n\n            ******************************************\n");
    printf(   "            *                                        *\n");
    printf(   "            *    Welcome to the potential evaluation  *\n");
    printf(   "            *    example program. This program finds  *\n");
    printf(   "            *    the gravitational potential energy   *\n");
    printf(   "            *    of a system of particles.            *\n");
    printf(   "            *                                        *\n");
    printf(   "            ******************************************\n");
}

/*********************** end of routine welcome *************************/
```

A-6.2 Include File `particle.h`

```
typedef struct particle{
  double x,y,z;
  double fx,fy,fz;
  double mass;
} OBJECT;
#define MAX_PARTICLES 128
#define INITIALIZE    1
#define FIND_POT      2
#define FIND_FORCE    3
#define OUTPUT_PART   4
#define OUTPUT_FORCE 5
#define STOP          6
#define JUMP        4
```

A-7 Matrix Multiplication

A-7.1 CUBIX Program

```
#include <cros.h>
#include <stdio.h>
#include "matmult.h"
#include "cubdefs.h"

#define m(r,c) *(matrix+row_local*nlocal+col_local)
#define m1(i,k) *(mat1+i*nlocal+k)
#define m2(k,j) *(mat2+k*nlocal+j)
#define m3(i,j) *(mat3+i*nlocal+j)

double AM[MAX_SIZE][MAX_SIZE],BM[MAX_SIZE][MAX_SIZE];
double CM[MAX_SIZE][MAX_SIZE];
int nproc,doc,procnum;
int xpos,ypos,upmask,dmask,lmask,rmask,file_status,std_flag=0,init_status;
int usize,nsize,nlocal,D;
FILE *fildat,*in_file,*out_file;

main()
{
    int command;

    in_file     = stdin;
    fildat      = stdin;
    out_file    = stdout;
    file_status = CLOSED;
    init_status = 0;

    welcome();

    get_param();

    decompose();

    while( (command=get_task()) != STOP ){
        switch(command){
                case INITIALIZE:
                        initialize(AM,BM);
                        break;
                case OUTPUT_MAT:
                        output_mat(AM,BM,CM);
                        break;
                case MAT_MULT:
                        mat_mult(AM,BM,CM);
```

```
                            break;
              }
      }
      printf("\n\nFinished\n\n");
      exit(0);
}


/*************************** end of routine main ***************************/
decompose()
{
      int coord[2];

      if(doc&1){
          printf("\n\n*** Dimension of hypercube must be even ***\n\n");
          exit(1);
      }
      D = 1<<(doc/2);

      coord[0] = D;
      coord[1] = D;
      gridinit(2,coord);
      gridcoord(procnum,coord);
      xpos  = coord[0];
      ypos  = coord[1];
      lmask = gridchan(procnum,0,-1);
      rmask = gridchan(procnum,0,1);
      upmask = gridchan(procnum,1,-1);
      dmask = gridchan(procnum,1,1);
}


/************************* end of routine decompose *************************/
disk_mat(amat,bmat)
double *amat,*bmat;
{
      FILE *setup_in();

      if(file_status==CLOSED) fildat = setup_in("containing the matrices");

      get_disk_mat(amat,fildat);
      get_disk_mat(bmat,fildat);
}


/************************* end of routine disk_mat *************************/
get_disk_mat(matrix,data_file)
double *matrix;
FILE *data_file;
{
```

```
     int row,row_block,row_local,col,col_block,col_local;
     double val;

     for(row=0;row<nsize;++row){
     row_block = row/nlocal;
         row_local = row%nlocal;
         for(col=0;col<nsize;++col){
             col_block = col/nlocal;
             col_local = col%nlocal;
             if(row<usize && col<usize) fscanf(fildat,"%lf",&val);
             else val = 0.0;
             if(col_block==xpos && row_block==ypos) m(r,c) = val;
         }
     }
}

/*********************** end of routine get_disk_mat ***********************/
int get_task()
{
     int task;
     char input[5];

     for(;;){
         printf("\n\nPlease choose one of the following :\n");
         printf("   1...to initialize the matrices A and B\n");
         printf("   2...to multiply A and B\n");
         printf("   3...to output the matrices A, B, and C\n");
         printf("   4...to terminate the program\n==> ");
         scanf("%s",input);
         task = atoi(input);

         if(task>0 && task<5) break;
         else printf("\n\n**** Invalid input - try again ****\n");
     }
     return task;
}

/*********************** end of routine get_task ***********************/
initialize(amat,bmat)
double *amat,*bmat;
{
     int iopt;
     char input[5];

     for(;;){
         printf("\n\nPlease give the order of the matrices ==> ");
         scanf("%s",input);
```

```
        usize = atoi(input);

        nlocal = (usize-1)/D + 1;
        nsize  = D*nlocal;
        if(nlocal>0 && nlocal<MAX_SIZE) break;
        else printf("\n\n**** Invalid input - try again ****\n");
    }

    for(;;){
        printf("\n\nPlease select one of the following :\n");
        printf("    1...to key in matrices on standard input\n");
        printf("    2...to generate random matrices\n");
        printf("    3...to read in matrices from disk file\n==> ");
        scanf("%s",input);
        iopt = atoi(input);

        if(iopt>0 && iopt<4) break;
        else printf("\n\n**** Invalid input - try again ****\n");
    }

    if(iopt==1){
        key_in_mat(amat,"matrix A");
        key_in_mat(bmat,"matrix B");
    }
    else if(iopt==2) random_mat(amat,bmat);
    else disk_mat(amat,bmat);

    init_status = 1;
}

/*********************** end of routine initialize ***********************/
key_in_mat(matrix,chrmat)
double *matrix;
char *chrmat;
{
    int row,row_block,row_local,col,col_block,col_local;
    double val;

    for(row=0;row<nsize;++row){
      row_block = row/nlocal;
      row_local = row%nlocal;
      if(row<usize)
         printf("\n\nPlease key in the %d numbers for row %d of %s ==> ",
                  usize,row,chrmat);
      for(col=0;col<nsize;++col){
        col_block = col/nlocal;
        col_local = col%nlocal;
```

```
                    if(row<usize && col<usize) scanf("%lf",&val);
                    else val = 0.0;
                    if(col_block==xpos && row_block==ypos) m(r,c) = val;
                        }
                }
        }

/*********************** end of routine key_in_mat ************************/
list_matrix(matrix)
double *matrix;
{
        int row,row_block,row_local,col,col_block,col_local;
        int numel,lines_per_row,line;

        fmulti(stdout);

        numel = (xpos==(D-1)) ? (usize-(D-1)*nlocal) : nlocal;
        lines_per_row  = (usize-1)/10 + 1;
        for(row=0,line=0;row<usize;++row){
            row_block = row/nlocal;
            row_local = row%nlocal;
            line += lines_per_row;
            if(line>=20){
                line = 0;
                fsingl(stdout);
                dw_pause();
                fmulti(stdout);
            }
            for(col_block=0,col=0;col_block<D;++col_block){
                if(col_block==xpos && row_block==ypos){
                    for(col_local=0;col_local<numel;++col_local){
                        printf("%7.4f%c",m(r,c),(col%10==9) ? '\n' : ' ');
                        col++;
                    }
                    if(col%10!=0 && col_block==(D-1)) printf("\n");
                }
                else col += nlocal;
                fflush(stdout);
            }
        }
        fsingl(stdout);
        if(line!=0) dw_pause();
}

/*********************** end of routine list_matrix ***********************/
```

```
mat_mult(amat,bmat,cmat)
double *amat,*bmat,*cmat;
{
    int step,i;
    double tmat[MAX_SIZE][MAX_SIZE];

    if(check_init()<0) return;

    for(i=0;i<nlocal*nlocal;++i) cmat[i] = 0.0;

    for(step=0;step<D;++step){
        pipe_A(amat,tmat,step);
        multiply(tmat,bmat,cmat);
        roll_B(bmat);
    }
}


/*********************** end of routine mat_mult ************************/
multiply(mat1,mat2,mat3)
double *mat1,*mat2,*mat3;
{
    int i,j,k;
    double sum;

    for(i=0;i<nlocal;++i){
        for(j=0;j<nlocal;++j){
            sum = m3(i,j);
            for(k=0;k<nlocal;++k) sum += m1(i,k)*m2(k,j);
            m3(i,j) = sum;
        }
    }
}


/*********************** end of routine multiply ************************/
output_mat(amat,bmat,cmat)
double *amat,*bmat,*cmat;
{
    int iopt;
    char input[5];

    if(check_init()<0) return;

    for(;;){
        printf("\n\nPlease choose one of the following :\n");
        printf("   1...to output matrix A\n");
        printf("   2...to output matrix B\n");
        printf("   3...to output matrix C\n");
```

```
                printf("    4...to quit this menu\n==> ");
                scanf("%s",input);
                iopt=atoi(input);
                if(iopt==1) list_matrix(amat);
                else if(iopt==2) list_matrix(bmat);
                else if(iopt==3) list_matrix(cmat);
                else if(iopt==4) break;
                else printf("\n\n**** Invalid input - try again ****\n");
        }
}


/************************* end of routine output_mat ************************/
pipe_A(matrix,copymat,step)
double *matrix,*copymat;
int step;
{
        int j,offset,last_pos,nbytes;

        nbytes = nlocal*nlocal*sizeof(double);
        offset = ypos+step;
        if(offset>=D) offset -= D;
        last_pos = offset-1;
        if(last_pos<0) last_pos += D;

        if(xpos==offset){
                for(j=0;j<nlocal*nlocal;++j) copymat[j] = matrix[j];
                cwrite(copymat,rmask,nbytes);
        }
        else if(xpos==last_pos) cread(copymat,lmask,0,nbytes);
        else cread(copymat,lmask,rmask,nbytes);
}


/*************************** end of routine pipe_A **************************/
random_mat(amat,bmat)
double *amat,*bmat;
{
        char input[5];
        int seed;

        for(;;){
                printf("\n\nPlease give a seed integer ==> ");
                scanf("%s",input);
                seed = atoi(input);
                if(seed>0) break;
                else printf("\n\n****invalid input - try again\n");
        }
        prand_setB(seed,0,0);
```

```
        ran_matrix(amat);
        ran_matrix(bmat);
}


/*********************** end of routine random_mat ***********************/
ran_matrix(matrix)
double *matrix;
{
        int row,row_block,row_local,col,col_block,col_local;
        double val,prandS();

        for(row=0;row<nsize;++row){
            row_block = row/nlocal;
            row_local = row%nlocal;
            for(col=0;col<nsize;++col){
                col_block = col/nlocal;
                col_local = col%nlocal;
                val = (col<usize && row<usize) ? prandS()-0.5 : 0.0;
                if(col_block==xpos && row_block==ypos) m(r,c) = val;
            }
        }
}


/*********************** end of routine ran_matrix ***********************/
roll_B(matrix)
double *matrix;
{
        int nbytes;

        nbytes = nlocal*nlocal*sizeof(double);
        cshift(matrix,dmask,nbytes,matrix,upmask,nbytes);
}


/*********************** end of routine roll_B ***********************/
welcome()
{
        printf("\n\n        *****************************************\n");
        printf(  "        *                                       *\n");
        printf(  "        *    Welcome to the matrix multiplication *\n");
        printf(  "        *    example program. This program finds  *\n");
        printf(  "        *    the product C=AB                     *\n");
        printf(  "        *                                       *\n");
        printf(  "        *****************************************\n");
}


/*********************** end of routine welcome ***********************/
```

A-7.2 Include File `matmult.h`

```
#define MAX_SIZE 30
#define INITIALIZE 1
#define MAT_MULT   2
#define OUTPUT_MAT 3
#define STOP       4
```

A-8 Fast Fourier Transforms

A-8.1 CUBIX Program

```c
#include <cros.h>
#include <stdio.h>
#include "fftdef.h"
#include "cubdefs.h"

int doc,procnum,nproc;
int std_flag=0,com_size,glob_start,nlocal,p,q,q_minus_p;
COMPLEX indata[MAXSIZE];
char IO_buf[4096];

main()
{
    int command,npts;

    com_size = sizeof(COMPLEX);
    welcome();

    get_param();

    while((command=get_task()) != STOP){
        switch(command){
            case INITIALIZE:
                npts = initialize(indata);
                break;
            case FFT_REC:
                fft_2(npts,1,indata);
                break;
            case FFT_ITER:
                fft_3(npts,indata);
                break;
            case INVERT_PERM:
                global_reverse(indata,npts,com_size);
                break;
            case OUTPUT:
                output_results(indata,npts);
                break;
        }
    }
    printf("\nFinished\n");
    exit(0);
}


/*************************** end of routine main ***************************/
```

```
COMPLEX c_diff(x,y)
COMPLEX x,y;
{
    COMPLEX result;

    result.re = x.re - y.re;
    result.im = x.im - y.im;

    return (result);
}

/*************************** end of routine c_diff **************************/
COMPLEX c_prod(x,y)
COMPLEX x,y;
{
    COMPLEX result;

    result.re = x.re*y.re - x.im*y.im;
    result.im = x.im*y.re + x.re*y.im;

    return (result);
}

/*************************** end of routine c_prod **************************/
COMPLEX c_root_unity(k,n)
int k,n;
{
    float fac;
    COMPLEX result;
    double cos(),sin();

    fac = 2.0*pi*(float)k/(float)n;

    result.re = cos((double)fac);
    result.im = sin((double)fac);

    return (result);
}

/********************** end of routine c_root_unity ***********************/
COMPLEX c_sum(x,y)
COMPLEX x,y;
{
    COMPLEX result;

    result.re = x.re + y.re;
    result.im = x.im + y.im;
```

```
        return (result);
}


/************************** end of routine c_sum **************************/
fft_2(Nx,increm,x)
int Nx,increm;
COMPLEX x[];
{
    if(Nx==1) return;
    else if(Nx <= nproc){
        fft_2(Nx/2,2*increm,x);
        fft_c_comm(Nx,x);
        return;
    }
    else{
        fft_2(Nx/2,2*increm,x);
        fft_2(Nx/2,2*increm,x+increm);
        fft_c_2(Nx,increm,x);
        return;
    }
}


/************************** end of routine fft_2 **************************/
fft_3(Nx,x)
int Nx;
COMPLEX x[];
{
    int i,bit_num,increm;

    increm = Nx/2;
    Nx     = 2;
    for(bit_num=(p+q-1);bit_num>=0;--bit_num){
        if(bit_num>=q) for(i=0;i<nlocal;++i) fft_c_comm(Nx,x+i);
        else for(i=0;i<increm;++i) fft_c_2(Nx,increm,x+i);
        Nx     *= 2;
        increm /= 2;
    }
}


/************************** end of routine fft_3 **************************/
fft_c_2(Nx,increm,y)
int Nx,increm;
COMPLEX y[];
{
    int pair_location,index,permute(),min_loc,max_loc;
    COMPLEX *evenptr,*oddptr,val_odd,val_even,c_expon,term2;
```

```
    COMPLEX c_root_unity(),c_sum(),c_prod(),c_diff();

    evenptr = y;
    oddptr  = y+increm;

    min_loc = procnum*Nx/(2*nproc);
    max_loc = min_loc + Nx/(2*nproc);

    for(pair_location=min_loc;pair_location<max_loc;++pair_location){
        val_odd  = *oddptr;
        val_even = *evenptr;
        index    = permute(pair_location,Nx/2);
        c_expon  = c_root_unity(index,Nx);
        term2    = c_prod(c_expon,val_odd);
        *oddptr  = c_diff(val_even,term2);
        *evenptr = c_sum(val_even,term2);
        evenptr += 2*increm;
        oddptr  += 2*increm;
    }
}


/************************** end of routine fft_c_2 **************************/
fft_c_comm(Nx,y)
int Nx;
COMPLEX *y;
{
    int proc_increm,location,pair_location,index,loc_is_odd;
    COMPLEX c_val,c_expon,term2;
    COMPLEX c_root_unity(),c_prod(),c_sum(),c_diff();

    proc_increm   = nproc/Nx;
    location      = procnum/proc_increm;
    loc_is_odd    = location&1;
    pair_location = location/2;

    cshift(&c_val,proc_increm,com_size,y,proc_increm,com_size);

    index = permute(pair_location,Nx/2);
    c_expon = c_root_unity(index,Nx);

    if(loc_is_odd){
        term2 = c_prod(c_expon,*y);
        *y    = c_diff(c_val,term2);
    }
    else{
        term2 = c_prod(c_expon,c_val);
        *y    = c_sum(*y,term2);
```

```
    }
}

/*********************** end of routine fft_c_comm *************************/
get_input(x,Nx)
COMPLEX x[];
int Nx;
{
    int iopt;
    char input[5];

    for(;;){
        printf("\n\nPlease select data to be transformed:\n");
        printf("   1...top-hat function\n");
        printf("   2...ramp function\n");
        printf("   3...triangle function\n");
        printf("   4...data from file\n==> ");
        if(std_flag) fflush(stdout);
        scanf("%s",input);
        iopt = atoi(input);

        if(iopt==1) top_hat_fun(x,Nx);
        else if(iopt==2) ramp_fun(x,Nx);
        else if(iopt==3) triangle_fun(x,Nx);
        else if(iopt==4) read_input(x,Nx);
        if(iopt>0 && iopt < 5) break;
        else printf("\n\n*** Invalid input - try again ***\n");
    }
}

/*********************** end of routine get_input *************************/
int get_task()
{
    int task;
    char input[5];

    for(;;){
        printf("\n\nPlease choose one of the following:\n");
        printf("   1...to set up data to be transformed\n");
        printf("   2...to find the FFT using the recursive algorithm\n");
        printf("   3...to find the FFT using the iterative algorithm\n");
        printf("   4...to send data to bit-reversed positions\n");
        printf("   5...to output the data array\n");
        printf("   6...to terminate program\n==> ");
        if(std_flag) fflush(stdout);
        scanf("%s",input);
        task = atoi(input);
```

```
            if(task>0 && task<7) break;
            else printf("\n\n*** Invalid input - try again ***\n");
    }
    return task;
}

/************************* end of routine get_task *************************/
int initialize(x)
COMPLEX *x;
{
    int numpt;
    char input[5];

    for(;;){
        printf("\n\nPlease give the number of data points ==> ");
        if(std_flag) fflush(stdout);
        scanf("%s",input);
        numpt  = atoi(input);
        nlocal = numpt/nproc;
        if(nlocal<1 || nlocal>MAXSIZE)
            printf("\n\n*** Invalid input - try again ***\n");
        else break;
    }

    p           = intlog2(nproc);
    q           = intlog2(nlocal);
    q_minus_p  = q-p;
    glob_start = procnum*nlocal;

    get_input(x,numpt);

    return numpt;
}

/********************* end of initialize routine *********************/

int intlog2(n)
int n;
{
    int answer;

    answer = 0;
    while(n>1){
        answer += 1;
        n /= 2;
    }
    return (answer);
```

```
    }

/*************************** end of routine intlog2 ***************************/
output_results(x,Nx)
COMPLEX x[];
int Nx;
{
    int i,j,k,lines;

    fmulti(stdout);
    lines = 0;
    for(i=0,k=0;i<nproc;++i){
        for(j=0;j<nlocal;++j,k++){
            if(procnum==i){
                printf("(%11.3e,%11.3e) ",x[j].re,x[j].im);
                if(k%3==2 || k==(Nx-1)) printf("\n");
            }
            if(k%3==2) lines++;
            if(lines>20){
                fsingl(stdout);
                dw_pause();
                fmulti(stdout);
                lines = 0;
            }
        }
        fflush(stdout);
    }
    fsingl(stdout);
}


/*********************** end of routine output_results ***********************/
int permute(l,m)
int l,m;
{
    if(m==1) return l;
    else return((l&1) ? (m>>1) + permute(l>>1,m>>1) : permute(l>>1,m>>1) );
}


/*************************** end of routine permute ***************************/
ramp_fun(x,Nx)
COMPLEX x[];
int Nx;
{
    int i,j;
    float slope;

    slope = 1.0/(float)(Nx-1);
```

```
        for(i=0,j=glob_start;i<nlocal;++i,++j){
            x[i].re = j*slope;
            x[i].im = 0.0;
        }
}


/************************* end of routine ramp_fun *************************/
read_input(x,Nx)
COMPLEX x[];
int Nx;
{
        int i,j,block_no;
        float x_real,x_imaginary;
        FILE *data_file,*setup_in();

        data_file = setup_in("containing the data to be transformed");

        for(i=0,j=0;i<Nx;++i){
            fscanf(data_file,"%f %f",&x_real,&x_imaginary);
            block_no = i/nlocal;
            if(procnum==block_no){
                x[j].re = x_real;
                x[j].im = x_imaginary;
                j++;
            }
        }
}


/************************* end of routine read_input *************************/
top_hat_fun(x,Nx)
COMPLEX x[];
int Nx;
{
        int i,j,nlow,nhigh;

        nlow  = Nx/4;
        nhigh = 3*nlow;
        for(i=0,j=glob_start;i<nlocal;++i,++j){
            x[i].re = (j>=nlow && j<nhigh) ? 1.0 : 0.0;
            x[i].im = 0.0;
        }
}


/************************* end of routine top_hat_fun *************************/
triangle_fun(x,Nx)
COMPLEX x[];
int Nx;
```

```
{
    int i,j,k,nhalf;
    float slope;

    nhalf = Nx/2;
    slope = 2.0/(float)(Nx-1);

    for(i=0,j=glob_start;i<nlocal;++i,++j){
        k = (j>=nhalf) ? Nx-1-j : j;
        x[i].re = k*slope;
        x[i].im = 0.0;
    }
}

/*********************** end of routine triangle_fun ***********************/
welcome()
{
    setbuffer(stdout,IO_buf,4096);
    std_flag = 1;

    printf("\n\n\t*********************************************");
    printf( "\n\t*                                          *");
    printf( "\n\t*      Welcome to the fft example program.  *");
    printf( "\n\t*                                          *");
    printf( "\n\t*  This program allows the use of both the  *");
    printf( "\n\t*  recursive and iterative algorithms.      *");
    printf( "\n\t*                                          *");
    printf( "\n\t*********************************************\n");

}

/************************* end of routine welcome *************************/
```

A-8.2 Include File fftdef.h

```
typedef struct { double re,im; } COMPLEX;
float pi = 3.1415927;
#define MAXSIZE 512
#define INITIALIZE  1
#define FFT_REC     2
#define FFT_ITER    3
#define INVERT_PERM 4
#define OUTPUT      5
#define STOP        6
```

A-9 The Generation of Random Numbers

A-9.1 CUBIX Program

```
#include <cros.h>
#include <stdio.h>
#include "randef.h"

int nproc,doc,procnum;
int std_flag=0;
char IO_buf[4096];

main()
{
    int command;

    welcome();

    get_param();

    while((command=get_task())!=STOP){
        switch(command){
            case LIST_NOS:
                list_nos();
                break;
            case INTEGRATE:
                mc_integrate();
                break;
            case FIND_PI:
                find_pi();
                break;
        }
    }
    printf("\n\nFinished\n\n");
    exit(0);
}

/************************* end of routine main *************************/
find_pi()
{
    int trials,i,add_double();
    double x,y,pi,score,rdoub,prandB(),prandS();
    char input[5];

    init_random(2);

    printf("\n\nPlease give the number of trials per processor ==> ");
```

```c
        if(std_flag) fflush(stdout);
        scanf("%s",input);
        trials = atoi(input);

        score = 0.0;
        for(i=0;i<trials;++i){
            rdoub  = prandS();
            x      = 2.0*rdoub - 1.0;
            rdoub  = prandB();
            y      = 2.0*rdoub - 1.0;
            if((x*x+y*y)<1.0) score++;
        }

        pi = 4.0*score/(double)(trials*nproc);
        combine(&pi,add_double,sizeof(double),1);

        fmulti(stdout);
        if(procnum==0) printf("\n\nAfter %d trials the value of PI is %10.8f",
                   nproc*trials,pi);
        fsingl(stdout);
}

/************************* end of routine find_pi *************************/
int get_task()
{
        int task;
        char input[5];

        for(;;){
            printf("\n\nPlease choose one of the following:");
            printf( "\n   1...to list a set of random numbers");
            printf( "\n   2...to evaluate a Monte-Carlo integral");
            printf( "\n   3...to evaluate PI by a Monte-Carlo method");
            printf( "\n   4...to terminate the program\n==> ");
            if(std_flag) fflush(stdout);
            scanf("%s",input);
            task = atoi(input);
            if(task>0 && task<5) break;
            else printf("\n\n**** Invalid input - try again ****\n");
        }
        return task;
}

/************************* end of routine get_task *************************/
int init_random(skip)
int skip;
{
```

```
    int seed;
    char input[5];

    printf("\n\nPlease give an integer seed ==> ");
    if(std_flag) fflush(stdout);
    scanf("%s",input);
    seed = atoi(input);

    prand_setB(seed,skip,procnum);
}

/*********************** end of routine initialize ***********************/
list_nos()
{
    int nmax,npts,nlocal,nleft,i,j;
    double prandB();
    char input[5];

    init_random(1);

    printf("\n\nPlease give the number of random numbers to list ==> ");
    if(std_flag) fflush(stdout);
    scanf("%s",input);
    npts = atoi(input);

    nlocal = npts/nproc;
    nleft  = npts%nproc;
    nmax   = nlocal + 1;
    nlocal = (procnum<nleft) ? nmax : nlocal;

    fmulti(stdout);
    for(i=0,j=procnum;i<nmax;++i,j += nproc){
        if(i<nlocal) printf("%6.4f%c",prandB(),(j%10==9) ? '\n' : ' ');
        fflush(stdout);
    }
    fsingl(stdout);
    printf("\n");
}

/*********************** end of routine list_nos ***********************/
mc_integrate()
{
    int trials,i,add_double();
    double integral,score,rdoub,prandB();
    char input[8];

    init_random(1);
```

```
    printf("\n\nPlease give the number of trials per processor ==> ");
    if(std_flag) fflush(stdout);
    scanf("%s",input);
    trials = atoi(input);

    score = 0.0;
    for(i=0;i<trials;++i){
        rdoub  = prandB();
        score += rdoub*rdoub;
    }

    integral = score/(double)(nproc*trials);
    combine((char *)&integral,add_double,sizeof(double),1);

    fmulti(stdout);
    if(procnum==0) printf("\n\nAfter %d trials the integral is %10.8f",
                    nproc*trials,integral);
    fsingl(stdout);
}

/********************* end of routine mc_integrate *********************/
welcome()
{
    setbuffer(stdout,IO_buf,4096);
    std_flag = 1;

    printf("\n\n\t**********************************************");
    printf(  "\n\t*                                            *");
    printf(  "\n\t*    Welcome to the random numbers program.  *");
    printf(  "\n\t*                                            *");
    printf(  "\n\t*  This program allows the user to list a set *");
    printf(  "\n\t*  of random numbers, and to evaluate an      *");
    printf(  "\n\t*  integral and PI using Monte Carlo methods. *");
    printf(  "\n\t*                                            *");
    printf(  "\n\t**********************************************\n");

}

/********************* end of routine welcome *********************/
```

A-9.2 Include File randef.h

```
#define LIST_NOS    1
#define INTEGRATE   2
#define FIND_PI     3
#define STOP        4
```

A-10 The Medium-Range Force Problem

A-10.1 CUBIX Program

```c
#include <cros.h>
#include <stdio.h>
#include "ljdef.h"
#include "cubdefs.h"

int nout;

int nproc,doc,procnum;
LIST *cell_arr[NCELL_X][NCELL_Y];
PARTICLE part_arr[MAX_PART];
double x_lower_left,x_upper_right,y_lower_left,y_upper_right;
double cell_sizex,cell_sizey,energy,sigma,sigma_squared,u0;
double xlo,ylo,xsize,ysize;
int nmax,xpos,ypos,ncells_x,ncells_y,ntotal,nlocal,bc,n_edge_parts;
int rtchan,lfchan,upchan,dnchan,std_flag=0,file_status;
int part_size = sizeof(PARTICLE);
int list_size = sizeof(LIST);
int size_int  = sizeof(int);
int size_double = sizeof(double);
FILE *fildat,*in_file,*out_file;
char IO_buf[4096];

main()
{
    int command;

    bc           = NON_PERIODIC;
    in_file      = stdin;
    fildat       = stdin;
    out_file     = stdout;
    file_status  = CLOSED;

    welcome();

    get_param();

    decompose();

    while( (command=get_task()) != STOP ){
        switch(command){
            case INITIALIZE:
                initialize();
                break;
```

```
                    case FIND_ENERGY:
                        compute_energy();
                        break;
                    case OUTPUT_PART:
                        output_particles();
                        break;
                }
            }
            printf("\nFinished\n");
            exit(0);
        }


/************************** end of routine main **************************/
abort_prog()
{
    int message,denom;

    denom   = 0;
    message = -99;
}


/************************* end of routine abort_prog *************************/
bound_exchg()
{
    int cellx,celly;

    n_edge_parts = 0;

    for(celly=0;celly<(ncells_y+2);++celly)
        list_exchange(rtchan,cell_arr[ncells_x+1][celly],lfchan,
                cell_arr[1][celly]);

    for(celly=0;celly<(ncells_y+2);++celly)
        list_exchange(lfchan,cell_arr[0][celly],rtchan,
                cell_arr[ncells_x][celly]);

    for(cellx=0;cellx<(ncells_x+2);++cellx)
        list_exchange(upchan,cell_arr[cellx][ncells_y+1],dnchan,
                cell_arr[cellx][1]);

    for(cellx=0;cellx<(ncells_x+2);++cellx)
        list_exchange(dnchan,cell_arr[cellx][0],upchan,
                cell_arr[cellx][ncells_y]);
}


/************************* end of routine bound_exchg *************************/
```

```
check_val(nval,nmin,nmax,s)
int nval,nmin,nmax;
char s[80];
{
    int check,add_int();

    check = (nval>=nmin && nval<=nmax) ? 0 : 1;
    combine(&check,add_int,size_int,1);
    if(check){
        printf("\n\n%s - program terminated\n\n",s);
        exit(1);
    }
}


/************************* end of routine check_val *************************/
compute_energy()
{
    int i,cellx,celly;
    LIST *make_list(),*rest(),*listp;
    PARTICLE *contents(),*partp;
    double add_double();

    energy = 0.0;
    for(cellx=0;cellx<(ncells_x+2);++cellx)
        for(celly=0;celly<(ncells_y+2);++celly)
            cell_arr[cellx][celly] = make_list();


    for(i=0;i<nlocal;++i){
        cellx = 1 + (int)((part_arr[i].x - x_lower_left)/cell_sizex);
        celly = 1 + (int)((part_arr[i].y - y_lower_left)/cell_sizey);
        insert(&(part_arr[i]),cell_arr[cellx][celly]);
    }

    bound_exchg();

    for(cellx=1;cellx<(ncells_x+1);++cellx){
        for(celly=1;celly<(ncells_y+1);++celly){
            listp = cell_arr[cellx][celly];
            while(!is_empty(listp)){
                partp = contents(listp);
                interact(partp,cellx,celly);
                listp = rest(listp);
            }
        }
    }
```

```
        for(cellx=0;cellx<(ncells_x+2);++cellx){
            for(celly=0;celly<(ncells_y+2);++celly){
                while(!is_empty(cell_arr[cellx][celly]))
                    delete_list(cell_arr[cellx][celly]);
                unmake_list(cell_arr[cellx][celly]);
            }
        }
        combine(&energy,add_double,size_double,1);

        fmulti(stdout);
        if(procnum==0)
            printf("\n\nThe energy of the %d particles is %e\n",ntotal,energy);
        fsingl(stdout);
    }


/********************** end of routine compute_energy **********************/
PARTICLE *contents(listp)
LIST *listp;
{
    if(is_empty(listp)) abort_prog();
    else return (listp->next->part);
}


/************************* end of routine contents *************************/
decompose()
{
    int coord[2],np[2],nprocs_x,nprocs_y;

    nprocs_x = nprocs_y = 1;
    if(nproc>1){
        for(;;){
            printf("\n\nPlease give the number of processors");
            printf("\n     1...in the x direction");
            printf("\n     2...in the y direction\n\n==> ");
            if(std_flag) fflush(stdout);
            scanf("%d%d",&nprocs_x,&nprocs_y);

            if(nprocs_x*nprocs_y == nproc) break;
            else printf("\n\nTotal number of processors must equal %4d",
                nproc);
        }
    }

    np[0] = nprocs_x;
    np[1] = nprocs_y;

    gridinit(2,np);
```

```
    upchan = gridchan(procnum,1,1);
    dnchan = gridchan(procnum,1,-1);
    rtchan = gridchan(procnum,0,1);
    lfchan = gridchan(procnum,0,-1);

    gridcoord(procnum,coord);

    xpos = coord[0];
    ypos = coord[1];
    if(bc==NON_PERIODIC){
        if(xpos==0)             lfchan = 0;
        if(xpos==(nprocs_x-1))  rtchan = 0;
        if(ypos==0)             dnchan = 0;
        if(ypos==(nprocs_y-1))  upchan = 0;
    }
}

/*********************** end of routine decompose ***********************/
delete_list(listp)
LIST *listp;
{
    LIST *kill;
    int is_empty();

    if(is_empty(listp)) abort_prog();
    else{
        kill = listp->next;
        listp->next = kill->next;
        free((char *)kill);
    }
}

/*********************** end of routine delete_list ***********************/
get_particles(option)
int option;
{
    double x,y,prandS();
    int np,xbin,ybin;

    nlocal=0;
    for(np=0;np<ntotal;++np){
        if(option==2 && fildat!=stdin) fscanf(fildat,"%lf %lf",&x,&y);
        else if(option==3){
                x = prandS();
                y = prandS();
        }
```

```
            else{
                    printf("\n\nPlease give the x and y co-ordinates ");
                    printf("for particle %d ==> ",np+1);
                    if(std_flag) fflush(stdout);
                        scanf("%lf %lf",&x,&y);
            }

            xbin = (int)((x-xlo)/xsize);
            ybin = (int)((y-ylo)/ysize);
            if(xbin==xpos && ybin==ypos){
                if(nlocal<MAX_PART){
                        part_arr[nlocal].x    = x;
                        part_arr[nlocal].y    = y;
                }
                nlocal++;
            }
        }
        check_val(nlocal,-1,MAX_PART,"Too many particles");
}

/*********************** end of routine get_particles **********************/
int get_task()
{
        int task;
        char input[5];

        for(;;){
                printf("\n\nPlease choose one of the following :\n");
                printf("    1...to initialize a new particle configuration\n");
                printf("    2...to evaluate the interaction energy\n");
                printf("    3...to output particle positions\n");
                printf("    4...to terminate the program\n==> ");
                if(std_flag) fflush(stdout);

                scanf("%s",input);

                task = atoi(input);

                if(task>0 && task<5) break;
                else printf("\n\n**** Invalid input - try again ****\n");
        }
        return task;
}

/*********************** end of routine get_task **************************/
```

```c
initialize()
{
    int option1,seed;
    char input[5];
    FILE *setup_in();

    printf("\n\nPlease give the length scale, sigma ==> ");
    if(std_flag) fflush(stdout);
    scanf("%lf",&sigma);

    printf("\n\nPlease give the potential scaling factor, U0 ==> ");
    if(std_flag) fflush(stdout);
    scanf("%lf",&u0);

    printf("\n\nPlease give the number of cells per processor");
    printf("\n     1...in the x direction\n     2...in the y direction");
    printf("\n\n==> ");
    if(std_flag) fflush(stdout);
    scanf("%d%d",&ncells_x,&ncells_y);

    sigma_squared = sigma*sigma;
    cell_sizex    = 3.0*sigma;
    cell_sizey    = 3.0*sigma;
    xsize = ncells_x*cell_sizex;
    ysize = ncells_y*cell_sizey;

    for(;;){
        printf("\n\nPlease choose one of the following:\n");
        printf("   1...to input particles from terminal\n");
        printf("   2...to input particles from a disk file\n");
        printf("   3...to generate random particles\n");
        printf("   4...to exit this menu\n==> ");
        if(std_flag) fflush(stdout);

        scanf("%s",input);

        option1 = atoi(input);

        if(option1>0 && option1<5) break;
        else printf("\n\n**** Invalid input - try again\n");
    }
    if(option1==4) return;
    else if(option1!=3){
        printf("\n\nPlease give the minimum x & y values of the domain ==> ");
        if(std_flag) fflush(stdout);
        scanf("%lf%lf",&xlo,&ylo);
    }
```

```
    if(option1==2 && fildat==stdin)
        fildat = setup_in("containing particle data");
    else if(option1==3){
        printf("\n\nPlease give a seed integer ==> ");
        if(std_flag) fflush(stdout);
        scanf("%d",&seed);
        prand_setB(seed,0,0);
        xlo = 0.0;
        ylo = 0.0;
    }

    if(option1==2 && fildat!=stdin)
        fscanf(fildat,"%s",input);
    else{
        printf("\n\nPlease give the total number of particles ==> ");
        if(std_flag) fflush(stdout);
        scanf("%s",input);
    }
    ntotal = atoi(input);

    get_particles(option1);

    x_lower_left  = xpos*xsize + xlo;
    y_lower_left  = ypos*ysize + ylo;
    x_upper_right = (xpos+1)*xsize + xlo;
    y_upper_right = (ypos+1)*ysize + ylo;
}

/*********************** end of routine initialize ***********************/
insert(partp,listp)
PARTICLE *partp;
LIST *listp;
{
    LIST *new;
    char *malloc();

    new = (LIST *)malloc(list_size);
    new->next = listp->next;
    new->part = partp;
    listp->next = new;
}

/*********************** end of routine insert ***********************/
interact(partp,cx,cy)
PARTICLE *partp;
int cx,cy;
```

```
{
    int xi,yi;
    double potential();
    PARTICLE *newpart,*contents();
    LIST *listp,*rest();

    for(xi=(cx-1);xi<=(cx+1);++xi){
        for(yi=(cy-1);yi<=(cy+1);++yi){
            listp = cell_arr[xi][yi];
            while(!is_empty(listp)){
                newpart = contents(listp);
                if(  (newpart->x > partp->x) ||
                    ((newpart->x==partp->x)  &&
                    (newpart->y > partp->y)) )
                    energy += potential(partp,newpart);
                listp = rest(listp);
            }
        }
    }
}

/*********************** end of routine interact **************************/
int is_empty(listp)
LIST *listp;
{
    return (listp->next == (LIST *)0);
}

/************************ end of routine is_empty *************************/
list_exchange(inchan,inlist,outchan,outlist)
int inchan,outchan;
LIST *inlist,*outlist;
{
    static PARTICLE edge_particle[MAX_EDGE];
    PARTICLE *inbuf,*outbuf,*contents();
    LIST *rest();
    int i,inspace,nbytes,nin;

    outbuf = &edge_particle[n_edge_parts];
    inbuf  = outbuf;
    nout   = 0;

    if(outchan!=0){
        while(!is_empty(outlist)){
            nout++;
            if(nout+n_edge_parts>MAX_EDGE) break;
            outbuf[nout-1] = *contents(outlist);
```

```
                outlist = rest(outlist);
            }
        }

        check_val(nout+n_edge_parts,-1,MAX_EDGE,"Too many edge particles");

        inspace = (MAX_EDGE - n_edge_parts)*part_size;

        nbytes = cshift(inbuf,inchan,inspace,outbuf,outchan,nout*part_size);

        nin = nbytes/part_size;
        for(i=0;i<nin;++i) insert(&inbuf[i],inlist);

        n_edge_parts += nin;
}

/*********************** end of routine list_exchange *********************/
LIST *make_list()
{
    LIST *ret;
    char *malloc();

    ret = (LIST *)malloc(list_size);

    ret->next = (LIST *)0;
    ret->part = (PARTICLE *)0;

    return ret;
}

/************************* end of routine make_list ***********************/
output_particles()
{
    int np,npts,i,j,xbin,ybin;
    FILE *setup_out();

    if(file_status==CLOSED){
        out_file=setup_out("mrCUB.c");
        setbuffer(out_file,IO_buf,4096);
    }

    fprintf(out_file,"\n\nNumber        x                y");
    fprintf(out_file,"        Processor    xbin      ybin\n");
    fmulti(out_file);
    for(i=0,np=1;i<nproc;++i){
        if(procnum==i) npts=nlocal;
        broadcast(&npts,i,nproc-1,size_int);
```

```
        for(j=0;j<npts;++j,++np){
            if(procnum==i){
                xbin = (int)((part_arr[j].x-xlo)/cell_sizex);
                ybin = (int)((part_arr[j].y-ylo)/cell_sizey);
                fprintf(out_file,"%4d %15.5e %15.5e %7d%10d%10d\n",np,
                        part_arr[j].x,part_arr[j].y,i,xbin,ybin);
            }
            if(out_file==stdout && np%21==0 && np!=ntotal){
                    fsingl(out_file);
                    dw_pause();
                    fmulti(out_file);
            }
            else if(out_file!=stdout && np%21==0) fflush(out_file);
        }
        fflush(out_file);
    }
    fsingl(out_file);
    if(out_file==stdout) dw_pause();
}


/********************* end of routine output_particles *********************/
double potential(p1,p2)
PARTICLE *p1,*p2;
{
    double x1,x2,y1,y2,diff_x,diff_y,dist_squared,sig_over_d2,sig_over_d6;

    x1 = p1->x;
    x2 = p2->x;
    y1 = p1->y:
    y2 = p2->y;

    diff_x = x2-x1;
    diff_y = y2-y1;

    dist_squared = diff_x*diff_x + diff_y*diff_y;
    if(dist_squared==0.0 || dist_squared >= 9.0*sigma_squared) return 0.0;

    sig_over_d2 = sigma_squared/dist_squared;
    sig_over_d6 = sig_over_d2*sig_over_d2*sig_over_d2;

    return u0*(sig_over_d6-1.0)*sig_over_d6/4.0;
}


/*********************** end of routine potential ***********************/
LIST *rest(listp)
LIST *listp;
{
```

```
        int is_empty();

        if(is_empty(listp)) abort_prog();
        else return (listp->next);
    }


/*************************** end of routine rest **************************/
unmake_list(listp)
LIST *listp;
{
        int is_empty();

        if(is_empty(listp)) free((char *)listp);
        else abort_prog();
    }


/************************ end of routine unmake_list *********************/
welcome()
{
        setbuffer(stdout,IO_buf,4096);
        std_flag = 1;

        printf("\n\n        ****************************************\n");
        printf(      "        *                                      *\n");
        printf(      "        *   Welcome to the potential evaluation *\n");
        printf(      "        *   example program. This program finds *\n");
        printf(      "        *   the potential energy of a system of *\n");
        printf(      "        *   particles interacting via a Lennard *\n");
        printf(      "        *   Jones potential.                    *\n");
        printf(      "        *                                      *\n");
        printf(      "        ****************************************\n");
    }


/*********************** end of routine welcome ************************/
output_list(listp)
LIST *listp;
{
        PARTICLE *ptemp;
        LIST *ltemp;
        int np;

        np = 0;
        ltemp = listp;

        while(ltemp->next != (LIST *)0){
            np++;
            ptemp = ltemp->next->part;
```

```
        printf("\n%6d %15.6e %15.6e %6d",np,ptemp->x,ptemp->y,procnum);
            ltemp = ltemp->next;
        }
}


/************************* end of routine output_list ************************/
output_part2()
{
    int i,j;

    fmulti(stdout);
    for(i=1;i<ncells_x+1;++i)
        for(j=1;j<ncells_y+1;++j) output_list(cell_arr[i][j]);
    fsingl(stdout);
}


/************************ end of routine output_part2 ***********************/
```

A-10.2 Include File ljdef.h

```
    #define INITIALIZE  1
    #define FIND_ENERGY 2
    #define OUTPUT_PART 3
    #define STOP        4
    #define NCELL_X 50
    #define NCELL_Y 50
    #define MAX_PART 200
    #define MAX_EDGE  40
    #define PERIODIC     0
    #define NON_PERIODIC 1
    typedef struct particle{
      double x,y;
    } PARTICLE;
    typedef struct list{
        PARTICLE *part;
        struct list *next;
    } LIST;
```

A-11 WaTor – an Ecological Simulation

A-11.1 CUBIX Program

```
#include <cros.h>
#include <stdio.h>
#include "wator.h"
#include "cubdefs.h"

int nproc,doc,procnum;
int file_status=CLOSED,std_flag=0;

char IO_buf[4096];
FILE *in_file,*out_file;
LIST *cell_arr[NCELL_X][NCELL_Y];
OCC ocean[MAX_OCC+2][MAX_OCC+2];
int xsize,ysize,ncells_x,ncells_y,cell_sizex,cell_sizey;
int fish_size = sizeof(FISH);
int list_size = sizeof(LIST);
int update_number,num_min,num_shark,breed_min,breed_shark,starve_shark;
int backup_status,output_level;
int lfchan,rtchan,upchan,dnchan,nprocs,nprocx,nprocy,coord[2];
int n_edge_send,n_edge_return,stdout_status,outfile_status;
FISH edge_send[MAX_EDGE],edge_return[MAX_EDGE];

main()
{
    FILE *setup_out();
    int nsweeps,i;

    stdout_status  = SINGLE;
    in_file        = stdin;

    get_param();

    welcome();

    ask_questions();

    out_file = setup_out("watorCUB.c");
    if(std_flag) fflush(stdout);

    xsize = ncells_x*cell_sizex;
    ysize = ncells_y*cell_sizey;

    update_number = 0;
    backup_status = MID_OF_LIST;
```

```
        setup_grid();

        setup_problem();

        output_results();

        nsweeps = 0;
        while(nsweeps>=0){

            printf("\n\nPlease give the number of sweeps (-ve to end) ==> ");
            fflush(stdout);
            scanf("%d",&nsweeps);

            for(i=0;i<nsweeps;++i){
                update_number++;
                move_fish();
            }

            output_results();
        }

        printf("\nFinished\n");
        exit(0);
}


/*************************** end of routine main ***************************/
ask_questions()
{
        char input[10];

        printf("\n\nDo you want commentary? (y/n) ==> ");
        fflush(stdout);
        scanf("%s",input);

        if(strcmp("y",input) ==0 || strcmp("Y",input) == 0) output_level = COM;
        else output_level = MIN;

        printf("\n\nPlease give the initial number of minnows and sharks ==> ");
        fflush(stdout);
        scanf("%d%d",&num_min,&num_shark);

        printf("\n\nPlease give the breeding age of minnows and sharks ==> ");
        fflush(stdout);
        scanf("%d%d",&breed_min,&breed_shark);

        printf("\n\nPlease give the shark starvation age ==> ");
```

```
        fflush(stdout);
        scanf("%d",&starve_shark);

        printf("\n\nPlease give the number of cells per processor ");
        printf("in the x direction ==> ");
        fflush(stdout);
        scanf("%d",&ncells_x);

        printf("\n\nPlease give the number of cells per processor ");
        printf("in the y direction ==> ");
        fflush(stdout);
        scanf("%d",&ncells_y);

        printf("\n\nPlease give the number of grid points per cell ");
        printf("in the x direction ==> ");
        fflush(stdout);
        scanf("%d",&cell_sizex);

        printf("\n\nPlease give the number of grid points per cell ");
        printf("in the y direction ==> ");
        fflush(stdout);
        scanf("%d",&cell_sizey);
}

/*********************** end of routine ask_questions ***********************/
setup_problem()
{
        int seed;

        printf("\n\nPlease give a random number seed ==> ");
        fflush(stdout);
        scanf("%d",&seed);

        prand_setB(seed,2,procnum);

        setup_ocean();
        setup_f_list();

        printf("\nThe fish list has been set up\n");

        setup_fish(num_min,MINNOW);
        setup_fish(num_shark,SHARK);

        printf("\n\nThe fish are all in position\n");
}

/*********************** end of routine setup_problem ***********************/
```

```
setup_ocean()
{
    int i,j;

    for(i=0;i<xsize+2;++i){
        for(j=0;j<ysize+2;++j){
            ocean[i][j].what_sort = NOFISH;
            ocean[i][j].f_list    = (LIST *)NULL;
        }
    }
}


/*********************** end of routine setup_ocean ***********************/
setup_f_list()
{
    int i,j;
    LIST *make_list();

    for(i=0;i<ncells_x;++i)
        for(j=0;j<ncells_y;++j)
            cell_arr[i][j] = make_list();
}


/*********************** end of routine setup_f_list ***********************/
setup_fish(number,type)
int number,type;
{
    int mask,xval,yval,xy[2],x_coord,y_coord,i,xtemp,ytemp,cellx,celly;
    int count,num_fish,global_iadd();
    double prandS(),prandB();

    mask  = nprocs - 1;
    count = 0;
    num_fish = 0;

    while(num_fish<number){
        xtemp = 1 + (int)(prandS()*(double)(nprocx*xsize));
        ytemp = 1 + (int)(prandB()*(double)(nprocy*ysize));
        for(i=0;i<nprocs;++i){
            xy[0] = xtemp;
            xy[1] = ytemp;
            broadcast(xy,i,mask,2*sizeof(int));
            x_coord = (int)((xy[0]-1)/xsize);
            y_coord = (int)((xy[1]-1)/ysize);
            if(x_coord==coord[0] && y_coord==coord[1]){
                xval = xy[0] - xsize*coord[0];
                yval = xy[1] - ysize*coord[1];
```

```
                    if(ocean[xval][yval].what_sort == NOFISH){
                        create_fish(xval,yval,type);
                        count++;
                    }
                }
            num_fish = count;
            combine(&num_fish,global_iadd,sizeof(int),1);
            if(num_fish == number) break;
        }
    }
}

/*********************** end of routine setup_fish ***********************/
create_fish(nx,ny,type)
int nx,ny,type;
{
    int cellx,celly;
    LIST *listp;
    FISH ichy;

    ichy.x_pos   = nx;
    ichy.y_pos   = ny;
    ichy.f_type  = type;
    ichy.f_age   = 0;
    ichy.last_ate = 0;
    ichy.itno    = update_number;

    cellx = (nx-1)/cell_sizex;
    celly = (ny-1)/cell_sizey;

    listp = cell_arr[cellx][celly];
    insert(&ichy,listp);

    ocean[nx][ny].what_sort = type;
    ocean[nx][ny].f_list    = listp->next;
}

/*********************** end of routine create_fish ***********************/
remove_from_list(listp)
LIST *listp;
{
    listp->prev->next = listp->next;
    if(listp->next != (LIST *)NULL) listp->next->prev = listp->prev;
}

/********************* end of routine remove_from_list *********************/
```

```
    change_list(listp,list_new)
    LIST *listp,*list_new;
    {
        LIST *temp_list;

        temp_list = listp->next;

        remove_from_list(listp->next);

        if(list_new->next != (LIST *)NULL) list_new->next->prev = temp_list;
        temp_list->next = list_new->next;
        temp_list->prev = list_new;
        list_new->next = temp_list;
        list_new->prev = (LIST *)NULL;
    }


/************************* end of routine change_list *************************/
    remove_fish(nx,ny)
    int nx,ny;
    {
        LIST *listp;

        listp = ocean[nx][ny].f_list;
        remove_from_list(listp);
        free((char*)listp);

        ocean[nx][ny].what_sort = NOFISH;
        ocean[nx][ny].f_list    = (LIST *)NULL;
    }


/************************* end of routine remove_fish *************************/
    LIST *move_location(listp,xnew,ynew,nx,ny)
    LIST *listp;
    int xnew,ynew,nx,ny;
    {
        LIST *list_new,*backup();
        int breed,cellx,celly,cellx_new,celly_new,type;
        int check_breed();

        type = listp->next->swimmer.f_type;

        listp->next->swimmer.x_pos = xnew;
        listp->next->swimmer.y_pos = ynew;

        breed = check_breed(listp);

        cellx     = (nx-1)/cell_sizex;
```

```
        celly    = (ny-1)/cell_sizey;
        cellx_new = (xnew-1)/cell_sizex;
        celly_new = (ynew-1)/cell_sizey;

        ocean[xnew][ynew].what_sort = type;
        ocean[xnew][ynew].f_list    = listp->next;

        if(BORDER){
            remove_from_list(listp->next);
            listp = backup(listp);
        }
        else if(NEW_CELL){
            list_new = cell_arr[cellx_new][celly_new];
            change_list(listp,list_new);
        }

        if(breed){
            if(output_level == COM) fprintf(out_file,"  and its breeding");
            create_fish(nx,ny,type);
        }
        else{
            ocean[nx][ny].what_sort = NOFISH;
            ocean[nx][ny].f_list    = (LIST *)NULL;
        }
        return listp;
}


/***** ****************** end of routine move_location **********************/
age_fish(listp)
LIST *listp;
{
        listp->next->swimmer.last_ate++;
        listp->next->swimmer.f_age++;
        listp->next->swimmer.itno++;
}


/************************** end of routine age_fish ************************/
unage_fish(listp)
LIST *listp;
{
        listp->next->swimmer.last_ate--;
        listp->next->swimmer.f_age--;
        listp->next->swimmer.itno--;
}


/************************** end of routine unage_fish **********************/
```

```
int check_breed(listp)
LIST *listp;
{
    int age,type,breed_age;

    age  = listp->next->swimmer.f_age;
    type = listp->next->swimmer.f_type;
    breed_age = (type == SHARK) ? breed_shark : breed_min;

    return (age>=breed_age);
}
```

/*********************** end of routine check_breed ***********************/

```
border_ocean(type,xtemp,ytemp,listp)
LIST *listp;
int type,xtemp,ytemp;
{
    if(xtemp == 1){
        ocean[xsize+1][ytemp].what_sort = type;
        ocean[xsize+1][ytemp].f_list    = listp->next;
    }
    else if(xtemp == xsize){
        ocean[0][ytemp].what_sort = type;
        ocean[0][ytemp].f_list    = listp->next;
    }
    else if(ytemp == 1){
        ocean[xtemp][ysize+1].what_sort = type;
        ocean[xtemp][ysize+1].f_list    = listp->next;
    }
    else if(ytemp == ysize){
        ocean[xtemp][0].what_sort = type;
        ocean[xtemp][0].f_list    = listp->next;
    }
}
```

/*********************** end of routine border_ocean ***********************/
```
welcome()
{
    setbuffer(stdout,IO_buf,4096);
    std_flag = 1;
    printf("\n\n          ******************************************");
    printf("  \n          *                                        *");
    printf("  \n          *    Welcome to the watery world of WaTor!  *");
    printf("  \n          *                                        *");
    printf("  \n          ******************************************\n");
}
```

```
/*************************** end of routine welcome ***************************/
int is_empty(listp)
LIST *listp;
{
    return (listp->next == (LIST *)NULL);
}


/*************************** end of routine is_empty ***************************/
LIST *rest(listp)
LIST *listp;
{
    int is_empty();

    if(is_empty(listp)) printf("\n\nError in routine rest\n");
    else if(backup_status == TOP_OF_LIST){
        backup_status = MID_OF_LIST;
        return listp;
    }
    else return (listp->next);
}


/*************************** end of routine rest ***************************/
LIST *backup(listp)
LIST *listp;
{
    int is_empty();

    if(listp->prev == (LIST *)NULL){
        backup_status = TOP_OF_LIST;
        return listp;
    }
    else{
        backup_status = MID_OF_LIST;
        return (listp->prev);
    }
}


/*************************** end of routine backup ***************************/
insert(fishp,listp)
FISH *fishp;
LIST *listp;
{
    LIST *new;
    char *malloc();

    new = (LIST *)malloc(list_size);
```

```
        new->swimmer = *fishp;
        if(listp->next != (LIST *)NULL) listp->next->prev = new;
        new->next = listp->next;
        new->prev = listp;
        listp->next = new;
        listp->prev = (LIST *)NULL;
}

/************************** end of routine insert ***************************/
delete_entry(listp)
LIST *listp;
{
    LIST *kill;
    int is_empty();

    if(is_empty(listp)) printf("\n\nError in routine delete\n");
    else{
        kill = listp->next;
        listp->next = kill->next;
        free((char *)kill);
    }
}

/*********************** end of routine delete_entry ***********************/
LIST *make_list()
{
    LIST *ret;
    char *malloc();

    ret = (LIST *)malloc(list_size);
    ret->next = (LIST *)NULL;
    ret->prev = (LIST *)NULL;
    return ret;
}

/************************** end of routine make_list ***********************/
unmake_list(listp)
LIST *listp;
{
    int is_empty();

    if(is_empty(listp)) free((char *)listp);
    else printf("\n\nError in routine unmake_list\n");
}

/*********************** end of routine unmake_list ***********************/
```

```
list_cells()
{
    int cellx,celly,proc;
    char input[10];

    for(;;){
        for(;;){
            printf("\n\nPlease give the processor number ==> ");
            fflush(stdout);
            scanf("%s",input);
            proc = atoi(input);
            if(proc<0 || proc>=nprocs){
                printf("\n\n**** In valid processor number ");
                printf("- please re-select ****\n");
            }
            else break;
        }
        for(;;){
            printf("\n\nPlease give the x and y");
            printf("co-ordinates of the cell ==> ");
            fflush(stdout);
            scanf("%d%d",&cellx,&celly);
            if(cellx<0 || cellx>=ncells_x || celly<0 || celly>=ncells_y)
            printf("\n\nNo such cell - please re-select\n");
            else break;
        }

        list_a_cell(cellx,celly,proc);

        printf("\n\nAnother cell? (y/n) ==> ");
        fflush(stdout);
        scanf("%s",input);

        if(strcmp("y",input) !=0 && strcmp("Y",input) != 0) break;
    }
}

/*********************** end of routine list_cells ***********************/
list_a_cell(cellx,celly,proc)
int cellx,celly,proc;
{
    int empty_flag,task,ok,okay;
    LIST *listp,*rest(),*backup();
    FISH ichy;
    char input[40];

    fmulti(out_file);
```

```
        empty_flag = 0;
        if(procnum == proc){
            listp = cell_arr[cellx][celly];
            if(is_empty(listp)) {
                fprintf(out_file,"\n\nThis cell is empty\n");
                empty_flag = 1;
            }
        }
        fsingl(out_file);
        broadcast(&empty_flag,proc,nprocs-1,sizeof(int));
        if(empty_flag) return;

        for(;;){
            printf("\n\nPlease select one of the following :\n");
            printf( "\n    1...to list next fish");
            printf( "\n    2...to list previous fish");
            printf( "\n    3...to quit this list\n\n==> ");
            fflush(stdout);

            scanf("%s",input);

            task = atoi(input);

            fmulti(out_file);
            if(out_file != stdout) fmulti(stdout);
            if(procnum==proc){
                if(task==1){
                    if(is_empty(listp))
                        printf("\n\nYou're at the end of the list\n");
                    else{
                        ichy = listp->next->swimmer;
                        list_fish(&ichy);
                        listp = rest(listp);
                    }
                }
                else if(task==2){
                    if(listp->prev->prev == (LIST *)NULL)
                        printf("\n\nYou're at the top of the list\n");
                    else{
                        ichy = listp->prev->swimmer;
                        list_fish(&ichy);
                        listp = backup(listp);
                    }
                }
            }
            if(out_file != stdout) fsingl(stdout);
            fsingl(out_file);
```

```
            if(task==3) break;
            else if (task !=1 && task !=2)
                printf("\n\n**** Invalid input - try again ****\n");
    }
}


/*********************** end of routine list_a_cell ***********************/
list_fish(ichy)
FISH *ichy;
{
    int xtemp,ytemp;

    xtemp = ichy->x_pos + xsize*coord[0];
    ytemp = ichy->y_pos + ysize*coord[1];

    fprintf(out_file,"\n\nFish x co-ordinate  = %6d",xtemp);
    fprintf(out_file,"\nFish y co-ordinate  = %6d",ytemp);
    if(ichy->f_type == MINNOW)
        fprintf(out_file,"\nFish type           = MINNOW");
    else{
        fprintf(out_file,"\nFish type           =  SHARK");
        fprintf(out_file,"\nTime shark last ate = %6d",ichy->last_ate);
    }
    fprintf(out_file,"\nAge of fish         = %6d",ichy->f_age);
    fprintf(out_file,"\nUpdate number       = %6d\n",ichy->itno);
}


/*********************** end of routine list_fish ***********************/
set_output_level()
{
    char input[40];
    int atoi(),ok;

    ok=0;
    while(!ok){
        printf("\n\nPlease select level of output :\n");
        printf(" \n    1...minimal output");
        printf(" \n    2...input data listed");
        printf(" \n    3...cell contents listed");
        printf(" \n    4...both (2) and (3) above\n\n==> ");
        fflush(stdout);

        scanf("%s",input);

        output_level = atoi(input);

        if(output_level>0 && output_level<5) ok = 1;
```

```
            else printf("\n**** Invalid input - try again ****\n");
    }
}

/********************* end of routine set_output_level *********************/
move_fish()
{
    LIST *listp;
    int cellx,celly;

    for(cellx=0;cellx<ncells_x;++cellx)
        for(celly=0;celly<ncells_y;++celly){
            listp = cell_arr[cellx][celly];
            if(!INSIDE) send_bound(cellx,celly);
            update_fish(listp,cellx,celly);
            if(!INSIDE) return_bound(cellx,celly);
        }
}

/************************* end of routine move_fish ************************/
output_results()
{
    int task;


    for(;;){
        printf("\n\nPlease choose one of the following :\n");
        printf( "\n    1...to list contents of a cell");
        printf( "\n    2...to display a patch of ocean");
        printf( "\n    3...to quit this menu");
        printf("\n\n==> ");
        fflush(stdout);
        scanf("%d",&task);

        if(task==1) list_cells();
        else if(task==2) list_ocean();
        else if(task==3) break;
        else printf("\n\n**** Invalid input - try again ****");
    }
}

/********************* end of routine output_results *********************/
list_ocean()
{
    int minx,miny,maxx,maxy,i,j,k,type,proc,which_proc(),xoc,yoc;

    printf("\n\nPlease define the rectangle you want to look at :\n");
```

```
printf(  "\n            minimum x, maximum x ==> ");
fflush(stdout);
scanf("%d%d",&minx,&maxx);
printf("\n\n          minimum y, maximum y ==> ");
fflush(stdout);
scanf("%d%d",&miny,&maxy);
fprintf(out_file,"\n");

if(out_file == stdout) getchar();

for(i=minx;i<=maxx+1;++i){
    fprintf(out_file,"--");
    if(2*(i-minx)>=SCREEN_WIDTH) break;
}


fprintf(out_file,"\n");

for(j=maxy,k=0;j>=miny;--j){
    fprintf(out_file,"|");
    for(i=minx;i<=maxx;++i,++k){
        if(2*(i-minx)>=SCREEN_WIDTH) break;
        proc = which_proc(i,j);
        fmulti(out_file);
        if(procnum == proc){
            xoc  = i - coord[0]*xsize;
            yoc  = j - coord[1]*ysize;
            type = ocean[xoc][yoc].what_sort;
            if(type == NOFISH) fprintf(out_file," ");
            else if(type == SHARK) fprintf(out_file,"S ");
            else fprintf(out_file,"M ");
        }
        if(k%100==99) fflush(out_file);
    }
    fsingl(out_file);
    fprintf(out_file,"|\n");
    if(out_file==stdout && (maxy-j)%20==19 && j!=miny) dw_pause();
}

fsingl(out_file);
for(i=minx;i<=maxx+1;++i){
    fprintf(out_file,"--");
    if(2*(i-minx)>=SCREEN_WIDTH) break;
}

fprintf(out_file,"\nUpdate number %d",update_number);

if(out_file == stdout) dw_pause();
```

```c
}

/************************* end of routine list_ocean *************************/
int which_proc(i,j)
int i,j;
{
    int px,py;

    px = (i-1)/xsize;
    py = (j-1)/ysize;

    if(px == coord[0] && py == coord[1]) return procnum;
    else return -1;
}

/************************* end of routine which_proc *************************/
update_fish(listp,cellx,celly)
LIST *listp;
int cellx,celly;
{
  FISH ichy;
  LIST *eat_minnow(),*rest(),*move_location();
  int done,starve,type,xtemp,ytemp,nx,ny,dir,give_dir(),xnew,ynew;
  int add_int(),fcount,xmw,ymw;

  fcount = 0;
  done   = 0;
  if(output_level == COM) fmulti(out_file);

  while(!is_empty(listp)){
     fcount++;
     age_fish(listp);
     ichy = listp->next->swimmer;
     if(ichy.itno != update_number){
        unage_fish(listp);
        listp = rest(listp);
        continue;
     }
     starve = ichy.last_ate;
     type   = ichy.f_type;
     nx     = ichy.x_pos;
     ny     = ichy.y_pos;
     xtemp  = nx + xsize*coord[0];
     ytemp  = ny + ysize*coord[1];
     if(type==SHARK){
        if(starve>starve_shark){
           if(output_level == COM){
```

```
                    fprintf(out_file,"\nShark at (%d,%d) ",xtemp,ytemp);
                    fprintf(out_file,"has starved to death");
                }
                listp = backup(listp);
                remove_fish(nx,ny);
            }
            else{
                dir = give_dir(nx,ny,MINNOW);
                if(dir>=0){
                    dirtoxy(dir,nx,ny,&xnew,&ynew);
                    if(output_level == COM){
                        xmw = xnew+xsize*coord[0];
                        ymw = ynew+ysize*coord[1];
                        fprintf(out_file,"\nShark at (%d,%d) ",xtemp,temp);
                        fprintf(out_file,"is eating minnow at (%d,%d)",xmw,ymw);
                    }
                    listp = eat_minnow(listp,xnew,ynew,nx,ny);
                }
                else{
                    dir = give_dir(nx,ny,NOFISH);
                    if(dir>=0){
                        xmw = xnew+xsize*coord[0];
                        ymw = ynew+ysize*coord[1];
                        dirtoxy(dir,nx,ny,&xnew,&ynew);
                        if(output_level == COM){
                            fprintf(out_file,"\nShark is moving from ");
                            fprintf(out_file,"(%d,%d) to (%d,%d)",xtemp,ytemp,xmw,ymw);
                        }
                        listp=move_location(listp,xnew,ynew,nx,ny);
                    }
                }
            }
        }
        else{
            dir = give_dir(nx,ny,NOFISH);
            if(dir>=0){
                dirtoxy(dir,nx,ny,&xnew,&ynew);
                if(output_level == COM){
                    xmw = xnew+xsize*coord[0]
                    ymw = ynew+ysize*coord[1];
                    fprintf(out_file,"\nMinnow is moving from ");
                    fprintf(out_file,"(%d,%d) to (%d,%d)",xtemp,ytemp,xmw,ymw);
                }
                listp = move_location(listp,xnew,ynew,nx,ny);
            }
        }
        if((output_level == COM) && (fcount%6==5)){
```

```
            done    = 0;
            combine(&done,add_int,sizeof(int),1);
            fflush(out_file);
        }
    }
    if(output_level == COM){
        while(done!=nprocs){
            done = 1;
            combine(&done,add_int,sizeof(int),1);
            fflush(out_file);
        }
        fsingl(out_file);
        fprintf(out_file,"\n");
    }
}


/*********************** end of routine update_fish ***********************/
LIST *eat_minnow(listp,xnew,ynew,nx,ny)
LIST *listp;
int xnew,ynew,nx,ny;
{
    LIST *food;

    food = ocean[xnew][ynew].f_list;
    ocean[xnew][ynew].what_sort = SHARK;

    food->swimmer.f_type = SHARK;
    food->swimmer.last_ate = 0;
    food->swimmer.f_age    = listp->next->swimmer.f_age;
    food->swimmer.itno     = listp->next->swimmer.itno;

    if(listp->next->swimmer.f_age >= breed_shark){
        if(output_level == COM)
            fprintf(out_file,"   and it's breeding");
        listp->next->swimmer.last_ate = 0;
        listp->next->swimmer.f_age    = 0;
    }
    else{
        listp = backup(listp);
        remove_fish(nx,ny);
    }
    return listp;
}


/*********************** end of routine eat_minnow ***********************/
```

```
int give_dir(x,y,type)
int x,y,type;
{
    int numposs,poss[4];
    double prandS();

    numposs = 0;
    if(ocean[x+1][y].what_sort == type) poss[numposs++] = 0;
    if(ocean[x-1][y].what_sort == type) poss[numposs++] = 1;
    if(ocean[x][y+1].what_sort == type) poss[numposs++] = 2;
    if(ocean[x][y-1].what_sort == type) poss[numposs++] = 3;

    if(numposs>0) return poss[(long)(numposs*prandS())];
    else return -1;
}

/************************* end of routine give_dir *************************/
dirtoxy(dir,x,y,pxnew,pynew)
int dir,x,y,*pxnew,*pynew;
{
    switch(dir){
        case 0:
                *pxnew = x+1;
                *pynew = y;
                break;
        case 1:
                *pxnew = x-1;
                *pynew = y;
                break;
        case 2:
                *pxnew = x;
                *pynew = y+1;
                break;
        case 3:
                *pxnew = x;
                *pynew = y-1;
                break;
    }
}

/************************* end of routine dirtoxy *************************/
send_bound(cellx,celly)
int cellx,celly;
{
    n_edge_send = 0;

    if(LEFT_EDGE)   ystrip_exchg(0,xsize,lfchan,rtchan,cellx,celly,SEND);
```

```
        if(RIGHT_EDGE)  ystrip_exchg(xsize+1,1,rtchan,lfchan,cellx,celly,SEND);
        if(TOP_EDGE)    xstrip_exchg(ysize+1,1,upchan,dnchan,cellx,celly,SEND);
        if(BOTTOM_EDGE) xstrip_exchg(0,ysize,dnchan,upchan,cellx,celly,SEND);
}


/************************* end of routine send_bound *************************/
return_bound(cellx,celly)
int cellx,celly;
{
        n_edge_return = 0;

        if(LEFT_EDGE)
                ystrip_exchg(xsize,0,rtchan,lfchan,cellx,celly,RETURN);
        if(RIGHT_EDGE)
                ystrip_exchg(1,xsize+1,lfchan,rtchan,cellx,celly,RETURN);
        if(TOP_EDGE)
                xstrip_exchg(1,ysize+1,dnchan,upchan,cellx,celly,RETURN);
        if(BOTTOM_EDGE)
                xstrip_exchg(ysize,0,upchan,dnchan,cellx,celly,RETURN);
}


/************************* end of routine return_bound *************************/
ystrip_exchg(xval_to,xval_from,inchan,outchan,cellx,celly,dir)
int xval_to,xval_from,inchan,outchan,cellx,celly,dir;
{
        int cx,cy,nx,ny,oc,oc_start,oc_end,i,nin,nout,n_edge;
        LIST *listp;
        OCC oc_temp;
        FISH *outbuf,*inbuf,ichy;

        if(dir == SEND) outbuf = &edge_send[n_edge_send];
        else outbuf = &edge_return[n_edge_return];

        inbuf = outbuf;
        nout  = 0;

        oc_start = 1 + celly*cell_sizey;
        oc_end   = oc_start + cell_sizey;
        for(oc=oc_start;oc<oc_end;++oc){
            if(dir == SEND) ocean[xval_to][oc].what_sort = NOFISH;
            if(dir == RETURN && ocean[xval_to][oc].what_sort != NOFISH)
                remove_fish(xval_to,oc);
            oc_temp = ocean[xval_from][oc];
            if(oc_temp.what_sort != NOFISH){
                listp = oc_temp.f_list;
                outbuf[nout++] = listp->swimmer;
            }
```

```
      }

      n_edge = (dir == SEND) ? n_edge_send : n_edge_return;
      nin = exchange_fish(inchan,inbuf,outchan,outbuf,nout,n_edge);

      for(i=0;i<nin;++i){
          ichy = inbuf[i];
          nx   = ichy.x_pos;
          ny   = ichy.y_pos;
          if(nx == 0) ichy.x_pos = xsize;
          if(nx == (xsize+1)) ichy.x_pos = 1;
          ocean[xval_to][ny].what_sort = ichy.f_type;
          if(dir == SEND)
              ocean[xval_to][ny].f_list    = (LIST *)(&inbuf[i]);
          else{
              cx = (ichy.x_pos-1)/cell_sizex;
              cy = (ichy.y_pos-1)/cell_sizey;
              listp = cell_arr[cx][cy];
              insert(&ichy,listp);
              ocean[xval_to][ny].f_list = listp->next;
          }
      }

      if(dir == SEND) n_edge_send += nin;
      else n_edge_return += nin;
}

/*********************** end of routine ystrip_exchg ***********************/
xstrip_exchg(yval_to,yval_from,inchan,outchan,cellx,celly,dir)
int yval_to,yval_from,inchan,outchan,cellx,celly,dir;
{
      int cx,cy,nx,ny,oc,oc_start,oc_end,i,nin,nout,n_edge;
      LIST *listp;
      OCC oc_temp;
      FISH *outbuf,*inbuf,ichy;

      if(dir == SEND) outbuf = &edge_send[n_edge_send];
      else outbuf = &edge_return[n_edge_return];

      inbuf  = outbuf;
      nout   = 0;

      oc_start = 1 + cellx*cell_sizex;
      oc_end   = oc_start + cell_sizex;
      for(oc=oc_start;oc<oc_end;++oc){
              if(dir == SEND) ocean[oc][yval_to].what_sort = NOFISH;
              if(dir == RETURN && ocean[oc][yval_to].what_sort != NOFISH)
```

```
                remove_fish(oc,yval_to);
        oc_temp = ocean[oc][yval_from];
        if(oc_temp.what_sort != NOFISH){
            listp = oc_temp.f_list;
            outbuf[nout++] = listp->swimmer;
        }
    }

    n_edge = (dir == SEND) ? n_edge_send : n_edge_return;
    nin = exchange_fish(inchan,inbuf,outchan,outbuf,nout,n_edge);

    for(i=0;i<nin;++i){
        ichy = inbuf[i];
        nx    = ichy.x_pos;
        ny    = ichy.y_pos;
        if(ny == 0) ichy.y_pos = ysize;
        if(ny == (ysize+1)) ichy.y_pos = 1;
        ocean[nx][yval_to].what_sort = ichy.f_type;
        if(dir == SEND)
            ocean[nx][yval_to].f_list    = (LIST *)(&inbuf[i]);
        else{
            cx = (ichy.x_pos-1)/cell_sizex;
            cy = (ichy.y_pos-1)/cell_sizey;
            listp = cell_arr[cx][cy];
            insert(&ichy,listp);
            ocean[nx][yval_to].f_list = listp->next;
        }
    }

    if(dir == SEND) n_edge_send += nin;
    else n_edge_return += nin;
}


/*********************** end of routine xstrip_exchg ***********************/
int exchange_fish(inchan,inbuf,outchan,outbuf,nout,n_edge)
int inchan,outchan,nout,n_edge;
FISH *inbuf,*outbuf;
{
    int inspace,nbytes;

    if((nout+n_edge)>MAX_EDGE){
        discard_edge_fish();
        nout = MAX_EDGE - n_edge;
    }

    inspace = (MAX_EDGE - n_edge)*fish_size;
```

```
    nbytes = cshift(inbuf,inchan,inspace,outbuf,outchan,nout*fish_size);

    return nbytes/fish_size;
}


/*********************** end of routine exchange_fish ***********************/
discard_edge_fish()
{
    if(stdout_status == SINGLE) fmulti(stdout);
    printf("\n\nToo many edge fish in processor %2d",procnum);
    printf(". Some will be discarded\n");
    if(stdout_status == SINGLE) fsingl(stdout);
}


/********************** end of routine discard_edge_fish ********************/
setup_grid()
{
    int log2_next(),nprocs_x,nprocs_y,ok,logx,logy,np[2];

    ok = 0;
    while(!ok){
    printf("\n\nPlease give the number of processors in the x");
    printf(" direction ==> ");
    fflush(stdout);
    scanf("%d",&nprocs_x);

    printf("\n\nPlease give the number of processors in the y");
    printf(" direction ==> ");
    fflush(stdout);
    scanf("%d",&nprocs_y);

    printf("\n");
    logx = log2_next(nprocs_x);
    logy = log2_next(nprocs_y);

    if((logx+logy)>(int)doc){
        printf("\n\nAn array of %d X %d ",nprocs_x,nprocs_y);
        printf("processors cannot be mapped ");
        printf("onto a hypercube of dimension %d\n",doc);
    }
    else if((logx+logy)<(int)doc){
        printf("\n\nSome processors will be idle. Please increase");
        printf(" the size of the array of processors\n");
    }
    else{
        ok = 1;
        nprocx = 1<<logx;
```

```
        nprocy = 1<<logy;
        if(nprocs_x != nprocx || nprocs_y != nprocy){
            printf("\n\nTo avoid idle processors the size of ");
            printf("the array of processors\n");
            printf("has been increased to %d X %d\n",nprocx,nprocy);
        }
    }

    nprocs = 1<<doc;

    np[0] = nprocx;
    np[1] = nprocy;

    gridinit(2,np);

    upchan = gridchan(procnum,1,1);
    dnchan = gridchan(procnum,1,-1);
    rtchan = gridchan(procnum,0,1);
    lfchan = gridchan(procnum,0,-1);

    gridcoord(procnum,coord);

    printf("\n\nThe computer is now configured as a ");
    printf("%d X %d array of processors\n",nprocx,nprocy);
    fflush(stdout);
    }

}

/*********************** end of routine setup_grid ***********************/
int global_iadd(p1,p2,size)
int *p1,*p2,size;
{
    *p1 += *p2;

    return 0;
}

/*********************** end of routine global_iadd ***********************/
```

A-11.2 Include File wator.h

```
typedef struct fish{
    int f_type,f_age,last_ate,x_pos,y_pos,itno;
} FISH;
typedef struct list{
    FISH swimmer;
    struct list *prev;
    struct list *next;
} LIST;
typedef struct occ{
    int what_sort;
    struct list *f_list;
} OCC;

#define SCREEN_WIDTH 72
#define NCELL_X 64
#define NCELL_Y 64
#define NOFISH  0
#define MINNOW  1
#define SHARK   2
#define MAX_OCC 64
#define INSIDE (cellx!=0&&cellx!=(ncells_x-1)&&celly!=0&&celly!=(ncells_y-1))
#define LEFT_EDGE   (cellx == 0)
#define RIGHT_EDGE  (cellx == (ncells_x-1))
#define TOP_EDGE    (celly == (ncells_y-1))
#define BOTTOM_EDGE (celly == 0)
#define BORDER (xnew==0 || xnew==(xsize+1) || ynew==0 || ynew==(ysize+1))
#define NEW_CELL (cellx != cellx_new || celly != celly_new)
#define SEND    0
#define RETURN 1
#define MAX_EDGE 200
#define COM 1
#define MIN 0
#define TOP_OF_LIST 0
#define MID_OF_LIST 1
#define SINGLE 0
#define MULTI  1
```

A-12 Distributed Sorting Algorithms

A-12.1 CUBIX Program

```c
#include <cros.h>
#include <stdio.h>
#include "sortdef.h"
#include "cubdefs.h"

#define min(A,B) ((A) > (B) ? (B) : (A))
#define max(A,B) ((A) > (B) ? (A) : (B))

int szarray[MAX_PROCS];
int nproc,doc,procnum;
int std_flag=0,file_status;
int ntotal,n_per_proc[MAX_PROCS];
FILE *fildat,*in_file,*out_file;
char IO_buf[4096];

main()
{
    int command,nitems,order_flag,nsample;
    TYPE items[MAX_ITEMS+2];

    in_file     = stdin;
    fildat      = stdin;
    out_file    = stdout;
    file_status = CLOSED;

    welcome();

    get_param();

    while( (command=get_task()) != STOP ){
        switch(command){
            case INITIALIZE:
                nitems = initialize(items);
                order_flag = 1;
                break;
            case BITONIC:
                par_bitonic(items,nitems);
                order_flag = 1;
                break;
            case SHELL_SORT:
                par_shellsort(items,nitems);
                order_flag = 0;
                break;
```

```
            case QUICK_SORT:
                nsample = sample_size();
                nitems = par_quicksort(items,nitems,nsample);
                order_flag = 2;
                break;
            case OUTPUT:
                output_data(items,nitems,order_flag);
                break;
        }
    }
    printf("\n\nFinished\n");
    exit(0);
}


/*************************** end of routine main **************************/
int and_int(p1,p2,size)
int *p1,*p2,size;
{
    *p1 &= *p2;
    return 0;
}


/************************** end of routine and_int ************************/
bitonic_merge(items,nitems)
TYPE *items;
int nitems;
{
    int i,j,parity,ithbit,jthbit;
    TYPE item2[MAX_ITEMS+2];

    ASNKEY(item2[0],NEGINF)
    ASNKEY(item2[nitems+1],POSINF)

    parity=0;          /* an array toggle */
    for(i=1;i<=doc;++i){
        ithbit = (procnum>>i)&1;
        for(j=i-1;j>=0;--j){
            jthbit = (procnum>>j)&1;
            if(ithbit^jthbit){
                if(parity)cmp_ex_hi(item2,items,nitems,1<<j);
                else      cmp_ex_hi(items,item2,nitems,1<<j);
            }
            else{
                if(parity) cmp_ex_low(item2,items,nitems,1<<j);
                else       cmp_ex_low(items,item2,nitems,1<<j);
            }
            parity = 1-parity;    /* toggle arrays */
```

```
            }
        }

        if(parity) for(i=0;i<nitems;++i) ASNKEY(items[i],item2[i+1])
        else        for(i=0;i<nitems;++i) ASNKEY(items[i],items[i+1])
}


/*********************** end of routine bitonic_merge ***********************/
int cmp_ex_hi(old_list,new_list,nitems,mask)
TYPE *old_list,*new_list;
int nitems,mask;
{
    int i,j,k,nrec,nbytes,tsize,in_space,index,done;
    TYPE comm_buf[COM_SIZE];

    done    = 1;
    if(!mask) return done;
    tsize   = sizeof(TYPE);
    in_space = NBUF*tsize;
    index   = 1;
    nbytes  = min(in_space,(nitems+1)*tsize);
    nrec = cshift(comm_buf,mask,in_space,old_list+index,mask,nbytes)/tsize;

    j = nrec-1;
    i = nitems;
    for(k=nitems;k>=1;--k) {
        if(COMPARE(old_list[i],comm_buf[j]) >= 0){
            ASNKEY(new_list[k],old_list[i])
            --i;
        }
        else{
            ASNKEY(new_list[k],comm_buf[j])
            done = 0;
            if(j == 0){
                index = min(nitems+1,index+NBUF);
                nbytes = min(in_space,(nitems+2-index)*tsize);
                nrec = cshift(comm_buf,mask,in_space,
                              old_list+index,mask,nbytes)/tsize;
                j = nrec-1;
            }
            else j--;
        }
    }
    return done;
}


/*********************** end of routine cmp_ex_hi ***********************/
```

```
int cmp_ex_low(old_list,new_list,nitems,mask)
TYPE *old_list,*new_list;
int nitems,mask;
{
    int i,j,k,nrec,nbytes,tsize,in_space,index,done;
    TYPE comm_buf[COM_SIZE];

    done     = 1;
    if(!mask) return done;
    tsize    = sizeof(TYPE);
    in_space = NBUF*tsize;
    index    = max(0,(nitems-NBUF+1));
    nbytes   = min(in_space,(nitems+1)*tsize);
    nrec = cshift(comm_buf,mask,in_space,old_list+index,mask,nbytes)/tsize;

    i = 1;
    j = 0;
    for(k=1;k<=nitems;++k){
        if(COMPARE(old_list[i],comm_buf[j]) <= 0){
            ASNKEY(new_list[k],old_list[i])
            ++i;
        }
        else{
            ASNKEY(new_list[k],comm_buf[j])
            done = 0;
            if(j == nrec-1){
                nbytes = min(in_space,max(1,index)*tsize);
                index  = max(0,index-NBUF);
                nrec = cshift(comm_buf,mask,in_space,
                            old_list+index,mask,nbytes)/tsize;
                j = 0;
            }
            else j++;
        }
    }
    return done;
}

/*********************** end of routine cmp_ex_low ***********************/
int distrib(items,nitems,nsample)
int nitems,nsample;
TYPE *items;
{
    TYPE sample[MAX_SAMPLE],splitting_keys[MAX_KEYS];
    int p,mask,chan,tsize;

    tsize = sizeof(TYPE);
```

```
    sample_data(items,nitems,sample,nsample);
    par_bitonic(sample,nsample);
    concat(sample,tsize,splitting_keys,tsize,szarray);

    for(p=mask=nproc/2,chan=doc-1;chan>=0;mask/=2,--chan){
        if(procnum&mask){
            nitems = highdist(items,nitems,chan,splitting_keys[p]);
            p += mask/2;
        }
        else{
            nitems =  lowdist(items,nitems,chan,splitting_keys[p]);
            p -= mask/2;
        }
    }
    return nitems;
}


/*************************** end of routine distrib ***************************/
int file_data(items)
TYPE *items;
{
    int i,npts,nleft,nmin,proc;
    TYPE temp_item;
    FILE *setup_in();

    fildat = setup_in("containing data to be sorted");

    do{
        printf("\n\nPlease give total number of items to be sorted ==> ");
        scanf("%d",&ntotal);
        nmin   = ntotal/nproc;
    } while((nmin+1)>=MAX_ITEMS);
    nleft  = ntotal%nproc;

    for(proc=0;proc<nproc;++proc){
        npts= (proc < nleft) ? 1+nmin : nmin;
        n_per_proc[proc] = npts;
        for(i=0;i<npts;++i){
            READ_ITEM(fildat,temp_item)
            if(proc==procnum) ASNKEY(items[i],temp_item)
        }
    }
    return ( (procnum < nleft) ? 1+nmin : nmin );
}


/*********************** end of routine file_data ************************/
```

```
int get_task()
{
    int task;
    char input[5];

    for(;;){
        printf("\n\nPlease choose one of the following :\n");
        printf("    1...to initialize data to be sorted\n");
        printf("    2...to sort data using the bitonic algorithm\n");
        printf("    3...to sort data using the shellsort algorithm\n");
        printf("    4...to sort data using the quicksort algorithm\n");
        printf("    5...to output data\n");
        printf("    6...to terminate the program\n==> ");
        if(std_flag) fflush(stdout);

        scanf("%s",input);

        task = atoi(input);

        if(task>0 && task<7) break;
        else printf("\n\n**** Invalid input - try again ****\n");
    }
    return task;
}

/************************* end of routine get_task *************************/
int highdist(items,nitems,chan,key)
int nitems,chan;
TYPE *items,key;
{
    int i,j,mask,num_in,nbytes,in_space,tsize;

    tsize = sizeof(TYPE);

    ASNKEY(items[0],POSINF)
    ASNKEY(items[nitems+1],NEGINF)

    i = 1;
    j = nitems;
    while(i<j){
        while(COMPARE(items[i],key) >  0) ++i;
        while(COMPARE(items[j],key) <= 0) --j;
        if(i<j) SWAP(items[i],items[j]);
    }

    nbytes = tsize*(nitems-i+1);
    in_space = (MAX_ITEMS+2-i)*tsize;
```

```
    mask    = 1<<chan;
    num_in = cshift(items+i,mask,in_space,items+i,mask,nbytes)/tsize;

    return (i+num_in-1);
}


/*********************** end of routine highdist ***********************/
int initialize(items)
TYPE *items;
{
    int option,nitems;
    char input[5];

    for(;;){
        printf("\n\nPlease indicate type of input data :\n");
        printf("   1...Data read from standard input\n");
        printf("   2...Data read from file\n");
        printf("   3...Use random data\n\n==> ");
        if(std_flag) fflush(stdout);
        scanf("%s",input);
        option = atoi(input);

        if(option>0 && option<4) break;
        else printf("\n\n**** Invalid input - try again ****\n");
    }
    if(option==1)      nitems = standard_data(items);
    else if(option==2) nitems = file_data(items);
    else if(option==3) nitems = random_data(items);

    return nitems;
}


/*********************** end of routine initialize ***********************/
insertion(low,high,item)
TYPE *item;
int low,high;
{
    int i,j,k;
    TYPE temp;

    for(i=low+1; i<=high; ++i) {
        if(COMPARE(item[i],item[i-1]) < 0){
            for(j=i-2; COMPARE(item[i],item[j])<0; --j)
                ;
            ASNKEY(temp,item[i])
            for(k=i; k>j+1; --k) ASNKEY(item[k],item[k-1])
            ASNKEY(item[j+1],temp)
```

```
            }
        }
}

/*********************** end of routine insertion ***********************/
int lowdist(items,nitems,chan,key)
int nitems,chan;
TYPE *items,key;
{
    int i,j,mask,num_in,nbytes,in_space,tsize;

    tsize = sizeof(TYPE);
    ASNKEY(items[0],NEGINF)
    ASNKEY(items[nitems+1],POSINF)

    i = 1;
    j = nitems;
    while(i<j){
        while(COMPARE(items[i],key) <= 0) ++i;
        while(COMPARE(items[j],key) >  0) --j;
        if(i<j) SWAP(items[i],items[j]);
    }

    nbytes = tsize*(nitems-i+1);
    in_space = (MAX_ITEMS+2-i)*tsize;
    mask   = 1<<chan;
    num_in = cshift(items+i,mask,in_space,items+i,mask,nbytes)/tsize;

    return (i+num_in-1);
}

/*********************** end of routine lowdist ***********************/
output_data(items,nitems,order_flag)
int nitems,order_flag;
TYPE *items;
{
    int i,ntot,proc,npts,nlines,order;
    FILE *setup_out();

    if(file_status==CLOSED) out_file = setup_out("sortCUB.c");

    if(order_flag) order = procnum;
    else {
        gridinit(1,&nproc);
        gridcoord(procnum,&order);
    }
```

```
        if(order_flag==2)
            concat(&nitems,sizeof(int),n_per_proc,sizeof(int),szarray);

        nlines = 0;
        printf("\n");
        fmulti(out_file);
        for(proc=0,ntot=0;proc<nproc;++proc){
            npts = n_per_proc[proc];
            for(i=0;i<npts;++i,++ntot){
                if(proc==order){
                    WRITE_ITEM(out_file,items[i])
                    if(ntot%N_PER_LINE==(N_PER_LINE-1)){
                        fprintf(out_file,"\n");
                        nlines++;
                    }
                }
                else if(ntot%N_PER_LINE==(N_PER_LINE-1)) nlines++;
                if(nlines%20==19 && out_file==stdout){
                    nlines=0;
                    fsingl(out_file);
                    dw_pause();
                    fmulti(out_file);
                }
            }
            fflush(out_file);
        }
        fsingl(out_file);
        if(nlines>10 && out_file==stdout) dw_pause();
}

/*********************** end of routine output_data ***********************/
par_bitonic(items,nitems)
int nitems;
TYPE *items;
{
    int i;

    for(i=nitems-1;i>=0;--i) ASNKEY(items[i+1],items[i])
    ASNKEY(items[0],NEGINF)
    ASNKEY(items[nitems+1],POSINF)

    quicksort(1,nitems,items);
    insertion(1,nitems,items);
    bitonic_merge(items,nitems);
}

/*********************** end of routine par_bitonic ***********************/
```

```
int par_quicksort(items,nitems,nsample)
int nitems,nsample;
TYPE *items;
{
    int i;

    for(i=nitems-1;i>=0;--i) ASNKEY(items[i+1],items[i])

    nitems = distrib(items,nitems,nsample);

    ASNKEY(items[0],NEGINF)
    ASNKEY(items[nitems+1],POSINF)

    quicksort(1,nitems,items);
    insertion(1,nitems,items);
    for(i=0;i<nitems;++i) ASNKEY(items[i],items[i+1])

    return nitems;
}

/*********************** end of routine par_quicksort **********************/
par_shellsort(items,nitems)
int nitems;
TYPE *items;
{
    int i;

    for(i=nitems-1;i>=0;--i) ASNKEY(items[i+1],items[i])
    ASNKEY(items[0],NEGINF)
    ASNKEY(items[nitems+1],POSINF)

    quicksort(1,nitems,items);
    insertion(1,nitems,items);

    shell_merge(items,nitems);
}

/*********************** end of routine par_shellsort **********************/
quicksort(low,high,item)
int low,high;
TYPE *item;
{
    int i,j;
    TYPE k;

        i = low+1;
        j = high;
```

```
                /* partition via R. Sedgwick's way; Knuth V3, pp.114 */
        ASNKEY(k,item[low])
        while(i<j){
            while(COMPARE(item[i],k) <= 0)
                ++i;
            while(COMPARE(item[j],k) > 0)
                --j;
            if(i<j) SWAP(item[i],item[j])
        }
        if(j>low) SWAP(item[low],item[j])
                /* quicksort only down to lists of size M - after */
                /* that, do a straight insertion sort - see */
                /* Knuth V3, pp. 116 */
        if(j-1-low > M)
            quicksort(low,j-1,item);
        if(high-i > M)
            quicksort(i,high,item);
}

/************************ end of routine quicksort ************************/
int random_data(items)
TYPE *items;
{
    int i,proc,npts,nitems,iseed,nleft,nmin;
    TYPE temp_item;

    do{
        printf("\n\nPlease give total number of items to be sorted ==> ");
        if(std_flag) fflush(stdout);
        scanf("%d",&ntotal);
        nmin    = ntotal/nproc;
    } while ((nmin+1)>=MAX_ITEMS);

    printf("\n\nPlease give a seed integer ==> ");
    if(std_flag) fflush(stdout);
    scanf("%d",&iseed);
    prand_setB(iseed,0,0);

    nleft  = ntotal%nproc;
    nitems = (procnum < nleft) ? 1+nmin : nmin;

    for(proc=0;proc<nproc;++proc){
        npts= (proc < nleft) ? 1+nmin : nmin;
        n_per_proc[proc] = npts;
        for(i=0;i<npts;++i){
            RANDOM_ITEM(temp_item)
            if(proc==procnum) ASNKEY(items[i],temp_item)
```

```
            }
        }
        return nitems;
    }


/************************ end of routine random_data *********************/
sample_data(items,nitems,sample,nsample)
int nitems,nsample;
TYPE *items,*sample;
{
    int i,j;
    double prandB();

    prand_setB(12345,1,procnum);

    for(i=0;i<nsample;++i){
        j = (int)(prandB()*(double)(nitems-1));
        sample[i] = items[j+1];
    }
}


/************************ end of routine sample_data *********************/
int sample_size()
{
    int nsample;
    double sqrt();

    printf("\n\nPlease give sample size per processor");
    printf(" (-ve for sqrt(m)) ==> ");
    if(std_flag) fflush(stdout);
    scanf("%d",&nsample);

    if(nsample<0)  nsample = ((int)sqrt((double)ntotal))/nproc;
    if(nsample==0) nsample = 1;

    printf("\n\nThe sample size is %d items per processor\n",nsample);
    if(std_flag) fflush(stdout);

    return nsample;
}


/*********************** end of routine sample_size *********************/
shell_merge(items,nitems)
TYPE *items;
int nitems;
{
    TYPE item2[MAX_ITEMS+2];
```

```c
int i,parity,done,zero_bit,ringpos,next_mask,prev_mask,d1,d2,and_int();

gridinit(1,&nproc);
gridcoord(procnum,&ringpos);
next_mask = (ringpos==(nproc-1)) ? 0 : gridchan(procnum,0,1);
prev_mask = (ringpos==0) ? 0 : gridchan(procnum,0,-1);

ASNKEY(item2[0],NEGINF)
ASNKEY(item2[nitems+1],POSINF)

parity=0;          /* an array toggle */
for(i=(doc-1);i>=0;--i){
    if((ringpos>>i)&1){
        if(parity)cmp_ex_hi(item2,items,nitems,1<<i);
        else       cmp_ex_hi(items,item2,nitems,1<<i);
    }
    else{
        if(parity) cmp_ex_low(item2,items,nitems,1<<i);
        else       cmp_ex_low(items,item2,nitems,1<<i);
    }
    parity = 1-parity;    /* toggle arrays */
}

zero_bit = ringpos&1;
done = 0;
while(!done){
    if(zero_bit){
        if(parity) d1=cmp_ex_hi(item2,items,nitems,prev_mask);
        else       d1=cmp_ex_hi(items,item2,nitems,prev_mask);
        if(prev_mask) parity = 1-parity;
        if(parity) d2=cmp_ex_low(item2,items,nitems,next_mask);
        else       d2=cmp_ex_low(items,item2,nitems,next_mask);
        if(next_mask) parity = 1-parity;
    }
    else{
        if(parity) d1=cmp_ex_low(item2,items,nitems,next_mask);
        else       d1=cmp_ex_low(items,item2,nitems,next_mask);
        if(next_mask) parity = 1-parity;
        if(parity) d2=cmp_ex_hi(item2,items,nitems,prev_mask);
        else       d2=cmp_ex_hi(items,item2,nitems,prev_mask);
        if(prev_mask) parity = 1-parity;
    }
    done = d1&d2;
    combine(&done,and_int,sizeof(int),1);
}

if(parity) for(i=0;i<nitems;++i) ASNKEY(items[i],item2[i+1])
```

```
        else        for(i=0;i<nitems;++i) ASNKEY(items[i],items[i+1])
}


/*********************** end of routine shell_merge ***********************/
int standard_data(items)
TYPE *items;
{
    int i,j,nitems,npts;
    TYPE temp_item;

    for(i=0,ntotal=0;i<nproc;++i){
        printf("\n\nPlease give number of items in processor %d ==> ",i);
        if(std_flag) fflush(stdout);
        scanf("%d",&npts);
        n_per_proc[i] = npts;
        for(j=0;j<npts;++j,++ntotal){
            printf("\n\nPlease key in item number %d ==> ",j+1);
            if(std_flag) fflush(stdout);
            READ_ITEM(stdin,temp_item)
            if(procnum==i) ASNKEY(items[j],temp_item)
        }
        if(procnum==i) nitems=npts;
    }
    return nitems;
}


/*********************** end of routine standard_data ***********************/
welcome()
{
    setbuffer(stdout,IO_buf,4096);
    std_flag = 1;

    printf("\n\n\t********************************************\n");
    printf(   "\t*                                          *\n");
    printf(   "\t*  Welcome to the sorting example program.  *\n");
    printf(   "\t*  This program will sort data using the    *\n");
    printf(   "\t*  Bitonic, Shellsort and Quicksort methods *\n");
    printf(   "\t*                                          *\n");
    printf(   "\t********************************************\n");
}


/*********************** end of routine welcome ***********************/
```

A-12.2 Include File sortdef.h

```
#define INITIALIZE 1
#define BITONIC    2
#define SHELL_SORT 3
#define QUICK_SORT 4
#define OUTPUT     5
#define STOP       6
#define MAX_ITEMS 500
#define MAX_SAMPLE 50
#define MAX_KEYS   64
#define MAX_PROCS  64
#define N_PER_LINE 10
#define M 6
#define NEGINF -10000
#define POSINF  10000
#define NBUF       2
#define COM_SIZE 100

#define TYPE int

#define READ_ITEM(F,I)   (  fscanf((F),"%d",&(I)) );
#define WRITE_ITEM(F,I)  ( fprintf((F),"%6d",(I)) );

#define RANDOM_ITEM(I) { double prandS(); (I) = (TYPE)(9999.0*prandS()); }

#define ASNKEY(I,J)      ( (I) = (J) );

#define COMPARE(I,J)     ( (I)-(J) )

#define SWAP(I,J) { TYPE temp; ASNKEY(temp,I) ASNKEY(I,J) ASNKEY(J,temp) }
```

A-13 Global Scalar Products

A-13.1 CUBIX Program

```c
#include <cros.h>
#include <stdio.h>
#include "cubdefs.h"
#include "addvdef.h"

int doc,nproc,procnum;
int std_flag=0;
char IO_buf[4096];

main()
{
    int nvec,task;
    double vectors[MAXSIZ],tmp[MAXSIZ];

    file_status = CLOSED;
    out_file   = stdout;
    in_file    = stdin;

    welcome();

    get_param();

    while((task=get_task())!=STOP){

        printf("\n\nPlease give the number of vectors ==> ");
        if(std_flag) fflush(stdout);
        scanf("%d",&nvec);

        setup_vectors(vectors,nvec);

        addvec(vectors,tmp,nvec);

        output_results(vectors,nvec);
    }
    printf("\nFinished\n");

    exit(0);
}

/*************************** end of routine main ***************************/
```

```c
int addvec(buf,tmp,P)
double buf[],tmp[];
int P;
{
    int d,j,error,mask,chan,size,block,offset,recv,send,recvn,sendn;

    error = 0;
    mask = chan = 1;
    size = sizeof(double);
    block = 2;
    offset = size<<1;

    for(d=0;d<doc;++d){
        recv    = procnum&mask;
        send    = recv^chan;
        recvn   = (P+mask-recv)>>(d+1);
        sendn   = (P+mask-send)>>(d+1);
        if( vshift(tmp+recv,chan,size,offset,recvn,
                    buf+send,chan,size,offset,sendn) == -1 ) error= -1;
        for(j=recv;j<P; j += block) buf[j] += tmp[j];
        block   = block<<1;
        offset = offset<<1;
        chan    = chan<<1;
        mask    = mask|chan;
    }

    chan    = 1<<(doc-1);
    mask    = nproc-1;
    offset = size<<doc;
    block   = 1<<doc;

    for(d=(doc-1);d>=0;--d){
        send    = procnum&mask;
        recv    = send^chan;
        sendn   = (P+mask-send)>>(d+1);
        recvn   = (P+mask-recv)>>(d+1);
        if( vshift(buf+recv,chan,size,offset,recvn,
                    buf+send,chan,size,offset,sendn) == -1 ) error= -1;
        mask    = mask&(~chan);
        block   = block>>1;
        offset = offset>>1;
        chan    = chan>>1;
    }
    return error;
}
```

```
/*********************** end of routine addvec ***************************/
```

```
int get_task()
{
    char ctemp[4];
    int task;

    for(;;){
        printf("\nPlease select one of the following :");
        printf("\n   1...to set up new vectors");
        printf("\n   2...to terminate program");
        printf("\n\n==> ");
        if(std_flag) fflush(stdout);
        scanf("%s",ctemp);

        task = atoi(ctemp);

        if(task>0 && task<3) break;
        else printf("\n\n**** Invalid input - try again ****");
    }

    return task;
}

/*********************** end of routine get_task ************************/
list_proc(sums,nvec,p,lptr)
double sums[];
int p,*lptr,nvec;
{
    int j,lines;

    lines = *lptr;

    fmulti(out_file);

    if(p==procnum){
        fprintf(out_file,"\n\nProcessor number %d\n",p);
        lines += 3;
        for(j=0;j<nvec;++j,++lines){
            fprintf(out_file,"\nVector number %3d sums to %12.4f",
                j,sums[j]);
        }
        fprintf(out_file,"\n");
    }
    else lines += 3+nvec;

    fflush(out_file);
    fsingl(out_file);
    if(lines>15){
```

```
            lines = 0;
            if(out_file==stdout) dw_pause();
        }
        *lptr = lines;
    }


/************************** end of routine list_proc **************************/
list_vec(sums,nvec,vec,lptr)
double sums[];
int vec,*lptr,nvec;
{
    int lines;

    lines = *lptr;

    fprintf(out_file,"\n\nVector number %d\n",vec);

    fmulti(out_file);

    fprintf(out_file,"%12.4f%c",copy_vec[vec],(procnum%6==5) ? '\n' : ' ');
    fflush(out_file);
    fsingl(out_file);
    fprintf(out_file,"\nSum = %12.4f\n",sums[vec]);
    lines += nproc/5 + 5;
    if(lines>15){
        lines = 0;
        if(out_file==stdout) dw_pause();
    }
    *lptr = lines;
}


/************************** end of routine list_vec **************************/
out_proc(sums,nvec)
double sums[];
int nvec;
{
    int i,proc,lines;

    proc = 0;
    while(proc>=0){
        printf("\n\nPlease give the processor number (-ve to end,");
        printf(" >(nproc-1) for all) ==> ");
        if(std_flag) fflush(stdout);
        scanf("%d",&proc);
        lines = 0;
        if(proc>(nproc-1))
            for(i=0;i<nproc;++i)
```

```
                          list_proc(sums,nvec,i,&lines);
             else if(proc>=0) list_proc(sums,nvec,proc,&lines);
    }
}


/************************** end of routine out_proc **************************/
output_results(sums,nvec)
double sums[];
int nvec;
{
    int ok,response;
    char input[10];
    FILE *setup_out();

    if(file_status==CLOSED){
        out_file = setup_out("addvCUB.c");
        if(out_file!=stdout) setbuffer(out_file,IO_buf,BUFLEN);
    }
    ok = 0;
    while(!ok){
        printf("\n\nPlease select one of the following :");
        printf(  "\n   1...for output for specified processors");
        printf(  "\n   2...for output for specified vectors");
        printf(  "\n   3...to quit this menu\n\n==> ");
        if(std_flag) fflush(stdout);

        scanf("%s",input);
        response = atoi(input);

        switch(response){
          case 1:
            out_proc(sums,nvec);
            break;
          case 2:
            out_vec(sums,nvec);
            break;
          case 3:
            ok = 1;
            break;
          default:
            printf("\n\n**** Invalid input - try again ****\n");
            break;
        }
    }
}


/********************** end of routine output_results **********************/
```

```
out_vec(sums,nvec)
double sums[];
int nvec;
{
    int i,vec,lines;

    vec = 0;
    while(vec>=0){
        printf("\n\nPlease give the vector number (-ve to end,");
        printf(" >(nvec-1) for all) ==> ");
        if(std_flag) fflush(stdout);
        scanf("%d",&vec);

        lines = 0;
        if(vec>(nvec-1))
            for(i=0;i<nvec;++i)
                list_vec(sums,nvec,i,&lines);
        else if(vec>=0) list_vec(sums,nvec,vec,&lines);
    }
}

/*************************** end of routine out_vec ***************************/
setup_vectors(vectors,nvec)
double vectors[];
int nvec;
{
    int i,seed,response;
    char input[10];
    FILE *fildat,*setup_in();
    double prandB();

    for(;;){
        printf("\n\nPlease choose one of the following :");
        printf( "\n   1...random vectors");
        printf( "\n   2...vectors read from terminal");
        printf( "\n   3...vectors read from file");
        printf( "\n   4...demonstration vectors\n\n==> ");
        if(std_flag) fflush(stdout);
        scanf("%s",input);

        response = atoi(input);

        if(response >0 && response <5) break;
        else printf("\n\n**** Invalid input - try again ****");
    }
    switch(response){
        case 1:
```

```
            printf("\n\nPlease give random number seed integer ==> ");
            if(std_flag) fflush(stdout);
            scanf("%d",&seed);

            prand_setB(seed,1,procnum);
            for(i=0;i<nvec;++i) vectors[i] = prandB();
            break;
        case 2:
            for(i=0;i<nvec;++i){
                printf("\n\nPlease enter %d numbers for vector %d :",nproc,i);
                if(std_flag) fflush(stdout);
                fmulti(stdin);
                scanf("%lf",&vectors[i]);
                fsingl(stdin);
            }
            break;
        case 3:
            fildat = setup_in("containing input vectors");
            fmulti(fildat);
            for(i=0;i<nvec;++i){
                fscanf(fildat,"%lf",&vectors[i]);
            }
            fsingl(fildat);
            break;
        case 4:
            for(i=0;i<nvec;++i) vectors[i] = (double)(i + procnum);
            break;
    }
    for(i=0;i<nvec;++i) copy_vec[i] = vectors[i];
}


/*************************** end of routine setup **************************/
welcome()
{
    setbuffer(stdout,IO_buf,4096);
    std_flag = 1;

    printf("\n\n\t*******************************************\n");
    printf(  "\t*                                         *\n");
    printf(  "\t*    Welcome to the addvec example program.  *\n");
    printf(  "\t*    This program sums vectors distributed   *\n");
    printf(  "\t*    across the hypercube.                 *\n");
    printf(  "\t*                                         *\n");
    printf(  "\t*******************************************\n");
}


/*************************** end of routine welcome **************************/
```

A-13.2 Include File addvdef.h

```
#define STOP   2
#define MAXSIZ 500
#define BUFLEN 2048
int file_status;
double copy_vec[MAXSIZ];
char iobuf[BUFLEN];
FILE *in_file,*out_file;
```

A-14 LU Decomposition and the Solution of Linear Systems

A-14.1 CUBIX Program

```
#include <cros.h>
#include <stdio.h>
#include "cubdefs.h"
#include "bandef.h"

int doc,nproc,procnum;
int std_flag=0;
char IO_buf[2048];

int nb,user_nb,D,user_n,user_m,row_blocks,b_col_blocks,half_w,n1,n11,n,m;
int A_col_blocks,j_blocks,input_option,jptr[MAXBLOCKS];
int row_pos,col_pos,up,down,left,right,file_status,i_off,j_off;
int PK,PI,PJ,left_of_diag,right_of_diag,tsize;
int do_pivot,A_max_blocks,krow;
int corner_proc[MAX_D+1],isize,j_plus,kend,kstart,ny,nx,over;
TYPE bspace[BMAX],L[MAXBLOCKS],U[MAXBLOCKS],bk[BMAXBLOCKS];
TYPE combuf[MAXBLOCKS];
int nblocks[MAXBLOCKS],rowno[MAXBLOCKS],blockno[MAXBLOCKS];
FILE *fildat,*out_file,*in_file,*pfile;
TYPE Aspace[AMAX];

main()
{
    int command;

    file_status = CLOSED;
    in_file     = stdin;
    pfile       = stdout;

    tsize = sizeof(TYPE);
    isize = sizeof(int);

    welcome();

    get_param();

    if(doc&1){
        printf("\n\n **** Cube dimension must be even ****\n\n");
        exit(1);
    }

    decompose();
```

```
    while( (command=get_task()) != STOP ){
        switch(command){
            case INITIALIZE:
                initialize();
                break;
            case LIST_MAT:
                list_matrices();
                break;
            case SOLVE:
                find_solution();
                break;
        }
    }
    printf("\nFinished\n");
    exit(0);
}


/*************************** end of routine main ***************************/
ask_questions()
{
    char input[5];
    int seed,i,max_blocks;
    FILE *setup_in(),*setup_out();

    if(file_status==CLOSED) out_file = setup_out("bandCUB.c");

    fprintf(pfile,"\n\nPlease give the order of the matrix ==> ");
    if(std_flag && (pfile==stdout)) fflush(stdout);
    scanf("%d",&user_n);
    fprintf(pfile,"\n\nPlease give the band-width (must be odd) ==> ");
    if(std_flag && (pfile==stdout)) fflush(stdout);
    scanf("%d",&user_m);
    fprintf(pfile,"\n\nPlease give the number of right-hand sides ==> ");
    if(std_flag && (pfile==stdout)) fflush(stdout);
    scanf("%d",&user_nb);

    init_pivot();

    row_blocks   = (user_n-1)/D + 1;
    b_col_blocks = (user_nb-1)/D + 1;
    j_blocks     = row_blocks + 2;
    j_plus       = -(j_blocks-1);
    nb           = D*b_col_blocks;
    n            = D*row_blocks;
    half_w       = user_m/2;
    n1           = half_w/D;
    n11          = n1 + 1;
```

```
m            = 2*D*n11 - 1;
kend         = n-m/2-1;
kstart       = m/2+1;
over         = -1;
A_col_blocks = 2*n11 + 1;
A_max_blocks = do_pivot ? 3*n11 + 1 : 2*n11+1;

max_blocks = A_max_blocks>b_col_blocks ? A_max_blocks : b_col_blocks;
for(i=0;i<max_blocks;++i) jptr[i] = i*j_blocks;

if(A_max_blocks*j_blocks>AMAX){
    printf("\n\nInsufficient space for the A matrix - ");
    printf("run abandoned\n\n");
    exit(1);
}
if(b_col_blocks*j_blocks>BMAX || b_col_blocks>BMAXBLOCKS){
    printf("\n\nInsufficient space for the b matrix - ");
    printf("run abandoned\n\n");
    exit(1);
}
if(max_blocks>MAXBLOCKS){
    printf("\n\nToo many blocks (band_width/D too large) - ");
    printf("run abandoned\n\n");
    exit(1);
}
if(D>MAX_D){
    printf("\n\nToo many processors (D too large) - ");
    printf("run abandoned\n\n");
    exit(1);
}

for(;;){
    fprintf(pfile,"\n\nPlease select one of the following :");
    fprintf(pfile, "\n   1...to read in matrices from file");
    fprintf(pfile, "\n   2...to use random numbers");
    fprintf(pfile, "\n   3...to run standard demo\n==> ");
    if(std_flag && (pfile==stdout)) fflush(stdout);
    scanf("%s",input);

    input_option = atoi(input);

    if(input_option>0 && input_option<4) break;
    else printf("\n\n**** Invalid input - try again ****\n");
}

if(input_option==1) fildat = setup_in("containing the data");
else if(input_option==2){
```

```
            fprintf(pfile,"\n\nPlease give seed integer ==> ");
            if(std_flag && (pfile==stdout)) fflush(stdout);
            scanf("%d",&seed);
            prand_setB(seed,0,0);
    }


    fprintf(out_file,"\n\n*********************************************");
    fprintf(out_file,"\n\nNumber of processors = %d",nproc);
    fprintf(out_file,"\n\nTemplate is %2d by %2d processors",D,D);
    fprintf(out_file,"\n\nRequested order of matrix A = %d,",user_n);
    fprintf(out_file," actual order = %d\n",n);
    fprintf(out_file,"\nRequested band-width of matrix A = %d",user_m);
    fprintf(out_file,", actual band-width = %d\n\n",m);
    fprintf(out_file,"Requested number of right-hand sides = %d,",user_nb);
    fprintf(out_file," actual number of right-hand sides = %d\n",nb);

    if(input_option==1)
        fprintf(out_file,"\nInput matrices read from file\n");
    else if(input_option==2){
        fprintf(out_file,"\nInput matrices are random, ");
        fprintf(out_file,"seed integer = %d\n",seed);
    }
    else fprintf(out_file,"\nStandard demonstration used\n");
    fflush(out_file);
}


/*********************** end of routine ask_questions ***********************/
back_bottom(bl)
int bl;
{
    int i,j,start_index;
    TYPE x;

    if(do_pivot) broadcast(&nx,corner_proc[PI%D+1],nproc-1,isize);
    else nx = krow<kstart ? krow/D+1 : n11;

    ny = nx;

    split_pipe(&x,L,left,right,ny*tsize,D-PJ,D);

    x = 1.0/L[0];
    for(j=0;j<b_col_blocks;++j) b(bl,0,j) *= x;
    v_to_c(combuf,bspace+bl,j_blocks,b_col_blocks);
    split_pipe(combuf,&x,up,down,b_col_blocks*tsize,0,D);

    start_index = -(ny-1);
    for(j=0;j<b_col_blocks;++j){
```

```
        x = b(bl,0,j);
        for(i=start_index;i<0;++i) b(bl,i,j) -= x*L[(-i)];
    }
}


/************************* end of routine back_bottom *************************/
back_corner(bl)
int bl;
{
    int i,j,start_index;
    TYPE x;

    if(do_pivot){
        nx = nblocks[PK];
        broadcast(&nx,corner_proc[PI%D+1],nproc-1,isize);
    }
    else nx = krow<kstart ? krow/D+1 : n11;

    ny = nx;

    v_to_c(combuf,Aspace+jptr[j_off]+i_off,j_blocks-1,ny);
    split_pipe(combuf,&x,left,right,ny*tsize,0,D);

    x = 1.0/(a(0,0));
    for(j=0;j<b_col_blocks;++j) b(bl,0,j) *= x;
    v_to_c(combuf,bspace+bl,j_blocks,b_col_blocks);
    split_pipe(combuf,&x,up,down,b_col_blocks*tsize,0,D);

    start_index = -(ny-1);
    for(j=0;j<b_col_blocks;++j){
        x = b(bl,0,j);
        for(i=start_index;i<0;++i) b(bl,i,j) -= x*a(i,0);
    }
}


/************************* end of routine back_corner *************************/
back_middle(bl)
int bl;
{
    int i,j,start_index;
    TYPE x;

    if(do_pivot) broadcast(&nx,corner_proc[PI%D+1],nproc-1,isize);
    else nx = krow<kstart ? krow/D+1 : n11;

    ny = nx;
```

```
        split_pipe(&x,L,left,right,ny*tsize,D-PJ,D);

        split_pipe(&x,bk,up,down,b_col_blocks*tsize,D-PI,D);

        start_index = -(ny-1);
        for(j=0;j<b_col_blocks;++j){
            x = bk[j];
            for(i=start_index;i<=0;++i) b(bl,i,j) -= x*L[(-i)];
        }
    }

/*********************** end of routine back_middle ***********************/
back_right(bl)
int bl;
{
        int i,j,start_index;
        TYPE x;

        if(do_pivot) broadcast(&nx,corner_proc[PI%D+1],nproc-1,isize);
        else nx = krow<kstart ? krow/D+1 : n11;

        ny = nx;

        v_to_c(combuf,Aspace+jptr[j_off]+i_off,j_blocks-1,ny);
        split_pipe(combuf,&x,left,right,ny*tsize,0,D);

        split_pipe(&x,bk,up,down,b_col_blocks*tsize,D-PI,D);

        start_index = -(ny-1);
        for(j=0;j<b_col_blocks;++j){
            x = bk[j];
            for(i=start_index;i<=0;++i) b(bl,i,j) -= x*a(i,0);
        }
    }

/*********************** end of routine back_right ***********************/
back_sub()
{
        int bl;

        PK = (PI==PJ) ? (row_blocks-1) : 2*(row_blocks-1);

        for(krow=(n-1);krow>=0;--krow){

            bl = (krow+PI)/D;
            lock(PK);
```

```
            if(PI==D && PJ==D) back_corner(bl);
            else if(PI==D)      back_bottom(bl);
            else if(PJ==D)      back_right(bl);
            else                back_middle(bl);

            PI = (PI==D) ? 1 : PI+1;
            PJ = (PJ==D) ? 1 : PJ+1;
            if(PI==1 || PJ==1) PK--;
        }
    }


/*********************** end of routine back_sub ***********************/
column_list()
{
    int i,j,k,row_block_no,col_block_no,proc_row;
    int proc_col,b_offset,row_min,row_max,col_min,col_max;
    TYPE value;

    fprintf(pfile,"\n\nPlease the minimum and maximum row numbers ==> ");
    if(std_flag && (pfile==stdout)) fflush(stdout);
    scanf("%d %d",&row_min,&row_max);
    if(row_min<0 || row_min>=user_n) row_min = 0;
    if(row_max<0 || row_max>=user_n) row_max = user_n-1;
    if(row_min>row_max){
        i       = row_min;
        row_min = row_max;
        row_max = i;
    }

    fprintf(pfile,"\n\nPlease give the minimum and maximum ");
    fprintf(pfile,"vector numbers ==> ");
    if(std_flag && (pfile==stdout)) fflush(stdout);
    scanf("%d %d",&col_min,&col_max);
    if(col_min<0 || col_min>=user_nb) col_min = 0;
    if(col_max<0 || col_max>=user_nb) col_max = user_nb-1;
    if(col_min>col_max){
        i       = col_min;
        col_min = col_max;
        col_max = i;
    }

    fmulti(out_file);

    for(j=col_min;j<=col_max;++j){
        col_block_no = j/D;
        proc_col     = col_block_no*D + col_pos;
        for(i=row_min;i<=row_max;++i){
```

```
            k           = i - row_min;
            row_block_no = i/D;
            proc_row     = D*row_block_no + row_pos;
            b_offset     = jptr[col_block_no] + row_block_no+1;
            if(i==proc_row && j==proc_col){
                value = *(bspace + b_offset);
                if(k==0)
                    fprintf(out_file,"Vector number %d\n",j);
                fprintf(out_file,"%9.3e%c",value,
                    (k%7==6 || i==row_max) ? '\n':' ');
            }
            fflush(out_file);
        }
    }
    fsingl(out_file);

    fprintf(out_file,"\nMATRIX b. ");
    fprintf(out_file,"Results for area defined by (%d,%d) to (%d,%d)",
            row_min,col_min,row_max,col_max);

    if(out_file == stdout) dw_pause();
}


/*********************** end of routine column_list ***********************/
c_to_v(outbuf,inbuf,off_items,nitems)
TYPE *inbuf,*outbuf;
int off_items,nitems;
{
    int i,j;

    for(i=0,j=0;j<nitems;i += off_items,++j) *(outbuf+i) = *(inbuf+j);
}

/************************** end of routine c_to_v **************************/
decompose()
{
    int coord[2];

    D = 1<<(doc/2);
    coord[0] = D;
    coord[1] = D;
    gridinit(2,coord);
    gridcoord(procnum,coord);
    col_pos = coord[0];
    row_pos = coord[1];
    left    = gridchan(procnum,0,-1);
    right   = gridchan(procnum,0,1);
```

```
        up      = gridchan(procnum,1,-1);
        down    = gridchan(procnum,1,1);

        PI = row_pos+1;
        PJ = col_pos+1;

        left_of_diag  = (col_pos<row_pos);
        right_of_diag = (col_pos>row_pos);
}

/************************** end of routine decompose ************************/
int divide(x,d)
int x,d;
{
        int result;

        result = x/d;
        if(x<0 && d*result != x) result -= 1;
        return result;
}

/************************** end of routine divide **************************/
find_pivot(p_row,piv_I)
int *p_row,*piv_I;
{
        TYPE pivot,cand_el,a_abs,atemp;
        int i,cand_row;

        if(PJ==1){
                pivot = - 0.1e+30;
                *piv_I = 0;
                for(i=0;i<ny;++i){
                        atemp = a(i,0);
                        a_abs = atemp > 0.0 ? atemp : -atemp;
                        if(a_abs>pivot){
                                pivot = a_abs;
                                *piv_I = i;
                        }
                }
                if(PI==1){
                        *p_row = 1;
                        for(i=2;i<=D;++i){
                                cread(&cand_el,down,0,tsize);
                                cread(&cand_row,down,0,isize);
                                if(cand_el>pivot){
                                        pivot = cand_el;
                                        *piv_I = cand_row;
```

```
                              *p_row = i;
                      }
               }
               blockno[PK] = *piv_I;
               rowno[PK]   = *p_row;
       }
       else{
               cwrite(&pivot,up,tsize);
               cwrite(piv_I,up,isize);
               if(PI != D){
                       for(i=PI+1;i<=D;++i){
                               cread(&cand_el,down,up,tsize);
                               cread(&cand_row,down,up,isize);
                       }
               }
       }
   }
   broadcast(p_row,corner_proc[PI],nproc-1,isize);
   broadcast(piv_I,corner_proc[PI],nproc-1,isize);
}


/*********************** end of routine find_pivot ***********************/
find_solution()
{
   int task;
   char input[5];

   for(;;){
       fprintf(pfile,"\n\nPlease choose one of the following :");
       fprintf(pfile, "\n   1...to do LU decomposition");
       fprintf(pfile, "\n   2...to do forward reduction");
       fprintf(pfile, "\n   3...to do back substitution");
       fprintf(pfile, "\n   4...to do all of the above");
       fprintf(pfile, "\n   5...to quit this menu\n==> ");
       if(std_flag && (pfile==stdout)) fflush(stdout);
       scanf("%s",input);
       task = atoi(input);
       if(task==1)     LU_decompose();
       else if(task==2) forward();
       else if(task==3) back_sub();
       else if(task==4){LU_decompose(); forward(); back_sub();}
       else if(task==5) break;
       else printf("\n\n**** Invalid input - try again ****\n");
   }
}


/*********************** end of routine find_solution ***********************/
```

```
forward()
{
    int bl;

    PK = 0;
    for(krow=0;krow<n;++krow){

        bl = (krow+PI-1)/D+1;
        lock(PK);

        if(do_pivot) pivot_B(bl);

        ny = krow>=kend ? (n-krow-1)/D+1 : n11;

        if(PI==1 && PJ==1) for_corner(bl);
        else if(PI==1)     for_top(bl);
        else if(PJ==1)     for_left(bl);
        else               for_middle(bl);

        PI = (PI==1) ? D : PI-1;
        PJ = (PJ==1) ? D : PJ-1;
        if(PI==D || PJ==D) PK++;
    }
}

/*************************** end of routine forward ***************************/
for_corner(bl)
int bl;
{
    int i,j;
    TYPE x;

    v_to_c(combuf,bspace+bl,j_blocks,b_col_blocks);
    split_pipe(combuf,&x,down,up,b_col_blocks*tsize,0,D);
    v_to_c(combuf,Aspace+jptr[j_off]+i_off,j_plus,ny);
    split_pipe(combuf,&x,right,left,ny*tsize,0,D);

    for(j=0;j<b_col_blocks;++j){
        x = b(bl,0,j);
        for(i=1;i<ny;++i) b(bl,i,j) -= x*a(i,0);
    }
}

/************************* end of routine for_corner *************************/
for_left(bl)
int bl;
{
```

```
    int i,j;
    TYPE x;

    split_pipe(&x,bk,down,up,b_col_blocks*tsize,PI-1,D);
    v_to_c(combuf,Aspace+jptr[j_off]+i_off,j_plus,ny);
    split_pipe(combuf,&x,right,left,ny*tsize,0,D);

    for(j=0;j<b_col_blocks;++j){
        x = bk[j];
        for(i=0;i<ny;++i) b(bl,i,j) -= x*a(i,0);
    }
}


/************************** end of routine for_left **************************/
for_middle(bl)
int bl;
{
    int i,j;
    TYPE x;

    split_pipe(&x,bk,down,up,b_col_blocks*tsize,PI-1,D);
    split_pipe(&x,L,right,left,ny*tsize,PJ-1,D);

    for(j=0;j<b_col_blocks;++j){
        x = bk[j];
        for(i=0;i<ny;++i) b(bl,i,j) -= x*L[i];
    }
}


/************************* end of routine for_middle *************************/
for_top(bl)
int bl;
{
    int i,j;
    TYPE x;

    v_to_c(combuf,bspace+bl,j_blocks,b_col_blocks);
    split_pipe(combuf,&x,down,up,b_col_blocks*tsize,0,D);
    split_pipe(&x,L,right,left,ny*tsize,PJ-1,D);

    for(j=0;j<b_col_blocks;++j){
        x = b(bl,0,j);
        for(i=1;i<ny;++i) b(bl,i,j) -= x*L[i];
    }
}


/************************** end of routine for_top **************************/
```

```
int get_task()
{
    char input[4],task;

    for(;;){
        fprintf(pfile,"\n\nPlease choose one of the following :");
        fprintf(pfile, "\n   1...to initialize a problem");
        fprintf(pfile, "\n   2...to list input/output matrices");
        fprintf(pfile, "\n   3...to find the solution");
        fprintf(pfile, "\n   4...to terminate the program\n==> ");
        if(std_flag && (pfile==stdout)) fflush(stdout);
        scanf("%s",input);

        task = atoi(input);

        if(task>0 && task<5) break;
        else fprintf(pfile,"\n\n**** Invalid input - try again ****");
    }

    return task;
}

/************************* end of routine get_task *************************/
int initialize()
{
    int i;

    for(i=0;i<AMAX;++i) *(Aspace+i) = 0.0;
    for(i=0;i<BMAX;++i) *(bspace+i) = 0.0;

    ask_questions();
    load_A();
    load_b();

    return 0;
}

/************************* end of routine initialize *************************/
init_pivot()
{
    char input[5];
    int i,coord[2];

    fprintf(pfile,"\n\nDo you want pivoting? (y/n) ==> ");
    if(std_flag && (pfile==stdout)) fflush(stdout);
    scanf("%s",input);
    if(strcmp("Y",input)==0 || strcmp("y",input)==0){
```

```
            do_pivot = 1;
            for(i=0;i<D;++i){
                coord[0] = i;
                coord[1] = i;
                corner_proc[PI] = gridproc(coord);
                PI = PI==1 ? D : PI-1;
            }
        }
        else do_pivot = 0;
    }


/************************ end of routine init_pivot ************************/
list_b()
{
    int list_option;
    char input[5];

    for(;;){
        fprintf(pfile,"\n\nPlease choose one of the following :");
        fprintf(pfile, "\n   1...to list b by columns\n");
        fprintf(pfile," 2...to list b by processor\n");
        fprintf(pfile," 3...to quit this menu\n ==> ");
        if(std_flag&&(pfile==stdout)) fflush(stdout);
        scanf("%s",input);
        list_option = atoi(input);

        if(list_option==1) column_list();
        else if(list_option==2) list_proc(1);
        else if(list_option==3) break;
        else printf("\n\n **** Invalid input - try again ****\n");
    }
}

/************************** end of routine list_b **************************/
list_matrices()
{
    int opt;
    char input[5];

    for(;;){
        fprintf(pfile,"\n\nPlease choose one of the following :\n");
        fprintf(pfile," \n   1...to list the matrix A");
        fprintf(pfile," \n   2...to list the matrix b");
        fprintf(pfile," \n   3...to quit this menu\n==> ");
        if(std_flag&&(pfile==stdout)) fflush(stdout);
        scanf("%s",input);
        opt = atoi(input);
```

```
            if(opt==1) list_A();
            else if(opt==2) list_b();
            else if(opt==3) break;
            else printf("\n\n **** Invalid input - try again ****\n");
      }
}

/*********************** end of routine list_matrices *********************/
list_proc(A_or_b)
int A_or_b;
{
    int proc,i,j,k,row_min,row_max,col_min,col_max;
    TYPE value;

    for(;;){
        fprintf(pfile,"\n\nPlease give the processor number ");
        fprintf(pfile,"(-ve to end) ==> ");
        if(std_flag&&(pfile==stdout)) fflush(stdout);
        scanf("%d",&proc);

        if(proc<0) break;
        if(proc>=nproc){
            printf("\n\n**** Invalid input - try again ****\n");
            continue;
        }
        fprintf(pfile,"\n\nPlease give the minimum and ");
        fprintf(pfile,"maximum row numbers ==> ");
        if(std_flag&&(pfile==stdout)) fflush(stdout);
        scanf("%d %d",&row_min,&row_max);

        row_min = (row_min<0) ? 0 : row_min;
        row_max = (row_max>=row_blocks) ? (row_blocks-1) : row_max;

        fprintf(pfile,"\n\nPlease give the minimum and ");
        fprintf(pfile,"maximum column numbers ==> ");
        if(std_flag&&(pfile==stdout)) fflush(stdout);
        scanf("%d %d",&col_min,&col_max);

        col_min = (col_min<0) ? 0 : col_min;
        if(A_or_b==0)
            col_max = (col_max>=A_max_blocks) ? (A_max_blocks-1): col_max;
        else
            col_max = (col_max>=b_col_blocks) ? (b_col_blocks-1): col_max;

        fmulti(out_file);
        if(proc==procnum){
```

```
        for(i=row_min;i<=row_max;++i){
            fprintf(out_file,"\nRow number %d\n",i);
            for(j=col_min,k=0;j<=col_max;++j,++k){
                if(A_or_b==0) value = *(Aspace+jptr[j]+i+1);
                else value = *(bspace+jptr[j]+i+1);
                fprintf(out_file,"%9.3e%c",value,(k%7==6) ? '\n' : ' ');
            }
        }
        if(A_or_b==0){
            fprintf(out_file,"\n\nThe matrix A as stored in");
            fprintf(out_file," processor %d.",procnum);
        }
        else{
            fprintf(out_file,"\n\nThe matrix b as stored in");
            fprintf(out_file," processor %d.",procnum);
        }
        fprintf(out_file," Area defined by (%d,%d) and (%d,%d)",
                row_min,col_min,row_max,col_max);
    }
    fsingl(out_file);
    if(out_file==stdout) dw_pause();
  }
}


/*********************** end of routine list_proc ***********************/
load_A()
{
    int jmax,i,j,i_offset,j_offset,row_block_no,col_block_no,proc_row;
    int proc_col,A_offset,j_shift;
    TYPE value,next_A();

    jmax = D*A_max_blocks;

    for(i=0;i<n;++i){
        row_block_no = i/D;
        proc_row     = D*row_block_no + row_pos;
        i_offset     = i;
        j_shift      = (row_block_no - n11)*D;
        for(j=0;j<jmax;++j){
            col_block_no = j/D;
            A_offset     = jptr[col_block_no] + row_block_no +1;
            j_offset     = j_shift + j;
            if(j_offset<0 || j_offset>=n) value = 0.0;
            else value = next_A(i_offset,j_offset);
            proc_col     = j_shift + col_block_no*D + col_pos;
            if(i_offset==proc_row && j_offset==proc_col)
                *(Aspace + A_offset) = value;
```

```
            }
        }
    }

/*************************** end of routine load_A ***************************/
load_b()
{
    int i,j,jmax,row_block_no,col_block_no,proc_row,proc_col,j_shift;
    TYPE value,next_b();

    jmax = D*b_col_blocks;

    for(j=0;j<jmax;++j){
        col_block_no = j/D;
        proc_col     = D*col_block_no + col_pos;
        j_shift      = jptr[col_block_no];
        for(i=0;i<n;++i){
            row_block_no = i/D;
            proc_row     = D*row_block_no + row_pos;
            if(j>=user_nb || i>=user_n) value = 0.0;
            else value = next_b(i,j);
            if(proc_col==j && proc_row==i)
                *(bspace+j_shift+row_block_no+1) = value;
        }
    }
}

/*************************** end of routine load_b ***************************/
lock(x)
int x;
{
    if(left_of_diag){
        i_off = 1 + divide(x,2);
        j_off = n11 + mod(x,2);
    }
    else if(right_of_diag){
        i_off = 1 + divide(x+1,2);
        j_off = n11 - mod(x,2);
    }
    else{
        i_off = 1 + x;
        j_off = n11;
    }
}

/*************************** end of routine lock ***************************/
```

```
LU_corner()
{
    int i,j,p_row,piv_I;
    TYPE x;

    ny = krow>=kend ? (n-krow-1)/D+1 : n11;

    if(do_pivot){
        find_pivot(&p_row,&piv_I);
        pivot_A(p_row,piv_I);
    }
    else{
        nx = ny;
        v_to_c(combuf,Aspace+jptr[j_off]+i_off,j_blocks,nx);
        split_pipe(combuf,&x,down,up,nx*tsize,0,D);
    }

    x = 1.0/(a(0,0));
    for(i=1;i<ny;++i) a(i,0) *= x;

    v_to_c(combuf,Aspace+jptr[j_off-1]+1+i_off,j_plus,ny-1);
    split_pipe(combuf,&x,right,left,(ny-1)*tsize,0,D);

    for(j=1;j<nx;++j) combuf[j] = a(0,j);

    for(i=1;i<ny;++i){
        x = a(i,0);
        for(j=1;j<nx;++j) a(i,j) -= x*combuf[j];
    }
}

/************************* end of routine LU_corner ************************/
LU_decompose()
{
    PK = 0;
    for(krow=0;krow<n;++krow){

        lock(PK);

        if(PI==1 && PJ==1) LU_corner();
        else if(PI==1)    LU_top();
        else if(PJ==1)    LU_left();
        else              LU_middle();

        PI'= (PI==1) ? D : PI-1;
        PJ = (PJ==1) ? D : PJ-1;
        if(PI==D || PJ==D) PK++;
```

```
    }
}

/********************** end of routine LU_decompose **********************/
LU_left()
{
    int i,j,p_row,piv_I;
    TYPE x;

    ny = krow>=kend ? (n-krow-1)/D+1 : n11;

    if(do_pivot){
        find_pivot(&p_row,&piv_I);
        pivot_A(p_row,piv_I);
    }
    else{
        nx = ny;
        split_pipe(&x,U,down,up,nx*tsize,PI-1,D);
    }

    x = U[0] = 1.0/U[0];

    for(i=0;i<ny;++i) a(i,0) *= U[0];

    v_to_c(combuf,Aspace+jptr[j_off]+i_off,j_plus,ny);
    split_pipe(combuf,&x,right,left,ny*tsize,0,D);

    for(i=0;i<ny;++i){
        x = a(i,0);
        for(j=1;j<nx;++j) a(i,j) -= x*U[j];
    }
}

/************************** end of routine LU_left **************************/
LU_middle()
{
    int i,j,p_row,piv_I;
    TYPE x;

    ny = krow>=kend ? (n-krow-1)/D+1 : n11;

    if(do_pivot){
        find_pivot(&p_row,&piv_I);
        pivot_A(p_row,piv_I);
    }
    else{
        nx = ny;
```

```
                split_pipe(&x,U,down,up,nx*tsize,PI-1,D);
        }

        split_pipe(&x,L,right,left,ny*tsize,PJ-1,D);

        for(i=0;i<ny;++i){
            x = L[i];
            for(j=0;j<nx;++j) a(i,j) -= x*U[j];
        }
}

/************************* end of routine LU_middle *************************/
LU_top()
{
        int i,j,p_row,piv_I;
        TYPE x;

        ny = krow>=kend ? (n-krow-1)/D+1 : n11;

        if(do_pivot){
            find_pivot(&p_row,&piv_I);
            pivot_A(p_row,piv_I);
        }
        else{
            nx = ny;
            v_to_c(combuf,Aspace+jptr[j_off]+i_off,j_blocks,nx);
            split_pipe(combuf,&x,down,up,nx*tsize,0,D);
        }

        split_pipe(&x,&L[1],right,left,(ny-1)*tsize,PJ-1,D);

        for(j=0;j<nx;++j) combuf[j] = a(0,j);

        for(i=1;i<ny;++i){
            x = L[i];
            for(j=0;j<nx;++j) a(i,j) -= x*combuf[j];
        }
}

/************************* end of routine LU_top *************************/
matrix_list(option)
int option;
{
        int i,j,k,i_offset,j_offset,row_block_no,col_block_no,proc_row;
        int proc_col,A_offset,j_shift,row_min,row_max,col_min,col_max;
        int col_lo,col_hi;
        TYPE value;
```

```
fprintf(pfile,"\n\nPlease the minimum and maximum row numbers ==> ");
if(std_flag && (pfile==stdout)) fflush(stdout);
scanf("%d %d",&row_min,&row_max);
if(row_min<0 || row_min>=user_n) row_min = 0;
if(row_max<0 || row_max>=user_n) row_max = user_n-1;
if(row_min>row_max){
    i       = row_min;
    row_min = row_max;
    row_max = i;
}

fprintf(pfile,"\n\nPlease the minimum and maximum column numbers ==> "
        );
if(std_flag && (pfile==stdout)) fflush(stdout);
scanf("%d %d",&col_min,&col_max);
if(col_min<0 || col_min>=user_n) col_min = 0;
if(col_max<0 || col_max>=user_n) col_max = user_n-1;
if(col_min>col_max){
    i       = col_min;
    col_min = col_max;
    col_max = i;
}
col_lo = col_min;
col_hi = col_max;

fmulti(out_file);

for(i=row_min;i<=row_max;++i){
    row_block_no = i/D;
    proc_row     = D*row_block_no + row_pos;
    i_offset     = i;
    j_shift      = (row_block_no - n11)*D;
    if(option==UPPER) col_lo = (col_min>i) ? col_min : i;
    if(option==LOWER) col_hi = (col_max>i) ? i : col_max;
    for(j_offset=col_lo;j_offset<=col_hi;++j_offset){
        k           = j_offset - col_lo;
        j           = j_offset - j_shift;
        col_block_no = divide(j,D);
        A_offset    = jptr[col_block_no] + row_block_no + 1;
        proc_col    = j_shift + col_block_no*D + col_pos;
        if(i_offset==proc_row && j_offset==proc_col){
            if(option==LOWER && i==j_offset) value = 1.0;
            else if(col_block_no<0 ||
                col_block_no>=A_max_blocks) value = 0.0;
            else value = *(Aspace + A_offset);
            if(k==0) fprintf(out_file,"Row number %d\n",i);
```

```
                    fprintf(out_file,"%9.3e%c",value,
                           (k%7==6 || j_offset==col_hi) ? '\n':' ');
                }
                fflush(out_file);
        }
    }
    fsingl(out_file);

    switch(option){
        case FULL:
            fprintf(out_file,"\nFULL MATRIX. ");
            break;
        case UPPER:
            fprintf(out_file,"\nUPPER-TRIANGULAR MATRIX. ");
            break;
        case LOWER:
            fprintf(out_file,"\nLOWER-TRIANGULAR MATRIX. ");
            break;
    }

    fprintf(out_file,"Results for area defined by (%d,%d) to (%d,%d)",
                row_min,col_min,row_max,col_max);

    if(out_file == stdout) dw_pause();
}

/*********************** end of routine matrix_list ***********************/
int mod(x,d)
{
    int result;

    if(x<0) result = (-x)%d;
    else    result = x%d;

    return result;
}

/**************************** end of routine mod ****************************/
TYPE next_A(row,col)
int row,col;
{
    TYPE value;
    double prandS();
    float ftemp;

    if(col>=user_n || row>=user_n) value = (row==col) ? 1.0 : 0.0;
    else if(col<(row-half_w) || col>(row+half_w)) value = 0.0;
```

```
        else{
            switch(input_option){
                case MFILE:
                    if(fildat==stdin){
                        fprintf(pfile,"\nGive A value ==> ");
                        if(std_flag&&(pfile==stdout)) fflush(pfile);
                    }
                    fscanf(fildat,"%f",&ftemp);
                    value = (TYPE)ftemp;
                    break;
                case RANDOM:
                    value = (TYPE)prandS();
                    break;
                case DEMO:
                    if(row==col) value = 3.792882;
                    else if(col==(row-half_w)||col==(row+half_w))
                        value = -1.0;
                    else if(col==(row-1)||col==(row+1))
                        value = -1.0;
                    else    value = 0.0;
                    break;
            }
        }
    return value;
}


/************************* end of routine next_A *************************/
TYPE next_b(row,col)
int row,col;
{
    TYPE value;
    double prandS();
    float ftemp;

    switch(input_option){
        case MFILE:
            if(fildat==stdin){
                fprintf(pfile,"\nGive b value ==> ");
                if(std_flag&&(pfile==stdout)) fflush(pfile);
            }
            fscanf(fildat,"%f",&ftemp);
            value = (TYPE)ftemp;
            break;
        case RANDOM:
            value = (TYPE)prandS();
            break;
        case DEMO:
```

```
                value = 1.0;
                break;
        }
        return value;
}


/************************* end of routine next_b *************************/
list_A()
{
        int list_option;
        char input[5];

        for(;;){
            fprintf(pfile,"\n\nPlease choose one of the following :");
            fprintf(pfile, "\n   1...to list A as a full matrix\n");
            fprintf(pfile,"   2...to list A as an upper-triangular matrix\n");
            fprintf(pfile,"   3...to list A as a lower-triangular matrix\n");
            fprintf(pfile,"   4...to list A by processor\n");
            fprintf(pfile,"   5...to quit this menu\n ==> ");
            if(std_flag && (pfile==stdout)) fflush(stdout);
            scanf("%s",input);
            list_option = atoi(input);

            if(list_option>0 && list_option<4) matrix_list(list_option);
            else if(list_option==4) list_proc(0);
            else if(list_option==5) break;
            else printf("\n\n **** Invalid input - try again ****\n");
        }
}


/************************* end of routine list_A *************************/
pivot_A(piv_proc_row,piv_block)
int piv_proc_row,piv_block;
{
        int j,ntemp,piv_row,ringpos;
        TYPE dummy;

        piv_row = D*piv_block + piv_proc_row - 1;
        ntemp   = m/2+piv_row+1;
        if(ntemp<(D*nx-1) && krow>0) ntemp = D*nx-1;
        ntemp   = (ntemp-1)/D+1;
        nx      = krow>=kend ? ny : ntemp;

        if(D*nx>over-krow+1){
            for(j=over+1;j<=(D*nx+krow-1);++j)
                if(col_pos==j%D && row_pos==j%D)
                    nblocks[j/D] = (j-krow)/D+1;
```

```
        over = D*nx+krow-1;
}

if (piv_proc_row>1){
    if(piv_proc_row>D/2){
        if(PI==1){
            v_to_c(combuf,Aspace+jptr[j_off]+i_off,
                    j_blocks,nx);
            cwrite(combuf,up,tsize*nx);
        }
        else if(PI>piv_proc_row)
            cread(U,down,up,tsize*nx);
        else if(PI==piv_proc_row)
            cread(U,down,0,tsize*nx);
    }
    else{
        if(PI==1){
            v_to_c(combuf,Aspace+jptr[j_off]+i_off,
                    j_blocks,nx);
            cwrite(combuf,down,tsize*nx);
        }
        else if(PI<piv_proc_row)
            cread(U,up,down,tsize*nx);
        else if(PI==piv_proc_row)
            cread(U,up,0,tsize*nx);
    }
    if(PI==piv_proc_row){
        v_to_c(combuf,Aspace+jptr[j_off-piv_block]+i_off+
                piv_block,j_blocks,nx);
        split_pipe(combuf,&dummy,down,up,tsize*nx,0,D);
        for(j=0;j<nx;++j){
            a(piv_block,j) = U[j];
            U[j]   = combuf[j];
        }
    }
    else{
        ringpos = PI-piv_proc_row;
        if(PI<piv_proc_row) ringpos += D;
        if(PI == 1){
          split_pipe(&dummy,combuf,down,up,tsize*nx,ringpos,D);
          c_to_v(Aspace+jptr[j_off]+i_off,combuf,j_blocks,nx);
        }
        else split_pipe(&dummy,U,down,up,tsize*nx,ringpos,D);
    }
}
else{
    if(piv_block != 0 && PI==1){
```

```
                    for(j=0;j<=nx;++j){
                        dummy          = a(0,j);
                        a(0,j)          = a(piv_block,j);
                        a(piv_block,j) = dummy;
                    }
                }
                if(PI==1){
                    v_to_c(combuf,Aspace+jptr[j_off]+i_off,j_blocks,nx);
                    split_pipe(combuf,&dummy,down,up,nx*tsize,0,D);
                }
                else split_pipe(&dummy,U,down,up,nx*tsize,PI-1,D);
            }
        }


/*************************** end of routine pivot_A **************************/
pivot_B(bl)
int bl;
{
    int p_row,piv_I,j;
    TYPE dummy;

    if(PI==1 && PJ==1){
        p_row = rowno[PK];
        piv_I = blockno[PK];
    }

    broadcast(&p_row,corner_proc[PI],nproc-1,isize);
    broadcast(&piv_I,corner_proc[PI],nproc-1,isize);

    if (p_row>1){
        if(p_row>D/2){
            if(PI==1){
                v_to_c(combuf,bspace+bl,j_blocks,b_col_blocks);
                cwrite(combuf,up,b_col_blocks*tsize);
                cread(combuf,up,0,tsize*b_col_blocks);
                c_to_v(bspace+bl,combuf,j_blocks,b_col_blocks);
            }
            else if(PI>p_row){
                cread(combuf,down,up,tsize*b_col_blocks);
                cread(combuf,up,down,tsize*b_col_blocks);
            }
            else if(PI==p_row){
                cread(U,down,0,tsize*b_col_blocks);
                v_to_c(combuf,bspace+bl+piv_I,j_blocks,b_col_blocks);
                cwrite(combuf,down,b_col_blocks*tsize);
                c_to_v(bspace+bl+piv_I,U,j_blocks,b_col_blocks);
            }
```

```
            }
            else{
                if(PI==1){
                        v_to_c(combuf,bspace+bl,j_blocks,b_col_blocks);
                        cwrite(combuf,down,b_col_blocks*tsize);
                        cread(combuf,down,0,tsize*b_col_blocks);
                        c_to_v(bspace+bl,combuf,j_blocks,b_col_blocks);
                }
                else if(PI<p_row){
                        cread(combuf,up,down,tsize*b_col_blocks);
                        cread(combuf,down,up,tsize*b_col_blocks);
                }
                else if(PI==p_row){
                        cread(U,up,0,tsize*b_col_blocks);
                        v_to_c(combuf,bspace+bl+piv_I,j_blocks,
                                        b_col_blocks);
                        cwrite(combuf,up,b_col_blocks*tsize);
                        c_to_v(bspace+bl+piv_I,U,j_blocks,b_col_blocks);
                }
            }
        }
        else{
            if(piv_I != 0 && PI==1){
                for(j=0;j<b_col_blocks;++j){
                    dummy           = b(bl,0,j);
                    b(bl,0,j)       = b(bl,piv_I,j);
                    b(bl,piv_I,j) = dummy;
                }
            }
        }
    }
}

/************************ end of routine pivot_B ************************/
split_pipe(outbuf,inbuf,clk_mask,anti_clk_mask,nbytes,ringpos,nring)
char *outbuf,*inbuf;
int clk_mask,anti_clk_mask,nbytes,ringpos,nring;
{
    if(ringpos==0){
        cwrite(outbuf,clk_mask,nbytes);
        cwrite(outbuf,anti_clk_mask,nbytes);
    }
    else if(ringpos<nring/2)
        cread(inbuf,anti_clk_mask,clk_mask,nbytes);
    else if(ringpos>nring/2)
        cread(inbuf,clk_mask,anti_clk_mask,nbytes);
    else if(ringpos==nring/2){
        cread(inbuf,anti_clk_mask,0,nbytes);
```

```
                cread(inbuf,clk_mask,0,nbytes);
         }
   }


   /************************* end of routine split_pipe ************************/
   v_to_c(outbuf,inbuf,off_items,nitems)
   TYPE *inbuf,*outbuf;
   int off_items,nitems;
   {
        int i,j;

        for(i=0,j=0;j<nitems;i += off_items,++j) *(outbuf+j) = *(inbuf+i);
   }


   /************************** end of routine v_to_c ***************************/
   welcome()
   {
        setbuffer(stdout,IO_buf,2048);
        std_flag = 1;
        printf("\n\n   ***********************************************");
        printf(  "\n   *                                               *");
        printf(  "\n   *  Welcome to the banded matrix solver. This    *");
        printf(  "\n   *  solves the equation Ax=b, where A is a banded *");
        printf(  "\n   *  matrix.                                      *");
        printf(  "\n   *                                               *");
        printf(  "\n   ***********************************************\n");
   }


   /************************* end of routine welcome ************************/
```

A-14.2 Include File bandef.h

```
   #define INITIALIZE 1
   #define LIST_MAT   2
   #define SOLVE      3
   #define STOP       4
   #define LU         1
   #define FORWARD    2
   #define BACK_SUB   3
   #define MFILE      1
   #define RANDOM     2
   #define DEMO       3
   #define FULL       1
   #define UPPER      2
   #define LOWER      3
   #define a(i,j) *(Aspace+jptr[j_off+j-i]+i+i_off)
   #define b(k,i,j) *(bspace+jptr[j]+i+k)
```

```
#define TYPE double
#define MAXBLOCKS  100
#define BMAXBLOCKS 100
#define AMAX 1000
#define BMAX 500
#define MAX_D 8
```

A-15 Subcube Management Utilities

A-15.1 CUBIX Program

```
#include <cros.h>
#include <stdio.h>

#define PARTITION 1
#define RESTORE   2
#define CURRENT   3
#define RESTRICT  4
#define STOP      5

int sc_id,level;
int nproc,procnum,doc,std_flag=0;
char IO_buf[4096];

main()
{
    int sc_number, command;

    get_param();

    welcome();

    sc_number = -1;
    while((command=get_task()) != STOP){
        switch(command){
            case PARTITION:
                run_partition(sc_number);
                sc_number = -1;
                break;
            case RESTORE:
                run_restore(sc_number);
                sc_number = -1;
                break;
            case CURRENT:
                run_show();
                sc_number = -1;
                break;
            case RESTRICT:
                sc_number = restrict();
                break;
            default:
                printf("\n\n**** Invalid input ****\n");
                break;
        }
```

```
    }
    printf("\n\nFinished\n\n");
    exit(0);
}


/*************************** end of routine main ***************************/
int get_number(string)
char string[72];
{
    int iresp;
    char input[5];

    for(;;){
        printf("\n\nPlease give %s ==> ",string);
        if(std_flag) fflush(stdout);
        scanf("%s",input);
        iresp = atoi(input);
        if(iresp>=0) break;
        else printf("\n\n*** Invalid input - try again ***\n");
    }
    return iresp;
}


/************************* end of routine get_number ************************/
int get_task()
{
    int task;
    char input[5];

    for(;;){
        printf("\n\nPlease choose one of the following:\n");
        printf("   1...to partition the current subcube\n");
        printf("   2...to restore a previous subcube\n");
        printf("   3...to show details of the current subcube\n");
        printf("   4...to restrict next task to a given subcube\n");
        printf("   5...to terminate program\n==> ");
        if(std_flag) fflush(stdout);
        scanf("%s",input);
        task = atoi(input);
        if(task>0 && task<6) break;
        else printf("\n\n*** Invalid input - try again ***\n");
    }
    return task;
}


/************************* end of routine get_task *************************/
```

```
int restrict()
{
    int sc_number;

    printf("\n\nPlease give ID of subcube to which instruction ");
    printf("applies (<0 for all) ==> ");
    scanf("%d",&sc_number);

    return sc_number;
}

/*********************** end of routine restrict ********************/

run_partition(sc_num)
int sc_num;
{
    int scmask;

    scmask = get_number("the mask of the new mapping");
    if((sc_num==-1)||(sc_num==sc_id)) sc_id = partition_subcube(scmask);
}

/*********************** end of routine run_partition ********************/
run_restore(sc_num)
int sc_num;
{
    level = get_number("the generation number");
    if((sc_num==-1)||(sc_num==sc_id)) sc_id = restore_subcube(level);
    sc_id = restore_subcube(level);
}

/*********************** end of routine run_restore ********************/
run_show()
{
    struct cubenv env;
    int iproc;

    cparam(&env);

    for(iproc=0;iproc<nproc;++iproc){
        fmulti(stdout);
        if(iproc==procnum){
            printf("\n\n****** CURRENT SUBCUBE MAPPING FOR ");
            printf("PROCESSOR %d ******\n",procnum);
            printf("\nID # of current subcube      = %d",sc_id);
            printf("\nGeneration # of current subcube = %d",level);
            printf("\nNode # in current subcube    = %d",env.procnum);
```

```
                printf("\nDimension of current subcube    = %d",env.doc);
                printf("\n# of nodes in current subcube    = %d",env.nproc);
            }
        fflush(stdout);
        fsingl(stdout);
        printf("\n");
        dw_pause();
    }
}


/*********************** end of routine show_current ***********************/
welcome()
{
    setbuffer(stdout,IO_buf,4096);
    std_flag = 1;

    printf("\n\n\t*************************************");
    printf(  "\n\t*                                 *");
    printf(  "\n\t*  Welcome to the subcube management  *");
    printf(  "\n\t*        utilities example program.   *");
    printf(  "\n\t*                                 *");
    printf(  "\n\t*************************************\n");

}


/************************** end of routine welcome **************************/
```

A-16 The *comutil* Routines

A-16.1 CUBIX Program

```c
#include <cros.h>
#include <stdio.h>
#include "utildef.h"
#include "cubdefs.h"

char IO_buf[4096];
int nproc,doc,procnum;
int std_flag=0,file_status;
FILE *in_file,*out_file;
int ntotal,lab_size=sizeof(LABEL);

main()
{
    int i,npts,nsend,source,dest,nbytes,max_bytes,ir,nlabels,command;
    int labfun();
    LABEL labdat[MAX_LABELS];

    file_status = CLOSED;
    in_file     = stdin;
    out_file    = stdout;

    welcome();

    get_param();

    while((command=get_task()) != STOP){
        switch(command){
            case INITIALIZE:
                nlabels = initialize(labdat);
                break;
            case GLOBAL_REVERSE:
                ir=global_reverse(labdat,ntotal,lab_size);
                check_retval(ir);
                break;
            case INDEX:
                ir=indexx(labdat,ntotal,lab_size);
                check_retval(ir);
                break;
            case TRANSPOSE:
                nbytes    = nlabels*lab_size;
                max_bytes = MAX_LABELS*lab_size;
                ir=transpose(labdat,nbytes,max_bytes);
                check_retval(ir);
```

```
                    nlabels = ir/lab_size;
                    break;
            case TRANSFER:
                    source = get_proc(0);
                    dest  = get_proc(1);
                    ir    = transfer(labdat,source,dest,nlabels,
                                     lab_size,MAX_LABELS);
                    check_retval(ir);
                    if(ir>=0) nlabels = ir;
                    break;
            case SCATTER:
                    source = get_proc(0);
                    ir=scatter(labdat,source,nlabels,lab_size,
                               MAX_LABELS);
                    check_retval(ir);
                    if(ir>0)
                        nlabels = (nlabels>nsend) ? nlabels:nsend;
                    break;
            case EXPAND:
                    npts = nlabels/nproc;
                    ir=expand(labdat+procnum,labdat,
                        nproc*lab_size,npts,lab_size);
                    check_retval(ir);
                    break;
            case CONCAT:
                    ir=expand(labdat,labdat,0,1,lab_size);
                    check_retval(ir);
                    break;
            case FOLD:
                    ir=fold(labdat,labfun,lab_size,nlabels);
                    check_retval(ir);
                    break;
            case OUTPUT:
                    output_results(labdat,nlabels);
                    break;
            }
        }
    printf("\n\nFinished\n\n");
    exit(0);
}


/*************************** end of routine main ****************************/
check_retval(ir)
int ir;
{
    int add_int(),check_err;
```

```
        check_err = (ir<0 && ir!=-99) ? 1 : 0;
        combine(&check_err,add_int,sizeof(int),1);

        if(check_err){
            fmulti(out_file);
            if(ir<0) fprintf(out_file,"\nThe return value in processor %d is %d",
                        procnum,ir);
            fsingl(out_file);
        }
    }

/*********************** end of routine check_retval ***********************/
int get_proc(i)
int i;
{
    int proc;
    char input[5];

    for(;;){
        if(i==0)
            printf("\n\nPlease choose the source processor ==> ");
        else
            printf("\n\nPlease choose the destination processor ==> ");
        if(std_flag) fflush(stdout);
        scanf("%s",input);
        proc = atoi(input);
        if(proc>=0 && proc<nproc) break;
        else printf("\n\n*** Invalid input - try again ***\n");
    }
    return proc;
}

/************************* end of routine get_procs *************************/
int get_task()
{
    int task;
    char input[5];

    for(;;){
            printf("\n\nPlease choose one of the following:\n");
            printf("    1...to initialize a set of labels\n");
            printf("    2...to transform the data using GLOBAL_REVERSE\n");
            printf("    3...to transform the data using INDEX\n");
            printf("    4...to transform the data using TRANSPOSE\n");
            printf("    5...to transform the data using TRANSFER\n");
            printf("    6...to transform the data using SCATTER\n");
            printf("    7...to transform the data using EXPAND\n");
```

```
                  printf("  8...to transform the data using CONCAT\n");
                  printf("  9...to transform the data using FOLD\n");
                  printf("  10...to output the data\n");
                  printf("  11...to terminate program\n==> ");
            if(std_flag) fflush(stdout);
            scanf("%s",input);
            task = atoi(input);
            if(task>0 && task<12) break;
            else printf("\n\n*** Invalid input - try again ***\n");
      }
      return task;
}


/*********************** end of routine get_task ************************/
int initialize(x)
LABEL x[];
{
      int i,nmin,nleft,nlocal;
      char input[5];

      for(;;){
            printf("\n\nPlease give the total number of labels ==> ");
            if(std_flag) fflush(stdout);
            scanf("%s",input);
            ntotal = atoi(input);
            nmin   = ntotal/nproc;
            nleft  = ntotal%nproc;
            nlocal = (procnum<nleft) ? nmin+1 : nmin;
            if(nmin<1 || nmin>MAX_LABELS || (nleft!=0&&nmin>=MAX_LABELS))
                  printf("\n\n*** Invalid input - try again ***\n");
            else break;
      }

      for(i=0;i<nlocal;++i){
            x[i].proc  = procnum;
            x[i].index = i;
      }

      return nlocal;
}

/******************** end of initialize routine ********************/

int labfun(p1,p2,size)
LABEL *p1,*p2;
int size;
{
```

```
        p1->index += p2->index;
        return 0;
}


/********************* end of labfun routine **************************/

output_results(x,nlab)
LABEL x[];
int nlab;
{
    int i,p,lines,nout;
    FILE *setup_out();

    if(file_status==CLOSED) out_file = setup_out("utilCUB.c");

    for(;;){
        printf("\n\nPlease give the processor number (-ve to end)==> ");
        if(std_flag) fflush(stdout);
        scanf("%d",&p);
        if(p<0 || p>=nproc) break;
        nout = nlab;
        broadcast(&nout,p,nproc-1,sizeof(int));
        fmulti(out_file);
        lines = 0;
        for(i=0;i<nout;++i){
            if(procnum==p)
                    fprintf(out_file,"\n(%4d,%4d) maps to (%4d,%4d)",
                            x[i].proc,x[i].index,p,i);
            lines++;
            if(lines>20){
                if(out_file==stdout) fsingl(stdout);
                dw_pause();
                if(out_file==stdout) fmulti(stdout);
                lines = 0;
            }
        }
        fsingl(out_file);
    }
}


/********************* end of routine output_results *******************/
welcome()
{
    setbuffer(stdout,IO_buf,4096);
    std_flag = 1;

    printf("\n\n\t*******************************************");
```

```
printf( "\n\t*                                        *");
printf( "\n\t*  Welcome to general-purpose communication  *");
printf( "\n\t*        utilities example program.        *");
printf( "\n\t*                                        *");
printf( "\n\t*  This program demonstrates the use of the  *");
printf( "\n\t*  routines global_reverse, transpose, index, *");
printf( "\n\t*  scatter, fold, expand, and transfer.      *");
printf( "\n\t*                                        *");
printf( "\n\t*********************************************\n");

}


/************************* end of routine welcome *************************/
```

A-16.2 Include File utildef.h

```
typedef struct { int proc, index;} LABEL;
#define MAX_LABELS     1000
#define INITIALIZE        1
#define GLOBAL_REVERSE    2
#define INDEX             3
#define TRANSPOSE         4
#define TRANSFER          5
#define SCATTER           6
#define EXPAND            7
#define CONCAT            8
#define FOLD              9
#define OUTPUT           10
#define STOP             11
```

A-17 The Crystal Router

A-17.1 CUBIX Program

```c
#include <cros.h>
#include <stdio.h>
#include <crdef.h>
#include "cubdefs.h"

#define MAX_DEST 256
#define MESS_LEN 512
#define SETUP_MESSAGES  1
#define LIST_MESSAGES   2
#define SEND_MESSAGES   3
#define GET_MESSAGES    4
#define CHANGE_BUFFER   5
#define CLEAR_MESSAGES  6
#define ERROR_MESSAGES  7
#define STOP            8

int nproc,doc,procnum;

main()
{
    int task,resp,get_task();

    welcome();

    get_param();

    while( (task=get_task()) != STOP ){
        switch(task){
            case SETUP_MESSAGES:
                resp = write_mail();
                break;
            case LIST_MESSAGES:
                resp = list_messages();
                break;
            case SEND_MESSAGES:
                resp = crystal_router();
                break;
            case GET_MESSAGES:
                resp = read_mail();
                break;
            case CHANGE_BUFFER:
                resp = set_mail_buffers();
                break;
```

```
                    case CLEAR_MESSAGES:
                        resp = clear_messages();
                        break;
                    case ERROR_MESSAGES:
                        resp = error_messages(stdout);
                        break;
            }
        }
        printf("\n\nFinished\n\n");
        exit(0);
}

/*********************** end of routine main ***************************/
int get_task()
{
        int ok,task;
        char input[4];

        ok = 0;
        while(!ok){
            printf("\n\nPlease choose one of the following :\n");
            printf( "    1...to create some messages\n");
            printf( "    2...to list one of the message buffers\n");
            printf( "    3...to send messages to their destinations\n");
            printf( "    4...to read some of the received messages\n");
            printf( "    5...to change size of message buffers\n");
            printf( "    6...to clear one of the message buffers\n");
            printf( "    7...to list error messages, if any\n");
            printf( "    8...to terminate the program\n\n==> ");

            scanf("%s",input);
            printf("\n");

            task = atoi(input);

            if(task>0 && task<9) ok = 1;
            else printf("\n**** Invalid input - try again ****\n");
        }
        return task;
}

/********************** end of routine get_task ************************/
welcome()
{
        printf("\n\n\t****************************************************\n");
        printf(    "\t*                                                *\n");
        printf(    "\t*    Welcome to the CUBIX version of the         *\n");
```

```
     printf(    "\t*     crystal router demonstration program.        *\n");
     printf(    "\t*                                                   *\n");
     printf(    "\t**************************************************\n");
}


/************************ end of routine welcome ************************/
int write_mail()
{
    int ntemp,destination,source,nbytes,resp,dest[MAX_DEST],ndest;
    char message[80];

    for(;;){
        printf("\n\nPlease give the source processor");
        printf(" ( -ve to end ) ==> ");
        scanf("%d",&source);
        if(source<0) break;
        ndest = 0;
        for(;;){
            printf("\n\nPlease give the destination processor");
            printf(" ( -ve to end ) ==> ");
            scanf("%d",&destination);
            if(destination<0) break;
            dest[ndest] = destination;
            ndest++;
        }
        getchar();
        printf("\n\nMessage (< 78 characters) ==> ");
        gets(message);
        if(procnum==source){
            nbytes = strlen(message) + 1;
            ntemp  = nbytes/4;
            if ( nbytes%4 != 0 ) nbytes = 4*(ntemp + 1);
            else nbytes = 4*ntemp;
            resp = send_message(message,nbytes,ndest,dest);
        }
    }
    return resp;
}


/********************** end of routine write_mail **********************/
int list_messages()
{
    int buf_id,resp;
    char input[10];

    resp = 0;
    for(;;){
```

```
        printf("\n\nPlease select the buffer you want to list :\n");
        printf(    "   1...the buffer of outgoing messages\n");
        printf(    "   2...the buffer of received messages\n");
        printf(    "   3...to quit this menu\n==> ");
        scanf("%s",input);
        printf("\n");

        buf_id = atoi(input);
        if( buf_id==1 )
            resp = list_buffer(out_start_ptr,out_bytes,OUT);
        else if( buf_id==2 )
            resp = list_buffer(in_start_ptr,in_bytes,IN);
        else if( buf_id==3 ) break;
        else printf("\n\n**** Invalid input - try again ****\n");
    }
    return resp;
}


/********************* end of routine list_messages *********************/
int list_buffer(start_ptr,total_bytes,in_out)
char *start_ptr;
int total_bytes,in_out;
{
    int proc,message_number,bytes,dest,src,message_size,status,nbytes;
    int i,j,ndest;
    char c,input[5],status_string[8],*buf_ptr;

    printf("\n\n     ************************************");
    printf(  "\n        ");
    if(in_out==OUT)
        printf("\n      Listing of buffer of outgoing messages");
    else
        printf("\n      Listing of buffer of received messages");
    printf("\n\n     ************************************");

    for(;;){
        printf("\n\nPlease give the processor ( -ve to end ) ==> ");
        scanf("%s",input);
        proc = atoi(input);
        if(proc<0)break;
        fmulti(stdout);
        if(procnum==proc){
            if(total_bytes==0)
                printf("\n\nThe buffer of processor %d is empty",proc);
            else{
                buf_ptr = start_ptr;
                bytes   = 0;
```

```
                    message_number = 1;
                    while(bytes<total_bytes){
                        ndest  = *((int *)buf_ptr);
                        src    = *((int *)(buf_ptr+isize));
                        nbytes = *((int *)(buf_ptr+2*isize));
                        status = *((int *)(buf_ptr+3*isize));
                        if(status==CURRENT)
                            strcpy(status_string,"CURRENT");
                        else
                            strcpy(status_string,"OLD");
                        header_size  = (4+ndest)*isize;
                        message_size = nbytes + header_size;
                        buf_ptr += 4*isize;
                        printf("\nMessage number %d from processor %d",
                                    message_number,src);
                        printf(", nbytes = %d, status = %s\n",
                                    nbytes,status_string);
                        printf("Destination processors :");
                        for(i=0,j=4;i<ndest;++i,j++){
                            dest = *((int *)buf_ptr);
                            c = (j%10==9 || i==(ndest-1)) ? '\n' : ' ';
                            printf("%6d%c",dest,c);
                            buf_ptr += isize;
                        }
                        printf("%s\n",buf_ptr);
                        bytes    += message_size;
                        buf_ptr += nbytes;
                        message_number++;
                    }
                }
            }
            fsingl(stdout);
        }
        return 0;
    }


    /*********************** end of routine list_buffer **********************/
    int read_mail()
    {
        int nbytes,source,resp,mess_proc,any;
        char input[10],buf[MESS_LEN];

        any = ANY;
        for(;;){
          printf("\n\nPlease give processor number for reading messages");
          printf(" ( -ve to end ) ==> ");
          scanf("%s",input);
```

```
        mess_proc = atoi(input);
        if(mess_proc<0) break;
        for(;;){
           printf("\n\nPlease give the source processor");
           printf(" ( %d = any, -ve = end ) ==> ",any);
           scanf("%s",input);
           source = atoi(input);
           if(source<0) break;
           if(source<nproc || source==ANY){
                fmulti(stdout);
                if(procnum==mess_proc){
                     resp = get_message(buf,&source,&nbytes);
                     if(resp>=0) print_mess(buf,source,nbytes,resp);
                }
                fsingl(stdout);
           }
           else printf("\n\n**** Invalid input - try again ****\n");
        }
     }
     return 0;
}


/*********************** end of routine read_mail() ***********************/
int print_mess(buf,source,nbytes,istat)
char *buf;
int source,nbytes,istat;
{
     switch(istat){
        case 0:
           printf("\n\nMessage from processor %d to processor %d :\n%s\n",
                      source,procnum,buf);
           break;
        case 1:
           printf("\n\nThere are no messages for processor %d\n",procnum);
           break;
        case 2:
           printf("\n\nNo message of the requested type has been");
           printf(" sent to processor %d\n",procnum);
           break;
        case 3:
           printf("\n\nAll the messages have been read for processor %d\n",
                      procnum);
     }
     return 0;
}


/*********************** end of routine print_mess ***********************/
```

```c
int set_mail_buffers()
{
    int resp,buf_id,buf_size;
    char input[5];

    resp = 0;

    for(;;){
        printf("\n\nPlease choose one of the following :\n");
        printf(    "    1...to change the outgoing message buffer\n");
        printf(    "    2...to change the received message buffer\n");
        printf(    "    3...to quit this menu\n\n==> ");

        scanf("%s",input);
        buf_id = atoi(input);

        if(buf_id==3) break;
        else if(buf_id==1){
            printf("\n\nPlease give buffer size in bytes ==> ");
            scanf("%d",&buf_size);
            resp = set_cr_buf(buf_size,OUT);
        }
        else if(buf_id==2){
            printf("\n\nPlease give buffer size in bytes ==> ");
            scanf("%d",&buf_size);
            resp = set_cr_buf(buf_size,IN);
        }
        else printf("\n\n**** Invalid input - try again ****\n");
    }
    printf("\n");

    return resp;
}

/********************* end of routine set_mail_buffers *********************/
int clear_messages()
{
    int resp,buf_id;
    char input[5];

    resp = 0;

    for(;;){
        printf("\n\nPlease choose one of the following :\n");
        printf(    "    1...to clear the outgoing message buffer\n");
        printf(    "    2...to clear the received message buffer\n");
        printf(    "    3...to quit this menu\n\n==> ");
```

```
        scanf("%s",input);
        buf_id = atoi(input);

        if(buf_id==3) break;
        else if(buf_id==1) resp = clear_cr_buf(OUT);
        else if(buf_id==2) resp = clear_cr_buf(IN);
        else printf("\n\n**** Invalid input - try again ****\n");
    }
    printf("\n");

    return resp;
}
/*********************** end of routine clear_messages ***********************/
```

A-18 The Crystal Accumulator

A-18.1 CUBIX Program

```
#include <stdio.h>
#include <cros.h>

#define TYPE int
#define INITIALIZE 1
#define SETUP_DBUF 2
#define OUTPUT     3
#define STOP       4
#define M          6

int procnum,doc,nproc,std_flag=0,init_status=0;

TYPE *Vx,*Sx;
int *qx,*px,*Sindex;
typedef struct { int cm,qorder; TYPE element; } DSTRUCT;
int *nmask,nd,dstruct_size=sizeof(DSTRUCT);

main()
{
    int command,nV,nS,nbytes,add_int();
    TYPE identity;

    get_param();
    nbytes = sizeof(TYPE);
    while((command=get_task())!=STOP){
        switch(command){
            case INITIALIZE:
                nV = initialize(nbytes,&identity);
                break;
            case SETUP_DBUF:
                nS = crystal_accumulator(Vx,Sx,add_int,
                        nbytes,nV,qx,px,Sindex,identity,nV);
                break;
            case OUTPUT:
                output_results(Vx,Sx,qx,px,Sindex,nV,nS,identity);
                break;
        }
    }
    printf("\n\nFinished\n\n");
    exit(0);
}


/*************************** end of routine main ***************************/
```

```
int crystal_accumulator(V,S,func,nbytes,nitems,q,p,Sind,identity,
                                data_buf_size)
TYPE *V,*S,identity;
int nitems,nbytes,*q,*p,*Sind,data_buf_size,(*func)();
{
    DSTRUCT *data1_buf,*data2_buf;
    char *malloc();
    int i,toggle,nrec,nsend,nkeep,inspace;

    data1_buf = (DSTRUCT *)malloc((data_buf_size+2)*dstruct_size);
    if(data1_buf==(DSTRUCT *)NULLPTR) return -1;

    nitems = set_up_data_buf(data1_buf,V,nitems,q,p,identity);

    data2_buf = (DSTRUCT *)malloc(data_buf_size*dstruct_size);
    if(data2_buf==(DSTRUCT *)NULLPTR) return -1;

    nbytes = sizeof(DSTRUCT);
    toggle = 1;
    for(i=(doc-1);i>=0;--i){
        if(toggle) nsend = high_pts(data1_buf,nitems,i);
        else       nsend = high_pts(data2_buf,nitems,i);
        nkeep   = nitems-nsend;
        inspace = (data_buf_size-nkeep)*nbytes;
        if(toggle){
            nrec    = cshift(data1_buf+nkeep,1<<i,inspace,
                        data1_buf+nkeep,1<<i,nsend*nbytes)/nbytes;
            nitems  = merge_lists(data2_buf,data1_buf,nkeep,
                        data1_buf+nkeep,nrec,i,func);
        }
        else{
            nrec    = cshift(data2_buf+nkeep,1<<i,inspace,
                        data2_buf+nkeep,1<<i,nsend*nbytes)/nbytes;
            nitems  = merge_lists(data1_buf,data2_buf,nkeep,
                        data2_buf+nkeep,nrec,i,func);
        }
        toggle = 1-toggle;
    }

    if(toggle)
        for(i=0;i<nitems;++i){
            S[i]    = data1_buf[i].element;
            Sind[i] = data1_buf[i].qorder;
        }
    else
        for(i=0;i<nitems;++i){
            S[i]    = data2_buf[i].element;
```

```
            Sind[i] = data2_buf[i].qorder;
        }

    free(data1_buf);
    free(data2_buf);

    return nitems;
}

/******************** end of routine crystal_accumulator ********************/
int high_pts(dbuf,nitems,step)
DSTRUCT *dbuf;
int nitems,step;
{
    int i,mask,nsend;

    mask  = 1<<step;
    nsend = 0;
    for(i=(nitems-1);i>=0;--i){
        if(dbuf[i].cm < mask) break;
        nsend++;
    }

    return nsend;
}

/*************************** end of routine high_pts **************************/
int initialize(nbytes,identity)
TYPE *identity;
int nbytes;
{
    int nlist,itemp,i,nitems,seed,*perm_list;
    double sparcity,temp,prandS(),prandB();
    char *malloc();

    if(init_status){
        free(qx);
        free(px);
        free(Vx);
        free(Sx);
        free(Sindex);
    }

    printf("\n\nPlease give the length of the vector ==> ");
    scanf("%d",&nitems);

    printf("\n\nPlease give the value of the identity element ==> ");
```

```
    scanf("%d",identity);

    printf("\n\nPlease give the sparcity of the vector ==> ");
    scanf("%lf",&sparcity);

    printf("\n\nPlease give a seed to generate q and p ==> ");
    scanf("%d",&seed);

    prand_setB(seed,0,procnum);

    qx = (int *)malloc(sizeof(int)*nitems);
    px = (int *)malloc(sizeof(int)*nitems);
    Sindex = (int *)malloc(sizeof(int)*nitems);
    perm_list = (int *)malloc(sizeof(int)*nitems);
    Vx = (TYPE *)malloc(sizeof(int)*nitems);
    Sx = (TYPE *)malloc(sizeof(int)*nitems);

    for(i=0;i<nitems;++i) perm_list[i] = i;
    nlist = nitems;
    for(i=0;i<nitems;++i){
        itemp = (int)(prandS()*(double)nlist);
        qx[i] = perm_list[itemp];
        perm_list[itemp] = perm_list[--nlist];
    }
    free(perm_list);

    for(i=0;i<nitems;++i) px[i] = (int)(prandS()*(double)nproc);

    printf("\n\nPlease give a seed to generate V ==> ");
    scanf("%d",&seed);

    prand_setB(seed,2,procnum);

    for(i=0;i<nitems;++i){
        temp = prandS();
        if(temp<sparcity){
            temp = prandB();
            Vx[i] = *identity;
        }
        else Vx[i] = (TYPE)(2.0+prandB()*(double)nitems);
    }
    init_status = 1;

    return nitems;
}

/*********************** end of routine initialize ***********************/
```

```
int get_task()
{
    int task;

    printf("\n\nPlease choose one of the following :\n");
    printf("      1...to initialize a new set of vectors\n");
    printf("      2...to run the crystal accumulator\n");
    printf("      3...to output data\n");
    printf("      4...to terminate program\n==> ");

    scanf("%d",&task);

    return task;
}

/************************* end of routine get_task *************************/
list_input(V,q,p,nitems,identity)
TYPE *V,identity;
int *p,*q,nitems;
{
    int i,iproc;

    printf("\n\nThe length of the vectors to be merged is %d",nitems);
    printf("\n\n The identity element is %f",(float)identity);

    printf("\n\nThe vector q mapping indices of V to those of S is:\n");
    for(i=0;i<nitems;++i) printf("%6d%c",q[i],(i%10==9) ? '\n' : ' ');

    printf("\n\nThe vector p mapping indices of S to processors is :\n");
    for(i=0;i<nitems;++i) printf("%6d%c",p[i],(i%10==9) ? '\n' : ' ');

    dw_pause();
    fmulti(stdout);
    for(iproc=0;iproc<nproc;++iproc){
        if(procnum==iproc)
    printf("\n\nThe data vector V for processor %d is :\n",procnum);
        for(i=0;i<nitems;++i){
            if(procnum==iproc)
                printf("%6d%c",V[i],(i%10==9) ? '\n' : ' ');
            if(i%50==49) fflush(stdout);
        }
        fsingl(stdout);dw_pause();fmulti(stdout);
    }
    fsingl(stdout);
}

/************************* end of routine list_input *************************/
```

```
list_output(S,Sind,nS)
TYPE *S;
int *Sind,nS;
{
    int i,nlist,iproc;

    fmulti(stdout);
    for(iproc=0;iproc<nproc;++iproc){
        if(procnum==iproc){
            nlist = nS;
            printf("\n\nThe data vector S for processor %d is :\n",procnum);
        }
        fflush(stdout);
        broadcast(&nlist,iproc,nproc-1,sizeof(int));
        for(i=0;i<nlist;++i){
            if(procnum==iproc) printf("(%4d,%4d)%c",
                    S[i],Sind[i],(i%6==5) ? '\n' : ' ');
            if(i%30==29) fflush(stdout);
        }
        fsingl(stdout);dw_pause();fmulti(stdout);
    }
    fsingl(stdout);
}

/********************** end of routine list_output **********************/
list_data_buf(dbuf,nitems)
DSTRUCT *dbuf;
int nitems;
{
    int iproc,i,j,k;

    for(iproc=0;iproc<nproc;++iproc){
        fmulti(stdout);
        if(iproc==procnum){
            printf("\n\nThe data buffer for processor %d is :\n",procnum);
            for(i=0;i<nitems;++i){
                printf("\ncmask = %6d, qorder = %6d, data_buf = %6d",
                dbuf[i].cm,dbuf[i].qorder,dbuf[i].element);
            }
        }
        fflush(stdout);
        fsingl(stdout);
        dw_pause();
    }
}

/********************** end of routine list_data_buf **********************/
```

```
DSTRUCT make_struct(a,b,c)
int a,b;
TYPE c;
{
    DSTRUCT x;

    x.cm      = a;
    x.qorder  = b;
    x.element = c;

    return x;
}


/*********************** end of routine make_struct ***********************/
int merge_lists(new_list,cur_list,cur_items,insert_list,in_items,step,cfunc)
DSTRUCT *new_list,*cur_list,*insert_list;
int cur_items,in_items,step,(*cfunc)();
{
    int i,j,k,m,new_cm,new_q,cur_cm,cur_q,in_cm,in_q;
    TYPE in_el,cur_el;
    DSTRUCT make_struct();

    i = 0;
    j = 0;
    k = 0;

    while((j<cur_items)&&(k<in_items)){
        in_cm  = insert_list[k].cm - (1<<step);
        in_q   = insert_list[k].qorder;
        in_el  = insert_list[k].element;
        cur_cm = cur_list[j].cm;
        cur_q  = cur_list[j].qorder;
        cur_el = cur_list[j].element;

        if(cur_cm<in_cm){
            new_list[i] = cur_list[j];
            j++;
        }
        else if(cur_cm==in_cm){
            if(cur_q<in_q){
                new_list[i] = cur_list[j];
                j++;
            }
            else if(cur_q==in_q){
                (*cfunc)(&cur_el,&in_el,sizeof(TYPE));
                new_list[i] = make_struct(cur_cm,cur_q,cur_el);
                j++;
```

```
                    k++;
                }
                else{
                    new_list[i] = make_struct(in_cm,in_q,in_el);
                    k++;
                }
            }
            else{
                new_list[i] = make_struct(in_cm,in_q,in_el);
                k++;
            }

            i++;
        }

        if(j<cur_items){
            for(m=j;m<cur_items;++m){
                new_list[i] = cur_list[m];
                i++;
            }
        }
        else if(k<in_items){
            for(m=k;m<in_items;++m){
                in_cm = insert_list[m].cm - (1<<step);
                in_q  = insert_list[m].qorder;
                in_el = insert_list[m].element;
                new_list[i] = make_struct(in_cm,in_q,in_el);
                i++;
            }
        }

        return i;
}

/************************* end of routine merge_lists *************************/
output_results(V,S,q,p,Sind,nV,nS,identity)
TYPE *V,*S,identity;
int *q,*p,*Sind,nV,nS;
{
        int opt;

        for(;;){
            printf("\n\nPlease choose one of the following :\n");
            printf("      1...to list the input data\n");
            printf("      2...to list the output data\n");
            printf("      3...to quit this menu\n ==> ");
            scanf("%d",&opt);
```

```
        if(opt==3) break;
        else if(opt==1) list_input(V,q,p,nV,identity);
        else if(opt==2) list_output(S,Sind,nS);
        else printf("\n\n *** Invalid input - try again ***\n");
    }
}


/*********************** end of routine output_results **********************/
int set_up_data_buf(dbuf,V,nitems,q,p,identity)
TYPE *V,identity;
DSTRUCT *dbuf;
int nitems,*q,*p;
{
    int iproc,i,mask;
    char *malloc();

    nmask = (int *)malloc(sizeof(int)*nproc);
    for(i=0;i<nproc;++i) nmask[i] = 0;

    nd = 0;
    for(i=0;i<nitems;++i){
        if(V[i]!=identity){
            nd++;
            mask = p[q[i]]^procnum;
            dbuf[nd].cm      = mask;
            dbuf[nd].qorder  = q[i];
            dbuf[nd].element = V[i];
            nmask[mask]++;
        }
    }
    dbuf[0].cm      =  0;
    dbuf[0].qorder = -1;
    dbuf[0].element= (TYPE)0;
    dbuf[nd+1].cm      = nproc;
    dbuf[nd+1].qorder = 0;
    dbuf[nd+1].element= (TYPE)0;

    quicksort(1,nd,dbuf);
    insertion(1,nd,dbuf);

    for(i=0;i<nd;++i) dbuf[i] = dbuf[i+1];

    return nd;
}


/*********************** end of routine set_up_data_buf **********************/
```

```
insertion(low,high,item)
DSTRUCT *item;
int low,high;
{
    int i,j,k;
    DSTRUCT temp;

    for(i=low+1; i<=high; ++i) {
        if(compare_keys(item[i],item[i-1]) < 0){
            for(j=i-2; compare_keys(item[i],item[j])<0; --j)
                ;
            temp=item[i];
            for(k=i; k>j+1; --k)
                item[k]=item[k-1] ;
            item[j+1]=temp;
        }
    }
}

/*********************** end of routine insertion ***********************/
quicksort(low,high,item)
int low,high;
DSTRUCT *item;
{
    int i,j;
    DSTRUCT k,dtemp;

        i = low+1;
        j = high;
        /* partition via R. Sedgwick's way; Knuth V3, pp.114 */
    k = item[low];
    while(i<j){
        while(compare_keys(item[i],k) <= 0) ++i;
        while(compare_keys(item[j],k) > 0)   --j;
        if(i<j) swap_items(&item[i],&item[j]);
    }
    if(j>low) swap_items(&item[low],&item[j]);
            /* quicksort only down to lists of size M - after */
            /* that, do a straight insertion sort - see */
            /* Knuth V3, pp. 116 */
    if(j-1-low > M)
        quicksort(low,j-1,item);
    if(high-i > M)
        quicksort(i,high,item);
}

/*********************** end of routine quicksort ***********************/
```

```
int compare_keys(d1,d2)
DSTRUCT d1,d2;
{
    if(d1.cm>d2.cm) return 1;
    else if(d1.cm==d2.cm){
        if(d1.qorder>d2.qorder) return 1;
        else if(d1.qorder==d2.qorder) return 0;
        else return -1;
    }
    else return -1;
}


/*********************** end of routine compare_keys ***********************/
swap_items(d1,d2)
DSTRUCT *d1,*d2;
{
    DSTRUCT dtemp;

    dtemp = *d1;
    *d1   = *d2;
    *d2   = dtemp;
}


/*********************** end of routine swap_items ***********************/
```

B

Appendix B:
Fortran Application Programs

This appendix lists the Fortran source code for the application programs described in Chapter 8. Most of the algorithms are also dealt with in Volume 1. For the C code a library of commonly-used routines has been developed (see App. A-1). A similar library has not yet been developed for the Fortran code. In addition, the *submap* utilities described in Chap. 5 have not yet been implemented in Fortran. Therefore, in order to ensure that the section numbers in this appendix agree with the corresponding sections of Chap. 8, sections B-1 and B-15 have been omitted, Although a reasonable effort has been made to ensure that the code is correct and reliable, there are, no doubt, bugs. If you encounter any bugs, or have constructive suggestions for improving the code, please write to the address given in Appendix G. When filing a bug report, please give full details of the problem and the input data.

B-2 The One-Dimensional Wave Equation: CPNODE Version

B-2.1 CP Program

```
      PROGRAM WAVFCP
      INTEGER INITIA, UPDATE, OUTPUT, QUIT
      PARAMETER (INITIA=1, UPDATE=2, OUTPUT=3, QUIT=4)
      PARAMETER ( MAXSIZ=500 )
      INTEGER PROCNU, DOC, NPROC, MYPOS, LCHAN, RCHAN
      COMMON/EXTCOM/ PROCNU, DOC, NPROC, MYPOS, LCHAN, RCHAN
      COMMON/NPTCOM/ NMIN, NLEFT, NTOT
      INTEGER TASK

      CALL DOWNLD('waveNODE')

10    CALL GETASK(TASK)
      IF (TASK.NE.QUIT) THEN
          IF(TASK.EQ.INITIA) THEN
              CALL INITCP
          ELSEIF (TASK.EQ.UPDATE) THEN
              CALL DOSTEP
          ELSEIF (TASK.EQ.OUTPUT) THEN
              CALL OUTRES
          ENDIF
          GOTO 10
      ENDIF

      STOP
      END
C
CCCCCCCCCCCCCCCCCCCCCCCCCCCCCCC END OF PROGRAM WAVFCP CCCCCCCCCCCCCCCCCCCCCCCCCCCCCCC
C
      SUBROUTINE DOWNLD(PRGNAM)
      CHARACTER*8 PRGNAM
      INTEGER PROCNU, DOC, NPROC, MYPOS, LCHAN, RCHAN
      COMMON/EXTCOM/ PROCNU, DOC, NPROC, MYPOS, LCHAN, RCHAN

      PRINT *,' '
         PRINT *,' Please give the dimension of the hypercube '
      READ(*,*)DOC

      CALL KCUBEL(DOC,PRGNAM)
      NPROC = 2**DOC

      RETURN
      END
C
```

```
CCCCCCCCCCCCCCCCCCCCCCCCCCCC END OF PROGRAM DOWNLD CCCCCCCCCCCCCCCCCCCCCCCCCCCCC
C
      SUBROUTINE GETASK(TASK)
      INTEGER INITIA, UPDATE, OUTPUT, QUIT
      PARAMETER ( INITIA=1, UPDATE=2, OUTPUT=3, QUIT=4 )
      PARAMETER ( ISIZE=4 )
      INTEGER TASK, STATUS
      CHARACTER*1 RESP

10    WRITE(*,100)
      READ(*,200) RESP
      IF (RESP.EQ.'1') THEN
          TASK = INITIA
      ELSEIF (RESP.EQ.'2') THEN
          TASK = UPDATE
      ELSEIF (RESP.EQ.'3') THEN
          TASK = OUTPUT
      ELSEIF (RESP.EQ.'4') THEN
          TASK = QUIT
      ELSE
          WRITE(*,101)
          GOTO 10
      ENDIF

      STATUS = KBCSTC(TASK,ISIZE)

      RETURN

100   FORMAT(/' Please select one of the following:'/
     #'    1...to initialize a new problem'/
     #'    2...to do some updates'/
     #'    3...to output solution'/
     #'    4...to terminate program'/)
101   FORMAT(/'**** Invalid input-please try again ****'/)
200   FORMAT(A)

      END
C
CCCCCCCCCCCCCCCCCCCCCCCCCCCC END OF ROUTINE GETASK CCCCCCCCCCCCCCCCCCCCCCCCCCCCC
C
      SUBROUTINE INITCP
      PARAMETER ( MAXSIZ = 500 )
      INTEGER PROCNU, DOC, NPROC, MYPOS, LCHAN, RCHAN
      COMMON/EXTCOM/ PROCNU, DOC, NPROC, MYPOS, LCHAN, RCHAN
      COMMON/NPTCOM/ NMIN, NLEFT, NTOT
      INTEGER DSIZE, STATUS
      DOUBLE PRECISION DELT, PI
```

```
      PARAMETER ( PI=3.14159265, DSIZE=8, ISIZE=4 )

10    WRITE(*,100)
      READ(*,*)NTOT
      NMIN = NTOT/NPROC
      NLEFT = MOD( NTOT, NPROC )
      IF(NMIN.GE.MAXSIZ) THEN
          WRITE(*,101)
          GOTO 10
      ENDIF

      WRITE(*,102)
      READ(*,*) DELT

      STATUS = KBCSTC( NTOT, ISIZE)
      STATUS = KBCSTC( DELT, DSIZE)

      RETURN

100   FORMAT(/' Please give the number of points'/)
101   FORMAT(/' **** Too many points specified ****'/)
102   FORMAT(/' Please give the time advance parameter'/)

      END
C
CCCCCCCCCCCCCCCCCCCCCCCCCCCCC END OF ROUTINE INITCP CCCCCCCCCCCCCCCCCCCCCCCCCCCCCC
C
      SUBROUTINE DOSTEP
      INTEGER ISIZE, CHECK, STATUS
      PARAMETER ( ISIZE = 4 )

      WRITE(*,100)
      READ(*,*)NSTEP
      STATUS = KBCSTC(NSTEP,ISIZE)

      STATUS = KCOMBC(CHECK,ISIZE,1)
      IF(CHECK.EQ.0) THEN
          PRINT *,NSTEP,' updates completed'
      ELSE
          PRINT *,' An error occured in update'
      ENDIF

      RETURN

100   FORMAT(/' Please give the number of time steps'/)

      END
```

```
C
CCCCCCCCCCCCCCCCCCCCCCCCCCCCCC END OF ROUTINE DOSTEP CCCCCCCCCCCCCCCCCCCCCCCCCCCCCC
C
      SUBROUTINE OUTRES
      PARAMETER ( MAXSIZ = 500 )
      INTEGER PROCNU, DOC, NPROC, MYPOS, LCHAN, RCHAN
      COMMON/EXTCOM/ PROCNU, DOC, NPROC, MYPOS, LCHAN, RCHAN
      COMMON/NPTCOM/ NMIN, NLEFT, NTOT
      DOUBLE PRECISION VALUES(0:MAXSIZ+1)
      PARAMETER ( MAXPRC = 16 )
      INTEGER BUFMAP(MAXPRC+1), DSIZE
      PARAMETER ( DSIZE = 8 )

      MAXBYT = (NMIN+1)*DSIZE
      DO 10 I = 0, NPROC-1
          NPTS = NMIN
          IF(I.LT.NLEFT) NPTS = NMIN+1
          STATUS = KMDUMP(VALUES(1),MAXBYT,BUFMAP)
          DO 20 J=1,NPTS,10
              KMAX = MIN0(9,NPTS-J)
              WRITE(*,100)(VALUES(J+K),K=0,KMAX)
20            CONTINUE
10        CONTINUE

      RETURN

100   FORMAT(10F7.3)

      END
C
CCCCCCCCCCCCCCCCCCCCCCCCCCCCCC END OF ROUTINE OUTRES CCCCCCCCCCCCCCCCCCCCCCCCCCCCCC
C
```

B-2.2 NODE Program

```
      PROGRAM WAVFCP
      INTEGER INITIA, UPDATE, OUTPUT, QUIT
      PARAMETER (INITIA=1, UPDATE=2, OUTPUT=3, QUIT=4)
      PARAMETER ( MAXSIZ=500 )
      INTEGER PROCNU, DOC, NPROC, MYPOS, LCHAN, RCHAN
      COMMON/EXTCOM/ PROCNU, DOC, NPROC, MYPOS, LCHAN, RCHAN
      COMMON/NPTCOM/ NMIN, NLEFT, NTOT
      INTEGER TASK

      CALL DOWNLD('waveNODE')
```

```
10    CALL GETASK(TASK)
      IF (TASK.NE.QUIT) THEN
          IF(TASK.EQ.INITIA) THEN
               CALL INITCP
          ELSEIF (TASK.EQ.UPDATE) THEN
               CALL DOSTEP
          ELSEIF (TASK.EQ.OUTPUT) THEN
               CALL OUTRES
          ENDIF
          GOTO 10
      ENDIF

      STOP
      END
C
CCCCCCCCCCCCCCCCCCCCCCCCCCCCCC END OF PROGRAM WAVFCP CCCCCCCCCCCCCCCCCCCCCCCCCCCCCC
C
      SUBROUTINE DOWNLD(PRGNAM)
      CHARACTER*8 PRGNAM
      INTEGER PROCNU, DOC, NPROC, MYPOS, LCHAN, RCHAN
      COMMON/EXTCOM/ PROCNU, DOC, NPROC, MYPOS, LCHAN, RCHAN

      PRINT *,' '
         PRINT *,' Please give the dimension of the hypercube '
      READ(*,*)DOC

      CALL KCUBEL(DOC,PRGNAM)
      NPROC = 2**DOC

      RETURN
      END
C
CCCCCCCCCCCCCCCCCCCCCCCCCCCCCC END OF PROGRAM DOWNLD CCCCCCCCCCCCCCCCCCCCCCCCCCCCCC
C
      SUBROUTINE GETASK(TASK)
      INTEGER INITIA, UPDATE, OUTPUT, QUIT
      PARAMETER ( INITIA=1, UPDATE=2, OUTPUT=3, QUIT=4 )
      PARAMETER ( ISIZE=4 )
      INTEGER TASK, STATUS
      CHARACTER*1 RESP

10    WRITE(*,100)
      READ(*,200) RESP
      IF (RESP.EQ.'1') THEN
          TASK = INITIA
      ELSEIF (RESP.EQ.'2') THEN
          TASK = UPDATE
```

```
      ELSEIF (RESP.EQ.'3') THEN
          TASK = OUTPUT
      ELSEIF (RESP.EQ.'4') THEN
          TASK = QUIT
      ELSE
          WRITE(*,101)
          GOTO 10
      ENDIF

      STATUS = KBCSTC(TASK,ISIZE)

      RETURN

 100  FORMAT(/' Please select one of the following:'/
     #'    1...to initialize a new problem'/
     #'    2...to do some updates'/
     #'    3...to output solution'/
     #'    4...to terminate program'/)
 101  FORMAT(/'**** Invalid input-please try again ****'/)
 200  FORMAT(A)

      END
C
CCCCCCCCCCCCCCCCCCCCCCCCCCCCCC END OF ROUTINE GETASK CCCCCCCCCCCCCCCCCCCCCCCCCCCCCC
C
      SUBROUTINE INITCP
      PARAMETER ( MAXSIZ = 500 )
      INTEGER PROCNU, DOC, NPROC, MYPOS, LCHAN, RCHAN
      COMMON/EXTCOM/ PROCNU, DOC, NPROC, MYPOS, LCHAN, RCHAN
      COMMON/NPTCOM/ NMIN, NLEFT, NTOT
      INTEGER DSIZE, STATUS
      DOUBLE PRECISION DELT, PI
      PARAMETER ( PI=3.14159265, DSIZE=8, ISIZE=4 )

 10   WRITE(*,100)
      READ(*,*)NTOT
      NMIN = NTOT/NPROC
      NLEFT = MOD( NTOT, NPROC )
      IF(NMIN.GE.MAXSIZ) THEN
          WRITE(*,101)
          GOTO 10
      ENDIF

      WRITE(*,102)
      READ(*,*) DELT

      STATUS = KBCSTC( NTOT, ISIZE)
```

```fortran
      STATUS = KBCSTC( DELT, DSIZE)

      RETURN

100   FORMAT(/' Please give the number of points'/)
101   FORMAT(/' **** Too many points specified ****'/)
102   FORMAT(/' Please give the time advance parameter'/)

      END
C
CCCCCCCCCCCCCCCCCCCCCCCCCCCCCCC END OF ROUTINE INITCP CCCCCCCCCCCCCCCCCCCCCCCCCCCCCCC
C
      SUBROUTINE DOSTEP
      INTEGER ISIZE, CHECK, STATUS
      PARAMETER ( ISIZE = 4 )

      WRITE(*,100)
      READ(*,*)NSTEP
      STATUS = KBCSTC(NSTEP,ISIZE)

      STATUS = KCOMBC(CHECK,ISIZE,1)
      IF(CHECK.EQ.0) THEN
          PRINT *,NSTEP,' updates completed'
      ELSE
          PRINT *,' An error occured in update'
      ENDIF

      RETURN

100   FORMAT(/' Please give the number of time steps'/)

      END
C
CCCCCCCCCCCCCCCCCCCCCCCCCCCCCCC END OF ROUTINE DOSTEP CCCCCCCCCCCCCCCCCCCCCCCCCCCCCCC
C
      SUBROUTINE OUTRES
      PARAMETER ( MAXSIZ = 500 )
      INTEGER PROCNU, DOC, NPROC, MYPOS, LCHAN, RCHAN
      COMMON/EXTCOM/ PROCNU, DOC, NPROC, MYPOS, LCHAN, RCHAN
      COMMON/NPTCOM/ NMIN, NLEFT, NTOT
      DOUBLE PRECISION VALUES(0:MAXSIZ+1)
      PARAMETER ( MAXPRC = 16 )
      INTEGER BUFMAP(MAXPRC+1), DSIZE
      PARAMETER ( DSIZE = 8 )

      MAXBYT = (NMIN+1)*DSIZE
      DO 10 I = 0, NPROC-1
```

```
         NPTS = NMIN
         IF(I.LT.NLEFT) NPTS = NMIN+1
         STATUS = KMDUMP(VALUES(1),MAXBYT,BUFMAP)
         DO 20 J=1,NPTS,10
             KMAX = MINO(9,NPTS-J)
             WRITE(*,100)(VALUES(J+K),K=0,KMAX)
20           CONTINUE
10       CONTINUE

      RETURN

100  FORMAT(10F7.3)

      END
C
CCCCCCCCCCCCCCCCCCCCCCCCCCCCCC END OF ROUTINE OUTRES CCCCCCCCCCCCCCCCCCCCCCCCCCCCCC
C
```

B-3 The One-Dimensional Wave Equation: CUBIX Version

```
      PROGRAM WAVCUB
      INTEGER INITIA, UPDATE, OUTPUT, QUIT
      PARAMETER (INITIA=1, UPDATE=2, OUTPUT=3, QUIT=4)
      PARAMETER ( MAXSIZ=500 )
      INTEGER PROCNU, DOC, NPROC, MYPOS, LCHAN, RCHAN
      COMMON/EXTCOM/ PROCNU, DOC, NPROC, MYPOS, LCHAN, RCHAN
      DOUBLE PRECISION VALUES(0:MAXSIZ+1)
      DOUBLE PRECISION OLDVAL(0:MAXSIZ+1), NEWVAL(0:MAXSIZ+1)
      COMMON/VALCOM/ VALUES, OLDVAL, NEWVAL
      COMMON/NPTCOM/ NMIN, NLEFT, NTOT
      INTEGER TASK,LEN
      DOUBLE PRECISION DELT
      INTEGER STDOUT
      PARAMETER ( STDOUT = 6 )

#ifndef SEQ
      BUFFER(UNIT=STDOUT,SIZE=2048)
#endif
      CALL GPARAM
      CALL DECOMP

10    CALL GETASK(TASK)
      IF (TASK.NE.QUIT) THEN
          IF(TASK.EQ.INITIA) THEN
              CALL INITZE( LEN, DELT)
          ELSEIF (TASK.EQ.UPDATE) THEN
              CALL DOSTEP(LEN,DELT)
          ELSEIF (TASK.EQ.OUTPUT) THEN
              CALL OUTRES
          ENDIF
          GOTO 10
      ENDIF

      STOP
      END
C
CCCCCCCCCCCCCCCCCCCCCCCCCCCCCCC END OF PROGRAM WAVCUB CCCCCCCCCCCCCCCCCCCCCCCCCCCCCCCC
C
      SUBROUTINE GPARAM
      INTEGER PROCNU, DOC, NPROC, MYPOS, LCHAN, RCHAN
      COMMON/EXTCOM/ PROCNU, DOC, NPROC, MYPOS, LCHAN, RCHAN
      INTEGER ENV(5)

      CALL KPARAM( ENV )
```

```
      DOC=ENV(1)
      PROCNU=ENV(2)
      NPROC=ENV(3)

      RETURN
      END
C
CCCCCCCCCCCCCCCCCCCCCCCCCCCCCC END OF PROGRAM GPARAM CCCCCCCCCCCCCCCCCCCCCCCCCCCCCC
C
      SUBROUTINE DECOMP
      INTEGER PROCNU, DOC, NPROC, MYPOS, LCHAN, RCHAN
      COMMON/EXTCOM/ PROCNU, DOC, NPROC, MYPOS, LCHAN, RCHAN
      INTEGER STATUS

      STATUS = KGRDIN( 1, NPROC )
      STATUS = KGRDCO( PROCNU, MYPOS )

      LCHAN = KGRDCH( PROCNU, 0, -1)
      RCHAN = KGRDCH( PROCNU, 0, 1)
      IF (MYPOS.EQ.0) LCHAN = 0
      IF (MYPOS.EQ.(NPROC-1)) RCHAN = 0

      RETURN
      END
C
CCCCCCCCCCCCCCCCCCCCCCCCCCCCCC END OF ROUTINE DECOMP CCCCCCCCCCCCCCCCCCCCCCCCCCCCCC
C
      SUBROUTINE GETASK(TASK)
      INTEGER INITIA, UPDATE, OUTPUT, QUIT
      PARAMETER ( INITIA=1, UPDATE=2, OUTPUT=3, QUIT=4 )
      INTEGER TASK
      CHARACTER*1 RESP

10    CONTINUE
      WRITE(*,100)
      WRITE(*,102)
#ifndef SEQ
      FLUSH(*)
#endif
      READ(*,200) RESP
      IF (RESP.EQ.'1') THEN
          TASK = INITIA
      ELSEIF (RESP.EQ.'2') THEN
          TASK = UPDATE
      ELSEIF (RESP.EQ.'3') THEN
          TASK = OUTPUT
      ELSEIF (RESP.EQ.'4') THEN
```

```fortran
              TASK = QUIT
      ELSE
          WRITE(*,101)
          GOTO 10
      ENDIF

      RETURN

100 FORMAT(/' Please select one of the following:'/
   #          ' 1...to initialize a new problem'/
   #          ' 2...to do some updates')
102 FORMAT( ' 3...to output solution'/
   #          ' 4...to terminate program'/)
101 FORMAT(/'**** Invalid input-please try again ****'/)
200 FORMAT(A)

      END
C
CCCCCCCCCCCCCCCCCCCCCCCCCCCCCC END OF ROUTINE GETASK CCCCCCCCCCCCCCCCCCCCCCCCCCCCCC
C
      SUBROUTINE INITZE( LEN, DELT )
      INTEGER LEN
      DOUBLE PRECISION DELT
      PARAMETER ( MAXSIZ = 500 )
      INTEGER PROCNU, DOC, NPROC, MYPOS, LCHAN, RCHAN
      COMMON/EXTCOM/ PROCNU, DOC, NPROC, MYPOS, LCHAN, RCHAN
      DOUBLE PRECISION VALUES(0:MAXSIZ+1)
      DOUBLE PRECISION OLDVAL(0:MAXSIZ+1), NEWVAL(0:MAXSIZ+1)
      COMMON/VALCOM/ VALUES, OLDVAL, NEWVAL
      COMMON/NPTCOM/ NMIN, NLEFT, NTOT
      DOUBLE PRECISION PI, FAC, X
      PARAMETER ( PI=3.14159265 )

10    CONTINUE
      WRITE(*,100)
#ifndef SEQ
      FLUSH(*)
#endif
      READ(*,*)NTOT
      NMIN = NTOT/NPROC
      NLEFT = MOD( NTOT, NPROC )
      IF(NMIN.GE.MAXSIZ) THEN
          WRITE(*,101)
#ifndef SEQ
          FLUSH(*)
#endif
          GOTO 10
```

```
        ENDIF

        FAC = 2.0*PI
        K = 0
        DO 20 I = 0, NPROC-1
            NPTS = NMIN
            IF(I.LT.NLEFT) NPTS = NMIN+1
            IF (MYPOS.EQ.I) THEN
                LEN = NPTS
                DO 30 J = 1, NPTS
                    X = DBLE(K)/DBLE(NTOT-1)
                    VALUES(J) = DSIN(FAC*X)
                    K = K+1
30              CONTINUE
            ELSE
                K = K+NPTS
            ENDIF
20          CONTINUE

        WRITE(*,102)
#ifndef SEQ
        FLUSH(*)
#endif
        READ(*,*) DELT

        DO 40 I = 1, LEN
40          OLDVAL(I) = VALUES(I)

        RETURN

100 FORMAT(/' Please give the number of points'/)
101 FORMAT(/' **** Too many points specified ****'/)
102 FORMAT(/' Please give the time advance parameter'/)

        END
C
CCCCCCCCCCCCCCCCCCCCCCCCCCCCCCC END OF ROUTINE INITZE CCCCCCCCCCCCCCCCCCCCCCCCCCCCCCC
C
        SUBROUTINE DOSTEP( LEN, DEL )
        INTEGER LEN
        DOUBLE PRECISION DEL
        INTEGER PROCNU, DOC, NPROC, MYPOS, LCHAN, RCHAN
        COMMON/EXTCOM/ PROCNU, DOC, NPROC, MYPOS, LCHAN, RCHAN
        PARAMETER ( MAXSIZ = 500 )
        DOUBLE PRECISION VALUES(0:MAXSIZ+1)
        DOUBLE PRECISION OLDVAL(0:MAXSIZ+1), NEWVAL(0:MAXSIZ+1)
        COMMON/VALCOM/ VALUES, OLDVAL, NEWVAL
```

```
      DOUBLE PRECISION C, DELX, PFAC
      INTEGER DSIZE, STATUS
      PARAMETER ( DSIZE = 8 )

      WRITE(*,100)
#ifndef SEQ
      FLUSH(*)
#endif
      READ(*,*)NSTEP

      C  = 1.0
      DELX = 1.0
      PFAC = (C*DEL/DELX)**2

      DO 20 I = 0, NSTEP-1
          STATUS = KCSHIF( VALUES(0),     LCHAN, DSIZE,
     #                     VALUES(LEN),   RCHAN, DSIZE )
          STATUS = KCSHIF( VALUES(LEN+1), RCHAN, DSIZE,
     #                     VALUES(1),     LCHAN, DSIZE )
          DO 30 J = 1, LEN
              IF(MYPOS.EQ.0.AND.J.EQ.1) THEN
                  NEWVAL(J) = 0.0
              ELSEIF (MYPOS.EQ.(NPROC-1).AND.J.EQ.LEN) THEN
                  NEWVAL(J)=0.0
              ELSE
                  T1 = 2.0*VALUES(J) - OLDVAL(J)
                  T2 = VALUES(J+1)-2.0*VALUES(J)+VALUES(J-1)
                  NEWVAL(J) =  T1 + T2*PFAC
              ENDIF
30        CONTINUE

          DO 40 J = 1, LEN
              OLDVAL(J) = VALUES(J)
40            VALUES(J) = NEWVAL(J)

20      CONTINUE

      RETURN

100  FORMAT(/' Please give the number of time steps'/)

      END
C
CCCCCCCCCCCCCCCCCCCCCCCCCCCCCCC END OF ROUTINE DOSTEP CCCCCCCCCCCCCCCCCCCCCCCCCCCCCCC
C
      SUBROUTINE OUTRES
      PARAMETER ( MAXSIZ = 500 )
```

```fortran
      INTEGER PROCNU, DOC, NPROC, MYPOS, LCHAN, RCHAN
      COMMON/EXTCOM/ PROCNU, DOC, NPROC, MYPOS, LCHAN, RCHAN
      DOUBLE PRECISION VALUES(0:MAXSIZ+1)
      DOUBLE PRECISION OLDVAL(0:MAXSIZ+1), NEWVAL(0:MAXSIZ+1)
      COMMON/VALCOM/ VALUES, OLDVAL, NEWVAL
      COMMON/NPTCOM/ NMIN, NLEFT, NTOT
      INTEGER STDOUT
      PARAMETER ( STDOUT = 6 )

#ifndef SEQ
      MULTIPLE( STDOUT )
#endif

      K = 0
      DO 10 I = 0, NPROC-1
          NPTS = NMIN
          IF(I.LT.NLEFT) NPTS = NMIN+1
          DO 20 J = 1, NPTS,10
              IF(MYPOS.EQ.I) THEN
                  KMAX = MIN0(9,NPTS-J)
                  WRITE(*,100) (VALUES(J+K),K=0,KMAX)
              ENDIF
#ifndef SEQ
              IF(MOD(K,60).EQ.59) THEN
                  FLUSH(STDOUT)
              ENDIF
#endif
20            CONTINUE
#ifndef SEQ
              FLUSH(STDOUT)
#endif
10        CONTINUE

#ifndef SEQ
      SINGLE( STDOUT )
#endif

      RETURN
100           FORMAT(10F7.3)
101           FORMAT(' ')

      END
C
CCCCCCCCCCCCCCCCCCCCCCCCCCCCCCCC END OF ROUTINE OUTRES CCCCCCCCCCCCCCCCCCCCCCCCCCCCCCCC
C
```

B-4 The Laplace Equation and the Finite Difference Method

B-4.1 CUBIX Program

```fortran
      PROGRAM LAPLACE
      PARAMETER (MAX=50)
      COMMON/PROC/NPROC,IDOC,IPNUM
      DOUBLE PRECISION VALUES(0:MAX+1,0:MAX+1)
      DOUBLE PRECISION OMEGA,VALMIN,VALMAX,VSTEP
      COMMON/VAL/VALUES,OMEGA,VALMIN,VALMAX,VSTEP
      COMMON/COMM/NY,NPROCX,NPROCY,ILCHAN,IRCHAN,IUCHAN,IDCHAN,IPOS(0:1)
      COMMON/BLOCK/IUSEST,NXPTS,NYPTS,ILPTS,IRPTS,ITPTS,IBPTS,NXTOT,NYTO
      COMMON/INFO/IBC(0:MAX+1,0:MAX+1),IYBYTE,IXBYTE,NITER
      INTEGER STDOUT
      PARAMETER (STDOUT=6)

#ifndef SEQ
      BUFFER(UNIT=STDOUT,SIZE=512)
#endif
      INITST=0
      CALL GPARAM
      CALL DECOMP
10    CALL GETJOB(JOB)
      IF (JOB.NE.4) THEN
          IF (JOB.EQ.1) THEN
              CALL INITLZ
              INITST=1
          ELSE IF (JOB.EQ.2.AND.INITST.NE.0) THEN
              PRINT *
              PRINT *
              PRINT *,'Please give the number of update cycles.'
#ifndef SEQ
              FLUSH(6)
#endif
              READ *,ICYCLE
              CALL UPDATE(ICYCLE)
          ELSE IF (JOB.EQ.3.AND.INITST.NE.0) THEN
              CALL OUTPUT
          ENDIF
          GOTO 10
      ENDIF

      STOP
      END
C
CCCCCCCCCCCCCCCCCCCCCCCCCCCCCCC END OF PROGRAM LAPLACE CCCCCCCCCCCCCCCCCCCCCCCCCCCCCCC
C
```

```
      SUBROUTINE GPARAM
      COMMON /PROC/NPROC,IDOC,IPNUM
      INTEGER ENV(5)

      CALL KPARAM(ENV)
      IDOC=ENV(1)
      IPNUM=ENV(2)
      NPROC=ENV(3)

      RETURN
      END
C
CCCCCCCCCCCCCCCCCCCCCCCCCCCCCCC END OF ROUTINE GPARAM CCCCCCCCCCCCCCCCCCCCCCCCCCCCCCC
C
      SUBROUTINE GETJOB(JOB)

      PRINT *
      PRINT *
      PRINT *,'Please select one of the following :'
      PRINT *,'  1..to read in bc''s and initialize problem'
      PRINT *,'  2..to perform update cycles'
      PRINT *,'  3..to output results'
      PRINT *,'  4..to terminate the program'
#ifndef SEQ
      FLUSH(6)
#endif
      READ *,JOB

      RETURN
      END
C
CCCCCCCCCCCCCCCCCCCCCCCCCCCCCCC END OF ROUTINE GETJOB CCCCCCCCCCCCCCCCCCCCCCCCCCCCCCC
C
      SUBROUTINE DECOMP
      COMMON/PROC/NPROC,IDOC,IPNUM
      COMMON/COMM/NY,NPROCX,NPROCY,ILCHAN,IRCHAN,IUCHAN,IDCHAN,IPOS(0:1)
      COMMON/BLOCK/IUSEST,NXPTS,NYPTS,ILPTS,IRPTS,ITPTS,IBPTS,NXTOT,NYTO
      INTEGER NUM(0:1),STDOUT,USED
      PARAMETER (STDOUT=6,USED=0,NOTUSE=1)

10    CONTINUE
      PRINT *
      PRINT *
      PRINT *,'Please give the # of processors in the x-direction.'
#ifndef SEQ
      FLUSH(6)
#endif
```

```
      READ *,NPROCX
      PRINT *,'Please give the # of processors in the y-direction.'
#ifndef SEQ
      FLUSH(6)
#endif
      READ *,NPROCY
      LOGX=LG2NXT(NPROCX)
      LOGY=LG2NXT(NPROCY)
      IF (2**(LOGX+LOGY).GT.NPROC) THEN
          PRINT *
          PRINT *,'*** Too many processors specified ***'
          GOTO 10
      ENDIF
      PRINT *
      PRINT *
      NX=2**LOGX
      NY=2**LOGY
20    IF (NX*NY.NE.NPROC) THEN
          NX=NX*2
          GOTO 20
      ENDIF
      NUM(0)=NY
      NUM(1)=NX
      IDUMMY=KGRDIN(2,NUM)
      IDUMMY=KGRDCO(IPNUM,IPOS)
      IF (IPOS(1).GT.NPROCX-1.OR.IPOS(0).GT.NPROCY-1) THEN
          IUSEST=NOTUSE
      ELSE
          IUSEST=USED
      ENDIF
      ILCHAN=KGRDCH(IPNUM,1,-1)
      IRCHAN=KGRDCH(IPNUM,1,1)
      IDCHAN=KGRDCH(IPNUM,0,-1)
      IUCHAN=KGRDCH(IPNUM,0,1)
      IF (IPOS(1).EQ.0) ILCHAN=0
      IF (IPOS(1).EQ.NPROCX-1) IRCHAN=0
      IF (IPOS(0).EQ.0) IDCHAN=0
      IF (IPOS(0).EQ.NPROCY-1) IUCHAN=0
#ifndef SEQ
      MULTIPLE(STDOUT)
#endif
      DO 30 I=0,NY-1
          DO 40 J=0,NX-1
              IF (I.EQ.IPOS(0).AND.J.EQ.IPOS(1)) THEN
                  IF (IUSEST.EQ.USED) THEN
                      WRITE (*,100)I,J,IPNUM
                  ELSE
```

```
                      WRITE (*,101)I,J,IPNUM
                  ENDIF
              ENDIF
#ifndef SEQ
              FLUSH(STDOUT)
#endif
40            CONTINUE
30        CONTINUE
#ifndef SEQ
      SINGLE(STDOUT)
#endif

      RETURN
100 FORMAT('Location (',I1,',',I1,') is processor ',I1,' :used')
101 FORMAT('Location (',I1,',',I1,') is processor ',I1,' :not used')
      END
C
CCCCCCCCCCCCCCCCCCCCCCCCCCCCCC END OF ROUTINE DECOMP CCCCCCCCCCCCCCCCCCCCCCCCCCCCCC
C
      FUNCTION LG2NXT(N)

      I=N
      J=0
10    IF (I.GT.1) THEN
          J=J+1
          I=I/2
          GOTO 10
      ENDIF
      IF (N.GT.2**J) J=J+1
      LG2NXT=J

      RETURN
      END
C
CCCCCCCCCCCCCCCCCCCCCCCCCCCCCC END OF ROUTINE LG2NXT CCCCCCCCCCCCCCCCCCCCCCCCCCCCCC
C
      SUBROUTINE CLEAN(BUF,IDIR,ICOLOR)
      PARAMETER (MAX=50)
      DOUBLE PRECISION BUF(0:MAX-1)
      DOUBLE PRECISION VALUES(0:MAX+1,0:MAX+1),OMEGA,VALMIN,VALMAX,VSTEP
      COMMON/VAL/VALUES,OMEGA,VALMIN,VALMAX,VSTEP
      COMMON/BLOCK/IUSEST,NXPTS,NYPTS,ILPTS,IRPTS,ITPTS,IBPTS,NXTOT,NYTO
      INTEGER RIGHT,BOTTOM,TOP,RED
      PARAMETER (LEFT=0,RIGHT=1,BOTTOM=2,TOP=3,RED=1)

      IF (IDIR.EQ.LEFT) THEN
          IF (ICOLOR.EQ.RED) THEN
```

```
                IOFFS=0
                NPTS=IBPTS
            ELSE
                IOFFS=IBPTS
                NPTS=ITPTS
            ENDIF
            DO 10 I=1,NPTS
                VALUES(I+IOFFS,0)=BUF(I-1)
10              CONTINUE
        ENDIF
        IF (IDIR.EQ.RIGHT) THEN
            IF (ICOLOR.EQ.RED) THEN
                IOFFS=IBPTS
                NPTS=ITPTS
            ELSE
                IOFFS=0
                NPTS=IBPTS
            ENDIF
            DO 20 I=1,NPTS
                VALUES(I+IOFFS,NXPTS+1)=BUF(I-1)
20              CONTINUE
        ENDIF
        IF (IDIR.EQ.BOTTOM) THEN
            IF (ICOLOR.EQ.RED) THEN
                IOFFS=0
                NPTS=ILPTS
            ELSE
                IOFFS=ILPTS
                NPTS=IRPTS
            ENDIF
            DO 30 I=1,NPTS
                VALUES(0,I+IOFFS)=BUF(I-1)
30              CONTINUE
        ENDIF
        IF (IDIR.EQ.TOP) THEN
            IF (ICOLOR.EQ.RED) THEN
                IOFFS=ILPTS
                NPTS=IRPTS
            ELSE
                IOFFS=0
                NPTS=ILPTS
            ENDIF
            DO 40 I=1,NPTS
                VALUES(NYPTS+1,I+IOFFS)=BUF(I-1)
40              CONTINUE
        ENDIF
```

```
      RETURN
      END
C
CCCCCCCCCCCCCCCCCCCCCCCCCCCCCC END OF ROUTINE CLEAN CCCCCCCCCCCCCCCCCCCCCCCCCCCCCC
C
      SUBROUTINE GETEDG(BUF,ICOLOR)
      PARAMETER (MAX=50)
      DOUBLE PRECISION BUF(0:MAX-1)
      COMMON/COMM/NY,NPROCX,NPROCY,ILCHAN,IRCHAN,IUCHAN,
     #  IDCHAN,IPOS(0:1)
      COMMON/INFO/IBC(0:MAX+1,0:MAX+1),IYBYTE,IXBYTE,NITER
      INTEGER RIGHT,BOTTOM,TOP
      PARAMETER (LEFT=0,RIGHT=1,BOTTOM=2,TOP=3)

      CALL GETRDY(BUF,LEFT,ICOLOR)
      IDUMMY=KCSHIF(BUF,IRCHAN,IYBYTE,BUF,ILCHAN,IYBYTE)
      CALL CLEAN(BUF,RIGHT,ICOLOR)

      CALL GETRDY(BUF,RIGHT,ICOLOR)
      IDUMMY=KCSHIF(BUF,ILCHAN,IYBYTE,BUF,IRCHAN,IYBYTE)
      CALL CLEAN(BUF,LEFT,ICOLOR)

      CALL GETRDY(BUF,TOP,ICOLOR)
      IDUMMY=KCSHIF(BUF,IDCHAN,IXBYTE,BUF,IUCHAN,IYBYTE)
      CALL CLEAN(BUF,BOTTOM,ICOLOR)

      CALL GETRDY(BUF,BOTTOM,ICOLOR)
      IDUMMY=KCSHIF(BUF,IUCHAN,IXBYTE,BUF,IDCHAN,IYBYTE)
      CALL CLEAN(BUF,TOP,ICOLOR)

      RETURN
      END
C
CCCCCCCCCCCCCCCCCCCCCCCCCCCCCC END OF ROUTINE GETEDG CCCCCCCCCCCCCCCCCCCCCCCCCCCCCC
C
      INTEGER FUNCTION GETLVL(XVAL)
      DOUBLE PRECISION XVAL
      PARAMETER (MAX=50)
      DOUBLE PRECISION VALUES(0:MAX+1,0:MAX+1),OMEGA,VALMIN,VALMAX,VSTEP
      COMMON/VAL/VALUES,OMEGA,VALMIN,VALMAX,VSTEP

      IRESUL=IDINT((XVAL-VALMIN)/VSTEP)
      IF (IRESUL.GT.15) IRESUL=15
      IF (IRESUL.LT.0) IRESUL=0
      GETLVL=IRESUL

      RETURN
```

```
      END
C
CCCCCCCCCCCCCCCCCCCCCCCCCCCCCC END OF ROUTINE GETVAL CCCCCCCCCCCCCCCCCCCCCCCCCCCCCC
C
      SUBROUTINE GETRDY(BUF,IDIR,ICOLOR)
      PARAMETER (MAX=50)
      DOUBLE PRECISION BUF(0:MAX-1)
      DOUBLE PRECISION VALUES(0:MAX+1,0:MAX+1),OMEGA,VALMIN,VALMAX,VSTEP
      COMMON/VAL/VALUES,OMEGA,VALMIN,VALMAX,VSTEP
      COMMON/BLOCK/IUSEST,NXPTS,NYPTS,ILPTS,IRPTS,ITPTS,IBPTS,NXTOT,NYTO
      INTEGER RIGHT,BOTTOM,TOP,RED
      PARAMETER (LEFT=0,RIGHT=1,BOTTOM=2,TOP=3,RED=1)

      IF (IDIR.EQ.LEFT) THEN
          IF (ICOLOR.EQ.RED) THEN
              IOFFS=IBPTS
              NPTS=ITPTS
          ELSE
              IOFFS=0
              NPTS=IBPTS
          ENDIF
          DO 10 I=1,NPTS
              BUF(I-1)=VALUES(I+IOFFS,1)
 10           CONTINUE
      ENDIF
      IF (IDIR.EQ.RIGHT) THEN
          IF (ICOLOR.EQ.RED) THEN
              IOFFS=0
              NPTS=IBPTS
          ELSE
              IOFFS=IBPTS
              NPTS=ITPTS
          ENDIF
          DO 20 I=1,NPTS
              BUF(I-1)=VALUES(I+IOFFS,NXPTS)
 20           CONTINUE
      ENDIF
      IF (IDIR.EQ.BOTTOM) THEN
          IF (ICOLOR.EQ.RED) THEN
              IOFFS=ILPTS
              NPTS=IRPTS
          ELSE
              IOFFS=0
              NPTS=ILPTS
          ENDIF
          DO 30 I=1,NPTS
              BUF(I-1)=VALUES(1,I+IOFFS)
```

```
30              CONTINUE
     ENDIF
     IF (IDIR.EQ.TOP) THEN
         IF (ICOLOR.EQ.RED) THEN
             IOFFS=0
             NPTS=ILPTS
         ELSE
             IOFFS=ILPTS
             NPTS=IRPTS
         ENDIF
         DO 40 I=1,NPTS
             BUF(I-1)=VALUES(NYPTS,I+IOFFS)
40           CONTINUE
     ENDIF

     RETURN
     END
C
CCCCCCCCCCCCCCCCCCCCCCCCCCCCCC END OF ROUTINE GETRDY CCCCCCCCCCCCCCCCCCCCCCCCCCCCCC
C
     SUBROUTINE INITLZ
     PARAMETER (MAX=50)
     DOUBLE PRECISION VALUES(0:MAX+1,0:MAX+1)
     DOUBLE PRECISION OMEGA,VALMIN,VALMAX,VSTEP
     COMMON/VAL/VALUES,OMEGA,VALMIN,VALMAX,VSTEP
     COMMON/COMM/NY,NPROCX,NPROCY,ILCHAN,IRCHAN,IUCHAN,IDCHAN,IPOS(0:1)
     COMMON/BLOCK/IUSEST,NXPTS,NYPTS,ILPTS,IRPTS,ITPTS,IBPTS,NXTOT,NYTO
     COMMON/INFO/IBC(0:MAX+1,0:MAX+1),IYBYTE,IXBYTE,NITER
     DOUBLE PRECISION LEDGE,REDGE,BEDGE,TEDGE,BVAL
     INTEGER XHALF,YHALF,ROW,COL,RLOCAL,CLOCAL
     INTEGER RIGHT,BOTTOM,TOP,RED,BLACK,EDGE,DBLSIZ
     PARAMETER (LEFT=0,RIGHT=1,BOTTOM=2,TOP=3,DBLSIZ=8)
     PARAMETER (INTERI=0,RED=1,BLACK=2,EDGE=3)
     LOGICAL TLOG1, TLOG2, TLOG3

10   CONTINUE
     PRINT *
     PRINT *
     PRINT *,'Please give the number of points per processor in ',
     #   'the x-direction.'
#ifndef SEQ
     FLUSH(6)
#endif
     READ *,NXPTS
     PRINT *,'Please give the number of points per processor in ',
     #   'the y-direction.'
#ifndef SEQ
```

```
      FLUSH(6)
#endif
      READ *,NYPTS
      TLOG1 = (NXPTS.LT.2).OR.(NXPTS.GT.MAX)
      TLOG2 = (NYPTS.LT.2).OR.(NYPTS.GT.MAX)
      IF (TLOG1 .OR. TLOG2) THEN
          PRINT *
          PRINT *,'*** Invalid number of points ***'
          GOTO 10
      ENDIF
      NXTOT=NXPTS*NPROCX
      NYTO=NYPTS*NPROCY
      IXBYTE=NXPTS*DBLSIZ
      IYBYTE=NYPTS*DBLSIZ
      NITER=0
      PRINT *
      PRINT *,'Please give the SOR parameter, omega.'
#ifndef SEQ
      FLUSH(6)
#endif
      READ *,OMEGA
      ILPTS=NXPTS/2
      IRPTS=NXPTS-ILPTS
      IBPTS=NYPTS/2
      ITPTS=NYPTS-IBPTS
      DO 20 I=1,NYPTS
          IF (I.GT.IBPTS) THEN
              YHALF=TOP
          ELSE
              YHALF=BOTTOM
          ENDIF
          TLOG1 = YHALF.EQ.BOTTOM
          DO 30 J=1,NXPTS
              VALUES(I,J)=0.0
              IF (J.GT.ILPTS) THEN
                  XHALF=RIGHT
              ELSE
                  XHALF=LEFT
              ENDIF
              TLOG2 = (XHALF.EQ.RIGHT).AND.TLOG1
              TLOG3 = (XHALF.EQ.LEFT ).AND.(.NOT.TLOG1)
              IF (TLOG2 .OR. TLOG3) THEN
                  IBC(I,J)=BLACK
              ELSE
                  IBC(I,J)=RED
              ENDIF
30            CONTINUE
```

```
20      CONTINUE
    PRINT *
    PRINT *,'Give the left, right, bottom, and top edge values.'
#ifndef SEQ
    FLUSH(6)
#endif
    READ *,LEDGE,REDGE,BEDGE,TEDGE
    PRINT *
    PRINT *,'Give the number of fixed interior grid points.'
#ifndef SEQ
    FLUSH(6)
#endif
    READ *,NBC
    PRINT *
    DO 40 I=0,NBC-1
        PRINT *,'Give column, row, and boundary value for point',I
#ifndef SEQ
        FLUSH(6)
#endif
        READ *,ICOL,IROW,BVAL
        ROW=IROW/NYPTS
        COL=ICOL/NXPTS
        IF (IPOS(0).EQ.ROW.AND.IPOS(1).EQ.COL) THEN
            RLOCAL=IROW-NYPTS*ROW+1
            CLOCAL=ICOL-NXPTS*COL+1
            IBC(RLOCAL,CLOCAL)=INTERI
            VALUES(RLOCAL,CLOCAL)=BVAL
        ENDIF
40      CONTINUE
    IF (IPOS(0).EQ.0) THEN
        DO 50 I=1,NXPTS
            IBC(1,I)=EDGE
            VALUES(1,I)=BEDGE
50          CONTINUE
    ENDIF
    IF (IPOS(0).EQ.NPROCY-1) THEN
        DO 60 I=1,NXPTS
            IBC(NYPTS,I)=EDGE
            VALUES(NYPTS,I)=TEDGE
60          CONTINUE
    ENDIF
    IF (IPOS(1).EQ.0) THEN
        DO 70 I=1,NYPTS
            IBC(I,1)=EDGE
            VALUES(I,1)=LEDGE
70          CONTINUE
    ENDIF
```

```
      IF (IPOS(1).EQ.NPROCX-1) THEN
          DO 80 I=1,NYPTS
              IBC(I,NXPTS)=EDGE
              VALUES(I,NXPTS)=REDGE
80            CONTINUE
      ENDIF

      RETURN
      END
C
CCCCCCCCCCCCCCCCCCCCCCCCCCCCCCC END OF ROUTINE INITLZ CCCCCCCCCCCCCCCCCCCCCCCCCCCCCCC
C
      SUBROUTINE LSTVAL
      COMMON/COMM/NY,NPROCX,NPROCY,ILCHAN,IRCHAN,IUCHAN,IDCHAN,IPOS(0:1)
      COMMON/BLOCK/IUSEST,NXPTS,NYPTS,ILPTS,IRPTS,ITPTS,IBPTS,NXTOT,NYTO
      INTEGER XMIN,XMAX,YMIN,YMAX,ROW,COL,RLOCAL,CLOCAL,COUNT,STDOUT
      PARAMETER (STDOUT=6)
      LOGICAL TLOG

      CALL SAREA(XMIN,XMAX,YMIN,YMAX)
#ifndef SEQ
      MULTIPLE(STDOUT)
#endif
      DO 10 I=YMIN,YMAX
          COUNT=XMIN
          ROW=I/NYPTS
          RLOCAL=I-ROW*NYPTS
          K=0
          DO 20 J=XMIN,XMAX
              COUNT=COUNT+1
              COL=J/NXPTS
              CLOCAL=J-COL*NXPTS
              TLOG  = (IPOS(0).EQ.ROW).AND.(IPOS(1).EQ.COL)
              IF (TLOG) CALL OUTVAL(I,J,K,XMIN,XMAX,RLOCAL,CLOCAL)
              IF (COUNT.EQ.NXPTS) THEN
                  COUNT=0
#ifndef SEQ
                  FLUSH(STDOUT)
#endif
              ENDIF
              K=K+1
20            CONTINUE
#ifndef SEQ
          IF (COUNT.NE.0) THEN
              FLUSH(STDOUT)
          ENDIF
#endif
```

```
10        CONTINUE
#ifndef SEQ
     SINGLE(STDOUT)
#endif
     PRINT *
     WRITE (*,100)YMIN,XMIN,YMAX,XMAX

     RETURN
100  FORMAT('Area defined by (',I2,',',I2,') and (',I2,',',I2,')')
     END
C
CCCCCCCCCCCCCCCCCCCCCCCCCCCCCC END OF ROUTINE LSTVAL CCCCCCCCCCCCCCCCCCCCCCCCCCCCCC
C
     SUBROUTINE MINMAX(XMIN,XMAX)
     DOUBLE PRECISION XMIN,XMAX
     PARAMETER (MAX=50)
     DOUBLE PRECISION VALUES(0:MAX+1,0:MAX+1),OMEGA,VALMIN,VALMAX,VSTEP
     COMMON/VAL/VALUES,OMEGA,VALMIN,VALMAX,VSTEP
     COMMON/BLOCK/IUSEST,NXPTS,NYPTS,ILPTS,IRPTS,ITPTS,IBPTS,NXTOT,NYTO
     EXTERNAL MINDBL,MAXDBL
     DOUBLE PRECISION LOW,HIGH,VAL
     INTEGER DBLSIZ,USED
     PARAMETER (DBLSIZ=8,USED=0)

     LOW=0.1D+30
     HIGH=-0.1D+30
     IF (IUSEST.EQ.USED) THEN
         DO 10 I=1,NYPTS
             DO 20 J=1,NXPTS
                 VAL=VALUES(I,J)
                 IF (VAL.LT.LOW) LOW=VAL
                 IF (VAL.GT.HIGH) HIGH=VAL
20               CONTINUE
10           CONTINUE
     ENDIF
     XMIN=LOW
     XMAX=HIGH
     CALL KCOMBI(XMIN,MINDBL,DBLSIZ,1)
     CALL KCOMBI(XMAX,MAXDBL,DBLSIZ,1)

     RETURN
     END
C
CCCCCCCCCCCCCCCCCCCCCCCCCCCCCC END OF ROUTINE MINMAX CCCCCCCCCCCCCCCCCCCCCCCCCCCCCC
C
     FUNCTION MINDBL(D1,D2,ISIZE)
     DOUBLE PRECISION D1,D2
```

```fortran
      IF (D1.GT.D2) D1=D2
      MINDBL=0

      RETURN
      END
C
CCCCCCCCCCCCCCCCCCCCCCCCCCCCCC END OF ROUTINE MINDBL CCCCCCCCCCCCCCCCCCCCCCCCCCCCCC
C
      FUNCTION MAXDBL(D1,D2,ISIZE)
      DOUBLE PRECISION D1,D2

      IF (D1.LT.D2) D1=D2
      MAXDBL=0

      RETURN
      END
C
CCCCCCCCCCCCCCCCCCCCCCCCCCCCCC END OF ROUTINE MAXDBL CCCCCCCCCCCCCCCCCCCCCCCCCCCCCC
C
      SUBROUTINE OUTPUT

10    CONTINUE
      PRINT *
      PRINT *
      PRINT *,'Please select one of the following:'
      PRINT *,'  1..to list current values'
      PRINT *,'  2..to plot current values'
      PRINT *,'  3..to plot mesh point type'
      PRINT *,'  4..to quit this menu'
#ifndef SEQ
      FLUSH(6)
#endif
      READ *,JOB
      IF (JOB.NE.4) THEN
          IF (JOB.EQ.1) CALL LSTVAL
          IF (JOB.EQ.2.OR.JOB.EQ.3) CALL PLOT(JOB)
          GOTO 10
      ENDIF

      RETURN
      END
C
CCCCCCCCCCCCCCCCCCCCCCCCCCCCCC END OF ROUTINE OUTPUT CCCCCCCCCCCCCCCCCCCCCCCCCCCCCC
C
      SUBROUTINE OUTVAL(I,J,K,XMIN,XMAX,RLOCAL,CLOCAL)
      INTEGER XMIN,XMAX,RLOCAL,CLOCAL
```

```
      PARAMETER (MAX=50)
      DOUBLE PRECISION VALUES(0:MAX+1,0:MAX+1),OMEGA,VALMIN,VALMAX,VSTEP
      COMMON/VAL/VALUES,OMEGA,VALMIN,VALMAX,VSTEP

      IF (J.EQ.XMIN) THEN
          PRINT *,'Row number ',I
      ENDIF
      WRITE(*,100)VALUES(RLOCAL+1,CLOCAL+1)
      IF (J.EQ.XMAX.OR.MOD(J-XMIN,6).EQ.5) THEN
          WRITE(*,101)
      ENDIF

      RETURN
#ifndef XENIX
100   FORMAT(2X,E10.4$)
#else
100   FORMAT(2X,E10.4\)
#endif
101   FORMAT(' ')
      END
C
CCCCCCCCCCCCCCCCCCCCCCCCCCCCCC END OF ROUTINE OUTVAL CCCCCCCCCCCCCCCCCCCCCCCCCCCCC
C
      SUBROUTINE PLTMSH(RLOCAL,CLOCAL)
      INTEGER RLOCAL,CLOCAL
      PARAMETER (MAX=50)
      COMMON/INFO/IBC(0:MAX+1,0:MAX+1),IYBYTE,IXBYTE,NITER
      CHARACTER*1 MTYPE(0:3)
      INTEGER STDOUT
      PARAMETER (STDOUT=6)

      MTYPE(0)=' '
      MTYPE(1)='R'
      MTYPE(2)='B'
      MTYPE(3)='E'
      IVAL=IBC(RLOCAL+1,CLOCAL+1)
      IF (IVAL.GT.3) THEN
          PRINT *
      ELSE
          WRITE(*,100)MTYPE(IVAL)
      ENDIF

      RETURN
#ifndef XENIX
100   FORMAT(A2$)
#else
100   FORMAT(A2\)
```

```
#endif
      END
C
CCCCCCCCCCCCCCCCCCCCCCCCCCCCC END OF ROUTINE PLTMSH CCCCCCCCCCCCCCCCCCCCCCCCCCCCCC
C
      SUBROUTINE PLOT(JOB)
      PARAMETER (MAX=50)
      DOUBLE PRECISION VALUES(0:MAX+1,0:MAX+1),OMEGA,VALMIN,
     #  VALMAX,VSTEP
      COMMON/VAL/VALUES,OMEGA,VALMIN,VALMAX,VSTEP
      COMMON/COMM/NY,NPROCX,NPROCY,ILCHAN,IRCHAN,IUCHAN,
     #  IDCHAN,IPOS(0:1)
      COMMON/BLOCK/IUSEST,NXPTS,NYPTS,ILPTS,IRPTS,ITPTS,IBPTS,
     #  NXTOT,NYTO
      COMMON/INFO/IBC(0:MAX+1,0:MAX+1),IYBYTE,IXBYTE,NITER
      INTEGER XMIN,XMAX,YMIN,YMAX,ROW,COL,RLOCAL,CLOCAL,COUNT,STDOUT
      PARAMETER (STDOUT=6)

      CALL SAREA(XMIN,XMAX,YMIN,YMAX)
#ifndef SEQ
      MULTIPLE(STDOUT)
#endif
      IF (JOB.EQ.2) CALL SETUPR
      DO 10 I=YMAX,YMIN,-1
          COUNT=MOD(XMIN,NXPTS)
          ROW=I/NYPTS
          RLOCAL=I-ROW*NYPTS
          DO 20 J=XMIN,XMAX
              COUNT=COUNT+1
              COL=J/NXPTS
              CLOCAL=J-COL*NXPTS
              IF (IPOS(0).EQ.ROW.AND.IPOS(1).EQ.COL) THEN
                  IF (JOB.EQ.3) THEN
                      CALL PLTMSH(RLOCAL,CLOCAL)
                  ELSE
                      CALL PLTVAL(RLOCAL,CLOCAL)
                  ENDIF
                  IF(J.EQ.XMAX) THEN
                      PRINT *
                  ENDIF
              ENDIF
              IF (COUNT.EQ.NXPTS) THEN
                  COUNT=0
#ifndef SEQ
                  FLUSH(STDOUT)
#endif
              ENDIF
```

```
20              CONTINUE
#ifndef SEQ
        IF (COUNT.NE.0) THEN
                FLUSH(STDOUT)
        ENDIF
#endif
10      CONTINUE
#ifndef SEQ
    SINGLE(STDOUT)
#endif
    PRINT *
    WRITE(*,100)YMIN,XMIN,YMAX,XMAX
    IF (JOB.EQ.2) THEN
        PRINT *
        WRITE (*,101)NITER
        WRITE (*,102)VALMIN,VALMAX,VSTEP
    ENDIF
#ifndef SEQ
    FLUSH(6)
#endif

    RETURN
100 FORMAT('Area defined by (',I2,',',I2,') and (',I2,',',I2,')')
101 FORMAT('Iteration ',I4)
102 FORMAT('Min=',E11.4E2,5X,'Max=',E11.4E2,5X,'Step=',E11.4E2)
    END
C
CCCCCCCCCCCCCCCCCCCCCCCCCCCCCCC END OF ROUTINE PLOT CCCCCCCCCCCCCCCCCCCCCCCCCCCCCCCC
C
    SUBROUTINE PLTVAL(RLOCAL,CLOCAL)
    INTEGER RLOCAL,CLOCAL,GETLVL
    PARAMETER (MAX=50)
    DOUBLE PRECISION VALUES(0:MAX+1,0:MAX+1),OMEGA,VALMIN,VALMAX,VSTEP
    COMMON/VAL/VALUES,OMEGA,VALMIN,VALMAX,VSTEP

    IVAL=GETLVL(VALUES(RLOCAL+1,CLOCAL+1))
    IF (IVAL.LT.10) THEN
        WRITE(*,100)IVAL
    ELSE
        WRITE(*,101)CHAR(IVAL+87)
    ENDIF

    RETURN
#ifndef XENIX
100 FORMAT(I2$)
101 FORMAT(A2$)
#else
```

```fortran
100   FORMAT(I2\)
101   FORMAT(A2\)
#endif
      END
C
CCCCCCCCCCCCCCCCCCCCCCCCCCCCCC END OF ROUTINE PLTVAL CCCCCCCCCCCCCCCCCCCCCCCCCCCCCC
C
      SUBROUTINE SAREA(XMIN,XMAX,YMIN,YMAX)
      INTEGER XMIN,XMAX,YMIN,YMAX
      COMMON/COMM/NY,NPROCX,NPROCY,ILCHAN,IRCHAN,IUCHAN,IDCHAN,IPOS(0:1)
      COMMON/BLOCK/IUSEST,NXPTS,NYPTS,ILPTS,IRPTS,ITPTS,IBPTS,NXTOT,NYTO

10    CONTINUE
      PRINT *
      PRINT *,'Please give the minimum and maximun column numbers.'
#ifndef SEQ
      FLUSH(6)
#endif
      READ *,XMIN,XMAX
      IF (XMIN.LT.0.OR.XMAX.LT.0) THEN
          XMIN=0
          XMAX=NXTOT-1
      ELSE IF (XMAX.GE.NXTOT.OR.XMIN.GT.XMAX) THEN
          PRINT *
          PRINT *,'*** Invalid input - try again ***'
          GOTO 10
      ENDIF
20    CONTINUE
      PRINT *,'Please give the minimum and maximun row numbers.'
#ifndef SEQ
      FLUSH(6)
#endif
      READ *,YMIN,YMAX
      IF (YMIN.LT.0.OR.YMAX.LT.0) THEN
          YMIN=0
          YMAX=NYTO-1
      ELSE IF (YMAX.GE.NYPTS*NY.OR.YMIN.GT.YMAX) THEN
          PRINT *
          PRINT *,'*** Invalid input - try again ***'
          PRINT *
          GOTO 20
      ENDIF

      RETURN
      END
C
CCCCCCCCCCCCCCCCCCCCCCCCCCCCCC END OF ROUTINE SAREA CCCCCCCCCCCCCCCCCCCCCCCCCCCCCC
```

```
C
      SUBROUTINE SETUPR
      PARAMETER (MAX=50)
      DOUBLE PRECISION VALUES(0:MAX+1,0:MAX+1),OMEGA,VALMIN,VALMAX,VSTEP
      COMMON/VAL/VALUES,OMEGA,VALMIN,VALMAX,VSTEP

      CALL MINMAX(VALMIN,VALMAX)
      VSTEP=(VALMAX-VALMIN)/16.0

      RETURN
      END
C
CCCCCCCCCCCCCCCCCCCCCCCCCCCCC END OF ROUTINE SETUPR CCCCCCCCCCCCCCCCCCCCCCCCCCCCCC
C
      SUBROUTINE UPDATE(ICYCLE)
      PARAMETER (MAX=50)
      DOUBLE PRECISION VALUES(0:MAX+1,0:MAX+1),OMEGA,VALMIN,VALMAX,VSTEP
      COMMON/VAL/VALUES,OMEGA,VALMIN,VALMAX,VSTEP
      COMMON/BLOCK/IUSEST,NXPTS,NYPTS,ILPTS,IRPTS,ITPTS,IBPTS,NXTOT,NYTO
      COMMON/INFO/IBC(0:MAX+1,0:MAX+1),IYBYTE,IXBYTE,NITER
      INTEGER RED,BLACK
      PARAMETER (RED=1,BLACK=2,NOTUSE=1)
      DOUBLE PRECISION EDGBUF(0:MAX-1),A,B

      IF (IUSEST.EQ.NOTUSE) RETURN
      A=OMEGA/4.0
      B=(1.0-OMEGA)
      DO 10 I=0,ICYCLE-1
          NITER=NITER+1
          CALL GETEDG(EDGBUF,RED)
          DO 20 J=1,NYPTS
              DO 30 K=1,NXPTS
                  IF (IBC(J,K) .EQ. RED) THEN
                      A1 = VALUES(J,K-1)+VALUES(J-1,K)
                      A1 = A1+VALUES(J,K+1)+VALUES(J+1,K)
                       B1 = VALUES(J,K)
                      VALUES(J,K)=A*A1+B*B1
                  ENDIF
30                CONTINUE
20            CONTINUE
          CALL GETEDG(EDGBUF,BLACK)
          DO 40 J=1,NYPTS
              DO 50 K=1,NXPTS
                  IF (IBC(J,K) .EQ. BLACK) THEN
                      A1 = VALUES(J,K-1)+VALUES(J-1,K)
                      A1 = A1+VALUES(J,K+1)+VALUES(J+1,K)
                       B1 = VALUES(J,K)
```

```
                     VALUES(J,K)=A*A1+B*B1
                 ENDIF
50                   CONTINUE
40               CONTINUE
10        CONTINUE

     RETURN
     END
C
CCCCCCCCCCCCCCCCCCCCCCCCCCCCCC END OF ROUTINE UPDATE CCCCCCCCCCCCCCCCCCCCCCCCCCCCCC
C
```

B-5 The Laplace Equation and the Finite Element Method

B-5.1 Cubix Program

```
      PROGRAM FEMPAR
      PARAMETER (NROW=10)
      PARAMETER (MAXNOD=(NROW+2)*(NROW+2))
      PARAMETER (MAXELM=(NROW+1)*(NROW+1))
      INTEGER EDGE(4,MAXELM), NGHBOR(9,MAXNOD), PROCNU
      REAL KE(MAXNOD,MAXNOD), PHI(MAXNOD), B(MAXNOD)
      LOGICAL BND(MAXNOD),YOURS(MAXNOD),INTR(MAXNOD)

      CALL SETELT(NPROC,PROCNU,MX,MY)

      PRINT *, ' '
      PRINT *, 'Numbering elements and nodes and setting boundary values ...'
      CALL IDELEM(EDGE,NGHBOR,BND,YOURS,NROW,PHI,NPROC,MX,MY)

      A = 0.25
      C = 0.25

      PRINT *, ' '
      PRINT *, 'Computing the stiffness matrix ...'
      CALL STIFF(KE,EDGE,A,C)

      PRINT *, ' '
      PRINT *, 'Computing the force terms ...'
      CALL GETBND(BND,NGHBOR,KE,INTR,PHI,B,NPROC)

      ALLOW = 0.0001

      PRINT *, ' '
      PRINT *, 'How many iterations?'
      READ  *, ITER
      PRINT *, 'Give Allowance'
      READ  *, ALLOW

      CALL CONGRA(KE,PHI,B,INTR,BND,YOURS,NGHBOR,ITER,ALLOW)

      PRINT *, ' '
      WRITE(*,100) ITER
      PRINT *, ' '
  100 FORMAT('                        Total number of iterations:',I3)

      CALL DUMP(PROCNU,NPROC,MX,MY,NROW,PHI)
      STOP
```

```fortran
      END
C
CCCCCCCCCCCCCCCCCCCCCCCCCCCCCCC END OF PROGRAM FEMPAR CCCCCCCCCCCCCCCCCCCCCCCCCCCCCCC
C
      SUBROUTINE SETELT(NPROC,PROCNU,MX,MY)
      INTEGER PROCNU,DOC,ENV(5),NUMDIM(2),MYPOST(2)
      INTEGER LMASK,RMASK,DMASK,UMASK
      COMMON /CUBE/ LMASK,RMASK,DMASK,UMASK

      CALL MESAGE()
      CALL KPARAM(ENV)
      DOC   = ENV(1)
      PROCNU= ENV(2)
      NPROC = ENV(3)
      NPROCX= 2**(DOC/2)
      NPROCY= 2**(DOC/2)

      NUMDIM(1) = NPROCY
      NUMDIM(2) = NPROCX

      CALL KGRDIN(2,NUMDIM)

      CALL KGRDCO(PROCNU,MYPOST)
      MX = MYPOST(2)
      MY = MYPOST(1)

      LMASK = KGRDCH(PROCNU,1,-1)
      RMASK = KGRDCH(PROCNU,1, 1)
      DMASK = KGRDCH(PROCNU,0, 1)
      UMASK = KGRDCH(PROCNU,0,-1)

      IF(MYPOST(2) .EQ. 0)          LMASK = 0
      IF(MYPOST(2) .EQ. (NPROCX-1)) RMASK = 0
      IF(MYPOST(1) .EQ. 0)          UMASK = 0
      IF(MYPOST(1) .EQ. (NPROCY-1)) DMASK = 0

#ifndef SEQ
      MULTIPLE(6)
#endif
      WRITE(6,100) PROCNU, MYPOST(2), MYPOST(1)
100   FORMAT(' Processor ', I2,' is working on region [X=',I1,' Y=',I1,']')
#ifndef SEQ
      SINGLE(6)
#endif

      RETURN
      END
```

```
C
CCCCCCCCCCCCCCCCCCCCCCCCCCCCC END OF ROUTINE SETELT CCCCCCCCCCCCCCCCCCCCCCCCCCCCC
C
      SUBROUTINE IDELEM(EDGE,NGHBOR,BND,YOURS,NROW,PHI,NPROC,MX,MY)
      INTEGER EDGE(4,*), NGHBOR(9,*)
      REAL PHI(*)
      LOGICAL BND(*),YOURS(*)

      NPROCH = NPROC/2
      MPROCH = NPROCH-1

      MROW   = NROW+1
      MAXELM = MROW**2
      MAXNOD = (NROW+2)**2

      DO 12 I=1,MAXNOD
          PHI(I)   = 0.0
          YOURS(I) = .FALSE.
          BND(I)   = .FALSE.
12        CONTINUE

      DO 5 I=1,NROW+2
          YOURS(I) = .TRUE.
5         CONTINUE
      DO 6 I=MAXNOD-NROW-1,MAXNOD
          YOURS(I) = .TRUE.
6         CONTINUE
      DO 7 I=NROW+2,MAXNOD-NROW-2,NROW+2
          YOURS(I) = .TRUE.
          YOURS(I+1)=.TRUE.
7         CONTINUE

      DO 10 I=1,MAXELM
          J = (I-1)/MROW+I
          K = J+MROW+1
          EDGE(1,I) = J
          EDGE(2,I) = J+1
          EDGE(3,I) = K
          EDGE(4,I) = K+1

          NGHBOR(5,J) = J
          NGHBOR(6,J) = J+1
          NGHBOR(8,J) = K
          NGHBOR(9,J) = K+1

          NGHBOR(4,J+1) = J
          NGHBOR(5,J+1) = J+1
```

```
                 NGHBOR(7,J+1) = K
                 NGHBOR(8,J+1) = K+1

                 NGHBOR(2,K) = J
                 NGHBOR(3,K) = J+1
                 NGHBOR(5,K) = K
                 NGHBOR(6,K) = K+1

                 NGHBOR(1,K+1) = J
                 NGHBOR(2,K+1) = J+1
                 NGHBOR(4,K+1) = K
                 NGHBOR(5,K+1) = K+1
10               CONTINUE

         IF (MY .EQ. 0) THEN
             DO 20 I=1,NROW+2
                 BND(I) = .TRUE.
                 PHI(I) = 1.0
20               CONTINUE
             DO 21 I=2,NROW+1
                 YOURS(I) = .FALSE.
21               CONTINUE
             IF (MX .EQ. 0) THEN
                 DO 22 I=1,MAXNOD-NROW-2,NROW+2
                     YOURS(I) = .FALSE.
22                   CONTINUE
             ENDIF
             IF (MX .EQ. MPROCH) THEN
                 DO 23 I=NROW+2,MAXNOD-NROW-2,NROW+2
                     YOURS(I) = .FALSE.
23                   CONTINUE
             ENDIF
         ENDIF

         IF (MY .EQ. MPROCH) THEN
             DO 30 I=MAXNOD-NROW-1,MAXNOD
                 BND(I) = .TRUE.
                 PHI(I) = -1.0
30               CONTINUE
             DO 31 I=MAXNOD-NROW,MAXNOD-1
                 YOURS(I) = .FALSE.
31               CONTINUE
             IF (MX .EQ. 0) THEN
                 DO 32 I=NROW+3,MAXNOD,NROW+2
                     YOURS(I) = .FALSE.
32                   CONTINUE
             ENDIF
```

```
              IF (MX .EQ. MPROCH) THEN
                  DO 33 I=2*(NROW+2),MAXNOD,NROW+2
                      YOURS(I) = .FALSE.
   33                 CONTINUE
              ENDIF
          ENDIF

          DELPHI = 2.0/(NROW*NPROCH+1)
          PHIREF = 1.0-DELPHI*MY*NROW

          IF (MX .EQ. 0) THEN
              DO 40 I=1,MAXNOD,NROW+2
                  BND(I)   = .TRUE.
                  PHI(I)   = -REAL(I/(NROW+2))*DELPHI+PHIREF
   40             CONTINUE
              IF ((MY .NE. 0) .OR. (MY .NE. MPROCH)) THEN
                  DO 41 I=NROW+3,MAXNOD-NROW-2,NROW+2
                      YOURS(I) = .FALSE.
   41                 CONTINUE
              ENDIF
          ENDIF

          IF (MX .EQ. MPROCH) THEN
              DO 50 I=NROW+2,MAXNOD,NROW+2
                  BND(I)   = .TRUE.
                  PHI(I)   = -REAL((I-1)/(NROW+2))*DELPHI+PHIREF
   50             CONTINUE
              IF ((MY .NE. 0) .OR. (MY .NE. MPROCH)) THEN
                  DO 51 I=2*(NROW+2),MAXNOD-NROW-2,NROW+2
                      YOURS(I) = .FALSE.
   51                 CONTINUE
              ENDIF
          ENDIF

          RETURN
          END
C
CCCCCCCCCCCCCCCCCCCCCCCCCCCCCCCC END OF ROUTINE IDELEM CCCCCCCCCCCCCCCCCCCCCCCCCCCCCCCC
C
      SUBROUTINE STIFF(KE,EDGE,A,B)
      PARAMETER (NROW=10)
      PARAMETER (MAXNOD=(NROW+2)*(NROW+2),MAXELM=(NROW+1)*(NROW+1))
      REAL    KE(MAXNOD,MAXNOD),KN(4,4),XK(4),YK(4)
      INTEGER EDGE(4,*)
      DATA (XK(I),I=1,4) /-1.0,1.0,-1.0,1.0/
      DATA (YK(I),I=1,4) /1.0,1.0,-1.0,-1.0/
```

```
      R = A/B

      DO 5 I=1,4
         DO 5 J=I,4
            TEMP1   = 0.25*R*XK(I)*XK(J)+0.25/R*YK(I)*YK(J)
            TEMP2   = XK(I)*XK(J)*YK(I)*YK(J)*(R+1.0/R)/12.0
            KN(I,J) = TEMP1 + TEMP2
5           CONTINUE

      DO 10 ID=1,MAXELM
         I = EDGE(1,ID)
         J = EDGE(2,ID)
         K = EDGE(3,ID)
         L = EDGE(4,ID)
         KE(I,I) = KE(I,I)+KN(1,1)
         KE(I,J) = KE(I,J)+KN(1,2)
         KE(J,I) = KE(I,J)
         KE(I,K) = KE(I,K)+KN(1,3)
         KE(K,I) = KE(I,K)
         KE(I,L) = KE(I,L)+KN(1,4)
         KE(L,I) = KE(I,L)
         KE(J,J) = KE(J,J)+KN(2,2)
         KE(J,K) = KE(J,K)+KN(2,3)
         KE(K,J) = KE(J,K)
         KE(J,L) = KE(J,L)+KN(2,4)
         KE(L,J) = KE(J,L)
         KE(K,K) = KE(K,K)+KN(3,3)
         KE(K,L) = KE(K,L)+KN(3,4)
         KE(L,K) = KE(K,L)
         KE(K,K) = KE(K,K)+KN(4,4)
10       CONTINUE

      RETURN
      END
C
CCCCCCCCCCCCCCCCCCCCCCCCCCCCCCC END OF ROUTINE STIFF CCCCCCCCCCCCCCCCCCCCCCCCCCCCCCC
C
      SUBROUTINE GETBND(BND,NGHBOR,KE,INTR,PHI,B,NPROC)
      PARAMETER (NROW=10)
      PARAMETER (MAXNOD=(NROW+2)*(NROW+2))
      INTEGER NGHBOR(9,*)
      REAL KE(MAXNOD,MAXNOD),B(*),PHI(*)
      LOGICAL BND(*),INTR(*),LOGT1,LOGT2

      NPROCH = NPROC/2

      N1 = NROW+2
```

```
        N2 = (NROW+2)*(NROW+1)

        DO 10 I=1,MAXNOD
           B(I)  = 0.0
           LOGT1 = (I .LE. N1) .OR. (I .GT. N2)
           LOGT2 = (MOD(I-1,N1) .EQ. 0) .OR. (MOD(I,N1) .EQ. 0)
           IF( LOGT1 .OR. LOGT2 ) THEN
                INTR(I) = .FALSE.
           ELSE
                INTR(I) = .TRUE.
           ENDIF

           IF (INTR(I)) THEN
                DO 20 K=1,9
                   J = NGHBOR(K,I)
                   IF (BND(J)) B(I) = B(I)-KE(I,J)*PHI(J)
20                 CONTINUE
           ENDIF
10         CONTINUE

      RETURN
      END
C
CCCCCCCCCCCCCCCCCCCCCCCCCCCCCCC END OF ROUTINE GETBND CCCCCCCCCCCCCCCCCCCCCCCCCCCCCCC
C
      SUBROUTINE CONGRA(KE,X,B,INTR,BND,YOURS,NGHBOR,K,ALLOW)
      PARAMETER (NROW=10)
      PARAMETER (MAXNOD=(NROW+2)*(NROW+2),MAXELM=(NROW+1)*(NROW+1))
      INTEGER NGHBOR(9,*)
      REAL    KE(MAXNOD,MAXNOD),X(*),B(*)
      REAL Q(MAXNOD),R(MAXNOD),P(MAXNOD),NEWNOM
      LOGICAL BND(*),INTR(*),YOURS(*)

      MROW = NROW+2
      ILOW = MROW+2
      IHIH = MAXNOD-MROW-1
      MSTOP= K/2

      DO 12 I=1,MAXNOD
         P(I) = 0.0
         R(I) = 0.0
         Q(I) = 0.0
12       CONTINUE

      DO 10 I=ILOW,IHIH
         IF (INTR(I)) THEN
              R(I) = B(I)
```

```
              P(I) = B(I)
          ENDIF
10        CONTINUE

      OLDNOM = SCALAR(R,R,MAXNOD,INTR)

      DO 100 M=1,K
          CALL COMMUN(P,NROW)

          DO 30 I=ILOW,IHIH
              IF (.NOT. INTR(I)) GOTO 30
              Q(I) = 0.0
              DO 35 L=1,9
                  J = NGHBOR(L,I)
                  IF ((J .EQ. 0) .OR. (BND(J))) GOTO 35
                  Q(I)=KE(I,J)*P(J)+Q(I)
35                CONTINUE
30            CONTINUE

          NEWNOM = SCALAR(P,Q,MAXNOD,INTR)

          ALPHA = OLDNOM/NEWNOM

          DO 40 I=ILOW,IHIH
              IF (.NOT. INTR(I)) GOTO 40
              X(I) = X(I)+ALPHA*P(I)
              R(I) = R(I)-ALPHA*Q(I)
40            CONTINUE

          NEWNOM = SCALAR(R,R,MAXNOD,INTR)

          BETA = NEWNOM/OLDNOM

          IF(M .GE. MSTOP) THEN
              IF (ABS(NEWNOM-OLDNOM) .LE. ALLOW) GOTO 99
          ENDIF

          OLDNOM = NEWNOM

          DO 50 I=ILOW,IHIH
              IF (.NOT. INTR(I)) GOTO 50
              P(I) = R(I)+BETA*P(I)
50            CONTINUE

100       CONTINUE

99    CONTINUE
```

```
      IF (M .LT. K) K = M

      RETURN
      END
C
CCCCCCCCCCCCCCCCCCCCCCCCCCCCCC END OF ROUTINE CONGRA CCCCCCCCCCCCCCCCCCCCCCCCCCCCCC
C
      FUNCTION SCALAR(A,B,N,INTR)
      REAL A(*),B(*)
      LOGICAL INTR(*)
      EXTERNAL ADD

      RN = 0.0
      DO 10 I=1,N
          IF (INTR(I)) RN = RN+A(I)*B(I)
10        CONTINUE

      IERR = KCOMBI(RN,ADD,4,1)
      SCALAR = RN

      RETURN
      END
C
CCCCCCCCCCCCCCCCCCCCCCCCCCCCCC END OF ROUTINE SCALAR CCCCCCCCCCCCCCCCCCCCCCCCCCCCCC
C
      FUNCTION ADD(X,Y,SIZE)
      INTEGER  ADD,SIZE
      X = X+Y
      ADD = 0
      RETURN
      END
C
C CCCCCCCCCCCCCCCCCCCCCCCCC END OF ROUTINE ADD CCCCCCCCCCCCCCCCCCCCCCCCC
C
      SUBROUTINE COMMUN(P,NROW)
      REAL P(*)
      INTEGER LMASK,RMASK,DMASK,UMASK
      COMMON /CUBE/ LMASK,RMASK,DMASK,UMASK

      MROW = NROW+2
      MAXNOD=MROW**2
      IROW = MROW+1
      JROW = 2*MROW
      LROW = MAXNOD-MROW+1
      J    = JROW-1
      K    = MROW+2
```

```
      IERR = KVSHIF(P(IROW),LMASK,4,MROW*4,MROW,P(J),RMASK,4,MROW*4,NROW)
      IERR = KVSHIF(P(JROW),RMASK,4,MROW*4,MROW,P(K),LMASK,4,MROW*4,NROW)

      IERR = KCSHIF(P(LROW),DMASK,MROW*4,P(IROW),UMASK,MROW*4)
      IERR = KCSHIF(P,UMASK,MROW*4,P(LROW-MROW),DMASK,MROW*4)

      RETURN
      END
C
C CCCCCCCCCCCCCCCCCCCCCCCC END OF ROUTINE COMMUN CCCCCCCCCCCCCCCCCCCCCCC
C
      SUBROUTINE MESAGE()
      PRINT *, ' '
      PRINT *, 'This is a Laplace equation solver in a rectangular region.'
      PRINT *, ' '
      PRINT *, '   IDELEM sets up the arrays for elements and nodes'
      PRINT *, '   STIFF computes the stiffness matrix.'
      PRINT *, '   GETBND computes the force terms.'
      PRINT *, '   CONGRA finds the solution vector.'
      PRINT *, ' '
      PRINT *, '   Some parameters are:'
      PRINT *, ' '
      PRINT *, '   DOC:    cube dimension (PLEASE set to 2 or 4)'
      PRINT *, '   MAXNOD: number of nodes.'
      PRINT *, '   MAXELM: number of elements.'
      PRINT *, '   ALLOW:  Allowance for terminating update'
      PRINT *, ' '

      RETURN
      END
C
C CCCCCCCCCCCCCCCCCCCCCCCCCCCCCC END OF ROUTINE MESAGE CCCCCCCCCCCCCCCCCCCCCCCCCCCCCC
C
      SUBROUTINE DUMP(PROCNU,NPROC,MX,MY,NROW,PHI)
      INTEGER PROCNU
      REAL PHI(*)

#ifndef SEQ
      MULTIPLE(6)
#endif

      DO 30 MYPROC=0,NPROC-1
         IF (PROCNU .EQ. MYPROC) THEN
             PRINT *, ' '
             WRITE(*,101) PROCNU,MX,MY
         ENDIF
#ifndef SEQ
```

```
      FLUSH(6)
#endif
        DO 40 J=2,NROW-1
            MSTART=(J-1)*(NROW+2)+2
            MFINI = MSTART+NROW-1
            IF (PROCNU .EQ. MYPROC) THEN
                WRITE(6,102) (PHI(K),K=MSTART,MFINI)
            ENDIF
#ifndef SEQ
    FLUSH(6)
#endif
40              CONTINUE
30        CONTINUE

#ifndef SEQ
    SINGLE(6)
#endif

101 FORMAT(' Processor #:',I2,' Quadrant:[',I2,',',I2,']')
102 FORMAT(10F8.4)

    RETURN
    END
C
CCCCCCCCCCCCCCCCCCCCCCCCCCCCCC END OF ROUTINE DUMP CCCCCCCCCCCCCCCCCCCCCCCCCCCCCC
C
```

B-6 The Long-Range Force Problem

B-6.1 CUBIX Program

```
      PROGRAM LRANGE
      PARAMETER (MAX=50)
      DOUBLE PRECISION OBJARR(7,0:MAX-1),OBJCPY(7,0:MAX-1)
      COMMON /ARR/OBJARR,OBJCPY
      COMMON /PROC/NPROC,IDOC,IPNUM
      COMMON /COMM/IRPOS,ICCLOK,ICLOCK
      COMMON /BLOCK/NLEFT,NMIN,NLOCAL,NTOTAL

      INZFLG=0
      CALL WELCOM
      CALL GPARAM
      CALL RING
10    CALL GETJOB(JOB)
      IF (JOB.NE.5) THEN
          IF (JOB.EQ.1) THEN
              CALL INITLZ
              INZFLG=1
              IFFLAG=0
          ELSE IF (JOB.EQ.2.AND.INZFLG.NE.0) THEN
              CALL GETPOT
          ELSE IF (JOB.EQ.3.AND.INZFLG.NE.0) THEN
              CALL OUTPAR
          ELSE IF (JOB.EQ.4.AND.INZFLG.NE.0) THEN
              IF (IFFLAG.EQ.0) THEN
                  CALL LRFOR(NLOCAL)
                  IFFLAG=1
              ENDIF
              CALL OUTFOR
          ENDIF
          GOTO 10
      ENDIF

      STOP
      END
C
CCCCCCCCCCCCCCCCCCCCCCCCCCCCCC END OF PROGRAM LRANGE CCCCCCCCCCCCCCCCCCCCCCCCCCCCCC
C
      SUBROUTINE GPARAM
      COMMON /PROC/NPROC,IDOC,IPNUM
      INTEGER ENV(5)

      CALL KPARAM(ENV)
      IDOC=ENV(1)
```

```
      IPNUM=ENV(2)
      NPROC=ENV(3)

      RETURN
      END
C
CCCCCCCCCCCCCCCCCCCCCCCCCCCCCCC END OF ROUTINE GPARAM CCCCCCCCCCCCCCCCCCCCCCCCCCCCCCC
C
      SUBROUTINE WELCOM

#ifndef SEQ
      BUFFER(UNIT=6,SIZE=512)
#endif
      PRINT *
      PRINT *,'**********************************************'
      PRINT *,'*                                            *'
      PRINT *,'*      Welcome to the potential evaluation   *'
      PRINT *,'*      example program.  This program finds  *'
      PRINT *,'*      the gravitational potential energy    *'
      PRINT *,'*      of a system of particles.             *'
      PRINT *,'*                                            *'
      PRINT *,'**********************************************'
      PRINT *
      PRINT *
#ifndef SEQ
      FLUSH(6)
#endif

      RETURN
      END
C
CCCCCCCCCCCCCCCCCCCCCCCCCCCCCCC END OF ROUTINE WELCOM CCCCCCCCCCCCCCCCCCCCCCCCCCCCCCC
C
      SUBROUTINE RING
      COMMON /PROC/NPROC,IDOC,IPNUM
      COMMON /COMM/IRPOS,ICCLOK,ICLOCK

      IDUMMY=KGRDIN(1,NPROC)
      IDUMMY=KGRDCO(IPNUM,IRPOS)
      ICCLOK=KGRDCH(IPNUM,0,-1)
      ICLOCK=KGRDCH(IPNUM,0,1)

      RETURN
      END
C
CCCCCCCCCCCCCCCCCCCCCCCCCCCCCCC END OF ROUTINE RING CCCCCCCCCCCCCCCCCCCCCCCCCCCCCCC
C
```

```fortran
      SUBROUTINE GETJOB(JOB)

      PRINT *
      PRINT *
      PRINT *,'Please select one of the following :'
      PRINT *,'  1..to initialize a new particle configuration'
      PRINT *,'  2..to evaluate the potential'
      PRINT *,'  3..to output particle positions and masses'
      PRINT *,'  4..to output force on each particle'
      PRINT *,'  5..to terminate the program'
#ifndef SEQ
      FLUSH(6)
#endif
      READ *,JOB

      RETURN
      END
C
CCCCCCCCCCCCCCCCCCCCCCCCCCCCCC END OF ROUTINE GETJOB CCCCCCCCCCCCCCCCCCCCCCCCCCCCCC
C
      SUBROUTINE INITLZ
      COMMON /PROC/NPROC,IDOC,IPNUM
      COMMON /COMM/IRPOS,ICCLOK,ICLOCK
      COMMON /BLOCK/NLEFT,NMIN,NLOCAL,NTOTAL
      PARAMETER (MAX=50)

10    CONTINUE
      PRINT *
      PRINT *
      PRINT *,'Please choose one of the following:'
      PRINT *,'  1..to input particles from terminal'
      PRINT *,'  2..to generate random particles'
      PRINT *,'  3..to exit this menu'
#ifndef SEQ
      FLUSH(6)
#endif
      READ *,METHOD
      IF (METHOD.NE.1.AND.METHOD.NE.3.AND.METHOD.NE.2) GOTO 10
      IF (METHOD.EQ.3) GOTO 99
      IF (METHOD.EQ.2) THEN
         PRINT *
         PRINT *,'Please give a seed integer.'
#ifndef SEQ
         FLUSH(6)
#endif
         READ *,ISEED
         CALL PRSETB(ISEED,4,IRPOS)
```

```
      ENDIF
20    CONTINUE
      PRINT *
      PRINT *,'Please give the total number of particles.'
#ifndef SEQ
      FLUSH(6)
#endif
      READ *,NTOTAL
      PRINT *
      NMIN=(NTOTAL-1)/NPROC
      IF ((NMIN+1).GT.MAX) THEN
          PRINT *
          PRINT *,'*** Too many particles - try again ***'
          GOTO 20
      ENDIF
      NLEFT=NTOTAL-NMIN*NPROC
      IF (IRPOS.LT.NLEFT) THEN
          NLOCAL=NMIN+1
      ELSE
          NLOCAL=NMIN
      ENDIF
      CALL GETPAR(METHOD)

99    RETURN
      END
C
CCCCCCCCCCCCCCCCCCCCCCCCCCCCCCCC END OF ROUTINE INITLZ CCCCCCCCCCCCCCCCCCCCCCCCCCCCCCCC
C
      SUBROUTINE GETPAR(METHOD)
      PARAMETER (MAX=50)
      DOUBLE PRECISION OBJARR(7,0:MAX-1),OBJCPY(7,0:MAX-1)
      COMMON /ARR/OBJARR,OBJCPY
      INTEGER X,Y,Z,FX,FY,FZ
      PARAMETER (X=1,Y=2,Z=3,MASS=4,FX=5,FY=6,FZ=7)
      COMMON /COMM/IRPOS,ICCLOK,ICLOCK
      COMMON /BLOCK/NLEFT,NMIN,NLOCAL,NTOTAL
      DOUBLE PRECISION VX,VY,VZ,VMASS

      IF (METHOD.EQ.2) THEN
          CALL RANPAR
      ELSE
          INDEX=0
          DO 10 NP=0,NTOTAL-1
              PRINT *,'Please give the x, y, & z coordinates',
     #                        'and mass for particle ',NP+1
#ifndef SEQ
              FLUSH(6)
```

```
#endif
                READ *,VX,VY,VZ,VMASS
                IF (NP.LT.(NMIN+1)*NLEFT) THEN
                    IPOS=NP/(NMIN+1)
                ELSE
                    IPOS=(NP-NLEFT)/NMIN
                ENDIF
                IF (IRPOS.EQ.IPOS) THEN
                    OBJARR(X,INDEX)=VX
                    OBJARR(Y,INDEX)=VY
                    OBJARR(Z,INDEX)=VZ
                    OBJARR(MASS,INDEX)=VMASS
                    OBJARR(FX,INDEX)=0.0
                    OBJARR(FY,INDEX)=0.0
                    OBJARR(FZ,INDEX)=0.0
                    INDEX=INDEX+1
                ENDIF
10          CONTINUE
        ENDIF

        RETURN
        END
C
CCCCCCCCCCCCCCCCCCCCCCCCCCCCCCC END OF ROUTINE GETPAR CCCCCCCCCCCCCCCCCCCCCCCCCCCCCCC
C
      DOUBLE PRECISION FUNCTION LRPAR(NRES)
      PARAMETER (MAX=50)
      DOUBLE PRECISION OBJARR(7,0:MAX-1),OBJCPY(7,0:MAX-1)
      COMMON /ARR/OBJARR,OBJCPY
      INTEGER X,Y,Z,FX,FY,FZ
      PARAMETER (X=1,Y=2,Z=3,MASS=4,FX=5,FY=6,FZ=7)
      COMMON /PROC/NPROC,IDOC,IPNUM
      DOUBLE PRECISION SUM,LRSYMP

      MOVERS=NRES
      DO 10 I=0,NRES-1
          OBJCPY(X,I)=OBJARR(X,I)
          OBJCPY(Y,I)=OBJARR(Y,I)
          OBJCPY(Z,I)=OBJARR(Z,I)
          OBJCPY(MASS,I)=OBJARR(MASS,I)
          OBJCPY(FX,I)=OBJARR(FX,I)
          OBJCPY(FY,I)=OBJARR(FY,I)
          OBJCPY(FZ,I)=OBJARR(FZ,I)
10    CONTINUE
      SUM=0.0
      DO 20 ISTEP=0,NPROC-1
          SUM=SUM+LRSYMP(NRES,MOVERS,ISTEP)
```

```
          CALL ROTATE(MOVERS)
20    CONTINUE
      LRPAR=SUM

      RETURN
      END
C
CCCCCCCCCCCCCCCCCCCCCCCCCCCCCCC END OF ROUTINE LRPAR CCCCCCCCCCCCCCCCCCCCCCCCCCCCCCC
C
      DOUBLE PRECISION FUNCTION LRSYMP(N1,N2,ISTEP)

      DOUBLE PRECISION SUM,PAIRP
      INTEGER SHOULD

      SUM=0.0
      IF (N1.LT.N2) THEN
          MIN=N1
      ELSE
          MIN=N2
      ENDIF
      DO 10 I=0,MIN-1
          IF (SHOULD(I,ISTEP).NE.0) SUM=SUM+PAIRP(I,I)
          DO 20 J=I+1,N2-1
              SUM=SUM+PAIRP(I,J)
20        CONTINUE
10    CONTINUE
      LRSYMP=SUM

      RETURN
      END
C
CCCCCCCCCCCCCCCCCCCCCCCCCCCCCCC END OF ROUTINE LRSYMP CCCCCCCCCCCCCCCCCCCCCCCCCCCCCCC
C
      DOUBLE PRECISION FUNCTION PAIRP(I1,I2)
      PARAMETER (MAX=50)
      DOUBLE PRECISION OBJARR(7,0:MAX-1),OBJCPY(7,0:MAX-1)
      COMMON /ARR/OBJARR,OBJCPY
      INTEGER X,Y,Z,FX,FY,FZ
      PARAMETER (X=1,Y=2,Z=3,MASS=4,FX=5,FY=6,FZ=7)

      DOUBLE PRECISION DIFFX,DIFFY,DIFFZ,SQUARE

      DIFFX=OBJARR(X,I1)-OBJCPY(X,I2)
      DIFFY=OBJARR(Y,I1)-OBJCPY(Y,I2)
      DIFFZ=OBJARR(Z,I1)-OBJCPY(Z,I2)
      SQUARE=DIFFX**2+DIFFY**2+DIFFZ**2
      IF (SQUARE.EQ.0) THEN
```

```
          PAIRP=0.0
      ELSE
          PAIRP=-OBJARR(MASS,I1)*OBJCPY(MASS,I2)/DSQRT(SQUARE)
      ENDIF

      RETURN
      END
C
CCCCCCCCCCCCCCCCCCCCCCCCCCCCCCC END OF ROUTINE PAIRP CCCCCCCCCCCCCCCCCCCCCCCCCCCCCCCC
C
      INTEGER FUNCTION SHOULD(I,ISTEP)
      COMMON /PROC/NPROC,IDOC,IPNUM
      COMMON /COMM/IRPOS,ICCLOK,ICLOCK

      IF (ISTEP.LT.NPROC/2) THEN
          SHOULD=0
      ELSE IF (ISTEP.GT.NPROC/2) THEN
          SHOULD=1
      ELSE IF (IRPOS.LT.NPROC/2) THEN
          SHOULD=IZEVEN(I)
      ELSE
          SHOULD=IZODD(I)
      ENDIF

      RETURN
      END
C
CCCCCCCCCCCCCCCCCCCCCCCCCCCCCCC END OF ROUTINE SHOULD CCCCCCCCCCCCCCCCCCCCCCCCCCCCCCCC
C
      FUNCTION IZEVEN(I)

      IF (MOD(I,2).EQ.0) THEN
        IZEVEN=1
      ELSE
        IZEVEN=0
      ENDIF

      RETURN
      END
C
CCCCCCCCCCCCCCCCCCCCCCCCCCCCCCCC END OF ROUTINE IZEVEN CCCCCCCCCCCCCCCCCCCCCCCCCCCCCCCC
C
      FUNCTION IZODD(I)

      IF (MOD(I,2).EQ.0) THEN
          IZODD=0
      ELSE
```

```
            IZODD=1
      ENDIF

      RETURN
      END
C
CCCCCCCCCCCCCCCCCCCCCCCCCCCCCC END OF ROUTINE IZODD CCCCCCCCCCCCCCCCCCCCCCCCCCCCCC
C
      SUBROUTINE GETPOT
      COMMON /BLOCK/NLEFT,NMIN,NLOCAL,NTOTAL
      INTEGER DBLSIZ,ADDBLE
      EXTERNAL ADDBLE
      PARAMETER (DBLSIZ=8)
      DOUBLE PRECISION POT,LRPAR

      POT=LRPAR(NLOCAL)
      IDUMMY=KCOMBI(POT,ADDBLE,DBLSIZ,1)
      PRINT *
      PRINT *
      WRITE(*,100)NTOTAL,POT
#ifndef SEQ
      FLUSH(6)
#endif

      RETURN
100   FORMAT('The potential of the ',I3,' particles is ',E13.5)
      END
C
CCCCCCCCCCCCCCCCCCCCCCCCCCCCCC END OF ROUTINE GETPOT CCCCCCCCCCCCCCCCCCCCCCCCCCCCCC
C
      INTEGER FUNCTION ADDBLE(D1,D2,ISIZE)
      DOUBLE PRECISION D1,D2

      D1=D1+D2
      ADDBLE=0

      RETURN
      END
C
CCCCCCCCCCCCCCCCCCCCCCCCCCCCCC END OF ROUTINE ADDBLE CCCCCCCCCCCCCCCCCCCCCCCCCCCCCC
C
      SUBROUTINE LRFOR(NRES)
      PARAMETER (MAX=50)
      DOUBLE PRECISION OBJARR(7,0:MAX-1),OBJCPY(7,0:MAX-1)
      COMMON /ARR/OBJARR,OBJCPY
      INTEGER X,Y,Z,FX,FY,FZ
      PARAMETER (X=1,Y=2,Z=3,MASS=4,FX=5,FY=6,FZ=7)
```

```
      COMMON /PROC/NPROC,IDOC,IPNUM

      MOVERS=NRES
      DO 10 I=0,NRES-1
          OBJCPY(X,I)=OBJARR(X,I)
          OBJCPY(Y,I)=OBJARR(Y,I)
          OBJCPY(Z,I)=OBJARR(Z,I)
          OBJCPY(MASS,I)=OBJARR(MASS,I)
          OBJCPY(FX,I)=OBJARR(FX,I)
          OBJCPY(FY,I)=OBJARR(FY,I)
          OBJCPY(FZ,I)=OBJARR(FZ,I)
10    CONTINUE
      DO 30 ISTEP=0,NPROC-1
          CALL LRF2(NRES,MOVERS,ISTEP)
          CALL ROTATE(MOVERS)
30    CONTINUE
      CALL RECOMB(NRES)

      RETURN
      END
C
CCCCCCCCCCCCCCCCCCCCCCCCCCCCCCCC END OF ROUTINE LRFOR CCCCCCCCCCCCCCCCCCCCCCCCCCCCCCCC
C
      SUBROUTINE LRF2(N1,N2,ISTEP)
      INTEGER SHOULD

      IF (N1.LT.N2) THEN
          MIN=N1
      ELSE
          MIN=N2
      ENDIF
      DO 10 I=0,MIN-1
          IF (SHOULD(I,ISTEP).NE.0) CALL PAIRF(I,I)
          DO 20 J=I+1,N2-1
              CALL PAIRF(I,J)
20        CONTINUE
10    CONTINUE

      RETURN
      END
C
CCCCCCCCCCCCCCCCCCCCCCCCCCCCCCCC END OF ROUTINE LRF2 CCCCCCCCCCCCCCCCCCCCCCCCCCCCCCCC
C
      SUBROUTINE PAIRF(I1,I2)
      PARAMETER (MAX=50)
      DOUBLE PRECISION OBJARR(7,0:MAX-1),OBJCPY(7,0:MAX-1)
      COMMON /ARR/OBJARR,OBJCPY
```

```
      INTEGER X,Y,Z,FX,FY,FZ
      PARAMETER (X=1,Y=2,Z=3,MASS=4,FX=5,FY=6,FZ=7)

      DOUBLE PRECISION FACTOR,DIST,DIFFX,DIFFY,DIFFZ,SQUARE
      DOUBLE PRECISION FORCEX,FORCEY,FORCEZ

      DIFFX=OBJARR(X,I1)-OBJCPY(X,I2)
      DIFFY=OBJARR(Y,I1)-OBJCPY(Y,I2)
      DIFFZ=OBJARR(Z,I1)-OBJCPY(Z,I2)
      SQUARE=DIFFX**2+DIFFY**2+DIFFZ**2
      IF (SQUARE.NE.0.0) THEN
          DIST=DSQRT(SQUARE)
          FACTOR=OBJARR(MASS,I1)*OBJCPY(MASS,I2)/(DIST*SQUARE)
          FORCEX=FACTOR*DIFFX
          FORCEY=FACTOR*DIFFY
          FORCEZ=FACTOR*DIFFZ
          OBJARR(FX,I1)=OBJARR(FX,I1)-FORCEX
          OBJARR(FY,I1)=OBJARR(FY,I1)-FORCEY
          OBJARR(FZ,I1)=OBJARR(FZ,I1)-FORCEZ
          OBJCPY(FX,I2)=OBJCPY(FX,I2)+FORCEX
          OBJCPY(FY,I2)=OBJCPY(FY,I2)+FORCEY
          OBJCPY(FZ,I2)=OBJCPY(FZ,I2)+FORCEZ
      ENDIF

      RETURN
      END
C
CCCCCCCCCCCCCCCCCCCCCCCCCCCCCCC END OF ROUTINE PAIRF CCCCCCCCCCCCCCCCCCCCCCCCCCCCCCC
C
      SUBROUTINE RECOMB(N)
      PARAMETER (MAX=50)
      DOUBLE PRECISION OBJARR(7,0:MAX-1),OBJCPY(7,0:MAX-1)
      COMMON /ARR/OBJARR,OBJCPY
      INTEGER X,Y,Z,FX,FY,FZ
      PARAMETER (X=1,Y=2,Z=3,MASS=4,FX=5,FY=6,FZ=7)

      DO 10 I=0,N-1
          OBJARR(FX,I)=OBJARR(FX,I)+OBJCPY(FX,I)
          OBJARR(FY,I)=OBJARR(FY,I)+OBJCPY(FY,I)
          OBJARR(FZ,I)=OBJARR(FZ,I)+OBJCPY(FZ,I)
10    CONTINUE

      RETURN
      END
C
CCCCCCCCCCCCCCCCCCCCCCCCCCCCCCC END OF ROUTINE RECOMB CCCCCCCCCCCCCCCCCCCCCCCCCCCCCCC
C
```

```
      SUBROUTINE ROTATE(NARR)
      PARAMETER (MAX=50)
      DOUBLE PRECISION OBJARR(7,0:MAX-1),OBJCPY(7,0:MAX-1)
      COMMON /ARR/OBJARR,OBJCPY
      COMMON /COMM/IRPOS,ICCLOK,ICLOCK
      COMMON /BLOCK/NLEFT,NMIN,NLOCAL,NTOTAL
      INTEGER DBLSIZ
      PARAMETER (DBLSIZ=8)

      NBYTES=NARR*(7*DBLSIZ)
      ISPACE=(NMIN+1)*(7*DBLSIZ)
      NREC=KCSHIF(OBJCPY,ICLOCK,ISPACE,OBJCPY,ICCLOK,NBYTES)
      NARR=NREC/(7*DBLSIZ)

      RETURN
      END
C
CCCCCCCCCCCCCCCCCCCCCCCCCCCCCCC END OF ROUTINE ROTATE CCCCCCCCCCCCCCCCCCCCCCCCCCCCCCC
C
      SUBROUTINE OUTFOR
      PARAMETER (MAX=50)
      DOUBLE PRECISION OBJARR(7,0:MAX-1),OBJCPY(7,0:MAX-1)
      COMMON /ARR/OBJARR,OBJCPY
      INTEGER X,Y,Z,FX,FY,FZ
      PARAMETER (X=1,Y=2,Z=3,MASS=4,FX=5,FY=6,FZ=7)
      COMMON /PROC/NPROC,IDOC,IPNUM
      COMMON /COMM/IRPOS,ICCLOK,ICLOCK
      COMMON /BLOCK/NLEFT,NMIN,NLOCAL,NTOTAL
      INTEGER STDOUT,DBLSIZ,ADDBLE
      EXTERNAL ADDBLE
      PARAMETER (STDOUT=6,DBLSIZ=8)
      DOUBLE PRECISION SUMX,SUMY,SUMZ

      PRINT *
      PRINT *
      PRINT *,'Number   x force        y force        z force'
#ifndef SEQ
      MULTIPLE(STDOUT)
#endif
      SUMX=0.0
      SUMY=0.0
      SUMZ=0.0
      NP=1
      DO 10 I=0,NPROC-1
          IF (I.LT.NLEFT) THEN
              NPTS=NMIN+1
          ELSE
```

```
                NPTS=NMIN
                       ENDIF
            DO 20 J=0,NPTS-1
                IF (IRPOS.EQ.I) THEN
                     WRITE(*,100)NP,OBJARR(FX,J),OBJARR(FY,J),OBJARR(FZ,J)
                     SUMX=SUMX+OBJARR(FX,J)
                     SUMY=SUMY+OBJARR(FY,J)
                     SUMZ=SUMZ+OBJARR(FZ,J)
                ENDIF
#ifndef SEQ
                IF (MOD(J,7).EQ.6) THEN
            FLUSH(STDOUT)
                ENDIF
                IF (MOD(NP,20).EQ.19) THEN
                     SINGLE(STDOUT)
                     CALL DWPAUS(0)
                     MULTIPLE(STDOUT)
                ENDIF
#else
            IF (MOD(NP,20).EQ.19) CALL DWPAUS(0)
#endif
            NP=NP+1
20          CONTINUE
#ifndef SEQ
            FLUSH(STDOUT)
#endif
10  CONTINUE
#ifndef SEQ
     SINGLE(STDOUT)
#endif
     IDUMMY=KCOMBI(SUMX,ADDBLE,DBLSIZ,1)
     IDUMMY=KCOMBI(SUMY,ADDBLE,DBLSIZ,1)
     IDUMMY=KCOMBI(SUMZ,ADDBLE,DBLSIZ,1)
     PRINT *,'         ---------      ---------      ---------'
     WRITE (*,101)SUMX,SUMY,SUMZ
#ifndef SEQ
     FLUSH(6)
#endif

     RETURN
100 FORMAT(1X,I4,3E15.5)
101 FORMAT(5X,3E15.5)
     END
C
CCCCCCCCCCCCCCCCCCCCCCCCCCCCCC END OF ROUTINE OUTFOR CCCCCCCCCCCCCCCCCCCCCCCCCCCCCC
C
     SUBROUTINE OUTPAR
```

```
      PARAMETER (MAX=50)
      DOUBLE PRECISION OBJARR(7,0:MAX-1),OBJCPY(7,0:MAX-1)
      COMMON /ARR/OBJARR,OBJCPY
      INTEGER X,Y,Z,FX,FY,FZ
      PARAMETER (X=1,Y=2,Z=3,MASS=4,FX=5,FY=6,FZ=7)
      COMMON /PROC/NPROC,IDOC,IPNUM
      COMMON /COMM/IRPOS,ICCLOK,ICLOCK
      COMMON /BLOCK/NLEFT,NMIN,NLOCAL,NTOTAL
      INTEGER STDOUT
      PARAMETER (STDOUT=6)


      PRINT *
      PRINT *
      PRINT *,'Number       x             y           z',
     #        '              mass'
#ifndef SEQ
      MULTIPLE(STDOUT)
#endif
      NP=1
      DO 10 I=0,NPROC-1
          IF (I.LT.NLEFT) THEN
              NPTS=NMIN+1
          ELSE
              NPTS=NMIN
          ENDIF
          DO 20 J=0,NPTS-1
              IF (IRPOS.EQ.I) THEN
          WRITE(*,100)NP,OBJARR(X,J),OBJARR(Y,J),OBJARR(Z,J),
     #                    OBJARR(MASS,J)
              ENDIF
#ifndef SEQ
              IF (MOD(J,7).EQ.6) THEN
                    FLUSH(STDOUT)
              ENDIF
              IF (MOD(NP,20).EQ.19) THEN
                    SINGLE(STDOUT)
                    CALL DWPAUS(0)
                    MULTIPLE(STDOUT)
              ENDIF
#else
              IF (MOD(NP,20).EQ.19) CALL DWPAUS(0)
#endif
              NP=NP+1
20        CONTINUE
#ifndef SEQ
          FLUSH(STDOUT)
#endif
```

```
10    CONTINUE
#ifndef SEQ
      SINGLE(STDOUT)
#endif

      RETURN
100   FORMAT(1X,I4,4E15.5)
      END
C
CCCCCCCCCCCCCCCCCCCCCCCCCCCCC END OF ROUTINE OUTPAR CCCCCCCCCCCCCCCCCCCCCCCCCCCCCC
C
      SUBROUTINE RANPAR
      PARAMETER (MAX=50)
      DOUBLE PRECISION OBJARR(7,0:MAX-1),OBJCPY(7,0:MAX-1)
      COMMON /ARR/OBJARR,OBJCPY
      INTEGER X,Y,Z,FX,FY,FZ
      PARAMETER (X=1,Y=2,Z=3,MASS=4,FX=5,FY=6,FZ=7)
      COMMON /BLOCK/NLEFT,NMIN,NLOCAL,NTOTAL
      DOUBLE PRECISION RANDS,RANDB

      DO 10 I=0,NLOCAL-1
          OBJARR(X,I)=RANDS()
          OBJARR(Y,I)=RANDS()
          OBJARR(Z,I)=RANDS()
          OBJARR(MASS,I)=RANDB()
          OBJARR(FX,I)=0.0
          OBJARR(FY,I)=0.0
          OBJARR(FY,I)=0.0
10    CONTINUE

      RETURN
      END
C
CCCCCCCCCCCCCCCCCCCCCCCCCCCCC END OF ROUTINE RANPAR CCCCCCCCCCCCCCCCCCCCCCCCCCCCCC
C
      SUBROUTINE PRSETB(ISEED,ISKIP,IORDER)
      COMMON /RAN/IRAND0,IRAND1,IAS0,IAS1,ICS0,ICS1,IAB0,IAB1,ICB0,ICB1
      SAVE /RAN/
      INTEGER ENV(5)
      PARAMETER (MULT0=20077,MULT1=16838,IADD0=12345,IADD1=0)
      PARAMETER (IPOW16=2**16)

      ISEED0=MOD(ISEED,IPOW16)
      ISEED1=ISEED/IPOW16
      CALL KPARAM(ENV)
      NPROC=ENV(3)
      IAB0=1
```

```
      IAB1=0
      ICB0=0
      ICB1=0
      DO 10 I=0,ISKIP*(NPROC-1)
          CALL LMULT(J0,J1,IAB0,IAB1,MULT0,MULT1)
          IAB0 = J0
          IAB1 = J1
          CALL LMULT(J0,J1,ICB0,ICB1,MULT0,MULT1)
          CALL LADD(ICB0,ICB1,J0,J1,IADD0,IADD1)
          IF (I.EQ.(ISKIP*IORDER)) THEN
              CALL LMULT(J0,J1,ISEED0,ISEED1,IAB0,IAB1)
              CALL LADD(IRAND0,IRAND1,J0,J1,ICB0,ICB1)
          ENDIF
10    CONTINUE
      IAS0=MULT0
      IAS1=MULT1
      ICS0=IADD0
      ICS1=IADD1

      RETURN
      END
C
CCCCCCCCCCCCCCCCCCCCCCCCCCCCCCCC END OF ROUTINE PRSETB CCCCCCCCCCCCCCCCCCCCCCCCCCCCCCCC
C
      DOUBLE PRECISION FUNCTION RANDB()
      COMMON /RAN/IRAND0,IRAND1,IAS0,IAS1,ICS0,ICS1,IAB0,IAB1,ICB0,ICB1
      DOUBLE PRECISION DIVFAC,POW16
      PARAMETER (DIVFAC=2.147483648D9,POW16=6.5536D4)

      RANDB=(DFLOAT(IRAND0)+POW16*DFLOAT(IRAND1))/DIVFAC
      CALL LMULT(J0,J1,IRAND0,IRAND1,IAB0,IAB1)
      CALL LADD(IRAND0,IRAND1,J0,J1,ICB0,ICB1)

      RETURN
      END
C
CCCCCCCCCCCCCCCCCCCCCCCCCCCCCCCCC END OF ROUTINE RANDB CCCCCCCCCCCCCCCCCCCCCCCCCCCCCCCCC
C
      DOUBLE PRECISION FUNCTION RANDS()
      COMMON /RAN/IRAND0,IRAND1,IAS0,IAS1,ICS0,ICS1,IAB0,IAB1,ICB0,ICB1
      DOUBLE PRECISION DIVFAC,POW16
      PARAMETER (DIVFAC=2.147483648D9,POW16=6.5536D4)

      RANDS=(DFLOAT(IRAND0)+POW16*DFLOAT(IRAND1))/DIVFAC
      CALL LMULT(J0,J1,IRAND0,IRAND1,IAS0,IAS1)
      CALL LADD(IRAND0,IRAND1,J0,J1,ICS0,ICS1)
```

```
      RETURN
      END
C
CCCCCCCCCCCCCCCCCCCCCCCCCCCCCC END OF ROUTINE RANDS CCCCCCCCCCCCCCCCCCCCCCCCCCCCCC
C
      SUBROUTINE LADD(I0,I1,J0,J1,K0,K1)
      PARAMETER (IPOW16=2**16,IPOW15=2**15)

      I0=MOD(K0+J0,IPOW16)
      I1=MOD((K0+J0)/IPOW16+K1+J1,IPOW15)

      RETURN
      END
C
CCCCCCCCCCCCCCCCCCCCCCCCCCCCCC END OF ROUTINE LADD CCCCCCCCCCCCCCCCCCCCCCCCCCCCCCC
C
      SUBROUTINE LMULT(I0,I1,J0,J1,K0,K1)
      PARAMETER (IPOW30=2**30,IPOW16=2**16,IPOW15=2**15)

      K = K0*J0
      IF(K.LT.0) K = (K+IPOW30)+IPOW30
      I0=MOD(K,IPOW16)
      L = K0*J1+K1*J0
      IF(L.LT.0) L = (L+IPOW30)+IPOW30
      K = K/IPOW16+L
      IF(K.LT.0) K = (K+IPOW30)+IPOW30
      I1=MOD(K,IPOW15)

      RETURN
      END
C
CCCCCCCCCCCCCCCCCCCCCCCCCCCCCC END OF ROUTINE LMULT CCCCCCCCCCCCCCCCCCCCCCCCCCCCCC
C
      SUBROUTINE DWPAUS(IDUMMY)
      CHARACTER*1 C

10    CONTINUE
      WRITE(*,100)
#ifndef SEQ
      FLUSH(6)
#endif
      READ(*,101)C
      IF(C.NE.'c'.AND.C.NE.'C') GOTO 10

      RETURN
100   FORMAT(/' <<<< Please enter c to continue >>>> ==> ')
101   FORMAT(A1)
```

```
      END
C
CCCCCCCCCCCCCCCCCCCCCCCCCCCC END OF ROUTINE DWPAUS CCCCCCCCCCCCCCCCCCCCCCCCCCCC
C
```

B-7 Matrix Multiplication

B-7.1 CUBIX Program

```
      PROGRAM MATRIX
      PARAMETER (NDIM=4,LBTE=4)
      REAL A(NDIM,NDIM),B(NDIM,NDIM),C(NDIM,NDIM)

      CALL SETELT()

      CALL INPUT(A,B)

      PRINT *, 'Beginning Matrix Multiplication'
      CALL MATMUL(A,B,C)
      PRINT *, 'MATMUL is done!'

      CALL VIEWMT(A,B,C)

      STOP
      END
C
CCCCCCCCCCCCCCCCCCCCCCCCCCCCCC END OF PROGRAM MATRIX CCCCCCCCCCCCCCCCCCCCCCCCCCCCCC
C
      SUBROUTINE SETELT()
      INTEGER  ENV(5),DOC,PROCNU,DIM(2),MYPOST(2)
      INTEGER  RCHN,LCHN,UCHN,DCHN
      COMMON /CUBE/ RCHN,LCHN,UCHN,DCHN,MX,MY,NPROCX

      CALL KPARAM(ENV)
      DOC = ENV(1)
      PROCNU=ENV(2)
      NPROC =ENV(3)

      DIM(1)=2**(DOC/2)
      DIM(2)=NPROC/DIM(1)
      NPROCX=DIM(2)
      N=NPROCX

      CALL KGRDIN(2,DIM)
      CALL KGRDCO(PROCNU,MYPOST)

      MX=MYPOST(2)
      MY=MYPOST(1)
      RCHN=KGRDCH(PROCNU,1, 1)
      LCHN=KGRDCH(PROCNU,1,-1)
      UCHN=KGRDCH(PROCNU,0,-1)
      DCHN=KGRDCH(PROCNU,0, 1)
```

```fortran
      RETURN
      END
C
CCCCCCCCCCCCCCCCCCCCCCCCCCCCCCC END OF ROUTINE SETELT CCCCCCCCCCCCCCCCCCCCCCCCCCCCCCC
C
      SUBROUTINE MATMUL(A,B,C)
      PARAMETER (NDIM=4,LBTE=4)
      REAL A(NDIM,NDIM),B(NDIM,NDIM),C(NDIM,NDIM),D(NDIM,NDIM)
      INTEGER RCHN,LCHN,UCHN,DCHN
      LOGICAL ISENT
      COMMON /CUBE/ RCHN,LCHN,UCHN,DCHN,MX,MY,NPROCX

      DO 10 KC=0,NPROCX-1
      CALL PIPEA(A,D,KC,ISENT)

      IF (ISENT) THEN
          DO 20 J=1,NDIM
              DO 20 I=1,NDIM
                  DO 20 K=1,NDIM
                      C(I,J)=A(I,K)*B(K,J)+C(I,J)
20                CONTINUE
      ELSE
          DO 21 J=1,NDIM
              DO 21 I=1,NDIM
                  DO 21 K=1,NDIM
                      C(I,J)=D(I,K)*B(K,J)+C(I,J)
21                CONTINUE
      ENDIF

      CALL ROLLB(B)

10    CONTINUE

      RETURN
      END
C
CCCCCCCCCCCCCCCCCCCCCCCCCCCCCCC END OF ROUTINE MATMUL CCCCCCCCCCCCCCCCCCCCCCCCCCCCCCC
C
      SUBROUTINE PIPEA(A,D,KC,ISENT)
      PARAMETER  (NDIM=4,LBTE=4)
      INTEGER RCHN,LCHN,UCHN,DCHN
      REAL    A(NDIM,NDIM),D(NDIM,NDIM)
      LOGICAL ISENT
      COMMON /CUBE/ RCHN,LCHN,UCHN,DCHN,MX,MY,NPROCX

      IC = MODPOS(MX-KC,NPROCX)
```

```
      IF (MY .EQ. IC) THEN
          IERR = KCWRIT(A,RCHN,NDIM**2*LBTE)
          ISENT= .TRUE.
      ELSE
          IRCHN=RCHN
          IF (MX .EQ. MODPOS(MY-1+KC,NPROCX)) IRCHN=0
          IERR = KCREAD(D,LCHN,IRCHN,NDIM**2*LBTE)
          ISENT= .FALSE.
      END IF

      RETURN
      END
C
CCCCCCCCCCCCCCCCCCCCCCCCCCCCCCCC END OF ROUTINE PIPEA CCCCCCCCCCCCCCCCCCCCCCCCCCCCCCCC
C
      FUNCTION MODPOS(N,NPROCX)
      MODPOS=MOD(N,NPROCX)
      IF (N .LT. 0) MODPOS=MOD(N+NPROCX,NPROCX)
      RETURN
      END
C
CCCCCCCCCCCCCCCCCCCCCCCCCCCCCCCC END OF ROUTINE MODPOS CCCCCCCCCCCCCCCCCCCCCCCCCCCCCCCC
C
      SUBROUTINE ROLLB(B)
      PARAMETER  (NDIM=4,LBTE=4)
      INTEGER  RCHN,LCHN,UCHN,DCHN
      REAL     B(NDIM,NDIM)
      COMMON /CUBE/ RCHN,LCHN,UCHN,DCHN,MX,MY,NPROCX

      IERR=KCSHIF(B,DCHN,NDIM**2*LBTE,B,UCHN,NDIM**2*LBTE)

      RETURN
      END
C
CCCCCCCCCCCCCCCCCCCCCCCCCCCCCCCC END OF ROUTINE ROLLB CCCCCCCCCCCCCCCCCCCCCCCCCCCCCCCC
C
      SUBROUTINE INPUT(A,B)
      PARAMETER (NDIM=4,LBTE=4)
      CHARACTER MSG
      REAL     A(NDIM,NDIM),B(NDIM,NDIM)
      INTEGER  RCHN,LCHN,UCHN,DCHN,ENV(5),DOC
      COMMON /CUBE/ RCHN,LCHN,UCHN,DCHN,MX,MY,NPROCX

      PRINT *, ' '
      PRINT *, 'Select [D - demo], [F - file "INPUT.A and INPUT.B"]'
      READ(*,100) MSG
```

```
      IF ((MSG .NE. 'F') .AND. (MSG .NE. 'f')) THEN
         IC = MY*NDIM
         DO 10 I=1, NDIM
            IC = IC+1
            JC = MX*NDIM
            DO 10 J=1, NDIM
               JC = JC+1
               A(I,J)=IC*JC
               B(I,J)=A(I,J)
10             CONTINUE
      ELSE

C     This is the simplest input method and also the slowest one.
C     In order to speed up, you may prefer multiple read mode,
C     where each processor reads chunks of data in procnum order.

         OPEN(UNIT=8,FILE='INPUT.A',STATUS='OLD')
         OPEN(UNIT=9,FILE='INPUT.B',STATUS='OLD')

         CALL KPARAM(ENV)
         DOC = ENV(1)
         NMAX= 2**(DOC/2)

         DO 20 I=0,NDIM*NMAX-1
            IC = MOD(I,NDIM)+1
            DO 20 J=0,NDIM*NMAX-1
               READ(8,*) X
               READ(9,*) Y
               IF ((I/NDIM.EQ.MY) .AND. (J/NDIM.EQ.MX)) THEN
                  JC = MOD(J,NDIM)+1
                  A(IC,JC) = X
                  B(IC,JC) = Y
               ENDIF
20             CONTINUE

         CLOSE(8)
         CLOSE(9)

      ENDIF

      RETURN
100   FORMAT(A)
      END
C
CCCCCCCCCCCCCCCCCCCCCCCCCCCCCCCCC END OF ROUTINE INPUT CCCCCCCCCCCCCCCCCCCCCCCCCCCCCCCC
C
      SUBROUTINE VIEWMT(A,B,C)
```

```
      PARAMETER (NDIM=4,LBTE=4)
      CHARACTER MSG
      REAL A(NDIM,NDIM),B(NDIM,NDIM),C(NDIM,NDIM)

30    CONTINUE
      PRINT *, ' '
      PRINT *, 'Which matrix to view? A or B or C, else exit'
      READ(*,100) MSG
      IF ((MSG .EQ. 'A') .OR. (MSG .EQ. 'a')) THEN
          CALL OUTPUT(A)
      ELSEIF ((MSG .EQ. 'B') .OR. (MSG .EQ. 'b')) THEN
          CALL OUTPUT(B)
      ELSEIF ((MSG .EQ. 'C') .OR. (MSG .EQ. 'c')) THEN
          CALL OUTPUT(C)
      ELSE
          GOTO 99
      ENDIF
      GOTO 30

99    RETURN
100   FORMAT(A)
      END
C
CCCCCCCCCCCCCCCCCCCCCCCCCCCCCC END OF ROUTINE VIEWMT CCCCCCCCCCCCCCCCCCCCCCCCCCCCCC
C
      SUBROUTINE OUTPUT(C)
      PARAMETER (NDIM=4,LBTE=4)
      REAL     C(NDIM,NDIM)
      INTEGER  RCHN,LCHN,UCHN,DCHN
      COMMON /CUBE/ RCHN,LCHN,UCHN,DCHN,MX,MY,NPROCX

5     CONTINUE
      PRINT *, ' '
      PRINT *, '        Give X - Y coordinates of the subblock'
      PRINT *, '            Negative # breaks the loop'
      READ *, IX, IY
      PRINT *, ' '
      IF ((IX .LE. 0) .OR. (IY .LE. 0)) GOTO 99
      IX = IX-1
      IY = IY-1
#ifndef SEQ
      MULTIPLE(6)
#endif

      IF ((MX .EQ. IX) .AND. (MY .EQ. IY)) THEN
          DO 10 I=1,NDIM
              WRITE(6,100) (C(I,J), J=1,NDIM)
```

```
10          CONTINUE
      ENDIF

#ifndef SEQ
      FLUSH(6)
      SINGLE(6)
#endif
      GOTO 5

99    RETURN
100   FORMAT(4 F12.2)
      END
C
CCCCCCCCCCCCCCCCCCCCCCCCCCCCCC END OF ROUTINE OUTPUT CCCCCCCCCCCCCCCCCCCCCCCCCCCCCC
C
```

B-8 Fast Fourier Transforms

B-8.1 CUBIX Program

```
      PROGRAM FFT
      PARAMETER (MAX=512)
      COMMON /PROC/NPROC,IDOC,IPNUM
      COMMON /INFO/ICMPSZ,IGLBST,NLOCAL,IP,IQ,IQMINP
      COMPLEX CDATA(0:MAX-1)
      INTEGER GLBREV

      ICMPSZ=8

      CALL WELCOM
      CALL GPARAM
10    CALL GETJOB(JOB)
      IF (JOB.NE.5) THEN
          IF (JOB.EQ.1) THEN
              NPTS=INITLZ(CDATA)
          ELSE IF (JOB.EQ.2) THEN
              CALL FFT3(NPTS,CDATA)
          ELSE IF (JOB.EQ.3) THEN
              IDUMMY=GLBREV(CDATA,NPTS,ICMPSZ,NPROC-1,IDOC)
              CALL INVLCL(CDATA,NPTS)
          ELSE IF (JOB.EQ.4) THEN
              CALL OUTRES(CDATA,NPTS)
          ENDIF
          GOTO 10
      ENDIF

      STOP
      END
C
CCCCCCCCCCCCCCCCCCCCCCCCCCCCCCCCC END OF PROGRAM FFT CCCCCCCCCCCCCCCCCCCCCCCCCCCCCCCCC
C
      SUBROUTINE GPARAM
      COMMON /PROC/NPROC,IDOC,IPNUM
      INTEGER ENV(5)

      CALL KPARAM(ENV)
      IDOC=ENV(1)
      IPNUM=ENV(2)
      NPROC=ENV(3)

      RETURN
      END
C
```

```
CCCCCCCCCCCCCCCCCCCCCCCCCCCCCC END OF ROUTINE GPARAM CCCCCCCCCCCCCCCCCCCCCCCCCCCCCC
C
      SUBROUTINE WELCOM
      INTEGER STDOUT
      PARAMETER (STDOUT=6)

#ifndef SEQ
      BUFFER(UNIT=STDOUT,SIZE=2048)
#endif
      PRINT *
      PRINT *,'****************************************************'
      PRINT *,'*                                                  *'
      PRINT *,'*       Welcome to the fft example program.        *'
      PRINT *,'*                                                  *'
      PRINT *,'*       This program uses the iterative algorithm  *'
      PRINT *,'*                                                  *'
      PRINT *,'****************************************************'
      PRINT *
#ifndef SEQ
      flush(6)
#endif

      RETURN
      END
C
CCCCCCCCCCCCCCCCCCCCCCCCCCCCCC END OF ROUTINE WELCOM CCCCCCCCCCCCCCCCCCCCCCCCCCCCCC
C
      SUBROUTINE GETJOB(JOB)

      PRINT *
      PRINT *
      PRINT *,'Please select one of the following :'
      PRINT *,'  1..to set up data to be transformed'
      PRINT *,'  2..to find the FFT using the iterative algorithm'
      PRINT *,'  3..to send data to bit-reversed positions'
      PRINT *,'  4..to output the data array'
      PRINT *,'  5..to terminate the program'
#ifndef SEQ
      flush(6)
#endif
      READ *,JOB

      RETURN
      END
C
CCCCCCCCCCCCCCCCCCCCCCCCCCCCCC END OF ROUTINE GETJOB CCCCCCCCCCCCCCCCCCCCCCCCCCCCCC
C
```

```
      SUBROUTINE FFT3(M,X)
      PARAMETER (MAX=512)
      COMMON /INFO/ICMPSZ,IGLBST,NLOCAL,IP,IQ,IQMINP
      COMPLEX X(0:MAX-1)

      INCREM=M/2
      NX=2
      DO 10 IBIT=(IP+IQ-1),0,-1
          IF (IBIT.GE.IQ) THEN
              DO 20 I=0,NLOCAL-1
                  CALL FFTCOM(NX,X(I))
20                CONTINUE
          ELSE
              DO 30 I=0,INCREM-1
                  CALL FFTC2(NX,INCREM,X,I)
30                CONTINUE
          ENDIF
          NX=NX*2
          INCREM=INCREM/2
10        CONTINUE

      RETURN
      END
C
CCCCCCCCCCCCCCCCCCCCCCCCCCCCCCC END OF ROUTINE FFT3 CCCCCCCCCCCCCCCCCCCCCCCCCCCCCCC
C
      SUBROUTINE FFTC2(NX,INCREM,Y,INDX)
      PARAMETER (MAX=512)
      COMMON /PROC/NPROC,IDOC,IPNUM
      COMPLEX Y(0:MAX-1)
      INTEGER PAIRLC,EVNPTR,ODDPTR
      COMPLEX VALODD,VALEVN,CEXPON,TERM2
      PARAMETER (PI=3.1415927)

      EVNPTR=INDX
      ODDPTR=INDX+INCREM
      MINLOC=IPNUM*NX/(2*NPROC)
      MAXLOC=MINLOC+NX/(2*NPROC)
      DO 10 PAIRLC=MINLOC,MAXLOC-1
          VALODD=Y(ODDPTR)
          VALEVN=Y(EVNPTR)
          CALL PERMUT(PAIRLC,NX/2,INDEX)
          FAC=2.0*PI*INDEX/NX
          V1=COS(FAC)
          V2=SIN(FAC)
          CEXPON=CMPLX(V1,V2)
          TERM2=CEXPON*VALODD
```

```
        Y(ODDPTR)=VALEVN-TERM2
        Y(EVNPTR)=VALEVN+TERM2
        EVNPTR=EVNPTR+2*INCREM
        ODDPTR=ODDPTR+2*INCREM
10      CONTINUE

    RETURN
    END
C
CCCCCCCCCCCCCCCCCCCCCCCCCCCCCC END OF ROUTINE FFTC2 CCCCCCCCCCCCCCCCCCCCCCCCCCCCCC
C
    SUBROUTINE FFTCOM(NX,Y)
    PARAMETER (MAX=512)
    COMMON /PROC/NPROC,IDOC,IPNUM
    COMMON /INFO/ICMPSZ,IGLBST,NLOCAL,IP,IQ,IQMINP
    COMPLEX Y
    INTEGER PINCRE,PAIRLC
    COMPLEX CVAL,CEXPON,TERM2
    PARAMETER (PI=3.1415927)

    PINCRE=NPROC/NX
    LOCATN=IPNUM/PINCRE
    LISODD=JAND(LOCATN,1)
    PAIRLC=LOCATN/2
    CALL KCSHIF(CVAL,PINCRE,ICMPSZ,Y,PINCRE,ICMPSZ)
    CALL PERMUT(PAIRLC,NX/2,INDEX)
    FAC=2.0*PI*INDEX/NX
    V1=COS(FAC)
    V2=SIN(FAC)
    CEXPON=CMPLX(V1,V2)
    IF (LISODD.NE.0) THEN
        TERM2=CEXPON*Y
        Y=CVAL-TERM2
    ELSE
        TERM2=CEXPON*CVAL
        Y=Y+TERM2
    ENDIF

    RETURN
    END
C
CCCCCCCCCCCCCCCCCCCCCCCCCCCCCC END OF ROUTINE FFTCOM CCCCCCCCCCCCCCCCCCCCCCCCCCCCCC
C
    SUBROUTINE GETINP(X,NX)
    COMMON /INFO/ICMPSZ,IGLBST,NLOCAL,IP,IQ,IQMINP
    PARAMETER (MAX=512)
    COMPLEX X(0:MAX-1)
```

```
10    CONTINUE
      PRINT *
      PRINT *
      PRINT *,'Please select data to be transformed:'
      PRINT *,'  1..top-hat function'
      PRINT *,'  2..ramp function'
      PRINT *,'  3..triangle function'
#ifndef SEQ
      flush(6)
#endif
      READ *,IOPT
      IF (IOPT.EQ.1) THEN
          CALL TOPHAT(X,NX)
      ELSEIF (IOPT.EQ.2) THEN
          CALL RAMP(X,NX)
      ELSEIF (IOPT.EQ.3) THEN
          CALL TRIANG(X,NX)
      ELSE
          GOTO 10
      ENDIF

      RETURN
      END
C
CCCCCCCCCCCCCCCCCCCCCCCCCCCCCCC END OF ROUTINE GETINP CCCCCCCCCCCCCCCCCCCCCCCCCCCCCCC
C
      FUNCTION INITLZ(X)
      PARAMETER (MAX=512)
      COMMON /PROC/NPROC,IDOC,IPNUM
      COMMON /INFO/ICMPSZ,IGLBST,NLOCAL,IP,IQ,IQMINP
      COMPLEX X(0:MAX-1)

10    CONTINUE
      PRINT *
      PRINT *
      PRINT *,'Please give the number of data points.'
#ifndef SEQ
      flush(6)
#endif
      READ *,NUMPTS
      NLOCAL=NUMPTS/NPROC
      IF (NLOCAL.LT.1.OR.NLOCAL.GT.MAX) THEN
          PRINT *
          PRINT *,'*** Invalid input - try again ***'
          GOTO 10
      ENDIF
```

```
      IP=LOG2(NPROC)
      IQ=LOG2(NLOCAL)
      IQMINP=IQ-IP
      IGLBST=IPNUM*NLOCAL
      CALL GETINP(X,NUMPTS)
      INITLZ=NUMPTS

      RETURN
      END
C
CCCCCCCCCCCCCCCCCCCCCCCCCCCCCC END OF ROUTINE INITLZ CCCCCCCCCCCCCCCCCCCCCCCCCCCCCC
C
      FUNCTION LOG2(ISAVE)

      N=ISAVE
      NUMBER=0
10    IF (N.GT.1) THEN
            NUMBER=NUMBER+1
            N=N/2
            GOTO 10
      ENDIF
      LOG2=NUMBER

      RETURN
      END
C
CCCCCCCCCCCCCCCCCCCCCCCCCCCCCC END OF ROUTINE LOG2 CCCCCCCCCCCCCCCCCCCCCCCCCCCCCC
C
      SUBROUTINE INVLCL(X,NX)
      PARAMETER (MAX=512)
      COMMON /PROC/NPROC,IDOC,IPNUM
      COMMON /INFO/ICMPSZ,IGLBST,NLOCAL,IP,IQ,IQMINP
      COMPLEX X(0:MAX-1)
      COMPLEX TEMPX
      INTEGER GLOBLR,GLOBLI,SWAPI,BLOCKI,OTHERI

      CALL PERMUT(IPNUM,NPROC,LOFFST)
      DO 10 LOCALI=0,NLOCAL-1
          BLOCKI=MOD(LOCALI,NPROC)
          OTHERI=LOFFST+NPROC*(LOCALI/NPROC)
          CALL PERMUT(BLOCKI,NPROC,NUMBER)
          GLOBLI=NLOCAL*NUMBER+OTHERI
          CALL PERMUT(GLOBLI,NX,GLOBLR)
          SWAPI=MOD(GLOBLR,NLOCAL)
          IF (SWAPI.GT.LOCALI) THEN
                TEMPX=X(LOCALI)
                X(LOCALI)=X(SWAPI)
```

```
                X(SWAPI)=TEMPX
            ENDIF
10          CONTINUE

     RETURN
     END
C
CCCCCCCCCCCCCCCCCCCCCCCCCCCCCC END OF ROUTINE INVLCL CCCCCCCCCCCCCCCCCCCCCCCCCCCC
C
     INTEGER FUNCTION GLBREV(X,NX,NBYTES,ICBMSK,ICBDIM)
     LOGICAL ISODD
     PARAMETER (MAX=512)
     COMMON /PROC/NPROC,IDOC,IPNUM
     COMPLEX X(0:MAX-1)

     GLBREV=0
     NITEMS=(NX/NPROC)/NPROC
     IOFFST=NPROC*NBYTES
     DO 20 IROUTE=0,NPROC-1
         CALL PERMUT(JEOR(IROUTE,IPNUM),NPROC,LOFFST)
         DO 30 I=0,IDOC-1
             K = 2**I
             IF (ISODD(IROUTE/K)) THEN
                 CALL KVSHIF(X(LOFFST),K,NBYTES,IOFFST,NITEMS,
     #                              X(LOFFST),K,NBYTES,IOFFST,NITEMS)
             ENDIF
30          CONTINUE
20       CONTINUE

     RETURN
     END
C
CCCCCCCCCCCCCCCCCCCCCCCCCCCCCC END OF ROUTINE GLBREV CCCCCCCCCCCCCCCCCCCCCCCCCCCC
C
     SUBROUTINE OUTRES(X,NX)
     PARAMETER (MAX=512)
     COMMON /PROC/NPROC,IDOC,IPNUM
     COMMON /INFO/ICMPSZ,IGLBST,NLOCAL,IP,IQ,IQMINP
     COMPLEX X(0:MAX-1)
     INTEGER STDOUT
     PARAMETER (STDOUT=6)

     PRINT *
     PRINT *
#ifndef SEQ
     MULTIPLE(STDOUT)
#endif
```

```
          K = 0
          DO 10 I=0,NPROC-1
              DO 20 J=0,NLOCAL-1
                  IF (IPNUM.EQ.I) THEN
                      WRITE(*,100)X(J)
                      IF (MOD(K,3).EQ.2) THEN
                          WRITE(*,101)
                      ENDIF
                  ENDIF
                  IF(MOD(K,60).EQ.59) THEN
#ifndef SEQ
                      SINGLE(STDOUT)
#endif
                      CALL DWPAUS(0)
#ifndef SEQ
                      MULTIPLE(STDOUT)
#endif
                  ENDIF
                  K = K+1
20        CONTINUE
#ifndef SEQ
          FLUSH(STDOUT)
#endif
10        CONTINUE
#ifndef SEQ
      SINGLE(STDOUT)
#endif

      RETURN
#ifndef XENIX
100   FORMAT('(',E11.4,',',E11.4,') '$)
#else
100   FORMAT('(',E11.4,',',E11.4,') '\)
#endif
101   FORMAT(' ')
      END
C
CCCCCCCCCCCCCCCCCCCCCCCCCCCCCC END OF ROUTINE OUTRES CCCCCCCCCCCCCCCCCCCCCCCCCCCCCCCC
C
      SUBROUTINE RAMP(X,NX)
      PARAMETER (MAX=512)
      COMMON /INFO/ICMPSZ,IGLBST,NLOCAL,IP,IQ,IQMINP
      COMPLEX X(0:MAX-1)

      SLOPE=1.0/(NX-1)
      J=IGLBST
      DO 10 I=0,NLOCAL-1
```

```
             V=J*SLOPE
             X(I)=CMPLX(V,0.0)
             J=J+1
10           CONTINUE

      RETURN
      END
C
CCCCCCCCCCCCCCCCCCCCCCCCCCCCCCC END OF ROUTINE RAMP CCCCCCCCCCCCCCCCCCCCCCCCCCCCCCC
C
      SUBROUTINE TOPHAT(X,NX)
      PARAMETER (MAX=512)
      COMMON /INFO/ICMPSZ,IGLBST,NLOCAL,IP,IQ,IQMINP
      COMPLEX X(0:MAX-1)

      NLOW=NX/4
      NHIGH=3*NLOW
      J=IGLBST
      DO 10 I=0,NLOCAL-1
          IF (J.GE.NLOW.AND.J.LT.NHIGH) THEN
              X(I)=(1.0,0.0)
          ELSE
              X(I)=(0.0,0.0)
          ENDIF
          J=J+1
10        CONTINUE

      RETURN
      END
C
CCCCCCCCCCCCCCCCCCCCCCCCCCCCCCC END OF ROUTINE TOPHAT CCCCCCCCCCCCCCCCCCCCCCCCCCCCCCC
C
      SUBROUTINE TRIANG(X,NX)
      PARAMETER (MAX=512)
      COMMON /INFO/ICMPSZ,IGLBST,NLOCAL,IP,IQ,IQMINP
      COMPLEX X(0:MAX-1)

      NHALF=NX/2
      SLOPE=2.0/(NX-1)
      J=IGLBST
      DO 10 I=0,NLOCAL-1
          IF (J.GE.NHALF) THEN
              V=(NX-1-J)*SLOPE
          ELSE
              V=J*SLOPE
          ENDIF
          X(I)=CMPLX(V,0.0)
```

```
        J=J+1
10      CONTINUE

     RETURN
     END
C
CCCCCCCCCCCCCCCCCCCCCCCCCCCCC END OF ROUTINE TRIANG CCCCCCCCCCCCCCCCCCCCCCCCCCCCCCC
C
     SUBROUTINE PERMUT(L,M,IPERM)
     LOGICAL ISODD

     NBITS = LOG2(M)
     K     = L
     IPOW  = M/2
     IPERM = 0
     DO 10 I=1,NBITS
         IF (ISODD(K)) IPERM = IPERM+IPOW
         IPOW = IPOW/2
10       K     = K/2

     RETURN
     END
C
CCCCCCCCCCCCCCCCCCCCCCCCCCCCC END OF ROUTINE PERMUT CCCCCCCCCCCCCCCCCCCCCCCCCCCCCCC
C
     LOGICAL FUNCTION ISODD(I)

     IF(2*(I/2).EQ.I) THEN
         ISODD = .FALSE.
     ELSE
         ISODD = .TRUE.
     ENDIF

     RETURN
     END
C
CCCCCCCCCCCCCCCCCCCCCCCCCCCCCC END OF ROUTINE ISODD CCCCCCCCCCCCCCCCCCCCCCCCCCCCCCC
C
     SUBROUTINE DWPAUS(IDUMMY)
     CHARACTER*1 C

10   CONTINUE
     WRITE(*,100)
#ifndef SEQ
     FLUSH(6)
#endif
     READ(*,101)C
```

```
      IF(C.NE.'c'.AND.C.NE.'C') GOTO 10

      RETURN
#ifndef XENIX
100   FORMAT(/' <<<< Please enter c to continue >>>> ==> '$)
#else
100   FORMAT(/' <<<< Please enter c to continue >>>> ==> '\)
#endif
101   FORMAT(A1)
      END
C
CCCCCCCCCCCCCCCCCCCCCCCCCCCCC END OF ROUTINE DWPAUS CCCCCCCCCCCCCCCCCCCCCCCCCCCCC
C
      FUNCTION JAND(N,M)
      LOGICAL ISODD

      K = N
      L = M
      JAND = 0
      IPOW = 1
10    IF (K.GT.0.AND.L.GT.0) THEN
          IF (ISODD(K).AND.ISODD(L)) JAND = JAND+IPOW
          K = K/2
          L = L/2
          IPOW = 2*IPOW
          GOTO 10
      ENDIF

      RETURN
      END
C
CCCCCCCCCCCCCCCCCCCCCCCCCCCCCCC END OF ROUTINE JAND CCCCCCCCCCCCCCCCCCCCCCCCCCCCCC
C
      FUNCTION JIOR(N,M)
      LOGICAL ISODD

      K = N
      L = M
      JIOR = 0
      IPOW = 1
10    IF (K.GT.0.OR.L.GT.0) THEN
          IF (ISODD(K).OR.ISODD(L)) JIOR = JIOR+IPOW
          K = K/2
          L = L/2
          IPOW = 2*IPOW
          GOTO 10
      ENDIF
```

```
      RETURN
      END
C
CCCCCCCCCCCCCCCCCCCCCCCCCCCCCCC END OF ROUTINE JIOR CCCCCCCCCCCCCCCCCCCCCCCCCCCCCCC
C
      FUNCTION JEOR(N,M)
      LOGICAL ISODD,LK,LL

      K = N
      L = M
      JEOR = 0
      IPOW = 1
10    IF (K.GT.0.OR.L.GT.0) THEN
          LL = ISODD(L)
          LK = ISODD(K)
          IF((LK.AND.(.NOT.LL)).OR.((.NOT.LK).AND.LL)) JEOR=JEOR+IPOW
          K = K/2
          L = L/2
          IPOW = 2*IPOW
          GOTO 10
      ENDIF

      RETURN
      END
C
CCCCCCCCCCCCCCCCCCCCCCCCCCCCCCC END OF ROUTINE JEOR CCCCCCCCCCCCCCCCCCCCCCCCCCCCCCC
C
```

B-9 The Generation of Random Numbers

B-9.1 CUBIX Program

```
      PROGRAM RANDOM
      COMMON /PROC/NPROC,IDOC,IPNUM
      INTEGER GETJOB

      CALL WELCOM
      CALL GPARAM
10    JOB=GETJOB()
      IF (JOB.NE.4) THEN
          IF (JOB.EQ.1) THEN
          CALL LSTNOS
          ELSE IF (JOB.EQ.2) THEN
          CALL MCINTG
          ELSE IF (JOB.EQ.3) THEN
          CALL FINDPI
          ENDIF
          GOTO 10
      ENDIF

      STOP
      END
C
CCCCCCCCCCCCCCCCCCCCCCCCCCCCCC END OF PROGRAM RANDOM CCCCCCCCCCCCCCCCCCCCCCCCCCCCCC
C
      SUBROUTINE GPARAM
      COMMON /PROC/NPROC,IDOC,IPNUM
      INTEGER ENV(5)

      CALL KPARAM(ENV)
      IDOC=ENV(1)
      IPNUM=ENV(2)
      NPROC=ENV(3)

      RETURN
      END
C
CCCCCCCCCCCCCCCCCCCCCCCCCCCCCC END OF ROUTINE GPARAM CCCCCCCCCCCCCCCCCCCCCCCCCCCCCC
C
      SUBROUTINE WELCOM
      INTEGER STDOUT
      PARAMETER (STDOUT=6)

#ifndef SEQ
      BUFFER(UNIT=STDOUT,SIZE=4096)
```

```
#endif
      PRINT *
      PRINT *,'*********************************************************'
      PRINT *,'*                                                       *'
      PRINT *,'*        Welcome to the random numbers program.         *'
      PRINT *,'*                                                       *'
      PRINT *,'*        This program allows the user to list a set     *'
      PRINT *,'*        of random numbers, and to evaluate an          *'
      PRINT *,'*        integral and PI using Monte Carlo methods.     *'
      PRINT *,'*                                                       *'
      PRINT *,'*********************************************************'
      PRINT *

      RETURN
      END
C
CCCCCCCCCCCCCCCCCCCCCCCCCCCCCCC END OF ROUTINE WELCOM CCCCCCCCCCCCCCCCCCCCCCCCCCCCCCC
C
      INTEGER FUNCTION GETJOB()

      PRINT *
      PRINT *
      PRINT *,'Please select one of the following :'
      PRINT *,'  1..to list a set of random numbers'
      PRINT *,'  2..to evaluate a Monte-Carlo integral'
      PRINT *,'  3..to evaluate PI by a Monte-Carlo method'
      PRINT *,'  4..to terminate the program'
#ifndef SEQ
      FLUSH(6)
#endif
      READ *,JOB
      GETJOB=JOB

      RETURN
      END
C
CCCCCCCCCCCCCCCCCCCCCCCCCCCCCCC END OF ROUTINE GETJOB CCCCCCCCCCCCCCCCCCCCCCCCCCCCCCC
C
      SUBROUTINE FINDPI
      COMMON /PROC/NPROC,IDOC,IPNUM
      INTEGER STDOUT,ADDBLE,DBLSIZ
      PARAMETER (STDOUT=6,DBLSIZ=8)
      EXTERNAL ADDBLE
      DOUBLE PRECISION X,Y,PI,SCORE,RDOUB,RANDS,RANDB

      CALL INITRN(2)
      PRINT *
```

```
      PRINT *,'Please give the number of trials per processor.'
#ifndef SEQ
      FLUSH(STDOUT)
#endif
      READ *,ITRIAL
      PRINT *
      SCORE=0.0
      DO 10 I=0,ITRIAL-1
          RDOUB=RANDS()
          X=2.0*RDOUB-1.0
          RDOUB=RANDB()
          Y=2.0*RDOUB-1.0
          IF (X*X+Y*Y.LT.1.0) SCORE=SCORE+1.0
10        CONTINUE
      PI=4.0*SCORE/DFLOAT(ITRIAL*NPROC)
      CALL KCOMBI(PI,ADDBLE,DBLSIZ,1)
#ifndef SEQ
      MULTIPLE(STDOUT)
#endif
      IF (IPNUM.EQ.0) THEN
          WRITE(*,100)NPROC*ITRIAL,PI
      ENDIF
#ifndef SEQ
      SINGLE(STDOUT)
#endif

      RETURN
100 FORMAT('After ',I4,' trials the value of PI is ',F10.8)
      END
C
CCCCCCCCCCCCCCCCCCCCCCCCCCCCCCC END OF ROUTINE FINDPI CCCCCCCCCCCCCCCCCCCCCCCCCCCCCCC
C
      INTEGER FUNCTION ADDBLE(D1,D2,ISIZE)
      DOUBLE PRECISION D1,D2

      D1=D1+D2
      ADDBLE=0

      RETURN
      END
C
CCCCCCCCCCCCCCCCCCCCCCCCCCCCCCC END OF ROUTINE ADDBLE CCCCCCCCCCCCCCCCCCCCCCCCCCCCCCC
C
      SUBROUTINE INITRN(ISKIP)
      COMMON /PROC/NPROC,IDOC,IPNUM
      INTEGER STDOUT
      PARAMETER (STDOUT=6)
```

```
      PRINT *
      PRINT *
      PRINT *,'Please give an integer seed.'
#ifndef SEQ
      FLUSH(STDOUT)
#endif
      READ *,ISEED
      CALL PRSETB(ISEED,ISKIP,IPNUM)

      RETURN
      END
C
CCCCCCCCCCCCCCCCCCCCCCCCCCCCCCC END OF ROUTINE INITRN CCCCCCCCCCCCCCCCCCCCCCCCCCCCCCC
C
      SUBROUTINE LSTNOS
      COMMON /RAN/IRAND0,IRAND1,IAS0,IAS1,ICS0,ICS1,IAB0,IAB1,ICB0,ICB1
      SAVE /RAN/
      COMMON /PROC/NPROC,IDOC,IPNUM
      DOUBLE PRECISION RANDB
      INTEGER STDOUT
      PARAMETER (STDOUT=6)

      CALL INITRN(1)
      PRINT *
      PRINT *,'Please give the number of random points to list.'
#ifndef SEQ
      FLUSH(STDOUT)
#endif
      READ *,NPTS
      PRINT *
      NLOCAL=NPTS/NPROC
      NLEFT=MOD(NPTS,NPROC)
      NMAX=NLOCAL+1
      IF (IPNUM.LT.NLEFT) NLOCAL=NMAX
#ifndef SEQ
      MULTIPLE(STDOUT)
#endif
      J = IPNUM
      DO 10 I=0,NMAX-1
          IF(I.LT.NLOCAL) THEN
              WRITE(*,100)RANDB()
              IF (MOD(J,10).EQ.9) THEN
          WRITE(*,101)
              ENDIF
          ENDIF
#ifndef SEQ
```

```
          FLUSH(STDOUT)
#endif
          J = J+NPROC
10        CONTINUE
#ifndef SEQ
     SINGLE(STDOUT)
#endif

     RETURN
#ifndef XENIX
100 FORMAT(F7.4$)
#else
100 FORMAT(F7.4\)
#endif
101 FORMAT(' ')
     END
C
CCCCCCCCCCCCCCCCCCCCCCCCCCCCCC END OF ROUTINE LISNOS CCCCCCCCCCCCCCCCCCCCCCCCCCCCCC
C
     SUBROUTINE MCINTG
     COMMON /PROC/NPROC,IDOC,IPNUM
     INTEGER STDOUT,ADDBLE,DBLSIZ
     PARAMETER (STDOUT=6,DBLSIZ=8)
     EXTERNAL ADDBLE
     DOUBLE PRECISION INTEGR,SCORE,RDOUB,RANDB

     CALL INITRN(1)
     PRINT *
     PRINT *,'Please give the number of trials per processor.'
#ifndef SEQ
     FLUSH(STDOUT)
#endif
     READ *,ITRIAL
     PRINT *
     SCORE=0.0
     DO 10 I=0,ITRIAL-1
         RDOUB=RANDB()
         SCORE=SCORE+RDOUB*RDOUB
10        CONTINUE
     INTEGR=SCORE/DFLOAT(NPROC*ITRIAL)
     CALL KCOMBI(INTEGR,ADDBLE,DBLSIZ,1)
#ifndef SEQ
     MULTIPLE(STDOUT)
#endif
     IF (IPNUM.EQ.0) THEN
         WRITE(*,100)NPROC*ITRIAL,INTEGR
     ENDIF
```

```
#ifndef SEQ
      SINGLE(STDOUT)
#endif

      RETURN
100   FORMAT('After ',I4,' trials the integeral is ',F10.8)
      END
C
CCCCCCCCCCCCCCCCCCCCCCCCCCCCCCCC END OF ROUTINE MCINTG CCCCCCCCCCCCCCCCCCCCCCCCCCCCCCCC
C
      SUBROUTINE PRSETB(ISEED,ISKIP,IORDER)
      COMMON /RAN/IRAND0,IRAND1,IAS0,IAS1,ICS0,ICS1,IAB0,IAB1,ICB0,ICB1
      SAVE /RAN/

      INTEGER ENV(5)
      PARAMETER (MULT0=20077,MULT1=16838,IADD0=12345,IADD1=0)
      PARAMETER (IPOW16=2**16)

      ISEED0=MOD(ISEED,IPOW16)
      ISEED1=ISEED/IPOW16
      CALL KPARAM(ENV)
      NPROC=ENV(3)
      IAB0=1
      IAB1=0
      ICB0=0
      ICB1=0
      DO 10 I=0,ISKIP*(NPROC-1)
          CALL LMULT(J0,J1,IAB0,IAB1,MULT0,MULT1)
          IAB0 = J0
          IAB1 = J1
          CALL LMULT(J0,J1,ICB0,ICB1,MULT0,MULT1)
          CALL LADD(ICB0,ICB1,J0,J1,IADD0,IADD1)
          IF (I.EQ.(ISKIP*IORDER)) THEN
              CALL LMULT(J0,J1,ISEED0,ISEED1,IAB0,IAB1)
              CALL LADD(IRAND0,IRAND1,J0,J1,ICB0,ICB1)
          ENDIF
10        CONTINUE
      IAS0=MULT0
      IAS1=MULT1
      ICS0=IADD0
      ICS1=IADD1

      RETURN
      END
C
CCCCCCCCCCCCCCCCCCCCCCCCCCCCCCCC END OF ROUTINE PRSETB CCCCCCCCCCCCCCCCCCCCCCCCCCCCCCCC
C
```

```
      DOUBLE PRECISION FUNCTION RANDB()
      COMMON /RAN/IRAND0,IRAND1,IAS0,IAS1,ICS0,ICS1,IAB0,IAB1,ICB0,ICB1
      DOUBLE PRECISION DIVFAC,POW16
      PARAMETER (DIVFAC=2.147483648D9,POW16=6.5536D4)

      RANDB=(DFLOAT(IRAND0)+POW16*DFLOAT(IRAND1))/DIVFAC
      CALL LMULT(J0,J1,IRAND0,IRAND1,IAB0,IAB1)
      CALL LADD(IRAND0,IRAND1,J0,J1,ICB0,ICB1)

      RETURN
      END
C
CCCCCCCCCCCCCCCCCCCCCCCCCCCCCCCC END OF ROUTINE RANDB CCCCCCCCCCCCCCCCCCCCCCCCCCCCCCCC
C
      DOUBLE PRECISION FUNCTION RANDS()
      COMMON /RAN/IRAND0,IRAND1,IAS0,IAS1,ICS0,ICS1,IAB0,IAB1,ICB0,ICB1
      DOUBLE PRECISION DIVFAC,POW16
      PARAMETER (DIVFAC=2.147483648D9,POW16=6.5536D4)

      RANDS=(DFLOAT(IRAND0)+POW16*DFLOAT(IRAND1))/DIVFAC
      CALL LMULT(J0,J1,IRAND0,IRAND1,IAS0,IAS1)
      CALL LADD(IRAND0,IRAND1,J0,J1,ICS0,ICS1)

      RETURN
      END
C
CCCCCCCCCCCCCCCCCCCCCCCCCCCCCCCC END OF ROUTINE RANDS CCCCCCCCCCCCCCCCCCCCCCCCCCCCCCCC
C
      SUBROUTINE LADD(I0,I1,J0,J1,K0,K1)
      PARAMETER (IPOW16=2**16,IPOW15=2**15)

      I0=MOD(K0+J0,IPOW16)
      I1=MOD((K0+J0)/IPOW16+K1+J1,IPOW15)

      RETURN
      END
C
CCCCCCCCCCCCCCCCCCCCCCCCCCCCCCCC END OF ROUTINE LADD CCCCCCCCCCCCCCCCCCCCCCCCCCCCCCCCC
C
      SUBROUTINE LMULT(I0,I1,J0,J1,K0,K1)
      PARAMETER (IPOW30=2**30,IPOW16=2**16,IPOW15=2**15)

      K = K0*J0
      IF(K.LT.0) K = (K+IPOW30)+IPOW30
      I0=MOD(K,IPOW16)
      L = K0*J1+K1*J0
      IF(L.LT.0) L = (L+IPOW30)+IPOW30
```

```
      K = K/IPOW16+L
      IF(K.LT.0) K = (K+IPOW30)+IPOW30
      I1=MOD(K,IPOW15)

      RETURN
      END
C
CCCCCCCCCCCCCCCCCCCCCCCCCCCCCC END OF ROUTINE LMULT CCCCCCCCCCCCCCCCCCCCCCCCCCCCCC
C
```

B-10 The Medium-Range Force Problem

B-10.1 CUBIX Program

```
      PROGRAM LJPAR
      PARAMETER (MAXPAR=1024, NUMDOM=4)
      INTEGER DOMX(MAXPAR),DOMY(MAXPAR)
      INTEGER INVENT(MAXPAR,NUMDOM+2,NUMDOM+2),L(NUMDOM+2,NUMDOM+2)
      INTEGER RCHN,LCHN,UCHN,DCHN,IXMIN,IXMAX,IYMIN,IYMAX
      REAL    X(MAXPAR),Y(MAXPAR)
      LOGICAL EDGE(4)
      EXTERNAL IADD,FADD
      COMMON   X,Y,DOMX,DOMY,INVENT,L,IC,NUMPAR
      COMMON   /CHAN/ RCHN,LCHN,UCHN,DCHN,IXMIN,IXMAX,IYMIN,IYMAX,EDGE
      COMMON   /SCAL/ DELX,DELY,XSCA,YSCA,MAXX,MAXY,XMAX,YMAX

      CALL SETELT()

      SIGMA= 1.0
      S6   = SIGMA**6
      S9   = 9.*SIGMA**2

C     Edge lengths of a little square
      DELX = 3.03*SIGMA
      DELY = 3.03*SIGMA

      XSCA = 0.5*DELX
      YSCA = 0.5*DELY

C     Edge lengths of the local domain
      TOMX = REAL(NUMDOM)*DELX
      TOMY = REAL(NUMDOM)*DELY

C     Edge lengths of the whole domain
      XMAX = REAL(MAXX)*DELX
      YMAX = REAL(MAXY)*DELY

C     Global coordinates of the lower left corner of a processor's domain
      DXMIN=REAL(IXMIN-1)*DELX
      DYMIN=REAL(IYMIN-1)*DELY

      EMIN = 1.0E30

      PRINT *, 'How many particles per processor? < 1000'
      READ  *,  NUMPAR

      CALL PRNSET(13579)
```

```
       DO 5 I=1,NUMPAR
          X(I) = TOMX*PRAND()+DXMIN
          Y(I) = TOMY*PRAND()+DYMIN
5         CONTINUE

       DO 1000  IBIG=1,10

          ENERGY=0.
          JC   =0
          KBAD =0

          CALL UPDATE()
          NUMPAR=IC

C    Fill in the boundary patches
          CALL EXCHG()

          DO 20 I=1,NUMPAR

             DO 30 K=DOMY(I)-1,DOMY(I)+1
                KT = K+1

C    Screening out all the particles in the left domain
                DO 40 J=DOMX(I),DOMX(I)+1
                   JT = J+1

C    Pairing with resident particles in the domain (JT,KT)
                   DO 50 KK=1,L(JT,KT)
                      LL=INVENT(KK,JT,KT)
                      XT=X(LL)
                      YT=Y(LL)
                      XD=XT-X(I)
                      YD=YT-Y(I)

C    Screening out the particles on the left
       IF((XD.LT.0.).OR.(XD.EQ.0.).AND.(YD.LE.0.)) GOTO 50

C    Large number of particles are disqualified in this test.
       IF((XD.GT.DELX).OR.(YD.GT.DELY).OR.(YD.LT.-DELY)) GOTO 50

                      DIST = XD**2+YD**2
                      IF (DIST .GT. S9) GOTO 50
                      T6  = S6/DIST**3

C    If the distance is too close it is set to SIGMA (sort of cheating)
                      IF (T6 .GT. 1.0) THEN
```

```
                                T6  = 1.0
                                KBAD= KBAD+1
                          END IF

                          ENERGY = ENERGY+(T6**2-T6)
                          JC  =   JC+1

50                              CONTINUE
40                           CONTINUE
30                        CONTINUE
20                  CONTINUE

            IERR = KCOMBI(JC,IADD,4,1)
            IERR = KCOMBI(KBAD,IADD,4,1)
            IERR = KCOMBI(ENERGY,FADD,4,1)
            WRITE(*,100) JC, KBAD
            WRITE(*,101) ENERGY

            IF (ENERGY .GT. EMIN) GOTO 1000
            EMIN=ENERGY
            IMIN=IBIG

1000     CONTINUE

     WRITE(*,102) IMIN, EMIN

100  FORMAT(I8,' pairs have been counted.',I5,' of them are bad.')
101  FORMAT('Total Energy:',F16.8)
102  FORMAT('Minimum of L-J occurred at', I5,
     # 'th trial with Total Energy',F16.8)

     STOP
     END
C
CCCCCCCCCCCCCCCCCCCCCCCCCCCCCCCCC END OF PROGRAM LJPAR CCCCCCCCCCCCCCCCCCCCCCCCCCCCCCCCC
C
     FUNCTION IADD(I1,I2,ISIZE)
     INTEGER IADD,I1,I2,ISIZE
     I1=I1+I2
     IADD=0
     RETURN
     END
C
CCCCCCCCCCCCCCCCCCCCCCCCCCCCCCCCC END OF ROUTINE IADD CCCCCCCCCCCCCCCCCCCCCCCCCCCCCCCCC
C
     FUNCTION FADD(P1,P2,ISIZE)
     INTEGER  FADD,ISIZE
```

```
      REAL P1,P2
      P1=P1+P2
      FADD=0
      RETURN
      END
C
CCCCCCCCCCCCCCCCCCCCCCCCCCCCC END OF ROUTINE FADD CCCCCCCCCCCCCCCCCCCCCCCCCCCCCCC
C
      SUBROUTINE SETELT()
      PARAMETER (NUMDOM=4)
      INTEGER ENV(5),PROCN,COORD(2),NUMDIM(2),RCHN,LCHN,UCHN,DCHN
      LOGICAL EDGE(4)
      COMMON  /CHAN/ RCHN,LCHN,UCHN,DCHN,IXMIN,IXMAX,IYMIN,IYMAX,EDGE
      COMMON  /SCAL/ DELX,DELY,XSCA,YSCA,MAXX,MAXY,XMAX,YMAX

      CALL KPARAM(ENV)
      PROCN=ENV(2)
      NPROC=ENV(3)

      PRINT *, ' '
      WRITE(*,200) NPROC
 200  FORMAT('You are running a hypercube with',I3, ' processors.')
      PRINT *, ' '
      WRITE(*,201)
 201  FORMAT('Give the number of processors in the Y direction?')
      READ  *,  NUMDIM(1)

      NUMDIM(2)=NPROC/NUMDIM(1)
      CALL KGRDIN(2,NUMDIM)

      RCHN=KGRDCH(PROCN,1,1)
      LCHN=KGRDCH(PROCN,1,-1)
      UCHN=KGRDCH(PROCN,0,1)
      DCHN=KGRDCH(PROCN,0,-1)

      CALL KGRDCO(PROCN, COORD)

      IXMIN=COORD(2)*NUMDOM+1
      IYMIN=COORD(1)*NUMDOM+1
      IXMAX=IXMIN+NUMDOM-1
      IYMAX=IYMIN+NUMDOM-1

      MAXX=NUMDIM(2)*NUMDOM
      MAXY=NUMDIM(1)*NUMDOM

      IF (IXMAX .EQ. MAXX) EDGE(1) = .TRUE.
      IF (IYMAX .EQ. MAXY) EDGE(2) = .TRUE.
```

```
      IF (IXMIN .EQ. 1)    EDGE(3) = .TRUE.
      IF (IYMIN .EQ. 1)    EDGE(4) = .TRUE.

      PRINT *, ' '
      WRITE(*,101)
      WRITE(*,102) MAXX
      WRITE(*,103) MAXY
101   FORMAT('The global number of little squares are')
102   FORMAT('             ',I3,' in the X direction')
103   FORMAT('             ',I3,' in the Y direction')
      PRINT *, ' '
#ifndef SEQ
      MULTIPLE(6)
#endif
      WRITE(*,104) PROCN,COORD(2),COORD(1)
104   FORMAT('Processor',I3,' is located at [X=',I2,' Y=',I2,']')
      WRITE(*,105) IXMIN,IXMAX,IYMIN,IYMAX
105   FORMAT(' and working on global domains: X [',I2,
     #  ' -->',I2,'], Y [',I2,' -->',I2,']')
      PRINT *, ' '
#ifndef SEQ
      FLUSH(6)
      SINGLE(6)
#endif

      RETURN
      END
C
CCCCCCCCCCCCCCCCCCCCCCCCCCCCCCC END OF ROUTINE SETELT CCCCCCCCCCCCCCCCCCCCCCCCCCCCCC
C
      SUBROUTINE UPDATE()
      PARAMETER (MAXPAR=1024, NUMDOM=4)
      PARAMETER (NUMBUF=MAXPAR/NUMDOM)
      INTEGER DOMX(MAXPAR),DOMY(MAXPAR)
      INTEGER INVENT(MAXPAR,NUMDOM+2,NUMDOM+2),L(NUMDOM+2,NUMDOM+2)
      INTEGER RCHN,LCHN,UCHN,DCHN
      LOGICAL ISENT,LEFT,RIGHT,UP,DOWN,EDGE(4)
      LOGICAL TOLF,TORT,TOUP,TODN
      REAL X(MAXPAR),Y(MAXPAR)
      REAL IMPXR(NUMBUF),IMPXL(NUMBUF),IMPXD(NUMBUF),IMPXU(NUMBUF)
      REAL IMPYR(NUMBUF),IMPYL(NUMBUF),IMPYD(NUMBUF),IMPYU(NUMBUF)
      REAL EXPXR(NUMBUF),EXPXL(NUMBUF),EXPXD(NUMBUF),EXPXU(NUMBUF)
      REAL EXPYR(NUMBUF),EXPYL(NUMBUF),EXPYD(NUMBUF),EXPYU(NUMBUF)
      COMMON   X,Y,DOMX,DOMY,INVENT,L,IC,NUMPAR
      COMMON   /CHAN/ RCHN,LCHN,UCHN,DCHN,IXMIN,IXMAX,IYMIN,IYMAX,EDGE
      COMMON   /SCAL/ DELX,DELY,XSCA,YSCA,MAXX,MAXY,XMAX,YMAX
```

```fortran
      DO 5   J=1,NUMDOM+2
         DO 5   K=1,NUMDOM+2
            L(J,K)=0
5              CONTINUE

      IL=0
      IR=0
      IU=0
      ID=0
      IC=0

      RIGHT= EDGE(1)
      LEFT = EDGE(3)
      UP   = EDGE(2)
      DOWN = EDGE(4)

      DO 10 I=1, NUMPAR

C     These are global coordinates
         XT=X(I)+XSCA*(PRAND()-0.5)
         YT=Y(I)+YSCA*(PRAND()-0.5)

C     Global domain number of the particle
         IDXG=MINT(XT/DELX)+1
         IDYG=MINT(YT/DELY)+1

C     Finding the new home for the particle.
         IF (IDXG .LT. IXMIN) THEN
            TOLF = .TRUE.
         ELSE
            TOLF = .FALSE.
         ENDIF
         IF (IDXG .GT. IXMAX) THEN
            TORT = .TRUE.
         ELSE
            TORT = .FALSE.
         ENDIF
         IF (IDYG .LT. IYMIN) THEN
            TODN = .TRUE.
         ELSE
            TODN = .FALSE.
         ENDIF
         IF (IDYG .GT. IYMAX) THEN
            TOUP = .TRUE.
         ELSE
            TOUP = .FALSE.
         ENDIF
```

```
        ISENT=.FALSE.

        IF (TOLF) THEN
C   Queuing particles going left
            IF (TODN) GOTO 100
            IL=IL+1
            IF (LEFT) THEN
C   Particle going out of the global domain reenters at the other end.
                EXPXL(IL)=XT+XMAX
            ELSE
                EXPXL(IL)=XT
            END IF
            EXPYL(IL)=YT
            ISENT=.TRUE.
        ELSE
            IF (TORT) THEN
C   Queuing particles going right
                IF (TOUP) GOTO 100
                    IR=IR+1
                IF (RIGHT) THEN
                    EXPXR(IR)=XT-XMAX
                ELSE
                    EXPXR(IR)=XT
                END IF
                EXPYR(IR)=YT
                ISENT=.TRUE.
            END IF
        END IF

100     CONTINUE

        IF (TODN) THEN
C   Queuing particles going down
            IF (TORT) GOTO 10
            ID=ID+1
            IF (DOWN) THEN
                EXPYD(ID)=YT+YMAX
            ELSE
                EXPYD(ID)=YT
            END IF
            EXPXD(ID)=XT
            ISENT=.TRUE.
        ELSE
            IF (TOUP) THEN
C   Queuing particles going up
                IF (TOLF) GOTO 10
```

```
                    IU=IU+1
                    IF (UP) THEN
                         EXPYU(IU)=YT-YMAX
                    ELSE
                         EXPYU(IU)=YT
                    END IF
                    EXPXU(IU)=XT
                    ISENT=.TRUE.
                END IF
            END IF

            IF (.NOT. ISENT) CALL INSERT(XT,YT,IDXG,IDYG)

10          CONTINUE

C    Exchanging non-resident particles along the edges.

     NL=KCSHIF(IMPXL,LCHN,NUMPAR,EXPXR,RCHN,IR*4)
     NR=KCSHIF(IMPXR,RCHN,NUMPAR,EXPXL,LCHN,IL*4)
     ND=KCSHIF(IMPXD,DCHN,NUMPAR,EXPXU,UCHN,IU*4)
     NU=KCSHIF(IMPXU,UCHN,NUMPAR,EXPXD,DCHN,ID*4)
     NL=KCSHIF(IMPYL,LCHN,NUMPAR,EXPYR,RCHN,IR*4)
     NR=KCSHIF(IMPYR,RCHN,NUMPAR,EXPYL,LCHN,IL*4)
     ND=KCSHIF(IMPYD,DCHN,NUMPAR,EXPYU,UCHN,IU*4)
     NU=KCSHIF(IMPYU,UCHN,NUMPAR,EXPYD,DCHN,ID*4)

     IL=0
     IR=0
     IU=0
     ID=0
     NR=NR/4
     NL=NL/4
     NU=NU/4
     ND=ND/4

     DO 11 I=1,NR
         IDYG=MINT(IMPYR(I)/DELY)+1
         IF (IDYG .GT. IYMAX) THEN
C    Queuing to forward those particles destined to corner nodes
             IU=IU+1
             EXPXU(IU)=IMPXR(I)
             IF (UP) THEN
                  EXPYU(IU)=IMPYR(I)-YMAX
             ELSE
                  EXPYU(IU)=IMPYR(I)
             END IF
         ELSE
```

```
C    Collect its own particles
             IDXG=MINT(IMPXR(I)/DELX)+1
             CALL INSERT(IMPXR(I),IMPYR(I),IDXG,IDYG)
         END IF
11       CONTINUE

     DO 12 I=1,NL
         IDYG=MINT(IMPYL(I)/DELY)+1
         IF (IDYG .LT. IYMIN) THEN
             ID=ID+1
             EXPXD(ID)=IMPXL(I)
             IF (DOWN) THEN
                 EXPYD(ID)=IMPYL(I)+YMAX
             ELSE
                 EXPYD(ID)=IMPYL(I)
             END IF
         ELSE
             IDXG=MINT(IMPXL(I)/DELX)+1
             CALL INSERT(IMPXL(I),IMPYL(I),IDXG,IDYG)
         END IF
12       CONTINUE

     DO 13 I=1,NU
         IDXG=MINT(IMPXU(I)/DELX)+1
         IF (IDXG .LT. IXMIN) THEN
             IL=IL+1
             IF (RIGHT) THEN
                 EXPXL(IL)=IMPXU(I)-XMAX
             ELSE
                 EXPXL(IL)=IMPXU(I)
             END IF
             EXPYL(IL)=IMPYU(I)
         ELSE
             IDYG=MINT(IMPYU(I)/DELY)+1
             CALL INSERT(IMPXU(I),IMPYU(I),IDXG,IDYG)
         END IF
13       CONTINUE

     DO 14 I=1,ND
         IDXG=MINT(IMPXD(I)/DELX)+1
         IF (IDXG .GT. IXMAX) THEN
             IR=IR+1
             IF (LEFT) THEN
                 EXPXR(IR)=IMPXD(I)+XMAX
             ELSE
                 EXPXR(IR)=IMPXD(I)
             END IF
```

```
                  EXPYR(IR)=IMPYD(I)
            ELSE
                  IDYG=MINT(IMPYD(I)/DELY)+1
                  CALL INSERT(IMPXD(I),IMPYD(I),IDXG,IDYG)
            END IF
14          CONTINUE

C     Exchanging left-over particles
      NL=KCSHIF(IMPXL,LCHN,NUMPAR,EXPXR,RCHN,IR*4)
      NR=KCSHIF(IMPXR,RCHN,NUMPAR,EXPXL,LCHN,IL*4)
      ND=KCSHIF(IMPXD,DCHN,NUMPAR,EXPXU,UCHN,IU*4)
      NU=KCSHIF(IMPXU,UCHN,NUMPAR,EXPXD,DCHN,ID*4)
      NL=KCSHIF(IMPYL,LCHN,NUMPAR,EXPYR,RCHN,IR*4)
      NR=KCSHIF(IMPYR,RCHN,NUMPAR,EXPYL,LCHN,IL*4)
      ND=KCSHIF(IMPYD,DCHN,NUMPAR,EXPYU,UCHN,IU*4)
      NU=KCSHIF(IMPYU,UCHN,NUMPAR,EXPYD,DCHN,ID*4)

      NR=NR/4
      NL=NL/4
      NU=NU/4
      ND=ND/4

      DO 16 I=1,NR
            IDXG=MINT(IMPXR(I)/DELX)+1
            IDYG=MINT(IMPYR(I)/DELY)+1
            CALL INSERT(IMPXR(I),IMPYR(I),IDXG,IDYG)
16          CONTINUE

      DO 17 I=1,NL
            IDXG=MINT(IMPXL(I)/DELX)+1
            IDYG=MINT(IMPYL(I)/DELY)+1
            CALL INSERT(IMPXL(I),IMPYL(I),IDXG,IDYG)
17          CONTINUE

      DO 18 I=1,ND
            IDXG=MINT(IMPXD(I)/DELX)+1
            IDYG=MINT(IMPYD(I)/DELY)+1
            CALL INSERT(IMPXD(I),IMPYD(I),IDXG,IDYG)
18          CONTINUE

      DO 19 I=1,NU
            IDXG=MINT(IMPXU(I)/DELX)+1
            IDYG=MINT(IMPYU(I)/DELY)+1
            CALL INSERT(IMPXU(I),IMPYU(I),IDXG,IDYG)
19          CONTINUE

      RETURN
```

```
      END
C
CCCCCCCCCCCCCCCCCCCCCCCCCCCCC END OF ROUTINE UPDATE CCCCCCCCCCCCCCCCCCCCCCCCCCCCC
C
      SUBROUTINE INSERT(XD,YD,IDXG,IDYG)
      PARAMETER (MAXPAR=1024, NUMDOM=4)
      PARAMETER (NUMBUF=MAXPAR/NUMDOM)
      INTEGER DOMX(MAXPAR),DOMY(MAXPAR)
      INTEGER INVENT(MAXPAR,NUMDOM+2,NUMDOM+2),L(NUMDOM+2,NUMDOM+2)
      INTEGER RCHN,LCHN,UCHN,DCHN,IXMIN,IXMAX,IYMIN,IYMAX
      REAL    X(MAXPAR),Y(MAXPAR)
      LOGICAL EDGE(4)
      COMMON  X,Y,DOMX,DOMY,INVENT,L,IC,NUMPAR
      COMMON  /CHAN/ RCHN,LCHN,UCHN,DCHN,IXMIN,IXMAX,IYMIN,IYMAX,EDGE

      IC=IC+1
C     Global coordinates
      X(IC)=XD
      Y(IC)=YD
C     local domain number
      DOMX(IC)=IDXG-IXMIN+1
      DOMY(IC)=IDYG-IYMIN+1
      J=DOMX(IC)+1
      K=DOMY(IC)+1
C     Total number of particles in domain (J,K)
      L(J,K)=L(J,K)+1
      INVENT(L(J,K),J,K)=IC

      RETURN
      END
C
CCCCCCCCCCCCCCCCCCCCCCCCCCCCC END OF ROUTINE INSERT CCCCCCCCCCCCCCCCCCCCCCCCCCCCC
C
      SUBROUTINE EXCHG()
      PARAMETER (MAXPAR=1024, NUMDOM=4)
      PARAMETER (NUMBUF=MAXPAR/NUMDOM)
      INTEGER DOMX(MAXPAR),DOMY(MAXPAR)
      INTEGER INVENT(MAXPAR,NUMDOM+2,NUMDOM+2),L(NUMDOM+2,NUMDOM+2)
      INTEGER RCHN,LCHN,UCHN,DCHN,IXMIN,IXMAX,IYMIN,IYMAX
      REAL X(MAXPAR),Y(MAXPAR)
      REAL IMPXR(NUMBUF),IMPXL(NUMBUF),IMPXD(NUMBUF),IMPXU(NUMBUF)
      REAL IMPYR(NUMBUF),IMPYL(NUMBUF),IMPYD(NUMBUF),IMPYU(NUMBUF)
      REAL EXPXR(NUMBUF),EXPXL(NUMBUF),EXPXD(NUMBUF),EXPXU(NUMBUF)
      REAL EXPYR(NUMBUF),EXPYL(NUMBUF),EXPYD(NUMBUF),EXPYU(NUMBUF)
      REAL IMPXUR(NUMBUF),IMPXUL(NUMBUF),IMPXDR(NUMBUF),IMPXDL(NUMBUF)
      REAL IMPYUR(NUMBUF),IMPYUL(NUMBUF),IMPYDR(NUMBUF),IMPYDL(NUMBUF)
      LOGICAL LEFT,RIGHT,UP,DOWN,EDGE(4)
```

```
      COMMON  X,Y,DOMX,DOMY,INVENT,L,IC,NUMPAR
      COMMON  /CHAN/ RCHN,LCHN,UCHN,DCHN,IXMIN,IXMAX,IYMIN,IYMAX,EDGE
      COMMON  /SCAL/ DELX,DELY,XSCA,YSCA,MAXX,MAXY,XMAX,YMAX

      IL=0
      IR=0
      IU=0
      ID=0

      RIGHT= EDGE(1)
      LEFT = EDGE(3)
      UP   = EDGE(2)
      DOWN = EDGE(4)

      MUMDOM = NUMDOM+1
      DO 11 K=2,MUMDOM
          DO 12 I=1,L(2,K)-1
              IT=INVENT(I,2,K)
              IL=IL+1
              IF (LEFT) THEN
                  EXPXL(IL)=X(IT)+XMAX
              ELSE
                  EXPXL(IL)=X(IT)
              END IF
              EXPYL(IL)=Y(IT)
12            CONTINUE
11        CONTINUE

      DO 13 K=2,MUMDOM
          DO 14 I=1,L(MUMDOM,K)-1
              IT=INVENT(I,MUMDOM,K)
              IR=IR+1
              IF (RIGHT) THEN
                  EXPXR(IR)=X(IT)-XMAX
              ELSE
                  EXPXR(IR)=X(IT)
              END IF
              EXPYR(IR)=Y(IT)
14            CONTINUE
13        CONTINUE

      DO 15 J=2,MUMDOM
          DO 16 I=1,L(J,2)-1
              IT=INVENT(I,J,2)
              ID=ID+1
              IF (DOWN) THEN
                  EXPYD(ID)=Y(IT)+YMAX
```

```
              ELSE
                     EXPYD(ID)=Y(IT)
              END IF
              EXPXD(ID)=X(IT)
16            CONTINUE
15        CONTINUE

      DO 17 J=2,MUMDOM
          DO 18 I=1,L(J,MUMDOM)-1
              IT=INVENT(I,J,MUMDOM)
              IU=IU+1
              IF (UP) THEN
                     EXPYU(IU)=Y(IT)-YMAX
              ELSE
                     EXPYU(IU)=Y(IT)
              END IF
              EXPXU(IU)=X(IT)
18            CONTINUE
17        CONTINUE

      NL=KCSHIF(IMPXL,LCHN,NUMPAR,EXPXR,RCHN,IR*4)
      NR=KCSHIF(IMPXR,RCHN,NUMPAR,EXPXL,LCHN,IL*4)
      ND=KCSHIF(IMPXD,DCHN,NUMPAR,EXPXU,UCHN,IU*4)
      NU=KCSHIF(IMPXU,UCHN,NUMPAR,EXPXD,DCHN,ID*4)
      NL=KCSHIF(IMPYL,LCHN,NUMPAR,EXPYR,RCHN,IR*4)
      NR=KCSHIF(IMPYR,RCHN,NUMPAR,EXPYL,LCHN,IL*4)
      ND=KCSHIF(IMPYD,DCHN,NUMPAR,EXPYU,UCHN,IU*4)
      NU=KCSHIF(IMPYU,UCHN,NUMPAR,EXPYD,DCHN,ID*4)

      IL=0
      IR=0
      IU=0
      ID=0
      NL=NL/4
      NR=NR/4
      NU=NU/4
      ND=ND/4

      DO 21 I=1,NL
          IDYG=MINT(IMPYL(I)/DELY)+1
          IF (IDYG .EQ. IYMIN) THEN
              ID=ID+1
              EXPXD(ID)=IMPXL(I)
              IF (DOWN) THEN
                     EXPYD(ID)=IMPYL(I)+YMAX
              ELSE
                     EXPYD(ID)=IMPYL(I)
```

```
                        END IF
                ELSE
                        IDXG=MINT(IMPXL(I)/DELX)+1
                        CALL INSERT(IMPXL(I),IMPYL(I),IDXG,IDYG)
                END IF
21              CONTINUE

        DO 22 I=1,NR
                IDYG=MINT(IMPYR(I)/DELY)+1
                IF (IDYG .EQ. IYMAX) THEN
                        IU=IU+1
                        EXPXU(IU)=IMPXR(I)
                        IF (UP) THEN
                                EXPYU(IU)=IMPYR(I)-YMAX
                        ELSE
                                EXPYU(IU)=IMPYR(I)
                        END IF
                ELSE
                        IDXG=MINT(IMPXR(I)/DELX)+1
                        CALL INSERT(IMPXR(I),IMPYR(I),IDXG,IDYG)
                END IF
22              CONTINUE

        DO 23 I=1,ND
                IDXG=MINT(IMPXD(I)/DELX)+1
                IF (IDXG .EQ. IXMAX) THEN
                        IR=IR+1
                        IF (RIGHT) THEN
                                EXPXR(IR)=IMPXD(I)-XMAX
                        ELSE
                                EXPXR(IR)=IMPXD(I)
                        END IF
                        EXPYR(IR)=IMPYD(I)
                ELSE
                        IDYG=MINT(IMPYD(I)/DELY)+1
                        CALL INSERT(IMPXD(I),IMPYD(I),IDXG,IDYG)
                END IF
23              CONTINUE

        DO 24 I=1,NU
                IDXG=MINT(IMPXU(I)/DELX)+1
                IF (IDXG .EQ. IXMIN) THEN
                        IL=IL+1
                        IF (LEFT) THEN
                                EXPXL(IL)=IMPXU(I)+XMAX
                        ELSE
                                EXPXL(IL)=IMPXU(I)
```

```
                    END IF
                    EXPYL(IL)=IMPYU(I)
                ELSE
                    IDYG=MINT(IMPYU(I)/DELY)+1
                    CALL INSERT(IMPXU(I),IMPYU(I),IDXG,IDYG)
                END IF
24              CONTINUE

        NL=KCSHIF(IMPXDL,LCHN,NUMPAR,EXPXR,RCHN,IR*4)
        NR=KCSHIF(IMPXUR,RCHN,NUMPAR,EXPXL,LCHN,IL*4)
        ND=KCSHIF(IMPXDR,DCHN,NUMPAR,EXPXU,UCHN,IU*4)
        NU=KCSHIF(IMPXUL,UCHN,NUMPAR,EXPXD,DCHN,ID*4)
        NL=KCSHIF(IMPYDL,LCHN,NUMPAR,EXPYR,RCHN,IR*4)
        NR=KCSHIF(IMPYUR,RCHN,NUMPAR,EXPYL,LCHN,IL*4)
        ND=KCSHIF(IMPYDR,DCHN,NUMPAR,EXPYU,UCHN,IU*4)
        NU=KCSHIF(IMPYUL,UCHN,NUMPAR,EXPYD,DCHN,ID*4)

        NL=NL/4
        NR=NR/4
        NU=NU/4
        ND=ND/4

        DO 31 I=1,NL
            IDXG=MINT(IMPXDL(I)/DELX)+1
            IDYG=MINT(IMPYDL(I)/DELY)+1
            CALL INSERT(IMPXDL(I),IMPYDL(I),IDXG,IDYG)
31          CONTINUE

        DO 32 I=1,NR
            IDXG=MINT(IMPXUR(I)/DELX)+1
            IDYG=MINT(IMPYUR(I)/DELY)+1
            CALL INSERT(IMPXUR(I),IMPYUR(I),IDXG,IDYG)
32          CONTINUE

        DO 33 I=1,ND
            IDXG=MINT(IMPXDR(I)/DELX)+1
            IDYG=MINT(IMPYDR(I)/DELY)+1
            CALL INSERT(IMPXDR(I),IMPYDR(I),IDXG,IDYG)
33          CONTINUE

        DO 34 I=1,NU
            IDXG=MINT(IMPXUL(I)/DELX)+1
            IDYG=MINT(IMPYUL(I)/DELY)+1
            CALL INSERT(IMPXUL(I),IMPYUL(I),IDXG,IDYG)
34          CONTINUE

        RETURN
```

```
      END
C
CCCCCCCCCCCCCCCCCCCCCCCCCCCCCC END OF ROUTINE EXCHG CCCCCCCCCCCCCCCCCCCCCCCCCCCCCC
C
      FUNCTION MINT(X)
      REAL X
      IF (X .GT. 0.) THEN
          MINT=INT(X)
      ELSE
          MINT=INT(X)-1
      END IF
      RETURN
      END
C
CCCCCCCCCCCCCCCCCCCCCCCCCCCCCC END OF ROUTINE MINT CCCCCCCCCCCCCCCCCCCCCCCCCCCCCCC
C
      SUBROUTINE PRNSET(SEED)
      PARAMETER (MULT=1103515245, IADD=12345)
      INTEGER SEED, PROCNU, NPROC, IA, IC, IRAND, ENV(5)
      COMMON /CUBE/ PROCNU, NPROC, IA, IC, IRAND

      CALL KPARAM(ENV)
      PROCNU=ENV(2)
      NPROC =ENV(3)

      IA = 1
      IC = 0

      DO 10 I=0, NPROC-1
      IA = MPOS(MULT*IA)
      IC = MPOS(MULT*IC+IADD)
      IF (I .EQ. PROCNU) IRAND = MPOS(IA*SEED + IC)
10    CONTINUE

      RETURN
      END
C
CCCCCCCCCCCCCCCCCCCCCCCCCCCCCC END OF ROUTINE PRNSET CCCCCCCCCCCCCCCCCCCCCCCCCCCCCC
C
      FUNCTION PRAND()
      INTEGER PROCNU, NPROC, IA, IC, IRAND
      COMMON /CUBE/ PROCNU, NPROC, IA, IC, IRAND

      PRAND = REAL(IRAND)/(REAL(2147483647)+1.00)
      IRAND = MPOS(IA*IRAND+IC)
      RETURN
      END
```

```
C
CCCCCCCCCCCCCCCCCCCCCCCCCCCCC END OF ROUTINE PRAND CCCCCCCCCCCCCCCCCCCCCCCCCCCCC
C
      FUNCTION MPOS(I)
      IF (I .GE. 0) THEN
          MPOS=I
      ELSE
          MPOS=I-2147483648
      END IF
      RETURN
      END
C
CCCCCCCCCCCCCCCCCCCCCCCCCCCCC END OF ROUTINE MPOS CCCCCCCCCCCCCCCCCCCCCCCCCCCCC
C
```

B-11 WaTor – an Ecological Simulation

B-11.1 CUBIX Program

```
PROGRAM WATPAR
PARAMETER (MAXX=100,MAXY=100,MAXNUM=MAXX*MAXY)
INTEGER FISHX(MAXNUM), FISHY(MAXNUM), FSKIND(MAXNUM)
INTEGER BREED(MAXNUM), STARVE(MAXNUM),MESH(MAXX,MAXY)
INTEGER KX(5), KY(5), FBREED, SBREED, DEADAG, SFRACT
INTEGER DEADFS(MAXNUM), DEADNO
COMMON   FISHX,FISHY,FSKIND,BREED,STARVE,MESH
COMMON   /DIREC/ KX,KY
COMMON   /DEADS/ DEADNO,DEADFS,NEW,NEATEN
COMMON   /PARAM/ FBREED,SBREED,DEADAG
COMMON   /EXPID/ IL,IR,IU,ID
COMMON   /OUTPRC/ MOVEDI,MOVEDO

DATA (KX(I), I=1,5) /1,0,-1,0,0/
DATA (KY(I), I=1,5) /0,1,0,-1,0/

CALL SETELT()

NPER  =3
SFRACT=5
CALL PUTFIS(NOFISH,NPER,SFRACT)

PRINT *
PRINT *,'Age at which fish breed?'
READ *, FBREED
PRINT *,'Age at which sharks breed?'
READ *,SBREED
PRINT *,'Age at which sharks starve?'
READ *, DEADAG
PRINT *

DO  1 ITER=1,10
    NEATEN=0
    DO 10 IDFISH=2,1,-1

        DEADNO=0
        MOVEDI=0
        MOVEDO=0
        NEW=NOFISH
        IL=0
        IR=0
        IU=0
        ID=0
```

```
            CALL SNDBND()

            DO 20 I=1, NOFISH
                IF (FSKIND(I) .NE. IDFISH) GOTO 20
                CALL UPDATE(I)
20              CONTINUE

            CALL RTNBND(IDFISH)
            CALL RESOLV(IDFISH)
            CALL REARRN(NOFISH,IDFISH)

10          CONTINUE
1       CONTINUE

    END
C
CCCCCCCCCCCCCCCCCCCCCCCCCCCCC END OF PROGRAM WATPAR CCCCCCCCCCCCCCCCCCCCCCCCCCCCCC
C
    SUBROUTINE SETELT()
    INTEGER  ENV(5),DIM(2),MYPOST(2)
    INTEGER  PROCNU,MX,MY,UCHN,DCHN,LCHN,RCHN,NPROCX,NPROCY
    LOGICAL  EDGE(4)
    COMMON   /CUBE/ PROCNU,EDGE,UCHN,DCHN,LCHN,RCHN,NPROCX,NPROCY

    CALL KPARAM(ENV)
    NDOC   = ENV(1)
    PROCNU = ENV(2)
    NPROC  = ENV(3)

    DIM(1) = 2**(NDOC/2)
    DIM(2) = NPROC/DIM(1)
    NPROCX = DIM(2)
    NPROCY = DIM(1)
    CALL KGRDIN(2,DIM)
    CALL KGRDCO(PROCNU,MYPOST)
    MX     = MYPOST(2)
    MY     = MYPOST(1)
    UCHN   = KGRDCH(PROCNU,0, 1)
    DCHN   = KGRDCH(PROCNU,0,-1)
    RCHN   = KGRDCH(PROCNU,1, 1)
    LCHN   = KGRDCH(PROCNU,1,-1)

    IF (MX .EQ. 0) THEN
        LCHN=0
        EDGE(3)=.TRUE.
    ENDIF
```

```
      IF (MX .EQ. NPROCX-1) THEN
          RCHN=0
          EDGE(1)=.TRUE.
      ENDIF
      IF (MY .EQ. 0) THEN
          DCHN=0
          EDGE(4)=.TRUE.
      ENDIF
      IF (MY .EQ. NPROCY-1) THEN
          UCHN=0
          EDGE(2)=.TRUE.
      ENDIF

      RETURN
      END
C
CCCCCCCCCCCCCCCCCCCCCCCCCCCCCCC END OF ROUTINE SETELT CCCCCCCCCCCCCCCCCCCCCCCCCCCCCCC
C
      SUBROUTINE SNDBND()
      PARAMETER (MAXX=100,MAXY=100,MAXNUM=MAXX*MAXY)
      INTEGER  FISHX(MAXNUM), FISHY(MAXNUM), FSKIND(MAXNUM)
      INTEGER  BREED(MAXNUM), STARVE(MAXNUM),MESH(MAXX,MAXY)
      INTEGER  UBUF(MAXX),DBUF(MAXX),LBUF(MAXY),RBUF(MAXY)
      INTEGER  PROCNU,UCHN,DCHN,LCHN,RCHN,TMP(MAXX)
      LOGICAL  EDGE(4),LEFT,RIGHT,UP,DOWN
      COMMON   FISHX,FISHY,FSKIND,BREED,STARVE,MESH
      COMMON   /BUFF/ UBUF,DBUF,LBUF,RBUF
      COMMON   /CUBE/ PROCNU,EDGE,UCHN,DCHN,LCHN,RCHN,NPROCX,NPROCY

      RIGHT= EDGE(1)
      LEFT = EDGE(3)
      UP   = EDGE(2)
      DOWN = EDGE(4)

      LBTE = 4
      MBTE = MAXY*LBTE
      IF (.NOT. RIGHT) THEN
          DO 10 I=1,MAXY
          TMP(I)=FSKIND(MESH(MAXX,I))
10        CONTINUE
      END IF
      IERR=KCSHIF(LBUF,LCHN,MBTE,TMP,RCHN,MBTE)

      IF (.NOT. LEFT) THEN
          DO 20 I=1,MAXY
          TMP(I)=FSKIND(MESH(1,I))
20        CONTINUE
```

```
      END IF
      IERR=KCSHIF(RBUF,RCHN,MBTE,TMP,LCHN,MBTE)

      MBTE = MAXX*LBTE
      IF (.NOT. UP) THEN
          DO 30 I=1,MAXX
          TMP(I)=FSKIND(MESH(I,MAXY))
30        CONTINUE
      END IF
      IERR=KCSHIF(DBUF,DCHN,MBTE,TMP,UCHN,MBTE)

      IF (.NOT. DOWN) THEN
          DO 40 I=1,MAXX
          TMP(I)=FSKIND(MESH(I,1))
40        CONTINUE
      END IF
      IERR=KCSHIF(UBUF,UCHN,MBTE,TMP,DCHN,MBTE)

      RETURN
      END
C
CCCCCCCCCCCCCCCCCCCCCCCCCCCCCCC END OF ROUTINE SNDBND CCCCCCCCCCCCCCCCCCCCCCCCCCCCCCC
C
      SUBROUTINE UPDATE(IP)
      PARAMETER (MAXX=100,MAXY=100,MAXNUM=MAXX*MAXY)
      INTEGER FISHX(MAXNUM), FISHY(MAXNUM), FSKIND(MAXNUM)
      INTEGER BREED(MAXNUM), STARVE(MAXNUM),MESH(MAXX,MAXY)
      INTEGER FBREED,SBREED,DEADAG,CHKMOV,KX(5),KY(5)
      COMMON  FISHX,FISHY,FSKIND,BREED,STARVE,MESH
      COMMON  /DIREC/ KX,KY
      COMMON  /PARAM/ FBREED,SBREED,DEADAG

      ND=NXTDIR(IP)
      BREED(IP)=BREED(IP)+1
      IF (FSKIND(IP) .EQ. 1) THEN
          IF (ND .NE. 5) THEN
              MOVX=KX(ND)
              MOVY=KY(ND)
              IF (CHKMOV(IP,MOVX,MOVY) .NE. 0) GOTO 99
              NOWX=FISHX(IP)
              NOWY=FISHY(IP)
              CALL MVFISH(IP,MOVX,MOVY)
              IF (BREED(IP) .GE. FBREED) THEN
                  CALL MAKEFS(NOWX,NOWY,1)
                  BREED(IP)=0
              END IF
          END IF
```

```
        ELSE
            STARVE(IP)=STARVE(IP)+1
            IF (ND .NE. 5) THEN
                MOVX=KX(ND)
                MOVY=KY(ND)
                IF (CHKMOV(IP,MOVX,MOVY) .NE. 0) GOTO 99
                NOWX=FISHX(IP)
                NOWY=FISHY(IP)

            IF (MOVEAT(IP,MOVX,MOVY) .EQ. 1) STARVE(IP)=0

                IF (BREED(IP) .GE. SBREED) THEN
                    CALL MAKEFS(NOWX,NOWY,2)
                    BREED(IP)=0
                END IF

                IF (STARVE(IP) .GE. DEADAG) THEN
                    CALL REMFIS(IP)
                END IF
            ELSE
                IF (STARVE(IP) .GE. DEADAG) THEN
                    NOWX=FISHX(IP)
                    NOWY=FISHY(IP)
                    NBRD=BREED(IP)
                    CALL REMFIS(IP)
                    IF (NBRD .GE. SBREED) THEN
                        CALL MAKEFS(NOWX,NOWY,2)
                    END IF
                END IF
            END IF
        END IF
    END IF

99  RETURN
    END
C
CCCCCCCCCCCCCCCCCCCCCCCCCCCCCC END OF ROUTINE UPDATE CCCCCCCCCCCCCCCCCCCCCCCCCCCCCCC
C
    FUNCTION NXTDIR(IP)
    PARAMETER (MAXX=100,MAXY=100,MAXNUM=MAXX*MAXY)
    INTEGER  FISHX(MAXNUM), FISHY(MAXNUM), FSKIND(MAXNUM)
    INTEGER  BREED(MAXNUM), STARVE(MAXNUM),MESH(MAXX,MAXY)
    INTEGER  L(4),UBUF(MAXX),DBUF(MAXX),LBUF(MAXY),RBUF(MAXY)
    INTEGER  PROCNU,UCHN,DCHN,LCHN,RCHN
    LOGICAL  EDGE(4),LEFT,RIGHT,UP,DOWN
    COMMON   FISHX,FISHY,FSKIND,BREED,STARVE,MESH
    COMMON   /BUFF/ UBUF,DBUF,LBUF,RBUF
    COMMON   /CUBE/ PROCNU,EDGE,UCHN,DCHN,LCHN,RCHN,NPROCX,NPROCY
```

```
        IDFISH=FSKIND(IP)
        IX = FISHX(IP)
        IY = FISHY(IP)
        J  = 0
        IF (IX .EQ. MAXX) THEN
            IF ((.NOT. RIGHT).AND.(RBUF(IY) .LT. IDFISH)) THEN
                J=J+1
                L(J)=1
            END IF
        ELSE
            IF (FSKIND(MESH(IX+1,IY)) .LT. IDFISH) THEN
                J=J+1
                L(J)=1
            END IF
        END IF

        IF (IY .EQ. MAXY) THEN
            IF ((.NOT. UP).AND.(UBUF(IX) .LT. IDFISH)) THEN
                J=J+1
                L(J)=2
            END IF
        ELSE
            IF (FSKIND(MESH(IX,IY+1)) .LT. IDFISH) THEN
                J=J+1
                L(J)=2
            END IF
        END IF

        IF (IX .EQ. 1) THEN
            IF ((.NOT. LEFT) .AND. (LBUF(IY) .LT. IDFISH)) THEN
                J=J+1
                L(J)=3
            END IF
        ELSE
            IF (FSKIND(MESH(IX-1,IY)) .LT. IDFISH) THEN
                J=J+1
                L(J)=3
            END IF
        END IF

        IF (IY .EQ. 1) THEN
            IF ((.NOT. DOWN).AND.(DBUF(IX) .LT. IDFISH)) THEN
                J=J+1
                L(J)=4
            END IF
        ELSE
```

```
          IF (FSKIND(MESH(IX,IY-1)) .LT. IDFISH) THEN
              J=J+1
              L(J)=4
          END IF
      END IF

      IF (J .NE. 0) THEN
          NXTDIR=L(IRNDOM(J))
      ELSE
          NXTDIR=5
      END IF

      RETURN
      END
C
CCCCCCCCCCCCCCCCCCCCCCCCCCCCCC END OF ROUTINE NXTDIR CCCCCCCCCCCCCCCCCCCCCCCCCCCCCC
C
      FUNCTION IRNDOM(J)

      IR=IRAND()
      IRNDOM=MOD(IR,J)+1

      RETURN
      END
C
CCCCCCCCCCCCCCCCCCCCCCCCCCCCCC END OF ROUTINE IRNDOM CCCCCCCCCCCCCCCCCCCCCCCCCCCCCC
C
      SUBROUTINE MVFISH(IP,NX,NY)
      PARAMETER (MAXX=100,MAXY=100,MAXNUM=MAXX*MAXY)
      INTEGER  FISHX(MAXNUM), FISHY(MAXNUM), FSKIND(MAXNUM)
      INTEGER  BREED(MAXNUM), STARVE(MAXNUM),MESH(MAXX,MAXY)
      COMMON   FISHX,FISHY,FSKIND,BREED,STARVE,MESH

      MESH(FISHX(IP),FISHY(IP))=0
      FISHX(IP)=FISHX(IP)+NX
      FISHY(IP)=FISHY(IP)+NY
      MESH(FISHX(IP),FISHY(IP))=IP

      RETURN
      END
C
CCCCCCCCCCCCCCCCCCCCCCCCCCCCCC END OF ROUTINE MVFISH CCCCCCCCCCCCCCCCCCCCCCCCCCCCCC
C
      SUBROUTINE REMFIS(IP)
      PARAMETER (MAXX=100,MAXY=100,MAXNUM=MAXX*MAXY)
      INTEGER FISHX(MAXNUM), FISHY(MAXNUM), FSKIND(MAXNUM)
      INTEGER BREED(MAXNUM), STARVE(MAXNUM),MESH(MAXX,MAXY)
```

```
      INTEGER DEADFS(MAXNUM),DEADNO
      COMMON  FISHX,FISHY,FSKIND,BREED,STARVE,MESH
      COMMON  /DEADS/ DEADNO,DEADFS,NEW,NEATEN

      MESH(FISHX(IP),FISHY(IP))=0
      FSKIND(IP)=0
      DEADNO=DEADNO+1
      DEADFS(DEADNO)=IP

      RETURN
      END
C
CCCCCCCCCCCCCCCCCCCCCCCCCCCCCCC END OF ROUTINE REMFIS CCCCCCCCCCCCCCCCCCCCCCCCCCCCCCC
C
      SUBROUTINE MAKEFS(NX,NY,IDFISH)
      PARAMETER (MAXX=100,MAXY=100,MAXNUM=MAXX*MAXY)
      INTEGER FISHX(MAXNUM), FISHY(MAXNUM), FSKIND(MAXNUM)
      INTEGER BREED(MAXNUM), STARVE(MAXNUM),MESH(MAXX,MAXY)
      INTEGER DEADFS(MAXNUM),DEADNO
      COMMON  FISHX,FISHY,FSKIND,BREED,STARVE,MESH
      COMMON  /DEADS/ DEADNO,DEADFS,NEW,NEATEN

      NEW=NEW+1
      FISHX(NEW) =NX
      FISHY(NEW) =NY
      FSKIND(NEW)=IDFISH
      BREED(NEW) =0
      STARVE(NEW)=0
      MESH(NX,NY)=NEW

      RETURN
      END
C
CCCCCCCCCCCCCCCCCCCCCCCCCCCCCCC END OF ROUTINE MAKEFS CCCCCCCCCCCCCCCCCCCCCCCCCCCCCCC
C
      FUNCTION MOVEAT(IP,MOVX,MOVY)
      PARAMETER (MAXX=100,MAXY=100,MAXNUM=MAXX*MAXY)
      INTEGER FISHX(MAXNUM), FISHY(MAXNUM), FSKIND(MAXNUM)
      INTEGER BREED(MAXNUM), STARVE(MAXNUM),MESH(MAXX,MAXY)
      INTEGER DEADFS(MAXNUM),DEADNO
      COMMON  FISHX,FISHY,FSKIND,BREED,STARVE,MESH
      COMMON  /DEADS/ DEADNO,DEADFS,NEW,NEATEN

      NEWX=FISHX(IP)+MOVX
      NEWY=FISHY(IP)+MOVY
      K=MESH(NEWX,NEWY)
      MOVEAT=0
```

```fortran
      IF (FSKIND(K).LT.2) THEN
          IF (FSKIND(K).EQ.1) THEN
              CALL REMFIS(K)
              MOVEAT=1
              NEATEN=NEATEN+1
          END IF
          FISHX(IP)=NEWX
          FISHY(IP)=NEWY
          MESH(NEWX,NEWY)=IP
      ENDIF

      RETURN
      END
C
CCCCCCCCCCCCCCCCCCCCCCCCCCCCCCC END OF ROUTINE MOVEAT CCCCCCCCCCCCCCCCCCCCCCCCCCCCCCC
C
      FUNCTION CHKMOV(IP,MOVX,MOVY)
      PARAMETER (MAXX=100,MAXY=100,MAXNUM=MAXX*MAXY)
      INTEGER  CHKMOV
      INTEGER  LY(MAXX),LBR(MAXX),LST(MAXX),IL
      INTEGER  RY(MAXX),RBR(MAXX),RST(MAXX),IR
      INTEGER  UX(MAXX),UBR(MAXX),UST(MAXX),IU
      INTEGER  DX(MAXX),DBR(MAXX),DST(MAXX),ID
      INTEGER  FISHX(MAXNUM), FISHY(MAXNUM), FSKIND(MAXNUM)
      INTEGER  BREED(MAXNUM), STARVE(MAXNUM),MESH(MAXX,MAXY)
      COMMON   FISHX,FISHY,FSKIND,BREED,STARVE,MESH
      COMMON   /EXCL/ LY,LBR,LST
      COMMON   /EXCR/ RY,RBR,RST
      COMMON   /EXCU/ UX,UBR,UST
      COMMON   /EXCD/ DX,DBR,DST
      COMMON   /EXPID/ IL,IR,IU,ID

      CHKMOV = 0
      IX = FISHX(IP)
      IY = FISHY(IP)
      IF ((IX .EQ. 1) .AND. (MOVX .EQ. -1)) THEN
          IL=IL+1
          CALL MOVOUT(1,IX,IY,IL,LY,LBR,LST,IP)
          CHKMOV=1
          GOTO 99
      END IF

      IF ((IX .EQ. MAXX) .AND. (MOVX .EQ. 1)) THEN
          IR=IR+1
          CALL MOVOUT(1,IX,IY,IR,RY,RBR,RST,IP)
          CHKMOV=1
          GOTO 99
```

```
      END IF

      IF ((IY .EQ. 1) .AND. (MOVY .EQ. -1)) THEN
          ID=ID+1
          CALL MOVOUT(2,IX,IY,ID,DX,DBR,DST,IP)
          CHKMOV=1
          GOTO 99
      END IF

      IF ((IY .EQ. MAXY) .AND. (MOVY .EQ. 1)) THEN
          IU=IU+1
          CALL MOVOUT(2,IX,IY,IU,UX,UBR,UST,IP)
          CHKMOV=1
          GOTO 99
      END IF

99    RETURN
      END
C
CCCCCCCCCCCCCCCCCCCCCCCCCCCCCC END OF ROUTINE CHKMOV CCCCCCCCCCCCCCCCCCCCCCCCCCCCCC
C
      SUBROUTINE MOVOUT(K,IX,IY,IL,LY,LBR,LST,IP)
      PARAMETER (MAXX=100,MAXY=100,MAXNUM=MAXX*MAXY)
      INTEGER  LY(MAXX),LBR(MAXX),LST(MAXX)
      INTEGER  FISHX(MAXNUM), FISHY(MAXNUM), FSKIND(MAXNUM)
      INTEGER  BREED(MAXNUM), STARVE(MAXNUM),MESH(MAXX,MAXY)
      INTEGER  FBREED,SBREED,DEADAG
      COMMON   FISHX,FISHY,FSKIND,BREED,STARVE,MESH
      COMMON  /PARAM/ FBREED,SBREED,DEADAG
      COMMON  /OUTPRC/ MOVEDI,MOVEDO

      IF (K .EQ. 1) THEN
          LY(IL)=IY
      ELSE
          LY(IL)=IX
      END IF
      LBR(IL)=BREED(IP)
      LST(IL)=STARVE(IP)
      IDFISH=FSKIND(IP)
      CALL REMFIS(IP)
      MOVEDO=MOVEDO+1

      RETURN
      END
C
CCCCCCCCCCCCCCCCCCCCCCCCCCCCCC END OF ROUTINE MOVOUT CCCCCCCCCCCCCCCCCCCCCCCCCCCCCC
C
```

```fortran
      SUBROUTINE RTNBND(IDFISH)
      PARAMETER (MAXX=100,MAXY=100,MAXNUM=MAXX*MAXY)
      INTEGER  MRM(MAXX),MBR(MAXX),MST(MAXX)
      INTEGER  LY(MAXX),LBR(MAXX),LST(MAXX),IL
      INTEGER  RY(MAXX),RBR(MAXX),RST(MAXX),IR
      INTEGER  UX(MAXX),UBR(MAXX),UST(MAXX),IU
      INTEGER  DX(MAXX),DBR(MAXX),DST(MAXX),ID
      INTEGER  UBUF(MAXX),DBUF(MAXX),LBUF(MAXY),RBUF(MAXY)
      INTEGER  PROCNU,UCHN,DCHN,LCHN,RCHN
      INTEGER  FISHX(MAXNUM), FISHY(MAXNUM), FSKIND(MAXNUM)
      INTEGER  BREED(MAXNUM), STARVE(MAXNUM),MESH(MAXX,MAXY)
      LOGICAL  EDGE(4)
      COMMON   FISHX,FISHY,FSKIND,BREED,STARVE,MESH
      COMMON   /EXCL/ LY,LBR,LST
      COMMON   /EXCR/ RY,RBR,RST
      COMMON   /EXCU/ UX,UBR,UST
      COMMON   /EXCD/ DX,DBR,DST
      COMMON   /EXPID/ IL,IR,IU,ID
      COMMON   /BUFF/ UBUF,DBUF,LBUF,RBUF
      COMMON   /CUBE/ PROCNU,EDGE,UCHN,DCHN,LCHN,RCHN,NPROCX,NPROCY

      LBTE=4
      MBTE=MAXX*LBTE

      NRECV=KCSHIF(MRM,RCHN,MBTE,LY,LCHN,IL*LBTE)
      NRECV=KCSHIF(MBR,RCHN,MBTE,LBR,LCHN,IL*LBTE)
      IF (IDFISH .EQ. 2) NRECV=KCSHIF(MST,RCHN,MBTE,LST,LCHN,IL*LBTE)
      NRECV=NRECV/LBTE
      IL=0
      IX=MAXX
      DO 10 I=1,NRECV
          IY=MRM(I)
          IDFS=RBUF(IY)
          CALL PUTSND(IX,IY,IDFS,MBR(I),MST(I),IL,LY,LBR,LST,IDFISH)
10        CONTINUE

      NRECV=KCSHIF(MRM,DCHN,MBTE,UX,UCHN,IU*LBTE)
      NRECV=KCSHIF(MBR,DCHN,MBTE,UBR,UCHN,IU*LBTE)
      IF (IDFISH .EQ. 2) NRECV=KCSHIF(MST,DCHN,MBTE,UST,UCHN,IU*LBTE)
      NRECV=NRECV/LBTE
      IU=0
      IY=1
      DO 20 I=1,NRECV
          IX=MRM(I)
          IDFS=DBUF(IX)
          CALL PUTSND(IX,IY,IDFS,MBR(I),MST(I),IU,UY,UBR,UST,IDFISH)
20        CONTINUE
```

```
      NRECV=KCSHIF(MRM,LCHN,MBTE,RY,RCHN,IR*LBTE)
      NRECV=KCSHIF(MBR,LCHN,MBTE,RBR,RCHN,IR*LBTE)
      IF (IDFISH .EQ. 2) NRECV=KCSHIF(MST,LCHN,MBTE,RST,RCHN,IR*LBTE)
      NRECV=NRECV/LBTE
      IR=0
      IX=1
      DO 30 I=1,NRECV
          IY=MRM(I)
          IDFS=LBUF(IY)
          CALL PUTSND(IX,IY,IDFS,MBR(I),MST(I),IR,RY,RBR,RST,IDFISH)
30        CONTINUE

      NRECV=KCSHIF(MRM,UCHN,MBTE,DX,DCHN,ID*LBTE)
      NRECV=KCSHIF(MBR,UCHN,MBTE,DBR,DCHN,ID*LBTE)
      IF (IDFISH .EQ. 2) NRECV=KCSHIF(MST,UCHN,MBTE,DST,DCHN,ID*LBTE)
      NRECV=NRECV/LBTE
      ID=0
      IY=MAXY
      DO 40 I=1,NRECV
          IX=MRM(I)
          IDFS=UBUF(IX)
          CALL PUTSND(IX,IY,IDFS,MBR(I),MST(I),ID,DY,DBR,DST,IDFISH)
40        CONTINUE

      RETURN
      END
C
CCCCCCCCCCCCCCCCCCCCCCCCCCCCCC END OF ROUTINE RTNBND CCCCCCCCCCCCCCCCCCCCCCCCCCCCCC
C
      SUBROUTINE PUTSND(IX,IY,IDFS,IBR,IST,IR,RY,RBR,RST,IDFISH)
      PARAMETER (MAXX=100,MAXY=100,MAXNUM=MAXX*MAXY)
      INTEGER   FBREED,SBREED,DEADAG
      INTEGER   RY(MAXX),RBR(MAXX),RST(MAXX),IR
      INTEGER   FISHX(MAXNUM), FISHY(MAXNUM), FSKIND(MAXNUM)
      INTEGER   BREED(MAXNUM), STARVE(MAXNUM),MESH(MAXX,MAXY)
      INTEGER   DEADFS(MAXNUM), DEADNO
      COMMON    FISHX,FISHY,FSKIND,BREED,STARVE,MESH
      COMMON    /DEADS/ DEADNO,DEADFS,NEW,NEATEN
      COMMON    /PARAM/ FBREED,SBREED,DEADAG
      COMMON    /OUTPRC/ MOVEDI,MOVEDO

      NOLD=MESH(IX,IY)
      IF (FSKIND(NOLD) .LT. IDFS) THEN
          MOVEDI=MOVEDI+1
          NEW=NEW+1
          FISHX(NEW)=IX
```

```fortran
        FISHY(NEW)=IY
        FSKIND(NEW)=IDFS
        BREED(NEW)=IBR
        MESH(IX,IY)=NEW
        IF (IDFISH .EQ. 2) THEN
            IF (NOLD .EQ. 0) THEN
                IF (IST .GE. DEADAG) THEN
                    CALL REMFIS(NEW)
                    GOTO 99
                END IF
                STARVE(NEW)=IST
            ELSE
                CALL REMFIS(NOLD)
                NEATEN=NEATEN+1
                STARVE(NEW)=0
            END IF
        END IF
    ELSE
        IR=IR+1
        IF (IDFISH .EQ. 2) RST(IR)=IST
        RY(IR)=IY
        RBR(IR)=IBR
    END IF

99  RETURN
    END
C
CCCCCCCCCCCCCCCCCCCCCCCCCCCCCCC END OF ROUTINE PUTSND CCCCCCCCCCCCCCCCCCCCCCCCCCCCCCC
C
    SUBROUTINE RESOLV(IDFISH)
    PARAMETER (MAXX=100,MAXY=100,MAXNUM=MAXX*MAXY)
    INTEGER  MRM(MAXX),MBR(MAXX),MST(MAXX)
    INTEGER  LY(MAXY),LBR(MAXY),LST(MAXY),IL
    INTEGER  RY(MAXY),RBR(MAXY),RST(MAXY),IR
    INTEGER  UX(MAXX),UBR(MAXX),UST(MAXY),IU
    INTEGER  DX(MAXX),DBR(MAXX),DST(MAXY),ID
    INTEGER  FISHX(MAXNUM), FISHY(MAXNUM), FSKIND(MAXNUM)
    INTEGER  BREED(MAXNUM), STARVE(MAXNUM),MESH(MAXX,MAXY)
    INTEGER  PROCNU,UCHN,DCHN,LCHN,RCHN,NPROCX,NPROCY
    LOGICAL  EDGE(4)
    COMMON   FISHX,FISHY,FSKIND,BREED,STARVE,MESH
    COMMON   /EXCL/ LY,LBR,LST
    COMMON   /EXCR/ RY,RBR,RST
    COMMON   /EXCU/ UX,UBR,UST
    COMMON   /EXCD/ DX,DBR,DST
    COMMON   /EXPID/ IL,IR,IU,ID
    COMMON   /CUBE/ PROCNU,EDGE,UCHN,DCHN,LCHN,RCHN,NPROCX,NPROCY
```

```
      LBTE=4
      MBTE=MAXX*LBTE

      NRECV=KCSHIF(MRM,LCHN,MBTE,LY,RCHN,IL*LBTE)
      NRECV=KCSHIF(MBR,LCHN,MBTE,LBR,RCHN,IL*LBTE)
      IF (IDFISH .EQ. 2) NRECV=KCSHIF(MST,LCHN,MBTE,LST,RCHN,IL*LBTE)
      NRECV=NRECV/LBTE

      IX=1
      DO 10 I=1,NRECV
          IY=MRM(I)
          IF (MESH(IX,IY) .EQ. 0) THEN
              CALL PUTBAK(IX,IY,MBR(I),MST(I),IDFISH)
          ENDIF
10        CONTINUE

      NRECV=KCSHIF(MRM,UCHN,MBTE,UY,DCHN,IU*LBTE)
      NRECV=KCSHIF(MBR,UCHN,MBTE,UBR,DCHN,IU*LBTE)
      IF (IDFISH .EQ. 2) NRECV=KCSHIF(MST,UCHN,MBTE,UST,DCHN,IU*LBTE)
      NRECV=NRECV/LBTE
      IY=MAXY
      DO 20 I=1,NRECV
          IX=MRM(I)
          IF (MESH(IX,IY) .EQ. 0) THEN
              CALL PUTBAK(IX,IY,MBR(I),MST(I),IDFISH)
          ENDIF
20        CONTINUE

      NRECV=KCSHIF(MRM,RCHN,MBTE,RY,LCHN,IR*LBTE)
      NRECV=KCSHIF(MBR,RCHN,MBTE,RBR,LCHN,IR*LBTE)
      IF (IDFISH .EQ. 2) NRECV=KCSHIF(MST,RCHN,MBTE,RST,LCHN,IR*LBTE)
      NRECV=NRECV/LBTE
      IX=MAXX
      DO 30 I=1,NRECV
          IY=MRM(I)
          IF (MESH(IX,IY) .EQ. 0) THEN
              CALL PUTBAK(IX,IY,MBR(I),MST(I),IDFISH)
          ENDIF
30        CONTINUE

      NRECV=KCSHIF(MRM,DCHN,MBTE,DY,UCHN,ID*LBTE)
      NRECV=KCSHIF(MBR,DCHN,MBTE,DBR,UCHN,ID*LBTE)
      IF (IDFISH .EQ. 2) NRECV=KCSHIF(MST,DCHN,MBTE,DST,UCHN,ID*LBTE)
      NRECV=NRECV/LBTE
      IY=1
      DO 40 I=1,NRECV
```

```
            IX=MRM(I)
            IF (MESH(IX,IY) .EQ. 0) THEN
                CALL PUTBAK(IX,IY,MBR(I),MST(I),IDFISH)
            ENDIF
40          CONTINUE

        RETURN
        END
C
CCCCCCCCCCCCCCCCCCCCCCCCCCCCCCC END OF ROUTINE RESOLV CCCCCCCCCCCCCCCCCCCCCCCCCCCCCCC
C
        SUBROUTINE PUTBAK(IX,IY,IBR,IST,IDFISH)
        PARAMETER (MAXX=100,MAXY=100,MAXNUM=MAXX*MAXY)
        INTEGER  FISHX(MAXNUM), FISHY(MAXNUM), FSKIND(MAXNUM)
        INTEGER  BREED(MAXNUM), STARVE(MAXNUM),MESH(MAXX,MAXY)
        INTEGER  DEADFS(MAXNUM),DEADNO
        COMMON   FISHX,FISHY,FSKIND,BREED,STARVE,MESH
        COMMON  /DEADS/ DEADNO,DEADFS,NEW,NEATEN
        COMMON  /OUTPRC/ MOVEDI,MOVEDO

        MOVEDI=MOVEDI+1
        NEW = NEW+1
        FISHX(NEW) =IX
        FISHY(NEW) =IY
        FSKIND(NEW)=IDFISH
        BREED(NEW) =IBR
        STARVE(NEW)=IST
        MESH(IX,IY)=NEW

        RETURN
        END
C
CCCCCCCCCCCCCCCCCCCCCCCCCCCCCCC END OF ROUTINE PUTBAK CCCCCCCCCCCCCCCCCCCCCCCCCCCCCCC
C
        SUBROUTINE REARRN(NOFISH,IDFISH)
        PARAMETER (MAXX=100,MAXY=100,MAXNUM=MAXX*MAXY)
        INTEGER FISHX(MAXNUM), FISHY(MAXNUM), FSKIND(MAXNUM)
        INTEGER BREED(MAXNUM), STARVE(MAXNUM),MESH(MAXX,MAXY)
        INTEGER DEADFS(MAXNUM),DEADNO,DEAD
        COMMON   FISHX,FISHY,FSKIND,BREED,STARVE,MESH
        COMMON  /DEADS/ DEADNO,DEADFS,NEW,NEATEN
        COMMON  /OUTPRC/ MOVEDI,MOVEDO
        SAVE ICOUNT
        EXTERNAL ADD

        N1=(NEW-MOVEDI)-NOFISH
        DO 10 I=1,DEADNO
```

```
11        DEAD=DEADFS(I)
          IF (DEAD.GT.NEW.OR.FSKIND(DEAD).NE.0.OR.NEW.EQ.0) GOTO 10
          IF (FSKIND(NEW).EQ.0) THEN
               NEW=NEW-1
               GOTO 11
          ENDIF
          FISHX(DEAD) =FISHX(NEW)
          FISHY(DEAD) =FISHY(NEW)
          FSKIND(DEAD)=FSKIND(NEW)
          BREED(DEAD) =BREED(NEW)
          STARVE(DEAD)=STARVE(NEW)
          MESH(FISHX(DEAD),FISHY(DEAD))=DEAD
          FSKIND(NEW)=0
          NEW=NEW-1
10        CONTINUE

      ICOUNT = ICOUNT+1
      IF (IDFISH.EQ.2) THEN
          DEADNO=DEADNO-NEATEN
      ELSE
          DEADNO=DEADNO+NEATEN
      ENDIF
      N2=DEADNO-MOVEDO
      N3=MOVEDO-MOVEDI
      N4=0
      NOFISH=NEW
      DO 30 I=1,NOFISH
          IF (FSKIND(I).EQ.IDFISH) N4=N4+1
30        CONTINUE

      IERR=KCOMBI(N1,ADD,4,1)
      IERR=KCOMBI(N2,ADD,4,1)
      IERR=KCOMBI(N3,ADD,4,1)
      IERR=KCOMBI(N4,ADD,4,1)

      IF (IDFISH.EQ.1) THEN
          WRITE(*,100) N1,N2,N3,N4
          PRINT *
      ELSE
          PRINT *,'PERIOD:',ICOUNT/2+1
          WRITE(*,101) N1,N2,N3,N4
      ENDIF
      RETURN

100 FORMAT(I5,' fish born;                    ',I5,' fish eaten;'
    #          /I5,' fish caught by fisherman;    ',I5,' fish remain.')
101 FORMAT(I5,' sharks born;                   ',I5,' sharks starved;'
```

```
       #          /I5,' sharks caught by fisherman;   ',I5,' sharks remain.')

       END
C
CCCCCCCCCCCCCCCCCCCCCCCCCCCCCC END OF ROUTINE REARRN CCCCCCCCCCCCCCCCCCCCCCCCCCCCCC
C
       SUBROUTINE PUTFIS(NOFISH,NPER,SFRACT)
       PARAMETER (MAXX=100,MAXY=100,MAXNUM=MAXX*MAXY)
       INTEGER FISHX(MAXNUM), FISHY(MAXNUM), FSKIND(MAXNUM)
       INTEGER BREED(MAXNUM), STARVE(MAXNUM),MESH(MAXX,MAXY)
       COMMON  FISHX,FISHY,FSKIND,BREED,STARVE,MESH
       INTEGER SFRACT
       EXTERNAL ADD

       CALL IRNSET(7325)
       I=0
       DO 10 IX=1,100
           DO 10 IY=1,100
               KCNT=IRAND()
               IF (MOD(KCNT,NPER) .NE. 0) GOTO 10
               I=I+1
               IF (MOD(I,SFRACT) .EQ. 0) THEN
                   FSKIND(I)=2
                   N2=N2+1
               ELSE
                   FSKIND(I)=1
                   N1=N1+1
               END IF
               BREED(I) =0
               STARVE(I)=0
               FISHX(I) =IX
               FISHY(I) =IY
               MESH(IX,IY)=I
10             CONTINUE
       NOFISH=I

       PRINT *
       IERR=KCOMBI(N1,ADD,4,1)
       IERR=KCOMBI(N2,ADD,4,1)
       WRITE (*,100) N1,N2

100 FORMAT(I5,' fish and 'I4,' sharks created.')

       RETURN
       END
C
CCCCCCCCCCCCCCCCCCCCCCCCCCCCCC END OF ROUTINE PUTFIS CCCCCCCCCCCCCCCCCCCCCCCCCCCCCC
```

```
C
      SUBROUTINE IRNSET(SEED)
      PARAMETER (MULT=1103515245, IADD=12345)
      INTEGER SEED,PROCNU,UCHN,DCHN,LCHN,RCHN
      LOGICAL  EDGE(4)
      COMMON  /CUBE/ PROCNU,EDGE,UCHN,DCHN,LCHN,RCHN,NPROCX,NPROCY
      COMMON /RND/  IA, IC, IX

      NPROC = NPROCX*NPROCY
      IA = 1
      IC = 0

      DO 10 I=0, NPROC-1
          IA = MASK(MULT*IA)
          IC = MASK(MULT*IC+IADD)
          IF (I .EQ. PROCNU) IX = MASK(IA*SEED + IC)
10        CONTINUE

      RETURN
      END
C
CCCCCCCCCCCCCCCCCCCCCCCCCCCCCCCC END OF ROUTINE IRNSET CCCCCCCCCCCCCCCCCCCCCCCCCCCCCCCC
C
      FUNCTION IRAND()
      COMMON /RND/  IA, IC, IX

      IX = MASK(IA*IX+IC)
      IRAND = IX

      RETURN
      END
C
CCCCCCCCCCCCCCCCCCCCCCCCCCCCCCCC END OF ROUTINE IRAND CCCCCCCCCCCCCCCCCCCCCCCCCCCCCCCC
C
      FUNCTION MASK(I)

      IF (I .GE. 0) THEN
          MASK=I
      ELSE
          MASK=I-2147483648
      END IF

      RETURN
      END
C
CCCCCCCCCCCCCCCCCCCCCCCCCCCCCCCCC END OF ROUTINE MASK CCCCCCCCCCCCCCCCCCCCCCCCCCCCCCCC
C
```

```
      FUNCTION ADD(X,Y,SIZE)
      INTEGER ADD,X,Y,SIZE
      X=X+Y
      ADD=0
      RETURN
      END
C
CCCCCCCCCCCCCCCCCCCCCCCCCCCCCCC END OF ROUTINE ADD CCCCCCCCCCCCCCCCCCCCCCCCCCCCCCC
C
```

B-12 Distributed Sorting Algorithms

B-12.1 The Bitonic Sort Program

```
      PROGRAM BITSOR
      INTEGER A(512)

      PRINT *, ' '
      PRINT *, 'How many items/processor to sort?'
      READ  *,  NITEMS
      PRINT *, ' '
      PRINT *, 'Give communication packet size?'
      READ  *,  NBUF

      CALL INPUT(A,NITEMS)

      PRINT *, ' '
      PRINT *, 'Before Sorting:'
      CALL OUTPUT(A,NITEMS)

      CALL BITMRG(A,NITEMS,NBUF)

      PRINT *, ' '
      PRINT *, 'After Sorting:'
      CALL OUTPUT(A,NITEMS)

      STOP
      END
C
CCCCCCCCCCCCCCCCCCCCCCCCCCCCCCC END OF PROGRAM BITSOR CCCCCCCCCCCCCCCCCCCCCCCCCCCCCCC
C
      SUBROUTINE BITMRG(ARR,NITEMS,NBUF)
      PARAMETER   (MAXNUM=512, MAXBUF=64)
      INTEGER ARR(*),ENV(5),DOC,PROCNU,CMPEXH,CMPEXL
      INTEGER OLDLST(MAXNUM),NEWLST(MAXNUM)
      COMMON  /TEMP/ OLDLST,NEWLST

      DO 1 I=1,NITEMS-1
          IVAL = ARR(I)
          DO 2 J=I+1,NITEMS
              JVAL = ARR(J)
              IF (JVAL .LT. IVAL) THEN
                  ITEMP = IVAL
                  IVAL  = JVAL
                  ARR(J) = ITEMP
              ENDIF
2             CONTINUE
```

```
          ARR(I) = IVAL
1         CONTINUE

      DO 5 I=1,NITEMS
          OLDLST(I) = ARR(I)
          NEWLST(I) = ARR(I)
5         CONTINUE

      CALL KPARAM(ENV)
      DOC = ENV(1)
      PROCNU = ENV(2)

      DO 10 I=1, DOC
          J = I-1
          DO 20 K=1, I
              IF (KBIT(I,PROCNU) .NE. KBIT(J,PROCNU)) THEN
                  IERR=CMPEXH(J,NITEMS,NBUF)
              ELSE
                  IERR=CMPEXL(J,NITEMS,NBUF)
              END IF
              J = J-1
20            CONTINUE
10        CONTINUE

      DO 30 I=1,NITEMS
          ARR(I) = NEWLST(I)
30        CONTINUE

      RETURN
      END
C
CCCCCCCCCCCCCCCCCCCCCCCCCCCCCCCC END OF ROUTINE BITMRG CCCCCCCCCCCCCCCCCCCCCCCCCCCCCCCC
C
      FUNCTION KBIT(I, J)
      MBIT = J
      DO 10 IC=0, I-1
          MBIT = MBIT/2
10        CONTINUE
      KBIT = MOD(MBIT,2)
      RETURN
      END
C
CCCCCCCCCCCCCCCCCCCCCCCCCCCCCCCC END OF ROUTINE KBIT CCCCCCCCCCCCCCCCCCCCCCCCCCCCCCCC
C
      FUNCTION CMPEXH(NCHAN,NITEMS,NBUF)
      PARAMETER  (MAXNUM=512, MAXBUF=64)
      INTEGER CMPEXH
```

```
      INTEGER OLDLST(MAXNUM),NEWLST(MAXNUM),COMBUF(MAXBUF),COMHI
      COMMON  /TEMP/ OLDLST,NEWLST

      CALL SHELL(1,NITEMS)
      IBTE = 4
      KBLK = 1
      MAXBLK = NITEMS/NBUF
      KCMASK = 2**NCHAN
      NZ     = NBUF*IBTE

      IERR = KCSHIF(COMBUF,KCMASK,NBUF*IBTE,OLDLST,KCMASK,NBUF*IBTE)
      COMHI = COMBUF(1)


      J = 1
      I = NITEMS
      K = NITEMS
      DO 10 LC=1, NITEMS
          IF (OLDLST(I) .GE. COMBUF(J)) THEN
              NEWLST(K) = OLDLST(I)
              I = I-1
          ELSE
              NEWLST(K) = COMBUF(J)
              IF (J .EQ. NBUF) THEN
                  IF (KBLK .EQ. MAXBLK) GOTO 15
                  KO = KBLK*NBUF + 1
                  IERR = KCSHIF(COMBUF,KCMASK,NZ,
     #                          OLDLST(KO),KCMASK,NZ)
                  KBLK = KBLK+1
                  J = 1
              ELSE
                  J = J+1
              END IF
          END IF
          K = K-1
10        CONTINUE

15    CONTINUE

      DO 20 IC=1,NITEMS
          OLDLST(IC)=NEWLST(IC)
20        CONTINUE

      IF (OLDLST(1) .GE. COMHI) THEN
          CMPEXH = 1
      ELSE
          CMPEXH = 0
      END IF
```

```
      RETURN
      END
C
CCCCCCCCCCCCCCCCCCCCCCCCCCCCCC END OF ROUTINE CMPEXH CCCCCCCCCCCCCCCCCCCCCCCCCCCCCC
C
      FUNCTION CMPEXL(NCHAN,NITEMS,NBUF)
      PARAMETER  (MAXNUM=512, MAXBUF=64)
      INTEGER CMPEXL
      INTEGER OLDLST(MAXNUM),NEWLST(MAXNUM),COMBUF(MAXBUF),COMLOW
      COMMON  /TEMP/ OLDLST,NEWLST

      CALL SHELL(0,NITEMS)
      IBTE = 4
      KBLK = 1
      MAXBLK = NITEMS/NBUF
      KCMASK = 2**NCHAN
      NZ     = NBUF*IBTE

      IERR = KCSHIF(COMBUF,KCMASK,NBUF*IBTE,OLDLST,KCMASK,NBUF*IBTE)

      I = NITEMS
      J = 1
      DO 10 K=1, NITEMS
          IF (OLDLST(I) .LT. COMBUF(J)) THEN
              NEWLST(K) = OLDLST(I)
              I = I-1
          ELSE
              NEWLST(K) = COMBUF(J)
              IF (J .EQ. NBUF) THEN
                  IF (KBLK .EQ. MAXBLK) GOTO 15
                  KO = KBLK*NBUF + 1
                  IERR = KCSHIF(COMBUF,KCMASK,NZ,
     #                             OLDLST(KO),KCMASK,NZ)
                  KBLK = KBLK+1
                  J = 1
              ELSE
                  J = J+1
              END IF
          END IF
10        CONTINUE

15    CONTINUE
      COMLOW = COMBUF(NBUF)

      DO 20 IC=1,NITEMS
          OLDLST(IC)=NEWLST(IC)
20        CONTINUE
```

```
      IF (OLDLST(NITEMS) .LE. COMLOW) THEN
          CMPEXL = 1
      ELSE
          CMPEXL = 0
      END IF
      RETURN
      END
C
CCCCCCCCCCCCCCCCCCCCCCCCCCCCCC END OF ROUTINE CMPEXL CCCCCCCCCCCCCCCCCCCCCCCCCCCCCC
C
      SUBROUTINE SHELL(LH,NITEMS)
      PARAMETER   (MAXNUM=512, MAXBUF=64)
      INTEGER OLDLST(MAXNUM),NEWLST(MAXNUM)
      COMMON  /TEMP/ OLDLST,NEWLST

      NH=LOG2(NITEMS)
      M =NITEMS
      DO 10 NN=1,NH
          M=M/2
          K=NITEMS-M
          DO 20 J=1,K
              I=J
25            CONTINUE
              L=I+M
              IF (LH .EQ. 1) THEN
                  IF (OLDLST(L) .GE. OLDLST(I)) GOTO 20
              ELSE
                  IF (OLDLST(L) .LE. OLDLST(I)) GOTO 20
              END IF
              MT=OLDLST(I)
              OLDLST(I)=OLDLST(L)
              OLDLST(L)=MT
              I=I-M
              IF (I .GE. 1) GOTO 25
20            CONTINUE
10        CONTINUE

      RETURN
      END
C
CCCCCCCCCCCCCCCCCCCCCCCCCCCCCC END OF ROUTINE SHELL CCCCCCCCCCCCCCCCCCCCCCCCCCCCCC
C
      FUNCTION LOG2(N)

      IL=1
      DO 10 I=0,30
```

```
         IH=IL*2
         IF ((N .GE. IL) .AND. (N .LT. IH)) GOTO 99
         IL=IH
10       CONTINUE
99   LOG2 = I

     RETURN
     END
C
CCCCCCCCCCCCCCCCCCCCCCCCCCCCCCCC END OF ROUTINE LOG2 CCCCCCCCCCCCCCCCCCCCCCCCCCCCCCCC
C
     SUBROUTINE INPUT(A,NITEMS)
     PARAMETER  (MAXNUM=512, MAXBUF=64)
     INTEGER A(*), PRAND

     CALL PRNSET(12357)

     DO 10 I=1,NITEMS
         A(I) = PRAND()
10       CONTINUE

     RETURN
     END
C
CCCCCCCCCCCCCCCCCCCCCCCCCCCCCCCCC END OF ROUTINE INPUT CCCCCCCCCCCCCCCCCCCCCCCCCCCCCCCC
C
     SUBROUTINE OUTPUT(A,NITEMS)
     INTEGER A(*), ENV(5), PROCNU

     CALL KPARAM(ENV)
     PROCNU= ENV(2)
     NPROC = ENV(3)

#ifndef SEQ
     MULTIPLE(6)
     BUFFER(UNIT=6,SIZE=1024)
#endif

     DO 10 J=0,NPROC-1
         IF (PROCNU .EQ. J) THEN
             DO 20 I=1, NITEMS
                 PRINT *,  A(I)
20               CONTINUE
         END IF
#ifndef SEQ
         FLUSH(6)
#endif
```

```
10        CONTINUE

#ifndef SEQ
      SINGLE(6)
#endif

      RETURN
      END
C
CCCCCCCCCCCCCCCCCCCCCCCCCCCCC END OF ROUTINE OUTPUT CCCCCCCCCCCCCCCCCCCCCCCCCCCCCC
C
      SUBROUTINE PRNSET(SEED)
      PARAMETER (MULT=1103515245, IADD=12345)
      INTEGER SEED, PROCNU, NPROC, IA, IC, IRAND, ENV(5)
      COMMON /CUBE/ PROCNU, NPROC, IA, IC, IRAND

      CALL KPARAM(ENV)
      PROCNU = ENV(2)
      NPROC  = ENV(3)

      IA = 1
      IC = 0

      DO 10 I=0, NPROC-1
         IA = MPOS(MULT*IA)
         IC = MPOS(MULT*IC+IADD)
         IF (I .EQ. PROCNU) IRAND = MPOS(IA*SEED + IC)
10        CONTINUE

      RETURN
      END
C
CCCCCCCCCCCCCCCCCCCCCCCCCCCCC END OF ROUTINE PRNSET CCCCCCCCCCCCCCCCCCCCCCCCCCCCCC
C
      FUNCTION PRAND()
      INTEGER  PRAND
      INTEGER PROCNU, NPROC, IA, IC, IRAND
      COMMON /CUBE/ PROCNU, NPROC, IA, IC, IRAND

      IRAND = MPOS(IA*IRAND+IC)
      PRAND = MOD(IRAND,10000)
      RETURN
      END
C
CCCCCCCCCCCCCCCCCCCCCCCCCCCCCC END OF ROUTINE PRAND CCCCCCCCCCCCCCCCCCCCCCCCCCCCCC
C
      FUNCTION MPOS(I)
```

```fortran
      IF (I .GE. 0) THEN
          MPOS=I
      ELSE
          MPOS=I-2147483648
      END IF
      RETURN
      END
C
CCCCCCCCCCCCCCCCCCCCCCCCCCCCCCC END OF ROUTINE MPOS CCCCCCCCCCCCCCCCCCCCCCCCCCCCCCC
C
```

B-12.2 The Quicksort Program

```fortran
      PROGRAM QKSORT
      COMMON/CUBCOM/ IPROC, NPROC, NDOC
      PARAMETER ( MXVAL = 1023 )
      COMMON/SORCOM/ NPERP(0:MXVAL), ISZARY(0:MXVAL)
      PARAMETER ( MXITMS = 500 )
      INTEGER ITEMS(0:MXITMS+1)

      CALL GETPAR
10    CONTINUE
      ITASK = IGTASK(0)
      IF ( ITASK .EQ. 1 ) THEN
          CALL INITLZ(ITEMS,NTOTAL,NITEMS,MXITMS)
      ELSE IF (ITASK .EQ. 2 ) THEN
          NSAMPL = ISAMSZ(NTOTAL)
          CALL PARQUK(ITEMS,NITEMS,NSAMPL)
      ELSE IF (ITASK .EQ. 3) THEN
          CALL OUTDAT(ITEMS,NITEMS)
      ELSE IF (ITASK .EQ. 4) THEN
          GOTO 99
      ELSE
          PRINT *, '**** Invalid Input -- Try again ****'
      ENDIF

      GOTO 10
99    STOP
      END
C
CCCCCCCCCCCCCCCCCCCCCCCCCCCCCCC END OF PROGRAM QKSORT CCCCCCCCCCCCCCCCCCCCCCCCCCCCCCC
C
      SUBROUTINE BITMRG(ITEMS,NITEMS)
      INTEGER ITEMS(0:*), NITEMS
      PARAMETER ( INFNEG = -10000, INFPOS = 10000 )
      PARAMETER ( ISIZE = 4, MXITMS = 500 )
```

```
      INTEGER ITEMS2(0:MXITMS+1)
      LOGICAL TLOG1, TLOG2
      COMMON/CUBCOM/ IPROC, NPROC, NDOC

      ITEMS2(0)        = INFNEG
      ITEMS2(NITEMS+1) = INFPOS
      IPAR = 0
      DO 10 I=1,NDOC
          ITHBIT = MOD(IPROC/(2**I),2)
          DO 20 J=I-1,0,-1
              JP     = 2**J
              JTHBIT = MOD(IPROC/JP,2)
              TLOG1  = (ITHBIT .EQ. 1).AND.(JTHBIT .EQ. 0)
              TLOG2  = (ITHBIT .EQ. 0).AND.(JTHBIT .EQ. 1)
              IF ( TLOG1 .OR. TLOG2 ) THEN
                  IF ( IPAR .EQ. 1) THEN
                      CALL CMPEHI(ITEMS2,ITEMS,NITEMS,JP)
                  ELSE
                      CALL CMPEHI(ITEMS,ITEMS2,NITEMS,JP)
                  ENDIF
              ELSE
                  IF ( IPAR .EQ. 1) THEN
                      CALL CMPELO(ITEMS2,ITEMS,NITEMS,JP)
                  ELSE
                      CALL CMPELO(ITEMS,ITEMS2,NITEMS,JP)
                  ENDIF
              ENDIF
              IPAR = 1 - IPAR
20            CONTINUE
10        CONTINUE

      IF ( IPAR .EQ. 1 ) THEN
          DO 30 I=0,NITEMS-1
              ITEMS(I) = ITEMS2(I+1)
30        CONTINUE
      ELSE
          DO 40 I=0,NITEMS-1
              ITEMS(I) = ITEMS(I+1)
40        CONTINUE
      ENDIF

      RETURN
      END
C
CCCCCCCCCCCCCCCCCCCCCCCCCCCCCCC END OF ROUTINE BITMRG CCCCCCCCCCCCCCCCCCCCCCCCCCCCCCCC
C
      SUBROUTINE CMPEHI(OLIST,NLIST,NITEMS,MASK)
```

```
      INTEGER OLIST(0:*), NLIST(0:*), NITEMS, MASK
      PARAMETER ( ICOMSZ = 100, ISIZE = 4, NBUF = 2 )
      INTEGER ICOMBF(0:ICOMSZ-1)
      INTEGER INSPCE

      IF ( MASK .EQ. 0 ) RETURN
      INSPCE = NBUF*ISIZE
      NINDEX = 1
      NBYTES = MIN(INSPCE,(NITEMS+1)*ISIZE)
      NREC   = KCSHIF(ICOMBF,MASK,INSPCE,OLIST(NINDEX),MASK,NBYTES)/ISIZE

      J = NREC - 1
      I = NITEMS
      DO 10 K=NITEMS,1,-1
          IF ( (OLIST(I)-ICOMBF(J)) .GE. 0 ) THEN
              NLIST(K) = OLIST(I)
              I        = I - 1
          ELSE
              NLIST(K) = ICOMBF(J)
              IF ( J .EQ. 0 ) THEN
                  NINDEX = MIN(NITEMS+1,NINDEX+NBUF)
                  NBYTES = MIN(INSPCE,(NITEMS+2-NINDEX)*ISIZE)
                  IRESP  = KCSHIF(ICOMBF,MASK,INSPCE,
     #                            OLIST(NINDEX),MASK,NBYTES)
                  NREC   = IRESP/ISIZE
                  J      = NREC - 1
              ELSE
                  J      = J - 1
              ENDIF
          ENDIF
10        CONTINUE
      RETURN
      END
C
CCCCCCCCCCCCCCCCCCCCCCCCCCCCCC END OF ROUTINE CMPEHI CCCCCCCCCCCCCCCCCCCCCCCCCCCCCC
C
      SUBROUTINE CMPELO(OLIST,NLIST,NITEMS,MASK)
      INTEGER OLIST(0:*), NLIST(0:*), NITEMS, MASK
      PARAMETER ( ICOMSZ = 100, ISIZE = 4, NBUF = 2 )
      INTEGER ICOMBF(0:ICOMSZ-1)
      INTEGER INSPCE, KTEMP, NBYTES

      IF ( MASK .EQ. 0 ) RETURN
      INSPCE = NBUF*ISIZE
      NINDEX = MAX(0,NITEMS-NBUF+1)
      NBYTES = MIN(INSPCE,(NITEMS+1)*ISIZE)
      IRESP  = KCSHIF(ICOMBF,MASK,INSPCE,OLIST(NINDEX),MASK,NBYTES)
```

```
       NREC   = IRESP/ISIZE

       I = 1
       J = 0
       DO 10 K=1,NITEMS
           IF ( (OLIST(I)-ICOMBF(J)) .LE. 0 ) THEN
               NLIST(K) = OLIST(I)
               I        = I + 1
           ELSE
               NLIST(K) = ICOMBF(J)
               IF ( J .EQ. (NREC-1) ) THEN
                   KTEMP  = MAX(1,NINDEX)*ISIZE
                   NBYTES = MIN(INSPCE,KTEMP)
                   NINDEX = MIN(0,NINDEX-NBUF)
                   IRESP  = KCSHIF(ICOMBF,MASK,INSPCE,
      #                          OLIST(NINDEX),MASK,NBYTES)
                   NREC   = IRESP/ISIZE
                   J      = 0
               ELSE
                   J      = J + 1
               ENDIF
           ENDIF
10         CONTINUE
       RETURN
       END
C
CCCCCCCCCCCCCCCCCCCCCCCCCCCCCC END OF ROUTINE CMPELO CCCCCCCCCCCCCCCCCCCCCCCCCCCCCC
C
       FUNCTION IDSTRB(ITEMS,NITEMS,NSAMPL)
       INTEGER ITEMS(0:*), NITEMS, NSAMPL
       PARAMETER ( ISIZE = 4, MXKEYS = 64, MXSMPL = 50 )
       INTEGER SAMPLE(0:MXSMPL-1), KEYS(0:MXKEYS-1)
       COMMON/CUBCOM/ IPROC, NPROC, NDOC
       PARAMETER ( MXVAL = 1023 )
       COMMON/SORCOM/ NPERP(0:MXVAL), ISZARY(0:MXVAL)

       CALL SMDATA(ITEMS,NITEMS,SAMPLE,NSAMPL)
       CALL PARBIT(SAMPLE,NSAMPL)
       IRESP = KCONCA(SAMPLE,ISIZE,KEYS,ISIZE,ISZARY)

       MASK  = NPROC/2
       IP    = MASK
       ICHAN = NDOC - 1
10     CONTINUE
       IF ( ICHAN .GE. 0 ) THEN
           IF ( MOD(IPROC/MASK,2) .EQ. 1) THEN
               NITEMS = IHDIST(ITEMS,NITEMS,ICHAN,KEYS(IP))
```

```
              IP    = IP + MASK/2
          ELSE
              NITEMS = ILDIST(ITEMS,NITEMS,ICHAN,KEYS(IP))
              IP    = IP - MASK/2

          ENDIF
          ICHAN = ICHAN -1
          MASK  = MASK/2
          GOTO 10
      ENDIF
      IDSTRB = NITEMS

      RETURN
      END
C
CCCCCCCCCCCCCCCCCCCCCCCCCCCCCC END OF ROUTINE DISTRB CCCCCCCCCCCCCCCCCCCCCCCCCCCCCC
C

      SUBROUTINE EXSORT(ILO,IHI,ITEMS)
      INTEGER ITEMS(0:*), ILO, IHI

      DO 10 I=ILO,IHI-1
          IVAL = ITEMS(I)
          DO 20 J=I+1,IHI
              JVAL = ITEMS(J)
              IF ( IVAL .GT. JVAL ) THEN
                  ITEMS(I) = JVAL
                  ITEMS(J) = IVAL
                  IVAL     = JVAL
              ENDIF
20            CONTINUE
10        CONTINUE
      RETURN
      END
C
CCCCCCCCCCCCCCCCCCCCCCCCCCCCCC END OF ROUTINE EXSORT CCCCCCCCCCCCCCCCCCCCCCCCCCCCCC
C
      SUBROUTINE GETPAR
      COMMON/CUBCOM/ IPROC, NPROC, NDOC
      INTEGER IENV(5)

      CALL KPARAM(IENV)
      NDOC  = IENV(1)
      IPROC = IENV(2)
      NPROC = IENV(3)

      RETURN
```

```
      END
C
CCCCCCCCCCCCCCCCCCCCCCCCCCCCCCC END OF ROUTINE GETPAR CCCCCCCCCCCCCCCCCCCCCCCCCCCCCCC
C
      FUNCTION IGTASK(IDUMMY)
      INTEGER IDUMMY

      PRINT *, ' '
      PRINT *, 'Please choose one of the following:'
      PRINT *, '   1...to initialize data to be sorted'
      PRINT *, '   2...to sort data using the quicksort algorithm'
      PRINT *, '   3...to output the data'
      PRINT *, '   4...to terminate the program'

      READ *, IGTASK
      RETURN
      END
C
CCCCCCCCCCCCCCCCCCCCCCCCCCCCCCC END OF ROUTINE IGTASK CCCCCCCCCCCCCCCCCCCCCCCCCCCCCCC
C
      FUNCTION IHDIST(ITEMS,NITEMS,ICHAN,KEY)
      INTEGER ITEMS(0:*),NITEMS,ICHAN,KEY
      PARAMETER ( INFNEG = -10000, INFPOS = 10000 )
      PARAMETER ( ISIZE = 4, MXITMS = 500 )

      ITEMS(0)        = INFPOS
      ITEMS(NITEMS+1) = INFNEG

      I = 1
      J = NITEMS
10    CONTINUE
      IF ( I .LT. J ) THEN
20        CONTINUE
          IF( (ITEMS(I)-KEY) .GT. 0 ) THEN
              I = I + 1
              GO TO 20
          ENDIF
30        CONTINUE
          IF( (ITEMS(J)-KEY) .LE. 0 ) THEN
              J = J - 1
              GOTO 30
          ENDIF
          IF ( I .LT. J ) THEN
              ITEMP    = ITEMS(I)
              ITEMS(I) = ITEMS(J)
              ITEMS(J) = ITEMP
          ENDIF
```

```fortran
          GOTO 10
      ENDIF

      NBYTES = ISIZE*(NITEMS-I+1)
      INSPCE = ISIZE*(MXITMS+2-I)
      MASK   = 2**ICHAN
      NUMIN  = KCSHIF(ITEMS(I),MASK,INSPCE,ITEMS(I),MASK,NBYTES)/ISIZE

      IHDIST = I + NUMIN - 1
      RETURN
      END
C
CCCCCCCCCCCCCCCCCCCCCCCCCCCCCCC END OF ROUTINE IHDIST CCCCCCCCCCCCCCCCCCCCCCCCCCCCCCCC
C
      FUNCTION ILDIST(ITEMS,NITEMS,ICHAN,KEY)
      INTEGER ITEMS(0:*),NITEMS,ICHAN,KEY
      PARAMETER ( INFNEG = -10000, INFPOS = 10000 )
      PARAMETER ( ISIZE = 4, MXITMS = 500 )

      ITEMS(0)        = INFNEG
      ITEMS(NITEMS+1) = INFPOS

      I = 1
      J = NITEMS
10    CONTINUE
      IF ( I .LT. J ) THEN
20        CONTINUE
          IF( (ITEMS(I)-KEY) .LE. 0 ) THEN
              I = I + 1
              GO TO 20
          ENDIF
30        CONTINUE
          IF( (ITEMS(J)-KEY) .GT. 0 ) THEN
              J = J - 1
              GOTO 30
          ENDIF
          IF ( I .LT. J ) THEN
              ITEMP    = ITEMS(I)
              ITEMS(I) = ITEMS(J)
              ITEMS(J) = ITEMP
          ENDIF
          GOTO 10
      ENDIF

      NBYTES = ISIZE*(NITEMS-I+1)
      INSPCE = ISIZE*(MXITMS+2-I)
      MASK   = 2**ICHAN
```

```
      NUMIN  = KCSHIF(ITEMS(I),MASK,INSPCE,ITEMS(I),MASK,NBYTES)/ISIZE

      ILDIST = I + NUMIN - 1
      RETURN
      END
C
CCCCCCCCCCCCCCCCCCCCCCCCCCCCCC END OF ROUTINE ILDIST CCCCCCCCCCCCCCCCCCCCCCCCCCCCCC
C
      SUBROUTINE INITLZ(ITEMS,NTOTAL,NITEMS,NMAX)
      INTEGER ITEMS(0:*), NTOTAL, NITEMS, NMAX
      DOUBLE PRECISION PRANDS
      COMMON/CUBCOM/ IPROC, NPROC, NDOC
      PARAMETER ( MXVAL = 1023 )
      COMMON/SORCOM/ NPERP(0:MXVAL), ISZARY(0:MXVAL)

10    CONTINUE
      PRINT *, 'Please give the total number of items to be sorted'
      READ *, NTOTAL
      NMIN = NTOTAL/NPROC
      IF ( (NMIN+1) .GE. NMAX ) GOTO 10

      PRINT *, 'Please give a seed integer'
      READ *, ISEED
      CALL PRSETB(ISEED,0,0)

      NLEFT  = MOD(NTOTAL,NPROC)
      NITEMS = NMIN
      IF ( IPROC .LT. NLEFT ) NITEMS = NMIN + 1

      DO 20 I=0,NPROC-1
         NPTS = NMIN
         IF ( I .LT. NLEFT ) NPTS = NMIN + 1
         NPERP(I) = NPTS
         DO 30 J=0,NPTS-1
            PTEMP = SNGL(PRANDS(0))
            ITEMP = INT(PTEMP*9999.0)
            IF ( I .EQ. IPROC ) ITEMS(J) = ITEMP
30          CONTINUE
20       CONTINUE

      RETURN
      END
C
CCCCCCCCCCCCCCCCCCCCCCCCCCCCCC END OF ROUTINE INITLZ CCCCCCCCCCCCCCCCCCCCCCCCCCCCCC
C
      FUNCTION ISAMSZ(NTOTAL)
      INTEGER NTOTAL
```

```fortran
      COMMON/CUBCOM/ IPROC, NPROC, NDOC

      PRINT *, ' '
      PRINT *, 'Please give the sample size per processor (-1 for default)'
      READ *, ISAMSZ

      IF ( ISAMSZ .LT. 0 ) THEN
          ITEMP  = INT(SQRT(REAL(NTOTAL)))
          ISAMSZ = STEMP/NPROC
      ENDIF
      IF ( ISAMSZ .EQ. 0 ) ISAMSZ = 1

      RETURN
      END
C
CCCCCCCCCCCCCCCCCCCCCCCCCCCCCCCC END OF ROUTINE ISAMSZ CCCCCCCCCCCCCCCCCCCCCCCCCCCCCCCC
C
      SUBROUTINE OUTDAT(ITEMS,NITEMS)
      INTEGER ITEMS(0:*), NITEMS
      INTEGER STDOUT
      PARAMETER ( ISIZE = 4, STDOUT = 6 )
      PARAMETER ( MXVAL = 1023 )
      COMMON/SORCOM/ NPERP(0:MXVAL), ISZARY(0:MXVAL)
      COMMON/CUBCOM/ IPROC, NPROC, NDOC

      IRESP = KCONCA(NITEMS,ISIZE,NPERP,ISIZE,ISZARY)

      NLINES = 0
      PRINT *, ' '
#ifndef SEQ
      MULTIPLE(STDOUT)
#endif
      NTOT = 0
      DO 10 IP=0,NPROC-1
          NPTS = NPERP(IP)
          DO 20 I=0,NPTS-1
              IF( IP .EQ. IPROC ) THEN
                  PRINT *,ITEMS(I)
              ENDIF
#ifndef SEQ
              IF( (MOD(I,20) .EQ. 19).OR.(I .EQ. NPTS-1) ) THEN
                  FLUSH(STDOUT)
              ENDIF
#endif
20            CONTINUE
10        CONTINUE
#ifndef SEQ
```

```
      SINGLE(STDOUT)
#endif

      RETURN
      END
C
CCCCCCCCCCCCCCCCCCCCCCCCCCCCCC END OF ROUTINE OUTDAT CCCCCCCCCCCCCCCCCCCCCCCCCCCCCC
C
      SUBROUTINE PARBIT(ITEMS,NITEMS)
      INTEGER ITEMS(0:*), NITEMS
      PARAMETER ( INFNEG = -10000, INFPOS = 10000 )

      DO 10 I=NITEMS-1,0,-1
          ITEMS(I+1) = ITEMS(I)
10        CONTINUE
      ITEMS(0)        = INFNEG
      ITEMS(NITEMS+1) = INFPOS

      CALL EXSORT(1,NITEMS,ITEMS)
      CALL BITMRG(ITEMS,NITEMS)

      RETURN
      END
C
CCCCCCCCCCCCCCCCCCCCCCCCCCCCCC END OF ROUTINE PARBIT CCCCCCCCCCCCCCCCCCCCCCCCCCCCCC
C
      SUBROUTINE PARQUK(ITEMS,NITEMS,NSAMPL)
      INTEGER ITEMS(0:*), NITEMS, NSAMPL
      PARAMETER ( INFNEG = -10000, INFPOS = 10000 )

      DO 10 I=NITEMS-1,0,-1
          ITEMS(I+1) = ITEMS(I)
10        CONTINUE

      NITEMS = IDSTRB(ITEMS,NITEMS,NSAMPL)
      ITEMS(0)        = INFNEG
      ITEMS(NITEMS+1) = INFPOS
      CALL EXSORT(1,NITEMS,ITEMS)

      DO 20 I=0,NITEMS-1
          ITEMS(I) = ITEMS(I+1)
20        CONTINUE
      RETURN
      END
C
CCCCCCCCCCCCCCCCCCCCCCCCCCCCCC END OF ROUTINE PARQUK CCCCCCCCCCCCCCCCCCCCCCCCCCCCCC
C
```

```fortran
      SUBROUTINE SMDATA(ITEMS,NITEMS,ISAMPL,NSAMPL)
      INTEGER ITEMS(0:*), NITEMS, ISAMPL(0:*), NSAMPL
      DOUBLE PRECISION PRANDB
      COMMON /CUBCOM/ IPROC, NPROC, NDOC

      CALL PRSETB(12345,1,IPROC)

      DO 10 I=0,NSAMPL-1
          J = (NITEMS-1)*INT(PRANDB(0))
          ISAMPL(I) = ITEMS(J+1)
10        CONTINUE

      RETURN
      END
C
CCCCCCCCCCCCCCCCCCCCCCCCCCCCCCC END OF ROUTINE SMDATA CCCCCCCCCCCCCCCCCCCCCCCCCCCCCCC
C
      SUBROUTINE PRSETB(ISEED,ISKIP,IORDER)
      COMMON /RAN/IRAND0,IRAND1,IAS0,IAS1,ICS0,ICS1,IAB0,IAB1,ICB0,ICB1
      SAVE /RAN/

      INTEGER ENV(5)
      PARAMETER (MULT0=20077,MULT1=16838,IADD0=12345,IADD1=0)
      PARAMETER (IPOW16=2**16)

      ISEED0=MOD(ISEED,IPOW16)
      ISEED1=ISEED/IPOW16
      CALL KPARAM(ENV)
      NPROC=ENV(3)
      IAB0=1
      IAB1=0
      ICB0=0
      ICB1=0
      DO 10 I=0,ISKIP*(NPROC-1)
          CALL LMULT(J0,J1,IAB0,IAB1,MULT0,MULT1)
          IAB0 = J0
          IAB1 = J1
          CALL LMULT(J0,J1,ICB0,ICB1,MULT0,MULT1)
          CALL LADD(ICB0,ICB1,J0,J1,IADD0,IADD1)
          IF (I.EQ.(ISKIP*IORDER)) THEN
              CALL LMULT(J0,J1,ISEED0,ISEED1,IAB0,IAB1)
              CALL LADD(IRAND0,IRAND1,J0,J1,ICB0,ICB1)
          ENDIF
10        CONTINUE
      IAS0=MULT0
      IAS1=MULT1
      ICS0=IADD0
```

```
      ICS1=IADD1

      RETURN
      END
C
CCCCCCCCCCCCCCCCCCCCCCCCCCCCC END OF ROUTINE PRSETB CCCCCCCCCCCCCCCCCCCCCCCCCCCCC
C
      DOUBLE PRECISION FUNCTION PRANDB()
      COMMON /RAN/IRAND0,IRAND1,IAS0,IAS1,ICS0,ICS1,IAB0,IAB1,ICB0,ICB1
      DOUBLE PRECISION DIVFAC,POW16
      PARAMETER (DIVFAC=2.147483648D9,POW16=6.5536D4)
      SAVE /RAN/

      PRANDB=(DFLOAT(IRAND0)+POW16*DFLOAT(IRAND1))/DIVFAC
      CALL LMULT(J0,J1,IRAND0,IRAND1,IAB0,IAB1)
      CALL LADD(IRAND0,IRAND1,J0,J1,ICB0,ICB1)

      RETURN
      END
C
CCCCCCCCCCCCCCCCCCCCCCCCCCCCC END OF ROUTINE PRANDB CCCCCCCCCCCCCCCCCCCCCCCCCCCCC
C
      DOUBLE PRECISION FUNCTION PRANDS()
      COMMON /RAN/IRAND0,IRAND1,IAS0,IAS1,ICS0,ICS1,IAB0,IAB1,ICB0,ICB1
      DOUBLE PRECISION DIVFAC,POW16
      PARAMETER (DIVFAC=2.147483648D9,POW16=6.5536D4)
      SAVE /RAN/

      PRANDS=(DFLOAT(IRAND0)+POW16*DFLOAT(IRAND1))/DIVFAC
      CALL LMULT(J0,J1,IRAND0,IRAND1,IAS0,IAS1)
      CALL LADD(IRAND0,IRAND1,J0,J1,ICS0,ICS1)

      RETURN
      END
C
CCCCCCCCCCCCCCCCCCCCCCCCCCCCC END OF ROUTINE PRANDS CCCCCCCCCCCCCCCCCCCCCCCCCCCCC
C
      SUBROUTINE LADD(I0,I1,J0,J1,K0,K1)
      PARAMETER (IPOW16=2**16,IPOW15=2**15)

      I0=MOD(K0+J0,IPOW16)
      I1=MOD((K0+J0)/IPOW16+K1+J1,IPOW15)

      RETURN
      END
C
CCCCCCCCCCCCCCCCCCCCCCCCCCCCC END OF ROUTINE LADD CCCCCCCCCCCCCCCCCCCCCCCCCCCCC
```

```
C
      SUBROUTINE LMULT(I0,I1,J0,J1,K0,K1)
      PARAMETER (IPOW30=2**30,IPOW16=2**16,IPOW15=2**15)

      K = K0*J0
      IF(K.LT.0) K = (K+IPOW30)+IPOW30
      I0=MOD(K,IPOW16)
      L = K0*J1+K1*J0
      IF(L.LT.0) L = (L+IPOW30)+IPOW30
      K = K/IPOW16+L
      IF(K.LT.0) K = (K+IPOW30)+IPOW30
      I1=MOD(K,IPOW15)

      RETURN
      END
C
CCCCCCCCCCCCCCCCCCCCCCCCCCCCCCC END OF ROUTINE LMULT CCCCCCCCCCCCCCCCCCCCCCCCCCCCCCC
C
```

B-12.3 The Shell Sort Program

```
      PROGRAM SHLSOR
      INTEGER A(512), SHLMRG

      PRINT *, ' '
      PRINT *, 'How many items/processor to sort?'
      READ *,   NITEMS
      PRINT *, ' '
      PRINT *, 'Give communication packet size?'
      READ *,   NBUF

      CALL INPUT(A,NITEMS)

      PRINT *, ' '
      PRINT *, 'Before Sorting:'
      CALL OUTPUT(A,NITEMS)

      KCNT = SHLMRG(A,NITEMS,NBUF)

      WRITE(*,100) KCNT
100   FORMAT('MOPPING took', I3, ' steps.')

      PRINT *, ' '
      PRINT *, 'After Sorting:'
      CALL OUTPUT(A,NITEMS)
```

```
      STOP
      END
C
CCCCCCCCCCCCCCCCCCCCCCCCCCCCC END OF PROGRAM SHLSOR CCCCCCCCCCCCCCCCCCCCCCCCCCCCCC
C
      FUNCTION SHLMRG(ARRAY,NITEMS,NBUF)
      PARAMETER  (MAXNUM=512, MAXBUF=64)
      INTEGER SHLMRG, ARRAY(*)
      INTEGER ENV(5),DOC,PROCNU,MYPOST,CLKFOR,CLKBAK
      INTEGER CMPEXH,CMPEXL,DONEH,DONEL
      INTEGER OLDLST(MAXNUM),NEWLST(MAXNUM)
      COMMON  /TEMP/ OLDLST,NEWLST
      EXTERNAL MADD

      DO 3 I=1,NITEMS
          OLDLST(I) = ARRAY(I)
3         CONTINUE

      CALL KPARAM(ENV)
      DOC = ENV(1)
      PROCNU= ENV(2)
      NPROC = ENV(3)

      CALL KGRDIN(1,NPROC)
      IERR = KGRDCO(PROCNU,MYPOST)
      CLKFOR=KGRDCH(PROCNU,0, 1)
      CLKBAK=KGRDCH(PROCNU,0,-1)
      CLKFOR=LOG2(CLKFOR)
      CLKBAK=LOG2(CLKBAK)
      IF (MYPOST .EQ. 0) CLKBAK=-1
      IF (MYPOST .EQ. NPROC-1) CLKFOR=-1

      DO 10 I=DOC-1,0,-1
          IF (KBIT(I,MYPOST) .EQ. 1) THEN
              DONEH=CMPEXH(I,NITEMS,NBUF)
          ELSE
              DONEL=CMPEXL(I,NITEMS,NBUF)
          END IF
10        CONTINUE

      KCNT = 0
5     CONTINUE

      IF (KCNT .NE. 0) THEN
          IERR=KCOMBI(DONEL,MADD,4,1)
          IERR=KCOMBI(DONEH,MADD,4,1)
```

```
          IF (KCNT .EQ. 3) GOTO 20
          IF ((DONEH .EQ. NPROC-1) .AND. (DONEL .EQ. NPROC-1)) GOTO 20
      ENDIF

      IF (KBIT(0, MYPOST) .EQ. 1) THEN
          DONEH=CMPEXH(CLKBAK,NITEMS,NBUF)
          DONEL=CMPEXL(CLKFOR,NITEMS,NBUF)
      ELSE
          DONEL=CMPEXL(CLKFOR,NITEMS,NBUF)
          DONEH=CMPEXH(CLKBAK,NITEMS,NBUF)
      ENDIF

      KCNT = KCNT+1
      GOTO 5

20    CONTINUE

      SHLMRG = KCNT

      DO 25 I=1,NITEMS
          ARRAY(I) = OLDLST(I)
25        CONTINUE

      RETURN
      END
C
CCCCCCCCCCCCCCCCCCCCCCCCCCCCCCC END OF ROUTINE SHLMRG CCCCCCCCCCCCCCCCCCCCCCCCCCCCCCC
C
      FUNCTION MADD(I1,I2,ISIZE)
      I1 = I1+I2
      MADD = 0
      RETURN
      END
C
CCCCCCCCCCCCCCCCCCCCCCCCCCCCCCC END OF ROUTINE MADD CCCCCCCCCCCCCCCCCCCCCCCCCCCCCCCCC
C
      FUNCTION KBIT(I, J)
      MBIT = J
      DO 10 IC=0, I-1
          MBIT = MBIT/2
10        CONTINUE
      KBIT = MOD(MBIT,2)
      RETURN
      END
C
CCCCCCCCCCCCCCCCCCCCCCCCCCCCCCC END OF ROUTINE KBIT CCCCCCCCCCCCCCCCCCCCCCCCCCCCCCCCC
C
```

```
      FUNCTION CMPEXH(NCHAN,NITEMS,NBUF)
      PARAMETER  (MAXNUM=512, MAXBUF=64)
      INTEGER CMPEXH
      INTEGER OLDLST(MAXNUM),NEWLST(MAXNUM),COMBUF(MAXBUF),COMHI
      COMMON  /TEMP/ OLDLST,NEWLST

      CALL SHELL(1,NITEMS)
      IBTE = 4
      KBLK = 1
      MAXBLK = NITEMS/NBUF
      KCMASK = 2**NCHAN
      NZ     = NBUF*IBTE

      IERR = KCSHIF(COMBUF,KCMASK,NBUF*IBTE,OLDLST,KCMASK,NBUF*IBTE)
      COMHI = COMBUF(1)


      J = 1
      I = NITEMS
      K = NITEMS
      DO 10 LC=1, NITEMS
          IF (OLDLST(I) .GE. COMBUF(J)) THEN
              NEWLST(K) = OLDLST(I)
              I = I-1
          ELSE
              NEWLST(K) = COMBUF(J)
              IF (J .EQ. NBUF) THEN
                  IF (KBLK .EQ. MAXBLK) GOTO 15
                  IERR = KCSHIF(COMBUF,KCMASK,NZ,
     #                          OLDLST(KBLK*NBUF+1),KCMASK,NZ)
                  KBLK = KBLK+1
                  J = 1
              ELSE
                  J = J+1
              END IF
          END IF
          K = K-1
10        CONTINUE

15    CONTINUE

      DO 20 IC=1,NITEMS
          OLDLST(IC)=NEWLST(IC)
20        CONTINUE

      IF (OLDLST(1) .GE. COMHI) THEN
          CMPEXH = 1
      ELSE
```

```
          CMPEXH = 0
       END IF
       RETURN
       END
C
CCCCCCCCCCCCCCCCCCCCCCCCCCCCCC END OF ROUTINE CMPEXH CCCCCCCCCCCCCCCCCCCCCCCCCCCCCC
C
       FUNCTION CMPEXL(NCHAN,NITEMS,NBUF)
       PARAMETER  (MAXNUM=512, MAXBUF=64)
       INTEGER CMPEXL
       INTEGER OLDLST(MAXNUM),NEWLST(MAXNUM),COMBUF(MAXBUF),COMLOW
       COMMON  /TEMP/ OLDLST,NEWLST

       CALL SHELL(0,NITEMS)
       IBTE = 4
       KBLK = 1
       MAXBLK = NITEMS/NBUF
       KCMASK = 2**NCHAN
       NZ     = NBUF*IBTE

       IERR = KCSHIF(COMBUF,KCMASK,NBUF*IBTE,OLDLST,KCMASK,NBUF*IBTE)

       I = NITEMS
       J = 1
       DO 10 K=1, NITEMS
           IF (OLDLST(I) .LT. COMBUF(J)) THEN
               NEWLST(K) = OLDLST(I)
               I = I-1
           ELSE
               NEWLST(K) = COMBUF(J)
               IF (J .EQ. NBUF) THEN
                   IF (KBLK .EQ. MAXBLK) GOTO 15
                   IERR = KCSHIF(COMBUF,KCMASK,NZ,
      #                         OLDLST(KBLK*NBUF+1),KCMASK,NZ)
                   KBLK = KBLK+1
                   J = 1
               ELSE
                   J = J+1
               END IF
           END IF
10         CONTINUE

15    CONTINUE
      COMLOW = COMBUF(NBUF)

      DO 20 IC=1,NITEMS
          OLDLST(IC)=NEWLST(IC)
```

```
20          CONTINUE

       IF (OLDLST(NITEMS) .LE. COMLOW) THEN
            CMPEXL = 1
       ELSE
            CMPEXL = 0
       END IF
       RETURN
       END
C
CCCCCCCCCCCCCCCCCCCCCCCCCCCCCC END OF ROUTINE CMPEXL CCCCCCCCCCCCCCCCCCCCCCCCCCCCCC
C
       SUBROUTINE SHELL(LH,NITEMS)
       PARAMETER  (MAXNUM=512, MAXBUF=64)
       INTEGER OLDLST(MAXNUM),NEWLST(MAXNUM)
       COMMON  /TEMP/ OLDLST,NEWLST

       NH=LOG2(NITEMS)
       M =NITEMS
       DO 10 NN=1,NH
            M=M/2
            K=NITEMS-M
            DO 20 J=1,K
                I=J
25              CONTINUE
                L=I+M
                IF (LH .EQ. 1) THEN
                     IF (OLDLST(L) .GE. OLDLST(I)) GOTO 20
                ELSE
                     IF (OLDLST(L) .LE. OLDLST(I)) GOTO 20
                END IF
                MT=OLDLST(I)
                OLDLST(I)=OLDLST(L)
                OLDLST(L)=MT
                I=I-M
                IF (I .GE. 1) GOTO 25
20          CONTINUE
10      CONTINUE

       RETURN
       END
C
CCCCCCCCCCCCCCCCCCCCCCCCCCCCCC END OF ROUTINE SHELL CCCCCCCCCCCCCCCCCCCCCCCCCCCCCC
C
       FUNCTION LOG2(N)

       IL=1
```

```
      DO 10 I=0,30
          IH=IL*2
          IF ((N .GE. IL) .AND. (N .LT. IH)) GOTO 99
          IL=IH
10        CONTINUE
99   LOG2 = I

     RETURN
     END
C
CCCCCCCCCCCCCCCCCCCCCCCCCCCCCC END OF ROUTINE LOG2 CCCCCCCCCCCCCCCCCCCCCCCCCCCCCC
C
     SUBROUTINE INPUT(A,NITEMS)
     PARAMETER  (MAXNUM=512, MAXBUF=64)
     INTEGER A(*), PRAND

     CALL PRNSET(12357)

     DO 10 I=1,NITEMS
         A(I) = PRAND()
10       CONTINUE

     RETURN
     END
C
CCCCCCCCCCCCCCCCCCCCCCCCCCCCCC END OF ROUTINE INPUT CCCCCCCCCCCCCCCCCCCCCCCCCCCCCC
C
     SUBROUTINE OUTPUT(A,NITEMS)
     INTEGER A(*), ENV(5), PROCNU

     CALL KPARAM(ENV)
     PROCNU= ENV(2)
     NPROC = ENV(3)

     CALL KGRDIN(1,NPROC)
     IERR = KGRDCO(PROCNU,MYPOST)

#ifndef SEQ
     MULTIPLE(6)
     BUFFER(UNIT=6,SIZE=1024)
#endif

     DO 10 J=0,NPROC-1
         IF (MYPOST .EQ. J) THEN
             DO 20 I=1, NITEMS
                 PRINT *,  A(I)
20               CONTINUE
```

```
              END IF
     #ifndef SEQ
              FLUSH(6)
     #endif
     10       CONTINUE

     #ifndef SEQ
          SINGLE(6)
     #endif

          RETURN
          END
     C
     CCCCCCCCCCCCCCCCCCCCCCCCCCCCC END OF ROUTINE OUTPUT CCCCCCCCCCCCCCCCCCCCCCCCCCCCCC
     C
          SUBROUTINE PRNSET(SEED)
          PARAMETER (MULT=1103515245, IADD=12345)
          INTEGER SEED, PROCNU, NPROC, IA, IC, IRAND, ENV(5)
          COMMON /CUBE/ PROCNU, NPROC, IA, IC, IRAND

          CALL KPARAM(ENV)
          PROCNU = ENV(2)
          NPROC  = ENV(3)

          IA = 1
          IC = 0

          DO 10 I=0, NPROC-1
              IA = MPOS(MULT*IA)
              IC = MPOS(MULT*IC+IADD)
              IF (I .EQ. PROCNU) IRAND = MPOS(IA*SEED + IC)
     10       CONTINUE

          RETURN
          END
     C
     CCCCCCCCCCCCCCCCCCCCCCCCCCCCCC END OF ROUTINE PRNSET CCCCCCCCCCCCCCCCCCCCCCCCCCCCCC
     C
          FUNCTION PRAND()
          INTEGER  PRAND
          INTEGER PROCNU, NPROC, IA, IC, IRAND
          COMMON /CUBE/ PROCNU, NPROC, IA, IC, IRAND

          IRAND = MPOS(IA*IRAND+IC)
          PRAND = MOD(IRAND,10000)
          RETURN
          END
```

```
C
CCCCCCCCCCCCCCCCCCCCCCCCCCCCCC END OF ROUTINE PRAND CCCCCCCCCCCCCCCCCCCCCCCCCCCCCC
C
      FUNCTION MPOS(I)
      IF (I .GE. 0) THEN
          MPOS=I
      ELSE
          MPOS=I-2147483648
      END IF
      RETURN
      END
C
CCCCCCCCCCCCCCCCCCCCCCCCCCCCCC END OF ROUTINE MPOS CCCCCCCCCCCCCCCCCCCCCCCCCCCCCCC
C
```

B-13 Global Scalar Products

B-13.1 CUBIX Program

```
      PROGRAM ADDVEC
      INTEGER ENV(5), BIN(25), DOC, PROCNU, ADVECT
      REAL    VECTOR(100), BUF(200)
      COMMON /CUBENV/ DOC, PROCNU, NPROC

      CALL KPARAM(ENV)
      DOC=ENV(1)
      PROCNU=ENV(2)
      NPROC=ENV(3)

      PRINT *, 'Dimension of the vector?'
      READ  *, NDIM

      DO 10 I=1,NDIM
          VECTOR(I)=REAL(I)
10        CONTINUE

      IERR=ADVECT(VECTOR, BUF, NDIM)

      DO 20 I=1,NDIM
          BIN(I)=INT(VECTOR(I))
20        CONTINUE

#ifndef SEQ
      MULTIPLE(6)
#endif
      PRINT *,  PROCNU, (BIN(I),I=1,NDIM)
#ifndef SEQ
      FLUSH(6)
#endif

      END
C
CCCCCCCCCCCCCCCCCCCCCCCCCCCCCC END OF PROGRAM ADDVEC CCCCCCCCCCCCCCCCCCCCCCCCCCCCCC
C
      FUNCTION ADVECT(BUF, TMP, N)
      INTEGER ADVECT,DOC,PROCNU
      REAL    BUF(*), TMP(*)
      INTEGER D,ERROR,CHAN,SIZE,BLOCK,OFFSET,RECV,SEND,RECVN,SENDN
      COMMON /CUBENV/ DOC, PROCNU, NPROC

      MASK=1
      CHAN=1
```

588 Appendix B: Fortran Application Programs

```
        SIZE=4
        BLOCK=2
        OFFSET=SIZE*2

        DO 10 D=1, DOC
            RECV=KAND(PROCNU,MASK)
            SEND=KXOR(RECV,CHAN)
            RECVN=KRSHIF(N+MASK-RECV,D)
            SENDN=KRSHIF(N+MASK-SEND,D)
            ERROR=KVSHIF(TMP(RECV+1),CHAN,SIZE,OFFSET,RECVN,
     #                   BUF(SEND+1),CHAN,SIZE,OFFSET,SENDN)

            DO 20 J=RECV, N-1, BLOCK
                BUF(J+1)=TMP(J+1)+BUF(J+1)
20              CONTINUE

            CHAN=2*CHAN
            MASK=KIOR(MASK,CHAN)
            BLOCK=2*BLOCK
            OFFSET=2*OFFSET

10          CONTINUE

        CHAN=2**(DOC-1)
        MASK=NPROC-1
        OFFSET=KLSHIF(SIZE,DOC)

        D=DOC
        DO 30 I=1,DOC
            D=D-1
            SEND=KAND(PROCNU,MASK)
            RECV=KXOR(SEND,CHAN)
            SENDN=KRSHIF(N+MASK-SEND,D+1)
            RECVN=KRSHIF(N+MASK-RECV,D+1)

            ERROR=KVSHIF(BUF(RECV+1),CHAN,SIZE,OFFSET,RECVN,
     #                   BUF(SEND+1),CHAN,SIZE,OFFSET,SENDN)

            MASK=KAND(MASK,KCOM(CHAN))
            CHAN=CHAN/2
            OFFSET=OFFSET/2

30          CONTINUE

        ADVECT=0
        IF (ERROR .EQ. -1) ADVECT=-1
        RETURN
```

```
      END
C
CCCCCCCCCCCCCCCCCCCCCCCCCCCCC END OF ROUTINE ADVECT CCCCCCCCCCCCCCCCCCCCCCCCCCCCC
C
      FUNCTION KXOR(M,N)

      KXOR=0
      MT=M
      IF (MT .LT. 0) MT=MT-2147483648
      NT=N
      IF (NT .LT. 0) NT=NT-2147483648
      IP=1
      DO 10 I=1,31
          IN=MOD(NT,2)
          IM=MOD(MT,2)
          IC=IN+IM
          IF (IC .EQ. 2) IC=0
          KXOR=IP*IC+KXOR
          IP=2*IP
          NT=NT/2
          MT=MT/2
          IF ((NT .EQ. 0) .AND. (MT .EQ. 0)) GOTO 99
10        CONTINUE
99    CONTINUE
      IF ((M .GT. 0) .AND. (N .LT. 0)) KXOR = KXOR+2147483648
      IF ((M .LT. 0) .AND. (N .GT. 0)) KXOR = KXOR+2147483648
      RETURN
      END
C
CCCCCCCCCCCCCCCCCCCCCCCCCCCCCC END OF ROUTINE KXOR CCCCCCCCCCCCCCCCCCCCCCCCCCCCCC
C
      FUNCTION KIOR(M,N)

      KIOR=0
      MT=M
      IF (MT .LT. 0) MT=MT-2147483648
      NT=N
      IF (NT .LT. 0) NT=NT-2147483648
      IP=1
      DO 10 I=1,31
      IN=MOD(NT,2)
      IM=MOD(MT,2)
      IC=IN+IM
      IF (IC .EQ. 2) IC=1
      KIOR=IP*IC+KIOR
      IP=2*IP
      NT=NT/2
```

```fortran
      MT=MT/2
      IF ((NT .EQ. 0) .AND. (MT .EQ. 0)) GOTO 99
10    CONTINUE
99    CONTINUE
      IF ((M .LT. 0) .OR. (N .LT. 0)) KIOR = KIOR+2147483648
      RETURN
      END
C
CCCCCCCCCCCCCCCCCCCCCCCCCCCCCCC END OF ROUTINE KIOR CCCCCCCCCCCCCCCCCCCCCCCCCCCCCCC
C
      FUNCTION KAND(M,N)
      KAND=0
      MT=M
      IF (MT .LT. 0) MT=MT-2147483648
      NT=N
      IF (NT .LT. 0) NT=NT-2147483648
      IP=1
      DO 10 I=1,31
          IN=MOD(NT,2)
          IM=MOD(MT,2)
          IC=(IN+IM)/2
          KAND=IP*IC+KAND
          IP=2*IP
          NT=NT/2
          MT=MT/2
          IF ((NT .EQ. 0) .AND. (MT .EQ. 0)) GOTO 99
10        CONTINUE
99    CONTINUE
      IF ((M .LT. 0) .AND. (N .LT. 0)) KAND = KAND+2147483648
      RETURN
      END
C
CCCCCCCCCCCCCCCCCCCCCCCCCCCCCCC END OF ROUTINE KAND CCCCCCCCCCCCCCCCCCCCCCCCCCCCCCC
C
      FUNCTION KRSHIF(M,N)
      MT = M
      IF (MT .LT. 0) MT=MT-2147483648
      KRSHIF=MT/2**N
      IF (M .LT. 0) KRSHIF = KRSHIF+2**(31-N)
      RETURN
      END
C
CCCCCCCCCCCCCCCCCCCCCCCCCCCCCCC END OF ROUTINE KRSHIF CCCCCCCCCCCCCCCCCCCCCCCCCCCCCCC
C
      FUNCTION KLSHIF(M,N)
      MT = M
      IF (MT .LT. 0) MT=MT-2147483648
```

```
      IF (N .EQ. 0)  MT=M
      KLSHIF=MT*2**N
      RETURN
      END
C
CCCCCCCCCCCCCCCCCCCCCCCCCCCC END OF ROUTINE KLSHIF CCCCCCCCCCCCCCCCCCCCCCCCCCCCC
C
      FUNCTION KCOM(M)
      KCOM = -(M+1)
      RETURN
      END
C
CCCCCCCCCCCCCCCCCCCCCCCCCCCCCCC END OF ROUTINE KCOM CCCCCCCCCCCCCCCCCCCCCCCCCCCCC
C
```

B-14 LU Decomposition and the Solution of Linear Systems

B-14.1 CUBIX Program

```
      PROGRAM LUPAR
      PARAMETER ( MXBLKS = 100, MBBLKS = 100, IAMAX = 1000, IBMAX = 500 )
      PARAMETER ( MAXD   =   8 )
      REAL ASPACE(0:IAMAX-1), BSPACE(0:IBMAX-1)
      INTEGER JPTR(0:MXBLKS-1)
      COMMON/ABCOM/ ASPACE, BSPACE, JPTR
      REAL COMBUF(0:MXBLKS-1), L(0:MXBLKS-1), U(0:MXBLKS-1), BK(0:MBBLKS-1)
      INTEGER NBLOKS(0:MXBLKS-1), NROWNO(0:MXBLKS-1), NBLKNO(0:MXBLKS-1)
      COMMON/COMCOM/ COMBUF, L, U, BK, NBLOKS, NROWNO, NBLKNO
      COMMON/CUBCOM/ IPROC, NPROC, NDOC
      LOGICAL ILDIAG, IRDIAG
      COMMON/GRDCOM/ ID, ICPOS, IRPOS, ILEFT, IRIGHT, IUP, IDOWN,
     #               IP, JP, KP, KROW, IOFF, JOFF, ILDIAG, IRDIAG
      COMMON/PARCOM/ NX, NY, IRBLKS, IBCBLK, JBLKS, JPLUS, NB, N, IHALFW,
     #               N1, N11, M, KEND, KSTART, IOVER, IACBLK, IAMBLK
      COMMON/USRCOM/ IUSERN, IUSERM, IUSERB
      LOGICAL IDOPIV
      COMMON/PIVCOM/ ICPROC(0:MAXD), IDOPIV

      CALL WELCOM
      CALL GETPAR

      IF ( MOD(NDOC,2) .EQ. 1) THEN
          PRINT *, '*** Cube dimension must be even ***'
          PRINT *, '*** Program terminated          ***'
          STOP
      ENDIF

      CALL DECOMP
10    CONTINUE
      ITASK = IGTASK(0)
      IF ( ITASK .EQ. 1 ) THEN
          CALL INITLZ
      ELSEIF ( ITASK .EQ. 2 ) THEN
          CALL LISMAT
      ELSEIF ( ITASK .EQ. 3 ) THEN
          CALL FNDSOL
      ELSEIF ( ITASK .EQ. 4 ) THEN
          GOTO 99
      ELSE
          PRINT *, '*** Invalid input - try again ***'
      ENDIF
      GOTO 10
```

```
 99   STOP
      END
C
CCCCCCCCCCCCCCCCCCCCCCCCCCCCCCC END OF PROGRAM LUPAR CCCCCCCCCCCCCCCCCCCCCCCCCCCCCCC
C
      SUBROUTINE ASKQ
      LOGICAL ILDIAG, IRDIAG
      COMMON/GRDCOM/ ID, ICPOS, IRPOS, ILEFT, IRIGHT, IUP, IDOWN,
     #               IP, JP, KP, KROW, IOFF, JOFF, ILDIAG, IRDIAG
      COMMON/PARCOM/ NX, NY, IRBLKS, IBCBLK, JBLKS, JPLUS, NB, N, IHALFW,
     #               N1, N11, M, KEND, KSTART, IOVER, IACBLK, IAMBLK
      COMMON/USRCOM/ IUSERN, IUSERM, IUSERB
      COMMON/CUBCOM/ IPROC, NPROC, NDOC
      PARAMETER ( MXBLKS = 100, MBBLKS = 100, IAMAX = 1000, IBMAX = 500 )
      REAL ASPACE(0:IAMAX-1), BSPACE(0:IBMAX-1)
      INTEGER JPTR(0:MXBLKS-1)
      COMMON/ABCOM/ ASPACE, BSPACE, JPTR
      PARAMETER ( MAXD   =   8 )
      LOGICAL IDOPIV
      COMMON/PIVCOM/ ICPROC(0:MAXD), IDOPIV

      PRINT *, 'Please give the order of the matrix'
      READ  *, IUSERN
      PRINT *, 'Please give the band-width (must be odd)'
      READ  *, IUSERM
      PRINT *, 'Please give the number of right-hand sides'
      READ  *, IUSERB

      CALL INITPV

      IRBLKS = (IUSERN-1)/ID + 1
      IBCBLK = (IUSERB-1)/ID + 1
      JBLKS  = IRBLKS + 2
      JPLUS  = 1 - JBLKS
      NB     = ID*IBCBLK
      N      = ID*IRBLKS
      IHALFW = IUSERM/2
      N1     = IHALFW/ID
      N11    = N1 + 1
      M      = 2*ID*N11 - 1
      KEND   = N - M/2 -1
      KSTART = M/2 + 1
      IOVER  = -1
      IACBLK = 2*N11 + 1
      IAMBLK = IACBLK
```

```
      IF ( IDOPIV ) IAMBLK = 3*N11 + 1
      IMXBLK = IBCBLK
      IF ( IAMBLK .GT. IBCBLK ) IMXBLK = IAMBLK

      DO 10 I=0,IMXBLK-1
          JPTR(I) = I*JBLKS
10        CONTINUE

      IF ( IAMBLK*JBLCKS .GT. IAMAX ) THEN
          PRINT *, 'Insufficient space for the A matrix'
          PRINT *, 'Run abandoned.'
          STOP
      ENDIF
      IF ( IBCBLK*JBLCKS .GT. IBMAX .OR. IBCBLK .GT. MBBLKS ) THEN
          PRINT *, 'Insufficient space for the b matrix'
          PRINT *, 'Run abandoned.'
          STOP
      ENDIF
      IF ( IMXBLK .GT. MXBLKS ) THEN
          PRINT *, 'Too many blocks (bandwidth/D too large).'
          PRINT *, 'Run abandoned.'
          STOP
      ENDIF
      IF ( ID .GT. MAXD/2 ) THEN
          PRINT *, 'Too many processors (ID too large)'
          PRINT *, 'Run abandoned.'
          STOP
      ENDIF

      PRINT *, 'Please give a seed integer for the random numbers'
      READ  *, ISEED
      CALL PRSETB(ISEED,0,0)

      PRINT *, ' '
      PRINT *, '*********************************************'
      PRINT *, 'Number of processors = ',NPROC
      PRINT *, 'Template is ',ID,' by ',ID,' processors'
      PRINT *, 'Requested order of matrix A = ',IUSERN
      PRINT *, 'Actual order                = ',N
      PRINT *, 'Requested bandwidth of matrix A = ',IUSERM
      PRINT *, 'Actual bandwidth                = ',M
      PRINT *, 'Requested number of right-hand sides = ',IUSERB
      PRINT *, 'Actual number of right-hand sides    = ',NB
      PRINT *, 'Input matrices are random'
      PRINT *, '*********************************************'
      PRINT *, ' '
```

```
      RETURN
      END
C
CCCCCCCCCCCCCCCCCCCCCCCCCCCCCC END OF ROUTINE ASKQ CCCCCCCCCCCCCCCCCCCCCCCCCCCCCC
C
      SUBROUTINE BCKBTM(IBL)
      INTEGER IBL
      PARAMETER ( MXBLKS = 100, MBBLKS = 100, IAMAX = 1000, IBMAX = 500 )
      PARAMETER ( MAXD   =   8 )
      REAL ASPACE(0:IAMAX-1), BSPACE(0:IBMAX-1)
      INTEGER JPTR(0:MXBLKS-1)
      COMMON/ABCOM/ ASPACE, BSPACE, JPTR
      REAL COMBUF(0:MXBLKS-1), L(0:MXBLKS-1), U(0;MXBLKS-1), BK(0:MBBLKS-1)
      INTEGER NBLOKS(0:MXBLKS-1), NROWNO(0:MXBLKS-1), NBLKNO(0:MXBLKS-1)
      COMMON/COMCOM/ COMBUF, L, U, BK, NBLOKS, NROWNO, NBLKNO
      COMMON/CUBCOM/ IPROC, NPROC, NDOC
      LOGICAL ILDIAG, IRDIAG
      COMMON/GRDCOM/ ID, ICPOS, IRPOS, ILEFT, IRIGHT, IUP, IDOWN,
     #               IP, JP, KP, KROW, IOFF, JOFF, ILDIAG, IRDIAG
      COMMON/PARCOM/ NX, NY, IRBLKS, IBCBLK, JBLKS, JPLUS, NB, N, IHALFW,
     #               N1, N11, M, KEND, KSTART, IOVER, IACBLK, IAMBLK
      LOGICAL IDOPIV
      COMMON/PIVCOM/ ICPROC(0:MAXD), IDOPIV
      PARAMETER ( IFSIZE = 4, ISIZE = 4 )

      ITEMP = MOD(IP,ID) + 1
      IF ( IDOPIV ) THEN
          IRESP = KBROAD(NX,ICPROC(ITEMP),NPROC-1,ISIZE)
      ELSE
          NX = N11
          IF ( KROW .LT. KSTART ) NX = KROW/ID + 1
      ENDIF
      NY=NX

      CALL SPLITP(X,L,ILEFT,IRIGHT,NY*IFSIZE,ID-JP,ID)
      X = 1.0/L(0)

      DO 10 J=0,IBCBLK-1
          BSPACE(JPTR(J)+IBL) = X*BSPACE(JPTR(J)+IBL)
10        CONTINUE

      CALL VTOC(COMBUF,BSPACE(IBL),JBLKS,IBCBLK)
      CALL SPLITP(COMBUF,X,IUP,IDOWN,IBCBLK*IFSIZE,0,ID)

      ISTART = -(NY-1)
      DO 20 J=0,IBCBLK-1
          X = BSPACE(JPTR(J)+IBL)
```

```fortran
          DO 30 I=ISTART,-1
              ITEMP = JPTR(J) + IBL + I
              LTEMP = -I
              BSPACE(ITEMP) = BSPACE(ITEMP) - X*L(LTEMP)
30            CONTINUE
20        CONTINUE

      RETURN
      END
C
CCCCCCCCCCCCCCCCCCCCCCCCCCCCCC END OF ROUTINE BCKBTM CCCCCCCCCCCCCCCCCCCCCCCCCCCCCC
C
      SUBROUTINE BCKCRN(IBL)
      INTEGER IBL
      PARAMETER ( MXBLKS = 100, MBBLKS = 100, IAMAX = 1000, IBMAX = 500 )
      PARAMETER ( MAXD   =    8 )
      REAL ASPACE(0:IAMAX-1), BSPACE(0:IBMAX-1)
      INTEGER JPTR(0:MXBLKS-1)
      COMMON/ABCOM/ ASPACE, BSPACE, JPTR
      REAL COMBUF(0:MXBLKS-1), L(0:MXBLKS-1), U(0:MXBLKS-1), BK(0:MBBLKS-1)
      INTEGER NBLOKS(0:MXBLKS-1), NROWNO(0:MXBLKS-1), NBLKNO(0:MXBLKS-1)
      COMMON/COMCOM/ COMBUF, L, U, BK, NBLOKS, NROWNO, NBLKNO
      COMMON/CUBCOM/ IPROC, NPROC, NDOC
      LOGICAL ILDIAG, IRDIAG
      COMMON/GRDCOM/ ID, ICPOS, IRPOS, ILEFT, IRIGHT, IUP, IDOWN,
     #               IP, JP, KP, KROW, IOFF, JOFF, ILDIAG, IRDIAG
      COMMON/PARCOM/ NX, NY, IRBLKS, IBCBLK, JBLKS, JPLUS, NB, N, IHALFW,
     #               N1, N11, M, KEND, KSTART, IOVER, IACBLK, IAMBLK
      LOGICAL IDOPIV
      COMMON/PIVCOM/ ICPROC(0:MAXD), IDOPIV
      PARAMETER ( IFSIZE = 4, ISIZE = 4 )

      IF ( IDOPIV ) THEN
          NX    = NBLOKS(KP)
          ITEMP = MOD(IP,ID) + 1
          IRESP = KBROAD(NX,ICPROC(ITEMP),NPROC-1,ISIZE)
      ELSE
          NX = N11
          IF ( KROW .LT. KSTART ) NX = KROW/ID + 1
      ENDIF
      NY=NX

      ITEMP = JPTR(JOFF) + IOFF
      CALL VTOC(COMBUF,ASPACE(ITEMP),JBLKS-1,NY)
      CALL SPLITP(COMBUF,X,ILEFT,IRIGHT,NY*IFSIZE,0,ID)
      X = 1.0/ASPACE(ITEMP)
```

```
      DO 10 J=0,IBCBLK-1
          BSPACE(JPTR(J)+IBL) = X*BSPACE(JPTR(J)+IBL)
10        CONTINUE

      CALL VTOC(COMBUF,BSPACE(IBL),JBLKS,IBCBLK)
      CALL SPLITP(COMBUF,X,IUP,IDOWN,IBCBLK*IFSIZE,0,ID)

      ISTART = -(NY-1)
      DO 20 J=0,IBCBLK-1
          X = BSPACE(JPTR(J)+IBL)
          DO 30 I=ISTART,-1
              ITEMP = JPTR(J) + IBL + I
              LTEMP = JPTR(JOFF-I) + I + IOFF
              BSPACE(ITEMP) = BSPACE(ITEMP) - X*ASPACE(LTEMP)
30            CONTINUE
20        CONTINUE

      RETURN
      END
C
CCCCCCCCCCCCCCCCCCCCCCCCCCCCCC END OF ROUTINE BCKCRN CCCCCCCCCCCCCCCCCCCCCCCCCCCCCC
C
      SUBROUTINE BCKMID(IBL)
      INTEGER IBL
      PARAMETER ( MXBLKS = 100, MBBLKS = 100, IAMAX = 1000, IBMAX = 500 )
      PARAMETER ( MAXD   =   8 )
      REAL ASPACE(0:IAMAX-1), BSPACE(0:IBMAX-1)
      INTEGER JPTR(0:MXBLKS-1)
      COMMON/ABCOM/ ASPACE, BSPACE, JPTR
      REAL COMBUF(0:MXBLKS-1), L(0:MXBLKS-1), U(0:MXBLKS-1), BK(0:MBBLKS-1)
      INTEGER NBLOKS(0:MXBLKS-1), NROWNO(0:MXBLKS-1), NBLKNO(0:MXBLKS-1)
      COMMON/COMCOM/ COMBUF, L, U, BK, NBLOKS, NROWNO, NBLKNO
      COMMON/CUBCOM/ IPROC, NPROC, NDOC
      LOGICAL ILDIAG, IRDIAG
      COMMON/GRDCOM/ ID, ICPOS, IRPOS, ILEFT, IRIGHT, IUP, IDOWN,
     #               IP, JP, KP, KROW, IOFF, JOFF, ILDIAG, IRDIAG
      COMMON/PARCOM/ NX, NY, IRBLKS, IBCBLK, JBLKS, JPLUS, NB, N, IHALFW,
     #               N1, N11, M, KEND, KSTART, IOVER, IACBLK, IAMBLK
      LOGICAL IDOPIV
      COMMON/PIVCOM/ ICPROC(0:MAXD), IDOPIV
      PARAMETER ( IFSIZE = 4, ISIZE = 4 )

      ITEMP = MOD(IP,ID) + 1
      IF ( IDOPIV ) THEN
          IRESP = KBROAD(NX,ICPROC(ITEMP),NPROC-1,ISIZE)
      ELSE
          NX = N11
```

```
            IF ( KROW .LT. KSTART ) NX = KROW/ID + 1
         ENDIF
         NY=NX

         CALL SPLITP(X,L,ILEFT,IRIGHT,NY*IFSIZE,ID-JP,ID)
         CALL SPLITP(X,BK,IUP,IDOWN,IBCBLK*IFSIZE,ID-IP,ID)

         ISTART = -(NY-1)
         DO 20 J=0,IBCBLK-1
            X = BK(J)
            DO 30 I=ISTART,0
               ITEMP = JPTR(J) + IBL + I
               LTEMP = -I
               BSPACE(ITEMP) = BSPACE(ITEMP) - X*L(LTEMP)
30          CONTINUE
20       CONTINUE

         RETURN
         END
C
CCCCCCCCCCCCCCCCCCCCCCCCCCCCCCC END OF ROUTINE BCKMID CCCCCCCCCCCCCCCCCCCCCCCCCCCCCCC
C
      SUBROUTINE BCKRGT(IBL)
      INTEGER IBL
      PARAMETER ( MXBLKS = 100, MBBLKS = 100, IAMAX = 1000, IBMAX = 500 )
      PARAMETER ( MAXD   =    8 )
      REAL ASPACE(0:IAMAX-1), BSPACE(0:IBMAX-1)
      INTEGER JPTR(0:MXBLKS-1)
      COMMON/ABCOM/ ASPACE, BSPACE, JPTR
      REAL COMBUF(0:MXBLKS-1), L(0:MXBLKS-1), U(0:MXBLKS-1), BK(0:MBBLKS-1)
      INTEGER NBLOKS(0:MXBLKS-1), NROWNO(0:MXBLKS-1), NBLKNO(0:MXBLKS-1)
      COMMON/COMCOM/ COMBUF, L, U, BK, NBLOKS, NROWNO, NBLKNO
      COMMON/CUBCOM/ IPROC, NPROC, NDOC
      LOGICAL ILDIAG, IRDIAG
      COMMON/GRDCOM/ ID, ICPOS, IRPOS, ILEFT, IRIGHT, IUP, IDOWN,
     #               IP, JP, KP, KROW, IOFF, JOFF, ILDIAG, IRDIAG
      COMMON/PARCOM/ NX, NY, IRBLKS, IBCBLK, JBLKS, JPLUS, NB, N, IHALFW,
     #               N1, N11, M, KEND, KSTART, IOVER, IACBLK, IAMBLK
      LOGICAL IDOPIV
      COMMON/PIVCOM/ ICPROC(0:MAXD), IDOPIV
      PARAMETER ( IFSIZE = 4, ISIZE = 4 )

      ITEMP = MOD(IP,ID) + 1
      IF ( IDOPIV ) THEN
         IRESP = KBROAD(NX,ICPROC(ITEMP),NPROC-1,ISIZE)
      ELSE
         NX = N11
```

```
          IF ( KROW .LT. KSTART ) NX = KROW/ID + 1
      ENDIF
      NY=NX

      ITEMP = JPTR(JOFF) + IOFF
      CALL VTOC(COMBUF,ASPACE(ITEMP),JBLKS-1,NY)
      CALL SPLITP(COMBUF,X,ILEFT,IRIGHT,NY*IFSIZE,0,ID)
      CALL SPLITP(X,BK,IUP,IDOWN,IBCBLK*IFSIZE,ID-IP,ID)

      ISTART = -(NY-1)
      DO 20 J=0,IBCBLK-1
          X = BK(J)
          DO 30 I=ISTART,0
              ITEMP = JPTR(J) + IBL + I
              LTEMP = JPTR(JOFF-I) + I + IOFF
              BSPACE(ITEMP) = BSPACE(ITEMP) - X*ASPACE(LTEMP)
30            CONTINUE
20        CONTINUE

      RETURN
      END
C
CCCCCCCCCCCCCCCCCCCCCCCCCCCCCCC END OF ROUTINE BCKRGT CCCCCCCCCCCCCCCCCCCCCCCCCCCCCCC
C
      SUBROUTINE BCKSUB
      LOGICAL ILDIAG, IRDIAG
      COMMON/GRDCOM/ ID, ICPOS, IRPOS, ILEFT, IRIGHT, IUP, IDOWN,
     #               IP, JP, KP, KROW, IOFF, JOFF, ILDIAG, IRDIAG
      COMMON/PARCOM/ NX, NY, IRBLKS, IBCBLK, JBLKS, JPLUS, NB, N, IHALFW,
     #               N1, N11, M, KEND, KSTART, IOVER, IACBLK, IAMBLK

      KP = 2*(IRBLKS - 1)
      IF ( IP .EQ. JP ) KP = IRBLKS - 1

      DO 10 KROW=N-1,0,-1
          IBL = (KROW+IP)/ID
          CALL LOCK(KP)
          IF ( IP .EQ. ID .AND. JP .EQ. ID ) THEN
              CALL BCKCRN(IBL)
          ELSEIF ( IP .EQ. ID ) THEN
              CALL BCKBTM(IBL)
          ELSEIF ( JP .EQ. ID ) THEN
              CALL BCKRGT(IBL)
          ELSE
              CALL BCKMID(IBL)
          ENDIF
          IP = IP + 1
```

```
          IF ( IP .GT. ID ) IP = 1
          JP = JP + 1
          IF ( JP .GT. ID ) JP = 1
          IF ( IP .EQ. 1 .OR. JP .EQ. 1 ) KP = KP - 1
10        CONTINUE

      RETURN
      END
C
CCCCCCCCCCCCCCCCCCCCCCCCCCCCCC END OF ROUTINE BCKSUB CCCCCCCCCCCCCCCCCCCCCCCCCCCCCC
C
      SUBROUTINE COLLIS
      INTEGER STDOUT
      PARAMETER ( STDOUT = 6 )
      COMMON/PARCOM/ NX, NY, IRBLKS, IBCBLK, JBLKS, JPLUS, NB, N, IHALFW,
     #               N1, N11, M, KEND, KSTART, IOVER, IACBLK, IAMBLK
      COMMON/CUBCOM/ IPROC, NPROC, NDOC
      PARAMETER ( MXBLKS = 100, MBBLKS = 100, IAMAX = 1000, IBMAX = 500 )
      REAL ASPACE(0:IAMAX-1), BSPACE(0:IBMAX-1)
      INTEGER JPTR(0:MXBLKS-1)
      COMMON/ABCOM/ ASPACE, BSPACE, JPTR
      LOGICAL ILDIAG, IRDIAG
      COMMON/GRDCOM/ ID, ICPOS, IRPOS, ILEFT, IRIGHT, IUP, IDOWN,
     #               IP, JP, KP, KROW, IOFF, JOFF, ILDIAG, IRDIAG
      COMMON/USRCOM/ IUSERN, IUSERM, IUSERB

      PRINT *, 'Please give the minimum and maximum row numbers'
      READ  *,IRMIN,IRMAX
      IF ( IRMIN .LT. 0 .OR. IRMIN .GE. IUSERN ) IRMIN = 0
      IF ( IRMAX .LT. 0 .OR. IRMAX .GE. IUSERN ) IRMAX = IUSERN - 1
      IF ( IRMIN .GT. IRMAX ) THEN
          I     = IRMIN
          IRMIN = IRMAX
          IRMAX = I
      ENDIF

      PRINT *, 'Please give the minimum and maximum vector numbers'
      READ  *,ICMIN,ICMAX
      IF ( ICMIN .LT. 0 .OR. ICMIN .GE. IUSERB ) ICMIN = 0
      IF ( ICMAX .LT. 0 .OR. ICMAX .GE. IUSERB ) ICMAX = IUSERB - 1
      IF ( ICMIN .GT. ICMAX ) THEN
          I     = ICMIN
          ICMIN = ICMAX
          ICMAX = I
      ENDIF

#ifndef SEQ
```

```
      MULTIPLE(STDOUT)
#endif
      DO 10 J=ICMIN,ICMAX
          ICBNO  = J/ID
          IPRCOL = ICBNO*ID + ICPOS
          DO 20 I=IRMIN,IRMAX
              K      = I - IRMIN
              IRBNO  = I/ID
              IPRROW = ID*IRBNO + IRPOS
              IBOFF  = JPTR(ICBNO) + IRBNO + 1
              IF ( I .EQ. IPRROW .AND .J .EQ. IPRCOL ) THEN
                  VALUE = BSPACE(IBOFF)
                  IF ( K .EQ. 0 ) THEN
                      PRINT *, 'Vector number ',J
                  ENDIF
                  PRINT 100,VALUE
                  IF ( MOD(K,7) .EQ. 6 .OR. I .EQ. IRMAX ) THEN
                      PRINT *, ' '
                  ENDIF
              ENDIF
#ifndef SEQ
              FLUSH(STDOUT)
#endif
20            CONTINUE
10        CONTINUE
#ifndef SEQ
      SINGLE(STDOUT)
#endif
      PRINT *, ' '
      PRINT *, 'MATRIX B'
      PRINT *, 'Results for rows ',IRMIN,' to ',IRMAX
      PRINT *, '     and columns ',ICMIN,' to ',ICMAX
      CALL DWPAUS

      RETURN
#ifndef XENIX
100 FORMAT(E11.3$)
#else
100 FORMAT(E11.3\)
#endif
      END
C
CCCCCCCCCCCCCCCCCCCCCCCCCCCCCC END OF ROUTINE COLLIS CCCCCCCCCCCCCCCCCCCCCCCCCCCCCC
C
      SUBROUTINE CTOV(OBUF,IBUF,IOFFTM,NTM)
      REAL OBUF(0:*), IBUF(0:*)
      INTEGER IOFFTM, NTM
```

```fortran
      I = 0
      DO 10 J=0,NTM-1
          OBUF(I) = IBUF(J)
          I = I + IOFFTM
10        CONTINUE

      RETURN
      END
C
CCCCCCCCCCCCCCCCCCCCCCCCCCCCCCC END OF ROUTINE CTOV CCCCCCCCCCCCCCCCCCCCCCCCCCCCCCCCC
C
      SUBROUTINE DECOMP
      INTEGER ICOORD(0:1)
      COMMON/CUBCOM/ IPROC, NPROC, NDOC
      LOGICAL ILDIAG, IRDIAG
      COMMON/GRDCOM/ ID, ICPOS, IRPOS, ILEFT, IRIGHT, IUP, IDOWN,
     #               IP, JP, KP, KROW, IOFF, JOFF, ILDIAG, IRDIAG

      ID = 2**(NDOC/2)
      ICOORD(0) = ID
      ICOORD(1) = ID

      IRESP  = KGRDIN(2,ICOORD)
      IRESP  = KGRDCO(IPROC,ICOORD)
      ICPOS  = ICOORD(0)
      IRPOS  = ICOORD(1)
      ILEFT  = KGRDCH(IPROC,0,-1)
      IRIGHT = KGRDCH(IPROC,0, 1)
      IUP    = KGRDCH(IPROC,1,-1)
      IDOWN  = KGRDCH(IPROC,1, 1)

      IP = IRPOS + 1
      JP = ICPOS + 1

      ILDIAG = ICPOS .LT. IRPOS
      IRDIAG = ICPOS .GT. IRPOS

      RETURN
      END
C
CCCCCCCCCCCCCCCCCCCCCCCCCCCCCCC END OF ROUTINE DECOMP CCCCCCCCCCCCCCCCCCCCCCCCCCCCCCCC
C
      SUBROUTINE DWPAUS
      CHARACTER*1 INCHAR

10    CONTINUE
```

```
      PRINT *,'<<<<<<<<<<< Key in C to continue >>>>>>>>>>>>>>'
      READ *,INCHAR
      IF( INCHAR .NE. 'C' .AND. INCHAR .NE. 'c' ) GOTO 10

      RETURN
      END
C
CCCCCCCCCCCCCCCCCCCCCCCCCCCCC END OF ROUTINE DWPAUS CCCCCCCCCCCCCCCCCCCCCCCCCCCCC
C
      SUBROUTINE FNDPIV(IPROW,IPIV)
      PARAMETER ( MXBLKS = 100, MBBLKS = 100, IAMAX = 1000, IBMAX = 500 )
      PARAMETER ( MAXD  =   8 )
      REAL ASPACE(0:IAMAX-1), BSPACE(0:IBMAX-1)
      INTEGER JPTR(0:MXBLKS-1)
      COMMON/ABCOM/ ASPACE, BSPACE, JPTR
      REAL COMBUF(0:MXBLKS-1), L(0:MXBLKS-1), U(0:MXBLKS-1), BK(0:MBBLKS-1)
      INTEGER NBLOKS(0:MXBLKS-1), NROWNO(0:MXBLKS-1), NBLKNO(0:MXBLKS-1)
      COMMON/COMCOM/ COMBUF, L, U, BK, NBLOKS, NROWNO, NBLKNO
      COMMON/CUBCOM/ IPROC, NPROC, NDOC
      LOGICAL ILDIAG, IRDIAG
      COMMON/GRDCOM/ ID, ICPOS, IRPOS, ILEFT, IRIGHT, IUP, IDOWN,
     #               IP, JP, KP, KROW, IOFF, JOFF, ILDIAG, IRDIAG
      COMMON/PARCOM/ NX, NY, IRBLKS, IBCBLK, JBLKS, JPLUS, NB, N, IHALFW,
     #               N1, N11, M, KEND, KSTART, IOVER, IACBLK, IAMBLK
      LOGICAL IDOPIV
      COMMON/PIVCOM/ ICPROC(0:MAXD), IDOPIV
      PARAMETER ( IFSIZE = 4, ISIZE = 4 )

      IF ( JP .EQ. 1 ) THEN
          PIVOT = -0.1E+30
          IPIV  = 0
          DO 10 I=0,NY-1
              ATEMP = ASPACE(JPTR(JOFF-I)+I+IOFF)
              AABS  = ABS(ATEMP)
              IF ( AABS .GT. PIVOT ) THEN
                  PIVOT = AABS
                  IPIV  = I
              ENDIF
10        CONTINUE
          IF ( IP .EQ. 1 ) THEN
              IPROW = 1
              DO 20 I=2,ID
                  IRESP = KCREAD(CANDEL,IDOWN,0,IFSIZE)
                  IRESP = KCREAD(ICANDR,IDOWN,0,ISIZE)
                  IF ( CANDEL .GT. PIVOT ) THEN
                      PIVOT = CANDEL
                      IPIV  = ICANDR
```

```fortran
                         IPROW = I
                  ENDIF
20                CONTINUE
              NBLKNO(KP) = IPIV
              NROWNO(KP) = IPROW
        ELSE
              IRESP = KCWRIT(PIVOT,IUP,IFSIZE)
              IRESP = KCWRIT(IPIV,IUP,ISIZE)
              IF ( IP .NE. ID ) THEN
                  DO 30 I=IP+1,ID
                          IRESP = KCREAD(CANDEL,IDOWN,IUP,IFSIZE)
                          IRESP = KCREAD(ICANDR,IDOWN,IUP,ISIZE)
30                        CONTINUE
              ENDIF
        ENDIF
    ENDIF

    IRESP = KBROAD(IPROW,ICPROC(IP),NPROC-1,ISIZE)
    IRESP = KBROAD(IPIV, ICPROC(IP),NPROC-1,ISIZE)

    RETURN
    END
C
CCCCCCCCCCCCCCCCCCCCCCCCCCCCC END OF ROUTINE FNDPIV CCCCCCCCCCCCCCCCCCCCCCCCCCCCCCC
C
    SUBROUTINE FNDSOL

10  CONTINUE
    PRINT *, ' '
    PRINT *, 'Please choose one of the following:'
    PRINT *, '   1...to do LU decomposition'
    PRINT *, '   2...to do forward reduction'
    PRINT *, '   3...to do back substitution'
    PRINT *, '   4...to do all of the above'
    PRINT *, '   5...to quit this menu'
    READ  *, IOPT

    IF ( IOPT .EQ. 1 )THEN
        CALL LUDCMP
    ELSEIF ( IOPT .EQ. 2 ) THEN
        CALL FORWRD
    ELSEIF ( IOPT .EQ. 3 ) THEN
        CALL BCKSUB
    ELSEIF ( IOPT .EQ. 4 ) THEN
        CALL LUDCMP
        CALL FORWRD
        CALL BCKSUB
```

```fortran
      ELSEIF ( IOPT .EQ. 5 ) THEN
          RETURN
      ELSE
          PRINT *, ' '
          PRINT *, '*** Invalid input - try again ***'
      ENDIF
      GOTO 10

      END
C
CCCCCCCCCCCCCCCCCCCCCCCCCCCCCC END OF ROUTINE FNDSOL CCCCCCCCCCCCCCCCCCCCCCCCCCCCCC
C
      SUBROUTINE FORCRN(IBL)
      INTEGER IBL
      PARAMETER ( MXBLKS = 100, MBBLKS = 100, IAMAX = 1000, IBMAX = 500 )
      PARAMETER ( MAXD   =    8 )
      REAL ASPACE(0:IAMAX-1), BSPACE(0:IBMAX-1)
      INTEGER JPTR(0:MXBLKS-1)
      COMMON/ABCOM/ ASPACE, BSPACE, JPTR
      REAL COMBUF(0:MXBLKS-1), L(0:MXBLKS-1), U(0:MXBLKS-1), BK(0:MBBLKS-1)
      INTEGER NBLOKS(0:MXBLKS-1), NROWNO(0:MXBLKS-1), NBLKNO(0:MXBLKS-1)
      COMMON/COMCOM/ COMBUF, L, U, BK, NBLOKS, NROWNO, NBLKNO
      COMMON/CUBCOM/ IPROC, NPROC, NDOC
      LOGICAL ILDIAG, IRDIAG
      COMMON/GRDCOM/ ID, ICPOS, IRPOS, ILEFT, IRIGHT, IUP, IDOWN,
     #               IP, JP, KP, KROW, IOFF, JOFF, ILDIAG, IRDIAG
      COMMON/PARCOM/ NX, NY, IRBLKS, IBCBLK, JBLKS, JPLUS, NB, N, IHALFW,
     #               N1, N11, M, KEND, KSTART, IOVER, IACBLK, IAMBLK
      LOGICAL IDOPIV
      COMMON/PIVCOM/ ICPROC(0:MAXD), IDOPIV
      PARAMETER ( IFSIZE = 4 )

      CALL VTOC(COMBUF,BSPACE(IBL),JBLKS,IBCBLK)
      CALL SPLITP(COMBUF,X,IDOWN,IUP,IBCBLK*IFSIZE,0,ID)

      CALL VTOC(COMBUF,ASPACE(JPTR(JOFF)+IOFF),JPLUS,NY)
      CALL SPLITP(COMBUF,X,IRIGHT,ILEFT,NY*IFSIZE,0,ID)

      DO 10 J=0,IBCBLK-1
          X = BSPACE(JPTR(J)+IBL)
          DO 20 I=1,NY-1
              ITEMP = JPTR(J) + IBL + I
              JTEMP = JPTR(JOFF-I) + I + IOFF
              BSPACE(ITEMP) = BSPACE(ITEMP) - X*ASPACE(JTEMP)
20        CONTINUE
10    CONTINUE
```

```
      RETURN
      END
C
CCCCCCCCCCCCCCCCCCCCCCCCCCCCC END OF ROUTINE FORCRN CCCCCCCCCCCCCCCCCCCCCCCCCCCCC
C
      SUBROUTINE FORLFT(IBL)
      INTEGER IBL
      PARAMETER ( MXBLKS = 100, MBBLKS = 100, IAMAX = 1000, IBMAX = 500 )
      PARAMETER ( MAXD   =   8 )
      REAL ASPACE(0:IAMAX-1), BSPACE(0:IBMAX-1)
      INTEGER JPTR(0:MXBLKS-1)
      COMMON/ABCOM/ ASPACE, BSPACE, JPTR
      REAL COMBUF(0:MXBLKS-1), L(0:MXBLKS-1), U(0:MXBLKS-1), BK(0:MBBLKS-1)
      INTEGER NBLOKS(0:MXBLKS-1), NROWNO(0:MXBLKS-1), NBLKNO(0:MXBLKS-1)
      COMMON/COMCOM/ COMBUF, L, U, BK, NBLOKS, NROWNO, NBLKNO
      COMMON/CUBCOM/ IPROC, NPROC, NDOC
      LOGICAL ILDIAG, IRDIAG
      COMMON/GRDCOM/ ID, ICPOS, IRPOS, ILEFT, IRIGHT, IUP, IDOWN,
     #               IP, JP, KP, KROW, IOFF, JOFF, ILDIAG, IRDIAG
      COMMON/PARCOM/ NX, NY, IRBLKS, IBCBLK, JBLKS, JPLUS, NB, N, IHALFW,
     #               N1, N11, M, KEND, KSTART, IOVER, IACBLK, IAMBLK
      LOGICAL IDOPIV
      COMMON/PIVCOM/ ICPROC(0:MAXD), IDOPIV
      PARAMETER ( IFSIZE = 4 )

      CALL SPLITP(X,BK,IDOWN,IUP,IBCBLK*IFSIZE,IP-1,ID)

      CALL VTOC(COMBUF,ASPACE(JPTR(JOFF)+IOFF),JPLUS,NY)
      CALL SPLITP(COMBUF,X,IRIGHT,ILEFT,NY*IFSIZE,0,ID)

      DO 10 J=0,IBCBLK-1
          X = BK(J)
          DO 20 I=0,NY-1
              ITEMP = JPTR(J) + IBL + I
              JTEMP = JPTR(JOFF-I) + I + IOFF
              BSPACE(ITEMP) = BSPACE(ITEMP) - X*ASPACE(JTEMP)
20            CONTINUE
10        CONTINUE

      RETURN
      END
C
CCCCCCCCCCCCCCCCCCCCCCCCCCCCC END OF ROUTINE FORLFT CCCCCCCCCCCCCCCCCCCCCCCCCCCCC
C
      SUBROUTINE FORMID(IBL)
      INTEGER IBL
      PARAMETER ( MXBLKS = 100, MBBLKS = 100, IAMAX = 1000, IBMAX = 500 )
```

```
      PARAMETER ( MAXD   =   8 )
      REAL ASPACE(0:IAMAX-1), BSPACE(0:IBMAX-1)
      INTEGER JPTR(0:MXBLKS-1)
      COMMON/ABCOM/ ASPACE, BSPACE, JPTR
      REAL COMBUF(0:MXBLKS-1), L(0:MXBLKS-1), U(0:MXBLKS-1), BK(0:MBBLKS-1)
      INTEGER NBLOKS(0:MXBLKS-1), NROWNO(0:MXBLKS-1), NBLKNO(0:MXBLKS-1)
      COMMON/COMCOM/ COMBUF, L, U, BK, NBLOKS, NROWNO, NBLKNO
      COMMON/CUBCOM/ IPROC, NPROC, NDOC
      LOGICAL ILDIAG, IRDIAG
      COMMON/GRDCOM/ ID, ICPOS, IRPOS, ILEFT, IRIGHT, IUP, IDOWN,
     #              IP, JP, KP, KROW, IOFF, JOFF, ILDIAG, IRDIAG
      COMMON/PARCOM/ NX, NY, IRBLKS, IBCBLK, JBLKS, JPLUS, NB, N, IHALFW,
     #              N1, N11, M, KEND, KSTART, IOVER, IACBLK, IAMBLK
      LOGICAL IDOPIV
      COMMON/PIVCOM/ ICPROC(0:MAXD), IDOPIV
      PARAMETER ( IFSIZE = 4 )

      CALL SPLITP(X,BK,IDOWN,IUP,IBCBLK*IFSIZE,IP-1,ID)
      CALL SPLITP(X,L,IRIGHT,ILEFT,NY*IFSIZE,JP-1,ID)

      DO 10 J=0,IBCBLK-1
         X = BK(J)
         DO 20 I=0,NY-1
            ITEMP = JPTR(J) + IBL + I
            BSPACE(ITEMP) = BSPACE(ITEMP) - X*L(I)
20       CONTINUE
10    CONTINUE

      RETURN
      END
C
CCCCCCCCCCCCCCCCCCCCCCCCCCCCCC END OF ROUTINE FORMID CCCCCCCCCCCCCCCCCCCCCCCCCCCCCCCC
C
      SUBROUTINE FORTOP(IBL)
      INTEGER IBL
      PARAMETER ( MXBLKS = 100, MBBLKS = 100, IAMAX = 1000, IBMAX = 500 )
      PARAMETER ( MAXD   =   8 )
      REAL ASPACE(0:IAMAX-1), BSPACE(0:IBMAX-1)
      INTEGER JPTR(0:MXBLKS-1)
      COMMON/ABCOM/ ASPACE, BSPACE, JPTR
      REAL COMBUF(0:MXBLKS-1), L(0:MXBLKS-1), U(0:MXBLKS-1), BK(0:MBBLKS-1)
      INTEGER NBLOKS(0:MXBLKS-1), NROWNO(0:MXBLKS-1), NBLKNO(0:MXBLKS-1)
      COMMON/COMCOM/ COMBUF, L, U, BK, NBLOKS, NROWNO, NBLKNO
      COMMON/CUBCOM/ IPROC, NPROC, NDOC
      LOGICAL ILDIAG, IRDIAG
      COMMON/GRDCOM/ ID, ICPOS, IRPOS, ILEFT, IRIGHT, IUP, IDOWN,
     #              IP, JP, KP, KROW, IOFF, JOFF, ILDIAG, IRDIAG
```

```
      COMMON/PARCOM/ NX, NY, IRBLKS, IBCBLK, JBLKS, JPLUS, NB, N, IHALFW,
     #               N1, N11, M, KEND, KSTART, IOVER, IACBLK, IAMBLK
      LOGICAL IDOPIV
      COMMON/PIVCOM/ ICPROC(0:MAXD), IDOPIV
      PARAMETER ( IFSIZE = 4 )

      CALL VTOC(COMBUF,BSPACE(IBL),JBLKS,IBCBLK)
      CALL SPLITP(COMBUF,X,IDOWN,IUP,IBCBLK*IFSIZE,0,ID)
      CALL SPLITP(X,L,IRIGHT,ILEFT,NY*IFSIZE,JP-1,ID)

      DO 10 J=0,IBCBLK-1
          X = BSPACE(JPTR(J)+IBL)
          DO 20 I=1,NY-1
              ITEMP = JPTR(J) + IBL + I
              BSPACE(ITEMP) = BSPACE(ITEMP) - X*L(I)
20        CONTINUE
10    CONTINUE

      RETURN
      END
C
CCCCCCCCCCCCCCCCCCCCCCCCCCCCCC END OF ROUTINE FORTOP CCCCCCCCCCCCCCCCCCCCCCCCCCCCCC
C
      SUBROUTINE FORWRD
      PARAMETER ( MAXD  =   8 )
      LOGICAL ILDIAG, IRDIAG
      COMMON/GRDCOM/ ID, ICPOS, IRPOS, ILEFT, IRIGHT, IUP, IDOWN,
     #               IP, JP, KP, KROW, IOFF, JOFF, ILDIAG, IRDIAG
      COMMON/PARCOM/ NX, NY, IRBLKS, IBCBLK, JBLKS, JPLUS, NB, N, IHALFW,
     #               N1, N11, M, KEND, KSTART, IOVER, IACBLK, IAMBLK
      LOGICAL IDOPIV
      COMMON/PIVCOM/ ICPROC(0:MAXD), IDOPIV

      KP = 0

      DO 10 KROW=0,N-1
          IBL = (KROW+IP-1)/ID + 1
          CALL LOCK(KP)
          IF ( IDOPIV ) CALL PIVOTB(IBL)
          NY = N11
          IF ( KROW .GE. KEND ) NY = (N-KROW-1)/ID + 1
          IF ( IP .EQ. 1 .AND. JP .EQ. 1 ) THEN
              CALL FORCRN(IBL)
          ELSEIF ( IP .EQ. 1 ) THEN
              CALL FORTOP(IBL)
          ELSEIF ( JP .EQ. 1 ) THEN
              CALL FORLFT(IBL)
```

```
          ELSE
              CALL FORMID(IBL)
          ENDIF
          IP = IP - 1
          IF ( IP .EQ. 0 ) IP = ID
          JP = JP - 1
          IF ( JP .EQ. 0 ) JP = ID
          IF ( IP .EQ. ID .OR. JP .EQ. ID ) KP = KP + 1
10        CONTINUE

       RETURN
       END
C
CCCCCCCCCCCCCCCCCCCCCCCCCCCCCCC END OF ROUTINE FORWRD CCCCCCCCCCCCCCCCCCCCCCCCCCCCCCC
C
       SUBROUTINE GETPAR
       COMMON/CUBCOM/ IPROC, NPROC, NDOC
       INTEGER IENV(5)

       CALL KPARAM(IENV)
       NDOC  = IENV(1)
       IPROC = IENV(2)
       NPROC = IENV(3)

       RETURN
       END
C
CCCCCCCCCCCCCCCCCCCCCCCCCCCCCCC END OF ROUTINE GETPAR CCCCCCCCCCCCCCCCCCCCCCCCCCCCCCC
C
       FUNCTION IDIVID(N,K)
       INTEGER N, K
       IDIVID = N/K
       IF ( N .LT. 0 .AND. K*IDIVID .NE. N ) IDIVID = IDIVID - 1
       RETURN
       END
C
CCCCCCCCCCCCCCCCCCCCCCCCCCCCCCC END OF ROUTINE IDIVID CCCCCCCCCCCCCCCCCCCCCCCCCCCCCCC
C
       FUNCTION IGTASK(IDUMMY)
       INTEGER IDUMMY

       PRINT *, ' '
       PRINT *, 'Please choose one of the following:'
       PRINT *, '   1...to initialize a problem'
       PRINT *, '   2...to list input/output matrices'
       PRINT *, '   3...to find the solution'
       PRINT *, '   4...to terminate the program'
```

```
      READ *, IGTASK
      RETURN
      END
C
CCCCCCCCCCCCCCCCCCCCCCCCCCCCCC END OF ROUTINE IGTASK CCCCCCCCCCCCCCCCCCCCCCCCCCCCCC
C
      SUBROUTINE INITLZ
      PARAMETER ( MXBLKS = 100, MBBLKS = 100, IAMAX = 1000, IBMAX = 500 )
      REAL ASPACE(0:IAMAX-1), BSPACE(0:IBMAX-1)
      INTEGER JPTR(0:MXBLKS-1)
      COMMON/ABCOM/ ASPACE, BSPACE, JPTR

      DO 10 I=0,IAMAX-1
          ASPACE(I) = 0.0
10        CONTINUE

      DO 20 I=0,IBMAX-1
          BSPACE(I) = 0.0
20        CONTINUE

      CALL ASKQ
      CALL LOADA
      CALL LOADB

      RETURN
      END
C
CCCCCCCCCCCCCCCCCCCCCCCCCCCCCC END OF ROUTINE INITLZ CCCCCCCCCCCCCCCCCCCCCCCCCCCCCC
C
      SUBROUTINE INITPV
      INTEGER ICOORD(0:1)
      LOGICAL ILDIAG, IRDIAG
      COMMON/GRDCOM/ ID, ICPOS, IRPOS, ILEFT, IRIGHT, IUP, IDOWN,
     #               IP, JP, KP, KROW, IOFF, JOFF, ILDIAG, IRDIAG
      PARAMETER ( MAXD = 8 )
      LOGICAL IDOPIV
      COMMON/PIVCOM/ ICPROC(0:MAXD), IDOPIV
      CHARACTER*1 YORN

      PRINT *, 'Do you want pivoting (y/n) ?'
      READ  *, YORN
      IF ( YORN .EQ. 'Y' .OR. YORN .EQ. 'y' ) THEN
          IDOPIV = .TRUE.
          DO 10 I=0,ID-1
              ICOORD(0) = I
              ICOORD(1) = I
```

```
                ICPROC(IP) = KGRDPR(ICOORD)
                IP = IP - 1
                IF ( IP .EQ. 0 ) IP = ID
10              CONTINUE
        ELSE
            IDOPIV = .FALSE.
        ENDIF

        RETURN
        END
C
CCCCCCCCCCCCCCCCCCCCCCCCCCCCCCCC END OF ROUTINE INITPV CCCCCCCCCCCCCCCCCCCCCCCCCCCCCCC
C
        SUBROUTINE LISMAT

10      CONTINUE
        PRINT *, 'Please choose one of the following:'
        PRINT *, '   1...to list the matrix A'
        PRINT *, '   2...to list the matrix B'
        PRINT *, '   3...to quit this menu'
        READ  *, IOPT

        IF ( IOPT .EQ. 1 ) THEN
            CALL LISTA
        ELSEIF ( IOPT .EQ. 2 ) THEN
            CALL LISTB
        ELSEIF ( IOPT .EQ. 3 ) THEN
            RETURN
        ELSE
            PRINT *, '*** Invalid input - try again'
        ENDIF
        GOTO 10

        END
C
CCCCCCCCCCCCCCCCCCCCCCCCCCCCCCCC END OF ROUTINE LISMAT CCCCCCCCCCCCCCCCCCCCCCCCCCCCCCC
C
        SUBROUTINE LISPRC(IAB)
        INTEGER IAB
        INTEGER STDOUT
        PARAMETER ( STDOUT = 6 )
        COMMON/PARCOM/ NX, NY, IRBLKS, IBCBLK, JBLKS, JPLUS, NB, N, IHALFW,
     #                 N1, N11, M, KEND, KSTART, IOVER, IACBLK, IAMBLK
        COMMON/CUBCOM/ IPROC, NPROC, NDOC
        PARAMETER ( MXBLKS = 100, MBBLKS = 100, IAMAX = 1000, IBMAX = 500 )
        REAL ASPACE(0:IAMAX-1), BSPACE(0:IBMAX-1)
        INTEGER JPTR(0:MXBLKS-1)
```

```
      COMMON/ABCOM/ ASPACE, BSPACE, JPTR

10    CONTINUE
      PRINT *, ' '
      PRINT *, 'Please give the processor number ( -ve to end )'
      READ  *,KPROC

      IF ( KPROC .LT. 0 ) RETURN
      IF ( KPROC .GE. NPROC ) THEN
          PRINT *, ' '
          PRINT *, '*** Invalid input - try again ***'
          GOTO 10
      ENDIF

      PRINT *, 'Please give the minimum and maximum row numbers'
      READ  *,IRMIN,IRMAX
      IF ( IRMIN .LT. 0 ) IRMIN = 0
      IF ( IRMAX .GE. IRBLKS ) IRMAX = IRBLKS - 1

      PRINT *, 'Please give the minimum and maximum column numbers'
      READ  *,ICMIN,ICMAX
      IF ( ICMIN .LT. 0 ) ICMIN = 0
      IF ( IAB .EQ. 0 ) THEN
          IF ( ICMAX .GE. IAMBLK ) ICMAX = IAMBLK - 1
      ELSE
          IF ( ICMAX .GE. IBCBLK ) ICMAX = IBCBLK - 1
      ENDIF
#ifndef SEQ
      MULTIPLE(STDOUT)
#endif
      DO 20 I =IRMIN,IRMAX
          IF ( IPROC .EQ. KPROC ) THEN
              PRINT *,'Row number',I
          ENDIF
          K = 0
          DO 30 J=ICMIN,ICMAX
              IF ( IPROC .EQ. KPROC ) THEN
                  IF ( IAB .EQ. 0 ) THEN
                      VALUE = ASPACE(JPTR(J)+I+1)
                  ELSE
                      VALUE = BSPACE(JPTR(J)+I+1)
                  ENDIF
                  PRINT 100,VALUE
              ENDIF
              IF ( MOD(K,7) .EQ. 6 ) THEN
                  PRINT *,' '
                  FLUSH(STDOUT)
```

```
                ENDIF
                K = K + 1
30              CONTINUE
        IF ( IPROC .EQ. KPROC ) THEN
                PRINT *, ' '
        ENDIF
        FLUSH(STDOUT)
20      CONTINUE
#ifndef SEQ
    SINGLE(STDOUT)
#endif
    IF ( IAB .EQ. 0 ) THEN
        PRINT *, ' '
        PRINT *, 'The matrix A as stored in processor ',IPROC
    ELSE
        PRINT *, ' '
        PRINT *, 'The matrix B as stored in processor ',IPROC
    ENDIF

    PRINT *, 'Results for rows ',IRMIN,' to ',IRMAX
    PRINT *, '      and columns ',ICMIN,' to ',ICMAX
    CALL DWPAUS
    GOTO 10
#ifndef XENIX
100 FORMAT(E11.3$)
#else
100 FORMAT(E11.3\)
#endif
    END
C
CCCCCCCCCCCCCCCCCCCCCCCCCCCCCC END OF ROUTINE LISPRC CCCCCCCCCCCCCCCCCCCCCCCCCCCCCC
C
    SUBROUTINE LISTA

10  CONTINUE
    PRINT *, ' '
    PRINT *, 'Please choose one of the following:'
    PRINT *, '   1...to list A as a full matrix'
    PRINT *, '   2...to list A as an upper triangular matrix'
    PRINT *, '   3...to list A as an lower triangular matrix'
    PRINT *, '   4...to list A by processor'
    PRINT *, '   5...to quit this menu'
    READ  *, LOPT

    IF ( LOPT .GT. 0 .AND. LOPT .LT. 4 ) THEN
        CALL MATLIS(LOPT)
    ELSEIF ( LOPT .EQ. 4 ) THEN
```

```
          CALL LISPRC(0)
      ELSEIF ( LOPT .EQ. 5 ) THEN
          GOTO 99
      ELSE
          PRINT *, '*** Invalid input - try again'
      ENDIF
      GOTO 10

99    RETURN
      END
C
CCCCCCCCCCCCCCCCCCCCCCCCCCCCC END OF ROUTINE LISTA CCCCCCCCCCCCCCCCCCCCCCCCCCCCC
C
      SUBROUTINE LISTB

10    CONTINUE
      PRINT *, ' '
      PRINT *, 'Please choose one of the following:'
      PRINT *, '   1...to list B by columns'
      PRINT *, '   2...to list B by processor'
      PRINT *, '   3...to quit this menu'
      READ  *, LOPT

      IF ( LOPT .EQ. 1 ) THEN
          CALL COLLIS
      ELSEIF ( LOPT .EQ. 2 ) THEN
          CALL LISPRC(1)
      ELSEIF ( LOPT .EQ. 3 ) THEN
          GOTO 99
      ELSE
          PRINT *, '*** Invalid input - try again'
      ENDIF
      GOTO 10

99    RETURN
      END
C
CCCCCCCCCCCCCCCCCCCCCCCCCCCCC END OF ROUTINE LISTB CCCCCCCCCCCCCCCCCCCCCCCCCCCCC
C
      SUBROUTINE LOADA
      REAL NEXTA
      PARAMETER ( MXBLKS = 100, MBBLKS = 100, IAMAX = 1000, IBMAX = 500 )
      REAL ASPACE(0:IAMAX-1), BSPACE(0:IBMAX-1)
      INTEGER JPTR(0:MXBLKS-1)
      COMMON/ABCOM/ ASPACE, BSPACE, JPTR
      LOGICAL ILDIAG, IRDIAG
      COMMON/GRDCOM/ ID, ICPOS, IRPOS, ILEFT, IRIGHT, IUP, IDOWN,
```

```
#                   IP, JP, KP, KROW, IOFF, JOFF, ILDIAG, IRDIAG
      COMMON/PARCOM/ NX, NY, IRBLKS, IBCBLK, JBLKS, JPLUS, NB, N, IHALFW,
#                   N1, N11, M, KEND, KSTART, IOVER, IACBLK, IAMBLK

      JMAX = ID*IAMBLK
      DO 10 I=0,N-1
          IRBNO  = I/ID
          IPRROW = ID*IRBNO + IRPOS
          IOFFST = I
          JSHIFT = ID*(IRBNO-N11)
          DO 20 J=0,JMAX-1
              ICBNO  = J/ID
              IAOFF  = JPTR(ICBNO) + IRBNO + 1
              JOFFST = JSHIFT + J
              IF ( JOFFST .LT. 0 .OR. JOFFST .GE. N ) THEN
                  VALUE = 0.0
              ELSE
                  VALUE = NEXTA(IOFFST,JOFFST)
              ENDIF
              IPRCOL = JSHIFT + ICBNO*ID + ICPOS
              IF ( IOFFST .EQ. IPRROW .AND. JOFFST .EQ. IPRCOL)
#                 ASPACE(IAOFF) = VALUE
20            CONTINUE
10        CONTINUE

      RETURN
      END
C
CCCCCCCCCCCCCCCCCCCCCCCCCCCCCCC END OF ROUTINE LOADA CCCCCCCCCCCCCCCCCCCCCCCCCCCCCCC
C
      SUBROUTINE LOADB
      REAL NEXTB
      PARAMETER ( MXBLKS = 100, MBBLKS = 100, IAMAX = 1000, IBMAX = 500 )
      REAL ASPACE(0:IAMAX-1), BSPACE(0:IBMAX-1)
      INTEGER JPTR(0:MXBLKS-1)
      COMMON/ABCOM/ ASPACE, BSPACE, JPTR
      LOGICAL ILDIAG, IRDIAG
      COMMON/GRDCOM/ ID, ICPOS, IRPOS, ILEFT, IRIGHT, IUP, IDOWN,
#                   IP, JP, KP, KROW, IOFF, JOFF, ILDIAG, IRDIAG
      COMMON/PARCOM/ NX, NY, IRBLKS, IBCBLK, JBLKS, JPLUS, NB, N, IHALFW,
#                   N1, N11, M, KEND, KSTART, IOVER, IACBLK, IAMBLK
      COMMON/USRCOM/ IUSERN, IUSERM, IUSERB

      JMAX = ID*IBCBLK
      DO 10 J=0,JMAX-1
          ICBNO  = J/ID
          IPRCOL = ID*ICBNO + ICPOS
```

```
        JSHIFT = JPTR(ICBNO)
        DO 20 I=0,N-1
            IRBNO  = I/ID
            IPRROW = ID*IRBNO + IRPOS
            IF ( J .GE. IUSERB .OR. I .GE. IUSERN ) THEN
                VALUE = 0.0
            ELSE
                VALUE = NEXTB(I,J)
            ENDIF
            IF ( IPRCOL .EQ. J .AND. IPRROW .EQ. I)
     #          BSPACE(JSHIFT+IRBNO+1) = VALUE
20          CONTINUE
10      CONTINUE

        RETURN
        END
C
CCCCCCCCCCCCCCCCCCCCCCCCCCCCCCCC END OF ROUTINE LOADB CCCCCCCCCCCCCCCCCCCCCCCCCCCCCCCC
C
        SUBROUTINE LOCK(IX)
        INTEGER IX
        LOGICAL ILDIAG, IRDIAG
        COMMON/GRDCOM/ ID, ICPOS, IRPOS, ILEFT, IRIGHT, IUP, IDOWN,
     #                 IP, JP, KP, KROW, IOFF, JOFF, ILDIAG, IRDIAG
        COMMON/PARCOM/ NX, NY, IRBLKS, IBCBLK, JBLKS, JPLUS, NB, N, IHALFW,
     #                 N1, N11, M, KEND, KSTART, IOVER, IACBLK, IAMBLK

        IF ( ILDIAG ) THEN
            IOFF = 1   + IDIVID(IX,2)
            JOFF = N11 + MYMOD(IX,2)
        ELSEIF ( IRDIAG ) THEN
            IOFF = 1   + IDIVID(IX+1,2)
            JOFF = N11 - MYMOD(IX,2)
        ELSE
            IOFF = 1 + IX
            JOFF = N11
        ENDIF

        RETURN
        END
C
CCCCCCCCCCCCCCCCCCCCCCCCCCCCCCCC END OF ROUTINE LOCK CCCCCCCCCCCCCCCCCCCCCCCCCCCCCCCC
C
        SUBROUTINE LUCORN
        PARAMETER ( MXBLKS = 100, MBBLKS = 100, IAMAX = 1000, IBMAX = 500 )
        PARAMETER ( MAXD  =    8 )
        REAL ASPACE(0:IAMAX-1), BSPACE(0:IBMAX-1)
```

```
      INTEGER JPTR(0:MXBLKS-1)
      COMMON/ABCOM/ ASPACE, BSPACE, JPTR
      REAL COMBUF(0:MXBLKS-1), L(0:MXBLKS-1), U(0:MXBLKS-1), BK(0:MBBLKS-1)
      INTEGER NBLOKS(0:MXBLKS-1), NROWNO(0:MXBLKS-1), NBLKNO(0:MXBLKS-1)
      COMMON/COMCOM/ COMBUF, L, U, BK, NBLOKS, NROWNO, NBLKNO
      LOGICAL ILDIAG, IRDIAG
      COMMON/GRDCOM/ ID, ICPOS, IRPOS, ILEFT, IRIGHT, IUP, IDOWN,
     #               IP, JP, KP, KROW, IOFF, JOFF, ILDIAG, IRDIAG
      COMMON/PARCOM/ NX, NY, IRBLKS, IBCBLK, JBLKS, JPLUS, NB, N, IHALFW,
     #               N1, N11, M, KEND, KSTART, IOVER, IACBLK, IAMBLK
      LOGICAL IDOPIV
      COMMON/PIVCOM/ ICPROC(0:MAXD), IDOPIV
      PARAMETER ( IFSIZE = 4 )

      NY = N11
      IF ( KROW .GE. KEND ) NY = (N-KROW-1)/ID + 1

      IF ( IDOPIV ) THEN
          CALL FNDPIV(IPROW,IPIV)
          CALL PIVOTA(IPROW,IPIV)
      ELSE
          NX = NY
          CALL VTOC(COMBUF,ASPACE(JPTR(JOFF)+IOFF),JBLKS,NX)
          CALL SPLITP(COMBUF,X,IDOWN,IUP,NX*IFSIZE,0,ID)
      ENDIF

      ITEMP = JPTR(JOFF) + IOFF
      X     = 1.0/ASPACE(ITEMP)
      DO 10 I=1,NY-1
          ITEMP = JPTR(JOFF-I) + I + IOFF
          ASPACE(ITEMP) = X*ASPACE(ITEMP)
10        CONTINUE

      CALL VTOC(COMBUF,ASPACE(JPTR(JOFF-1)+1+IOFF),JPLUS,NY-1)
      CALL SPLITP(COMBUF,X,IRIGHT,ILEFT,(NY-1)*IFSIZE,0,ID)

      DO 20 J=1,NX-1
          COMBUF(J) = ASPACE(JPTR(JOFF+J)+IOFF)
20        CONTINUE

      DO 30 I=1,NY-1
          X = ASPACE(JPTR(JOFF-I)+I+IOFF)
          DO 40 J=1,NX-1
              ITEMP = JPTR(JOFF+J-I) + I + IOFF
              ASPACE(ITEMP) = ASPACE(ITEMP) - X*COMBUF(J)
40            CONTINUE
30        CONTINUE
```

```
      RETURN
      END
C
CCCCCCCCCCCCCCCCCCCCCCCCCCCC END OF ROUTINE LUCORN CCCCCCCCCCCCCCCCCCCCCCCCCCCCCC
C
      SUBROUTINE LULEFT
      PARAMETER ( MXBLKS = 100, MBBLKS = 100, IAMAX = 1000, IBMAX = 500 )
      PARAMETER ( MAXD   =   8 )
      REAL ASPACE(0:IAMAX-1), BSPACE(0:IBMAX-1)
      INTEGER JPTR(0:MXBLKS-1)
      COMMON/ABCOM/ ASPACE, BSPACE, JPTR
      REAL COMBUF(0:MXBLKS-1), L(0:MXBLKS-1), U(0:MXBLKS-1), BK(0:MBBLKS-1)
      INTEGER NBLOKS(0:MXBLKS-1), NROWNO(0:MXBLKS-1), NBLKNO(0:MXBLKS-1)
      COMMON/COMCOM/ COMBUF, L, U, BK, NBLOKS, NROWNO, NBLKNO
      LOGICAL ILDIAG, IRDIAG
      COMMON/GRDCOM/ ID, ICPOS, IRPOS, ILEFT, IRIGHT, IUP, IDOWN,
     #               IP, JP, KP, KROW, IOFF, JOFF, ILDIAG, IRDIAG
      COMMON/PARCOM/ NX, NY, IRBLKS, IBCBLK, JBLKS, JPLUS, NB, N, IHALFW,
     #               N1, N11, M, KEND, KSTART, IOVER, IACBLK, IAMBLK
      LOGICAL IDOPIV
      COMMON/PIVCOM/ ICPROC(0:MAXD), IDOPIV
      PARAMETER ( IFSIZE = 4 )

      NY = N11
      IF ( KROW .GE. KEND ) NY = (N-KROW-1)/ID + 1

      IF ( IDOPIV ) THEN
          CALL FNDPIV(IPROW,IPIV)
          CALL PIVOTA(IPROW,IPIV)
      ELSE
          NX = NY
          CALL SPLITP(X,U,IDOWN,IUP,NX*IFSIZE,IP-1,ID)
      ENDIF

      X    = 1.0/U(0)
      U(0) = X
      DO 10 I=0,NY-1
          ITEMP = JPTR(JOFF-I) + I + IOFF
          ASPACE(ITEMP) = U(0)*ASPACE(ITEMP)
10        CONTINUE

      CALL VTOC(COMBUF,ASPACE(JPTR(JOFF)+IOFF),JPLUS,NY)
      CALL SPLITP(COMBUF,X,IRIGHT,ILEFT,NY*IFSIZE,0,ID)

      DO 30 I=0,NY-1
          X = ASPACE(JPTR(JOFF-I)+I+IOFF)
```

```
          DO 40 J=1,NX-1
              ITEMP = JPTR(JOFF+J-I) + I + IOFF
              ASPACE(ITEMP) = ASPACE(ITEMP) - X*U(J)
40            CONTINUE
30        CONTINUE

      RETURN
      END
C
CCCCCCCCCCCCCCCCCCCCCCCCCCCC END OF ROUTINE LULEFT CCCCCCCCCCCCCCCCCCCCCCCCCCCCCCC
C
      SUBROUTINE LUMIDL
      PARAMETER ( MXBLKS = 100, MBBLKS = 100, IAMAX = 1000, IBMAX = 500 )
      PARAMETER ( MAXD   =    8 )
      REAL ASPACE(0:IAMAX-1), BSPACE(0:IBMAX-1)
      INTEGER JPTR(0:MXBLKS-1)
      COMMON/ABCOM/ ASPACE, BSPACE, JPTR
      REAL COMBUF(0:MXBLKS-1), L(0:MXBLKS-1), U(0:MXBLKS-1), BK(0:MBBLKS-1)
      INTEGER NBLOKS(0:MXBLKS-1), NROWNO(0:MXBLKS-1), NBLKNO(0:MXBLKS-1)
      COMMON/COMCOM/ COMBUF, L, U, BK, NBLOKS, NROWNO, NBLKNO
      LOGICAL ILDIAG, IRDIAG
      COMMON/GRDCOM/ ID, ICPOS, IRPOS, ILEFT, IRIGHT, IUP, IDOWN,
     #               IP, JP, KP, KROW, IOFF, JOFF, ILDIAG, IRDIAG
      COMMON/PARCOM/ NX, NY, IRBLKS, IBCBLK, JBLKS, JPLUS, NB, N, IHALFW,
     #               N1, N11, M, KEND, KSTART, IOVER, IACBLK, IAMBLK
      LOGICAL IDOPIV
      COMMON/PIVCOM/ ICPROC(0:MAXD), IDOPIV
      PARAMETER ( IFSIZE = 4 )

      NY = N11
      IF ( KROW .GE. KEND ) NY = (N-KROW-1)/ID + 1

      IF ( IDOPIV ) THEN
          CALL FNDPIV(IPROW,IPIV)
          CALL PIVOTA(IPROW,IPIV)
      ELSE
          NX = NY
          CALL SPLITP(X,U,IDOWN,IUP,NX*IFSIZE,IP-1,ID)
      ENDIF

      CALL SPLITP(X,L,IRIGHT,ILEFT,NY*IFSIZE,JP-1,ID)

      DO 30 I=0,NY-1
          X = L(I)
          DO 40 J=0,NX-1
              ITEMP = JPTR(JOFF+J-I) + I + IOFF
              ASPACE(ITEMP) = ASPACE(ITEMP) - X*U(J)
```

```
40          CONTINUE
30        CONTINUE

      RETURN
      END
C
CCCCCCCCCCCCCCCCCCCCCCCCCCCC END OF ROUTINE LUMIDL CCCCCCCCCCCCCCCCCCCCCCCCCCCCCCC
C
      SUBROUTINE LUTOP
      PARAMETER ( MXBLKS = 100, MBBLKS = 100, IAMAX = 1000, IBMAX = 500 )
      PARAMETER ( MAXD   =   8 )
      REAL ASPACE(0:IAMAX-1), BSPACE(0:IBMAX-1)
      INTEGER JPTR(0:MXBLKS-1)
      COMMON/ABCOM/ ASPACE, BSPACE, JPTR
      REAL COMBUF(0:MXBLKS-1), L(0:MXBLKS-1), U(0:MXBLKS-1), BK(0:MBBLKS-1)
      INTEGER NBLOKS(0:MXBLKS-1), NROWNO(0:MXBLKS-1), NBLKNO(0:MXBLKS-1)
      COMMON/COMCOM/ COMBUF, L, U, BK, NBLOKS, NROWNO, NBLKNO
      LOGICAL ILDIAG, IRDIAG
      COMMON/GRDCOM/ ID, ICPOS, IRPOS, ILEFT, IRIGHT, IUP, IDOWN,
     #               IP, JP, KP, KROW, IOFF, JOFF, ILDIAG, IRDIAG
      COMMON/PARCOM/ NX, NY, IRBLKS, IBCBLK, JBLKS, JPLUS, NB, N, IHALFW,
     #               N1, N11, M, KEND, KSTART, IOVER, IACBLK, IAMBLK
      LOGICAL IDOPIV
      COMMON/PIVCOM/ ICPROC(0:MAXD), IDOPIV
      PARAMETER ( IFSIZE = 4 )

      NY = N11
      IF ( KROW .GE. KEND ) NY = (N-KROW-1)/ID + 1

      IF ( IDOPIV ) THEN
          CALL FNDPIV(IPROW,IPIV)
          CALL PIVOTA(IPROW,IPIV)
      ELSE
          NX = NY
          CALL VTOC(COMBUF,ASPACE(JPTR(JOFF)+IOFF),JBLKS,NX)
          CALL SPLITP(COMBUF,X,IDOWN,IUP,NX*IFSIZE,0,ID)
      ENDIF

      CALL SPLITP(X,L(1),IRIGHT,ILEFT,(NY-1)*IFSIZE,JP-1,ID)

      DO 20 J=0,NX-1
          COMBUF(J) = ASPACE(JPTR(JOFF+J)+IOFF)
20        CONTINUE

      DO 30 I=1,NY-1
          X = L(I)
          DO 40 J=0,NX-1
```

```
                ITEMP = JPTR(JOFF+J-I) + I + IOFF
                ASPACE(ITEMP) = ASPACE(ITEMP) - X*COMBUF(J)
40           CONTINUE
30        CONTINUE

      RETURN
      END
C
CCCCCCCCCCCCCCCCCCCCCCCCCCCCCCC END OF ROUTINE LUTOP CCCCCCCCCCCCCCCCCCCCCCCCCCCCCCC
C
      SUBROUTINE LUDCMP
      LOGICAL ILDIAG, IRDIAG
      COMMON/GRDCOM/ ID, ICPOS, IRPOS, ILEFT, IRIGHT, IUP, IDOWN,
     #               IP, JP, KP, KROW, IOFF, JOFF, ILDIAG, IRDIAG
      COMMON/PARCOM/ NX, NY, IRBLKS, IBCBLK, JBLKS, JPLUS, NB, N, IHALFW,
     #               N1, N11, M, KEND, KSTART, IOVER, IACBLK, IAMBLK

      KP = 0
      DO 10 KROW=0,N-1
          CALL LOCK(KP)
          IF ( IP .EQ. 1 .AND. JP .EQ. 1 ) THEN
              CALL LUCORN
          ELSEIF ( IP .EQ. 1 ) THEN
              CALL LUTOP
          ELSEIF ( JP .EQ. 1 ) THEN
              CALL LULEFT
          ELSE
              CALL LUMIDL
          ENDIF
          IP = IP - 1
          IF ( IP .EQ. 0 ) IP = ID
          JP = JP - 1
          IF ( JP .EQ. 0 ) JP = ID
          IF ( IP .EQ. ID .OR. JP .EQ. ID ) KP = KP + 1
10        CONTINUE

      RETURN
      END
C
CCCCCCCCCCCCCCCCCCCCCCCCCCCCCCC END OF ROUTINE LUDCMP CCCCCCCCCCCCCCCCCCCCCCCCCCCCCCC
C
      SUBROUTINE MATLIS(IOPT)
      INTEGER IOPT
      INTEGER STDOUT
      PARAMETER ( STDOUT = 6 )
      PARAMETER ( IFULL = 1, IUPPER = 2, ILOWER = 3 )
      LOGICAL ILDIAG, IRDIAG
```

```
      COMMON/GRDCOM/ ID, ICPOS, IRPOS, ILEFT, IRIGHT, IUP, IDOWN,
     #              IP, JP, KP, KROW, IOFF, JOFF, ILDIAG, IRDIAG
      COMMON/PARCOM/ NX, NY, IRBLKS, IBCBLK, JBLKS, JPLUS, NB, N, IHALFW,
     #              N1, N11, M, KEND, KSTART, IOVER, IACBLK, IAMBLK
      COMMON/USRCOM/ IUSERN, IUSERM, IUSERB
      PARAMETER ( MXBLKS = 100, MBBLKS = 100, IAMAX = 1000, IBMAX = 500 )
      REAL ASPACE(0:IAMAX-1), BSPACE(0:IBMAX-1)
      INTEGER JPTR(0:MXBLKS-1)
      COMMON/ABCOM/ ASPACE, BSPACE, JPTR
      LOGICAL TLOG

      PRINT *, 'Please give the minimum and maximum row numbers'
      READ  *,IRMIN,IRMAX
      IF ( IRMIN .LT. 0 .OR. IRMIN .GE. IUSERN ) IRMIN = 0
      IF ( IRMAX .LT. 0 .OR. IRMAX .GE. IUSERN ) IRMAX = IUSERN - 1
      IF ( IRMIN .GT. IRMAX ) THEN
          IRTEMP = IRMIN
          IRMIN  = IRMAX
          IRMAX  = IRTEMP
      ENDIF

      PRINT *, 'Please give the minimum and maximum column numbers'
      READ  *,ICMIN,ICMAX
      IF ( ICMIN .LT. 0 .OR. ICMIN .GE. IUSERN ) ICMIN = 0
      IF ( ICMAX .LT. 0 .OR. ICMAX .GE. IUSERN ) ICMAX = IUSERN - 1
      IF ( ICMIN .GT. ICMAX ) THEN
          ICTEMP = ICMIN
          ICMIN  = ICMAX
          ICMAX  = ICTEMP
      ENDIF
      ICOLLO = ICMIN
      ICOLHI = ICMAX

#ifndef SEQ
      MULTIPLE(STDOUT)
#endif
      DO 10 I=IRMIN,IRMAX
          IRBNO  = I/ID
          IPRROW = ID*IRBNO + IRPOS
          IOFFST = I
          JSHIFT = ID*(IRBNO - N11)
          IF ( IOPT .EQ. IUPPER ) THEN
              ICOLLO = I
              IF ( ICMIN .GT. I ) ICOLLO = ICMIN
          ENDIF
          IF ( IOPT .EQ. ILOWER ) THEN
              ICOLHI = ICMAX
```

```
                    IF ( ICMAX .GT. I ) ICOLHI = I
              ENDIF
              DO 20 JOFFST=ICOLLO,ICOLHI
                    K      = JOFFST - ICOLLO
                    J      = JOFFST - JSHIFT
                    TLOG   = MOD(K,7) .EQ. 6 .OR. JOFFST .EQ. ICOLHI
                    ICBNO  = IDIVID(J,ID)
                    IAOFF  = JPTR(ICBNO) + IRBNO + 1
                    IPRCOL = JSHIFT + ICBNO*ID + ICPOS
                    IF ( IOFFST .EQ. IPRROW .AND. JOFFST .EQ. IPRCOL ) THEN
                        IF ( IOPT .EQ. ILOWER .AND. I .EQ.JOFFST ) THEN
                            VALUE = 1.0
                        ELSEIF ( ICBNO.LT.0 .OR. ICBNO.GE.IAMBLK ) THEN
                            VALUE = 0.0
                        ELSE
                            VALUE = ASPACE(IAOFF)
                        ENDIF
                        IF ( K .EQ. 0 ) THEN
                            PRINT *, 'Row number ',I
                        ENDIF
                        PRINT 100,VALUE
                        IF ( TLOG ) THEN
                            PRINT *, ' '
                        ENDIF
                    ENDIF
#ifndef SEQ
                    FLUSH(STDOUT)
#endif
20            CONTINUE
10        CONTINUE
#ifndef SEQ
        SINGLE(STDOUT)
#endif
        IF ( IOPT .EQ. IFULL ) THEN
            PRINT *, 'FULL MATRIX'
        ELSEIF ( IOPT .EQ. IUPPER ) THEN

                PRINT *, 'UPPER TRIANGULAR MATRIX'
        ELSEIF ( IOPT .EQ. ILOWER ) THEN
            PRINT *, 'LOWER TRIANGULAR MATRIX'
        ENDIF

        PRINT *, 'Results for rows ',IRMIN,' to ',IRMAX
        PRINT *, '      and columns ',ICMIN,' to ',ICMAX

        RETURN
```

```fortran
#ifndef XENIX
100 FORMAT(E11.3$)
#else
100 FORMAT(E11.3\)
#endif
    END
C
CCCCCCCCCCCCCCCCCCCCCCCCCCCCCC END OF ROUTINE MATLIS CCCCCCCCCCCCCCCCCCCCCCCCCCCCCC
C
    FUNCTION MYMOD(IX,JD)
    INTEGER IX, JD

    IF ( IX .LT. 0 ) THEN
        MYMOD = MOD((-IX),JD)
    ELSE
        MYMOD = MOD(IX,JD)
    ENDIF

    RETURN
    END
C
CCCCCCCCCCCCCCCCCCCCCCCCCCCCCC END OF ROUTINE MYMOD CCCCCCCCCCCCCCCCCCCCCCCCCCCCCC
C
    REAL FUNCTION NEXTA(IR,IC)
    INTEGER IR, IC
    DOUBLE PRECISION PRANDS
    COMMON/PARCOM/ NX, NY, IRBLKS, IBCBLK, JBLKS, JPLUS, NB, N, IHALFW,
   #               N1, N11, M, KEND, KSTART, IOVER, IACBLK, IAMBLK
    COMMON/USRCOM/ IUSERN, IUSERM, IUSERB

    IF ( IC .GE. IUSERN .OR. IR .GE. IUSERN ) THEN
        VALUE = 0.0
        IF ( IR .EQ. IC ) VALUE = 1.0
    ELSEIF ( IC .LT. (IR-IHALFW) .OR. IC .GT. (IR+IHALFW) ) THEN
        VALUE = 0.0
    ELSE
        VALUE = SNGL(PRANDS(0))
    ENDIF

    NEXTA = VALUE
    RETURN
    END
C
CCCCCCCCCCCCCCCCCCCCCCCCCCCCCC END OF ROUTINE NEXTA CCCCCCCCCCCCCCCCCCCCCCCCCCCCCC
C
    REAL FUNCTION NEXTB(IR,IC)
```

```
      INTEGER IR, IC
      DOUBLE PRECISION PRANDS

      NEXTB = SNGL(PRANDS(0))

      RETURN
      END
C
CCCCCCCCCCCCCCCCCCCCCCCCCCCCCCC END OF ROUTINE NEXTB CCCCCCCCCCCCCCCCCCCCCCCCCCCCCCC
C
      SUBROUTINE PIVOTA(IPVPRC,IPVBLK)
      INTEGER IPVPRC,IPVBLK
      PARAMETER ( MXBLKS = 100, MBBLKS = 100, IAMAX = 1000, IBMAX = 500 )
      PARAMETER ( MAXD   =    8 )
      REAL ASPACE(0:IAMAX-1), BSPACE(0:IBMAX-1)
      INTEGER JPTR(0:MXBLKS-1)
      COMMON/ABCOM/ ASPACE, BSPACE, JPTR
      REAL COMBUF(0:MXBLKS-1), L(0:MXBLKS-1), U(0:MXBLKS-1), BK(0:MBBLKS-1)
      INTEGER NBLOKS(0:MXBLKS-1), NROWNO(0:MXBLKS-1), NBLKNO(0:MXBLKS-1)
      COMMON/COMCOM/ COMBUF, L, U, BK, NBLOKS, NROWNO, NBLKNO
      COMMON/CUBCOM/ IPROC, NPROC, NDOC
      LOGICAL ILDIAG, IRDIAG
      COMMON/GRDCOM/ ID, ICPOS, IRPOS, ILEFT, IRIGHT, IUP, IDOWN,
     #               IP, JP, KP, KROW, IOFF, JOFF, ILDIAG, IRDIAG
      COMMON/PARCOM/ NX, NY, IRBLKS, IBCBLK, JBLKS, JPLUS, NB, N, IHALFW,
     #               N1, N11, M, KEND, KSTART, IOVER, IACBLK, IAMBLK
      COMMON/USRCOM/ IUSERN, IUSERM, IUSERB
      LOGICAL IDOPIV
      COMMON/PIVCOM/ ICPROC(0:MAXD), IDOPIV
      PARAMETER ( IFSIZE = 4 )

      IPVROW = ID*IPVBLK + IPVPRC - 1
      NTEMP  = M/2 + IPVROW + 1
      IF ( NTEMP .LT. (ID*NX-1) .AND. KROW .GT. 0 ) NTEMP = ID*NX - 1
      NTEMP  = (NTEMP-1)/ID + 1
      NX     = NTEMP
      IF ( KROW .GE. KEND ) NX = NY

      IF ( (ID*NX) .GT. (IOVER-KROW+1) ) THEN
          DO 10 J=IOVER+1,ID*NX+KROW-1
              IT = MOD(J,ID)
              IF ( ICPOS .EQ. IT .AND. IRPOS .EQ. IT ) THEN
                  NBLOKS(J/ID) = (J-KROW)/ID + 1
              ENDIF
10            CONTINUE
          IOVER = ID*NX + KROW - 1
      ENDIF
```

```
      IF ( IPVPRC .GT. 1) THEN
          IF ( IPVPRC .GT. ID/2 ) THEN
              IF ( IP .EQ. 1 ) THEN
                  IT = JPTR(JOFF) + IOFF
                  CALL VTOC(COMBUF,ASPACE(IT),JBLKS,NX)
                  IRESP = KCWRIT(COMBUF,IUP,IFSIZE*NX)
              ELSEIF ( IP .GT. IPVPRC ) THEN
                  IRESP = KCREAD(U,IDOWN,IUP,IFSIZE*NX)
              ELSEIF ( IP .EQ. IPVPRC ) THEN
                  IRESP = KCREAD(U,IDOWN,0,IFSIZE*NX)
              ENDIF
          ELSE
              IF ( IP .EQ. 1 ) THEN
                  IT = JPTR(JOFF) + IOFF
                  CALL VTOC(COMBUF,ASPACE(IT),JBLKS,NX)
                  IRESP = KCWRIT(COMBUF,IDOWN,IFSIZE*NX)
              ELSEIF ( IP .LT. IPVPRC ) THEN
                  IRESP = KCREAD(U,IUP,IDOWN,IFSIZE*NX)
              ELSEIF ( IP .EQ. IPVPRC ) THEN
                  IRESP = KCREAD(U,IUP,0,IFSIZE*NX)
              ENDIF
          ENDIF
          IF ( IP .EQ. IPVPRC ) THEN
              IT = JPTR(JOFF-IPVBLK) + IOFF + IPVBLK
              CALL VTOC(COMBUF,ASPACE(IT),JBLKS,NX)
              CALL SPLITP(COMBUF,X,IDOWN,IUP,IFSIZE*NX,0,ID)
              DO 20 J=0,NX-1
                  IT = JPTR(JOFF+J-IPVBLK) + IPVBLK + IOFF
                  ASPACE(IT) = U(J)
                  U(J)       = COMBUF(J)
20                CONTINUE
          ELSE
              IRINGP = IP - IPVPRC
              IF ( IP .LT. IPVPRC ) IRINGP = IRINGP + ID
              IF ( IP .EQ. 1 ) THEN
                  NS = IFSIZE*NX
                  CALL SPLITP(X,COMBUF,IDOWN,IUP,NS,IRINGP,ID)
                  IT = JPTR(JOFF) + IOFF
                  CALL CTOV(ASPACE(IT),COMBUF,JBLKS,NX)
              ELSE
                  NS = IFSIZE*NX
                  CALL SPLITP(X,U,IDOWN,IUP,NS,IRINGP,ID)
              ENDIF
          ENDIF
      ELSE
          IF ( IPVBLK .NE. 0 .AND. IP .EQ. 1 ) THEN
              DO 30 J=0,NX
```

```
                    IT = JPTR(JOFF+J-IPVBLK)+IPVBLK+IOFF
                    JT = JPTR(JOFF+J)+IOFF
                    X          = ASPACE(JT)
                    ASPACE(JT) = ASPACE(IT)
                    ASPACE(IT) = X
30                  CONTINUE
          ENDIF
          IF ( IP .EQ. 1 ) THEN
              IT = JPTR(JOFF) + IOFF
              CALL VTOC(COMBUF,ASPACE(IT),JBLKS,NX)
              CALL SPLITP(COMBUF,X,IDOWN,IUP,NX*IFSIZE,0,ID)
          ELSE
              CALL SPLITP(X,U,IDOWN,IUP,NX*IFSIZE,IP-1,ID)
          ENDIF
      ENDIF

      RETURN
      END
C
CCCCCCCCCCCCCCCCCCCCCCCCCCCCCCC END OF ROUTINE PIVOTA CCCCCCCCCCCCCCCCCCCCCCCCCCCCCC
C
      SUBROUTINE PIVOTB(IBL)
      INTEGER IBL
      PARAMETER ( MXBLKS = 100, MBBLKS = 100, IAMAX = 1000, IBMAX = 500 )
      PARAMETER ( MAXD  =    8 )
      REAL ASPACE(0:IAMAX-1), BSPACE(0:IBMAX-1)
      INTEGER JPTR(0:MXBLKS-1)
      COMMON/ABCOM/ ASPACE, BSPACE, JPTR
      REAL COMBUF(0:MXBLKS-1), L(0:MXBLKS-1), U(0:MXBLKS-1), BK(0:MBBLKS-1)
      INTEGER NBLOKS(0:MXBLKS-1), NROWNO(0:MXBLKS-1), NBLKNO(0:MXBLKS-1)
      COMMON/COMCOM/ COMBUF, L, U, BK, NBLOKS, NROWNO, NBLKNO
      COMMON/CUBCOM/ IPROC, NPROC, NDOC
      LOGICAL ILDIAG, IRDIAG
      COMMON/GRDCOM/ ID, ICPOS, IRPOS, ILEFT, IRIGHT, IUP, IDOWN,
     #              IP, JP, KP, KROW, IOFF, JOFF, ILDIAG, IRDIAG
      COMMON/PARCOM/ NX, NY, IRBLKS, IBCBLK, JBLKS, JPLUS, NB, N, IHALFW,
     #              N1, N11, M, KEND, KSTART, IOVER, IACBLK, IAMBLK
      LOGICAL IDOPIV
      COMMON/PIVCOM/ ICPROC(0:MAXD), IDOPIV
      PARAMETER ( ISIZE = 4, IFSIZE = 4 )

      IF ( IP .EQ. 1 .AND. JP .EQ. 1 ) THEN
          IPROW = NROWNO(KP)
          IPIV  = NBLKNO(KP)
      ENDIF

      IRESP = KBROAD(IPROW,ICPROC(IP),NPROC-1,ISIZE)
```

```
      IRESP = KBROAD(IPIV, ICPROC(IP),NPROC-1,ISIZE)

      NBYTES = IBCBLK*IFSIZE
      IF ( IPROW .GT. 1 ) THEN
          IF ( IPROW .GT. ID/2 ) THEN
              IF ( IP .EQ. 1 ) THEN
                  CALL VTOC(COMBUF,BSPACE(IBL),JBLKS,IBCBLK)
                  IRESP = KCWRIT(COMBUF,IUP,NBYTES)
                  IRESP = KCREAD(COMBUF,IUP,0,NBYTES)
                  CALL CTOV(BSPACE(IBL),COMBUF,JBLKS,IBCBLK)
              ELSEIF ( IP .GT. IPROW ) THEN
                  IRESP = KCREAD(COMBUF,IDOWN,IUP,NBYTES)
                  IRESP = KCREAD(COMBUF,IUP,IDOWN,NBYTES)
              ELSEIF ( IP .EQ. IPROW ) THEN
                  ITEMP = IBL + IPIV
                  IRESP = KCREAD(U,IDOWN,0,NBYTES)
                  CALL VTOC(COMBUF,BSPACE(ITEMP),JBLKS,IBCBLK)
                  IRESP = KCWRIT(COMBUF,IDOWN,NBYTES)
                  CALL CTOV(BSPACE(ITEMP),U,JBLKS,IBCBLK)
              ENDIF
          ELSE
              IF ( IP .EQ. 1 ) THEN
                  CALL VTOC(COMBUF,BSPACE(IBL),JBLKS,IBCBLK)
                  IRESP = KCWRIT(COMBUF,IDOWN,NBYTES)
                  IRESP = KCREAD(COMBUF,IDOWN,0,NBYTES)
                  CALL CTOV(BSPACE(IBL),COMBUF,JBLKS,IBCBLK)
              ELSEIF ( IP .GT. IPROW ) THEN
                  IRESP = KCREAD(COMBUF,IUP,IDOWN,NBYTES)
                  IRESP = KCREAD(COMBUF,IDOWN,IUP,NBYTES)
              ELSEIF ( IP .EQ. IPROW ) THEN
                  ITEMP = IBL + IPIV
                  IRESP = KCREAD(U,IUP,0,NBYTES)
                  CALL VTOC(COMBUF,BSPACE(ITEMP),JBLKS,IBCBLK)
                  IRESP = KCWRIT(COMBUF,IUP,NBYTES)
                  CALL CTOV(BSPACE(ITEMP),U,JBLKS,IBCBLK)
              ENDIF
          ENDIF
      ELSE
          IF ( IPIV .NE. 0 .AND. IP .EQ. 1 ) THEN
              DO 10 J=0,IBCBLK-1
                  ITEMP1 = JPTR(J) + IBL
                  ITEMP2 = ITEMP1 + IPIV
                  DUMMY  = BSPACE(ITEMP1)
                  BSPACE(ITEMP1) = BSPACE(ITEMP2)
                  BSPACE(ITEMP2) = DUMMY
10                CONTINUE
          ENDIF
```

```
      ENDIF

      RETURN
      END
C
CCCCCCCCCCCCCCCCCCCCCCCCCCCCC END OF ROUTINE PIVOTB CCCCCCCCCCCCCCCCCCCCCCCCCCCCC
C
      SUBROUTINE SPLITP(OBUF,IBUF,ICLKM,IACLKM,NBYTES,IRPOS,NRING)
      INTEGER OBUF(0:*),IBUF(0:*)
      INTEGER ICLKM, IACLKM, NBYTES, IRPOS, NRING

      IF ( IRPOS .EQ. 0 ) THEN
          IRESP = KCWRIT(OBUF,ICLKM, NBYTES)
          IRESP = KCWRIT(OBUF,IACLKM,NBYTES)
      ELSEIF ( IRPOS .LT. NRING/2 ) THEN
          IRESP = KCREAD(IBUF,IACLKM,ICLKM,NBYTES)
      ELSEIF ( IRPOS .GT. NRING/2 ) THEN
          IRESP = KCREAD(IBUF,ICLKM,IACLKM,NBYTES)
      ELSEIF ( IRPOS .EQ. NRING/2 ) THEN
          IRESP = KCREAD(IBUF,IACLKM,0,NBYTES)
          IRESP = KCREAD(IBUF,ICLKM, 0,NBYTES)
      ENDIF

      RETURN
      END
C
CCCCCCCCCCCCCCCCCCCCCCCCCCCCC END OF ROUTINE SPLITP CCCCCCCCCCCCCCCCCCCCCCCCCCCCC
C
      SUBROUTINE VTOC(OBUF,IBUF,IOTEMS,NITEMS)
      INTEGER OBUF(0:*), IBUF(0:*)
      INTEGER IOTEMS, NITEMS

      I = 0
      DO 10 J=0,NITEMS-1
          OBUF(J) = IBUF(I)
          I = I + IOTEMS
10        CONTINUE

      RETURN
      END
C
CCCCCCCCCCCCCCCCCCCCCCCCCCCCC END OF ROUTINE VTOC CCCCCCCCCCCCCCCCCCCCCCCCCCCCC
C
      SUBROUTINE WELCOM

      PRINT *, '   ****************************************'
      PRINT *, '   *                                      *'
```

```
      PRINT *, '   *  Welcome to the banded matrix solver.  *'
      PRINT *, '   *                                        *'
      PRINT *, '   *  This program solves Ax=b, where A is  *'
      PRINT *, '   *  a banded matrix.                      *'
      PRINT *, '   *                                        *'
      PRINT *, '   ******************************************'

      RETURN
      END
C
CCCCCCCCCCCCCCCCCCCCCCCCCCCCC END OF ROUTINE WELCOM CCCCCCCCCCCCCCCCCCCCCCCCCCCCC
C
      SUBROUTINE PRSETB(ISEED,ISKIP,IORDER)
      COMMON /RAN/IRAND0,IRAND1,IAS0,IAS1,ICS0,ICS1,IAB0,IAB1,ICB0,ICB1
      SAVE /RAN/

      INTEGER ENV(5)
      PARAMETER (MULT0=20077,MULT1=16838,IADD0=12345,IADD1=0)
      PARAMETER (IPOW16=2**16)

      ISEED0=MOD(ISEED,IPOW16)
      ISEED1=ISEED/IPOW16
      CALL KPARAM(ENV)
      NPROC=ENV(3)
      IAB0=1
      IAB1=0
      ICB0=0
      ICB1=0
      DO 10 I=0,ISKIP*(NPROC-1)
          CALL LMULT(J0,J1,IAB0,IAB1,MULT0,MULT1)
          IAB0 = J0
          IAB1 = J1
          CALL LMULT(J0,J1,ICB0,ICB1,MULT0,MULT1)
          CALL LADD(ICB0,ICB1,J0,J1,IADD0,IADD1)
          IF (I.EQ.(ISKIP*IORDER)) THEN
              CALL LMULT(J0,J1,ISEED0,ISEED1,IAB0,IAB1)
              CALL LADD(IRAND0,IRAND1,J0,J1,ICB0,ICB1)
          ENDIF
10        CONTINUE
      IAS0=MULT0
      IAS1=MULT1
      ICS0=IADD0
      ICS1=IADD1

      RETURN
      END
C
```

```
CCCCCCCCCCCCCCCCCCCCCCCCCCCCC END OF ROUTINE PRSETB CCCCCCCCCCCCCCCCCCCCCCCCCCCCCCC
C
      DOUBLE PRECISION FUNCTION PRANDB()
      COMMON /RAN/IRAND0,IRAND1,IAS0,IAS1,ICS0,ICS1,IAB0,IAB1,ICB0,ICB1
      DOUBLE PRECISION DIVFAC,POW16
      PARAMETER (DIVFAC=2.147483648D9,POW16=6.5536D4)
      SAVE /RAN/

      PRANDB=(DFLOAT(IRAND0)+POW16*DFLOAT(IRAND1))/DIVFAC
      CALL LMULT(J0,J1,IRAND0,IRAND1,IAB0,IAB1)
      CALL LADD(IRAND0,IRAND1,J0,J1,ICB0,ICB1)

      RETURN
      END
C
CCCCCCCCCCCCCCCCCCCCCCCCCCCCC END OF ROUTINE PRANDB CCCCCCCCCCCCCCCCCCCCCCCCCCCCCCC
C
      DOUBLE PRECISION FUNCTION PRANDS()
      COMMON /RAN/IRAND0,IRAND1,IAS0,IAS1,ICS0,ICS1,IAB0,IAB1,ICB0,ICB1
      DOUBLE PRECISION DIVFAC,POW16
      PARAMETER (DIVFAC=2.147483648D9,POW16=6.5536D4)
      SAVE /RAN/

      PRANDS=(DFLOAT(IRAND0)+POW16*DFLOAT(IRAND1))/DIVFAC
      CALL LMULT(J0,J1,IRAND0,IRAND1,IAS0,IAS1)
      CALL LADD(IRAND0,IRAND1,J0,J1,ICS0,ICS1)

      RETURN
      END
C
CCCCCCCCCCCCCCCCCCCCCCCCCCCCC END OF ROUTINE PRANDS CCCCCCCCCCCCCCCCCCCCCCCCCCCCCCC
C
      SUBROUTINE LADD(I0,I1,J0,J1,K0,K1)
      PARAMETER (IPOW16=2**16,IPOW15=2**15)

      I0=MOD(K0+J0,IPOW16)
      I1=MOD((K0+J0)/IPOW16+K1+J1,IPOW15)

      RETURN
      END
C
CCCCCCCCCCCCCCCCCCCCCCCCCCCCC END OF ROUTINE LADD CCCCCCCCCCCCCCCCCCCCCCCCCCCCCCCCC
C
      SUBROUTINE LMULT(I0,I1,J0,J1,K0,K1)
      PARAMETER (IPOW30=2**30,IPOW16=2**16,IPOW15=2**15)

      K = K0*J0
```

```
      IF(K.LT.0) K = (K+IPOW30)+IPOW30
      I0=MOD(K,IPOW16)
      L = K0*J1+K1*J0
      IF(L.LT.0) L = (L+IPOW30)+IPOW30
      K = K/IPOW16+L
      IF(K.LT.0) K = (K+IPOW30)+IPOW30
      I1=MOD(K,IPOW15)

      RETURN
      END
C
CCCCCCCCCCCCCCCCCCCCCCCCCCCCCC END OF ROUTINE LMULT CCCCCCCCCCCCCCCCCCCCCCCCCCCCCC
C
```

B-16 The *comutil* Routines

B-16.1 The *expand* Routine

```
      PROGRAM TSTEXP
      INTEGER ENV(5), DOC, PROCNU, EXPAND
      INTEGER VECTOR(100), BUF(200)
      COMMON /CUBENV/ DOC, PROCNU, NPROC

      CALL KPARAM(ENV)
      DOC=ENV(1)
      PROCNU=ENV(2)
      NPROC =ENV(3)

      PRINT *, ' '
      PRINT *, 'Dimension of the vector? < 100'
      READ  *, NDIM

      DO 10 I=1,NDIM
          VECTOR(I)=I*(PROCNU+1)
10        CONTINUE

      MULTIPLE(6)
      PRINT *, ' '
      WRITE(*,100) PROCNU
100   FORMAT('Before expanding processor',I2,' has')
      PRINT *, '         ', (VECTOR(I),I=1,NDIM)
      FLUSH(6)

      IERR=EXPAND(VECTOR, BUF, NDIM)

      PRINT *, ' '
      WRITE(*,200) PROCNU
200   FORMAT('After expanding processor',I2,' has')
      PRINT *, '         ', (VECTOR(I),I=1,NDIM)
      FLUSH(6)

      END

C
CCCCCCCCCCCCCCCCCCCCCCCCCCCCCC END OF PROGRAM TSTEXP CCCCCCCCCCCCCCCCCCCCCCCCCCCCCC
C
      FUNCTION EXPAND(BUF, TMP, N)
      INTEGER EXPAND,DOC,PROCNU
      REAL    BUF(*), TMP(*)
      INTEGER D,ERROR,CHAN,SIZE,OFFSET,RECV,SEND,RECVN,SENDN
      COMMON /CUBENV/ DOC, PROCNU, NPROC
```

```
      SIZE=4
      CHAN=2**(DOC-1)
      MASK=NPROC-1
      OFFSET=KLSHIF(SIZE,DOC)

      D=DOC
      DO 30 I=1,DOC
          D=D-1
          SEND=KAND(PROCNU,MASK)
          RECV=KXOR(SEND,CHAN)
          SENDN=KRSHIF(N+MASK-SEND,D+1)
          RECVN=KRSHIF(N+MASK-RECV,D+1)

          ERROR=KVSHIF(BUF(RECV+1),CHAN,SIZE,OFFSET,RECVN,
     #                 BUF(SEND+1),CHAN,SIZE,OFFSET,SENDN)

          MASK=KAND(MASK,KCOM(CHAN))
          CHAN=CHAN/2
          OFFSET=OFFSET/2

30        CONTINUE

      EXPAND=0
      IF (ERROR .EQ. -1) EXPAND=-1
      RETURN
      END
C
CCCCCCCCCCCCCCCCCCCCCCCCCCCCCC END OF ROUTINE EXPAND CCCCCCCCCCCCCCCCCCCCCCCCCCCCCC
C
      FUNCTION KXOR(M,N)
      KXOR=0
      MT=M
      IF (MT .LT. 0) MT=MT-2147483648
      NT=N
      IF (NT .LT. 0) NT=NT-2147483648
      IP=1
      DO 10 I=1,31
          IN=MOD(NT,2)
          IM=MOD(MT,2)
          IC=IN+IM
          IF (IC .EQ. 2) IC=0
          KXOR=IP*IC+KXOR
          IP=2*IP
          NT=NT/2
          MT=MT/2
          IF ((NT .EQ. 0) .AND. (MT .EQ. 0)) GOTO 99
```

```
10      CONTINUE
99   CONTINUE
     IF ((M .GT. 0) .AND. (N .LT. 0)) KXOR = KXOR+2147483648
     IF ((M .LT. 0) .AND. (N .GT. 0)) KXOR = KXOR+2147483648
     RETURN
     END
C
CCCCCCCCCCCCCCCCCCCCCCCCCCCCCC END OF ROUTINE KXOR CCCCCCCCCCCCCCCCCCCCCCCCCCCCCC
C
     FUNCTION KIOR(M,N)
     KIOR=0
     MT=M
     IF (MT .LT. 0) MT=MT-2147483648
     NT=N
     IF (NT .LT. 0) NT=NT-2147483648
     IP=1
     DO 10 I=1,31
         IN=MOD(NT,2)
         IM=MOD(MT,2)
         IC=IN+IM
         IF (IC .EQ. 2) IC=1
         KIOR=IP*IC+KIOR
         IP=2*IP
         NT=NT/2
         MT=MT/2
         IF ((NT .EQ. 0) .AND. (MT .EQ. 0)) GOTO 99
10      CONTINUE
99   CONTINUE
     IF ((M .LT. 0) .OR. (N .LT. 0)) KIOR = KIOR+2147483648
     RETURN
     END
C
CCCCCCCCCCCCCCCCCCCCCCCCCCCCCC END OF ROUTINE KIOR CCCCCCCCCCCCCCCCCCCCCCCCCCCCCC
C
     FUNCTION KAND(M,N)
     KAND=0
     MT=M
     IF (MT .LT. 0) MT=MT-2147483648
     NT=N
     IF (NT .LT. 0) NT=NT-2147483648
     IP=1
     DO 10 I=1,31
         IN=MOD(NT,2)
         IM=MOD(MT,2)
         IC=(IN+IM)/2
         KAND=IP*IC+KAND
         IP=2*IP
```

```
         NT=NT/2
         MT=MT/2
         IF ((NT .EQ. 0) .AND. (MT .EQ. 0)) GOTO 99
10       CONTINUE
99    CONTINUE
      IF ((M .LT. 0) .AND. (N .LT. 0)) KAND = KAND+2147483648
      RETURN
      END
C
CCCCCCCCCCCCCCCCCCCCCCCCCCCCCCC END OF ROUTINE KAND CCCCCCCCCCCCCCCCCCCCCCCCCCCCCCC
C
      FUNCTION KRSHIF(M,N)
      MT = M
      IF (MT .LT. 0) MT=MT-2147483648
      KRSHIF=MT/2**N
      IF (M .LT. 0) KRSHIF = KRSHIF+2**(31-N)
      RETURN
      END
C
CCCCCCCCCCCCCCCCCCCCCCCCCCCCCCC END OF ROUTINE KRSHIF CCCCCCCCCCCCCCCCCCCCCCCCCCCCCCC
C
      FUNCTION KLSHIF(M,N)
      MT = M
      IF (MT .LT. 0) MT=MT-2147483648
      IF (N .EQ. 0)  MT=M
      KLSHIF=MT*2**N
      RETURN
      END
C
CCCCCCCCCCCCCCCCCCCCCCCCCCCCCCC END OF ROUTINE KLSHIF CCCCCCCCCCCCCCCCCCCCCCCCCCCCCCC
C
      FUNCTION KCOM(M)
      KCOM = -(M+1)
      RETURN
      END
C
CCCCCCCCCCCCCCCCCCCCCCCCCCCCCCC END OF ROUTINE KCOM CCCCCCCCCCCCCCCCCCCCCCCCCCCCCCC
C
```

B-16.2 The *fold* Routine

```
      PROGRAM TSTFLD
      INTEGER ENV(5), DOC, PROCNU, FOLD
      INTEGER VECTOR(100), BUF(200)
      COMMON /CUBENV/ DOC, PROCNU, NPROC

      CALL KPARAM(ENV)
      DOC=ENV(1)
      PROCNU=ENV(2)
      NPROC =ENV(3)

      PRINT *, ' '
      PRINT *, 'Dimension of the vector? < 100'
      READ  *, NDIM

      DO 10 I=1,NDIM
          VECTOR(I)=I*(PROCNU+1)
10        CONTINUE

      MULTIPLE(6)
      PRINT *, ' '
      WRITE(*,100) PROCNU
100   FORMAT('Before folding processor',I2,' has')
      PRINT *, '         ', (VECTOR(I),I=1,NDIM)
      FLUSH(6)

      IERR=FOLD(VECTOR, BUF, NDIM)

      PRINT *, ' '
      WRITE(*,200) PROCNU
200   FORMAT('After folding processor',I2,' has')
      PRINT *, '         ', (VECTOR(I),I=1,NDIM)
      FLUSH(6)

      END

C
CCCCCCCCCCCCCCCCCCCCCCCCCCCCCC END OF PROGRAM TSTFLD CCCCCCCCCCCCCCCCCCCCCCCCCCCCCC
C
      FUNCTION FOLD(BUF, TMP, N)
      INTEGER FOLD,DOC,PROCNU
      REAL    BUF(*), TMP(*)
      INTEGER D,ERROR,CHAN,SIZE,BLOCK,OFFSET,RECV,SEND,RECVN,SENDN
      COMMON /CUBENV/ DOC, PROCNU, NPROC

      MASK=1
```

```
      CHAN=1
      SIZE=4
      BLOCK=2
      OFFSET=SIZE*2

      DO 10 D=1, DOC
          RECV=KAND(PROCNU,MASK)
          SEND=KXOR(RECV,CHAN)
          RECVN=KRSHIF(N+MASK-RECV,D)
          SENDN=KRSHIF(N+MASK-SEND,D)
          ERROR=KVSHIF(TMP(RECV+1),CHAN,SIZE,OFFSET,RECVN,
     #                 BUF(SEND+1),CHAN,SIZE,OFFSET,SENDN)

          DO 20 J=RECV, N-1, BLOCK
              BUF(J+1)=TMP(J+1)+BUF(J+1)
20            CONTINUE

          CHAN=2*CHAN
          MASK=KIOR(MASK,CHAN)
          BLOCK=2*BLOCK
          OFFSET=2*OFFSET

10        CONTINUE

      FOLD=0
      IF (ERROR .EQ. -1) FOLD=-1
      RETURN
      END
C
CCCCCCCCCCCCCCCCCCCCCCCCCCCCCCCC END OF ROUTINE FOLD CCCCCCCCCCCCCCCCCCCCCCCCCCCCCCCC
C
      FUNCTION KXOR(M,N)
      KXOR=0
      MT=M
      IF (MT .LT. 0) MT=MT-2147483648
      NT=N
      IF (NT .LT. 0) NT=NT-2147483648
      IP=1
      DO 10 I=1,31
          IN=MOD(NT,2)
          IM=MOD(MT,2)
          IC=IN+IM
          IF (IC .EQ. 2) IC=0
          KXOR=IP*IC+KXOR
          IP=2*IP
          NT=NT/2
          MT=MT/2
```

```
            IF ((NT .EQ. 0) .AND. (MT .EQ. 0)) GOTO 99
10          CONTINUE
99    CONTINUE
      IF ((M .GT. 0) .AND. (N .LT. 0)) KXOR = KXOR+2147483648
      IF ((M .LT. 0) .AND. (N .GT. 0)) KXOR = KXOR+2147483648
      RETURN
      END
C
CCCCCCCCCCCCCCCCCCCCCCCCCCCCCCC END OF ROUTINE KXOR CCCCCCCCCCCCCCCCCCCCCCCCCCCCCCC
C
      FUNCTION KIOR(M,N)
      KIOR=0
      MT=M
      IF (MT .LT. 0) MT=MT-2147483648
      NT=N
      IF (NT .LT. 0) NT=NT-2147483648
      IP=1
      DO 10 I=1,31
          IN=MOD(NT,2)
          IM=MOD(MT,2)
          IC=IN+IM
          IF (IC .EQ. 2) IC=1
          KIOR=IP*IC+KIOR
          IP=2*IP
          NT=NT/2
          MT=MT/2
          IF ((NT .EQ. 0) .AND. (MT .EQ. 0)) GOTO 99
10          CONTINUE
99    CONTINUE
      IF ((M .LT. 0) .OR. (N .LT. 0)) KIOR = KIOR+2147483648
      RETURN
      END
C
CCCCCCCCCCCCCCCCCCCCCCCCCCCCCCC END OF ROUTINE KIOR CCCCCCCCCCCCCCCCCCCCCCCCCCCCCCC
C
      FUNCTION KAND(M,N)
      KAND=0
      MT=M
      IF (MT .LT. 0) MT=MT-2147483648
      NT=N
      IF (NT .LT. 0) NT=NT-2147483648
      IP=1
      DO 10 I=1,31
          IN=MOD(NT,2)
          IM=MOD(MT,2)
          IC=(IN+IM)/2
          KAND=IP*IC+KAND
```

```
         IP=2*IP
         NT=NT/2
         MT=MT/2
         IF ((NT .EQ. 0) .AND. (MT .EQ. 0)) GOTO 99
10       CONTINUE
99    CONTINUE
      IF ((M .LT. 0) .AND. (N .LT. 0)) KAND = KAND+2147483648
      RETURN
      END
C
CCCCCCCCCCCCCCCCCCCCCCCCCCCCCC END OF ROUTINE KAND CCCCCCCCCCCCCCCCCCCCCCCCCCCCCCC
C
      FUNCTION KRSHIF(M,N)
      MT = M
      IF (MT .LT. 0) MT=MT-2147483648
      KRSHIF=MT/2**N
      IF (M .LT. 0) KRSHIF = KRSHIF+2**(31-N)
      RETURN
      END
C
CCCCCCCCCCCCCCCCCCCCCCCCCCCCCC END OF ROUTINE KRSHIF CCCCCCCCCCCCCCCCCCCCCCCCCCCCCC
C
      FUNCTION KLSHIF(M,N)
      MT = M
      IF (MT .LT. 0) MT=MT-2147483648
      IF (N .EQ. 0)  MT=M
      KLSHIF=MT*2**N
      RETURN
      END
C
CCCCCCCCCCCCCCCCCCCCCCCCCCCCCC END OF ROUTINE KLSHIF CCCCCCCCCCCCCCCCCCCCCCCCCCCCCC
C
      FUNCTION KCOM(M)
      KCOM = -(M+1)
      RETURN
      END
C
CCCCCCCCCCCCCCCCCCCCCCCCCCCCCC END OF ROUTINE KCOM CCCCCCCCCCCCCCCCCCCCCCCCCCCCCCC
C
```

B-16.3 The *global_reverse* Routine

```
      PROGRAM TSTGRV
      INTEGER ENV(5), PROCNU
      REAL F(2,1024)

      CALL KPARAM(ENV)
      PROCNU = ENV(2)

      PRINT *, ' '
      PRINT *, 'Give number of elements per processor and dimension of FFT'

      READ *, NELT,ND

      DO 10 I=0,2**ND-1
          J = IBITRV(I,ND)
          IF (J/NELT .EQ. PROCNU) THEN
              K = MOD(J,NELT)
              F(1,K+1) = I
          ENDIF
10        CONTINUE

      MULTIPLE(6)
      BUFFER(UNIT=6,SIZE=1024)

      MYREF = PROCNU*NELT

      DO 15 I=1,NELT
          WRITE(*,100) PROCNU, MYREF+I-1, F(1,I)
15        CONTINUE
      FLUSH(6)

      CALL GLOREV(NELT,ND,F)

      DO 20 I=1,NELT
          WRITE(*,100) PROCNU, MYREF+I-1, F(1,I)
20        CONTINUE
      FLUSH(6)

100   FORMAT(2I5, F8.2)
      STOP
      END
C
CCCCCCCCCCCCCCCCCCCCCCCCCCCCCCC END OF PROGRAM TSTGRV CCCCCCCCCCCCCCCCCCCCCCCCCCCCCCC
C
      SUBROUTINE GLOREV(NELT,ND,F)
      REAL F(2,1024),TMP(2,1024)
```

```
        INTEGER DOC,PROCNU,ENV(5),MAP(1024)

        CALL KPARAM(ENV)
        DOC   =ENV(1)
        PROCNU=ENV(2)
        NPROC =ENV(3)

        MASK = 1
        MYSIZE = 4*NPROC
        MYOFST = 8*NPROC
        MYITEM = NELT/NPROC
        MYPROC = PROCNU
        MAXPRO = NPROC/2
        IF (MOD(PROCNU,2) .EQ. 0) THEN
            MYRECV = NPROC/2
            MYSEND = NPROC/2
        ELSE
            MYRECV = 0
            MYSEND = 0
        ENDIF

        DO 10 I=1,DOC
            IERR = KVSHIF(F(1,MYRECV+1),MASK,MYSIZE,MYOFST,MYITEM,
     #                    F(1,MYSEND+1),MASK,MYSIZE,MYOFST,MYITEM)
            MASK   = 2*MASK
            MYSIZE = MYSIZE/2
            MYOFST = MYOFST/2
            MYITEM = MYITEM*2
            MYPROC = MYPROC/2
            MAXPRO = MAXPRO/2
            IF (MOD(MYPROC,2) .EQ. 0) THEN
                MYRECV = MAXPRO
                MYSEND = MAXPRO
            ELSE
                MYRECV = 0
                MYSEND = 0
            ENDIF
 10     CONTINUE

        CALL MAPING(NELT,ND,NPROC,MAP)

        DO 20 I=1,NELT
            TMP(1,MAP(I)) = F(1,I)
            TMP(2,MAP(I)) = F(2,I)
 20     CONTINUE
        DO 30 I=1,NELT
            F(1,I) = TMP(1,I)
```

```
         F(2,I) = TMP(2,I)
30   CONTINUE

     RETURN
     END
C
CCCCCCCCCCCCCCCCCCCCCCCCCCCCC END OF ROUTINE GLOREV CCCCCCCCCCCCCCCCCCCCCCCCCCCCCC
C
     SUBROUTINE MAPING(NELT,ND,NPROC,MAP)
     INTEGER MAP(*)

     IC = 0
     DO 10 I=0,NELT-1,NPROC
         J = IBITRV(I,ND)
         DO 20 K=1,NPROC
         IC = IC+1
         MAP(IC) = J+K
20       CONTINUE
10   CONTINUE

     RETURN
     END
C
CCCCCCCCCCCCCCCCCCCCCCCCCCCCC END OF ROUTINE MAPING CCCCCCCCCCCCCCCCCCCCCCCCCCCCCC
C
     FUNCTION IBITRV(NXELT, ND)
     IBITRV = 0
     NT = 2**ND
     NO = NXELT
     DO 10 I=1, ND
     IA = MOD(NO, 2)
     NO = NO/2
     NT = NT/2
     IBITRV = NT*IA + IBITRV
10   CONTINUE
     RETURN
     END
C
CCCCCCCCCCCCCCCCCCCCCCCCCCCCC END OF ROUTINE IBITRV CCCCCCCCCCCCCCCCCCCCCCCCCCCCCC
C
```

B-16.4 The *indexx* Routine

```
      PROGRAM TSTIND
      INTEGER ENV(5),VECTOR(100),PROCNU

      CALL KPARAM(ENV)
      NDOC=ENV(1)
      PROCNU=ENV(2)

      PRINT *, ' '
      PRINT *, 'Dimension of the vector? < 100'
      READ *, NDIM

      DO 10 I=1,NDIM
          VECTOR(I)=I*(PROCNU+1)
10        CONTINUE

      MULTIPLE(6)
      PRINT *, ' '
      WRITE(*,100) PROCNU
100   FORMAT('Before indexing processor',I2,' has')
      PRINT *, '           ', (VECTOR(I),I=1,NDIM)
      FLUSH(6)

      CALL INDEXX(VECTOR, NDIM, NDOC, PROCNU)

      PRINT *, ' '
      WRITE(*,200) PROCNU
200   FORMAT('After indexing processor',I2,' has')
      PRINT *, '           ', (VECTOR(I),I=1,NDIM)
      FLUSH(6)

      END
C
CCCCCCCCCCCCCCCCCCCCCCCCCCCCCC END OF PROGRAM TSTIND CCCCCCCCCCCCCCCCCCCCCCCCCCCCCCC
C
      SUBROUTINE INDEXX(D,M,NDOC,IPROC)
      INTEGER  D(*)

      NITEM= M/2
      MASK = 1
      NOFF = 2
      DO 10 ICHN=0,NDOC-1

          IB = MOD(KRSHIF(IPROC,ICHN),2)
          IF (IB .EQ. 0) THEN
              IERR=KVSHIF(D(MASK+1),MASK,MASK*4,NOFF*4,NITEM,
```

```
#                           D(MASK+1),MASK,MASK*4,NOFF*4,NITEM)
         ELSE
              IERR=KVSHIF(D(1),MASK,MASK*4,NOFF*4,NITEM,
#                           D(1),MASK,MASK*4,NOFF*4,NITEM)
         ENDIF

         MASK = 2*MASK
         NOFF = 2*NOFF
         NITEM= NITEM/2

10       CONTINUE
     RETURN
     END
C
CCCCCCCCCCCCCCCCCCCCCCCCCCCCCC END OF ROUTINE INDEXX CCCCCCCCCCCCCCCCCCCCCCCCCCCC
C
     FUNCTION KRSHIF(M,N)
     MT = M
     IF (MT .LT. 0) MT=MT-2147483648
     KRSHIF=MT/2**N
     IF (M .LT. 0) KRSHIF = KRSHIF+2**(31-N)
     RETURN
     END
C
CCCCCCCCCCCCCCCCCCCCCCCCCCCCCC END OF ROUTINE KRSHIF CCCCCCCCCCCCCCCCCCCCCCCCCCCC
C
     FUNCTION KLSHIF(M,N)
     MT = M
     IF (MT .LT. 0) MT=MT-2147483648
     IF (N .EQ. 0)  MT=M
     KLSHIF=MT*2**N
     RETURN
     END
C
CCCCCCCCCCCCCCCCCCCCCCCCCCCCCC END OF ROUTINE KLSHIF CCCCCCCCCCCCCCCCCCCCCCCCCCCC
C
```

B-16.5 The *scatter* Routine

```
     PROGRAM TSTSCT
     INTEGER V(12),ENV(5),PROCNU
     CALL KPARAM(ENV)
     PROCNU=ENV(2)
     NPROC =ENV(3)

     PRINT *, ' '
```

```
      PRINT *, 'What is the source processor?'
      READ  *, NSRC
      PRINT *, 'How many elements to scatter?'
      READ  *, NITEM

      IF (PROCNU .EQ. NSRC) THEN
          DO 10 I=1,12
              V(I)=I
10            CONTINUE
      ENDIF

      CALL SCATER(NSRC,V,NITEM,NPROC,PROCNU)

      MULTIPLE(6)
      WRITE(*,100) PROCNU, (V(J),J=1,12)
      FLUSH(6)
100   FORMAT(I4, 12 I3)

      END
C
CCCCCCCCCCCCCCCCCCCCCCCCCCCCC END OF PROGRAM TSTSCT CCCCCCCCCCCCCCCCCCCCCCCCCCCCC
C
      SUBROUTINE SCATER(SRC,X,M,NPROC,PROCNU)
      INTEGER X(*), TMP(512), HBIT, SRC, PROCNU, KUP(256)

      MUP = M/NPROC
      MRN = MOD(M,NPROC)
      DO 10 I=0,NPROC-1
          IF (I .LT. MRN) THEN
              KUP(I) = MUP+1
          ELSE
              KUP(I) = MUP
          ENDIF
10        CONTINUE

      MELT = NPROC
      MYPROC = KXOR(PROCNU,SRC)

      IF (PROCNU .EQ. SRC) THEN
          DO 20 I=MELT-1, 1, -1
              ICL = 2**LBIT(I)
              J = KXOR(I,SRC)
              IERR=KVWRIT(X(J+1),ICL,4,NPROC*4,KUP(J))
20            CONTINUE
      ELSE
          ICH = 2**HBIT(MYPROC)
          NPIPE=MELT/(ICH*2)-1
```

```
            DO 30 I=1, NPIPE
                ICL = 2**LBIT(I)
                IERR=KVREAD(TMP,ICH,ICH*ICL*2,4,4,100)
30              CONTINUE
            IERR=KVREAD(X(PROCNU+1),ICH,0,4,NPROC*4,KUP(PROCNU))
        ENDIF
        RETURN
        END
C
CCCCCCCCCCCCCCCCCCCCCCCCCCCCCCC END OF ROUTINE SCATER CCCCCCCCCCCCCCCCCCCCCCCCCCCCCCC
C
        FUNCTION LBIT(N)
        NT=N
        DO 10 I=0,10
            IF (MOD(NT,2) .EQ. 1) GOTO 99
            NT=NT/2
10          CONTINUE
99      LBIT=I
        RETURN
        END
C
CCCCCCCCCCCCCCCCCCCCCCCCCCCCCCC END OF ROUTINE LBIT CCCCCCCCCCCCCCCCCCCCCCCCCCCCCCC
C
        FUNCTION HBIT(N)
        INTEGER  HBIT
        NT=N
        DO 10 I=0,10
            IF (MOD(NT,2) .EQ. 1) HBIT=I
            NT=NT/2
10          CONTINUE
        IF (N .EQ. 0) HBIT=0
        RETURN
        END
C
CCCCCCCCCCCCCCCCCCCCCCCCCCCCCCC END OF ROUTINE HBIT CCCCCCCCCCCCCCCCCCCCCCCCCCCCCCC
C
        FUNCTION KXOR(M,N)
        KXOR=0
        MT=M
        IF (MT .LT. 0) MT=MT-2147483648
        NT=N
        IF (NT .LT. 0) NT=NT-2147483648
        IP=1
        DO 10 I=1,31
            IN=MOD(NT,2)
            IM=MOD(MT,2)
            IC=IN+IM
```

```
        IF (IC .EQ. 2) IC=0
        KXOR=IP*IC+KXOR
        IP=2*IP
        NT=NT/2
        MT=MT/2
        IF ((NT .EQ. 0) .AND. (MT .EQ. 0)) GOTO 99
10      CONTINUE
99   CONTINUE
     IF ((M .GT. 0) .AND. (N .LT. 0)) KXOR = KXOR+2147483648
     IF ((M .LT. 0) .AND. (N .GT. 0)) KXOR = KXOR+2147483648
     RETURN
     END
C
CCCCCCCCCCCCCCCCCCCCCCCCCCCCCCCCC END OF ROUTINE KXOR CCCCCCCCCCCCCCCCCCCCCCCCCCCCCCCCC
C
```

B-16.6 The *transfer* Routine

```
     PROGRAM TSTTRN
     INTEGER ENV(5), DOC, PROCNU
     INTEGER VECTOR(100)
     COMMON /CUBENV/ DOC, PROCNU, NPROC

     CALL KPARAM(ENV)
     DOC=ENV(1)
     PROCNU=ENV(2)
     NPROC =ENV(3)

     PRINT *, ' '
     PRINT *, 'Dimension of the vector? < 100'
     READ  *, NDIM
     PRINT *, 'Give Source and Destination Processor'
     READ *,  NSRC, NDST

     DO 10 I=1,NDIM
         VECTOR(I)=I*(PROCNU+1)
10       CONTINUE

     MULTIPLE(6)
     PRINT *, ' '
     WRITE(*,100) PROCNU
100  FORMAT('Before tranfering processor',I2,' has')
     PRINT *, '           ', (VECTOR(I),I=1,NDIM)
     FLUSH(6)

     CALL TRANSF(VECTOR,NDIM,NSRC,NDST)
```

```
      PRINT *, ' '
      WRITE(*,200) PROCNU
  200 FORMAT('After tranfering processor',I2,' has')
      PRINT *, '           ', (VECTOR(I),I=1,NDIM)
      FLUSH(6)

      END
C
CCCCCCCCCCCCCCCCCCCCCCCCCCCCCCC END OF PROGRAM TSTRN CCCCCCCCCCCCCCCCCCCCCCCCCCCCCCC
C
      SUBROUTINE TRANSF(V,M,NSRC,NDST)
      INTEGER V(*)
      INTEGER PROCNU, IMASK(10), ENV(5)

      LBTE = 4
      CALL KPARAM(ENV)
      NDOC = ENV(1)
      PROCNU = ENV(2)
      MASKOD = KXOR(NSRC,NDST)
      CALL ROUTER(IMASK,NH,MASKOD,NDOC)
      IFLAG = 0
      MODD = (M+1)/2
      MEVN = M/2
      IF (PROCNU .EQ. NSRC) THEN
          MASK1 = IMASK(1)
          MASK2 = IMASK(NH)
      ELSE
          IF (PROCNU .EQ. NDST) THEN
              MASK1 = IMASK(NH)
              MASK2 = IMASK(1)
          ELSE
              INTMED = NSRC
              DO 10 I=1,NH-1
                  INTMED=KXOR(IMASK(I),INTMED)
                  IF (PROCNU .EQ. INTMED) THEN
                      IRECV = IMASK(I)
                      ISEND = IMASK(I+1)
                      IFLAG = 1
                      GOTO 15
                  END IF
   10         CONTINUE

              INTMED = NSRC
              DO 20 I=NH,2,-1
                  INTMED=KXOR(IMASK(I),INTMED)
                  IF (PROCNU .EQ. INTMED) THEN
```

```
                        IRECV = IMASK(I)
                        ISEND = IMASK(I-1)
                        IFLAG = 2
                        GOTO 15
                    END IF
20                  CONTINUE

15              CONTINUE
            END IF
        END IF

        IF (PROCNU .EQ. NSRC) THEN
            DO 30 I=1,M
                IF (MOD(I-1,2) .EQ. 1) THEN
                    IERR = KCWRIT(V(I),MASK1,LBTE)
                ELSE
                    IERR = KCWRIT(V(I),MASK2,LBTE)
                END IF
30              CONTINUE
        ELSE
            IF (PROCNU .EQ. NDST) THEN
                DO 40 I=1,M
                    IF (MOD(I-1,2) .EQ. 1) THEN
                        IERR = KCREAD(V(I),MASK1,0,LBTE)
                    ELSE
                        IERR = KCREAD(V(I),MASK2,0,LBTE)
                    END IF
40                  CONTINUE
            ELSE
                IF (IFLAG .EQ. 1) THEN
                    DO 50 I=1,MODD
                        IERR = KCREAD(T,IRECV,ISEND,LBTE)
50                      CONTINUE
                ELSE
                    IF (IFLAG .EQ. 2) THEN
                        DO 60 I=1,MEVN
                        IERR = KCREAD(T,IRECV,ISEND,LBTE)
60                      CONTINUE
                    END IF
                END IF
            END IF
        END IF
    END IF
    RETURN
    END
C
CCCCCCCCCCCCCCCCCCCCCCCCCCCCCCC END OF ROUTINE TRANSF CCCCCCCCCCCCCCCCCCCCCCCCCCCCCCC
C
```

```
      SUBROUTINE ROUTER(IMASK,NH,MASKOD,NDOC)
      INTEGER IMASK(10)
      NT = MASKOD
      KC = 0
      DO 10 I=0,NDOC-1
          IF (MOD(NT,2) .EQ. 1) THEN
              KC = KC+1
              IMASK(KC) = 2**I
          END IF
          NT = NT/2
10        CONTINUE
      NH = KC
      RETURN
      END
C
CCCCCCCCCCCCCCCCCCCCCCCCCCCCCC END OF ROUTINE ROUTER CCCCCCCCCCCCCCCCCCCCCCCCCCCCCCC
C
      FUNCTION KXOR(M,N)
      KXOR=0
      MT=M
      IF (MT .LT. 0) MT=MT-2147483648
      NT=N
      IF (NT .LT. 0) NT=NT-2147483648
      IP=1
      DO 10 I=1,31
          IN=MOD(NT,2)
          IM=MOD(MT,2)
          IC=IN+IM
          IF (IC .EQ. 2) IC=0
          KXOR=IP*IC+KXOR
          IP=2*IP
          NT=NT/2
          MT=MT/2
          IF ((NT .EQ. 0) .AND. (MT .EQ. 0)) GOTO 99
10        CONTINUE
99    CONTINUE
      IF ((M .GT. 0) .AND. (N .LT. 0)) KXOR = KXOR+2147483648
      IF ((M .LT. 0) .AND. (N .GT. 0)) KXOR = KXOR+2147483648
      RETURN
      END
C
CCCCCCCCCCCCCCCCCCCCCCCCCCCCCC END OF ROUTINE KXOR CCCCCCCCCCCCCCCCCCCCCCCCCCCCCCC
C
```

B-16.7 The *transpose* Routine

```
PROGRAM TSTMTR
INTEGER A(4,4), ENV(5), COORD(2), NDIM(2), PROCNU

CALL KPARAM(ENV)
NDOC = ENV(1)
NDOCH = NDOC/2
PROCNU = ENV(2)
NDIM(1) = 2**NDOCH
NDIM(2) = NDIM(1)
CALL KGRDIN(2, NDIM)
CALL KGRDCO(PROCNU, COORD)
MX = COORD(1)
MY = COORD(2)

PRINT *, '         Before Transpose:'
MOFSTX = MX*4
MOFSTY = MY*4

MULTIPLE(6)
PRINT *, ' '
WRITE(*,101)
WRITE(*,102) 1+MOFSTX,2+MOFSTX,3+MOFSTX,4+MOFSTX

DO 10 I=1,4
    DO 15 J=1,4
        A(I,J) = 4*(2*MY+I-1)+2*MX+J
15        CONTINUE
    WRITE(*,100) PROCNU,I+MOFSTY,(A(I,J), J=1,4)
10      CONTINUE
100 FORMAT(I5 I7, 4 I8)
101 FORMAT('Procnum Row No. Col #1  Col #2  Col #3  Col #4')
102 FORMAT('       ',4 I8)
FLUSH(6)

CALL MTRANS(A,4,MX,MY,NDOCH,PROCNU)

SINGLE(6)
PRINT *, ' '
PRINT *, '         After Transpose'

MULTIPLE(6)
PRINT *, ' '
WRITE(*,101)
WRITE(*,102) 1+MOFSTX,2+MOFSTX,3+MOFSTX,4+MOFSTX
```

```
      DO 20 I=1,4
          WRITE(*,100) PROCNU,I+MOFSTY,(A(I,J), J=1,4)
20        CONTINUE
      FLUSH(6)

      STOP
      END
C
CCCCCCCCCCCCCCCCCCCCCCCCCCCCCC END OF PROGRAM TSTMTR CCCCCCCCCCCCCCCCCCCCCCCCCCCCCCCC
C
      SUBROUTINE MTRANS(A,N,MX,MY,NDOCH,PROCNU)
      INTEGER  A(4,4), TMP(4,4), PROCNU

      LBTE  = N*4
      MASKG = 2**NDOCH

      DO 10 ICHN=0, NDOCH-1
          MASK1 = 2**ICHN
          MASK2 = MASK1*MASKG
          IX = MOD(KRSHIF(MX,ICHN),2)
          IY = MOD(KRSHIF(MY,ICHN),2)
          IF (IX .EQ. IY) THEN
              DO 15 I=1,N
                  IERR=KCREAD(TMP(1,I), MASK2, MASK1, LBTE)
15                CONTINUE
          ELSE
              DO 25 I=1,N
                  IERR=KCWRIT(A(1,I), MASK2, LBTE)
                  IERR=KCREAD(A(1,I), MASK1, 0, LBTE)
25                CONTINUE
          END IF
10        CONTINUE

      DO 35 I=1,N
          DO 35 J=I+1,N
              MT = A(I,J)
              A(I,J) = A(J,I)
              A(J,I) = MT
35            CONTINUE

      RETURN
      END
C
CCCCCCCCCCCCCCCCCCCCCCCCCCCCCC END OF ROUTINE MTRANS CCCCCCCCCCCCCCCCCCCCCCCCCCCCCCCC
C
      FUNCTION KRSHIF(M,N)
      MT = M
```

```
      IF (MT .LT. 0) MT=MT-2147483648
      KRSHIF=MT/2**N
      IF (M .LT. 0) KRSHIF = KRSHIF+2**(31-N)
      RETURN
      END
C
CCCCCCCCCCCCCCCCCCCCCCCCCCCCCC END OF ROUTINE KRSHIF CCCCCCCCCCCCCCCCCCCCCCCCCCCCCC
C
      FUNCTION KLSHIF(M,N)
      MT = M
      IF (MT .LT. 0) MT=MT-2147483648
      IF (N .EQ. 0)  MT=M
      KLSHIF=MT*2**N
      RETURN
      END
C
CCCCCCCCCCCCCCCCCCCCCCCCCCCCCC END OF ROUTINE KLSHIF CCCCCCCCCCCCCCCCCCCCCCCCCCCCCC
C
```

B-17 The Crystal Router

B-17.1 CUBIX Program

```
      PROGRAM CROUTR
      PARAMETER (MAXITM=10,MAXBUF=80,NPROC=4)
      INTEGER ENV(5), PROCNU, DOC, CRYSRT
      INTEGER OTMAIL(MAXITM,NPROC), NITEM(NPROC), INMAIL(512)

      CALL KPARAM(ENV)
      DOC  = ENV(1)
      PROCNU= ENV(2)
      PRINT *, ' '
      IF (ENV(3) .NE. NPROC) THEN
          PRINT *, 'NPROC must be the same as in PARAMETER statement.'
          PRINT *, 'Program exiting ...'
          GOTO 99
      ENDIF

      DO 10 I=1,NPROC
      NITEM(I) = MOD(I-1,5) + 1
      DO 20 J=1,MAXITM
      OTMAIL(J,I) = I*J*(PROCNU+1)
20    CONTINUE
10    CONTINUE

      PRINT *, ' '
      MULTIPLE(6)
      DO 30 I=1,NPROC
      WRITE(*,100) PROCNU,I-1
      PRINT *, '    ',(OTMAIL(J,I),J=1,NITEM(I))
30    CONTINUE
      FLUSH(6)
100   FORMAT('Processor',I2,' sends to processor',I2)

      IERR = CRYSRT(OTMAIL,NITEM,INMAIL)

      PRINT *, ' '
      PRINT *, PROCNU,' received ',(INMAIL(K),K=1,IERR)
      FLUSH(6)

99    STOP
      END
C
CCCCCCCCCCCCCCCCCCCCCCCCCCCCCC END OF PROGRAM CROUTR CCCCCCCCCCCCCCCCCCCCCCCCCCCCCCC
C
      FUNCTION CRYSRT(OTMAIL,NITEM,INMAIL)
```

```
      PARAMETER (MAXITM=10,MAXBUF=80,NPROC=4)
      INTEGER  CRYSRT,PROCNU,NDOC,ERRFLG,ENV(5)
      INTEGER  OTMAIL(MAXITM,*),INMAIL(*),NITEM(*)
      INTEGER  COMBUF(MAXBUF),TMPBUF(MAXBUF*NPROC/2),TOMBUF(MAXBUF)
      INTEGER  ITHBIT(0:9,0:63),IHOLD(NPROC),TITEM(NPROC)
      INTEGER*2  AITEM(NPROC/2),BITEM(NPROC/2)
      INTEGER*2  CITEM(NPROC/2),DITEM(NPROC/2)
      LOGICAL  BREAK,CALLED,TLOG
      COMMON  /TOM/ CITEM,DITEM,COMBUF,AITEM,BITEM,TOMBUF,TMPBUF
      SAVE    IBITCK,ITHBIT,CALLED,IHOLD

      CALL KPARAM(ENV)
      NDOC  = ENV(1)
      PROCNU= ENV(2)
      NDOCP = NDOC-1
      MPROC = PROCNU+1
      LBTE = 4
      NBTE = NPROC*2
      MBTE = MAXBUF*LBTE+NBTE

      IF (IBITCK .NE. 1) IBITCK=KTHBIT(ITHBIT,NDOC,NPROC)

      IHU= 0
      K  = 0
      MC = 0
      NC = 0

      DO 10 I=1,NPROC
          IF (I .EQ. MPROC) THEN
              IF (NITEM(I) .EQ. 0) GOTO 10
              DO 20 K=1,NITEM(I)
                  INMAIL(K) = OTMAIL(K,I)
20                CONTINUE
              K = NITEM(I)
          ELSE
              IF (ITHBIT(0,PROCNU) .EQ. ITHBIT(0,I-1)) THEN
                  IF (.NOT. CALLED) THEN
                      IHU = IHU+1
                      IHOLD(I) = IHU
                      IHOLD(I) = (IHOLD(I)-1)*MAXBUF+1
                  ENDIF
                  IF(NITEM(I) .EQ. 0) GOTO 26
                  JLO = IHOLD(I)
                  JHI = JLO+NITEM(I)-1
                  JC  = 0
                  DO 25 J=JLO,JHI
                      JC = JC+1
```

```
                              TMPBUF(J) = OTMAIL(JC,I)
25                         CONTINUE
26                 TITEM(I) = NITEM(I)
            ELSE
                 IF (NITEM(I) .EQ. 0) GOTO 31
                 DO 30 J=1,NITEM(I)
                     MC = MC+1
                     TOMBUF(MC) = OTMAIL(J,I)
30                   CONTINUE
31               NC = NC+1
                 AITEM(NC) = NITEM(I)
                 BITEM(NC) = I
            END IF
        END IF
10      CONTINUE

     DO 40 IC=0,NDOCP
        IMASK = 2**IC
        IF (IC .NE. NDOCP) THEN
            IERR = KCSHIF(CITEM,IMASK,MBTE,AITEM,IMASK,MC*LBTE+NBTE)
        ELSE
            IERR = KCSHIF(INMAIL(K+1),IMASK,MBTE,TOMBUF,IMASK,MC*LBTE)
            K = K+IERR/4
            GOTO 99
        ENDIF

        IF (IERR .EQ. -1) ERRFLG = -1
        LC = 0
        MC = 0
        NC = 0
        ICP= IC+1

        DO 50 I=1,NPROC/2
            IF (DITEM(I) .EQ. -1) GOTO 51
            ID    = DITEM(I)
            TLOG  = ITHBIT(ICP,PROCNU) .EQ. ITHBIT(ICP,ID-1)
            BREAK = (CITEM(I) .EQ. 0)
            IF (ID .EQ. MPROC) THEN
                IF (BREAK) GOTO 50
                DO 60 J=K+1,K+CITEM(I)
                    LC = LC+1
                    INMAIL(J) = COMBUF(LC)
60                  CONTINUE
                K = K+CITEM(I)
            ELSE
                IF (TLOG) THEN
                    IF (BREAK) GOTO 50
```

```
                            JLO = IHOLD(ID)+TITEM(ID)
                            JHI = JLO+CITEM(I)-1
                            DO 65 J=JLO,JHI
                                LC = LC+1
                                TMPBUF(J) = COMBUF(LC)
      65                        CONTINUE
                            TITEM(ID) = TITEM(ID)+CITEM(I)
                    ELSE
                            IF (BREAK) GOTO 71
                            DO 70 J=MC+1,MC+CITEM(I)
                                LC = LC+1
                                TOMBUF(J) = COMBUF(LC)
      70                        CONTINUE
                            MC = MC+CITEM(I)
      71                    CONTINUE
                            IF (TITEM(ID) .EQ. 0) GOTO 76
                            JLO = IHOLD(ID)
                            JHI = JLO+TITEM(ID)-1
                            DO 75 J=JLO,JHI
                                MC = MC+1
                                TOMBUF(MC) = TMPBUF(J)
      75                        CONTINUE
      76                    NC = NC+1
                            AITEM(NC) = CITEM(I)+TITEM(ID)
                            BITEM(NC) = ID
                            TITEM(ID) = 0
                    ENDIF
                END IF
      50        CONTINUE
      51    NC = NC+1
           BITEM(NC) = -1

      40    CONTINUE

      99 IF (ERRFLG .EQ. -1) THEN
               CRYSRT = ERRFLG
           ELSE
               CRYSRT = K
           END IF
           CALLED = .TRUE.
           RETURN
           END
    C
    CCCCCCCCCCCCCCCCCCCCCCCCCCCCCC END OF ROUTINE CRYSRT CCCCCCCCCCCCCCCCCCCCCCCCCCCCCC
    C
           FUNCTION KTHBIT(ITHBIT,NDOC,NPROC)
           INTEGER ITHBIT(0:9,0:63)
```

```
        DO 10 I=0,NDOC-1
           DO 10 N=0,NPROC-1
               ITHBIT(I,N) = MOD(N/2**I,2)
10             CONTINUE
        KTHBIT=1
        RETURN
        END
C
CCCCCCCCCCCCCCCCCCCCCCCCCCCCC END OF ROUTINE KTHBIT CCCCCCCCCCCCCCCCCCCCCCCCCCCCC
C
```

B-18 The Crystal Accumulator

B-18.1 CUBIX Program

```
      PROGRAM CRYACC
      PARAMETER (NITEM=8)
      INTEGER  V(0:15),P(0:NITEM-1),Q(0:NITEM-1),VP(0:127,0:15)
      INTEGER  CRACUM,PROCNU,NDOC,ENV(5),S(0:NITEM-1)
      DATA (P(I),I=0,NITEM-1) /0,0,1,0,3,2,3,3/
      DATA (Q(I),I=0,NITEM-1) /2,4,5,3,1,7,0,6/
      DATA (VP(0,I),I=0,NITEM-1) /1,2,3,0,5,6,7,0/
      DATA (VP(1,I),I=0,NITEM-1) /0,2,3,0,0,6,0,8/
      DATA (VP(2,I),I=0,NITEM-1) /1,2,3,4,0,6,7,8/
      DATA (VP(3,I),I=0,NITEM-1) /0,0,3,4,0,6,7,8/

      CALL KPARAM(ENV)
      NDOC  = ENV(1)
      PROCNU= ENV(2)
      NPROC = ENV(3)

      PRINT *, ' '

      MULTIPLE(6)

      DO 5 I=0,NITEM-1
          V(I)=VP(PROCNU,I)
5         CONTINUE

      NC = CRACUM(V,P,Q,S)

      PRINT *, PROCNU,(S(I),I=0,NC-1)
      FLUSH(6)

99    STOP
      END
C
CCCCCCCCCCCCCCCCCCCCCCCCCCCCCCCC END OF PROGRAM CRYACC CCCCCCCCCCCCCCCCCCCCCCCCCCCCCCCC
C
      FUNCTION CRACUM(V,P,Q,S)
      PARAMETER (NITEM=8,MAXBUF=16)
      PARAMETER (MB=MAXBUF-1)
      INTEGER  V(0:15),P(0:NITEM-1),Q(0:NITEM-1)
      INTEGER  CRACUM,PROCNU,NDOC,ENV(5),S(0:NITEM-1)
      INTEGER  DEST(0:NITEM-1),LIST(0:NITEM-1)
      REAL     COMBUF(0:MB),TOMBUF(0:MB),TMPBUF(0:MB),INMAIL(0:MB)
      INTEGER  DOMBUF(0:MB),SOMBUF(0:MB),SMPBUF(0:MB),JNMAIL(0:MB)
      INTEGER  ITHBIT(0:6,0:127)
```

```
        SAVE      IBITCK,ITHBIT

        CALL KPARAM(ENV)
        NDOC  = ENV(1)
        PROCNU= ENV(2)
        NPROC = ENV(3)

        LBTE = 4
        MBTE = NITEM*LBTE

        IF (IBITCK .NE. 1) IBITCK=KTHBIT(ITHBIT,NDOC,NPROC)

        K  = 0
        MC = 0
        JC = 0

        DO 10 I=0,NITEM-1
            DEST(Q(I)) = P(I)
            IF (V(Q(I)) .EQ. 0) GOTO 10
            IF (P(I) .EQ. PROCNU) THEN
                INMAIL(K) = V(Q(I))
                JNMAIL(K) = Q(I)
                K = K+1
            ELSEIF (ITHBIT(0,PROCNU) .EQ. ITHBIT(0,P(I))) THEN
                TMPBUF(JC) = V(Q(I))
                SMPBUF(JC) = Q(I)
                JC = JC+1
            ELSE
                TOMBUF(MC) = V(Q(I))
                SOMBUF(MC) = Q(I)
                MC = MC+1
            ENDIF
10          CONTINUE

        IMASK = 1
        DO 40 ICP=1,NDOC
            IF (MC .GT. MAXBUF) THEN
                IERR = -1
                GOTO 99
            ENDIF
            IERR = KCSHIF(COMBUF,IMASK,MBTE,TOMBUF,IMASK,MC*LBTE)
            IERR = KCSHIF(DOMBUF,IMASK,MBTE,SOMBUF,IMASK,MC*LBTE)
            IMASK = IMASK*2

            MC    = 0
            MYBIT = ITHBIT(ICP,PROCNU)
```

```
        DO 50 I=0,IERR/4-1
            M = DOMBUF(I)
            NDEST = DEST(M)
            IF (PROCNU .EQ. NDEST) THEN
                DO 51 J=0,K-1
                    IF (JNMAIL(J) .EQ. M) GOTO 52
51                  CONTINUE
                INMAIL(K) = COMBUF(I)
                JNMAIL(K) = DOMBUF(I)
                K = K+1
                GOTO 50
52              INMAIL(J) = COMBUF(I)+INMAIL(J)

            ELSEIF (MYBIT .EQ. ITHBIT(ICP,NDEST)) THEN
                DO 53 J=0,JC-1
                    IF (SMPBUF(J) .EQ. M) GOTO 54
53                  CONTINUE
                TMPBUF(JC) = COMBUF(I)
                SMPBUF(JC) = DOMBUF(I)
                JC = JC+1
                GOTO 50
54              TMPBUF(J) = COMBUF(I)+TMPBUF(J)
            ELSE
                DO 55 J=0,JC-1
                    IF (SMPBUF(J) .EQ. M) GOTO 56
55                  CONTINUE
                TOMBUF(MC) = COMBUF(I)
                SOMBUF(MC) = DOMBUF(I)
                MC = MC+1
                GOTO 50
56              TOMBUF(MC) = COMBUF(I)+TMPBUF(J)
                SOMBUF(MC) = M
                MC = MC+1
                IF (J .LT. JC-1) THEN
                    TMPBUF(J) = TMPBUF(JC-1)
                    SMPBUF(J) = SMPBUF(JC-1)
                ENDIF
                JC = JC-1
            ENDIF
50          CONTINUE

        LC = 0
        DO 60 I=0,JC-1
            J=SMPBUF(I)
            NDEST=DEST(J)
            IF (J .NE. PROCNU) THEN
                IF (MYBIT .NE. ITHBIT(ICP,NDEST)) THEN
```

```
                    TOMBUF(MC) = TMPBUF(I)
                    SOMBUF(MC) = SMPBUF(I)
                    MC = MC+1
                    LIST(LC) = I
                    LC = LC+1
                 ENDIF
              ENDIF
60            CONTINUE
          DO 61 I=0,LC
              TMPBUF(LIST(I))=TMPBUF(JC-1)
              SMPBUF(LIST(I))=SMPBUF(JC-1)
              JC = JC-1
61            CONTINUE

40        CONTINUE

      IC = 0
      LC = 0
      DO 70 J=0,NITEM-1
          DO 70 M=0,K-1
              IF (IC .EQ. K) GOTO 99
              IF (JNMAIL(M) .EQ. Q(J)) THEN
                  S(IC) = INMAIL(M)
                  IC = IC+1
              ENDIF
70            CONTINUE
99   CRACUM = IC
      IF (IERR .EQ. -1) CRACUM = -1

      RETURN
      END
C
CCCCCCCCCCCCCCCCCCCCCCCCCCCCCC END OF ROUTINE CRACUM CCCCCCCCCCCCCCCCCCCCCCCCCCCCCC
C
      FUNCTION KTHBIT(ITHBIT,NDOC,NPROC)
      INTEGER ITHBIT(0:6,0:127)
      DO 10 I=0,NDOC-1
          DO 10 N=0,NPROC-1
              ITHBIT(I,N) = MOD(N/2**I,2)
10            CONTINUE
      KTHBIT=1
      RETURN
      END
C
CCCCCCCCCCCCCCCCCCCCCCCCCCCCCC END OF ROUTINE KTHBIT CCCCCCCCCCCCCCCCCCCCCCCCCCCCCC
C
```

C

Appendix C:
C Code For Tutorial Programs

This appendix lists the C source code for the tasks set in the Tutorial at the beginning of the book. Although a reasonable effort has been made to ensure that the code is correct and reliable, there are, no doubt, bugs. If you encounter any bugs, or have constructive suggestions for improving the code, please write to the address given in Appendix G. When filing a bug report, please give full details of the problem and the input data.

C-1 C Code For Tutorial Task 2.3

C-1.1 CP Program

```c
#include <stdio.h>
#include <cros.h>

#define MAX_PROCS 1024

int doc, nproc;

main()
{
    int intcp, iresp, i;
    int node_vals[MAX_PROCS], bufmap[MAX_PROCS+1];

    iresp = down_load("task23NODE");
    if (iresp<0){
        printf("\n\n**** An error occurred in cubeld ****\n");
        printf("  \n**** Program aborted            ****\n\n");
        exit(1);
    }

    printf("\n\nPlease give an integer ==> ");
    scanf("%d",&intcp);

    bcastcp(&intcp,sizeof(int));

    mdumpcp(node_vals,sizeof(int),bufmap);

    printf("\nValue in each node:\n");
    for(i=0;i<nproc;++i)
        printf("%d%c",node_vals[i],(i%20==19) ? '\n' : ' ');

    printf("\n\nFinished\n\n");
    exit(0);
}

/*************************** end of routine main ***************************/
int down_load(node_prog)
char *node_prog;
{
    printf("\n\nPlease give the dimension of the hypercube ==> ");
    scanf("%d",&doc);

    nproc   = 1<<doc;
    return (cubeld(doc,node_prog));
```

```
    }

    /************************** end of routine down_load *********************/
```

C-1.2 NODE Program

```c
    #include <stdio.h>
    #include <cros.h>

    main()
    {
        int intcp, iproc, isum;
        struct cubenv env;

        bcastelt(&intcp,sizeof(int));

        cparam(&env);

        iproc = env.procnum;
        isum  = iproc + intcp;

        dumpelt(&isum,sizeof(int));

        exit(0);
    }

    /************************** end of routine main **************************/
```

C-1.3 CUBIX Program

```c
    #include <stdio.h>
    #include <cros.h>

    main()
    {
        int intcp, iproc, isum;
        struct cubenv env;

        printf("\n\nPlease give an integer ==> ");
        scanf("%d",&intcp);

        cparam(&env);

        iproc = env.procnum;
        isum  = iproc + intcp;

        printf("\nValue in each node:\n");
```

```
        fmulti(stdout);
        printf("%d%c",isum,(iproc%20==19) ? '\n' : ' ');

        fsingl(stdout);
        printf("\n\nFinished\n\n");

        exit(0);
}

/*************************** end of routine main ***************************/
```

C-2 C Code For Tutorial Task 2.4

C-2.1 CP Program

```
#include <stdio.h>
#include <cros.h>

#define MAX_PROCS 1024

int doc, nproc;

main()
{
    int iresp, i;
    int input_vals[MAX_PROCS];
    int node_vals[MAX_PROCS], bufmap[MAX_PROCS+1];

    iresp = down_load("task24NODE");
    if (iresp<0){
        printf("\n\n**** An error occurred in cubeld ****\n");
        printf("  \n**** Program aborted              ****\n\n");
        exit(1);
    }

    printf("\n\nPlease give %2d integers ==> ",nproc);
    for(i=0;i<nproc;++i){
        scanf("%d",&input_vals[i]);
        bufmap[i+1] = sizeof(int);
    }
    bufmap[0] = nproc;

    printf("\nValues sent to nodes:\n");
    for(i=0;i<nproc;++i)
        printf("%d%c",input_vals[i],(i%20==19) ? '\n' : ' ');

    mloadcp(input_vals,bufmap);
    mdumpcp(node_vals,sizeof(int),bufmap);

    printf("\n\nValue in each node:\n");
    for(i=0;i<nproc;++i)
        printf("%d%c",node_vals[i],(i%20==19) ? '\n' : ' ');

    printf("\n\nFinished\n\n");
    exit(0);
}


/*************************** end of routine main ***************************/
```

```
int down_load(node_prog)
char *node_prog;
{
    printf("\n\nPlease give the dimension of the hypercube ==> ");
    scanf("%d",&doc);

    nproc   = 1<<doc;
    return (cubeld(doc,node_prog));
}
```

/************************* end of routine down_load *************************/

C-2.2 NODE Program

```
#include <stdio.h>
#include <cros.h>

main()
{
    int intcp, iproc, isum;
    struct cubenv env;

    loadelt(&intcp,sizeof(int));

    cparam(&env);

    iproc = env.procnum;
    isum  = iproc + intcp;

    dumpelt(&isum,sizeof(int));

    exit(0);
}
```

/*************************** end of routine main ***************************/

C-2.3 CUBIX Program

```
#include <stdio.h>
#include <cros.h>

main()
{
    int intcp, iproc, isum;
    struct cubenv env;

    cparam(&env);
```

```
        fmulti(stdin);
        printf("\n\nPlease give %2d integers ==> ",env.nproc);
        scanf("%d",&intcp);

        iproc = env.procnum;
        isum  = iproc + intcp;

        printf("\nValues sent to nodes:\n");
        fmulti(stdout);
        printf("%d%c",intcp,(iproc%20==19) ? '\n' : ' ');

        fsingl(stdout);
        printf("\nValue in each node:\n");
        fmulti(stdout);
        printf("%d%c",isum,(iproc%20==19) ? '\n' : ' ');

        fsingl(stdout);
        printf("\n\nFinished\n\n");
        exit(0);
}

/*************************** end of routine main ***************************/
```

C-3 C Code For Tutorial Task 2.5

C-3.1 CP Program

```
#include <stdio.h>
#include <cros.h>

#define MAX_PROCS 1024

int doc, nproc;

main()
{
    int iresp, i;
    int input_vals[MAX_PROCS];
    int node_vals[MAX_PROCS], bufmap[MAX_PROCS+1];
    float average;

    iresp = down_load("task25NODE");
    if (iresp<0){
        printf("\n\n**** An error occurred in cubeld ****\n");
        printf("  \n**** Program aborted             ****\n\n");
        exit(1);
    }

    printf("\n\nPlease give %2d integers ==> ",nproc);
    for(i=0;i<nproc;++i){
        scanf("%d",&input_vals[i]);
        bufmap[i+1] = sizeof(int);
    }
    bufmap[0] = nproc;

    printf("\nValues sent to nodes:\n");
    for(i=0;i<nproc;++i)
        printf("%d%c",input_vals[i],(i%20==19) ? '\n' : ' ');

    mloadcp(input_vals,bufmap);
    mdumpcp(node_vals,sizeof(int),bufmap);

    printf("\n\nValue in each node:\n");
    for(i=0;i<nproc;++i)
        printf("%d%c",node_vals[i],(i%20==19) ? '\n' : ' ');

    combcp(&average,sizeof(float),1);
    printf("\n\nAverage value over all nodes = %f",average);

    printf("\n\nFinished\n\n");
```

```
    exit(0);
}

/*************************** end of routine main ***************************/
int down_load(node_prog)
char *node_prog;
{
    printf("\n\nPlease give the dimension of the hypercube ==> ");
    scanf("%d",&doc);

    nproc   = 1<<doc;
    return (cubeld(doc,node_prog));
}

/************************** end of routine down_load **************************/
```

C-3.2 NODE Program

```
    #include <stdio.h>
    #include <cros.h>

    main()
    {
        int intcp, iproc, isum, float_add();
        float average;
        struct cubenv env;

        loadelt(&intcp,sizeof(int));

        cparam(&env);

        iproc = env.procnum;
        isum  = iproc + intcp;
        average = (float)isum/(float)env.nproc;

        dumpelt(&isum,sizeof(int));
        combelt(&average,float_add,sizeof(float),1);

        exit(0);
    }

/************************** end of routine main **************************/
    int float_add(p1,p2,size)
    float *p1, *p2;
    int size;
    {
        *p1 += *p2;
```

```
        return 0;
    }


/*************************** end of routine float_add ************************/
```

C-3.3 CUBIX Program

```
    #include <stdio.h>
    #include <cros.h>

    main()
    {
        int intcp, iproc, isum, float_add();
        float average;
        struct cubenv env;

        cparam(&env);

        fmulti(stdin);
        printf("\n\nPlease give %2d integers ==> ",env.nproc);
        scanf("%d",&intcp);

        iproc  = env.procnum;
        isum   = iproc + intcp;
        average = (float)isum/(float)env.nproc;

        printf("\nValues sent to nodes:\n");
        fmulti(stdout);
        printf("%d%c",intcp,(iproc%20==19) ? '\n' : ' ');

        fsingl(stdout);
        printf("\nValue in each node:\n");
        fmulti(stdout);
        printf("%d%c",isum,(iproc%20==19) ? '\n' : ' ');

        combine(&average,float_add,sizeof(float),1);

        fsingl(stdout);
        printf("\n\nAverage value over all nodes = %f",average);
        printf("\n\nFinished\n\n");
        exit(0);
    }


/*************************** end of routine main ***************************/
    int float_add(p1,p2,size)
    float *p1, *p2;
    int size;
```

```
{
    *p1 += *p2;
    return 0;
}

/************************** end of routine float_add **************************/
```

C-4 C Code For Tutorial Task 3.2

C-4.1 CP Program

```
#include <stdio.h>
#include <cros.h>

#define MAX_PROCS 1024
int doc, nproc;

main()
{
    int i, iresp, nloops;

    iresp = down_load("task32NODE");
    if (iresp<0){
        printf("\n\n**** An error occurred in cubeld ****\n");
        printf("  \n**** Program aborted            ****\n\n");
        exit(1);
    }

    printf("\n\nPlease give the number of loops ==> ");
    scanf("%d",&nloops);
    bcastcp(&nloops,sizeof(int));

    printf("\n\nAll integers are output in order of ");
    printf("increasing node number\n");

    printf("\n\nPosition in ring:\n");
    output_results();

    printf("\n\nNode number of clockwise neighboring node:\n");
    output_results();

    printf("\n\nNode number of anti-clockwise neighboring node:\n");
    output_results();

    printf("\n\nMask of channel in clockwise direction:\n");
    output_results();

    printf("\n\nMask of channel in anti-clockwise direction:\n");
    output_results();

    printf("\n\nMove node numbers %d steps around the ring:\n");
    for(i=0;i<nloops;++i){
        output_results();
        printf("\n");
```

```
    }

    printf("\n\nFinished\n\n");
    exit(0);
}

/*************************** end of routine main ***************************/
int down_load(node_prog)
char *node_prog;
{
    printf("\n\nPlease give the dimension of the hypercube ==> ");
    scanf("%d",&doc);

    nproc   = 1<<doc;
    return (cubeld(doc,node_prog));
}

/************************** end of routine down_load ***********************/
output_results()
{
    int i;
    int node_vals[MAX_PROCS], bufmap[MAX_PROCS+1];

    mdumpcp(node_vals,sizeof(int),bufmap);
    for(i=0;i<nproc;++i)
        printf("%d%c",node_vals[i],(i%20==19) ? '\n' : ' ');
}

/*********************** end of routine output_results ********************/
```

C-4.2 NODE Program

```
    #include <stdio.h>
    #include <cros.h>

    main()
    {
        int nloops, iproc, nproc, i, imove, isize=sizeof(int);
        int ring_pos, clk_node, anti_clk_node;
        int clk_pos, anti_clk_pos, clk_mask, anti_clk_mask;
        struct cubenv env;

        bcastelt(&nloops,isize);

        cparam(&env);
```

```
    iproc = env.procnum;
    nproc = env.nproc;

    gridinit(1,&nproc);
    gridcoord(iproc,&ring_pos);
    dumpelt(&ring_pos,isize);

    clk_pos      = (ring_pos==(nproc-1)) ?   0 : ring_pos+1;
    anti_clk_pos = (ring_pos==0) ?      nproc-1 : ring_pos-1;
    clk_node     = gridproc(&clk_pos);
    anti_clk_node = gridproc(&anti_clk_pos);
    dumpelt(&clk_node,isize);
    dumpelt(&anti_clk_node,isize);

    clk_mask      = gridchan(iproc,0, 1);
    anti_clk_mask = gridchan(iproc,0,-1);
    dumpelt(&clk_mask,isize);
    dumpelt(&anti_clk_mask,isize);

    imove = iproc;
    for(i=0;i<nloops;++i){
        cshift(&imove,anti_clk_mask,isize,&imove,clk_mask,isize);
        dumpelt(&imove,isize);
    }

    exit(0);
}
```

```
/*************************** end of routine main ***************************/
```

C-4.3 CUBIX Program

```
    #include <stdio.h>
    #include <cros.h>

    int iproc;

    main()
    {
        int nloops, nproc, i, imove, isize=sizeof(int);
        int ring_pos, clk_node, anti_clk_node;
        int clk_pos, anti_clk_pos, clk_mask, anti_clk_mask;
        struct cubenv env;

        printf("\n\nPlease give the number of loops ==> ");
        scanf("%d",&nloops);
```

```
        cparam(&env);

        iproc = env.procnum;
        nproc = env.nproc;

        gridinit(1,&nproc);
        gridcoord(iproc,&ring_pos);

        printf("\n\nAll integers are output in order of ");
        printf("increasing node number\n");

        printf("\n\nPosition in ring:\n");
        output_results(ring_pos);

        clk_pos       = (ring_pos==(nproc-1)) ?   0 : ring_pos+1;
        anti_clk_pos  = (ring_pos==0) ?     nproc-1 : ring_pos-1;
        clk_node      = gridproc(&clk_pos);
        anti_clk_node = gridproc(&anti_clk_pos);

        printf("\n\nNode number of clockwise neighboring node:\n");
        output_results(clk_node);

        printf("\n\nNode number of anti-clockwise neighboring node:\n");
        output_results(anti_clk_node);

        clk_mask      = gridchan(iproc,0, 1);
        anti_clk_mask = gridchan(iproc,0,-1);

        printf("\n\nMask of channel in clockwise direction:\n");
        output_results(clk_mask);

        printf("\n\nMask of channel in anti-clockwise direction:\n");
        output_results(anti_clk_mask);

        printf("\n\nMove node numbers %d steps around the ring:\n");
        imove = iproc;
        for(i=0;i<nloops;++i){
            cshift(&imove,anti_clk_mask,isize,&imove,clk_mask,isize);
            output_results(imove);
            printf("\n");
        }

        printf("\n\nFinished\n\n");
        exit(0);
}

/*************************** end of routine main ***************************/
```

```
output_results(ival)
int ival;
{
    fmulti(stdout);
    printf("%d%c",ival,(iproc%20==19) ? '\n' : ' ');
    fsingl(stdout);
}

/********************** end of routine output_results **********************/
```

C-5 C Code For Tutorial Task 3.3

C-5.1 CP Program

```c
#include <stdio.h>
#include <cros.h>

#define MAX_PROCS 1024
int doc, nproc;

main()
{
    int i, iresp, npx, npy;

    iresp = down_load("task33NODE");
    if (iresp<0){
        printf("\n\n**** An error occurred in cubeId ****\n");
        printf("  \n**** Program aborted           ****\n\n");
        exit(1);
    }

    printf("\n\nPlease give the number of nodes in the x-direction ==> ");
    scanf("%d",&npx);
    printf("\n\nPlease give the number of nodes in the y-direction ==> ");
    scanf("%d",&npy);

    if(npx*npy != nproc){
        printf("\n\n**** Invalid decomposition ****\n");
        printf("  \n**** Program aborted      ****\n\n");
        exit(1);
    }

    bcastcp(&npx,sizeof(int));
    bcastcp(&npy,sizeof(int));

    printf("\n\nAll integers are output in order of ");
    printf("increasing node number\n");

    printf("\n\nPosition in the x-direction\n");
    output_results();

    printf("\n\nPosition in the y-direction\n");
    output_results();

    printf("\n\nSum of node numbers in each row:\n");
    output_results();
```

```
    printf("\n\nSum of node numbers over all rows and columns:\n");
    output_results();

    printf("\n\nFinished\n\n");
    exit(0);
}


/*************************** end of routine main ***************************/
int down_load(node_prog)
char *node_prog;
{
    printf("\n\nPlease give the dimension of the hypercube ==> ");
    scanf("%d",&doc);

    nproc  = 1<<doc;
    return (cubeld(doc,node_prog));
}


/************************** end of routine down_load ***********************/
output_results()
{
    int i;
    int node_vals[MAX_PROCS], bufmap[MAX_PROCS+1];

    mdumpcp(node_vals,sizeof(int),bufmap);
    for(i=0;i<nproc;++i)
        printf("%d%c",node_vals[i],(i%20==19) ? '\n' : ' ');
}


/*********************** end of routine output_results ********************/
```

C-5.2 NODE Program

```
    #include <stdio.h>
    #include <cros.h>

    int isize = sizeof(int);

    main()
    {
        int irsum, isend, irec, iproc, nproc;
        int x_pos, y_pos, npx, npy, num[2], coord[2];
        int maskl, maskr, masku, maskd;
        struct cubenv env;

        bcastelt(&npx,isize);
```

```
        bcastelt(&npy,isize);
        num[0] = npx;
        num[1] = npy;

        cparam(&env);

        iproc = env.procnum;
        nproc = env.nproc;

        gridinit(2,num);
        gridcoord(iproc,coord);
        x_pos = coord[0];
        y_pos = coord[1];
        dumpelt(&x_pos,isize);
        dumpelt(&y_pos,isize);

        maskr = gridchan(iproc,0, 1);
        maskl = gridchan(iproc,0,-1);
        masku = gridchan(iproc,1, 1);
        maskd = gridchan(iproc,1,-1);

        irsum = pipe_sum(iproc,x_pos,npx-1,maskl,maskr);
        irsum = pipe_int(irsum,x_pos,npx-1,maskr,maskl);

        dumpelt(&irsum,isize);

        irsum = pipe_sum(irsum,y_pos,npy-1,maskd,masku);
        irsum = pipe_int(irsum,y_pos,npy-1,masku,maskd);

        dumpelt(&irsum,isize);

        exit(0);
}

/*************************** end of routine main ***************************/
int pipe_sum(ival,pos,end,in_mask,out_mask)
int ival, end, pos, in_mask, out_mask;
{
        int irec, irsum, isend;

        irsum = 0;
        if(pos==0){
            cwrite(&ival,out_mask,isize);
        }
        else if(pos==end){
            cread(&irec,in_mask,0,isize);
            irsum = irec + ival;
```

```
        }
        else{
            cread(&irec,in_mask,0,isize);
            isend = irec + ival;
            cwrite(&isend,out_mask,isize);
        }

        return irsum;

}

/************************** end of routine pipe_sum **************************/
int pipe_int(ival,pos,end,in_mask,out_mask)
int ival, end, pos, in_mask, out_mask;
{
    if(pos==end)    cwrite(&ival,out_mask,isize);
    else if(pos==0) cread(&ival,in_mask,0,isize);
    else            cread(&ival,in_mask,out_mask,isize);

    return ival;
}

/************************** end of routine pipe_int **************************/
```

C-5.3 CUBIX Program

```
#include <stdio.h>
#include <cros.h>

int iproc, isize = sizeof(int);

main()
{
    int irsum, isend, irec, nproc;
    int x_pos, y_pos, npx, npy, num[2], coord[2];
    int maskl, maskr, masku, maskd;
    struct cubenv env;

    printf("\n\nPlease give the number of nodes in the x-direction ==> ");
    scanf("%d",&npx);
    printf("\n\nPlease give the number of nodes in the y-direction ==> ");
    scanf("%d",&npy);

    num[0] = npx;
    num[1] = npy;

    cparam(&env);
```

```
    iproc = env.procnum;
    nproc = env.nproc;

    gridinit(2,num);
    gridcoord(iproc,coord);
    x_pos = coord[0];
    y_pos = coord[1];

    printf("\n\nAll integers are output in order of ");
    printf("increasing node number\n");

    printf("\n\nPosition in the x-direction\n");
    output_results(x_pos);

    printf("\n\nPosition in the y-direction\n");
    output_results(y_pos);

    maskr = gridchan(iproc,0, 1);
    maskl = gridchan(iproc,0,-1);
    masku = gridchan(iproc,1, 1);
    maskd = gridchan(iproc,1,-1);

    irsum = pipe_sum(iproc,x_pos,npx-1,maskl,maskr);
    irsum = pipe_int(irsum,x_pos,npx-1,maskr,maskl);

    printf("\n\nSum of node numbers in each row:\n");
    output_results(irsum);

    irsum = pipe_sum(irsum,y_pos,npy-1,maskd,masku);
    irsum = pipe_int(irsum,y_pos,npy-1,masku,maskd);

    printf("\n\nSum of node numbers over all rows and columns:\n");
    output_results(irsum);

    printf("\n\nFinished\n\n");
    exit(0);
}

/*************************** end of routine main ***************************/
int pipe_sum(ival,pos,end,in_mask,out_mask)
int ival, end, pos, in_mask, out_mask;
{
    int irec, irsum, isend;

    irsum = 0;
    if(pos==0){
        cwrite(&ival,out_mask,isize);
```

```
    }
    else if(pos==end){
        cread(&irec,in_mask,0,isize);
        irsum = irec + ival;
    }
    else{
        cread(&irec,in_mask,0,isize);
        isend = irec + ival;
        cwrite(&isend,out_mask,isize);
    }

    return irsum;
}

/*********************** end of routine pipe_sum ***********************/
int pipe_int(ival,pos,end,in_mask,out_mask)
int ival, end, pos, in_mask, out_mask;
{
    if(pos==end)    cwrite(&ival,out_mask,isize);
    else if(pos==0) cread(&ival,in_mask,0,isize);
    else            cread(&ival,in_mask,out_mask,isize);

    return ival;
}

/*********************** end of routine pipe_int ***********************/
output_results(ival)
int ival;
{
    fmulti(stdout);
    printf("%d%c",ival,(iproc%20==19) ? '\n' : ' ');
    fsingl(stdout);
}

/*********************** end of routine output_results ***********************/
```

C-6 C Code For Tutorial Task 3.4

C-6.1 CP Program

```
#include <stdio.h>
#include <cros.h>

#define MAX_PROCS 1024
int doc, nproc;

main()
{
    int i, iresp, npx, npy;

    iresp = down_load("task34NODE");
    if (iresp<0){
        printf("\n\n**** An error occurred in cubeld ****\n");
        printf("  \n**** Program aborted              ****\n\n");
        exit(1);
    }

    printf("\n\nPlease give the number of nodes in the x-direction ==> ");
    scanf("%d",&npx);
    printf("\n\nPlease give the number of nodes in the y-direction ==> ");
    scanf("%d",&npy);

    if(npx*npy != nproc){
        printf("\n\n**** Invalid decomposition ****\n");
        printf("  \n**** Program aborted       ****\n\n");
        exit(1);
    }

    bcastcp(&npx,sizeof(int));
    bcastcp(&npy,sizeof(int));

    printf("\n\nAll integers are output in order of ");
    printf("increasing node number\n");

    printf("\n\nPosition in the x-direction\n");
    output_results();

    printf("\n\nPosition in the y-direction\n");
    output_results();

    printf("\n\nSum of node numbers in each row:\n");
    output_results();
```

```
        printf("\n\nSum of node numbers over all rows and columns:\n");
        output_results();

        printf("\n\nFinished\n\n");
        exit(0);
}

/*************************** end of routine main ***************************/
int down_load(node_prog)
char *node_prog;
{
        printf("\n\nPlease give the dimension of the hypercube ==> ");
        scanf("%d",&doc);

        nproc    = 1<<doc;
        return (cubeld(doc,node_prog));
}

/************************** end of routine down_load **********************/
output_results()
{
        int i;
        int node_vals[MAX_PROCS], bufmap[MAX_PROCS+1];

        mdumpcp(node_vals,sizeof(int),bufmap);
        for(i=0;i<nproc;++i)
            printf("%d%c",node_vals[i],(i%20==19) ? '\n' : ' ');
}

/********************** end of routine output_results ********************/
```

C-6.2 NODE Program

```
    #include <stdio.h>
    #include <cros.h>

    int isize = sizeof(int);

    main()
    {
        int source, sc_mask;
        int irsum, isend, irec, iproc, nproc;
        int x_pos, y_pos, npx, npy, num[2], coord[2];
        int maskl, maskr, masku, maskd;
        struct cubenv env;
```

```
        bcastelt(&npx,isize);
        bcastelt(&npy,isize);
        num[0] = npx;
        num[1] = npy;

        cparam(&env);

        iproc = env.procnum;
        nproc = env.nproc;

        gridinit(2,num);
        gridcoord(iproc,coord);
        x_pos = coord[0];
        y_pos = coord[1];
        dumpelt(&x_pos,isize);
        dumpelt(&y_pos,isize);

        maskr = gridchan(iproc,0, 1);
        maskl = gridchan(iproc,0,-1);
        masku = gridchan(iproc,1, 1);
        maskd = gridchan(iproc,1,-1);

        irsum = pipe_sum(iproc,x_pos,npx-1,maskl,maskr);
        coord[0] = npx-1;
        coord[1] = y_pos;
        source   = gridproc(coord);
        sc_mask  = npx-1;
        broadcast(&irsum,source,sc_mask,isize);

        dumpelt(&irsum,isize);

        irsum = pipe_sum(irsum,y_pos,npy-1,maskd,masku);
        coord[0] = x_pos;
        coord[1] = npy-1;
        source   = gridproc(coord);
        sc_mask  = npx*(npy-1);
        broadcast(&irsum,source,sc_mask,isize);

        dumpelt(&irsum,isize);

        exit(0);
}


/*************************** end of routine main ***************************/
int pipe_sum(ival,pos,end,in_mask,out_mask)
int ival, end, pos, in_mask, out_mask;
{
```

```
    int irec, irsum, isend;

    irsum = 0;
    if(pos==0){
        cwrite(&ival,out_mask,isize);
    }
    else if(pos==end){
        cread(&irec,in_mask,0,isize);
        irsum = irec + ival;
    }
    else{
        cread(&irec,in_mask,0,isize);
        isend = irec + ival;
        cwrite(&isend,out_mask,isize);
    }

    return irsum;
}
```

```
/************************ end of routine pipe_sum ************************/
```

C-6.3 CUBIX Program

```
#include <stdio.h>
#include <cros.h>

int iproc, isize = sizeof(int);

main()
{
    int source, sc_mask;
    int irsum, isend, irec, nproc;
    int x_pos, y_pos, npx, npy, num[2], coord[2];
    int maskl, maskr, masku, maskd;
    struct cubenv env;

    printf("\n\nPlease give the number of nodes in the x-direction ==> ");
    scanf("%d",&npx);
    printf("\n\nPlease give the number of nodes in the y-direction ==> ");
    scanf("%d",&npy);

    num[0] = npx;
    num[1] = npy;

    cparam(&env);

    iproc = env.procnum;
```

```
        nproc = env.nproc;

        gridinit(2,num);
        gridcoord(iproc,coord);
        x_pos = coord[0];
        y_pos = coord[1];

        printf("\n\nAll integers are output in order of ");
        printf("increasing node number\n");

        printf("\n\nPosition in the x-direction\n");
        output_results(x_pos);

        printf("\n\nPosition in the y-direction\n");
        output_results(y_pos);

        maskr = gridchan(iproc,0, 1);
        maskl = gridchan(iproc,0,-1);
        masku = gridchan(iproc,1, 1);
        maskd = gridchan(iproc,1,-1);

        irsum = pipe_sum(iproc,x_pos,npx-1,maskl,maskr);
        coord[0] = npx-1;
        coord[1] = y_pos;
        source   = gridproc(coord);
        sc_mask  = npx-1;
        broadcast(&irsum,source,sc_mask,isize);

        printf("\n\nSum of node numbers in each row:\n");
        output_results(irsum);

        irsum = pipe_sum(irsum,y_pos,npy-1,maskd,masku);
        coord[0] = x_pos;
        coord[1] = npy-1;
        source   = gridproc(coord);
        sc_mask  = npx*(npy-1);
        broadcast(&irsum,source,sc_mask,isize);

        printf("\n\nSum of node numbers over all rows and columns:\n");
        output_results(irsum);

        printf("\n\nFinished\n\n");
        exit(0);
}


/*************************** end of routine main ***************************/
```

```
    int pipe_sum(ival,pos,end,in_mask,out_mask)
    int ival, end, pos, in_mask, out_mask;
    {
        int irec, irsum, isend;

        irsum = 0;
        if(pos==0){
            cwrite(&ival,out_mask,isize);
        }
        else if(pos==end){
            cread(&irec,in_mask,0,isize);
            irsum = irec + ival;
        }
        else{
            cread(&irec,in_mask,0,isize);
            isend = irec + ival;
            cwrite(&isend,out_mask,isize);
        }

        return irsum;
    }


/************************* end of routine pipe_sum *************************/
    int pipe_int(ival,pos,end,in_mask,out_mask)
    int ival, end, pos, in_mask, out_mask;
    {
        if(pos==end)    cwrite(&ival,out_mask,isize);
        else if(pos==0) cread(&ival,in_mask,0,isize);
        else            cread(&ival,in_mask,out_mask,isize);

        return ival;
    }


/************************* end of routine pipe_int *************************/
    output_results(ival)
    int ival;
    {
        fmulti(stdout);
        printf("%d%c",ival,(iproc%20==19) ? '\n' : ' ');
        fsingl(stdout);
    }


/********************** end of routine output_results **********************/
```

C-7 C Code For Tutorial Task 3.5

C-7.1 CP Program

```c
#include <stdio.h>
#include <cros.h>

#define MAX_PROCS 1024
int doc, nproc;

main()
{
    int n, i, iresp, npx, npy;
    double a, b, answer;

    iresp = down_load("task35NODE");
    if (iresp<0){
        printf("\n\n**** An error occurred in cubeld ****\n");
        printf("  \n**** Program aborted            ****\n\n");
        exit(1);
    }

    printf("\n\nPlease give the lower limit of the integral ==> ");
    scanf("%lf",&a);
    printf("\n\nPlease give the upper limit of the integral ==> ");
    scanf("%lf",&b);
    printf("\n\nPlease give the number of intervals ==> ");
    scanf("%d",&n);
    n = 2*((n+1)/2);

    bcastcp(&a,sizeof(double));
    bcastcp(&b,sizeof(double));
    bcastcp(&n,sizeof(int));

    combcp(&answer,sizeof(double),1);
    printf("\n\nThe integral is approximately %lf\n",answer);

    printf("\n\nFinished\n\n");
    exit(0);
}

/*************************** end of routine main ***************************/
int down_load(node_prog)
char *node_prog;
{
    printf("\n\nPlease give the dimension of the hypercube ==> ");
    scanf("%d",&doc);
```

```
        nproc    = 1<<doc;
        return (cubeld(doc,node_prog));
    }


    /************************* end of routine down_load ************************/
```

C-7.2 NODE Program

```c
    #include <stdio.h>
    #include <cros.h>
    #include <math.h>

    int isize = sizeof(int), fsize = sizeof(double);
    int iproc, nproc, pos;

    main()
    {
        int n, double_add();
        double a, b, integrand(), simpsons_rule(), local_int;
        struct cubenv env;

        bcastelt(&a,fsize);
        bcastelt(&b,fsize);
        bcastelt(&n,isize);

        cparam(&env);

        iproc = env.procnum;
        nproc = env.nproc;

        gridinit(1,&nproc);
        gridcoord(iproc,&pos);

        local_int = simpsons_rule(a,b,n,integrand);
        combelt(&local_int,double_add,fsize,1);

        exit(0);
    }


    /************************* end of routine main ****************************/
    double simpsons_rule(a,b,n,func)
    double a, b;
    int n;
    double (*func)();
    {
        int start, nlocal, nleft,i;
```

```
        double sum, odd_sum, even_sum, h;

        h = (b-a)/(double)n;
        nlocal = (n+1)/nproc;
        nleft  = (n+1)%nproc;
        if(pos<nleft){
            nlocal = nlocal + 1;
            start  = nlocal*pos;
        }
        else    start  = nlocal*pos + nleft;

        even_sum = 0.0;
        for(i=0;i<nlocal;i += 2) even_sum += func(a+h*(double)(i+start));
        odd_sum = 0.0;
        for(i=1;i<nlocal;i += 2) odd_sum  += func(a+h*(double)(i+start));

        if( (start&1)==0 ) sum = 2.0*even_sum + 4.0*odd_sum;
        else               sum = 4.0*even_sum + 2.0*odd_sum;

        if (pos==0)        sum -= func(a);
        if (pos==(nproc-1)) sum -= func(b);

        sum *= h/3.0;

        return sum;
}


/********************** end of routine simpsons_rule **********************/
double integrand(x)
double x;
{
    double sinx;

    sinx = sin(x);
    return (1.0/sqrt(1.0-0.5*sinx*sinx));
}


/************************ end of routine integrand ************************/
int double_add(p1,p2,size)
double *p1, *p2;
int size;
{
    *p1 += *p2;
    return 0;
}


/*********************** end of routine double_add ***********************/
```

C-7.3 CUBIX Program

```c
#include <stdio.h>
#include <cros.h>
#include <math.h>

int isize = sizeof(int), fsize = sizeof(double);
int iproc, nproc, pos;

main()
{
    int n, double_add();
    double a, b, integrand(), simpsons_rule(), local_int;
    struct cubenv env;

    printf("\n\nPlease give the lower limit of the integral ==> ");
    scanf("%lf",&a);
    printf("\n\nPlease give the upper limit of the integral ==> ");
    scanf("%lf",&b);
    printf("\n\nPlease give the number of intervals ==> ");
    scanf("%d",&n);
    n = 2*((n+1)/2);

    cparam(&env);

    iproc = env.procnum;
    nproc = env.nproc;

    gridinit(1,&nproc);
    gridcoord(iproc,&pos);

    local_int = simpsons_rule(a,b,n,integrand);
    combine(&local_int,double_add,fsize,1);

    printf("\n\nThe integral is approximately %lf\n",local_int);

    printf("\n\nFinished\n\n");
    exit(0);
}

/*************************** end of routine main ***************************/
double simpsons_rule(a,b,n,func)
double a, b;
int n;
double (*func)();
{
    int start, nlocal, nleft,i;
```

```
        double sum, odd_sum, even_sum, h;

        h = (b-a)/(double)n;
        nlocal = (n+1)/nproc;
        nleft  = (n+1)%nproc;
        if(pos<nleft){
            nlocal = nlocal + 1;
            start  = nlocal*pos;
        }
        else    start  = nlocal*pos + nleft;

        even_sum = 0.0;
        for(i=0;i<nlocal;i += 2) even_sum += func(a+h*(double)(i+start));
        odd_sum = 0.0;
        for(i=1;i<nlocal;i += 2) odd_sum  += func(a+h*(double)(i+start));

        if( (start&1)==0 ) sum = 2.0*even_sum + 4.0*odd_sum;
        else               sum = 4.0*even_sum + 2.0*odd_sum;

        if (pos==0)         sum -= func(a);
        if (pos==(nproc-1)) sum -= func(b);

        sum *= h/3.0;

        return sum;
}


/********************** end of routine simpsons_rule **********************/
double integrand(x)
double x;
{
        double sinx;

        sinx = sin(x);
        return (1.0/sqrt(1.0-0.5*sinx*sinx));
}


/*********************** end of routine integrand **********************/
int double_add(p1,p2,size)
double *p1, *p2;
int size;
{
        *p1 += *p2;
        return 0;
}


/********************** end of routine double_add **********************/
```

D

Appendix D:
Fortran Code For Tutorial Programs

This appendix lists the Fortran source code for the tasks set in the Tutorial at the beginning of the book. Although a reasonable effort has been made to ensure that the code is correct and reliable, there are, no doubt, bugs. If you encounter any bugs, or have constructive suggestions for improving the code, please write to the address given in Appendix G. When filing a bug report, please give full details of the problem and the input data.

D-1 Fortran Code For Tutorial Task 2.3

D-1.1 CP Program

```
      PROGRAM TCP23
      PARAMETER ( ISIZE = 4, MAXPRC = 1024, MAXPP = 1025 )
      INTEGER NODVLS(MAXPRC), IBFMAP(MAXPP)
      COMMON/CUBCOM/ IPROC, NPROC

      PRINT *, ' '
      IRESP = DOWNLD("task23NODE")
      IF (IRESP .LT. 0) THEN
          PRINT *, '**** An error occurred in KCUBLD ****'
          PRINT *, '**** Program aborted            ****'
          STOP
      ENDIF

      PRINT *, ' '
      PRINT *, 'Please give an integer:'
      READ  *, INTCP

      IRESP = KBCSTC(INTCP,ISIZE)

      IRESP = KMDUMP(NODVLS,ISIZE,IBFMAP)

      PRINT *, ' '
      PRINT *, 'Value in each node:'
      WRITE(*,100) (NODVLS(I),I=1,NPROC)

      PRINT *, ' '
      PRINT *, 'Finished'
      PRINT *, ' '

      STOP
100   FORMAT(20I6)
      END
C
CCCCCCCCCCCCCCCCCCCCCCCCCCCCCCCC END OF PROGRAM TCP23 CCCCCCCCCCCCCCCCCCCCCCCCCCCCCCCC
C
      INTEGER FUNCTION DOWNLD(PRGNAM)
      CHARACTER*10 PRGNAM
      COMMON/CUBCOM/ IPROC, NPROC

      PRINT *, 'Please give the dimension of the hypercube:'
      READ  *, NDOC

      NPROC  = 2**NDOC
```

```
      DOWNLD = KCUBEL(NDOC,PRGNAM)

      RETURN
      END
C
CCCCCCCCCCCCCCCCCCCCCCCCCCCCCCCC END OF ROUTINE DOWNLD CCCCCCCCCCCCCCCCCCCCCCCCCCCCCCCC
C
```

D-1.2 NODE Program

```
      PROGRAM TND23
      PARAMETER ( ISIZE = 4 )
      INTEGER IENV(5)

      IRESP = KBCSTE(INTCP,ISIZE)

      CALL KPARAM(IENV)

      IPROC = IENV(2)
      ISUM  = IPROC + INTCP

      IRESP = KDUMPE(ISUM,ISIZE)

      STOP
      END
C
CCCCCCCCCCCCCCCCCCCCCCCCCCCCCCCC END OF PROGRAM TND23 CCCCCCCCCCCCCCCCCCCCCCCCCCCCCCCC
C
```

D-1.3 CUBIX Program

```
      PROGRAM TND23
      INTEGER STDOUT
      PARAMETER ( STDOUT = 6 )
      INTEGER IENV(5)

      PRINT *, ' '
      PRINT *, 'Please give an integer:'
      READ  *, INTCP

      CALL KPARAM(IENV)

      IPROC = IENV(2)
      ISUM  = IPROC + INTCP
```

```
      PRINT *, ' '
      PRINT *, 'Value in each node:'
      MULTIPLE(STDOUT)
      PRINT *, ISUM

      SINGLE(STDOUT)
      PRINT *, ' '
      PRINT *, 'Finished'
      PRINT *, ' '

      STOP
      END
C
CCCCCCCCCCCCCCCCCCCCCCCCCCCCCC END OF PROGRAM TND23 CCCCCCCCCCCCCCCCCCCCCCCCCCCCCC
C
```

D-2 Fortran Code For Tutorial Task 2.4

D-2.1 CP Program

```
      PROGRAM TCP24
      PARAMETER ( ISIZE = 4, MAXPRC = 1024, MAXPP = 1025 )
      INTEGER INPUTV(MAXPRC)
      INTEGER NODVLS(MAXPRC), IBFMAP(MAXPP)
      COMMON/CUBCOM/ IPROC, NPROC

      PRINT *, ' '
      IRESP = DOWNLD("task24NODE")
      IF (IRESP .LT. 0) THEN
          PRINT *, '**** An error occurred in KCUBLD ****'
          PRINT *, '**** Program aborted            ****'
          STOP
      ENDIF

      PRINT *, ' '
      PRINT *, 'Please give ',NPROC,' integers (1 per line):'
      DO 10 I=1,NPROC
          READ *, INPUTV(I)
          IBFMAP(I+1) = ISIZE
10        CONTINUE
      IBFMAP(1) = NPROC

      PRINT *, ' '
      PRINT *, 'Values sent to nodes:'
      WRITE(*,100) (INPUTV(I),I=1,NPROC)

      IRESP = KMLOAD(INPUTV,IBFMAP)
      IRESP = KMDUMP(NODVLS,ISIZE,IBFMAP)

      PRINT *, 'Value in each node:'
      WRITE(*,100) (NODVLS(I),I=1,NPROC)

      PRINT *, ' '
      PRINT *, 'Finished'
      PRINT *, ' '

      STOP
100   FORMAT(20I6)
      END
C
CCCCCCCCCCCCCCCCCCCCCCCCCCCCCCC END OF PROGRAM TCP24 CCCCCCCCCCCCCCCCCCCCCCCCCCCCCCC
C
```

```
      INTEGER FUNCTION DOWNLD(PRGNAM)
      CHARACTER*10 PRGNAM
      COMMON/CUBCOM/ IPROC, NPROC

      PRINT *, 'Please give the dimension of the hypercube:'
      READ *, NDOC

      NPROC = 2**NDOC
      DOWNLD = KCUBEL(NDOC,PRGNAM)

      RETURN
      END
C
CCCCCCCCCCCCCCCCCCCCCCCCCCCCCCC END OF ROUTINE DOWNLD CCCCCCCCCCCCCCCCCCCCCCCCCCCCCCC
C
```

D-2.2 NODE Program

```
      PROGRAM TND24
      PARAMETER ( ISIZE = 4 )
      INTEGER IENV(5)

      IRESP = KLOADE(INTCP,ISIZE)

      CALL KPARAM(IENV)

      IPROC = IENV(2)
      ISUM  = IPROC + INTCP

      IRESP = KDUMPE(ISUM,ISIZE)

      STOP
      END
C
CCCCCCCCCCCCCCCCCCCCCCCCCCCCCCC END OF PROGRAM TND24 CCCCCCCCCCCCCCCCCCCCCCCCCCCCCCCC
C
```

D-2.3 CUBIX Program

```
      PROGRAM TND24
      INTEGER STDIN, STDOUT
      PARAMETER ( STDIN = 5, STDOUT = 6 )
      INTEGER IENV(5)

      CALL KPARAM(IENV)
```

```
      PRINT *, ' '
      PRINT *, 'Please give ',IENV(3),' integers (1 per line):'
      MULTIPLE(STDIN)
      READ  *,INTCP

      IPROC = IENV(2)
      ISUM  = IPROC + INTCP

      PRINT *, ' '
      PRINT *, 'Values sent to nodes:'
      MULTIPLE(STDOUT)
      PRINT *, INTCP

      SINGLE(STDOUT)
      PRINT *, ' '
      PRINT *, 'Value in each node:'
      MULTIPLE(STDOUT)
      PRINT *, ISUM

      SINGLE(STDOUT)
      PRINT *, ' '
      PRINT *, 'Finished'

      STOP
      END
C
CCCCCCCCCCCCCCCCCCCCCCCCCCCCCC END OF PROGRAM TND24 CCCCCCCCCCCCCCCCCCCCCCCCCCCCCC
C
```

D-3 Fortran Code For Tutorial Task 2.5

D-3.1 CP Program

```
      PROGRAM TCP25
      PARAMETER ( IFSIZE = 4, ISIZE = 4, MAXPRC = 1024, MAXPP = 1025 )
      INTEGER INPUTV(MAXPRC)
      INTEGER NODVLS(MAXPRC), IBFMAP(MAXPP)
      COMMON/CUBCOM/ IPROC, NPROC

      PRINT *, ' '
      IRESP = DOWNLD("task25NODE")
      IF (IRESP .LT. 0) THEN
          PRINT *, '**** An error occurred in KCUBLD ****'
          PRINT *, '**** Program aborted            ****'
          STOP
      ENDIF

      PRINT *, ' '
      PRINT *, 'Please give ',NPROC,' integers (1 per line):'
      DO 10 I=1,NPROC
          READ *, INPUTV(I)
          IBFMAP(I+1) = ISIZE
10        CONTINUE
      IBFMAP(1) = NPROC

      PRINT *, ' '
      PRINT *, 'Values sent to nodes:'
      WRITE(*,100) (INPUTV(I),I=1,NPROC)

      IRESP = KMLOAD(INPUTV,IBFMAP)
      IRESP = KMDUMP(NODVLS,ISIZE,IBFMAP)

      PRINT *, ' '
      PRINT *, 'Value in each node:'
      WRITE(*,100) (NODVLS(I),I=1,NPROC)

      IRESP = KCOMBC(AVRAGE,IFSIZE,1)
      PRINT *, ' '
      PRINT *, 'Average value over all nodes = ',AVRAGE

      PRINT *, ' '
      PRINT *, 'Finished'
      PRINT *, ' '

      STOP
100   FORMAT(20I6)
```

```
      END
C
CCCCCCCCCCCCCCCCCCCCCCCCCCCCCC END OF PROGRAM TCP25 CCCCCCCCCCCCCCCCCCCCCCCCCCCCCC
C
      INTEGER FUNCTION DOWNLD(PRGNAM)
      CHARACTER*10 PRGNAM
      COMMON/CUBCOM/ IPROC, NPROC

      PRINT *, 'Please give the dimension of the hypercube:'
      READ  *, NDOC

      NPROC  = 2**NDOC
      DOWNLD = KCUBEL(NDOC,PRGNAM)

      RETURN
      END
C
CCCCCCCCCCCCCCCCCCCCCCCCCCCCCC END OF ROUTINE DOWNLD CCCCCCCCCCCCCCCCCCCCCCCCCCCCCC
C
```

D-3.2 NODE Program

```
      PROGRAM TND25
      PARAMETER ( IFSIZE = 4, ISIZE = 4 )
      INTEGER IENV(5)
      EXTERNAL IFADD

      IRESP = KLOADE(INTCP,ISIZE)

      CALL KPARAM(IENV)

      IPROC  = IENV(2)
      ISUM   = IPROC + INTCP
      AVRAGE = REAL(ISUM)/REAL(IENV(3))

      IRESP = KDUMPE(ISUM,ISIZE)
      IRESP = KCOMBE(AVRAGE,IFADD,IFSIZE,1)

      STOP
      END
C
CCCCCCCCCCCCCCCCCCCCCCCCCCCCCC END OF PROGRAM TND25 CCCCCCCCCCCCCCCCCCCCCCCCCCCCCC
C
      FUNCTION IFADD(F1,F2,NSIZE)
      F1 = F1+F2
      IFADD = 0
```

```
      RETURN
      END
C
CCCCCCCCCCCCCCCCCCCCCCCCCCCCCC END OF PROGRAM IFADD CCCCCCCCCCCCCCCCCCCCCCCCCCCCCC
C
```

D-3.3 CUBIX Program

```
      PROGRAM TND25
      INTEGER STDIN, STDOUT
      PARAMETER ( STDIN = 5, STDOUT = 6 )
      PARAMETER ( IFSIZE = 4 )
      INTEGER IENV(5)
      EXTERNAL IFADD

      CALL KPARAM(IENV)

      PRINT *, ' '
      PRINT *, 'Please give ',IENV(3),' integers (1 per line):'
      MULTIPLE(STDIN)
      READ  *,INTCP

      IPROC  = IENV(2)
      ISUM   = IPROC + INTCP
      AVRAGE = REAL(ISUM)/REAL(IENV(3))

      PRINT *, ' '
      PRINT *, 'Values sent to nodes:'
      MULTIPLE(STDOUT)
      PRINT *, INTCP

      SINGLE(STDOUT)
      PRINT *, ' '
      PRINT *, 'Value in each node:'
      MULTIPLE(STDOUT)
      PRINT *, ISUM

      IRESP = KCOMBI(AVRAGE,IFADD,IFSIZE,1)

      SINGLE(STDOUT)
      PRINT *, ' '
      PRINT *, 'Average value over all nodes = ',AVRAGE

      PRINT *, ' '
      PRINT *, 'Finished'
      PRINT *, ' '
```

```
      STOP
      END
C
CCCCCCCCCCCCCCCCCCCCCCCCCCCCCC END OF PROGRAM TND25 CCCCCCCCCCCCCCCCCCCCCCCCCCCCCC
C
      FUNCTION IFADD(F1,F2,NSIZE)
      F1 = F1+F2
      IFADD = 0
      RETURN
      END
C
CCCCCCCCCCCCCCCCCCCCCCCCCCCCCC END OF PROGRAM IFADD CCCCCCCCCCCCCCCCCCCCCCCCCCCCCC
C
```

D-4 Fortran Code For Tutorial Task 3.2

D-4.1 CP Program

```
PROGRAM TCP32
PARAMETER ( ISIZE = 4 )
COMMON/CUBCOM/ IPROC, NPROC

PRINT *, ' '
IRESP = DOWNLD("task32NODE")
IF (IRESP .LT. 0) THEN
    PRINT *, '**** An error occurred in KCUBLD ****'
    PRINT *, '**** Program aborted              ****'
    STOP
ENDIF

PRINT *, ' '
PRINT *, 'Please give the number of loops:'
READ *, NLOOPS

IRESP = KBCSTC(NLOOPS,ISIZE)

PRINT *, ' '
PRINT *, 'All integers are output in order of increasing node number'

PRINT *, ' '
PRINT *, 'Position in ring:'
CALL OUTRES

PRINT *, ' '
PRINT *, 'Node number of clockwise neighboring node:'
CALL OUTRES

PRINT *, ' '
PRINT *, 'Node number of anti-clockwise neighboring node:'
CALL OUTRES

PRINT *, ' '
PRINT *, 'Mask of channel in clockwise direction:'
CALL OUTRES

PRINT *, ' '
PRINT *, 'Mask of channel in anti-clockwise direction:'
CALL OUTRES

PRINT *, ' '
PRINT *, 'Move node numbers ',NLOOPS,' steps around the ring:'
```

```
      DO 10 I=1,NLOOPS
         CALL OUTRES
10       CONTINUE

      PRINT *, ' '
      PRINT *, 'Finished'
      PRINT *, ' '

      STOP
      END
C
CCCCCCCCCCCCCCCCCCCCCCCCCCCCCC END OF PROGRAM TCP32 CCCCCCCCCCCCCCCCCCCCCCCCCCCCCC
C
      INTEGER FUNCTION DOWNLD(PRGNAM)
      CHARACTER*10 PRGNAM
      COMMON/CUBCOM/ IPROC, NPROC

      PRINT *, 'Please give the dimension of the hypercube:'
      READ  *, NDOC

      NPROC = 2**NDOC
      DOWNLD = KCUBEL(NDOC,PRGNAM)

      RETURN
      END
C
CCCCCCCCCCCCCCCCCCCCCCCCCCCCCC END OF ROUTINE DOWNLD CCCCCCCCCCCCCCCCCCCCCCCCCCCCC
C
      SUBROUTINE OUTRES
      PARAMETER ( ISIZE = 4, MAXPRC = 1024, MAXPP = 1025 )
      INTEGER NODVLS(MAXPRC), IBFMAP(MAXPP)
      COMMON/CUBCOM/ IPROC, NPROC

      IRESP = KMDUMP(NODVLS,ISIZE,IBFMAP)
      WRITE(*,100) (NODVLS(I),I=1,NPROC)

      RETURN
100   FORMAT(20I6)
      END
C
CCCCCCCCCCCCCCCCCCCCCCCCCCCCCC END OF ROUTINE OUTRES CCCCCCCCCCCCCCCCCCCCCCCCCCCCC
C
```

D-4.2 NODE Program

```fortran
      PROGRAM TND32
      PARAMETER ( ISIZE = 4 )
      INTEGER IENV(5)

      IRESP  = KBCSTE(NLOOPS,ISIZE)

      CALL KPARAM(IENV)

      IPROC  = IENV(2)
      NPROC  = IENV(3)

      IRESP  = KGRDIN(1,NPROC)
      IRESP  = KGRDCO(IPROC,IRPOS)
      IRESP  = KDUMPE(IRPOS,ISIZE)

      ICLKP  = IRPOS + 1
      IF ( IRPOS .EQ. (NPROC-1) ) ICLKP = 0
      IACLKP = IRPOS - 1
      IF ( IRPOS .EQ. 0 ) IACLKP = NPROC - 1
      ICLKN  = KGRDPR(ICLKP)
      IACLKN = KGRDPR(IACLKP)
      IRESP  = KDUMPE(ICLKN,ISIZE)
      IRESP  = KDUMPE(IACLKN,ISIZE)

      ICLKM  = KGRDCH(IPROC,0, 1)
      IACLKM = KGRDCH(IPROC,0,-1)
      IRESP  = KDUMPE(ICLKM,ISIZE)
      IRESP  = KDUMPE(IACLKM,ISIZE)

      IMOVE = IPROC
      DO 10 I=1,NLOOPS
          IRESP = KCSHIF(IMOVE,IACLKM,ISIZE,IMOVE,ICLKM,ISIZE)
          IRESP = KDUMPE(IMOVE,ISIZE)
10        CONTINUE

      STOP
      END
C
CCCCCCCCCCCCCCCCCCCCCCCCCCCCCCCCC END OF PROGRAM TND32 CCCCCCCCCCCCCCCCCCCCCCCCCCCCCCCCC
C
```

D-4.3 CUBIX Program

```
PROGRAM TND32
PARAMETER ( ISIZE = 4 )
INTEGER IENV(5)
COMMON/CUBCOM/ IPROC, NPROC

PRINT *, ' '
PRINT *, 'Please give the number of loops:'
READ *, NLOOPS

CALL KPARAM(IENV)

IPROC = IENV(2)
NPROC = IENV(3)

IRESP = KGRDIN(1,NPROC)
IRESP = KGRDCO(IPROC,IRPOS)

PRINT *, ' '
PRINT *, 'Position in ring:'
CALL OUTRES(IRPOS)

ICLKP  = IRPOS + 1
IF ( IRPOS .EQ. (NPROC-1) ) ICLKP = 0
IACLKP = IRPOS - 1
IF ( IRPOS .EQ. 0 ) IACLKP = NPROC - 1
ICLKN  = KGRDPR(ICLKP)
IACLKN = KGRDPR(IACLKP)

PRINT *, ' '
PRINT *, 'Node number of clockwise neighboring node:'
CALL OUTRES(ICLKN)

PRINT *, ' '
PRINT *, 'Node number of anti-clockwise neighboring node:'
CALL OUTRES(IACLKN)

ICLKM  = KGRDCH(IPROC,0, 1)
IACLKM = KGRDCH(IPROC,0,-1)

PRINT *, ' '
PRINT *, 'Mask of channel in clockwise direction:'
CALL OUTRES(ICLKM)

PRINT *, ' '
PRINT *, 'Mask of channel in anti-clockwise direction:'
```

```fortran
      CALL OUTRES(IACLKM)

      PRINT *, ' '
      PRINT *, 'Move node numbers ',NLOOPS,' steps around the ring:'
      IMOVE = IPROC
      DO 10 I=1,NLOOPS
          PRINT *, 'Step Number ',I
          IRESP = KCSHIF(IMOVE,IACLKM,ISIZE,IMOVE,ICLKM,ISIZE)
          CALL OUTRES(IMOVE)
10        CONTINUE

      PRINT *, ' '
      PRINT *, 'Finished'
      PRINT *, ' '

      STOP
      END
C
CCCCCCCCCCCCCCCCCCCCCCCCCCCCCCC END OF PROGRAM TND32 CCCCCCCCCCCCCCCCCCCCCCCCCCCCCCC
C
      SUBROUTINE OUTRES(IVAL)
      INTEGER IVAL
      INTEGER STDOUT
      PARAMETER ( STDOUT = 6 )
      COMMON/CUBCOM/ IPROC, NPROC

      MULTIPLE(STDOUT)
      PRINT *, '     Node ',IPROC,':      ',IVAL
      SINGLE(STDOUT)

      RETURN
      END
C
CCCCCCCCCCCCCCCCCCCCCCCCCCCCCCC END OF ROUTINE OUTRES CCCCCCCCCCCCCCCCCCCCCCCCCCCCCCC
C
```

D-5 Fortran Code For Tutorial Task 3.3

D-5.1 CP Program

```
PROGRAM TCP33
PARAMETER ( ISIZE = 4 )
COMMON/CUBCOM/ IPROC, NPROC

PRINT *, ' '
IRESP = DOWNLD("task33NODE")
IF (IRESP .LT. 0) THEN
    PRINT *, '**** An error occurred in KCUBLD ****'
    PRINT *, '**** Program aborted               ****'
    STOP
ENDIF

PRINT *, ' '
PRINT *, 'Please give the number of nodes in the x-direction:'
READ *, NPX
PRINT *, ' '
PRINT *, 'Please give the number of nodes in the y-direction:'
READ *, NPY

IF ( NPX*NPY .NE. NPROC ) THEN
    PRINT *, '**** Invalid decomposition ****'
    PRINT *, '**** Program aborted       ****'
    STOP
ENDIF

IRESP = KBCSTC(NPX,ISIZE)
IRESP = KBCSTC(NPY,ISIZE)

PRINT *, ' '
PRINT *, 'All integers are output in order of increasing node number'

PRINT *, ' '
PRINT *, 'Position in the x-direction:'
CALL OUTRES

PRINT *, ' '
PRINT *, 'Position in the y-direction:'
CALL OUTRES

PRINT *, ' '
PRINT *, 'Sum of node numbers in each row:'
CALL OUTRES
```

```fortran
      PRINT *, ' '
      PRINT *, 'Sum of node numbers over all rows and columns:'
      CALL OUTRES

      PRINT *, ' '
      PRINT *, 'Finished'
      PRINT *, ' '

      STOP
      END
C
CCCCCCCCCCCCCCCCCCCCCCCCCCCCCCC END OF PROGRAM TCP33 CCCCCCCCCCCCCCCCCCCCCCCCCCCCCCC
C
      INTEGER FUNCTION DOWNLD(PRGNAM)
      CHARACTER*10 PRGNAM
      COMMON/CUBCOM/ IPROC, NPROC

      PRINT *, 'Please give the dimension of the hypercube:'
      READ  *, NDOC

      NPROC  = 2**NDOC
      DOWNLD = KCUBEL(NDOC,PRGNAM)

      RETURN
      END
C
CCCCCCCCCCCCCCCCCCCCCCCCCCCCCCC END OF ROUTINE DOWNLD CCCCCCCCCCCCCCCCCCCCCCCCCCCCCCC
C
      SUBROUTINE OUTRES
      PARAMETER ( ISIZE = 4, MAXPRC = 1024, MAXPP = 1025 )
      INTEGER NODVLS(MAXPRC), IBFMAP(MAXPP)
      COMMON/CUBCOM/ IPROC, NPROC

      IRESP = KMDUMP(NODVLS,ISIZE,IBFMAP)
      WRITE(*,100) (NODVLS(I),I=1,NPROC)

      RETURN
 100  FORMAT(20I6)
      END
C
CCCCCCCCCCCCCCCCCCCCCCCCCCCCCCC END OF ROUTINE OUTRES CCCCCCCCCCCCCCCCCCCCCCCCCCCCCCC
C
```

D-5.2 NODE Program

```
      PROGRAM TND33
      PARAMETER ( ISIZE = 4 )
      INTEGER NUM(2), ICOORD(2)
      INTEGER IENV(5)

      IRESP = KBCSTE(NPX,ISIZE)
      IRESP = KBCSTE(NPY,ISIZE)
      NUM(1) = NPX
      NUM(2) = NPY

      CALL KPARAM(IENV)

      IPROC = IENV(2)
      NPROC = IENV(3)

      IRESP = KGRDIN(2,NUM)
      IRESP = KGRDCO(IPROC,ICOORD)
      IXPOS = ICOORD(1)
      IYPOS = ICOORD(2)
      IRESP = KDUMPE(IXPOS,ISIZE)
      IRESP = KDUMPE(IYPOS,ISIZE)

      MASKR = KGRDCH(IPROC,0, 1)
      MASKL = KGRDCH(IPROC,0,-1)
      MASKU = KGRDCH(IPROC,1, 1)
      MASKD = KGRDCH(IPROC,1,-1)

      IRSUM = IPSUM(IPROC,IXPOS,NPX-1,MASKL,MASKR)
      IRSUM = IPINT(IRSUM,IXPOS,NPX-1,MASKR,MASKL)

      IRESP = KDUMPE(IRSUM,ISIZE)

      IRSUM = IPSUM(IRSUM,IYPOS,NPY-1,MASKD,MASKU)
      IRSUM = IPINT(IRSUM,IYPOS,NPY-1,MASKU,MASKD)

      IRESP = KDUMPE(IRSUM,ISIZE)

      STOP
      END
C
CCCCCCCCCCCCCCCCCCCCCCCCCCCCCC END OF PROGRAM TND33 CCCCCCCCCCCCCCCCCCCCCCCCCCCCCC
C
      FUNCTION IPSUM(IVAL,IPOS,IEND,IMASK,OMASK)
      INTEGER IVAL, IPOS, IEND, IMASK, OMASK
      PARAMETER ( ISIZE = 4 )
```

```
      IPSUM = IVAL
      IF ( IPOS .EQ. 0 ) THEN
          IRESP = KCWRIT(IVAL,OMASK,ISIZE)
      ELSEIF ( IPOS .EQ. IEND ) THEN
          IRESP = KCREAD(IREC,IMASK,0,ISIZE)
          IPSUM = IREC + IVAL
      ELSE
          IRESP = KCREAD(IREC,IMASK,0,ISIZE)
          ISEND = IREC + IVAL
          IRESP = KCWRIT(ISEND,OMASK,ISIZE)
      ENDIF

      RETURN
      END
C
CCCCCCCCCCCCCCCCCCCCCCCCCCCCCC END OF ROUTINE IPSUM CCCCCCCCCCCCCCCCCCCCCCCCCCCCCC
C
      FUNCTION IPINT(IVAL,IPOS,IEND,IMASK,OMASK)
      INTEGER IVAL, IPOS, IEND, IMASK, OMASK
      PARAMETER ( ISIZE = 4 )

      IF ( IPOS .EQ. IEND ) THEN
          IRESP = KCWRIT(IVAL,OMASK,ISIZE)
      ELSEIF ( IPOS .EQ. 0 ) THEN
          IRESP = KCREAD(IVAL,IMASK,0,ISIZE)
      ELSE
          IRESP = KCREAD(IVAL,IMASK,OMASK,ISIZE)
      ENDIF

      IPINT = IVAL

      RETURN
      END


C
CCCCCCCCCCCCCCCCCCCCCCCCCCCCCC END OF ROUTINE IPINT CCCCCCCCCCCCCCCCCCCCCCCCCCCCCC
C
```

D-5.3 CUBIX Program

```
PROGRAM TND33
INTEGER NUM(2), ICOORD(2)
INTEGER IENV(5)
COMMON/CUBCOM/ IPROC, NPROC

PRINT *, ' '
PRINT *, 'Please give the number of nodes in the x-direction:'
READ *, NPX
PRINT *, ' '
PRINT *, 'Please give the number of nodes in the y-direction:'
READ *, NPY
NUM(1) = NPX
NUM(2) = NPY

CALL KPARAM(IENV)

IPROC = IENV(2)
NPROC = IENV(3)

IF ( NPX*NPY .NE. NPROC ) THEN
    PRINT *, '**** Invalid decomposition ****'
    PRINT *, '**** Program aborted        ****'
    STOP
ENDIF

IRESP = KGRDIN(2,NUM)
IRESP = KGRDCO(IPROC,ICOORD)
IXPOS = ICOORD(1)
IYPOS = ICOORD(2)

PRINT *, ' '
PRINT *, 'Position in the x-direction:'
CALL OUTRES(IXPOS)

PRINT *, ' '
PRINT *, 'Position in the y-direction:'
CALL OUTRES(IYPOS)

MASKR = KGRDCH(IPROC,0, 1)
MASKL = KGRDCH(IPROC,0,-1)
MASKU = KGRDCH(IPROC,1, 1)
MASKD = KGRDCH(IPROC,1,-1)

IRSUM = IPSUM(IPROC,IXPOS,NPX-1,MASKL,MASKR)
IRSUM = IPINT(IRSUM,IXPOS,NPX-1,MASKR,MASKL)
```

```fortran
      PRINT *, ' '
      PRINT *, 'Sum of node numbers in each row:'
      CALL OUTRES(IRSUM)

      IRSUM = IPSUM(IRSUM,IYPOS,NPY-1,MASKD,MASKU)
      IRSUM = IPINT(IRSUM,IYPOS,NPY-1,MASKU,MASKD)

      PRINT *, ' '
      PRINT *, 'Sum of node numbers over all rows and columns:'
      CALL OUTRES(IRSUM)

      PRINT *, ' '
      PRINT *, 'Finished'
      PRINT *, ' '

      STOP
      END
C
CCCCCCCCCCCCCCCCCCCCCCCCCCCCC END OF PROGRAM TND33 CCCCCCCCCCCCCCCCCCCCCCCCCCCCCCC
C
      FUNCTION IPSUM(IVAL,IPOS,IEND,IMASK,OMASK)
      INTEGER IVAL, IPOS, IEND, IMASK, OMASK
      PARAMETER ( ISIZE = 4 )

      IPSUM = IVAL
      IF ( IPOS .EQ. 0 ) THEN
          IRESP = KCWRIT(IVAL,OMASK,ISIZE)
      ELSEIF ( IPOS .EQ. IEND ) THEN
          IRESP = KCREAD(IREC,IMASK,0,ISIZE)
          IPSUM = IREC + IVAL
      ELSE
          IRESP = KCREAD(IREC,IMASK,0,ISIZE)
          ISEND = IREC + IVAL
          IRESP = KCWRIT(ISEND,OMASK,ISIZE)
      ENDIF

      RETURN
      END
C
CCCCCCCCCCCCCCCCCCCCCCCCCCCCC END OF ROUTINE IPSUM CCCCCCCCCCCCCCCCCCCCCCCCCCCCCCC
C
      FUNCTION IPINT(IVAL,IPOS,IEND,IMASK,OMASK)
      INTEGER IVAL, IPOS, IEND, IMASK, OMASK
      PARAMETER ( ISIZE = 4 )

      IF ( IPOS .EQ. IEND ) THEN
```

```
            IRESP = KCWRIT(IVAL,OMASK,ISIZE)
        ELSEIF ( IPOS .EQ. 0 ) THEN
            IRESP = KCREAD(IVAL,IMASK,0,ISIZE)
        ELSE
            IRESP = KCREAD(IVAL,IMASK,OMASK,ISIZE)
        ENDIF

        IPINT = IVAL

        RETURN
        END

C
CCCCCCCCCCCCCCCCCCCCCCCCCCCC END OF ROUTINE IPINT CCCCCCCCCCCCCCCCCCCCCCCCCCCCC
C
        SUBROUTINE OUTRES(IVAL)
        INTEGER IVAL
        INTEGER STDOUT
        PARAMETER ( STDOUT = 6 )
        COMMON/CUBCOM/ IPROC, NPROC

        MULTIPLE(STDOUT)
        PRINT *, '    Node ',IPROC,':    ',IVAL
        SINGLE(STDOUT)

        RETURN
        END
C
CCCCCCCCCCCCCCCCCCCCCCCCCCCCC END OF ROUTINE OUTRES CCCCCCCCCCCCCCCCCCCCCCCCCCCC
C
```

D-6 Fortran Code For Tutorial Task 3.4

D-6.1 CP Program

```
PROGRAM TCP34
PARAMETER ( ISIZE = 4 )
COMMON/CUBCOM/ IPROC, NPROC

PRINT *, ' '
IRESP = DOWNLD("task34NODE")
IF (IRESP .LT. 0) THEN
    PRINT *, '**** An error occurred in KCUBLD ****'
    PRINT *, '**** Program aborted          ****'
    STOP
ENDIF

PRINT *, ' '
PRINT *, 'Please give the number of nodes in the x-direction:'
READ *, NPX
PRINT *, ' '
PRINT *, 'Please give the number of nodes in the y-direction:'
READ *, NPY

IF ( NPX*NPY .NE. NPROC ) THEN
    PRINT *, '**** Invalid decomposition ****'
    PRINT *, '**** Program aborted      ****'
    STOP
ENDIF

IRESP = KBCSTC(NPX,ISIZE)
IRESP = KBCSTC(NPY,ISIZE)

PRINT *, ' '
PRINT *, 'All integers are output in order of increasing node number'

PRINT *, ' '
PRINT *, 'Position in the x-direction:'
CALL OUTRES

PRINT *, ' '
PRINT *, 'Position in the y-direction:'
CALL OUTRES

PRINT *, ' '
PRINT *, 'Sum of node numbers in each row:'
CALL OUTRES
```

```
      PRINT *, ' '
      PRINT *, 'Sum of node numbers over all rows and columns:'
      CALL OUTRES

      PRINT *, ' '
      PRINT *, 'Finished'
      PRINT *, ' '

      STOP
      END
C
CCCCCCCCCCCCCCCCCCCCCCCCCCCCC END OF PROGRAM TCP34 CCCCCCCCCCCCCCCCCCCCCCCCCCCCC
C
      INTEGER FUNCTION DOWNLD(PRGNAM)
      CHARACTER*10 PRGNAM
      COMMON/CUBCOM/ IPROC, NPROC

      PRINT *, 'Please give the dimension of the hypercube:'
      READ *, NDOC

      NPROC = 2**NDOC
      DOWNLD = KCUBEL(NDOC,PRGNAM)

      RETURN
      END
C
CCCCCCCCCCCCCCCCCCCCCCCCCCCCC END OF ROUTINE DOWNLD CCCCCCCCCCCCCCCCCCCCCCCCCCCCC
C
      SUBROUTINE OUTRES
      PARAMETER ( ISIZE = 4, MAXPRC = 1024, MAXPP = 1025 )
      INTEGER NODVLS(MAXPRC), IBFMAP(MAXPP)
      COMMON/CUBCOM/ IPROC, NPROC

      IRESP = KMDUMP(NODVLS,ISIZE,IBFMAP)
      WRITE(*,100) (NODVLS(I),I=1,NPROC)

      RETURN
 100  FORMAT(20I6)
      END
C
CCCCCCCCCCCCCCCCCCCCCCCCCCCCC END OF ROUTINE OUTRES CCCCCCCCCCCCCCCCCCCCCCCCCCCCC
C
```

D-6.2 NODE Program

```
PROGRAM TND33
PARAMETER ( ISIZE = 4 )
INTEGER NUM(2), ICOORD(2)
INTEGER IENV(5)

IRESP  = KBCSTE(NPX,ISIZE)
IRESP  = KBCSTE(NPY,ISIZE)
NUM(1) = NPX
NUM(2) = NPY

CALL KPARAM(IENV)

IPROC  = IENV(2)
NPROC  = IENV(3)

IRESP  = KGRDIN(2,NUM)
IRESP  = KGRDCO(IPROC,ICOORD)
IXPOS  = ICOORD(1)
IYPOS  = ICOORD(2)
IRESP  = KDUMPE(IXPOS,ISIZE)
IRESP  = KDUMPE(IYPOS,ISIZE)

MASKR  = KGRDCH(IPROC,0, 1)
MASKL  = KGRDCH(IPROC,0,-1)
MASKU  = KGRDCH(IPROC,1, 1)
MASKD  = KGRDCH(IPROC,1,-1)

IRSUM  = IPSUM(IPROC,IXPOS,NPX-1,MASKL,MASKR)
ICOORD(1) = NPX - 1
ICOORD(2) = IYPOS
ISORCE = KGRDPR(ICOORD)
MASKSC = NPX - 1
IRESP  = KBROAD(IRSUM,ISORCE,MASKSC,ISIZE)

IRESP  = KDUMPE(IRSUM,ISIZE)

IRSUM  = IPSUM(IRSUM,IYPOS,NPY-1,MASKD,MASKU)
ICOORD(1) = IXPOS
ICOORD(2) = NPY - 1
ISORCE = KGRDPR(ICOORD)
MASKSC = NPX*(NPY-1)
IRESP  = KBROAD(IRSUM,ISORCE,MASKSC,ISIZE)

IRESP  = KDUMPE(IRSUM,ISIZE)
```

```
      STOP
      END
C
CCCCCCCCCCCCCCCCCCCCCCCCCCCCCC END OF PROGRAM TND33 CCCCCCCCCCCCCCCCCCCCCCCCCCCCC
C
      FUNCTION IPSUM(IVAL,IPOS,IEND,IMASK,OMASK)
      INTEGER IVAL, IPOS, IEND, IMASK, OMASK
      PARAMETER ( ISIZE = 4 )

      IPSUM = IVAL
      IF ( IPOS .EQ. 0 ) THEN
          IRESP = KCWRIT(IVAL,OMASK,ISIZE)
      ELSEIF ( IPOS .EQ. IEND ) THEN
          IRESP = KCREAD(IREC,IMASK,0,ISIZE)
          IPSUM = IREC + IVAL
      ELSE
          IRESP = KCREAD(IREC,IMASK,0,ISIZE)
          ISEND = IREC + IVAL
          IRESP = KCWRIT(ISEND,OMASK,ISIZE)
      ENDIF

      RETURN
      END
C
CCCCCCCCCCCCCCCCCCCCCCCCCCCCCC END OF ROUTINE IPSUM CCCCCCCCCCCCCCCCCCCCCCCCCCCCC
C
```

D-6.3 CUBIX Program

```
      PROGRAM TND33
      PARAMETER ( ISIZE = 4)
      INTEGER NUM(2), ICOORD(2)
      INTEGER IENV(5)
      COMMON/CUBCOM/ IPROC, NPROC

      PRINT *, ' '
      PRINT *, 'Please give the number of nodes in the x-direction:'
      READ *, NPX
      PRINT *, ' '
      PRINT *, 'Please give the number of nodes in the y-direction:'
      READ *, NPY
      NUM(1) = NPX
      NUM(2) = NPY

      CALL KPARAM(IENV)
```

```
IPROC  = IENV(2)
NPROC  = IENV(3)

IF ( NPX*NPY .NE. NPROC ) THEN
    PRINT *, '**** Invalid decomposition ****'
    PRINT *, '**** Program aborted        ****'
    STOP
ENDIF

IRESP  = KGRDIN(2,NUM)
IRESP  = KGRDCO(IPROC,ICOORD)
IXPOS  = ICOORD(1)
IYPOS  = ICOORD(2)

PRINT *, ' '
PRINT *, 'Position in the x-direction:'
CALL OUTRES(IXPOS)

PRINT *, ' '
PRINT *, 'Position in the y-direction:'
CALL OUTRES(IYPOS)

MASKR  = KGRDCH(IPROC,0, 1)
MASKL  = KGRDCH(IPROC,0,-1)
MASKU  = KGRDCH(IPROC,1, 1)
MASKD  = KGRDCH(IPROC,1,-1)

IRSUM  = IPSUM(IPROC,IXPOS,NPX-1,MASKL,MASKR)
ICOORD(1) = NPX - 1
ICOORD(2) = IYPOS
ISORCE = KGRDPR(ICOORD)
MASKSC = NPX - 1
IRESP  = KBROAD(IRSUM,ISORCE,MASKSC,ISIZE)

PRINT *, ' '
PRINT *, 'Sum of node numbers in each row:'
CALL OUTRES(IRSUM)

IRSUM  = IPSUM(IRSUM,IYPOS,NPY-1,MASKD,MASKU)
ICOORD(1) = IXPOS
ICOORD(2) = NPY - 1
ISORCE = KGRDPR(ICOORD)
MASKSC = NPX*(NPY-1)
IRESP  = KBROAD(IRSUM,ISORCE,MASKSC,ISIZE)

PRINT *, ' '
PRINT *, 'Sum of node numbers over all rows and columns:'
```

```
      CALL OUTRES(IRSUM)

      PRINT *, ' '
      PRINT *, 'Finished'
      PRINT *, ' '

      STOP
      END
C
CCCCCCCCCCCCCCCCCCCCCCCCCCCCCC END OF PROGRAM TND33 CCCCCCCCCCCCCCCCCCCCCCCCCCCCCC
C
      FUNCTION IPSUM(IVAL,IPOS,IEND,IMASK,OMASK)
      INTEGER IVAL, IPOS, IEND, IMASK, OMASK
      PARAMETER ( ISIZE = 4 )

      IPSUM = IVAL
      IF ( IPOS .EQ. 0 ) THEN
          IRESP = KCWRIT(IVAL,OMASK,ISIZE)
      ELSEIF ( IPOS .EQ. IEND ) THEN
          IRESP = KCREAD(IREC,IMASK,0,ISIZE)
          IPSUM = IREC + IVAL
      ELSE
          IRESP = KCREAD(IREC,IMASK,0,ISIZE)
          ISEND = IREC + IVAL
          IRESP = KCWRIT(ISEND,OMASK,ISIZE)
      ENDIF

      RETURN
      END
C
CCCCCCCCCCCCCCCCCCCCCCCCCCCCCC END OF ROUTINE IPSUM CCCCCCCCCCCCCCCCCCCCCCCCCCCCCC
C
      SUBROUTINE OUTRES(IVAL)
      INTEGER IVAL
      INTEGER STDOUT
      PARAMETER ( STDOUT = 6 )
      COMMON/CUBCOM/ IPROC, NPROC

      MULTIPLE(STDOUT)
      PRINT *, '     Node ',IPROC,':      ',IVAL
      SINGLE(STDOUT)

      RETURN
      END
C
CCCCCCCCCCCCCCCCCCCCCCCCCCCCCC END OF ROUTINE OUTRES CCCCCCCCCCCCCCCCCCCCCCCCCCCCCC
C
```

D-7 Fortran Code For Tutorial Task 3.5

D-7.1 CP Program

```
      PROGRAM TCP35
      PARAMETER ( IDSIZE = 8, ISIZE = 4 )
      DOUBLE PRECISION A, B, ANSWER
      COMMON/CUBCOM/ IPROC, NPROC

      PRINT *, ' '
      IRESP = DOWNLD("task35NODE")
      IF (IRESP .LT. 0) THEN
          PRINT *, '**** An error occurred in KCUBLD ****'
          PRINT *, '**** Program aborted              ****'
          STOP
      ENDIF

      PRINT *, ' '
      PRINT *, 'Please give the lower limit of the integral:'
      READ *, A
      PRINT *, ' '
      PRINT *, 'Please give the upper limit of the integral:'
      READ *, B
      PRINT *, ' '
      PRINT *, 'Please give the number of intervals:'
      READ *, N
      N = 2*((N+1)/2)

      IRESP = KBCSTC(A,IDSIZE)
      IRESP = KBCSTC(B,IDSIZE)
      IRESP = KBCSTC(N,ISIZE)

      IRESP = KCOMBC(ANSWER,IDSIZE,1)

      PRINT *, ' '
      PRINT *, 'The integral is approximately ',ANSWER

      PRINT *, ' '
      PRINT *, 'Finished'
      PRINT *, ' '

      STOP
      END
C
CCCCCCCCCCCCCCCCCCCCCCCCCCCCCCC END OF PROGRAM TCP35 CCCCCCCCCCCCCCCCCCCCCCCCCCCCCCC
C
```

```
        INTEGER FUNCTION DOWNLD(PRGNAM)
        CHARACTER*10 PRGNAM
        COMMON/CUBCOM/ IPROC, NPROC

        PRINT *, 'Please give the dimension of the hypercube:'
        READ  *, NDOC

        NPROC  = 2**NDOC
        DOWNLD = KCUBEL(NDOC,PRGNAM)

        RETURN
        END
C
CCCCCCCCCCCCCCCCCCCCCCCCCCCCCC END OF ROUTINE DOWNLD CCCCCCCCCCCCCCCCCCCCCCCCCCCCCC
C
```

D-7.2 NODE Program

```
        PROGRAM TND35
        PARAMETER ( IDSIZE = 8, ISIZE = 4 )
        DOUBLE PRECISION A, B, FUNINT, SIMPSN, SUMLOC
        INTEGER IENV(5)
        COMMON/CUBCOM/ IPROC,NPROC,IPOS
        EXTERNAL IDADD, FUNINT

        IRESP  = KBCSTE(A,IDSIZE)
        IRESP  = KBCSTE(B,IDSIZE)
        IRESP  = KBCSTE(N,ISIZE)

        CALL KPARAM(IENV)

        IPROC  = IENV(2)
        NPROC  = IENV(3)

        IRESP  = KGRDIN(1,NPROC)
        IRESP  = KGRDCO(IPROC,IPOS)

        SUMLOC = SIMPSN(A,B,N,FUNINT)
        IRESP  = KCOMBE(SUMLOC,IDADD,IDSIZE,1)

        STOP
        END
C
CCCCCCCCCCCCCCCCCCCCCCCCCCCCCC END OF PROGRAM TND35 CCCCCCCCCCCCCCCCCCCCCCCCCCCCCC
C
```

```fortran
      DOUBLE PRECISION FUNCTION SIMPSN(A,B,N,FUNC)
      DOUBLE PRECISION A,B,FUNC
      INTEGER N
      DOUBLE PRECISION H, SUM, OSUM, ESUM
      COMMON/CUBCOM/ IPROC,NPROC,IPOS
      EXTERNAL FUNC

      H     = (B-A)/DBLE(N)

      NLOCAL = (N+1)/NPROC
      NLEFT  = MOD(N+1,NPROC)
      IF ( IPOS .LT. NLEFT ) THEN
          NLOCAL = NLOCAL + 1
          ISTART = NLOCAL*IPOS
      ELSE
          ISTART = NLOCAL*IPOS + NLEFT
      ENDIF

      ESUM  = 0.D0
      DO 10 I=0,NLOCAL-1,2
          ESUM = ESUM + FUNC(A+H*DBLE(I+ISTART))
10        CONTINUE

      OSUM  = 0.D0
      DO 20 I=1,NLOCAL-1,2
          OSUM = OSUM + FUNC(A+H*DBLE(I+ISTART))
20        CONTINUE

      IF ( MOD(ISTART,2) .EQ. 0 ) THEN
          SUM = 2.D0*ESUM + 4.D0*OSUM
      ELSE
          SUM = 4.D0*ESUM + 2.D0*OSUM
      ENDIF

      IF ( IPOS .EQ. 0 )          SUM = SUM - FUNC(A)
      IF ( IPOS .EQ. (NPROC-1) ) SUM = SUM - FUNC(B)

      SIMPSN = SUM*H/3.D0

      RETURN
      END
C
CCCCCCCCCCCCCCCCCCCCCCCCCCCCCCC END OF ROUTINE SIMPSN CCCCCCCCCCCCCCCCCCCCCCCCCCCC
C
      DOUBLE PRECISION FUNCTION FUNINT(X)
      DOUBLE PRECISION X
      DOUBLE PRECISION SINX
```

```
      SINX  = DSIN(X)
      FUNINT = 1.D0/DSQRT(1.D0-SINX*SINX/2.D0)

      RETURN
      END
C
CCCCCCCCCCCCCCCCCCCCCCCCCCCCCC END OF ROUTINE FUNINT CCCCCCCCCCCCCCCCCCCCCCCCCCCCCC
C
      FUNCTION IDADD(D1,D2,NSIZE)
      DOUBLE PRECISION D1, D2
      INTEGER NSIZE

      D1 = D1 + D2
      IDADD = 0

      RETURN
      END
C
CCCCCCCCCCCCCCCCCCCCCCCCCCCCCC END OF ROUTINE IDADD CCCCCCCCCCCCCCCCCCCCCCCCCCCCCC
C
```

D-7.3 CUBIX Program

```
      PROGRAM TND35
      PARAMETER ( IDSIZE = 8 )
      DOUBLE PRECISION A, B, FUNINT, SIMPSN, ANSWER
      INTEGER IENV(5)
      COMMON/CUBCOM/ IPROC,NPROC,IPOS
      EXTERNAL IDADD, FUNINT

      PRINT *, ' '
      PRINT *, 'Please give the lower limit of the integral:'
      READ *, A
      PRINT *, ' '
      PRINT *, 'Please give the upper limit of the integral:'
      READ *, B
      PRINT *, ' '
      PRINT *, 'Please give the number of intervals:'
      READ *, N
      N = 2*((N+1)/2)

      CALL KPARAM(IENV)

      IPROC  = IENV(2)
      NPROC  = IENV(3)
```

```fortran
      IRESP  = KGRDIN(1,NPROC)
      IRESP  = KGRDCO(IPROC,IPOS)

      ANSWER = SIMPSN(A,B,N,FUNINT)
      IRESP  = KCOMBI(ANSWER,IDADD,IDSIZE,1)

      PRINT *, ' '
      PRINT *, 'The integral is approximately ',ANSWER

      PRINT *, ' '
      PRINT *, 'Finished'
      PRINT *, ' '

      STOP
      END
C
CCCCCCCCCCCCCCCCCCCCCCCCCCCCCC END OF PROGRAM TND35 CCCCCCCCCCCCCCCCCCCCCCCCCCCCCC
C
      DOUBLE PRECISION FUNCTION SIMPSN(A,B,N,FUNC)
      DOUBLE PRECISION A,B,FUNC
      INTEGER N
      DOUBLE PRECISION H, SUM, OSUM, ESUM
      COMMON/CUBCOM/ IPROC,NPROC,IPOS
      EXTERNAL FUNC

      H      = (B-A)/DBLE(N)

      NLOCAL = (N+1)/NPROC
      NLEFT  = MOD(N+1,NPROC)
      IF ( IPOS .LT. NLEFT ) THEN
           NLOCAL = NLOCAL + 1
           ISTART = NLOCAL*IPOS
      ELSE
           ISTART = NLOCAL*IPOS + NLEFT
      ENDIF

      ESUM  = 0.D0
      DO 10 I=0,NLOCAL-1,2
           ESUM = ESUM + FUNC(A+H*DBLE(I+ISTART))
10         CONTINUE

      OSUM  = 0.D0
      DO 20 I=1,NLOCAL-1,2
           OSUM = OSUM + FUNC(A+H*DBLE(I+ISTART))
20         CONTINUE

      IF ( MOD(ISTART,2) .EQ. 0 ) THEN
```

```
          SUM = 2.D0*ESUM + 4.D0*OSUM
      ELSE
          SUM = 4.D0*ESUM + 2.D0*OSUM
      ENDIF

      IF ( IPOS .EQ. 0 )          SUM = SUM - FUNC(A)
      IF ( IPOS .EQ. (NPROC-1) ) SUM = SUM - FUNC(B)

      SIMPSN = SUM*H/3.D0

      RETURN
      END
C
CCCCCCCCCCCCCCCCCCCCCCCCCCCCCCC END OF ROUTINE SIMPSN CCCCCCCCCCCCCCCCCCCCCCCCCCCCCCC
C
      DOUBLE PRECISION FUNCTION FUNINT(X)
      DOUBLE PRECISION X
      DOUBLE PRECISION SINX

      SINX   = DSIN(X)
      FUNINT = 1.D0/DSQRT(1.D0-SINX*SINX/2.D0)

      RETURN
      END
C
CCCCCCCCCCCCCCCCCCCCCCCCCCCCCCC END OF ROUTINE FUNINT CCCCCCCCCCCCCCCCCCCCCCCCCCCCCCC
C
      FUNCTION IDADD(D1,D2,NSIZE)
      DOUBLE PRECISION D1, D2
      INTEGER NSIZE

      D1 = D1 + D2
      IDADD = 0

      RETURN
      END
C
CCCCCCCCCCCCCCCCCCCCCCCCCCCCCCC END OF ROUTINE IDADD CCCCCCCCCCCCCCCCCCCCCCCCCCCCCCC
C
```

E

Appendix E:
The CrOS III Utility Library

This appendix lists the source code for the *comutil*, *crystal_router*, *prand*, and *submap* utilities for which the manual pages are given in Appendix F. Since the Fortran versions of these utilities have not yet been implemented, only the C code is given here.

E-1 The *comutil* Routines

E-1.1 The *expand* Routine

```
#include <cros.h>

int expand(x,y,step,nitems,nbytes)
char *x,*y;
int step,nitems,nbytes;
{
    int j,dest,proc,num_procs,i,offset,mask,size;
    int resp,send_offset,recv_offset,error;
    struct cubenv env;

    if(nitems<0) return -1;

    cparam(&env);
    proc      = env.procnum;
    num_procs = env.nproc;

    for(i=0;i<nitems;++i){
        offset = (proc+i*num_procs)*nbytes;
        for(j=0;j<nbytes;++j) *(y+j+offset) = *(x+j+i*step);
    }

    offset = num_procs*nbytes;
    size   = nbytes;
    mask   = num_procs-1;
    error  = nitems;
    for(i=0;i<env.doc;++i){
        dest = (1<<i)^proc;
        send_offset = (proc&mask)*nbytes;
        recv_offset = (dest&mask)*nbytes;
        resp = vshift(y+recv_offset,1<<i,size,offset,nitems,
                      y+send_offset,1<<i,size,offset,nitems);
        if (resp<0) error = -1;
        size = size<<1;
        mask = mask<<1;
    }
    return error;
}

/*********************** end of routine expand ***********************/
```

E-1.2 The *fold* Routine

```
#include <cros.h>

#define MAX_TEMP 512

int fold(x,func,nbytes,nitems)
char *x;
int (*func)(),nitems,nbytes;
{
    int j,dest,i,offset,mask,chan,flag,block,send,recv,sendn,recvn;
    int proc;
    struct cubenv env;
    char y[MAX_TEMP],*tmp,*malloc();

    if(nitems<=0) return -1;
    if(nbytes<=0) return -1;

    cparam(&env);
    proc     = env.procnum;

    if(nitems*nbytes>MAX_TEMP){
        tmp = malloc(nitems*nbytes);
        if(tmp==NULLPTR) return -1;
        flag = 1;
    }
    else{
        tmp  = y;
        flag = 0;
    }

    offset = nbytes<<1;
    mask    = chan = 1;
    block  = 2;
    for(i=0;i<env.doc;++i){
        recv = proc&mask;
        send = recv^chan;
        recvn = (nitems+mask-recv)>>(i+1);
        sendn = (nitems+mask-send)>>(i+1);
        vshift(tmp+recv*nbytes,1<<i,nbytes,offset,recvn,
                x+send*nbytes,  1<<i,nbytes,offset,sendn);
        for(j=recv;j<nitems;j += block)
            (*func)(x+j*nbytes,tmp+j*nbytes,nbytes);
        block  = block<<1;
        offset = offset<<1;
        chan   = chan<<1;
        mask   = mask|chan;
```

```
        }
        if(flag) free(tmp);

        return 0;
}
/*********************** end of rou14ztine fold ***********************/
```

E-1.3 The *global_reverse* Routine

```
#include <cros.h>

int global_reverse(x,Nx,nbytes)
char *x;
int Nx,nbytes;
{
    char tempx,*p1,*p2;
    int ibit,proc,num_procs,i,offset,local_offset,nq,nitems;
    int j,route,error,resp;
    int global_index,global_rev,swap_index,block_index,other_index;
    struct cubenv env;

    if(Nx<=0) return -1;

    cparam(&env);
    proc     = env.procnum;
    num_procs = env.nproc;

    nq = Nx/num_procs;
    if(nq*num_procs != Nx) return -2;

    nitems = nq/num_procs;
    if(!nitems) return -3;

    offset = num_procs*nbytes;
    error  = 0;
    for(route=0;route<num_procs;++route){
        local_offset = nbytes*permute(route^proc,num_procs);
        for(i=0;i<env.doc;++i)
            if((route>>i)&1){
            resp = vshift(x+local_offset,1<<i,nbytes,offset,nitems,
                          x+local_offset,1<<i,nbytes,offset,nitems);
            if (resp<0) error = -1;
        }
    }
    if (error<0) return error;
```

```
        local_offset = permute(proc,num_procs);
        for(i=0;i<nq;++i){
            block_index  = i%num_procs;
            other_index  = local_offset + num_procs*(i/num_procs);
            global_index = nq*permute(block_index,num_procs) + other_index;
            global_rev   = permute(global_index,Nx);
            swap_index   = global_rev%nq;
            if(swap_index>i){
                p1 = x+i*nbytes;
                p2 = x+swap_index*nbytes;
                for(j=0;j<nbytes;++j){
                    tempx = *p1;
                    *p1++ = *p2;
                    *p2++ = tempx;
                }
            }
        }

        return 0;
    }


/********************* end of routine global_reverse *********************/
```

E-1.4 The *indexx* Routine

```
    #include <cros.h>

    int indexx(x,Nx,nbytes)
    char *x;
    int Nx,nbytes;
    {
        int nq,nitems,block,i,proc,num_procs,nex;
        int error,ibit,block_size,offset,local_offset,resp;
        struct cubenv env;

        if(Nx<=0) return -1;

        cparam(&env);
        proc      = env.procnum;
        num_procs = env.nproc;

        nq = Nx/num_procs;
        if(nq*num_procs != Nx) return -2;

        nitems = nq/num_procs;
        if(!nitems) return -3;
```

```
        block = 1;
        nex   = nq/2;
        error = 0;
        for(i=0;i<env.doc;++i){
            ibit        = (proc>>i)&1;
            block_size  = block*nbytes;
            offset      = 2*block_size;
            local_offset = (1-ibit)*block_size;
            resp = vshift(x+local_offset,1<<i,block_size,offset,nex,
                          x+local_offset,1<<i,block_size,offset,nex);
            if(resp<0) error = -1;
            block = block<<1;
            nex   = nex>>1;
        }

        return error;
    }
    /*************************** end of routine indexx ***************************/
```

E-1.5 The *bcast* Routine

```
    #include <cros.h>

    int bcast(x,source,nbytes)
    char *x;
    int source,nbytes;
    {
        int proc,num_procs,rbit,proc_trans,chanr,chanw,mask_trans;
        struct cubenv env;

        if(nbytes<0) return -1;

        cparam(&env);
        proc      = env.procnum;
        num_procs = env.nproc;

        if(source<0 || source>num_procs) return -1;

        proc_trans = proc^source;

        if(proc_trans==0){
            mask_trans = num_procs-1;
            return (cwrite(x,mask_trans,nbytes));
        }
        else{
```

```
            rbit  = lowest_bit_no(proc_trans);
            chanr = 1<<rbit;
            chanw = chanr-1;
            return (cread(x,chanr,chanw,nbytes));
        }
    }


    /*********************** end of routine bcast **********************/
```

E-1.6 The *scatter* Routine

```c
    #include <cros.h>

    int scatter(x,source,nlocal,nbytes,max_elements)
    char *x;
    int source,nlocal,nbytes,max_elements;
    {
        int error,proc,num_procs,cl,ch,npipes;
        int itrans,proc_trans,i,nloop,nitems,resp,local_offset,offset;
        struct cubenv env;

        if(nbytes<0) return -1;

        cparam(&env);
        proc      = env.procnum;
        num_procs = env.nproc;

        if(source<0 || source>=num_procs) return -2;

        error      = 0;
        proc_trans = source^proc;
        offset     = nbytes*num_procs;
        nloop      = num_procs<nlocal ? num_procs : nlocal;
        if(proc_trans==0){
            for(i=(nloop-1);i>0;--i){
                cl           = lowest_bit_no(i);
                itrans       = i^source;
                nitems       = (nlocal-itrans-1)/num_procs + 1;
                local_offset = itrans*nbytes;
                resp = vwrite(x+local_offset,1<<cl,nbytes,offset,nitems);
                if(resp<0) error = -1;
            }
        }
        else if(proc_trans<nlocal){
            ch     = highest_bit_no(proc_trans);
            npipes = nloop/(1<<(ch+1)) - 1;
```

```
        for(i=1;i<=npipes;++i){
            cl =lowest_bit_no(i)+1;
            vread(NULLPTR,1<<ch,1<<(cl+ch),nbytes,offset,max_elements);
            if(resp<0) error = -1;
        }
        resp = vread(x+nbytes*proc,1<<ch,0,nbytes,offset,max_elements);
        if(resp<0) error = -1;
    }
    return error;
}
/*************************** end of routine scatter **************************/
```

E-1.7 The *transfer* Routine

```
#include <cros.h>

int transfer(x,source,dest,nsend,nbytes,max_elements)
char *x;
int source,dest,nsend,nbytes,max_elements;
{
    int meven,modd,proc,route,proc_trans;
    int chr,clr,resp,cl,ch,num_procs,forward_chan,even_route,odd_route;
    struct cubenv env;

    if(source==dest) return nsend;
    if(nbytes<0) return -1;

    cparam(&env);
    proc      = env.procnum;
    num_procs = env.nproc;

    if(source<0 || source>=num_procs) return -2;
    if(dest<0 || dest>=num_procs) return -3;

    modd  = nsend/2;
    meven = (nsend+1)/2;

    route      = source^dest;
    proc_trans = source^proc;

    cl    = lowest_bit_no(route);
    ch    = highest_bit_no(route);
    clr   = lowest_bit_no(proc_trans);
    chr   = highest_bit_no(proc_trans);

    even_route = route&((1<<(chr+1))-1);
```

```
    odd_route  = route&((~0)<<clr);

    resp = -99;
    if(proc_trans==0){
        vwrite(x,1<<cl,nbytes,2*nbytes,meven);
        vwrite(x+nbytes,1<<ch,nbytes,2*nbytes,modd);
    }
    else if(proc_trans==route){
        resp  = vread(x,1<<ch,0,nbytes,2*nbytes,max_elements);
        resp += vread(x+nbytes,1<<cl,0,nbytes,2*nbytes,max_elements);
    }
    else if(proc_trans==even_route){
        forward_chan = lowest_bit_no(route-proc_trans);
        vread(NULLPTR,1<<chr,1<<forward_chan,nbytes,
                            2*nbytes,max_elements);
    }
    else if(proc_trans==odd_route){
        forward_chan = highest_bit_no(route-proc_trans);
        vread(NULLPTR,1<<clr,1<<forward_chan,nbytes,
                            2*nbytes,max_elements);
    }
    return resp;
}


/************************ end of routine transfer ************************/
```

E-1.8 The *transpose* Routine

```
#include <cros.h>

#define MAX_TEMP 1024

int transpose(x,nbytes,in_space)
char *x;
int nbytes,in_space;
{
    int ndoc,xbit,ybit,rec_bytes,D,ND,procx,procy,proc,num_procs,i;
    struct cubenv env;
    char y[MAX_TEMP];

    if(nbytes<0) return -1;

    cparam(&env);
    proc      = env.procnum;
    num_procs = env.nproc;
    ndoc      = env.doc;
```

```
        if(ndoc&1) return -3;

        D       = ndoc/2;
        ND      = 1<<D;
        procx = proc%ND;
        procy = proc/ND;
        rec_bytes = nbytes;

        for(i=0;i<D;++i){
            xbit = (procx>>i)&1;
            ybit = (procy>>i)&1;
            if(xbit != ybit){
                cwrite(x,1<<(i+D),nbytes);
                rec_bytes = cread(x,1<<i,0,in_space);
            }
            else{
                rec_bytes = cread(y,1<<(i+D),0,in_space);
                cwrite(y,1<<i,rec_bytes);
            }
        }
        return rec_bytes;
}


/*********************** end of routine transpose ***********************/
```

E-1.9 Auxiliary Routines

```
int highest_bit_no(x)
int x;
{
    int i;

    if(x==0) return -1;

    i=0;
    while(x=x>>1) i++;

    return i;
}

/********************* end of routine highest_bit_no *********************/

int lowest_bit_no(x)
int x;
{
```

```
        int i;

        if(x==0) return -1;

        i=0;
        while(!(x&1)){ i++; x = x>>1;}

        return i;
}

/*********************** end of routine lowest_bit_no **********************/
int permute(l,m)
int l,m;
{
    if(m==1) return l;
    else return((l&1) ? (m>>1) + permute(l>>1,m>>1) : permute(l>>1,m>>1) );
}

/*************************** end of routine permute *************************/
```

E-2 The *crystal_router* Routines

E-2.1 The *clear_cr_buf* Routine

```
#define IN      0
#define OUT     1

extern int   out_bytes, first_call, in_bytes, in_count;
extern char *out_buf_ptr, *out_start_ptr;
extern char *in_buf_ptr,  *in_start_ptr;

int clear_cr_buf(in_or_out)
int in_or_out;
{
    if(first_call) cr_init();

    if(in_or_out==IN){
        in_buf_ptr = in_start_ptr;
        in_bytes   = 0;
        in_count   = 0;
    }
    else if(in_or_out==OUT){
        out_buf_ptr = out_start_ptr;
        out_bytes   = 0;
    }

    return 0;
}

/*************************** end of routine clear_buf ***************************/
```

E-2.2 The *crystal_router* Routine

```
extern int   out_bytes, out_buf_size, com_bytes, com_buf_size;
extern int   in_bytes, in_count, cr_doc, first_call;
extern char *com_start_ptr, *out_start_ptr, *out_buf_ptr;
extern float hwm_out;

int crystal_router()
{
    int rec_bytes,d,resp,chan,read_bytes;
    float tempx;

    if(first_call) cr_init();

    resp = 0;
```

```
        compress_in_buf();
        resp += copy_to_in_buf(out_start_ptr,out_bytes);


        for(d=0;d<cr_doc;++d){
            chan = 1<<d;
            if(d>0) resp += compress_out_buf();
            resp += check_buffer(d);
            com_buf_size = out_buf_size - out_bytes;
            read_bytes = cshift(com_start_ptr,chan,com_buf_size,
                                com_start_ptr,chan,com_bytes);
            if(read_bytes<0){
                hwm_out = 1.0;
                rec_bytes = rescue_buf(com_start_ptr,com_buf_size);
                resp = -1;
                set_bit(4);
            }
            else{
                tempx = ((float)(out_bytes+read_bytes))/((float)out_buf_size);
                hwm_out = (tempx > hwm_out) ? tempx:hwm_out;
                rec_bytes = read_bytes;
            }
            resp += copy_to_in_buf(com_start_ptr,rec_bytes);
            out_bytes += rec_bytes;
            out_buf_ptr = out_start_ptr + out_bytes;
        }
        in_count = in_bytes;

        compress_out_buf();

        return (resp<0 ? -1 : 0);
    }

/*********************** end of routine crystal_router ***********************/
```

E-2.3 The *get_message* Routine

```
    #define CURRENT 0
    #define OLD     1
    #define ANY     999

    extern int    first_call, header_size, isize;
    extern int    cr_procnum, in_bytes, in_count;
    extern char *in_buf_ptr, *in_start_ptr;
```

```
int get_message(buf,source,nbytes)
char *buf;
int *source,*nbytes;
{
    int ncur,stemp,message_size,src,bytes,found,i,nb,dest,status;

    if(first_call) cr_init();

    if(in_count>=in_bytes){
        in_count = 0;
        in_buf_ptr = in_start_ptr;
    }

    if(in_bytes==0) return 1;

    bytes = 0;
    src = *source;
    ncur = 0;
    found = 0;
    header_size = 5*isize;
    while(bytes<in_bytes && !found){
        stemp  = *((int *)(in_buf_ptr+isize));
        nb     = *((int *)(in_buf_ptr+2*isize));
        status = *((int *)(in_buf_ptr+3*isize));
        dest   = *((int *)(in_buf_ptr+4*isize));
        message_size = nb + header_size;
        if(status==CURRENT){
          ncur++;
          if(dest==cr_procnum && (src==stemp || src==ANY)) found = 1;
        }
        if(!found){
            bytes += message_size;
            in_buf_ptr += message_size;
            in_count += message_size;
            if(in_count>=in_bytes) {
                in_count = 0;
                in_buf_ptr  = in_start_ptr;
            }
        }
    }
    if(!ncur) return 3;
    if(!found) return 2;

    *source = stemp;
    *nbytes = nb;
    *((int *)(in_buf_ptr+3*isize)) = OLD;
    in_buf_ptr += header_size;
```

```
        for(i=0;i<nb;++i) *buf++ = *in_buf_ptr++;
        in_count += message_size;

        return 0;
}
```

/*********************** end of routine get_message **********************/

E-2.4 The *rewindx* Routine

```
#define CURRENT 0
#define OLD     1

extern int    isize, header_size, in_bytes;
extern char *in_start_ptr;

rewindx()
{
    int bytes = 0, nb, *mess_stat;
    char *cptr;
    cptr = in_start_ptr;
    while(bytes<in_bytes){
            nb      = *((int *)(cptr+2*isize));
            mess_stat = ((int *)(cptr+3*isize));
            if(*mess_stat == OLD) *mess_stat = CURRENT;
            cptr    += nb+header_size;
            bytes += nb+header_size;
    }
}
```

/************************ end of routine rewindx *************************/

E-2.5 The *send_message* Routine

```
extern int    out_bytes, out_buf_size, first_call, header_size;
extern int    isize, cr_nproc, cr_procnum;
extern char *out_buf_ptr;
extern float hwm_out;

#define CURRENT 0

int send_message(buf,nbytes,ndest,dest)
char *buf;
int nbytes,ndest,*dest;
```

```
{
    int valid_dest,destination,i,resp,temp_bytes,message_size;
    float tempx;

    resp = 0;

    if(first_call) cr_init();

    if (nbytes<0){
        set_bit(2);
        return -1;
    }
    if(ndest<0){
        set_bit(0);
        return -1;
    }

    valid_dest = ndest;
    for(i=0;i<ndest;++i){
        destination = dest[i];
        if(destination<0 || destination>(cr_nproc-1)){
            set_bit(1);
            resp = -1;
            valid_dest--;
        }
    }
    if(valid_dest==0) return 0;

    header_size = (valid_dest + 4)*isize;
    message_size = nbytes + header_size;
    temp_bytes = out_bytes + message_size;
    if(temp_bytes<=out_buf_size){
        *((int *)out_buf_ptr)            = valid_dest;
        *((int *)(out_buf_ptr+isize))    = cr_procnum;
        *((int *)(out_buf_ptr+2*isize))  = nbytes;
        *((int *)(out_buf_ptr+3*isize))  = CURRENT;
        out_buf_ptr += 4*isize;
        for(i=0;i<valid_dest;++i){
            destination = dest[i];
            if(destination>=0 && destination<cr_nproc){
                *((int *)out_buf_ptr) = destination;
                out_buf_ptr += isize;
            }
        }
        for(i=0;i<nbytes;++i) *out_buf_ptr++ = *buf++;
        out_bytes = temp_bytes;
        tempx = ((float)out_bytes)/((float)out_buf_size);
```

```
                hwm_out = (tempx > hwm_out) ? tempx : hwm_out;
                return resp;
        }
        else{
                hwm_out   = 1.0;
                set_bit(3);
                return -1;
        }
}
```

```
/*********************** end of routine send_message ***********************/
```

E-2.6 The *set_cr_buf* Routine

```
#define IN   0
#define OUT  1

extern int    out_buf_size, out_bytes, first_call;
extern int    in_buf_size, in_count, in_bytes;
extern char *in_buf_ptr,  *in_start_ptr,  in_default_buf[];
extern char *out_buf_ptr, *out_start_ptr, out_default_buf[];

int set_cr_buf(buf_size,in_out)
int buf_size,in_out;
{
        char *new_ptr,*malloc();
        int i,resp;

        if(first_call) cr_init();

        resp = 0;

        new_ptr = malloc(buf_size);
        if(in_out==OUT){
            if(new_ptr==(char *)0){
                set_bit(7);
                return -1;
            }
            else{
                if(out_bytes>buf_size){
                    set_bit(9);
                    resp = -1;
                    out_bytes= rescue_buf(out_start_ptr,buf_size);
                }
                out_buf_ptr = new_ptr;
                for(i=0;i<out_bytes;++i)
```

```
                    *out_buf_ptr++ = *out_start_ptr++;
                    if(out_start_ptr != out_default_buf) free(out_start_ptr);
                    out_start_ptr = new_ptr;
                    out_buf_size = buf_size;
                }
            }
        else if(in_out==IN){
            if(new_ptr==(char *)0){
                set_bit(8);
                return -1;
            }
            else{
                if(in_bytes>buf_size){
                    set_bit(10);
                    resp = -1;
                    in_bytes= rescue_buf(in_start_ptr,buf_size);
                    if(in_count>buf_size) in_count = 0;
                }
                in_buf_ptr = new_ptr;
                for(i=0;i<in_bytes;++i)
                  *in_buf_ptr++ = *in_start_ptr++;
                if(in_start_ptr != in_default_buf) free(in_start_ptr);
                in_start_ptr = new_ptr;
                in_buf_size  = buf_size;
            }
        }

        return resp;
}


/************************* end of routine set_cr_buf *************************/
```

E-2.7 The *show_buf_usage* Routine

```
#include <stdio.h>
#include <cros.h>

#define IN   0
#define OUT  1

extern int   cr_procnum;
extern float hwm_in, hwm_out;

float show_buffer_usage(stream,in_out)
FILE *stream;
int in_out;
```

```
{
    float usage;

    if (in_out==IN)        usage = hwm_in;
       else if(in_out==OUT) usage = hwm_out;
       else                 usage = -1.0;

    if(stream != (FILE *)0){
       fmulti(stream);
       fprintf(stream,"\n");
       if (in_out==IN)
          fprintf(stream,"\nInput buffer usage for processor %d : %7.3f",
                  cr_procnum,usage);
       else if(in_out==OUT)
          fprintf(stream,"\nOutput buffer usage for processor %d : %7.3f",
                  cr_procnum,usage);
       else
          fprintf(stream,"\nInvalid buffer ID passed to show_buffer_usage");
       fprintf(stream,"\n");
       fsingl(stream);
    }
    return usage;
}

/******************** end of routine show_buffer_usage ********************/
```

E-2.8 The *zero_hwm* Routine

```
#define IN      0
#define OUT     1

extern float hwm_in, hwm_out;

int zero_hwm(in_out)
int in_out;
{
    if (in_out==IN){
        hwm_in = 0.0;
        return 0;
    } else if(in_out==OUT){
        hwm_out = 0.0;
        return 0;
    } else    return -1;
}

/************************ end of routine zero_hwm ************************/
```

E-2.9 Auxiliary Routines

```
extern int    com_bytes, com_buf_size, out_bytes, out_buf_size;
extern float hwm_out;
extern char *com_buf_ptr;

int add_to_com_buf(buf,nbytes)
char *buf;
int nbytes;
{
    int i,temp_bytes;
    float tempx;

    temp_bytes = com_bytes + nbytes;
    if(temp_bytes<=com_buf_size){
        for(i=0;i<nbytes;++i) *com_buf_ptr++ = *buf++;
        com_bytes = temp_bytes;
        tempx = (float)(out_bytes+com_bytes)/((float)out_buf_size);
        hwm_out = (tempx > hwm_out) ? tempx : hwm_out;
        return 0;
    }
    else{
        hwm_out = 1.0;
        set_bit(3);
        return -1;
    }
}

/********************** end of routine add_to_com_buf **********************/

#define OLD      1

extern int    com_bytes, com_buf_size, out_bytes, out_buf_size;
extern int    header_size, isize, cr_procnum;
extern char *com_buf_ptr,    *out_buf_ptr;
extern char *com_start_ptr, *out_start_ptr;

int check_buffer(dim)
int dim;
{
    int p4,ndest,status,bit,mask,message_size,dest,nbytes,resp,bytes;
    int cur_dest,i,*dest_ptr,sent,c_bytes,s4,err;
    char *start_ptr,*c_start;

    mask = 1<<dim;
```

```
    bit  = cr_procnum&mask;
    s4   = 4*isize;

    com_start_ptr = out_buf_ptr;
    out_buf_ptr   = out_start_ptr;
    com_buf_size  = out_buf_size - out_bytes;
    com_buf_ptr   = com_start_ptr;
    com_bytes     = 0;

    err  = 0;

    bytes = 0;
    while(bytes<out_bytes){
        resp  = 0;
        ndest = *((int *)out_buf_ptr);
        nbytes = *((int *)(out_buf_ptr+2*isize));
        status = *((int *)(out_buf_ptr+3*isize));
        header_size  = (4+ndest)*isize;
        message_size = nbytes + header_size;
        if(status==OLD){
            out_buf_ptr += message_size;
            bytes       += message_size;
            continue;
        }
        dest_ptr = (int *)(out_buf_ptr+4*isize);
        start_ptr= out_buf_ptr;
        cur_dest = ndest;
        sent     = 0;
        c_bytes  = com_bytes;
        c_start  = com_buf_ptr;
        for(i=0;i<ndest;++i){
            dest = *dest_ptr++;
            if(dest<0) cur_dest--;
            else if((dest&mask)^bit){
                p4 = (4+i)*isize;
                if(!sent){
                    resp = add_to_com_buf(out_buf_ptr,s4);
                    err += resp;
                    if(resp<0) break;
                }
                resp = add_to_com_buf(&dest,isize);
                err += resp;
                if(resp==0){
                    cur_dest--;
                    *((int *)(start_ptr+p4)) = -99;
                    sent++;
                }
            }
```

```
                    else break;
                }
            }
            if(!cur_dest) *((int *)(start_ptr+3*isize)) = OLD;
            if(sent && resp==0){
                resp = add_to_com_buf(out_buf_ptr+header_size,nbytes);
                err += resp;
                *((int *)c_start) = sent;
            }
            if(resp != 0){
                start_ptr += 4*isize;
                for(i=0;i<sent;++i){
                    dest = *((int *)(c_start+(4+i)*isize));
                    while(*((int *)start_ptr) != -99)
                        start_ptr += isize;
                    *((int *)start_ptr) = dest;
                }
                com_bytes   = c_bytes;
                com_buf_ptr = c_start;
            }
            out_buf_ptr += message_size;
            bytes       += message_size;
        }
        return (err<0 ? -1 : 0);
}


/*********************** end of routine check_buffer ***********************/

#define CURRENT 0

extern int isize;

char *compress(start_ptr,total_bytes)
int *total_bytes;
char *start_ptr;
{
        int j,ndest,nbytes,message_size,status,tot_bytes;
        int bytes;
        char *buf_ptr,*cur_buf_ptr;

        buf_ptr = cur_buf_ptr = start_ptr;
        tot_bytes    = 0;
        bytes        = 0;
        while(bytes< *total_bytes){
            ndest  = *((int *)buf_ptr);
            nbytes = *((int *)(buf_ptr+2*isize));
            status = *((int *)(buf_ptr+3*isize));
```

```
            message_size = nbytes + (4+ndest)*isize;
            if(status==CURRENT){
                tot_bytes += message_size;
                if(cur_buf_ptr != buf_ptr)
                    for(j=0;j<message_size;++j)
                        *cur_buf_ptr++ = *buf_ptr++;
                else{
                    cur_buf_ptr += message_size;
                    buf_ptr     += message_size;
                }
            }
            else buf_ptr += message_size;
            bytes += message_size;
    }

    *total_bytes = tot_bytes;

    return cur_buf_ptr;
}

/*********************** end of routine compress ***********************/

#define OLD 1

extern int    header_size, isize, in_bytes, in_buf_size, cr_procnum;
extern char *out_buf_ptr, *in_buf_ptr;
extern float hwm_in;

int copy_to_in_buf(start_ptr,total_bytes)
char *start_ptr;
int total_bytes;
{
    int temp_bytes,cur_dest,ndest,i,dest,nbytes,status,message_size,bytes;
    int j,p4,cpy_size,resp,source,*dest_ptr;
    float tempx;
    char *cpy_ptr,*buf_ptr;

    resp = 0;

    buf_ptr = start_ptr;

    bytes    = 0;
    while(bytes<total_bytes){
        ndest  = *((int *)buf_ptr);
        source = *((int *)(buf_ptr+isize));
        nbytes = *((int *)(buf_ptr+2*isize));
        status = *((int *)(buf_ptr+3*isize));
```

```
    header_size  = ( 4+ndest )*isize;
    message_size = nbytes + header_size;
    if(status==OLD){
        buf_ptr += message_size;
        bytes   += message_size;
        continue;
    }
    cpy_size = 5*isize + nbytes;
    cur_dest = ndest;
    dest_ptr = (int *)(buf_ptr + 4*isize);
    for(i=0;i<ndest;++i){
        cpy_ptr = buf_ptr + header_size;
        dest = *dest_ptr++;
        if(dest==cr_procnum){
            temp_bytes = in_bytes + cpy_size;
            if(temp_bytes<=in_buf_size){
                p4 = (4+i)*isize;
                *((int *)in_buf_ptr)          = 1;
                *((int *)(in_buf_ptr+isize))  = source;
                *((int *)(in_buf_ptr+2*isize))= nbytes;
                *((int *)(in_buf_ptr+3*isize))= status;
                *((int *)(in_buf_ptr+4*isize))= dest;
                in_buf_ptr += 5*isize;
                for(j=0;j<nbytes;++j)
                    *in_buf_ptr++ = *cpy_ptr++;
                *((int *)(buf_ptr+p4)) = -99;
                cur_dest--;
                in_bytes = temp_bytes;
                tempx = ((float)in_bytes)/((float)in_buf_size);
                hwm_in = (tempx>hwm_in) ? tempx : hwm_in;
            }
            else{
                hwm_in = 1.0;
                set_bit(6);
                resp = -1;
            }
        }
        else if(dest<0) cur_dest--;
    }
    if(!cur_dest) *((int *)(buf_ptr+3*isize)) = OLD;
    bytes   += message_size;
    buf_ptr += message_size;
}
return resp;
}


/********************* end of routine copy_to_in_buf *********************/
```

```
extern int    in_bytes;
extern char *in_buf_ptr, *in_start_ptr;

int compress_in_buf()
{
    int old_bytes;
    char *compress();

    old_bytes  = in_bytes;
    in_buf_ptr = compress(in_start_ptr,&in_bytes);

    return (old_bytes - in_bytes);

}

/********************** end of routine compress_in_buf *********************/

extern int    out_bytes;
extern char *out_buf_ptr, *out_start_ptr;

int compress_out_buf()
{
    int old_bytes;
    char *compress();

    old_bytes  = out_bytes;
    out_buf_ptr = compress(out_start_ptr,&out_bytes);

    return (old_bytes - out_bytes);

}

/********************** end of routine compress_out_buf *********************/

#include <cros.h>

#define IN_BUFSIZ   10000
#define OUT_BUFSIZ 10000

extern char *out_start_ptr,    *in_start_ptr;
extern char  out_default_buf[], in_default_buf[];
extern char *out_buf_ptr,       *in_buf_ptr;
extern int   out_buf_size, in_buf_size, out_bytes, in_bytes;
extern int   isize, in_count, cr_error, first_call;
extern int   cr_doc, cr_procnum, cr_nproc;
```

```
cr_init()
{
    struct cubenv crenv;

    out_start_ptr = out_default_buf;
    in_start_ptr  = in_default_buf;
    out_buf_size  = OUT_BUFSIZ;
    in_buf_size   = IN_BUFSIZ;
    isize         = sizeof(int);
    out_buf_ptr   = out_start_ptr;
    in_buf_ptr    = in_start_ptr;
    out_bytes     = 0;
    in_bytes      = 0;
    in_count      = 0;
    cr_error      = 0;
    first_call    = 0;

    cparam(&crenv);
    cr_doc   = crenv.doc;
    cr_procnum = crenv.procnum;
    cr_nproc = crenv.nproc;
}

/************************* end of routine cr_init *************************/

extern int isize;

int rescue_buf(start_ptr,max_bytes)
char *start_ptr;
int max_bytes;
{
    int nbytes,ndest,temp,bytes;
    char *buf_ptr;

    buf_ptr = start_ptr;
    bytes = 0;
    while(bytes<max_bytes){
        temp = bytes + 4*isize;
        if(temp>max_bytes) break;
        ndest  = *((int *)buf_ptr);
        nbytes = *((int *)(buf_ptr+2*isize));
        temp  += nbytes + ndest*isize;
        if(temp>max_bytes) break;
        bytes = temp;
        buf_ptr += nbytes + (ndest+4)*isize;
    }
    return bytes;
```

```
    }

/*********************** end of routine rescue_buf ***********************/

    extern int cr_error;

    set_bit(n)
    int n;
    {
        if(!(((cr_error>>n)&1))) cr_error += 1<<n;
    }

/*********************** end of routine set_bit ***********************/
```

E-2.10 The Include File crdef.h

```
    #define IN              0
    #define OUT             1
    #define CURRENT         0
    #define OLD             1
    #define IN_BUFSIZ   10000
    #define OUT_BUFSIZ  10000
    #define ANY           999

    int   cr_procnum,cr_doc,cr_nproc,cr_error,in_count;
    int   in_bytes,out_bytes,in_buf_size,out_buf_size;
    int   com_bytes,com_buf_size;
    int   isize,header_size,first_call=1;
    char *com_start_ptr,*com_buf_ptr;
    char *in_buf_ptr,*out_buf_ptr,*in_start_ptr,*out_start_ptr;
    char  in_default_buf[IN_BUFSIZ];
    char  out_default_buf[OUT_BUFSIZ];
    float hwm_in=0.0, hwm_out=0.0;
```

E-3 The *prand* Routines

E-3.1 The *prand_setB* Routine

```
#include <cros.h>

#define MULT (long)1103515245
#define ADD  (long)12345
#define MASK (long) (0x7fffffff)
#define TWOTO31 ((double)MASK+1.0)

long randx,A,C,a,c;

prand_setB(seed,nskip,order)
int seed,nskip,order;
{
    int i;
    struct cubenv env;

    cparam(&env);

    A     = 1;
    C     = 0;

    for(i=0;i<nskip*(env.nproc-1)+1;++i){
        A = (MULT*A)&MASK;
        C = (MULT*C+ADD)&MASK;
        if(i == nskip*order) randx = (A*seed + C)&MASK;
    }
    a = MULT;
    c = ADD;
}

/*********************** end of routine prandom_setB ***********************/
```

E-3.2 The *prandS* Routine

```
#define MASK (long) (0x7fffffff)
#define TWOTO31 ((double)MASK+1.0)

extern long randx,a,c;

double prandS()
{
    double retval;
```

```
    retval = randx/TWOTO31;
    randx = (a*randx+c)&MASK;
    return (retval);
}


/*************************** end of routine prandS **************************/
```

E-3.3 The *prandB* Routine

```
#define MASK (long) (0x7fffffff)
#define TWOTO31 ((double)MASK+1.0)

extern long randx,A,C;

double prandB()
{
    double retval;

    retval = randx/TWOTO31;
    randx = (A*randx+C)&MASK;
    return (retval);
}


/************************** end of routine prandB **************************/
```

E-4 The *submap* Routines

E-4.1 The *partition_subcube* Routine

```
#include "sys/crossys.h"
#include "subcube.h"

partition_subcube(mask)
int mask;
{
int id;

if ( subcube(SET_SUBCUBE,&mask) == ERROR )
    return(ERROR);
else {   (void)subcube(SID_SUBCUBE,&id);
    return(id);
    }
}
```

E-4.2 The *restore_subcube* Routine

```
#include "sys/crossys.h"
#include "subcube.h"

restore_subcube(lvl)
int lvl;
{
int id;

if ( subcube(LVL_SUBCUBE,&lvl) == ERROR )
    return(ERROR);
else {   (void)subcube(SID_SUBCUBE,&id);
    return(id);
    }
}
```

E-4.3 Auxiliary Routines

```
#include "sys/crossys.h"
#include "sys/debugsys.h"

#include "subcube.h"

#define MAX_S_LEVEL    _Maxdoc

typedef struct {
```

```
        int  subcube_id,
             parent_id,
             _nproc,
             _procnum,
             _doc,
             _subdoc,
             _legal_mask,
             _ihmask,
             _even_bits,
             _tocp,
             _brchan,
             _chan_i[_Maxdoc],
             _order[1<<_Maxdoc],
             _submask[1<<_Maxdoc];
        } SUB_STACK;

LOCAL SUB_STACK    mappings[MAX_S_LEVEL];

LOCAL    subcube_lvl = 0,        /* Level in subcube stack */
         subcube_id = 0;         /* ID of current subcube */

LOCAL void   push_cube(),
             pop_cube();

        /* subcube - Executive to control user subcubes */

subcube(cmd,arg)
int  cmd,
     *arg;
{
switch ( cmd ) {
    case SET_SUBCUBE:
        if ( *arg & ~(_nproc - 1) ) {
            errno = EBCHM;
            goto error;
            }
        block();
        push_cube(*arg);
        break;
    case REL_SUBCUBE:
        if ( *arg < 0 || *arg > subcube_lvl ) {
            errno = EBSLVL;
            goto error;
            }
        if ( *arg == subcube_lvl )
            break;
        pop_cube(*arg);
```

```
            block();
            break;
      case LVL_SUBCUBE:
            *arg = subcube_lvl;
            break;
      case SID_SUBCUBE:
            *arg = subcube_id;
            break;
      case PRC_SUBCUBE:
            *arg = _node;
            break;
      default:
            errno = EBSCMD;
            goto error;
      }
return(OK);

error:
      return(ERROR);
}

      /* push_cube - Increase level of subcubes on stack */

LOCAL void push_cube(mask)
int mask;
{
SUB_STACK      *map_p = &mappings[subcube_lvl++];

map_p->subcube_id = subcube_id;

map_p->_nproc = _nproc;
map_p->_procnum = _procnum;
map_p->_doc = _doc;
map_p->_subdoc = _subdoc;
map_p->_legal_mask = _legal_mask;
map_p->_even_bits = _even_bits;
map_p->_ihmask = _ihmask;
map_p->_brchan = _brchan;
map_p->_tocp = _tocp;
      {
      int chan = 0;

      for ( chan = 0 ; chan < _doc ; chan++ )
            (map_p->_chan_i)[chan] = _chan_i[chan];
      }
      {               /* Other arrays */
      int i;
```

```
        for ( i = 0 ; i < _nproc ; i++ ) {
            (map_p->_order)[i] = _order[i];
            (map_p->_submask)[i] = _submask[i];
            }
        }

        /* Find new _doc, _procnum */
    {
    int offset = 0,
        ndoc = 0,
        nprocnum = 0,
        subc_id = subcube_id << _doc,
        root = _procnum & ~mask,
        chan,
        nchan;

    _procnum -= root;

    for ( chan = nchan = 0 ; chan < _doc ; chan++, mask >>= 1 ) {
        if ( mask & 1 ) {
            _chan_i[nchan++] = chan;
            ndoc++;
            nprocnum |= (_procnum & (1<<chan)) >> offset;
            }
        else {   subc_id += (root & (1<<chan)) >> (chan - offset);
            offset++;
            }
        }

    subcube_id = subc_id;
    _procnum = nprocnum;
    _doc = ndoc;
    }

_setup2();
}

    /* pop_cube - Drop to a level of subcube decomposition */

LOCAL void pop_cube(lvl)
int lvl;
{
SUB_STACK    *map_p = &mappings[subcube_lvl = lvl];

subcube_id = map_p->subcube_id;
```

```
_nproc = map_p->_nproc;
_procnum = map_p->_procnum;
_doc = map_p->_doc;
_subdoc = map_p->_subdoc;
_legal_mask = map_p->_legal_mask;
_even_bits = map_p->_even_bits;
_ihmask = map_p->_ihmask;
_tocp = map_p->_tocp;
_brchan = map_p->_brchan;
    {               /* Channel masks */
    int  chan;

    for ( chan = 0 ; chan < _doc ; chan++ )
        _chan_i[chan] = (map_p->_chan_i)[chan];
    }
    {               /* Other arrays */
    int  i;

    for ( i = 0 ; i < _nproc ; i++ ) {
        _order[i] = (map_p->_order)[i];
        _submask[i] = (map_p->_submask)[i];
        }
    }
}
```

E-4.4 The Include File subcube.h

```
#define SET_SUBCUBE    01       /* Divide a subcube */
#define REL_SUBCUBE    02       /* recombine subcubes */
#define LVL_SUBCUBE    04       /* Return current level */
#define SID_SUBCUBE    010      /* Id of current subcube */
#define PRC_SUBCUBE    020      /* Get true processor number */
```

F

Appendix F:
Utility Library Manual Pages

This appendix presents the manual pages for the *comutil*, *crystal_router*, *prand*, and *submap* utilities. These utilities, together with the *cparam* and *gridmap* routines described in Appendix E of Volume 1, make up the CrOS III utility library. We expect more utilities, for example for performing fast Fourier transforms, linear algebra, and sorting, to be added to this library in the future. The *comutil*, *crystal_router*, and *submap* routines are described in Chap. 5 of this volume, and the *prand* routines are discussed in Chap. 12 of Volume 1. The source code for the routines presented in this Appendix is listed in Appendix E.

C NAME

comutil — utilities for performing global communication between nodes

C SYNOPSIS

```
int expand ( outbuf, inbuf, step, nbytes, nitems )
char *outbuf;
char *inbuf;
int step;
int nbytes;
int nitems;

int fold ( buf, func, nbytes, nitems )
char *buf;
int (*func)();
int nbytes;
int nitems;

int global_reverse ( buf, nbytes, nitems )
char *buf;
int nbytes;
int nitems;

int indexx ( buf, nbytes, nitems )
char *buf;
int nbytes;
int nitems;

int bcast ( buf, source, nbytes )
char *buf;
int source;
int nbytes;

int scatter ( buf, source, nitems, nbytes, max_items )
char *buf;
int source;
int nitems;
int nbytes;
int max_items;

int transfer ( buf, source, dest, nsend, pkt_size, max_send )
char *buf;
int source;
int dest;
int nsend;
int pkt_size;
int max_send;
```

```
int transpose ( buf, nbytes, max_bytes )
char *buf;
int nbytes;
max_bytes;
```

C DESCRIPTION

The routine *expand* may only be called in the nodes. The routine takes a block of data of length *nbytes* bytes from memory starting at address *outbuf* and concatenates it with the corresponding data from the other nodes so that all nodes contain the same concatenated data in the buffer *inbuf*. The concatenated data is stored in order of increasing node number. This procedure is then repeated for the data blocks beginning at addresses offset by $i * step$ items from *outbuf*, where $i = 1, 2, \ldots, (nitems - 1)$. In each case the data are appended to the data that have already been written to *inbuf*. If the hypercube has dimensional 0 then the *nitems* items in *outbuf* are copied to *inbuf*. The values of *nitems* and *nbytes* must be the same in all nodes.

The routine *fold* may only be called in the nodes. The routine *fold* takes *nitems* items, each of length *nbytes* bytes, starting at *buf* and combines them according to function *func*. The result of combining item number i over all the nodes overwrites item number i of *buf* in node number $i \bmod N_p$, where N_p is the number of nodes. Thus *fold* differs from *combine* since each combined quantity is stored in only one of the nodes, rather than in all of them. In node number P combined data is stored at locations $P + i * N_p$ of *buf*, where $i = 0, 1, \ldots, \lceil (nitems - P)/N_p \rceil - 1$. The value of items at other locations is left indeterminate.

The function *func*, which must be commutative and associative and takes three arguments, combines the data items in pairs. It combines the two data items indicated by its first two arguments, which are pointers to the two data items to be combined, and overwrites the data item indicated by its first argument with the result. The third argument of *func* is *nbytes*, which allows the possibility of using the same combining function on data items of different size.

The combining function *func*, and *nbytes* and *nitems* must be the same in all the nodes, and *fold* must be called with loose synchronicity.

The routine *global_reverse* may only be called in the nodes, and permutes the *nitems* items of a distributed array. The part of this array assigned to a particular node is stored in memory starting at *buf*. Each item is *nbytes* bytes long. The permutation is as follows. Item number i of *buf* in node P has global index $g = i + P * N_p$. This item is exchanged with the item whose global index is g_{rev}. If $q = \log_2(nitems)$, then g_{rev} is the number obtained by writing the q bits of g in reverse order. For example, if $nitems = 32$ and $g = 11$ (or 01011 in binary), then $g_{rev} = 26$ (or 11010 in binary).

The value of *nitems* must be a power of 2 and must not be less than N_p. Both *nitems* and *nbytes* must be the same in all nodes.

The routine *indexx* may only be called in the nodes, and permutes the *nitems* items of a distributed array. The part of this array assigned to a particular node is stored in memory starting at *buf*. Each item is *nbytes* bytes long. The permutation is as follows. Item number i of *buf* in node P has global index $g = i + P * N_p$. This item is exchanged with the item whose global index is g_{ind}. If $q = \log_2(nitems)$ then g can be represented by q binary digits. If $d = \log_2 N_p$ is the hypercube dimension, then g_{ind} is the number obtained by exchanging the upper d bits of g with the lower d bits. For example, if $nitems = 128$, $d = 3$ and $g = 11$ (or 0001011 in binary), then $g_{ind} = 56$ (or 0111000 in binary). Note how the lower 3 bits of g (011) have been exchanged with the upper 3 bits (000) to give g_{ind}.

The upper d bits of the global index of an item gives the number of the node in which that item is stored, while the lower $q - d$ bits give the local index at which the item is located in *buf*. Thus the item with local index $i = j + k * N_p$, where $0 \le j < N_p$, in node P is sent by *indexx* to node j where it is stored with local index $P + k * N$.

The value of *nitems* must be a power of 2 and must not be less than N_p. Both *nitems* and *nbytes* must be the same in all nodes.

The routine *scatter* may only be called in the nodes. The routine *scatter* takes *nitems*, starting at *buf*, from node number *source*, and scatters them amongst the other nodes. Each item is *nbytes* bytes long. Item number i of *buf* in node *source* is sent to node number $i \bmod N_p$ where it is stored as item number i of *buf*. The value of *max_items* gives the maximum number of items that will be received or forwarded by a node.

All nodes must have the same values of *source* and *nbytes*.

The routine *bcast* may only be called in the nodes. The routine *bcast* broadcasts *nbytes* bytes of data starting at the address *buf* from node *source* to all other nodes. In nodes other than the source node, *bcast* causes at most *nbytes* bytes of data to be read from the source node and placed in memory starting at *buf*. All nodes do not have to have the same value of *nbytes*.

It is guaranteed that *nbytes* will be written to all nodes; *bcast* will not return in the source node until all *nbytes* bytes of data have been written to and read by each node. However, it is not guaranteed that *nbytes* bytes will be read in the nodes other than the source node; the actual number of bytes read depends on the number written by the source node. A call to *bcast* must be complemented by a call to *bcast* in all other nodes. In addition, all must have the same value of *source*; otherwise deadlock will result.

If the value of *nbytes* is larger in the source node than in a receiving node, only the first *nbytes* bytes are placed in the receiving node's memory starting at *buf*. The remaining bytes are then read, so the corresponding call to *bcast* in the other nodes can return, but the extra bytes are lost and -1 is returned to indicate the error.

The routine *transfer* may only be called in the nodes. The routine *transfer* causes *nsend* packets of data starting at memory location *buf* in node *source* to be transferred to node *dest*. The packet size is *pkt_size* bytes. In the destination node packets are received and placed in memory starting at location *buf*. The maximum number of packets that will be received or forwarded by nodes other than the source node is *max_send*. All nodes must call *transfer* loosely synchronously with the same values of *source*, *dest*, and *pkt_size*.

The routine *transpose* may only be called in the nodes. Suppose the nodes are arranged as a square 2-dimensional grid, with the node in row μ and column ν being node number $\nu + \mu\sqrt{N_p}$, where N_p is the number of nodes. The routine *transpose* transposes the data stored on this grid of nodes, that is, *nbytes* bytes of data starting at memory location *buf* in the node at position (μ, ν) are exchanged with the corresponding data in the node at position (ν, μ). The maximum amount of data that each node is prepared to receive or forward is *max_bytes* bytes. The value of *max_bytes* need not be the same in all nodes, but must be no less than the maximum value of *nbytes* over all nodes. If no errors occur *transpose* returns the number of bytes received and stored in *buf*.

SEE ALSO

broadcast(2), combine(3)

FORTRAN SYNOPSIS

```
FUNCTION KEXPND ( OUTBUF, INBUF, ISTEP, NBYTES, NITEMS )
INTEGER OUTBUF(*)
INTEGER INBUF(*)
INTEGER ISTEP
INTEGER NBYTES
INTEGER NITEMS

FUNCTION KFOLD ( BUF, IFUNC, NBYTES, NITEMS )
INTEGER BUF(*)
INTEGER IFUNC
INTEGER NBYTES
INTEGER NITEMS

FUNCTION KGLOBR ( BUF, NBYTES, NITEMS )
INTEGER BUF(*)
INTEGER NBYTES
INTEGER NITEMS
```

FUNCTION KINDEX (BUF, NBYTES, NITEMS)
INTEGER BUF(*)
INTEGER NBYTES
INTEGER NITEMS

FUNCTION KSCATR (BUF, IPROC, NITEMS, NBYTES, MXITMS)
INTEGER BUF(*)
INTEGER IPROC
INTEGER NITEMS
INTEGER NBYTES
INTEGER MXITMS

FUNCTION KBCAST (BUF, IPROC, NBYTES)
INTEGER BUF(*)
INTEGER IPROC
INTEGER NBYTES

FUNCTION KTRNSF (BUF, ISOURC, IDEST, NSEND, IPKTSZ, MXSEND
INTEGER BUF(*)
INTEGER ISOURC
INTEGER IDEST
INTEGER NSEND
INTEGER IPKTSZ
INTEGER MXSEND

FUNCTION KTRNSP (BUF, NBYTES, MXBYTS)
INTEGER BUF(*)
INTEGER NBYTES
INTEGER MXBYTS

DIAGNOSTICS

If an error is encountered in any of the *submap* routines a value of -1 is
returned; otherwise 0 is returned. Possible sources of error are: (1) communication errors, (2) a bad buffer address, or (3) an invalid value of one or more
of the input arguments.

EXAMPLES

```
double x,bigbuf[MAX_PROCS];
status = expand(&x,bigbuf,0,sizeof(double),1);
```

The above example causes the value of x from each node to be concatenated
in node number order into the buffer *bigbuf*. Thus after the call, element
number P of *bigbuf* in every node is the value of x from node P.

```
double buf[3*MAX_PROCS];
status = expand(buf+procnum,buf,nproc,sizeof(double),3);
```

The above example causes element number $(P + i * N)$ of *buf* in all nodes
to be set equal to element number $(P + i * N)$ of *buf* from node P, where
$i = 0, 1, 2$.

```
double buf[MAX_PROCS];
status = scatter( buf, 3, 2*nproc, sizeof(double), 2*nproc );
```

The above example scatters the first $2N_p$ elements in the array buf in node number 3. Element numbers j and $j+N_p$ are sent to node j ($j = 0, 1, \ldots, N_p - 1$), where they are stored at the same positions in buf.

C NAME

#include <crdef.h>

int clear_cr_buf (in_or_out)
int in_or_out;

int crystal_router ( )

int error_messages (stream)
FILE *stream;

int get_message (buf, source, nbytes)
char *buf;
int *source;
int *nbytes;

void rewindx ( )

int send_message (buf, nbytes, ndest, dest)
char *buf;
int nbytes;
int ndest;
int *dest;

int set_cr_buf (buf_size, in_or_out)
int buf_size;
int in_or_out;

float show_buf_usage (stream, in_or_out)
FILE *stream;
int in_or_out;

int zero_hwm (in_or_out)

C DESCRIPTION

The *crystal_router* routines may only be called in the nodes, and the user must include the file crdef.h.

The routine *clear_cr_buf* discards all messages waiting to be sent or to be read in a node, depending on whether *in_or_out* has the value defined by the macro IN or the macro OUT.

The routine *crystal_router* causes all messages waiting to be sent to be transmitted to their respective destination nodes.

The routine *error_messages* may only be called in a CUBIX program. The *crystal_router* routines indicate an error by setting the appropriate bit in the integer *cr_error*. The routine *error_messages* checks the value of *cr_error* and if it is non-zero outputs error messages on the previously opened I/O stream

stream. The value of *cr_error* is then re-set to 0. If necessary the CUBIX I/O mode is set to multiple mode on entry to *error_messages*. Before returning the I/O mode is re-set to whatever it was on entry.

The routine *get_message* copies the next message in the received message buffer whose source node is indicated by the value stored at *source*, to the buffer *buf*. If the value of the quantity pointed to by *source* is that defined by the macro ANY, then the next message in the (circular) buffer is copied, regardless of the source node. The user must allocate the storage for the buffer *buf* and unpredictable errors may occur if this is too small. Once a message has been successfully read using *get_message* it is marked for deletion from the received message buffer. Such messages are physically removed, and the buffer compressed, at the start of the next call to *crystal_router*. On exit, if a message has been successfully read, *source* points to the node number of the source node, and *nbytes* to the number of bytes in the message.

The routine *rewindx* returns the state of the received message buffer to how it was immediately after the last call to the routine *crystal_router*. Usually a message can only be read once by a call to *get_message*, however *rewindx* allows messages to be read again by permitting a second pass to be made through the received message buffer.

The routine *send_message* causes *nbytes* of data starting at *buf* to be queued for transmission to each of the *ndest* nodes stored in the integer array *dest*. If *nbytes* is negative, or if the value of *ndest* or one of the destination nodes in *dest* is invalid, then the appropriate bit of *cr_error* is set and on return a value of -1 is returned. Invalid destination nodes are ignored. Insufficient space in the outgoing message buffer for the data also generates an error which causes a bit of *cr_error* to be set.

The routine *set_cr_buf* allows the user to change the sizes of the outgoing and received message buffers from their default values of 2048 bytes to *buf_size* bytes. The value of *in_or_out* must be one of the macro definitions IN or OUT, depending on which buffer is to be changed. If the system is unable to allocate the requested space then the appropriate bit of *cr_error* is set and a value of -1 is returned. In this case the message buffers are unchanged. If the requested space is successfully allocated then any messages in the old buffer are copied to the new buffer. If there is insufficient space for all the messages to be copied to the new buffer the appropriate bit of *cr_error* is set and a value of -1 is returned.

The routine *show_buffer_usage* returns the "high-water mark" for either the outgoing or received message buffer, depending on whether *in_or_out* has the value defined by the macro IN or the macro OUT. The high-water mark of a buffer is the highest level to which that buffer has been filled during previous calls to *crystal_router* routines, expressed as a fraction of the size of the buffer.

If the file pointer *stream* is not null, then in a CUBIX program high-water mark information is output on the I/O stream *stream*.

The routine *zero_hwm* sets the high-water mark for either the outgoing or received message buffer to zero, depending on whether *in_or_out* has the value defined by the macro IN or the macro OUT.

FORTRAN SYNOPSIS

```
FUNCTION KCLEAR ( INOUT )
INTEGER INOUT

FUNCTION KCROUT ( IDUMMY )
INTEGER IDUMMY

FUNCTION KEMESS ( LUNIT )
INTEGER LUNIT

FUNCTION KGMESS ( IBUF, ISOURC, NBYTES )
INTEGER IBUF(*)
INTEGER ISOURC
INTEGER NBYTES

FUNCTION KREWIN ( IDUMMY )
INTEGER IDUMMY

FUNCTION KSMESS ( IBUF, NBYTES, NDEST, IDEST )
INTEGER IBUF(*)
INTEGER NBYTES
INTEGER NDEST
INTEGER IDEST(*)

FUNCTION KSETCR ( IBUFSZ, INOUT)
INTEGER IBUFSZ
INTEGER INOUT

REAL FUNCTION SHOWBU ( LUNIT, INOUT )
INTEGER LUNIT
INTEGER INOUT

FUNCTION KZEROH ( INOUT )
INTEGER INOUT
```

FORTRAN DESCRIPTION

The use of the Fortran *crystal_router* routines closely follows that described above for the C version. The only significant difference is that in Fortran a unit number is used to specify an I/O stream. In the function SHOWBU a negative value for the unit number *LUNIT* suppresses the output of information about the high-water mark values.

DIAGNOSTICS

In general, the *crystal_router* routines return −1 in the event of an error; otherwise 0 is returned. In addition, the routines *crystal_router, get_message, send_message* and *set_cr_buf* provide an indication of the nature of the error by setting the appropriate bit of the integer *cr_error*. In a CUBIX program, a call to the routine *error_messages* will output messages describing any messages that have occurred.

C NAME

prand_setB, prandS, prandB — parallel random number generation routines.

C SYNOPSIS

void prand_setB (seed, nskip, order)
int seed;
int nskip;
int order;

double prandS ( )

double prandB ( )

C DESCRIPTION

Suppose a simulation requires a certain sequence of events to be modeled, and each event requires the generation of *nskip* random numbers. The N_p nodes of the concurrent computer are ordered by assigning to each a unique integer, *order*, in the range 0 to $N_p - 1$. Each node is responsible for handling the events numbered $order + i * N_p$ in the sequence, where $i = 0, i, 2, \ldots$.

The routine *prand_setB* initializes the routines *prandS* and *prandB* for generating random numbers for simulations of the type described above in such a way that each event in the sequence always receives the same set of *nskip* random numbers for a given seed integer, *seed*, regardless of the number of nodes. For each event the routine *prandS* must be used to generate the first $nskip - 1$ random numbers, and the last random number for the event must be generated by a call to *prandB*.

The *prand* routines use the linear congruential method for generating the random numbers uniformly distributed on the interval 0 to 1.

FORTRAN SYNOPSIS

SUBROUTINE PRSETB (ISEED, NSKIP, IORDER)
INTEGER ISEED
INTEGER NSKIP
INTEGER IORDER

DOUBLE PRECISION FUNCTION PRANDS (IDUMMY)
INTEGER IDUMMY

DOUBLE PRECISION FUNCTION PRANDB (IDUMMY)
INTEGER IDUMMY

DIAGNOSTICS

There are none. Possible sources of error are (1) an invalid value for an argument to *prandset_B*, or (2) calling *prandS* or *prandB* before calling *prand_setB*.

EXAMPLES

Suppose each event requires a point to be generated at random with uniform probability within the unit cube. Then we might write:

```
prandset_B ( 123, 3, procnum );
for(i=0; i<nevents; ++i){
    x = prandS();
    y = prandS();
    z = prandB();
    iresp = do_event(x,y,z);
}
```

Here **procnum** is the node number determined by a previous call to *cparam*. Each node processes **nevents** events by calling the routine **do_event**.

C NAME

submap — routines for subcube allocation and management within an application node program.

C SYNOPSIS

int partition_subcube (scmask)
int scmask;

int restore_subcube (level)
int level;

C DESCRIPTION

The routine *partition_subcube* may be called only from the nodes, and partitions the current hypercube as specified by the mask *scmask*. The partitioning is performed by discarding the channels of the current hypercube that correspond to zeros in the binary representation of *scmask*. Each of the resulting subcubes then act independently, and is assigned a unique ID number. The node and channel numbers within each subcube are reconfigured so that they are appropriate for that subcube, and for each node the current hypercube becomes the subcube that the node now lies in.

The routine *restore_subcube* may be called only from the nodes. This routine takes a set of subcubes and reconfigures them as a larger subcube. Suppose the successive partitioning of a hypercube is represented by a tree, then a level or generation number can be associated with each subcube which is the number of times the nodes in that subcube have called the routine *partition_subcube*. Thus the initial hypercube has level 0, and its children are at level 1, and so on. The argument *level* of *restore_subcube* specifies the level number of the restored subcube. Thus if all the descendants of the subcube which is to be restored call *restore_subcube* in loose synchrony with same argument *level*, then they will be reconfigured as the restored subcube.

FORTRAN SYNOPSIS

FUNCTION KPARTI (ISCMSK)
INTEGER ISCMSK

FUNCTION KRESTO (LEVEL)
INTEGER LEVEL

DIAGNOSTICS

If an error occurs in *partition_subcube* or in *restore_subcube* a value of -1 is returned. Otherwise the ID number of the subcube that the node is in is returned. Possible sources of error are providing an non-integer or negative value for *scmask* or *level*, or too large a value for *level*.

EXAMPLES

Suppose the hypercube dimension is 4. Consider the following code:

```
id = partition_subcube(5);
```

Since the binary representation of the mask 5 is 0101, this will partition the hypercube into four 2-dimensional subcubes by removing communication channels numbered 1. The first of the subcubes will contain the nodes numbered 0, 1, 4, and 5; the second nodes 2, 3, 6, and 7; the third nodes 8, 9, 12, and 13; and the fourth nodes 10, 11, 14, 15.

As an example of the use of *restore_subcube* suppose the hypercube dimension is 4. Consider the following code:

```
id1 = partition_subcube(7);
if (id1==0){
    id2 = partition_subcube(5);
    if (id2==0) iresp = iwork1();
    else        iresp = iwork2();
    id3 = restore_subcube(1);
    iresp = iwork3();
}
else{
    iresp = iwork4();
}
id4 = restore_subcube(0);
```

This code first of all partitions the hypercube into two 3-dimensional subcubes. Those nodes lying in the subcube with ID number 0 are then further partitioned into two 2-dimensional subcubes each of which performs a different task by calling either the function *iwork1* or *iwork2*. After this the two 2-dimensional subcubes are restored to level 1, so they now are configured as a single 3-dimensional subcube. This subcube then performs another task by calling the routine *iwork3*. Meanwhile the other 3-dimensional subcube produced by the initial call to *partition_subcube* performs yet another task by calling the routine *iwork4*. Finally all nodes call *restore_subcube* with argument 0. This reconfigures them once more as a single 4-dimensional hypercube.

BUGS

The subcubes will only be able to perform I/O independently on systems which can perform asynchronous message-passing.

G

Appendix G:
How To Get The Software

The hypercube simulator, *nsim*, and the application programs and utilities described in this volume and listed in Appendices A through E, may be obtained in computer-readable form by electronic mail. This is done by means of *citlib*, which is a file-server at Caltech for distributing software, documentation, and technical reports. *citlib* is based on the netlib program developed at Argonne National Laboratories. Requests should be addressed to:

> `citlib@klee.caltech.edu`   for INTERNET users
>
> `citlib@caltech.bitnet`   for BITNET users

The principal *citlib* command is `send`. The server will respond to a one-line message such as:

> `send help`

or,

> `send file_name for path_name`

by sending the requester a help file with detailed instructions about using the file-server, or the file `file_name` residing in the sub-directory `path_name`. If you wish to use *citlib* your first step should be to obtain a copy of the help file.

If you experience problems using *citlib*, or are unable to access it using electronic mail, please write to:

> Software For Concurrent Processors,
> Caltech Concurrent Computation Program,
> Mail Stop 206-49,
> California Institute of Technology,
> CA 91125, USA.

Electronic mail should be addressed to:

> `c3prequest@hamlet.caltech.edu`   for INTERNET users
>
> `c³prequest@hamlet`   for BITNET users

H

Appendix H:
A List of Suppliers

In this appendix we list some of the suppliers of hardware and software mentioned in this volume, along with others that we think may be of interest to readers. This list is provided as a convenience to readers, and should not be construed as an endorsement of any particular company or product. Companies that would like to be listed here in subsequent editions of the book should send their details to the address given at the end of Appendix G. A more complete directory of hardware and software suppliers for advanced architecture computers may be found in the inaugural issue of *Supercomputing Review*, edited by Norris Parker Smith (ISBN 1-871165-00-8).

H-1 Commercial Suppliers of Distributed Memory Computers

Active Memory Technologies, Inc.
16802 Aston Street
Irvine, CA 92714
Phone: (714) 261-8901

BBN Advanced Computers, Inc.
10 Fawcett Street
Cambridge, MA 02238
Phone: (617) 873-6000

Intel Scientific Computers, Inc.
15201 Northwest Greenbrier Parkway
Beaverton, OR 97006
Phone: (503) 629-7629

Meiko Scientific Corporation
400 Oyster Point Blvd.
Suite 523
South San Francisco, CA 94080
Phone: (415) 952-9900

Myrias Computer Corporation
1400 Woodloch Forest Drive
Suite 530
The Woodlands, TX 77380
Phone: (713) 363-2696

NCUBE Corporation
1825 Northwest 167th Place
Beaverton, OR 97006
Phone: (503) 629-5088 or (800) 35-NCUBE

Thinking Machines Corporation
245 First Street
Cambridge, MA 02142-1214
Phone: (617) 876-1111

H-2 Suppliers of Add-On Boards for PCs and Workstations

Computer System Architects,
950 North University Avenue
Provo, UT 84604
Phone: (801) 374-2300

Definicon Systems, Inc.
1100 Business Center Circle
Newbury Park, CA 91320
Phone: (805) 499-0652

Levco Sales, Inc.
6160 Lusk Blvd.
San Diego, CA 92121
Phone: (619) 457-2011

Meiko Scientific Corporation
400 Oyster Point Blvd.
Suite 523
South San Francisco, CA 94080
Phone: (415) 952-9900

MicroWay, Inc.
P. O. Box 79
Kingston, MA 02364
Phone: (617) 746-7361

NCUBE Corporation
1825 Northwest 167th Place
Beaverton, OR 97006
Phone: (503) 629-5088 or (800) 35-NCUBE

ParaSoft Corporation
27415 Trabuco Circle
Mission Viejo, CA 92692
Phone: (714) 380-9739

Topologix Inc.
4860 Ward Road
Denver, CO 80033
Phone: (303) 421-7700

H-3 Suppliers of Software for Distributed Memory Computers

ParaSoft Corporation
27415 Trabuco Circle
Mission Viejo, CA 92692
Phone: (714) 380-9739

Index

Contents Of Volume 1